D1145180

MANAGING ORGANIZATIONAL BEHAVIOR

Henry L. Tosi
University of Florida

John R. Rizzo
Western Michigan University

Stephen J. Carroll
University of Maryland

BLACKWELL
Business

Copyright © Henry L. Tosi, John R. Rizzo, Stephen J. Carroll 1994

First edition published 1986 by Pitman Publishing Inc., USA.
Second edition published 1990 by Harper Collins Publishers, Inc., USA.

First published 1994

Blackwell Publishers
238 Main Street
Cambridge, Massachusetts 02142
USA

108 Cowley Road
Oxford OX4 1JF
UK

Library of Congress Cataloging-in-Publication Data

Tosi, Henry L.
    Managing organizational behavior / Henry L. Tosi, John R. Rizzo,
Stephen J. Carroll. - - 3rd ed.
      p.   cm.
    Includes bibliographical references and index.
    ISBN 1-55786-551-5
    1. Organizational behavior. I. Rizzo, John R. II. Carroll,
Stephen J., 1930-   . III. Title.
HD58.7.T66 1993
658- -dc20   93-38203
                                          CIP

British Library Cataloguing in Publication Data

A CIP catalogue record for this book is available from the British Library.

Typeset in 10.5 point Garamond by Benchmark Productions.
Printed in the United States of America

This book is printed on acid-free paper

To Rosemary, Gayleen, and Donna

Contents

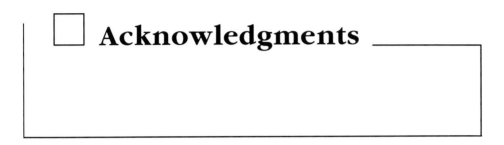

Acknowledgments

There are a number of people who have helped us in many ways in this edition and earlier ones. Each has been important and has added constructively to what we have done. Two, however, deserve special mention for the preparation of this edition. Gayleen Rollins worked very hard to develop a better test bank. Kim Smithson brought a high energy level, outstanding administrative skills, and a bright attitude to it. She was a great help to all of us.

We also relied very heavily on several people in the production of the manuscript. Bob St. Clair was the first publisher who liked the ideas we have in this book and helped get them into print. Bill Roberts, who is out there somewhere in the publishing business, gave us much help in getting the book where it is, and so did Carol Franco.

We received many useful reviewer suggestions which were integrated into the manuscript. We thank all for their help knowing that the rewards for their work are more intrinsic than extrinsic.

☐ Preface _____

This book is about the problem of managing people in organizations. We take the view that these issues can only be considered in terms of the interaction between human beings and the organizational context within which they work. Further, just as there are individual differences which help us to understand human behavior, there are differences in organizations which must be understood if we are to effectively manage resources, both human and technical. We are pleased that those who reviewed earlier editions of this book thought that this perspective was a strong point of the book.

Understanding the organization and its interaction with individual and group level factors is so important that we did two things to emphasize it. First, we placed most of the important ideas about the organizational context in the early part of the book. Second, there are constant references to and discussion of these contextual elements in the later parts of the text which discuss the psychological and sociological processes which occur in organizations.

ORGANIZATION OF THE BOOK

The framework of the book is fairly conventional, consistent with the ideas which are important and relevant today. We emphasize fundamental concepts about organizations, individuals, and groups in a section which we call the "building blocks of organization." One of these building blocks is dealt with in a set of chapters which discusses the organizational context. Chapter 2 describes how the environment and decisions made by managers result in the different types of organization design. In Chapter 3 the important contextual factor, organizational culture, is discussed in detail. In this chapter we show the embedded nature of organizational culture and how it affects so much of what happens in organizations. Chapter 18, which treats the broader social context within which organizations exist, shows why values differ across cultures and how these differences are reflected in what goes on in organizations.

The second building block is the "individual." In Chapters 4 and 5 we discuss perception, attitudes, personality, and judgment. Chapter 6 moves the person into the organization, as the processes of career choice, organizational socialization, and accommodating to work are treated in detail. Chapter 7 covers motivation theories, important to understand if one wishes to increase the willingness of members to work harder and perform better. Stress, at work and as a result of work, is the subject of Chapter 9. Here we show how stress develops, its costs to the organization, and how it can be managed.

The third building block is the "group." The pressures and processes that an individual experiences when interacting with others in a group are discussed in this section. In Chapters 10 and 11, group formation, development, and processes that occur in groups are considered. Chapter 14 describes many of the factors that lead to conflict in groups and organizations.

The second part of the book is devoted to "managerial processes." These are things that managers do to improve organizational effectiveness. Chapter 8 describes how motivational strategies are applied in organizations. Decision-making processes are discussed in Chapter 13. Interpersonal influence processes are the subject of the chapters on power and politics (Chapter 15) and leadership (Chapter 16). Chapter 17 discusses some ways to systematically change the organization and those who work in it.

NEW TO THIS EDITION

There are a number of changes that have been made in this edition. First, we have updated the research and theoretical developments in each chapter and substantially revised several others. For example, there is now an extensive discussion in each chapter of how cultural diversity affects organization in Chapter 6, *Careers in Organizations*. The motivation chapters have been extensively reorganized, as have been the chapters on organizational design (Chapter 2), organizational culture (Chapter 3), and power and politics (Chapter 15).

Second, in order to deal with the global aspects of behavioral issues in organizations, we have attempted to show with examples how the concepts are applicable in a wide range of national and cultural settings.

Third, the international focus is emphasized with a new chapter (Chapter 18) on cross national issues in organizational behavior.

Fourth, the book is a bit shorter, and we think tighter, than the previous edition because we have done two things. We eliminated two chapters, and we also deleted from the text the "hands-on" experiential activities in each chapter. These are, however, now available to the instructor in the instructor's manual. In fact, there is a richer selection of this type of material in the instructor's manual for those who prefer to use such pedagogical devices.

Fifth, we changed our approach to cases. In earlier editions there were two relatively short cases at the end of each chapter. For this edition we decided to include only one, but each is a longer, more involved case. This provides the instructor who prefers to use cases in teaching with a self-contained book, with both text and cases.

Sixth, we were fortunate to find Rolf Janke and Blackwell Publishers who were willing to take a risk with us on what we wanted to do in this edition. They, along with the three of us, believed that a trend was developing in publishing texts in organizational behavior in which form was more important than substance and that this was having several negative effects. One is that complicated and exaggerated production formats can draw attention to less important matters. A second is that these production values do not translate into either educational or economic benefits to students. The result of this thinking is a book that is very straightforward and simply produced which delivers sound basic content.

Finally, we worked very hard on the writing style so that it is not heavy or pedantic. We wanted to ensure that the ideas presented are easy to understand, with absolutely no compromise of the theory and empirical work which underlies the field.

Henry L. Tosi

John R. Rizzo

Stephen J. Carroll

Chapter 1

The Field of Organizational Behavior

In 1983, Oregon Steel Mills was close to bankruptcy. Japanese and Korean companies were selling higher-quality steel at lower prices. Demand for steel was down, and the company had just experienced a bitter strike [32]. The owners of Oregon Steel sold nearly all of the stock to the employees, who bought control to save their jobs. By 1988, the employee-owned company had reversed its profit position. This happened as a result of two things. First, the company had made substantial investments in new technology. Second, the management worked hard to change the adversary relationship that had existed between it and the workers. They eliminated the separate management profit-sharing plan as well as management status symbols such as reserved parking. They also put the work force on salaried compensation, just like the managers. The result was a 63 percent increase in productivity between 1983 and 1988. In 1983 it took 9.3 hours to produce a ton of steel. By 1988, it took only 3.4 labor hours.

In 1988, Oregon Steel made a public offering of its stock. The market value of the stock was $400 million, a dramatic increase from its pre-employee buyout market value of just $15 million. Many of the employees who bought the stock only to protect their jobs became millionaires [31]. In 1992, Oregon Steel agreed to a joint venture with Nucor to build a sheet steel mini-mill in the western United States, using the most advanced steel-making technology.

The turnaround at Oregon Steel was not easy. Technological and financial problems had to be solved, but so did many issues dealing with the personnel, both management and workers. One of the key factors to the project's success is that the management group and the work force at Oregon were able to overcome the "we-them" attitude which characterized the historical relationship and develop a cooperative organization culture.

This book is about the human problems faced by companies like Oregon Steel in managing performance. It is not enough to know about the technical, financial, and economic facets of work; managers must understand organizations, how they work, and the people in them. Any good manager knows that these are among the most difficult issues and that they are not well equipped to deal with them. Executives responsible for recruiting and developing managers say that people skills, as they are called, are the most important requirement for future managers [37].

Organizational behavior is the behavioral science that focuses on these issues. It is the study of human action in organizations. **Organizational behavior** is the systematic and scientific analysis of individuals, groups, and organizations; its purpose is to understand, predict, and improve the performance of individuals and, ultimately, the organizations in which they work. It draws concepts about individuals from psychology, concepts from groups are taken from sociology, and managerial themes are drawn from a wide range of disciplines that help us understand how to implement this knowledge in organizations.

BACKGROUND CONTEXT OF TODAY'S MANAGEMENT PROBLEMS

The case of Oregon Steel typifies some ways that companies have adapted to an environment that has changed, often subtly and imperceptibly but at other times extremely, over the past 30 years. First, American industrial superiority after World War II has eroded as countries worldwide developed strong economies. Second, the Vietnam era had tremendous political significance. The war was not financed properly, setting the groundwork for the hyperinflation of the 1970s. It disenchanted many and, many analysts believe, an era of self-indulgence began which eroded traditional work values [11]. Third, during the 1970s the status of women and minority groups changed. They began entering the work force in increasing numbers and demanded an end to the discrimination they had suffered in the past. Finally, in the early 1980s there was a period of sustained economic growth, but the residual effects were large national trade and budget deficits that continue to plague the economy to this day.

These are among the many forces which have led to circumstances that managers will face in the future. Some of the more important ones which have implications for managing organizations are changes in (1) the structure of industry, (2) the nature of the work force, and (3) the way organizations are structured and managed.

STRUCTURAL ECONOMIC ISSUES

Some aspects of United States industry are changing in important ways. The manufacturing sector is making continuing adjustments. The service economy is growing and will continue to do so. The relationships between unions and companies will never be as they were 20 years ago and, finally, one of the most important changes is the globalization of the firm.

Changes in the manufacturing sector. There have been significant changes in the mature manufacturing industries, located in the Northeast and Midwest United States, such as steel, basic metals, and the auto industry. These industries had serious productivity problems. Productivity had been declining rapidly, beginning in 1965, for several reasons. Not only were many production facilities old and inefficient, but the newer ones were less efficient than those in foreign countries. Foreign competitors of these industries began operating with relatively new plants, built since World War II. United States firms lagged in modernizing their plant and equipment, partly because foreign competition had not been a serious threat for so long. Lack of modern, efficient production facilities is a major cause of the quality problems that many American products suffer.

Responding to this has led to a restructuring of these industries. Many old plants have been closed, causing serious unemployment and economic problems in regions that were dependent on those plants. When plants have been renovated and made more efficient, there is often a large reduction in the work force, and the firms are also faced with the difficult task of retraining their labor force.

Some think that the manufacturing sector is now in a position to make a major recovery. Many of the problems have been worked out by market forces or through cooperation between managers, workers, and investors. If this growth occurs, it will mean a more robust manufacturing sector, but it will be very different from the post-war period.

Growth of the Service Sector.   The U.S. economy of the future will have a very large service component. The Hudson Institute estimates that manufacturing output by the year 2000 will be 17 percent of Gross National Product (GNP), dropping from around 21 percent of GNP in the late 1980s [20]. During the same period, the output of service industries should increase from 69 to 75 percent of GNP.

Such a shift has several implications for the work force [20]. One is that there will be substantial employment growth in small businesses. Another is that the number of part-time employees will grow. This may reduce direct wage and fringe benefit costs to employers and could give rise to more government programs to provide health care and retirement programs for workers who, in the past, had these benefits as part of their compensation packages in larger manufacturing firms.

The Role of Unions.   Union membership has been hurt by the decline in the basic industries where unionism has been important for many years. But something else seems to be operating. With pressures for increased productivity resulting in less labor-intensive operating facilities, management has become more aggressive. This could shift the balance of power in the direction of management. More companies are asking for, and getting, concessions from unions with respect to work rules and wages.

Regardless of the presence of unions, a firm has to pay the costs of maintaining an effective work force. Although most managers believe that it is an advantage for a plant to be non-union, it has been shown that while union wages are from 10 percent to 20 percent higher than in nonunion plants, unionized plants are 20 percent more productive [16]. In addition, many non-union plants offer competitive pay and benefits and have a "lifetime" employment perspective similar to that of Japanese plants [14].

Globalization.   Companies are beginning to compete in worldwide markets in different ways, and the nature of the competition itself is changing. In the past, each country was a separate producer and a separate market. Historically, products would be manufactured in the home country and then exported to foreign markets. For many years, for example, Nissan and Honda automobiles were built only in Japan and then shipped to the United States. Similarly, U.S. products were built here and exported. Firms are now locating manufacturing facilities in foreign countries. Now Nissan and Honda produce motor vehicles in the United States, General Electric builds small appliances in the Far East, and Sony has manufacturing facilities in the United States.

The multi-national firm must also consider cultural differences when it has units in different countries. Cultural values, attitudes, and beliefs will be reflected in managerial philosophies, organization structure, and motivational orientations. The challenge of the multi-national firm is to effectively integrate far flung and often culturally different units into an effective organization.

THE CHANGING CHARACTER OF THE WORK FORCE

The nature and structure of the work force will change. There will be major shifts in the age composition of the work force. The trend for women and minorities to enter the work force and to move into influential positions will continue. Finally, the values of the population from which the work force comes will be different.

Age Distribution.   There will be several changes in the work force by the year 2000 [20]. First, although the size of the work force will increase, the rate of growth will be less than in the past. Second, the number of younger workers (under 35) is going to decrease from 50 percent to 38 percent of the work force. The age group between 35 and 54 will expand dramatically. This group will constitute over 50 percent of the labor force, up from 38 percent in 1985. In addition, the number of workers over 55 will decline. Because of the increase in life span, there will be a large increase in the number of people over 65. The decrease in the working-age population may result in a shortage of labor by the year 2000.

The change in the age structure of the work force poses some interesting challenges. For instance, it is during the age period from the mid-20s to the mid-40s that people have traditionally advanced in a career. However, if organizations become smaller, requiring fewer managers, and if, at the same time, there are a large number of people in this age group, promotion channels in organizations may become clogged.

If a labor shortage occurs, as some predict, then there are economic incentives for companies to keep older employees working longer. However, changes in attitudes as well as organization practices may be necessary. Productivity actually increases with age, but older workers receive lower performance ratings [48], suggesting the existence of age stereotypes which might hinder retention of older workers.

Gender and ethnic makeup. The proportion of white males will decline as more women, Black Americans, Asians, Hispanics, Native Americans, and other minorities enter the work force. The cultures of organizations, which have been dominated by the values of white males, will slowly change as these others move into positions of power and influence.

Changes in Work Values. In the past 25 years, there have been several changes in the orientations of Americans toward work. Prior to 1960, the work ethic was dominant. Generally, most believed that hard work was good, that it would lead to success, and that one could be successful by finding a position in a good organization and doing the job well. By 1965, Americans had begun to shift away from this perspective toward one that the American value system was too materialistic, that the structure of social relationships was too rigid, and that there were more important things in life than work. The move was away from conservatism and more toward liberalism. By 1975, however, a more conservative attitude reemerged. People again valued work and success in much the same way as they had in the past. If there was a difference, it appears to be one that has been described nicely by Odiorne [35].

> People today are strongly committed to finding a lifestyle and then a job to support it, rather than the reverse, which was characteristic of the depression-raised generation before them. This calls for more participative styles of leadership, more listening, and considerable democracy in the workplace if these people are to be made more productive and creative.

CHANGES IN ORGANIZATION AND MANAGEMENT

The ways organizations are managed have been changing. Many companies, among them Ford, AT&T, General Motors, Anheuser-Busch, and Xerox, are finding better ways to capitalize on their human resources by redesigning the work to increase participation, using quality circles, and developing leaner organizations. In firms such as NCR, Donnelly Mirrors and Domino's Pizza employees are called "stakeholders" or "associates" to reflect a more egalitarian orientation. Some important themes that pervade these efforts include technological changes that affect work, changes in the nature of work, more delegation of task authority to lower organizational levels, and a general streamlining of the organization.

Technological changes and work. The technological revolution, based largely on advances in computers, will continue to have significant effects on the work place. Computers facilitate communications within and between organizations all over the world. It is simple to send electronic mail from one person to another when both are part of computer networks. Teleconferencing is made possible by computer networks. Those along a network, even though geographically dispersed, can hold a conference and send messages that all group members can read. Telefax machines transmit text materials instantly across telephone lines. In computer word processing, text material can be produced, edited, printed, and stored for later use rather easily.

Computer networks make telecommuting possible, where a person can work at home or in areas removed from the traditional office. For instance, a typist in a secretarial pool doesn't have to work in an office with several other typists but can have a word-processing terminal at home.

The integrated circuit and the silicon chip not only changed the computer industry, but have also changed the face of manufacturing. Machines can now be programmed to perform very complicated and exacting tasks, often with little or no human help. Currently, robots are welding and painting cars in Detroit and making computer chips in the Silicon Valley. Supermarkets have installed optical-scanning checkout devices which have changed the cashier's job but, more importantly, now permit managers to obtain information instantaneously about demand and inventory levels. Computer networks and optical-scanning devices are also used to validate credit cards at the point of purchase in retailing outlets of all kinds, and they have made it very simple for banks to use automatic teller machines.

Changes in the nature of work. Jobs in the future will require higher skill levels than in the past [20]. For example, those whose jobs are "computerized" must learn the new technology, as accountants who must be able to use computers for record keeping, data retrieval, and the design of information systems or typists who must use word processors.

There could also be more monitoring of work because of computers and computer networks. For example, in many large offices where clerical work is performed on networked computers, productivity reports are regularly produced from the information system itself and used to provide feedback to the workers. This impersonal and frequent monitoring certainly will increase the stress and pressure on workers, resulting in greater alienation.

Increased delegation. More people, both managers and workers, at lower organizational levels have increased authority. Many of the newer management approaches such as quality circles and participative approaches require extensive delegation of control. One approach to delegation is the creation of self-directed work groups. These groups can have responsibility for a large number of related tasks such as preparing daily work plans, training other team members, recommending pay increases for team members, and handling disciplinary problems.

To delegate, managers must trust the workers and take a hands-off approach. At the same time, workers must believe that managers will not violate the integrity of those areas which have been delegated to the group for decision making. This kind of relationship only develops when the work force is well informed about the operations of the firm and they feel secure that management is not hiding anything.

Leaner Management Structures. Today's intense competition has pressured many firms to create leaner, or flatter, organizations. The use of computers and the downsizing of firms driven by competitive forces have resulted in the need for fewer people to produce the same or more output. The estimates of worker displacement for such reasons range between four million and fifteen million blue-collar jobs [7].

This leads to a corresponding decrease in the need for managers. Many firms have flattened the organization structure, eliminating at least one layer of management in the organization structure and reducing the number of managers at other levels. These flatter, leaner structures not only result in a lower managerial wage bill, but they often are very convincing evidence to equity-holders that company presidents are taking forceful, effective action to deal with increasingly turbulent environments [41].

A FRAMEWORK FOR UNDERSTANDING ORGANIZATIONAL BEHAVIOR

The framework for this book is derived from our definition of organizational behavior—the scientific analysis of individuals and groups in the organizational context with the ultimate objective of improving organizational performance. Figure 1.1 shows this framework. In it can be seen the building blocks that focus on understanding individuals, groups, and organizations. It is with these elements that managers must work, so the second part of Figure 1.1 shows the managerial processes that lead to organization effectiveness.

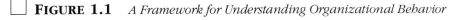 **FIGURE 1.1** *A Framework for Understanding Organizational Behavior*

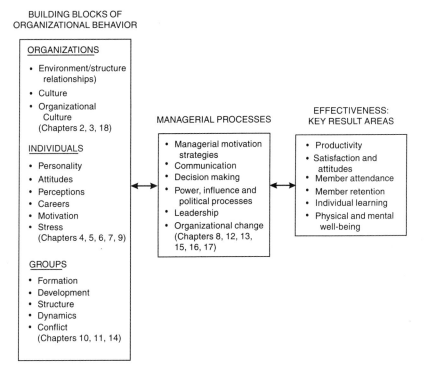

ORGANIZATION EFFECTIVENESS

There are several ways to judge effectiveness of organizations, as shown in Figure 1.1. Employee productivity is a critical factor that must be monitored, and organizations also must maintain some level of employee satisfaction in order to keep a work force. Attendance and retention are important because lateness, absences, and turnover can be very costly. An organization cannot survive and compete unless its employees improve and learn how to adapt to new forces. Finally, organizations should not want to manage in a way that threatens or damages the physical and mental health of its members.

These indicators of effectiveness spell the difference between success and failure. Yet managers cannot change any of these factors easily—productivity or job satisfaction does not improve because a manager wants them to. However, many factors that affect the different dimensions of effectiveness can be manipulated. For example, the organization structure can be changed, different performance appraisal approaches may be implemented, or leadership styles can be modified. Such actions change the odds that an organization will be effective.

THE BUILDING BLOCKS OF ORGANIZATIONS

To manage effectively, it is necessary to be knowledgeable about organizations, individuals, and groups.

The Organization. We explain some of the broader forces which affect human behavior patterns in organizations in three chapters. Chapter 2 describes the different types of organizational structures within which people work and how these structures are affected by the organization's relevant environment. The organization's culture is discussed in Chapter 3, and in Chapter 18 there is discussion of the effects of the broader cultural differences on individuals, groups, and organizations.

The Individual. Some essential aspects of people such as personality, perception, attitudes, and judgment are the topics of Chapters 4 and 5. In Chapter 6, we move the person into the work organization and examine the choice of career and the way individuals adjust to work. Chapter 7 is a discussion of several important theories of work motivation. Then, in Chapter 9 we show some of the problems that stress at work might create. Many issues are raised in this chapter about the importance of work to individuals and how the work setting can result in serious psychological and physiological reactions.

Groups. Individuals work with other people, and they are affected by them. The way that groups are formed and developed is discussed in Chapter 10. Chapter 11 shows how groups can affect individuals in them and how individuals affect groups.

MANAGERIAL PROCESSES

Managers do a variety of things to achieve organization effectiveness. Chapter 8 shows how managers can use the motivational theories discussed earlier. Communication is discussed in Chapter 12. In Chapter 13, we cover decision making from the perspective of individuals and groups. In Chapter 14, the causes of conflict and its resolution are discussed.

Ways that managers exercise power and influence are examined in Chapters 15 and 16. Power and political process are discussed in Chapter 15. Leadership is the subject of Chapter 16, which flows logically from the discussion of power and politics. The subject of Chapter 17 is organizational change and development. In it we describe ways that managers may attempt to change organization practices and member behavior when there is a need to do so.

A HISTORICAL OVERVIEW OF ORGANIZATIONAL BEHAVIOR

Organizational behavior began to emerge as a distinct area of research and academic specialization in the late 1950s and early 1960s. Since then, a somewhat unified body of knowledge and thinking has developed that falls under the general label **organizational behavior**, or **OB**. The study of organizational behavior developed from a convergence of several streams of management thinking and writing. Psychologists, sociologists, anthropologists, and other scientists studied worker and management problems from a behavioral perspective before 1960, and managers were concerned with human problems before then. But there is an important difference between then and now. Contemporary organizational behavior draws on several different perspectives and attempts to integrate them into a comprehensive body of knowledge.

ANTECEDENTS OF CONTEMPORARY ORGANIZATIONAL BEHAVIOR

Human beings have been concerned with effective ways to organize people and manage them since the dawn of civilization, but most thinking and writing was done in the context of political science, military theory, or religion [17]. Less attention was paid to the management of commercial activities in ancient times, perhaps because they were not the large-scale endeavors of the military, political, and religious organizations of the day.

The development of economic sciences and management practices began around the start of the seventeenth century. The Industrial Revolution and Adam Smith's writing on political economy are key marker events, particularly for most Western management thinkers. While there may be some debate about when serious thinking about management problems began, it is very clear that it became more important when the economic sectors of societies throughout the world became larger and more complicated.

Contemporary organizational behavior can trace its roots to the late nineteenth and early twentieth century. Four primary groups of ideas were very important forces in the formation of management theories and application: (1) the scientific management approach, (2) administrative theory, (3) industrial psychology, and (4) the human relations perspective.

The Scientific Management Approach. The **scientific management approach** focused on the lowest level of the organization—the worker and the boss. The basic question addressed was, "How can the job be designed most efficiently?" Many people were associated with the beginnings of scientific management, but the most prominent was Frederick W. Taylor—he was to become the "father of scientific management." Born to a well-to-do Philadelphia family but unable to complete college because of poor eyesight, Taylor took a job in industry as an apprentice at the Midvale Steel Company in 1878. He quickly rose through the ranks to become chief engineer in 1884 at the age of 28. Based on his experiences and studies, Taylor developed many ideas to increase efficiency and became widely sought as a consultant to other firms. His ideas, when applied, met with considerable success. Some of the more important ideas from the work of Taylor and others who pioneered scientific management are:

1. Current management practice was inefficient.
2. Management must adopt the scientific method in industry.
3. Specialization should be practiced.
4. Planning and scheduling are essential.
5. Proper selection should be done.
6. The standard method for a job should be found.
7. Standard times for each task should be established.
8. Wage incentives should be utilized.

The application of scientific management resulted in significant productivity increases. In the well-known shoveling experiment, Taylor found that the optimum-size shovel for handling material carried about 21 pounds of material. He was able to increase productivity from 16 to 59 tons of material shoveled per day while the number of shovelers needed per day was decreased from 500 to 140.

Such results were typical when scientific management was applied, and they led to a strong advocacy of scientific management methods. The analysis and redesign of work were widely applied in industry. As Daniel Bell says of this movement:

> . . . The prophet of modern work was Frederick W. Taylor, and the stopwatch was his rod. If any social upheaval can ever be attributed to one man, the logic of efficiency as a mode of life is due to Taylor. With "scientific management," as formulated by Taylor in 1893, we pass far beyond the old, rough computations of the division of labor and more into the division of time itself. . . . [4].

The emphasis on specialization, however, was to become one of the targets of critics of scientific management. They argued, as we will see, that specialization was ultimately inefficient but, more importantly, it did not allow people to achieve their full potential at work.

Administrative Theory. By the late 1920s, another perspective on management problems emerged. A number of writers began to analyze the work of managers and called their ideas **administrative theory**, which is concerned with understanding the basic task of management and developing guidelines, or principles, about how to manage effectively. Important ideas about managing that belong to the administrative school are (1) principles of management, (2) an emphasis on objectives, and (3) the functions of management. These became points of attack for critics of administrative theory.

Principles of management are general guides to handling problems that an executive encounters in work situations. They tell a manager what to do when faced with problems of designing an organization, making decisions, or dealing with people. One of the earliest and most important writers who developed these ideas was Henri Fayol (13). Fayol was a French businessman who wrote about effective management from his own experience. He differentiated management activities from technical activities, pointing out that managerial activities increased in importance and technical activities decreased in importance as one moved from the lowest to the highest level of an organization.

Fayol proposed 14 principles of management. He stressed the importance of specialization of labor to make the best use of human resources, although he warned that this could be carried too far. Principles of management were developed for nearly every phase of the managerial task. There were principles of leadership, of objectives, of single accountability, of unity, of command, of equity, and of exception. Drawn from real-world experiences, they were meant to facilitate high performance.

Principles can be, of course, useful guides to action. They give the manager somewhere to start when faced with a problem, and if they are not viewed too rigidly, they can be very helpful in finding a solution. Charles Perrow has said:

> Though the . . . theory was derided for presenting principles that were only proverbs, all the resources of organization theory and research have not managed to substitute better principles (or proverbs) for those ridiculed. . . . These principles have worked and are still working, for they address themselves to the very real problems of management [36].

An emphasis on objectives is another major theme of administrative theory. This emphasis is required to develop a rational relationship among organization activities. When goals are clearly defined and stated, other resources can be arranged in such a way as to maximize the possibility of attainment. Managers, the administrative theorists believed, would be able to select the best alternative from those available only when goals were known. Fayol and other administrative theorists stressed designing an organization in a rational and systematic way and then fitting individuals to it.

Management functions are those activities that all executives perform in whole or in part. The administrative theorists did the most extensive early analysis of the managerial functions of *planning*, *organizing*, and *controlling*. *Planning* is the determining, in advance of activity execution, what factors are required to achieve goals. The planning function defines the objective and determines what resources are necessary. *Organizing* is the function of acquiring and assembling resources in the proper relation to each other to achieve objectives. *Controlling* is ensuring that activities, when carried out, conform to plans, so that objectives are achieved.

Industrial Psychology. Around 1900, at about the same time that the scientific management movement began to gain impetus, **industrial psychology** began its growth. The driving initial force in this discipline was Hugo Munsterberg. Munsterberg's work was directed at finding the most effective and productive relationship between human and physical resources. According to Daniel Wren, a historian of management:

> Munsterberg's *Psychology and Industrial Efficiency* was directly related to Taylor's proposals and contained three broad parts: (1) "The best possible man," (2) "The best possible work," and (3) "The best possible effect. . . ." Munsterberg outlined

definite proposals for the use of tests in worker selection, for the application of research on learning in training industrial personnel, and for the study of psychological techniques which increased workers' motives and reduced fatigue. . . .

Taylor and others . . . had envisioned contributions from psychologists for research in the human factor. Munsterberg fitted into this scheme, and the ethic of scientific management was readily apparent in (1) the focus on the individual, (2) the emphasis on efficiency, and (3) the social benefits to be derived from the application of the scientific method [51].

An early success of industrial psychology was personnel selection for the U.S. Army in World War I. Faced with the problem of drafting, inducting, and placing millions of men, the Army sought the assistance of the American Psychological Association. A group of psychologists under the leadership of Walter Dill Scott responded [26]. To cope with the selection problem, the army Alpha Test was developed, and it proved "extremely valuable in placing draftees and is estimated to have saved . . . millions of dollars" [33].

After World War I, what had been learned and used for the military was applied in the private sector. Companies became increasingly concerned with personnel management problems. Sweeping changes in labor legislation in the 1930s increased management's concern with cost reduction through both industrial engineering and industrial psychology.

World War II had another major impact on industrial psychology. The same selection and placement problems of World War I existed, but by now psychologists had developed refined techniques to improve these processes. For instance, screening instruments were used to predict the probability of success at completing different types of military training. Because of the large-scale production effort to produce defense materials during World War II under conditions where workers had been lost to the armed services, new techniques for training employees had to be developed.

One of the more important results of World War II for psychology was the growth of interest in leadership. Major research projects were undertaken at Ohio State University and the University of Michigan in the late 1940s that have set the tone of research and theory to this date.

The Human Relations Perspective.   In the early years of the scientific management movement, behavioral scientists, like Munsterberg, were concerned with problems such as worker fatigue, boredom, and job design. Quite a different behavioral perspective emerged after the Hawthorne experiments at Western Electric in the late 1920s, which gave rise to the **human relations perspective** [40].

The Hawthorne experiments were carried out in the Hawthorne plant of Western Electric, an AT&T subsidiary in Cicero, Illinois. The Hawthorne Studies, started in 1927, were prompted by an experiment that was carried out by the company's engineers between 1924 and 1927. The engineers, in the best tradition of scientific management, were seeking the answers to industrial questions through research. They studied two groups of workers to determine the effects of different levels of illumination on worker performance. In one group the level of illumination was changed, while in the other it was not. They found that when illumination was increased, the level of performance increased. But productivity also increased when the level of illumination decreased, even down to the level of moonlight. Moreover, productivity also increased in the control group. These results seemed contrary to reason, and so the engineers examined other factors that might have affected the results. The workers were responding in a way that they thought the experimenters wanted and because they were the center of attention. The researchers concluded that how people were treated made an important difference in performance. Obviously the subjects were responding not to the level of light, but to the experiment itself and to their involvement in it. Since that time, this effect in research has been known as the Hawthorne Effect.

The studies that followed the experiment were conducted by a team of researchers headed by Elton Mayo and F.J. Roethlisberger, from Harvard University. They did several studies in the Hawthorne plant. One was a two-year study of a relay assembly group, in which they systematically varied working conditions. They found that no matter what changes were made, productivity increased. A second relay assembly study which examined the effects of wage incentives on performance led to the conclusion, perhaps unwisely, that group competition, not pay incentives, led to better performance. During a long-term interview research program, the researchers sought to delve more deeply into the causes of worker productivity through careful, in-depth discussions with employees. The researchers found that morale was improved when workers could air grievances, that complaints are often not objective statements of fact, and that worker satisfaction is influenced by how workers see themselves relative to others. Finally, the significant effects of work groups on performance and attitudes were demonstrated in the bank wiring room study.

The Hawthorne studies seemed to point out the importance of leadership practices and work-group pressures on employee satisfaction and performance. They downgraded the importance of economic incentives in worker motivation and stressed the importance of recognizing that employees react to a whole complex of forces, rather than to one factor alone.

Both the research methods and the conclusions of the Hawthorne studies have been questioned [5, 6, 22, 45]. For instance, it is said that the research had a management bias, striving to increase productivity without regard to the welfare of workers. Criticism has also been leveled at the research method, that results were misinterpreted [15]. For example, in the second relay assembly study, production actually increased with incentives, yet the researchers concluded that group rivalry was the cause. Some questioned the conclusion that management and workers have similar rather than contradictory objectives. Regardless of the merit of the criticisms, the research at Hawthorne had a significant impact on thinking about management problems. It provided the impetus for critics of the scientific management movement to argue that it was fruitless to attempt to develop a science of management without taking the human factor into account.

CONTEMPORARY ORGANIZATIONAL BEHAVIOR

In the late 1950s, three threads of change began to develop that were to be the basis of contemporary organization behavior. These were (1) criticisms of scientific management, (2) an attack on the administrative theory approach, and (3) changes in management education.

1. *Criticisms of Scientific Management.* Many felt that scientific management approaches were deficient [2, 30]. They argued that the rigid job specifications, rules, and polices that resulted from the assumptions and analytical methods of scientific management stifled the creativity, growth, development, and general effectiveness of the human side of the organization. Such restrictions on human activity, they said, were unproductive. More important, some felt that both scientific management and the administrative theory perspective failed to deal with ways to integrate the interests of workers with those of management, that scientific management approaches fostered divisiveness between management and workers.

2. *The Attack on Administrative Theory.* In the late 1950s and the 1960s, the management principles approach came under severe criticism from a new group of management writers. Critics such as March and Simon attacked these principles, calling them "proverbs" because they were based on observation, not research [28]. Management principles were also criticized because they were not consistent with other principles and because they were too rigid. Some critics rejected the principles approach because, they argued, principles told managers the "one best way" to manage and there was no one best way. This criticism is, of course, hollow, since there is no one best way to do anything. Proponents of the principles approach had recognized that not all cases would fall within the guidelines they prescribed, but critics generally failed to note these reservations. This attack on the management principles approach was an important stimulus to the development of current management approaches, and particularly to what we now call organizational behavior.

3. *Changes in Management Education.* A profound change also occurred in the approach to teaching management in university schools of business administration. In 1959 the Carnegie Report and the Gordon and Howell Report, both on business education, provided pressures for increased training and emphasis on quantitative analysis, organization theory, and human relations [38, 51].

   After publication of these reports, there was much less emphasis on functional areas such as marketing, finance, and accounting, though these functional and skill areas are still extremely important. The focus shifted toward the underlying disciplines of mathematics and psychology and those of functional areas [38].

Two distinct but related behavioral approaches resulted. One is a focus on organizations as the unit of analysis, called organization theory, in which individuals and groups are not prominent in the analysis. Organizational behavior is the second focus that flowed from the flux in the field, wherein the individual and the group are the main object of study, not organizations. Our view of contemporary organizational behavior contains both these perspectives.

Organization Theory. **Organization theory** is concerned with how an organization could be designed to operate more effectively to achieve objectives in a "rational" way. These theorists look at organization problems rather than at individual problems. This broad view was reflected in the work of Max Weber [49]. This German sociologist, whose emphasis was on bureaucracy, was an important influence on writing and theory about the study of organization. Weber's analysis considered organizations as part of a broader society. He described the characteristics of the bureaucracy, a form or organization that uses extensive formal rules and procedures to govern the job behavior of organization members. Weber felt that bureaucracy emphasized predictability of behavior and results and showed greater stability over time. He suggested that organizations naturally evolved toward this rational form.

Chester Barnard had a significant effect on organization theory [3]. Barnard developed the concept of the "informal organization" more fully and added much to the thinking about organizations with such concepts as "the linking pin," "the zone of indifference," and "the acceptance theory of authority."

Using concepts from Barnard, March and Simon integrated psychology, sociology, and economic theory in their book *Organizations* [28]. They felt that the existing research and theory about organization and management were inadequate, points that we have already made. March and Simon extended the Barnard view of the organization as a social system. Following Barnard, they presented a more elaborate motivational theory than the scientific management writers and the administrative theory writers. This approach emphasized individual decision making.

A very important development in the study of organizations is contingency theory. **Contingency theory** is based upon the idea that the management approach must be tailored to the situation. Critics of the administrative and scientific management theorists were correct when they said that there is no best way to manage, that "it all depended." But the critics never really told anyone how to proceed to develop a proper managerial strategy. It did all depend— but on what? Some of the answers began to emerge from a study of the Tennessee Valley Authority by Selznick [43]. In *TVA and the Grass Roots* he showed that the structure of any organization is affected by outside restraints, so that the organization develops both formal and informal systems that help it to adapt to the outside environment and thus to survive.

In 1961, Burns and Stalker published a study of British industry [36]. They found differences in the structures of the firms and traced these differences to the nature of the technology used and to the markets served. When the technological and market environments were uncertain, they found a loose organization. When the environment was more predictable, a traditional bureaucracy seemed to be more effective. Burns and Stalker specified more precisely than ever before what the internal structure should look like, given a certain kind of environment.

Another English study reported by Woodward, following the Burns and Stalker model, showed that the type of organizational structure used was related to a firm's economic performance when type of technology was taken into account [50].

Lawrence and Lorsch studied a highly effective and a less effective organization in three different environments, which differed with respect to rate of technological change for the products they produced, the production methods used, and environmental uncertainty [24]. In general, they concluded that organizations in a stable environment are more effective if they have more detailed procedures and a more centralized decision-making process, while organizations in an unstable environment should have decentralization, participation, and less emphasis on rules and standard procedures to be effective.

Organizational Behavior. Some of the early contributors to contemporary organizational behavior are Douglas McGregor, Chris Argyris, Rensis Likert, Ralph Stogdill, and Lyman Porter. Although others helped forge the discipline of organizational behavior as we know it today, the work of these scholars deserves special mention.

Douglas McGregor, in *The Human Side of Enterprise*, said that most managers make incorrect assumptions about those who work for them [30]. He called these assumptions, collectively, Theory X. **Theory X** assumed that people were lazy, that personal goals ran counter to the organization's, and that because of this, people had to be controlled externally. In a work context, this meant close supervision and guidance so that management could ensure high performance. **Theory Y** assumptions were based on greater trust in others. Human beings were more mature, self-motivated, and self-controlled than Theory X assumed. McGregor suggested that there was little need for either rigid organization or interpersonal controls.

Chris Argyris [1, 2] also made a strong case for reducing the amount of organizational control. He believed that many constraints placed by organization structure on human beings were self-defeating to organizational goals of effectiveness and efficiency. The thrust of his argument, along with McGregor's, is that the bureaucratic form of organization is incongruent with the basic needs of the healthy individual and that it treats lower organizational members like children. This fosters dependence and leads to the frustration of the highest-order human needs. This frustration expresses itself in lack of work involvement and antiorganizational activities such as sabotage.

In 1961 Rensis Likert, a psychologist, published *New Patterns of Management*, a book that was to have a powerful impact on thinking about human problems of management. Likert believed that "managers with the best record of performance in American business and government [were] in the process of pointing the way to an appreciably more effective system of management than now exists" [25]. He proposed that leaders (or managers) would be most effective using a supportive approach. This means that they must create a work environment in which the individual sees his "experiences (in terms of his values, goals, expectations and aspirations) as contributing to and maintaining his sense of personal worth and importance" [25]. Likert went on to detail the characteristics of managers and organizations that would be "supportive" to individuals and, hence, organizationally effective.

Another leadership researcher and psychologist, Ralph Stogdill, formulated a broad-ranging theory of individual behavior and group achievement [44]. Stogdill was one of the first to skillfully blend the results of social science research with some of the theories of administrative and scientific management.

Lyman Porter reported an important line of research beginning in the early 1960s [37]. This work examined how managers' needs, attitudes, and satisfactions were related to organization size, organization structure, and the nature of the position a person held. Porter's work is significant because it drew attention to the work setting and also demonstrated that such matters could be studied in a systematic, empirical way.

The work of these writers (and others whom we have not mentioned) is important because it broadened the scope of traditional behavioral approaches and introduced some of the critical factors that the scientific management writers and the administrative theorists had not addressed.

DEVELOPING KNOWLEDGE ABOUT ORGANIZATIONAL BEHAVIOR

Everyone has personal theories about how to manage or affect others, and these theories guide one's actions. For example, every professor has a theory about how to teach a class. It may be rather simple, such as, "Give the students challenging material, test them frequently, give them quick and accurate feedback, and they will learn." A manager may have a theory that workers perform better when they are highly paid. Both the professor and the manager probably developed their theories after many years of experience.

Student learning for the professor and worker performance for the manager are both dependent on other factors. For the student in the professor's theory, it is challenging work; for the manager, it is pay level for the workers. These can be changed or manipulated by the professor or the manager to affect performance. Challenge in the class can be high or low, depending on how difficult or easy the assignments are. Pay can be increased or decreased, or it can be tied to performance or not. In theory and research, those factors that can be manipulated are called **independent variables**, like class challenge or pay. Those factors that are the outcomes (performance or learning) are called **dependent variables**.

The difference between a manager and a researcher/theorist isn't (or shouldn't be) that the manager lacks interest in theory and research while a researcher has such an interest—it should be only that they do these things differently. Both must be systematic, cautious, and thoughtful about their observations and conclusions because both want to get the right answer.

THEORY AND ORGANIZATIONAL BEHAVIOR

Formulating a theory is a way of organizing knowledge about something. A **theory** is an abstraction of real life, a way of defining a system into variables and their relationships. It is a set of interrelated concepts, definitions, and propositions about relationships between the concepts. In this section we describe how theory is developed, tested, and changed. We will show this

17

process using the example of Management by Objectives (MBO) and goal setting, two very basic and popular concepts in organizational behavior. We have chosen these concepts because a broad, well-developed set of studies spanning over 25 years of organizational behavior history exists which illustrate the points nicely.

Developing Theoretical Concepts. A theory begins with a person observing some phenomena. These observations may be very imprecise, only the casual observations of an interested individual. From these observations, concepts or constructs emerge to help the person understand what is going on. A **concept (construct)** is a mental image, formed after observations have been made. It is developed after careful study of some phenomena. In the physical sciences "atom," "molecule," and "gravity" are examples of concepts. In the behavioral sciences "achievement needs," "self-esteem," "intelligence," and "status" are examples. Concepts are necessary to make sense of the world.

In a theory, concepts are tentatively related to other concepts. These tentative relationships are called **hypotheses**, conditional predictions about the relationship between two concepts or variables. They state how the concepts in a theory are related and form the basis for research efforts to test and refine the theory.

EARLY FORMULATIONS OF GOAL SETTING AND MANAGEMENT BY OBJECTIVES

A widely used and important concept in organizational behavior is that of a goal. A goal is some desired end state, someplace a person wants to be or a state he or she would like to attain. Much has been written on the importance of goals to managing effectively. One approach is Management by Objectives. In the mid-1950s, Peter Drucker wrote that he had observed that good, effective managers set specific goals for their subordinates and used them for performance appraisal [10]. Others, like McGregor and Odiorne, followed and expanded the ideas about how goals were related to performance [29, 34]. In the very popular book, *Management by Objectives*, Odiorne set out the definition and principles of MBO. Management by Objectives is a process in which managers and subordinates jointly identify common goals, define each individual's area of responsibility in terms of results expected, and use these measures as guides for assessing performance [34].

Management by Objectives is a complicated organizational process, but its key element is mutual goal setting and its effects are positive organizational outcomes. As described by these writers, it is not a theory in the strict sense of the term, but it is a loosely structured formulation of how performance can be affected by goals.

☐ **EARLY FORMULATIONS**
  OF GOAL SETTING . . .

In 1968, Locke reported a number of studies that he had done with others on the relationship of goals to performance [27]. From these studies and other work, he advanced a more formal theoretical statement, in which goal setting plays a very important part. He proposed an explanation of why goal setting works and what characteristics of goals are related to performance (see Chapters 7 and 8).

Testing Hypotheses. Once hypotheses are formed they can be tested. The results are used to accept or refute the hypotheses. To identify the nature of the relationship between two or more concepts, they must be put into operational terms and measured. But many concepts are quite difficult to measure. Consider intelligence. How is it to be measured? Performance on several problems with different levels of difficulty might be one way of operationalizing it. The concept of status might be measured by obtaining rankings of groups by members of other groups, by observing communication patterns, or by noting who influences whom.

☐ **SEVERAL HYPOTHESES**
  ABOUT THE EFFECTS OF GOALS

Odiorne's definition of MBO contains a number of suggestions about how goals are related to performance and individual responses [34]. These are easily translated into hypotheses that can be tested in research. Several studies have examined hypotheses about how goals are related to performance. One of these studies, by Carroll and Tosi, tested several hypotheses about goal setting suggested by the early writings about MBO [8]. Among those hypotheses tested were:

1. Goal clarity is related to higher performance.
2. Goal difficulty is related to higher performance.
3. Feedback about goal achievement is related to higher performance.
4. Participation in goal setting leads to higher performance and higher satisfaction.

Research often fails to support a theory because of weak concepts or because the operationalization of those concepts is inadequate or insufficient. The concept, as conceived in a theory, may be broader, richer, and more complex than the measurements to convert it into operational terms. This can be seen in the example below of the way "goal" has been operationalized in research.

If the hypothesis is correct, then the researcher would expect to find a certain relationship between concepts and variables. The researcher states—in the form of an hypothesis—what the theory predicts. The researcher then designs a study and research instruments, collects and analyzes data, and comes to certain conclusions about the validity of the hypothesis. The results may confirm or disprove the hypothesis. If the hypothesis is confirmed, it stays in the theory. If it is disproved, then the theory should be revised if the research was executed properly and if other research continues to provide evidence that disproves the hypothesis.

☐ OPERATIONALIZING GOALS

The different ways that goals have been studied illustrates the problem of measuring a concept. In some studies, a goal is conceived of as an assigned level of performance. Locke, for example, studied goals in an experimental laboratory [27]. To differentiate between the level of goal specificity, he had groups of students work on an addition task. They were to work simple addition problems and told to "do their best." Later all these subjects came back for further problem solving. Some were told again to "do your best," while others were given specific goals; for example, to solve 20 problems. This is one way to conceptualize the difference between general and specific goals.

Another approach to measuring goals was taken by Carroll and Tosi [8]. They asked a group of managers on a questionnaire to respond to the following questions:

1. To what extent were your performance goals clearly stated with respect to the results expected?
2. To what extent were your self-improvement goals clearly stated to you?

The managers responded in a five-point scale that ranged from "to a very great degree" to "not at all clearly stated." The responses to these two items were added together. A high score meant that a manager had "clear goals" and a low score meant that goals were "ambiguous."

Theory Revision.   When a properly tested hypothesis is disconfirmed, this suggests that the theory needs to be revised. However, results might be either positive or negative for many reasons other than that they represent the reality of the situation. All types of errors can creep in, such as weak concepts, poor measurements, bad design, and so forth. But there are ways to solve these problems, and if they are solved, a theory should be revised when there is a substantial amount of disconfirming evidence.

☐ A QUESTIONABLE HYPOTHESIS ABOUT PARTICIPATION

One important hypothesis about goals had to do with subordinate participation in goal setting. It was expected from the work of Odiorne and others [10, 29, 34] that managers who participated in setting goals would do better and have higher levels of job satisfaction than those who did not participate. Carroll and Tosi tested this hypothesis and found that subordinate participation in setting goals was not related to higher levels of perceived goal success or more favorable attitudes toward a superior or toward Management by Objectives [8]. Other researchers reached a similar conclusion [23].

☐ RECONSIDERATION OF THE ROLE OF PARTICIPATION IN GOAL SETTING

The evidence showing that participation in goal setting seemed to be less important than originally thought by Drucker, McGregor and Odiorne surprised Carroll and Tosi [8, 10, 29, 35].

When research results do not support a theory, at least two alternatives exist. One is to eliminate participation from the theory; the other is to attempt to explain why these results occurred by modifying the theory.

As originally formulated, the best hypothesis to test was that participation in all goals was desirable. This was not supported by Carroll and Tosi [8]. Further, other work that was not consistent with the hypothesis was done in laboratory settings [23]. Tosi, Rizzo, and Carroll have suggested a possible modification of the participation hypothesis [47]. They suggest participation might be effective in some work settings, but not in others. They suggested participation in goal setting was required when a person's job had certain characteristics:

1. The subordinate has high control and discretion over the work.
2. The subordinate is more competent in the task than the superior.

RESEARCH APPROACHES IN ORGANIZATIONAL BEHAVIOR

Research is only a way to view experiences in a systematic, logical, and controlled fashion to increase the likelihood that the conclusion drawn about a relationship between concepts is correct. Consistent research findings from several different techniques provide a basis for strong corroboration of a theory.

In this section we examine techniques for studying organizational behavior, using the concepts of goal setting and MBO, to show that a particular problem can be studied in many different ways.

Laboratory Research.   In **laboratory research**, the investigator attempts to minimize the effects of extraneous factors irrelevant to the problem by isolating the research setting from the ordinary situation in which the problem occurs. Then the variables are carefully manipulated under controlled conditions to determine their effect.

For instance, one way of studying how difficult goals affect job performance would be to ask a group of workers or managers how difficult their work goals are and then relate their answers to how well they do their job. But a person might respond to the question, "How difficult are your work goals?" in different ways. For example, does the person understand what is meant by "difficult" or "work goals"? The intent of the researcher might be, "Did your boss require you to produce 20 percent above standard for this week?" Perhaps the person interprets the question as meaning, "In general, how hard is your job?" To eliminate problems such as this, it may be desirable to perform the research in a laboratory. The laboratory study on goal setting, described in the following boxed insert, attempted to minimize such problems.

The most obvious criticisms of laboratory research are that (1) it is an artificial setting, (2) it generally uses subjects who are not representative of the group to whom we would wish to apply the results, and (3) the tasks are contrived, routine, simple, and meaningless. But there are some important advantages to work done in the laboratory. Situations can be isolated, and variables can be manipulated and controlled more easily than out of the laboratory. The researcher can come much closer to controlling conditions so as to eliminate the impact of extraneous factors, those other than the independent variables being manipulated.

Field Research.   Often the same kind of manipulation described under laboratory research is possible outside the laboratory, where the research is called a field experiment, as opposed to the field study in which there is no attempt made to control any variables. In a **field study**, the variables are observed to determine how they are related to one another. Field studies are perhaps the most common type of studies reported in the organizational behavior research literature. They can be defined as "ex post facto scientific inquiries aimed at discovering the relations and interactions among sociological [and] psychological . . . variables in real social structures" [21]. The researcher looks at sets of variables and how they are related to one another, generally at one point in time, using statistical measures of association such as correlation, difference tests, and analysis of variance.

In **field experiments**, the research is carried out in the actual setting instead of in a laboratory environment. However, some experimental controls may be present. In a field experiment, the researcher is able to systematically vary a condition in one setting while keeping it constant (to the extent possible) in another setting. Doing a field experiment requires that there be some identifiable and measurable change in the situation, some way to measure the

☐ STUDYING GOALS
IN THE LABORATORY

A laboratory study was done by Latham and Steele [23] to examine the motivational effects of goal setting on performance. The subjects were 72 college students who were assigned to one of six groups. These groups represented the experimental manipulation, or the different conditions that were to be studied. One condition was the nature of participation in goal setting (participative, assigned, do best), and the second was the nature of decision-making participation. This design is shown below.

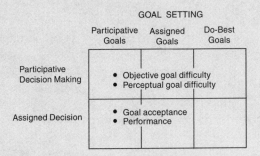

Here is how these conditions were made to differ. Those in participative decision-making groups decided how they would perform the experimental task, building a toy. They decided which of several toys to produce, how it was to be produced, and when to schedule breaks for the group. Those in the assigned decision groups were told which toy to make, how to make it, and when to take rest breaks.

The goal-setting condition was also varied. The participative goal group was asked to set their own difficult, specific, but attainable goals about how many toys would be produced. The assigned goal group was instructed how many toys to produce, and the do best groups were told, "Do as well as you can." The dependent variables in the study were goal acceptance and performance.

change, and some way to test hypotheses by comparing the results in the "experimental" case to results in a "control" situation [42].

The major problem with field research is that factors other than those that are being studied may affect the findings. There are many possible factors beyond the control and awareness of the researcher that may systematically bias the results. The real-world setting, however, gives field research a credibility for applications to problems far beyond that done in laboratory settings. This is especially true, we think, for research in organizational behavior, which must ultimately be translated into real-world application to be useful.

☐ A FIELD STUDY ON GOAL SETTING ───────────

One of the most extensive field studies on MBO was reported in an article by Tosi, Hunter, Chesser, Tartar, and Carroll [46]. They conducted this field study in the Black and Decker Company, a manufacturer of power tools and Tenneco, a large conglomerate. Over a hundred managers were surveyed by questionnaire in each company at three different times. The questionnaire contained measures of goal difficulty, goal clarity, participation in goal setting, satisfaction with work, satisfaction with MBO, perceived success at goal achievement, and several personality variables such as self-esteem and initiative.

When the data were collected, the scores to each of these measures were computed and correlated with one another. From this analysis, the authors were able to draw conclusions about how, for example, goal clarity was related to perceived success in the achievement of goals.

☐ A FIELD
EXPERIMENT ON GOAL SETTING ───────────

Erez, Early, and Hulin reported a field experiment on the effects of participation in goal setting and performance [12]. They divided workers in an animal laboratory into two groups. In one group, the employees jointly developed a method for monitoring the animals on a daily basis. When this was finished, they reached a consensus about a goal for the task. In the other group, which performed the same task, the goals were assigned to the workers.

Integrating Research Findings.   Consistent research findings from several studies, using different techniques, provide a basis for corroboration of the hypotheses in a theory. Sometimes, however, inconsistent findings emerge when the same concepts are researched. For example, some studies will show that degree of participation is related to goal acceptance, whereas others will show that it is not. One way to make sense out of a large body of research is to integrate the results with a technique called meta-analysis. **Meta-analysis** is a way to aggregate knowledge from several studies by counting the statistically significant findings, and then averaging statistical results [19]. Meta-analysis has been applied to MBO and goal-setting research. After analysis of several studies on goal setting, Guzzo, Jenne, and Katzell found that it had a positive effect on productivity [18]. Rodgers, Hunter, and Rogers analyzed the results of research on the relationship of MBO to job satisfaction and of studies about its relationship to productivity [39]. They concluded that the research showed both higher job satisfaction and higher productivity when MBO is implemented with top management support.

APPLICATION OF ORGANIZATIONAL RESEARCH

The ultimate question about the value of theory and research in organizational behavior is if it leads to improved levels of productivity, satisfaction, absenteeism, retention, learning, or member well-being (the effectiveness dimensions shown in Figure 1.1). An example of the way that research on MBO was used is reported by Carroll and Tosi [8]. When the initial data gathered in Black and Decker were analyzed, several things were found that were likely to hinder the effective utilization of MBO. As a result, a "diagnostic change program" was implemented. The objective was to increase the acceptance of MBO and improve the ways that managers used it. The change effort consisted of (1) feeding back the results of the research to the managers, (2) developing a more systematic approach to setting goals, and (3) changing the way goals were used in the evaluation process. As a result, there were several improvements. Goals were more clear to managers, and they sensed a much stronger level of top management support for the MBO effort. Similar useful and important applications of theory-supported research are reported elsewhere in this book, especially in Chapters 8 and 17. For example, positive reinforcement programs have produced some startling improvements in productivity; Total Quality Management (TQM) programs have been successful in improving quality levels in both manufacturing and service firms, and many firms have successfully become High Involvement Organizations.

SUMMARY

Organizational behavior is the study of human action in organizations. It is a systematic analysis of individual and group processes and characteristics. The objective of organizational behavior is to understand, predict, and improve the performance of individuals and organizations.

While concern with managing people is as old as human history, it is only recently that organizational behavior (OB) has been considered a separate field of study. Prior to the late 1950s, concern about managing human factors was found in writings on scientific management, administrative theory, industrial psychology, and the human relations approach. These writings were not based on solid research from the behavioral sciences, however, and the prescriptions for action made by many of the authors at this time were questionable to many. In the late 1950s, an evaluation of what was being taught in university schools of business administration pointed out the need for bringing to the attention of prospective managers information from the basic behavioral science disciplines, such as psychology, in addition to an improved understanding of mathematics. It was felt that answers to questions about the best way to manage human beings in organizational settings would be found through systematic research using the scientific method. This research should focus on individuals, groups, and organizations and how they interact to determine behavior in organizations. The field of organizational behavior then evolved. This field is a body of knowledge, still incomplete, derived from the research process of developing theory and theoretical concepts, developing hypotheses from these, testing these hypotheses, and then revising the theory as necessary. This book is an introduction to the present state of knowledge in this field, obviously being selective in what is covered, given the limitations of time and space.

☐ KEY CONCEPTS

Administrative theory	Hypotheses	Organization theory
Concept (construct)	Independent variables	Principles of management
Contingency theories	Industrial psychology	Scientific management approach
Dependent variables	Laboratory research	Theory
Field experiments	Management functions	Theory X
Field research	Meta-analysis	Theory Y
Field studies	Organizational behavior	
Human relations perspective		

☐ STUDY QUESTIONS

1. Our discussion of antecedents of management thinking begins with the period around 1900. It is obvious that there was much thinking about this subject before then. What are some early sources about organizing and managing people that you know about?
2. What would be the difference in a person's managerial approach if it was guided by scientific management principles as compared to being guided by concepts from organizational behavior?
3. What are the critical elements in the "administrative theory approach"?
4. What are the main forces that gave impetus to the development of current thinking about organizational behavior and management?
5. What are the differences between organizational theory and organizational behavior? Is this a useful distinction in studying organizations? In managing them?
6. Some think that managers should know about research and theory so that they can be intelligent consumers of it. What are some other reasons?

STUDY . . .

7. What are some hypotheses that you have about human behavior? Look in the index to determine if any of these topics are discussed in this book.
8. How would you test your hypotheses about human behavior?
9. What are the strengths and weaknesses of field studies and laboratory experiments?

CASE

TORONTO HOME BUILDERS: PART I

Glen Gannon wondered what he should do. Glen was a carpenter who, with one helper, has earned a reputation as a very skilled tradesman. He was happy in his work. He had control over his workday, which he liked because he could attend the various sports events in his hometown of Toronto, Canada. He was a follower of both the Toronto Blue Jays and the Toronto Argonauts. Two days ago, Kathy Mondlak called Glen to ask him if he would like to purchase Toronto Home Builders, Incorporated. Frank Mondlak, her father and the owner of Toronto Home Builders, died of a heart attack last month and she was anxious to sell the business to settle the estate. Toronto Home Builders, with its twenty-two workers, four trucks, several buildings, and equipment was a thriving business.

The chance to own his own company came at a lucky time for Glen. He could afford to buy Toronto Home Builders because his wife had recently inherited a relatively large sum of money and they were looking for a good investment. He liked the idea of investing in himself, but he worried about what this new job might require of him. He wondered if he would be happy in this new role. Could he get out to sports events as he did before? Certainly Frank Mondlak had never had time to really enjoy life. There was too much to consider.

QUESTIONS

1. If Glen buys Toronto Home Builders, how will his work change since he would now be a manager?
2. What are some of the inevitable personnel problems Glen is likely to experience if he buys Toronto Home Builders?
3. What are the things that Glen must manage if he wants to have an effective organization?

TORONTO HOME BUILDERS: PART II

In discussing the issue with his wife Betty, he realized that she had a great deal of fear about losing her inheritance if the business went sour. They decided that if the risk could be reduced by finding a partner they would buy the company.

Glen offered Doug Wilson, another carpenter and old friend, the opportunity to buy half of Toronto Home Builders. He knew that Doug, like he, was a competent carpenter and would be a valuable asset. He also knew that Doug could borrow the money needed for the investment from his parents.

QUESTION

1. What additional dimensions of organizational effectiveness does this partnership arrangement require?

TORONTO HOME BUILDERS: PART III

Glen and Doug decided to go ahead with the partnership, and they decided to specialize in home renovations including making houses bigger by building additions, installing outside decks, and installing new energy efficient windows. They began an aggressive effort to find new customers, primarily through ads in the local newspaper and handbills distributed in the Toronto area. Interest rates were low, home equity loans were becoming more popular, and many individuals found they could borrow money to make these home renovations. The business grew so fast that they had trouble keeping all the commitments they made to customers.

Glen began to work seven days a week and long hours each day. He had little time to go to the sports events he liked so much. He started to have a number of personnel problems . One of the most difficult problems was his partner, Doug. Doug was not as willing as Glen to work the long hours every day. He often showed up late on the job. Glen suspected this was because Doug, who drank heavily in the evening, had hangovers in the morning, making it tough to get started. There were also difficulties with the work force. Some of the carpenters, for example, often did not show up for work, forcing Glen and Doug to pitch in and do labor themselves. Glen believed that the problems with the carpenters were because (1) there was always work for them in the city and (2) some of them would take on individual projects of their own, for which they could earn more money than they were paid by Toronto Home Builders. Doug and Glen disagreed on how to handle the carpenters who failed to report to work. Glen thought he should be tough with them, while Doug was unwilling to criticize them when they were late or did not show up. Glen felt that he was being thought of by his employees as the "bad guy" while Doug was viewed as the "good guy".

TORONTO HOME BUILDERS . . .

The situation got worse as the problems continued. Doug and Glen had a number of heated arguments which resulted in Glen wanting to dissolve the partnership. The original partnership agreement was written to anticipate such a problem. It contained a clause that one could buy out the other by submitting an offer, in a letter, which was to be a price that the partner making the offer would agree to accept himself if the other refused to sell. Glen made an offer, and Doug accepted. He agreed to pay a lump sum amount, plus to continue to make annual payments to Doug for ten years, reflecting Doug's part in the development of Toronto Home Builders.

When the employees were informed of the agreement, six carpenters decided to leave Toronto Homes and start their own business. Glen was actually fairly happy about this since he decided that the remaining carpenters, managed correctly, could be as productive as the original 22, and if he could be more selective, taking the more profitable projects, profits might even improve.

Then the economic problems started. Over the next few years interest rates increased rapidly. This meant a significant drop in business for Toronto Home Builders. One problem was that Glen still owed Doug the regular payment to which they had agreed in the buyout. Glen had to cut back, which meant reducing the size of the work force. He wondered how he should go about laying off some of the carpenters. What factors should he consider in making such a decision? All of these problems were contributing to high stress for Glen. He found himself starting to yell at his wife and children more than he used to.

QUESTIONS

1. Based on Glen's responses to the various problems that he experienced, how would you describe his "theory of managing people?"
2. What dangers do you see for Glen from the stress he is experiencing? How is your answer here related to your own "theory" of dealing with stress?
3. Overall, what ideas about management and organizational behavior would have been useful to Glen to study before buying this business? Why?

REFERENCES

1. Argyris, C. *Personality and organization: The conflict between the system and the individual.* New York: Harper & Row, 1957.
2. Argyris, C. *Integrating the individual and the organization.* New York: John Wiley, 1964.

3. Barnard, C. *The functions of the executive.* Cambridge, MA: Harvard University Press, 1938.

4. Bell, D. *Work and its discontents. The cult of efficiency in America.* New York: League for Industrial Democracy, 1970.

5. Bendix, R., and Fisher, L.N. The perspectives of Elton Mayo. *Review of Economics And Statistics,* 1949, 31, 312-21.

6. Carey, A. The Hawthorne studies: A radical criticism. *American sociological Review,* 1967, 32, 408-16.

7. Carroll, S.J., and Schuler, R.S. Professional HRM: Changing functions and problems. In S.J. Carroll and R.S. Schuler, eds. *Human Resource Management in the 1980s.* Washington, D.C.: Bureau of National Affairs, 1983, 8-1 to 8-28.

8. Carroll, S.J., and Tosi, H.L. *Management by Objectives: Applications and research.* New York: Macmillan, 1973.

9. Davis, R.C. *The fundamentals of top management.* New York: Harper, 1951.

10. Drucker, P. *The practice of management.* New York: Harper, 1954.

11. Dyer, W.G., and Dyer, J.H. The M*A*S*H generation: Implications for future organization values. *Organization Dynamics,* 1984, 12, 66-79.

12. Erez, M., Early, P.C., and Hulin, C. The impact of participation on goal acceptance and participation. *The Academy of Management Journal,* 1985, 28(1), 50-66.

13. Fayol, H. *General and industrial management.* C. Storrs, trans. London: Sir Isaac Pitman & Sons, 1949.

14. Foulkes, F.K. *Personnel policies in large non-union companies.* Englewood Cliffs, NJ: Prentice-Hall 1980.

15. Franke, R., and Kaul, J. The Hawthorne experiments: First statistical interrelation. *American Sociological Review,* 1978, 43, 623-43.

16. Freeman, R., and Medoff, J. *What do unions do?* New York: Basic Books, 1984.

17. George, C.S. *The history of management thought.* Englewood Cliffs, NJ: Prentice-Hall, 1972.

18. Guzzo, R.A., Jenne, R.D. & Katzell, R.A. The effects of psychologically based intervention programs on worker productivity: A meta-analysis. *Personnel Psychology,* 1985, 38, 275-291.

19. Hunter, J.E., Schmidt, F.L., and Jackson, G.B. *Meta-analysis: Cumulating research findings across studies.* Beverly Hills, CA: Sage Publications, 1982.

20. Johnston, W.B., and Packer, A.E. *Workforce 2000: Work and workers for the 21st century.* Indianapolis, IN: Hudson Institute, 1987.

21. Kerlinger, F.N. *Foundations of behavioral research.* New York: Holt, Rinehart and Winston, 1986.

22. Kerr, C. What became of independent spirit? *Fortune,* 1953, 48, 110-11.

23. Latham, G.P., and Steele, T.P. The motivational effects of participation versus goal setting in performance. *Academy of Management Journal,* 1983, 3, 406-17.

24. Lawrence, P.R., and Lorsch, J.W. *Organization and environment: Managing differentiation and integration.* Homewood, IL: Richard D. Irwin, 1969.

25. Likert, R. *New patterns of management.* New York: McGraw-Hill, 1961.

26. Ling, C.C. *The management of personnel relations: History and origins.* Homewood, IL: Richard D. Irwin, 1965.

27. Locke, E.A. Toward a theory of task motivation and incentives. *Organization Behavior and Human Performance*, 1968, 3, 152-89.

28. March, G., and Simon, H. *Organizations*. New York: John Wiley, 1958.

29. McGregor, D. An uneasy look at performance appraisal. *Harvard Business Review*, 1957, 35, 89-94.

30. McGregor, D. *The human side of enterprise*. New York: McGraw-Hill, 1960.

31. Milbank, D. Here is one LBO deal where the workers became millionaires. *The Wall Street Journal*, October 27, 1992.

32. Miller, A. Joining the game: Some workers set up LBOs of their own and benefit greatly. *The Wall Street Journal*, December 12, 1988, A1(6).

33. Miner, J.B. *Personnel Psychology*. New York: Macmillan, 1969.

34. Odiorne, G.S. *Management by Objectives*. Los Angeles: Pitman, 1965.

35. Odiorne, G.S. HRM policy and program managements: A new look in the 1980s. In S.J. Carroll and R.S. Schuler, eds. *Human resource management in the 1980s*. Washington, D.C.: Bureau of National Affairs, 1983, 1,1–1,23.

36. Perrow, C. *Organizational analysis: A sociological view*. Belmont, CA: Wadsworth, 1970.

37. Porter, L.W. *Organizational patterns of managerial job attitudes*. New York: American Foundation for Management Research, 1964.

38. Porter, L.W., and McKibbin, L.E. *Management education and development: Drift or thrust into the 21st century*. New York: McGraw-Hill, 1988.

39. Rodgers, R., Hunter, J.E. & Rogers, D.L. Influence of top management commitment on Management by Objectives program success. *Journal of Applied Psychology*, 1993, 78, 151-155.

40. Roethlisberger, F.J., and Dickson, W.J. *Management and the worker*. Cambridge, MA: Harvard University Press, 1939.

41. Salancik, G.R., and Meindl, J.R. Corporate attributions as strategic illusions of management control. *Administrative Science Quarterly*, 1984, 29, 238-54.

42. Seashore, S.E. Field experiments in organizations. *Human Organization*, 1964, 23, 165-70.

43. Selznick, P. *TVA and the grass roots*. Berkeley: University of California Press, 1949.

44. Stogdill, R.M. *Individual behavior and group achievement*. New York: Oxford University Press, 1959.

45. Sykes, A.J.N. Economic interest and the Hawthorne researches. *Human Relations*, 1965, 18, 253-63.

46. Tosi, H.L., Hunter, J., Chesser, R., Tartar, J., and Carroll, S.J. How real are changes induced by Management by Objectives? *Administrative Science Quarterly*, 1976, 21, 278-305.

47. Tosi, H.L., Rizzo, J.R., & Carroll, S.J. Setting goals in Management by Objectives. *California Management Review*, 1970, 12(4), 70-78.

48. Waldman, D.A., and Avolio, B.M. A Meta-analysis of age differences in job performance. *Journal of Applied Psychology*, 1986. 71(1), 33-38.

49. Weber, M. *The theory of social and economic organization*. T. Parsons, trans. New York: Free Press, 1947.

50. Woodward, J. *Industrial organization*. London: Oxford University Press, 1965.

51. Wren, D. *The evolution of management thought*. New York: Ronald, 1972.

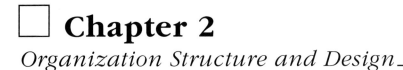

Chapter 2
Organization Structure and Design

The automotive divisions of Ford Motor Company, General Motors, Chrysler, Honda, Toyota, Fiat, and Volkswagen do exactly the same things—they design, manufacture, and sell automobiles. With few exceptions, probably unimportant, the same basic engineering technology is available to all of them. Further, within a similar price class, the basic mechanical configurations of cars, as well as the channels of distribution through which the cars are marketed, have very similar characteristics.

What is interesting is this: while the basic activities of these firms are very similar in terms of both the technological and market structure, these activities can be configured in different ways. This is the question of organization structure and design which is addressed in this chapter. For example, in these different companies, it is common that new product development is done by cross-functional teams which include design engineers, production engineers, manufacturing staff, marketing representatives among the team members. The idea is to develop the various components of the car simultaneously, which is more efficient than the older approach of developing them in a sequential way [18].

But while the cross-functional structures are a common approach to product design, there are very important differences in how these are organized in different firms. One difference lies in the size of the operation and the support staff. Firms in the United States used an average of 1,500 employees while Japanese manufacturers required only 250 workers and managers and achieved much better results [4]. Another is how these teams are linked to the top management of the firms. Japanese manufacturers use what Wheelwright and Clark call a "heavyweight approach" [18]. Heavyweight teams include a top manager. They have access to adequate resources and the most talented people in the firm, a clear sense of mission, and ownership in the project. The U.S. firms use a "lightweight approach." The cross functional team does not have such heavy involvement of top management and has less decision-making power than its Japanese counterparts.

This example illustrates an important point: Organizations which do the same things, whether it is to sell cars or sell women's clothes, can be organized in different ways. The choices that are made about how the activities, resources, and individuals are organized to achieve objectives can have a significant impact on how the work is done and on the effectiveness of the firm.

THE ORGANIZATION/ENVIRONMENT MODEL

An **organization** is a group of people, working toward objectives, which develops and maintains relatively stable and predictable behavior patterns, even though the individuals in the organization may change. Usually we describe organizations in terms of how they differ on three dimensions: complexity, formalization, and centralization [7]. These three factors vary across organizations, and it is these important differences which contribute to the patterns of behavior observed in organizations.

Complexity refers to the breadth of different activities, functions, jobs, and number of levels which exist in an organization. There are more coordination and control problems in more complex organizations because there are more task activities to perform, and there are alternative ways to design relationships. Complexity typically is greater in larger organizations.

Formalization refers to the existence of policies, procedures, and rules which constrain the choices of members. In a highly formalized organization, members' discretion and freedom of action are limited by the boundaries defined by these organizational devices. In less formalized organizations, there is more freedom of action and choice.

The term **centralization** refers to the distribution of power and authority [7]. Power and authority are maintained by those in higher organization positions in centralized organizations. In decentralized organizations, decision rights and responsibility are delegated to those at lower organization levels.

The patterns of complexity, formalization, and centralization are reflected in two factors: the organization structure and the organization culture (discussed in more detail in the following chapter). **Organization structure** refers to the relationship among the tasks performed by the members of the organization and can be seen in the forms of division of labor, departments, hierarchy, policies and rules, and coordination and control mechanisms. The organization culture is the set of dominant values, beliefs, attitudes, and norms that is the basis for justifying decisions and behavior. Just as organization structure influences behavioral stability, so does organization culture, but in a different way. Differences in organization culture explain why organizations in the same industry and with similar organization forms are different.

But the most obvious differences in behavior patterns are apparent between organizations that are not in the same or similar fields. Behavior patterns in hospitals are not the same as they are in department stores, and for more reasons beyond the fact that there are doctors and nurses in hospitals while there are salesclerks and managers in department stores. Behavior patterns also may vary between companies in the same industry — one day's observation of the women's departments at Sears and a high-fashion boutique will reveal many dissimilarities.

The Organization/Environment Model developed in this section is a way to understand why differences exist in organization structures across organizations of various types. It is a model which views organizations as systems which are dependent upon the environments within which they exist and of which they are a part. They interact with various environments and, in order to survive, must develop some sort of relationship with them.

☐ TECHNOLOGY AND ORGANIZATION "REENGINEERING"

The technology of computers and information processing is only now beginning to have a dramatic effect on the design of organizations. For many years, computers were simply high speed information processors. Organizations would invest in them and they would be used to move information more quickly along the same channels that were used to previously process the information. This was a waste of technology because it was underutilized. Today this has changed as information technology is being combined with organization redesign, leading to significant changes in the structures of firms. In the "reengineered organization" the existing structures, and the assumptions on which they are based, have been challenged and new ones are developed which take advantage of the technology. The result is that in organizations there are more interdisciplinary teams made up of members from marketing, finance, production, and engineering. Their focus is on getting the product to the customer. The role of technology in these reengineered organizations, which it is capable of performing very well, is to get information to those people who need it for decision making, allowing them to act quickly. The result is better decisions and, in many cases, a significant reduction in the number of people needed to do the work.

The premises of the model are straightforward. First, organizations must accommodate to the contexts (environments) within which they exist. Second, differences in the environments require different activities and different relationships among activities in order to survive. Third, managements have some flexibility, though constrained by the environment, to design these activities. These design decisions will have an impact on the effectiveness of the organization.

ORGANIZATION ENVIRONMENTS

The environment is a source of resources in the form of raw materials, financial resources, human resources, and information. These are imported into the organization, which then transforms them into products or services through different sorts of processes. These are then exchanged with other segments of the firms' environment, usually for revenues which are then used to maintain the organization system.

The **relevant environment** of an organization is made up of groups or institutions that provide immediate inputs, exert significant pressure on the way decisions are made in the organization, or make use of the organization's output. At any one time, some external organizations are closer and have a more significant effect on what goes on in a firm than do others. For instance, customers and suppliers are always interacting with a business organization. They constitute its most relevant environment. A sudden shift in the level of consumer demand may force internal organization changes, as when a slump in sales causes a firm to lay off workers.

Circumstances might develop that could change the relevant environment. When this causes sufficient pressure, the organization must adapt to it. When equal opportunity laws were passed, many firms had to change their hiring procedures as well as the criteria used for promotion. The relevant external environment of an organization may include, at least:

1. Markets
2. Suppliers
3. Unions
4. Competitors
5. Public pressure groups
6. Government agencies
7. Investors
8. Technology and science

An organization's environment may range from being relatively simple to being very complex [15]. It is simple when it contains a small number of relatively homogeneous sectors. For example, the market environment for a small firm which manufactures personal computers is relatively simple, though it might be very competitive. The environment is complex when it is composed of many heterogeneous sectors, such as would be the case for an engineering firm which specializes in the installation of manufacturing plants of different types and in different countries.

Environmental Sectors. We focus only on the market environment and the technological environment, two sectors which are very important to understanding the problems of managing most business organizations. There are two reasons for this. First, these are of traditional importance in the management of economic organizations. Customers in markets exchange their money for the firm's products and services and the firm must use the available technology to produce these outputs. Second, these two sectors are the primary focus of most theory and research.

The **market environment** is the particular set of individuals, groups, or institutions which make use of the organization's outputs. These outputs are values such as commodities, products, or services for which the market provides some sort of exchange in return. For business organizations this means products such as autos, computers, steel, television sets, bread, or the ideas and services which might be provided by advertising agencies, consulting firms, or travel agencies.

The **technological environment** has two components. The first is the techniques and the processes that the organization may use to produce the product or service. In this sense, technology refers to available methods and hardware. From the existing technology, some will be selected for use in the organization. What technology is used and how it is organized defines the form of the production subsystem. The production system of an organization cannot be any more advanced than the technology available, although it is possible that a firm does not use all available technology. For example, customer credit accounts in a large department store might be handled by computers, while the same function in a small specialty store might be performed manually.

Technology also refers to the ideas or knowledge underlying the production or the distribution of the product or service; that is, the way science is translated into useful applications.

Characteristics of the Environment.   The degree of change in the environment has major implications for the internal structure of the organization [2, 12], the type of individual who is likely to join it, and the perceptions, attitudes, and values of those in the organization. The most important effect of the environment is whether or not the organization structure takes on highly routine or nonroutine characteristics.

The degree of change is a continuum: at the opposite ends are (1) **stability** and (2) **volatility**. In the stable environment, changes are relatively small, occurring in small increments, with a small impact on the structure, processes, and output of the organization. Environmental changes are more likely to affect size dimensions (e.g., the amount of beer or insurance sold) rather than the kind of product. The number of employees in the organization may change, but the product and the way the product is made are unlikely to change significantly. If there is extensive investment in plant, equipment, and distribution methods, the method of adaptation can be short-term. This usually consists of reducing or increasing the work force rather than making changes in the product or the method of production. Large commercial bakeries use a fairly high-cost system of production, but the final product is still bread. Changes in technology may come rather slowly, but steadily. If there is a drop in demand, then the organization will probably not seek new products but lay off workers.

In a stable environment it is possible to make fairly accurate market predictions based on some relatively common indexes. For instance, the level of automobile sales may be predicted reasonably well if there are generally accurate data available about changes in population and income.

The volatile environment is likely to be turbulent, with more intense changes than in the stable environment. Changes are also more rapid and customers may change, and the level of demand may vary widely. The women's high-fashion market is an example. Product decisions of designers and manufacturers are based on predictions of customer tastes and preferences, and these are highly changeable.

When the technology is volatile, new concepts and ideas are being rapidly generated, and these new ideas affect either the way the production process is carried out or the nature of the processes themselves. The electronics industry, with breakthroughs in integrated circuits, transistors, and general miniaturization, illustrates how technology changes could affect the nature of a product as well as marketing strategies.

Such technological changes were instrumental in the recent problems of IBM. For many years, the mainstay of IBM's business was large, mainframe computers. But over the years, the computing capacity of microchips increased while costs of computing dropped as the price of a unit of processing power dropped. This led to more powerful personal computers and to price wars among personal computer manufacturers. With the development of networking, it was possible to link together these more powerful personal computers which sharply reduced the demand for mainframes. These developments increased the importance of software, a market which IBM had chosen not to develop.

ORGANIZATIONS AS SYSTEMS

The accommodation to the external environment is accomplished by the activities of different organization **subsystems** [8]. Organization subsystems are functionally related activities, not organization departments, per se. The main subsystems functions are to absorb inputs, transform them into outputs, transfer them to users, and coordinate all of these activities. The organization subsystems are (1) production, (2) boundary spanning, (3) adaptive, (4) maintenance, and (5) managerial [8].

Production Subsystems. The **production subsystem** is the technical core of the organization creating the product, service, or ideas that are consumed by the market [15]. Every organization has a production subsystem. In a business firm, the production system is the task-oriented work that creates the product or service—for example, an assembly line or tellers in a bank. In hospitals, the care facilities, operating rooms, and emergency services are different parts of the production subsystem.

Boundary Spanning Subsystems. **Boundary spanning subsystems** carry on transactions with the environment, procuring the input, disposing of the output, or assisting in these functions. The activities themselves are performed within the organization; they connect it with external points of contact. Selling, purchasing, recruiting, and acquiring capital resources are examples of boundary spanning activities.

Adaptive Subsystems. When the environment changes, the organization must change. **Adaptive subsystems** are those organization activities that monitor, or sense, the nature of the world in which the organization operates. Research and development is one kind of adaptive subsystem activities, as is lobbying to influence government policy that might affect the organization.

Maintenance Subsystems. **Maintenance subsystems** smooth out the problems of operating the other subsystems and serve to monitor their internal operation. One important function of the maintenance subsystem is to maintain high enough levels of motivation so that members continue to contribute. This is done by activities such as indoctrination, socialization, rewarding and punishing, training, and overseeing the compensation and performance appraisal systems. Setting standards for work, raw materials, and product or service quality are also maintenance functions.

Managerial Subsystems. "[**Managerial**] **subsystems**," say Katz and Kahn, "are the organized activities for controlling, coordinating, and directing the many subsystems of the structure. They represent another slice of the organizational pattern and . . . deal with coordination of subsystems and adjustment of the total system to its environment" [8]. The managerial subsystem activities focus on general policy and strategy to interact with the environment with the intent of ensuring long-term survival. The resolution of internal conflict between departments is also one of its functions, as is the use of the authority structure to disseminate directives.

GENERIC TYPES OF ORGANIZATIONS

The dynamics of the environment and organization subsystems can be integrated into the Organization/Environment Model, shown in Figure 2.1. It contains four generic types of organizations [17]. On one axis of Figure 2.1 is the technological dimension of the environment; the other axis is the market dimension. Both dimensions are characterized by levels of uncertainty, stability and volatility at the extremes. For simplicity, we have described four generic types of organizations which fall near the ends of both continue though it would be possible to describe organizations that would fall elsewhere. The four different generic organization types are:

1. The Mechanistic Organization

2. The Organic Organization

3. The Technology-Dominated (TDM) Mixed Organization

4. The Market-Dominated (MDM) Mixed Organization

These are called **generic organizations** because these are subsystem patterns and *not*, as you will see later, types of formal department structures. They are generic in the sense that they are underlying models for understanding organizations of various types. For example, one of the generic types is mechanistic, a form of highly bureaucratized system. It is possible to apply the mechanistic concept to large industrial firms, government agencies, and universities.

☐ **FIGURE 2.1**   *The Basic Relationship Between Environment and Types of Organizations*

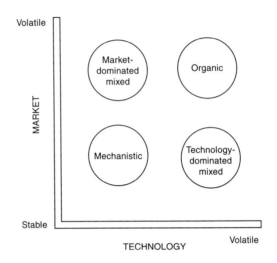

Each subsystem has a different type of interaction with the environment depending on its proximity to the organization boundary and the degree of environmental volatility. For example, adaptive subsystems and boundary spanning subsystems are in direct contact with the environment while the production activities tend to be more deeply embedded and buffered from it. Further, the form of the subsystem will be affected by the nature of the environment. When it is stable, the subsystem will take on routine characteristics. When it is volatile, the subsystem will have to be more flexible. This should have an effect on the nature or the internal relationships among the subsystems (production, adaptive, and so on) and the demand placed on organization members. These effects will depend upon whether or not the market or technology environments are stable or volatile. The different patterns of subsystem relationships in the generic organization types are summarized in Table 2.1 and discussed in more detail in the following section.

The Mechanistic Organization.   The **mechanistic organization** will exist whenever the market and the technology are stable and predictable, largely because it is efficient, and efficiency is required for survival [2].

In production subsystems, tasks are likely to be highly repetitive, with extreme division of labor. The work activities can be standard, narrow, relatively small, and simple.

The two major boundary-spanning activities are marketing and procurement. Marketing activities will be well defined and standardized because the market is relatively unchanging. This type of organization will have a great deal of influence over the distribution system. The procurement function will draw inputs from well-developed and well-defined sources. In large industries, such as the auto industry, firms may have captive suppliers. They can influence the suppliers' price and production techniques to such an extent that the supplier may well be considered as a subsidiary.

TABLE 2.1 Summary Table of Differences among Generic Types of Organizations

Organization Subsystem	Type of Organization			
	Mechanistic	**Organic**	**TD-Mixed**	**MD-Mixed**
Environmental characteristics	• Stable technology • Stable market	• Volatile technology • Volatile market	• Volatile technology • Stable market	• Stable technology • Volatile market
Production	• Repetitive work • High division of labor. • Low skill level • Jobs well defined	• Non-routine work • Intensive technology • Jobs loosely defined	• Intensive and mediating technologies • Highly skilled staff	• Long-linked and/or repetitive technology
Boundary-spanning	• Fixed distribution channels • Well-defined sources of supply	• Varied systems for distribution • Requires highly skilled individuals	• Fixed marketing channels • High prices in early product stages	• Distribution channels influenced by "style" changes • Promoters rather than salespersons
External-monitoring	• Simple system • Good information base • Set rules for interpreting environment	• Clinical skill required to judge changes • Very important function	• Extensive R & D • Clinical skills required for technological environment • Simple monitoring of market • R & D most influential	• Clinical skills required in marketing areas • Little R & D • Marketing most influential
Control	• Standardized budgeting • Historical costs and standards • Possible inversion of ends and means	• Evaluation based on projected best way • Minimal use of historical data	• Standard historical costs and standards in marketing function • More subjective evaluation in technical areas	• Subjective evaluation in marketing areas • Standard costs in technical and production areas
Managerial	• Centralized decision making • Rigid hierarchy • Conflict between higher and lower levels	• Decentralized decision making • Flexible structure and work assignments • Conflict between professionals	• Decentralized control in technical functions • Hierarchical control in marketing • Interface management problems	• Decentralized control in marketing function • Centralized control in other areas • Interface management problems

Adaptive subsystems in a stable environment will be relatively simple. There will be set rules for interpreting changes in the environment because from experience the organization will learn what parts of the environment it should monitor and how to adapt to them. It will have a fairly good information base to be used in making decisions. Usually it is possible to develop a fairly systematic procedure, which can be implemented when the environment changes. Since technological changes are relatively minimal, engineering and research and development activities focus on applications rather than on advancing the state of the art.

Maintenance subsystems will be fairly stable. Historically developed information that has achieved organizational acceptance and legitimacy will be used for control purposes. The focus of the maintenance subsystems will be on measuring performance outcomes. Because of the availability of much cost and other performance information, the tendency is to rely on "hard criteria." This type of information is usually centralized and controlled in the mechanistic organization. Since information is centralized in maintenance subsystems, those who work in these subsystems have a great deal of organization influence.

Managerial subsystems will have highly centralized managerial control located at the top of the organization. Information can be quickly collected and transmitted to the higher levels so that decisions can be made about operations at lower levels without requiring a great deal of involvement of managers at lower levels. There will be close control and monitoring of operations centralized at higher levels and lower-level discretion is likely to be relatively low.

The Organic Organization. The **organic organization** is found in volatile market and technological sectors [2]. In it the structure, relationships, and jobs are more loosely defined to facilitate the process of adapting to the changing environment.

The production subsystem is composed primarily of general-purpose technology. In essence, it is job-shop-oriented **intensive technology** so that the various production elements can be rearranged as the market or technology changes.

Boundary-spanning subsystems which get the product or service to customers, will vary from customer to customer. Channels of distribution will be unstructured and will change from time to time.

Those involved with the procurement function must constantly seek and find different types of raw materials and resources, because both the level and the type of raw material inputs will change from time to time.

Adaptive subsystems will be different from those in the mechanistic organic form. For the organization, the timing of information that might trigger internal changes will be highly variable. Thus, individual skill is essential to assess the environment and know how to change the organization, since it is practically impossible to specify in advance what aspect of the environment must be monitored.

Maintenance subsystems will be based on cost standards, since evaluation of performance will be based on forecasted estimates, not historical data. This means that performance control and evaluation will be more "subjective" and not so much based on "objective" performance measures. Performance indicators will have a greater focus on the manner in which individuals go about performing their work.

The managerial subsystem will be less structured than in other forms of organizations. Few policy guidelines will be used in the decision making process because the variability of the environment will preclude well-defined, set policies over time.

Individuals may be moved from project to project as the need for their skills arises, with a different authority structure for each one. They may work for more than one manager, depending on what needs to be done. Teams will be created to work on particular projects; when the project is completed, team members may move to different teams. This can cause problems unless the individual has a high tolerance for ambiguity and role conflict.

Organic organizations are likely to be relatively small compared with mechanistic forms. This small size facilitates adaptability to the environment. As an organization grows, however, it will begin to develop some degree of procedural rigidity and hierarchy, which may make adapting to environmental changes difficult.

Technology-Dominated Mixed Organizations. This generic type is called a **technology-dominated mixed (TDM)** organization because the major policy and strategy influence lies in the technological units. The major threat to survival and effectiveness stems from uncertainty in the technological environment. The market environment of these organizations is relatively stable. Therefore, it is important mainly to monitor the technological environment carefully and make changes in the organization system when necessary. The TDM organization will have market-related units with mechanistic characteristics, and technology-related units will be more loosely structured.

The production subsystem in a TDM organization will likely use general-purpose processes to increase the productive life expectancy of equipment. Personnel who work in the production subsystem are likely to be more skilled than those who work in production subsystems in mechanistic organizations.

Product distribution in boundary systems will be fairly stable. Products may change technologically, but they will be distributed as they had been before any new product developments. For example, there has been exceptional technological advancement in photography over the last 30 years. Instant cameras by Polaroid started a technological revolution. With the use of electronics, Nikon and Canon have developed camera systems with mechanisms which automatically adjust focus and shutter speed. Now there are disposable cameras which produce photos of very respectable quality and at a reasonable price. Yet, the channel of distribution for cameras has not changed greatly.

Adaptive subsystems which monitor the technological environment will differ from those which scan the market. Research and development will place more emphasis on advanced knowledge development than on pragmatic engineering issues. The market research activities will be fairly simple. They will probably focus on existing or easily collectible data and fairly widely accepted indicators to aid in decision making.

The maintenance subsystem faces a difficult problem of developing controls for major organizational units which have very different structural characteristics. The marketing segments of organization will have a more constrained "bureaucratic" structure because of the stable market, while those in the units interacting with the technological environment will have a more organic structure. This can lead to tensions between the units, as well as organizational conflict.

Managerial subsystems will likewise be different. The authority structure of a TDM organization will be different in the major organization units. For instance, in the marketing sector we would expect to find fairly well-defined job responsibilities, accountability to specific superiors for work, and limited discretion for decisions. On the other hand, those in the technological functions will have more freedom of action. The production subsystem is likely to be caught in the middle, between pressures from research and engineering to adopt newer production methods and the marketing unit's desire to maintain the product relatively as is.

Market-Dominated Mixed Organization. In **market-dominated mixed (MDM) organizations**, major strategic and policy influence will be from the marketing unit because of the need to stay in close touch with a constantly changing consumer or client group.

Production subsystems in MDM organizations will probably be programmed production tasks with low skill requirements. The performance of the production system will be measured by relatively objective cost measures.

Adaptive activities require little scientific research or development in the MDM organization because of the relatively placid technological external environment. Much effort will be expended in marketing research. Experience, intuition, and judgment will be more useful in determining markets than standard market information such as population data, income estimates, or traditional buying patterns. For instance, in the fashion or recording industry the clinical judgment of a designer or a record promoter is more crucial than a judgment made from more systematic market information.

Boundary spanning distribution systems will be simple. In general, product changes of an MDM firm will be style or design changes rather than changes in the product's function. Therefore, the acquisition of inputs will only be a significant problem when they may directly change the character of the output or if the market requires a product with different raw material requirements. When a fashion designer creates fashions with new materials that are successful in the market, the purchasing staff of the manufacturer will have to seek out new sources of supply.

Maintenance subsystems will be affected by the difference in types of environments. The flexible and varied nature of the marketing and distribution system will make collection of historical and relevant cost data difficult, since distribution patterns and systems may be changing. This will lead to performance measurement problems.

Managerial subsystems will have a hierarchical authority structure in the technical parts of the market-dominated firm. A looser authority structure will exist in the marketing and distribution sectors, which will have more individual discretion and freedom in decision making. Control systems to monitor changes in and adapt to the environment will be developed in such a way as to be triggered by decisions made in the marketing sector. It is highly likely that the head of this type of mixed organization will be someone with a marketing or sales background, and the tone of the firm will be set by those in marketing, since they are the ones with the knowledge and skill to deal with the volatile environment.

As in a technologically dominated firm, there will be problems in coordinating the organic and mechanistic segments of the organization. The well-defined structure of the technical sector may not only pose adjustment problems for the professionals who work in it but also may present difficulties when it is interrelated to the more organic organization structure in the marketing sector.

FORMAL ORGANIZATIONS: DESIGN AND STRUCTURE

We don't see a generic organization form such as the MDM type when we observe an organization or an organizational chart. Instead what we see is the formal organization, a configuration of major subunits usually called divisions or departments, terms which we use interchangeably in this book. **Departments** engage in a distinct, defined set of subsystem activities over which a manager has authority and responsibility for specific outcomes. For example, the subsystem activities in a university are embedded in colleges such as Law, Business, and Fine Arts, and the responsibility for the college is assigned to a dean. Companies which have multiple product lines, such as Proctor and Gamble, organize a large portion of their activities into product units such as detergents or dental hygiene products and assign responsibility to product managers.

The subsystems lie, so to speak, under the surface of the formal departments. For example, a shipping department responsible for packing, sorting, and delivering a product has to concern itself with boundary spanning activities (getting the product to the consumer), adaptive activities (knowing about changes in rates and tariffs that affect total costs), and maintenance activities (optimizing the relationship between shipping costs and customer satisfaction). Also, subsystem activities cut across departmental boundaries and link units to each other. The example of the cross-functional product development teams at the opening of this chapter illustrates different ways in which units which perform adaptive activities (such as engineering, marketing and finance groups) can be interconnected. Equally important, the example of the product development teams shows what happens when subsystem activities cut across departmental boundaries, increasing the interdependence between departments: there can be serious coordination problems.

Divisions and departments are created through two processes, structural differentiation and structural integration. **Structural differentiation** is the process of unbundling subsystem activities, separating a specific set of activities from others. For example, the production subsystem activities of the university are the total set of teaching activities. They may be differentiated, unbundled, in various ways to create colleges and departments. For example, it is common that most courses an accounting major takes are assigned to the School of Accounting and the courses for a music major are assigned to the Music Department.

Structural differentiation may be accomplished in different ways. Subunits may be organized on the basis of products (or services), the work performed (functions), projects, geographical location, and by type of customer. Not all of these are good options for every organization. Some are more logical and more effective than others, depending upon the environmental conditions and managerial preferences. These are discussed in more detail later.

Structural integration is necessary when the differentiation has occurred because of the need to coordinate the activities of different departments. It is the process of linking the differentiated subunits back together through authority, responsibility, and accountability relationships. Like the differentiation process, there are choices about the type and degree of integration. It is possible to create very tight and well defined linkages or leave them more loosely connected. The integration of the cross-functional development teams described in the opening of the chapter has been managed in different ways in the Japanese and U.S. firms. The "heavyweight" teams are tightly linked to top management, while the "lightweight" teams are not.

The set of decisions about how this is accomplished is usually called **organization design**. First, it calls for a process of creating the internal conditions which facilitate (1) accommodation to the environment and (2) the implementation of strategy by arranging the subsystem activities into organizational subunits and hierarchies. These are strategic decisions about where to locate the organization in the environment and the tactics for operating in that environment. For example, the market for women's clothes ranges from high fashion to conventional styles, and a firm may select a niche within that range. A firm such as The Limited sells somewhat expensive but more conventional women's clothing, whereas firms such as Armani and Gianni Versace focus most of their efforts in the high-fashion sector. The selection of a niche minimizes adaptation problems in the sense that management must focus on the particular characteristics of that environment but not on the more broad context. It allows the firm to develop a narrow rather than a broad set of competencies.

Second, decisions are then made which result in the organization structure. The first choice is about how the work will be differentiated, the *division of labor*. The second choice is how the work is then grouped into organizational subunits. This is the selection of the *form of departmentation*. Then relationships between the subunits are defined by the *distribution of authority*. The results of decisions about the form of organization and the distribution of authority create the hierarchical aspects of structures.

DIVISION OF LABOR AND TASK INTERDEPENDENCE

The **division of labor** is the way that work in organizations is subdivided and assigned to individuals as a job. Consider the following case. Suppose that Dennis McGathey decides to start his own company, Cabinets Unlimited. In the beginning, McGathey performs all the work tasks shown in Figure 2.2 and all the organization subsystems activities described earlier. When he sells cabinets, purchases materials, and delivers and installs cabinets, he is performing

◻ **BENETTON—A CASE OF**
   DIFFERENTIATION AND INTEGRATION

The way Benetton is organized is a good example of the differentiation and integration of subsystems. It is well known for its unique organization. The firm was created in 1965. Giuliana Benetton used borrowed knitting machinery to create colored sweaters which were then sold by her brother. The firm was family-owned until 1986 when shares were sold to the public. The company has seven factories in Italy and others in France, Spain, England, and the United States.

Part of the secret of the company's success is that they make sweaters by a special technique in undyed wool, then dye it quickly just before shipping. This gives the company considerable flexibility and speed in meeting customer needs, but requires very sophisticated coordination.

This coordination is complicated by changing demand and the Italian government. The Italian industrial system is quite rigid. The political and economic systems are very much intertwined. There are many government regulations which govern the work force. To avoid the inflexibility that this causes in an industry subject to very high international competitiveness, Benetton uses a rather unique system called a "network organization." Essentially, it subcontracts a great deal of its production and distribution. The 6,000 Benetton shops in over 100 countries are managed by private owners in partnership with Benetton.

There is a very advanced information system which supports the unique network relationships that make the company successful. The information system allows the company to keep in constant touch with 40 of its shops which it uses as test markets. The information enables the company to produce what is selling in particular markets. The company does not make manufacturing decisions until it has purchase orders in hand. Its manufacturing operations borrow from Japanese just-in-time techniques which give it speed and flexibility in responding to the ever-changing consumer demands characteristic of this industry.

It manages this network with a core group of 1,700 key employees who represent the company in its relationship with the more than 50,000 other workers who are part of the Benetton network but who are not directly on its payroll. The network is connected to Benetton by agents who are responsible for developing and controlling areas and regions for the company. These agents are carefully selected, trained, and indoctrinated with the company philosophy and values to work outside of the organization to manage this network. It has a very paternalistic orientation, with family members taking a very "hands on" approach in dealing with their employees.

boundary spanning activities. When he makes the cabinets, he does production subsystem tasks. The estimation and control of manufacturing costs are maintenance subsystems activities. If he is successful and Cabinets Unlimited is to grow and prosper, someone else must do some of the work. And when deciding what work he or she is to do, Dennis will want to arrange to have it done in such a way as to still make high-quality cabinets and maximize profits.

FIGURE 2.2   *Activities Required to Make and Sell Cabinets*

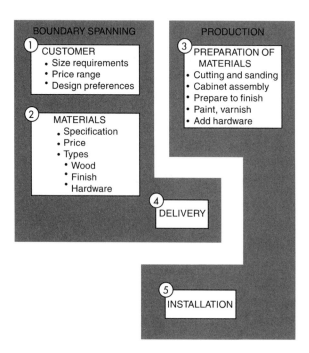

There are two different approaches to deciding how others will work, and they have different implications for what a person does in a task and how it is managed: the scientific management approach and the job enrichment approach (discussed later in Chapter 7). The differences between these two orientations are illustrated in Table 2.2. In scientific management, the philosophy is to make jobs simple, have few tasks assigned to a person, have the job supervised by someone other than the person doing it, give the worker little autonomy, and limit the amount of responsibility for the tasks. Jobs with these characteristics have low motivating potential. In the job enrichment approach, jobs are more complex. They consist of many tasks. The person controls the work more than in scientific management and has higher autonomy and more responsibility. Jobs designed this way have more motivation potential.

SPECIALIZATION OF WORK

The division of labor leads to **specialization**, which means that a person performs only some specific part of the whole job. For example, in Cabinets

Unlimited, McGathey may decide to hire a person whose only job is to sand and finish the cabinets prior to painting. That is a form of specialization called task specialization [16], or he may decide to hire another cabinetmaker who will perform all the cabinet-manufacturing tasks listed under number 3 in Figure 2.2. This type of specialization is called personal specialization [16]. The main difference between task specialization and personal specialization is that task specialization usually requires less knowledge and ability (see Figure 2.3).

☐ **TABLE 2.2**   Some Differences Between the Scientific Management and the Job Enrichment Approach

Scientific Management	←	Work Characteristic	→	Job Enrichment
Simplify	←	Basic philosophy toward work design	→	Increase complexity
Few	←	Number of tasks in a job	→	Many
By others	←	Supervision and control	→	Self
Low	←	Worker automony	→	High
Limited	←	Level of task responsibility	→	Increased
Low	←	Motivating potential of task	→	High

Task specialization occurs when a job is broken down into smaller components, or task elements. These activities are then grouped into jobs and generally assigned to different people. When task specialization is carried to extremes, the jobs will have the following characteristics:

1. *The work is more repetitive.* A person is doing only a small part of the complete task, so he or she is going to be doing it more times during the workday.

2. *The work cycle is shorter.* The work cycle is the time that elapses between the start of an activity and when it begins again. The work cycle for a professor is an academic term, perhaps a quarter or a semester. For a person working on a highly automated job, it may be as short as 30 seconds.

3. *The need for direct supervision decreases.* Because tasks are more simple and repetitive, they are easier to learn and to do. Therefore face-to-face supervision is not necessary in order to ensure that the job is done right. Generally, it is possible to tell if the work is done correctly by inspecting the output rather than through the time-consuming task of direct personal supervision.

☐ **FIGURE 2.3** *The Relationship Between Knowledge/Ability and the Different Types of Specialization*

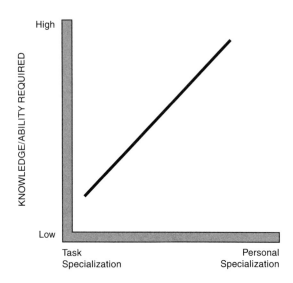

4. *The workers are less involved with their job.* High morale and motivation are especially difficult to maintain when the work is routine, repetitive, or highly programmed.

There is evidence that a greater percentage of workers in jobs with these characteristics are less satisfied and more bored than workers in those settings where the work is less routine and less repetitive [1, 11, 19]. Many individuals learn to accommodate to the routine work demands. Those who cannot adapt either leave or withdraw psychologically. Further, some employees in repetitive programmed jobs do not choose more complex jobs when given the opportunity to do so [10].

Task specialization may have some positive economic effects, such as increased efficiency, but some problems have been associated with it. These problems are:

> more subtle and pervasive, raising problems of individual autonomy, integrity, and self-realization. [A continuing issue] is a displacement from the intrinsic value of work to its by-products of income, security, prestige, and leisure. This displacement stems from the impersonality, the specialization and the group character of work in the typical big organization [13].

In Cabinets Unlimited the first stage of the task specialization process would be to separate most of the work of managing the company from the work of producing the cabinets. McGathey will continue to plan the direction of the company, make the financial decisions, and handle any problems with outside individuals or firms. He will hire someone to help with the operating tasks, most likely activities in the production subsystem.

For example, suppose Dennis decides that the most important tasks (the ones that the wants to do himself) are cutting and sanding, cabinet assembly, and finishing. He assigns a helper the remaining manufacturing tasks of initial preparation of wood, preparing the cabinets for finishing, and adding to the hardware. These are the simplest tasks, and they are much easier to learn. The new helper is a "task specialist."

The tasks might become even more specialized if business grows and Dennis builds a cabinet manufacturing plant. With more machinery, the tasks may become even more routine. The result might be a manufacturing process in

THE WAY WORKERS COPE WITH TASK SPECIALIZATION

One of the most insightful examples of how workers react to very narrowly specialized tasks is reported in a study called "Banana Time" [14]. This is a study of a group of machine operators who worked in a stamping department. Each worker was assigned to a single machine and stayed in the same spot all day long. The work was very repetitive; it was a simple sequence of placing the die in the machine, punching the start button, removing the part, and then beginning again. This work sequence took less than one minute.

The work area was not very pleasant. Though it was well lit, the walls of the room were bare. There were some windows, but they were barred and the view through them was the wall of a brick warehouse next to the plant.

From the company's point of view, the job was well defined and worker behavior was very predictable: place the die, punch the button, remove the part, place the die, punch the button . . .

The study revealed that the work was predictable but in more ways than the manner in which the job was defined. The workers did perform as they were supposed to, most of the time. However, to relieve the monotony and boredom, the workers had what they called "times" during the day, and each "time" had a particular theme.

The first "time" of the day was "Peach Time." One of the workers would yell "Peach Time!" and the machines would stop and the group would share peaches that had been brought for the day. There were other regular times: Banana Time, Window Time, Cake Time, and Pickup Time.

During these times, the workers talked about various themes, some serious and some not. Different workers had different roles. For example, "kidding themes" were usually started by the same two workers, and "serious themes" were usually started by the same three workers. The behavior patterns were so much a part of the workers' way of accommodating to their jobs that they became upset when, for example, one of the workers who usually started a "kidding theme" tried to start a "serious theme."

which a person does only one of the manufacturing tasks, say adding the hardware. This is shown in Figure 2.4. Each individual does fewer and fewer of the tasks necessary to make cabinets. One person may do nothing but screw handles onto doors all day.

FIGURE 2.4   *Assignment and Arrangement of Tasks in Making Cabinets*

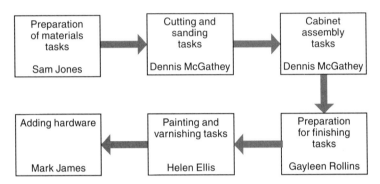

In some cases, the work is so complex and advanced that a great deal of skill and training are necessary to perform it. When the individual, not the work, is specialized, it is called **personal specialization** [16]. Typically, personal specialization is associated with occupations such as law and medicine. Those with skills in these fields tend to work in small organizations, quite often owned by the physician or attorney. Other personal specialists work in complex organizations. Scientific personnel, engineers, computer scientists, accountants, and human resource personnel are typical specialists found in larger organizations. Specialists are extremely important because they bring high levels of skills that are critical to the success of the organization.

Personal specialists usually invest a good deal of time, effort, training, and money in acquiring their skill. It takes money, years, and much effort to get through professional training such as medical school.

Consider what would happen at Cabinets Unlimited if Dennis decided to hire a personal specialist (another first-rate cabinetmaker) instead of specializing the task. Another cabinetmaker would perform all the manufacturing activities (Figure 2.2, group 3). Dennis and his new employee would each make complete cabinets. If business volume increased, it would be necessary to find more skilled cabinetmakers each time Dennis wished to increase production. This might be difficult if skilled craftspeople are in short supply, as well as being more expensive than task specialization.

Task Interdependence.   **Task interdependence** exists when several different tasks required to complete a project, product, or subassembly are performed by different people. When tasks are divided, task interdependence is one result. When tasks are highly interdependent, a person cannot complete a job until the work of someone else is finished. For example, there is a high level of task interdependence among workers in a can lid manufacturing plant. The manufacturing process starts with a large press that stamps out the round shell from a large roll of aluminum. The lid travels on a conveyer to a machine that curls the edge and attaches a sealing material to the lid, and then it moves to a machine that attaches an opening tab. From there it goes to a bagging machine. Lids are then bagged and sent to inventory. The high interdependence is illustrated in a comment of one worker who said, "When one of these machines stops, you get behind, and once you are behind, you never catch up. And most of the time it isn't even your fault."

There are three types of task interdependence: sequential, reciprocal, and pooled [15]. The work in the can lid plant is an example of **sequential task interdependence**, which exists when there are several tasks to be performed and they must be done in sequence. The work flows in a linear fashion through the production subsystem. An example of sequential interdependence is the organization of the jobs at Cabinets Unlimited shown in Figure 2.4.

Reciprocal task interdependence is when the tasks of two or more people are mutually dependent. Reciprocal task interdependence would exist at Cabinets Unlimited if a task specialist is hired and performs the tasks as shown in Figure 2.5. The cabinet must go back and forth between the two workers, and each depends on the other to get the job done right.

FIGURE 2.5 *Reciprocal Task Interdependence*

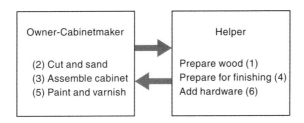

Figure 2.6 shows pooled task interdependence in Cabinets Unlimited. If Dennis McGathey hired four expert carpenters and assigned each the complete cabinetmaking task, there would be pooled task interdependence. **Pooled task interdependence** occurs when individuals in an organization work in a more autonomous fashion. What one does is not entirely dependent on the others, but organization success or failure depends on the unique contribution of each

FIGURE 2.6 *Pooled Task Interdependence*

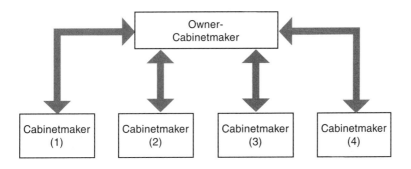

member. Some professionals often have this form of interdependent relation-ship. Law firms and medical clinics, for example, are set up so that each law-er or physician works with a high degree of autonomy.

EPARTMENTATION CHOICES

The next step in organization design is to group the differentiated tasks into departments. There are several bases for making these groupings. For exam-ple, activities may be grouped based on whether they (1) are related to the same product, (2) have similar skill requirements, (3) serve particular custom-ers or clients (4) are performed in a particular geographic area. Typical design choices and their implications are discussed on the following pages. It should be pointed out that some organization designs are better suited to certain generic organization types. For example, the mechanistic organization is likely to be more effective if the product or functional organization design is used, mixed-type organizations are suited to the matrix structure, while the organic generic form is likely to use the project organization structure.

Product Organizations and Functional Organizations.   In mechanistic organiza-tions, the organization subsystems will probably take either the product form or the functional form. In the **functional organization**, the major departments are grouped around similar work functions and responsibilities, such as accounting, purchasing, production, and personnel. These subunits are very similar to the organization's subsystems. Managers and workers are assigned to units that are responsible for similar tasks. Figure 2.7 shows a functional orga-nization for the Eagle Brewing Company. The manufacturing division is assigned the task of producing both beers that the company sells. A single brewery might produce American Eagle Beer for a period and then shift its production to Belken Brew. The marketing unit is responsible for selling both products. All the production work is the responsibility of one unit and all the marketing work is the function of another one.

FIGURE 2.7   *The Eagle Brewing Company as a Functional Organization*

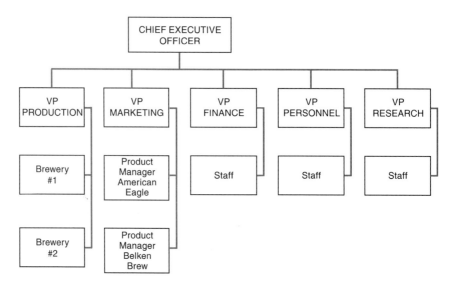

Most of the staff in departments of functional organizations will have similar training and work experience. This results in units with high levels of specialization in the functional activity, such as marketing. Because the work of each unit is so specialized, the functional form offers great opportunity for increasing operating efficiency, particularly of the production unit. Economies of scale can be more easily achieved because all the production activities are in one department.

This similarity of background should also lead to easier communication within the functional departments because the individuals will have a common frame of reference. For instance, the "jargon" will be more easily understood by the department members. On the other hand, there may be communication problems between groups because of the differences in their orientations. Coordinating units is one of the main problems of the functional organization. For instance, the marketing division would like to have a ready supply of both brands on hand at all times to meet customer demand. However, the manufacturing unit may wish to produce only one brand at a time and have very long production runs to minimize production costs. Each department's interest is best served by different goals (either long production runs or high inventories of both beers).

In **product departmentation**, departments are created around different products or services. Figure 2.8 shows the Eagle Brewing Company as a product organization. Each major unit (the American Eagle Division and the Belken

FIGURE 2.8   *Eagle Brewing as a Product Organization*

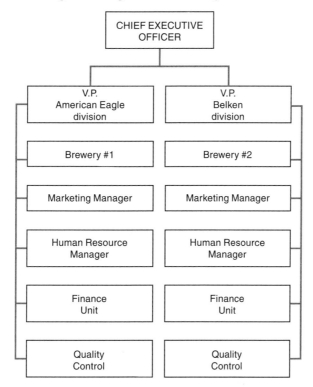

Brewing Division) has its own manufacturing operation, marketing, and so on. Each division is responsible for manufacturing and selling its own product, and each may be very autonomous. Note that *within* each product division there is considerable functional departmentation. The head of the American Eagle Division will have a production executive, a marketing executive, and other executives in charge of functional units within the product division. It is unlikely that any of them will interact frequently with his or her counterpart departments in the Belken Brewing Division.

The product organization simplifies some problems, but it creates others. For example, it is easier to develop control systems because production and selling costs can be allocated to the different products, which are almost completely the responsibility of a single unit. However, it is generally believed that costs are higher for a product organization because it does not offer the same economies of scale associated with grouping similar activities into functional units [5].

Though organizations are usually mixtures of two or more types of departmentation, a firm must choose a major form of departmental organization. Several factors must be considered that will affect the decision. Functional organizations differ from product organizations with respect to the issues listed in Table 2.3 [3, 5, 6, 9].

In the final analysis, the choice of one form over the other probably reflects the values of the organization's key decision makers. If they believe

☐ **TABLE 2.3**   Some Differences Between Functional and Product Organization

	Functional	**Product**
Unit communication and coordination issues		
Conflict between major subunits	Higher	Lower
Communication within subunits	Easier	Harder
Communication between subunits	Harder	Easier
Complexity of coordinating mechanisms	Higher	Lower
Human resource issues		
Technical knowledge applied to problems	Higher	Lower
Group and professional identification	Higher	Lower
Training ground for top management	Lower	Higher
Organization effectiveness issues		
Duplication of staff activities	Lower	Higher
Product Quality	Higher	Lower
Efficiency	Higher	Lower
Customer orientation	Lower	Higher
Concern with long-term issues	Lower	Higher

Source: A.C. Filley, *The Compleat Manager: What Works When* (Champaign, Ill.: Research Press, 1978). [5]

that the firm's goals can be maximized by emphasizing customer or client services, then the product form will probably be most effective. If internal effectiveness and control is more important, then the functional form is more likely to be effective [5]. We will have more to say about this in the next chapter.

The Matrix Organization.   The **matrix organization** works well for mixed organizations (TDM and MDM). The organization faces uncertainty in one or more environmental sectors and some certainty in others. The matrix organization integrates the activities of different specialists while at the same time maintaining specialized organizational units. In the matrix organization, technicians from specialized organizational units are assigned to one or more project teams to work together with other personnel.

The basic structure of the matrix organization is determined by which sector of the environment is stable and which is volatile. The specialists in the matrix organization tend to come from the organization segment that interacts with the volatile sector. Figure 2.9 illustrates a matrix organization with a technologically volatile environment (a TDM organization) for a hypothetical aerospace firm [6]. There are three functional units (production, design, and engin-

FIGURE 2.9   *A "Classic" Matrix Organization*

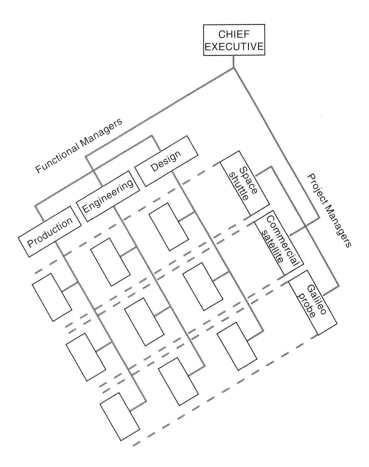

eering) and three projects in the firm (space shuttle, commercial satellite, and the Galileo probe). The functional departments of production, engineering, and design have a "project manager" from each project who assist them. The functional specialists (for example, production personnel) assigned to the space shuttle project report to both the production manager and the space shuttle project manager. In an MDM organization, such as the record company, the specialists would come from the marketing sectors. These specialists would be responsible for different areas of music such as classical, rock and roll, and country and western.

Matrix organization can result in both high technical performance and integration of diverse specialties at the same time. It demands a great deal of coordination and cooperation rather than competition. Matrix organization has the potential for harmful conflict since often diverse and contradictory objectives and values come together in it, creating a good deal of ambiguity and stress for the individuals involved.

People in the matrix organization may be accountable at the same time to both the project manager and the manager of the department to which they are assigned. The goals of these different managers may be incongruent. In the aerospace industry, for example, project managers tend to be concerned about meeting their own schedules and producing output within previously planned specifications. Specialized unit managers, on the other hand, are more concerned with high technical performance. Working under such circumstances is certainly stressful.

Project Organization. When the nature of the work changes rapidly due to changes in the environment, an organization must have a structural form that changes with it. A **project organization** form may be appropriate. A project is a series of related activities required to achieve an outcome, such as a new product or a plan for constructing a new building. Projects are generally unique; no two are the same, as are different brands of refrigerators or different makes of automobiles.

In a project organization individuals are assigned to one or more temporary teams that exist for the life of the project. The specific composition of the team is determined by the project needs. When different skills are needed for different projects, the composition of the team will change.

The Construction Real Estate Development Company, shown in Figure 2.10, is an example of project organization. Each house and each commercial building is a unique project, taking a different time to complete. Workers may be assigned to more than one project or moved among the different projects as needed. Each project will have a supervisor who is responsible for the execution of the project plan and must coordinate the construction and manage its capital and human resources. When a building project is completed, a new one will begin and it will have a different configuration of people and resources.

FIGURE 2.10   *Project Organization of a Consumer and Real Estate Development Company*

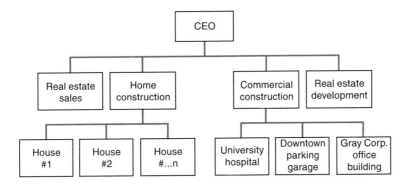

Other Forms of Departmentation.   There are other ways to differentiate and integrate organization subsystems. A firm may choose a geographical structure in which the major organization units are designated by geographical regions. Departmentation by customer type is another form. In this case, the classes of customers or clients would be the major organizing theme for departments.

THE DISTRIBUTION OF AUTHORITY

Authority is the right of decision and control a person has to perform tasks and to meet assigned responsibilities. To have authority means that a person can make decisions without having them approved by others. For workers, it refers to the control a person has over the work itself. For managers, authority refers to the rights of decision and command about the use of organization resources by themselves and by others for whom they have responsibility. It is necessary because tasks and the responsibility for their performance are dispersed throughout the organization by the process of division of labor. It is one mechanism for coordination and integration of the work of members.

Authority is distributed both horizontally and vertically in organizations. The horizontal distribution of authority is a function of the span of control and occurs through decisions that are made in the departmentation process. The span of control is the number of subordinates which report to a manager. It is affected by factors such as the subordinates' competence, the decision maker's philosophy about control, the nature of the work to be supervised and organization size and complexity. For given size organizations, the span of control will affect the structure and the number of levels. When the span of control is large, the horizontal dispersion of authority is greater and the organization will be flatter, In other words, it will have fewer organization levels. With a smaller span of control, there will be less horizontal distribution of authority and the organization will be tall, with more organization levels.

Centralization refers to the degree to which authority and power are distributed vertically in an organization [7]. Organizations are decentralized when most decisions are made by those at lower levels of the organization, guided by policies and procedures. They are highly centralized when decisions are made near the top of the organization hierarchy and the discretion of those at lower levels is constrained by formalized policies.

The distribution of authority within the departmental structure is governed by two factors. First, the generic type of organization, discussed earlier in this chapter, acts as a soft constraint on the authority structure in that it affects decisions about the degree of delegation [17]. For example, the authority structures of mechanistic and organic generic organization forms will differ because of the nature of the managerial subsystems in them. In mechanistic organizations, authority will be highly formalized, authority relationships will be clearly defined, and decision making will be more centralized. In organic organizations authority will be less clearly articulated in policies and practices, authority relationships will be less rigidly defined, and decision making will be more decentralized. Second, the organization's culture (discussed in the following chapter) will have effects on the distribution of authority. In cultures characterized by trust and confidence, authority will be more decentralized than when lack of trust is present.

SUMMARY

Organizations are defined as open systems which interact and transact with the environments within which they exist. From it they take in inputs, they transform them into products or services, then export these as a form of output. This is accomplished by subsystems, which have different functions relative to the environment. These subsystems will take on different forms, depending upon the character of the environment. We call these different forms generic organization types. If market and technological environments are stable, organizations take on mechanistic characteristics. They are more routine and bureaucratic. Organic organizations are found in volatile market and technological environments. They are more flexible, adaptable, and less bureaucratic. An organization in an environment with both stable and volatile sectors has an internal structure with both mechanistic and organic dimensions. When the technological environment is volatile and markets are stable it is called a technology-dominated mixed organization. Market-dominated mixed organizations are in stable technological and volatile market environments.

To create the structures that we see when observing organizations, the activities of these generic organizations are differentiated and integrated in the process of organization design. First the activities are divided into organization tasks. This is called the division of labor. These tasks are then grouped together into organizational subunits. This process is called departmentation and may lead to product-based structures, function-based structures, matrix structures or project structures. Then an authority structure is created to coordinate and control the activities.

☐ KEY CONCEPTS

Adaptive
    subsystems
Authority
Boundary spanning
    subsystems
Centralization
Complexity
Departments
Division of Labor
Formalization
Functional
    organization
Generic organizations
Intensive technologies
Maintenance
    subsystems
Managerial subsystems
Market
    environment
Market-dominated
    mixed
    organization

Matrix
    organization
Mechanistic
    organization
Organic
    organizations
Organization
Organization
    design
Organization
    structure
Personal
    specialization
Pooled task
    inter-
    dependence
Product
    organization
Production
    subsystems
Project
    organization

Reciprocal
    task inter-
    dependence
Relevant
    environment
Sequential task
    interdependence
Specialization
Stability
Structural differentiation
Structural
    integration
Subsystems
Task interdependence
Task specialization
Technological
    environment
Technology-dominated
    mixed organization
Volatility

☐ STUDY QUESTIONS

1. In stable technological and market environments, why is it possible to design the departmental structure of an organization in either the functional or the product form?
2. What would happen if an organization is in a stable market and stable technological environment and the form of departmentation chosen was "matrix"?
3. How do accounting control systems and performance measurement systems differ in the different types of organizations?
4. Why is it useful (if it is) to understand the difference between the concept of the "structure of subsystems" and the "structure of departments"?
5. How do the concepts of differentiation and integration explain organizational design choices?
6. Is the R & D function (an adaptive subsystem) more important to the effectiveness of a mechanistic or an organic organization? Explain.
7. What are the particular problems of managing "mixed organizations"? What are the important differences between the technology-dominated mixed and the market-dominated mixed organization?
8. Give some examples of organization subsystems that cross departmental boundaries.

61

☐ STUDY . . .

9. Compare the strengths and weaknesses of product and functional organizations.

10. What is the relationship between the division of labor and the concept of organization subsystems?

11. What is the difference between task specialization and personal specialization? Give some examples of highly professionalized jobs which illustrate that task specialization can exist in jobs other than "blue collar" jobs.

12. What is meant by the term "task interdependencies"? What are the different types of task interdependencies? Give some examples of each from your work experience. Are there different types of task interdependencies in different types of sports? Give some examples.

CASE

☐ APPLIED CHEMISTRY RESEARCH CORPORATION

TECAR Industries headquarters is in Chicago, Illinois. TECAR manufactures a variety of products in a number of different plants in various regions of the United States. Dana Hare, Vice President of Engineering of TECAR Industries, was asked to spend a few days at Applied Chemistry Research Corporation in Denver, Colorado, one of TECAR's newest acquisitions. She was to identify any serious problems at ACRC and recommend solutions to TECAR before the transition of management took place.

Hare visited ACRC in the fall. In obtaining background information about the company, Hare found that ACRC manufactured batteries for pacemakers, missiles, and calculators. The pacemaker batteries provided the bulk of the firm's profits. The company controlled more than 50 percent of the total world market for this type of battery.

Hare visited the production facilities for the manufacture of the batteries used in calculators and similar devices. She commented on the rather slow pace of the operators. The production supervisor, Norm Wingard, replied:

WINGARD: Well, in general, in this company we emphasize quality in the work we do. This is true in all of our manufacturing departments, but especially in the case of the pacemaker and missile batteries.

HARE: What types of production problems, if any, have you been having lately?

☐ APPLIED CHEMISTRY . . .

WINGARD: Lately I have been concerned about our line having to stop because of insufficient materials or components. All incoming material to this plant must be inspected by the receiving department for quality, and they seem to take their own sweet time for doing this. They don't seem to recognize that we must keep these lines going.

Hare next spoke with Joe Marcelle, Receiving Quality Control Manager.

HARE: What are your basic responsibilities?

MARCELLE: My basic responsibilities are to check all incoming materials before they get into production. We receive raw materials such as iodine, raw calcium, iron powder, various components of the battery that we subcontract out to other manufacturers, and also tools that we order for our production process. All of these items must be checked against the standards, specifications, or drawings that we have on file here. We must ensure that our specifications are met.

HARE: You include the specifications and drawings in the purchase order?

MARCELLE: Yes, that's right. Of course, sometimes after the vendor receives a purchase order, he will call me back and say that he cannot meet the specifications as they are unrealistic or even impossible. When that happens, I have to contact the engineer ordering the part, component, or tool to see if he agrees to a modification in what he wants so that the vendor can comply with the request.

HARE: How do you select your staff?

MARCELLE: I select inspectors on the basis of having a mechanical background and being a good observer. Inspectors must be alert and sensitive to small things. They must be able to spot a small deviation.

HARE: Do you employ both males and females?

MARCELLE: Yes, they are equally good at this job. My biggest problem now is a shortage of people. I need two people. One was transferred recently to another unit. It was a promotion for her. Another employee has been ill a long time. We keep him on payroll and cannot replace him yet. This has created a big problem for me. There is a hiring freeze in effect. What am I going to do?

HARE: Are your people specialists?

MARCELLE: Yes, they are. Many different jobs, though, are done by the inspectors, but each specializes in certain products.

☐ A<small>PPLIED</small> C<small>HEMISTRY</small> . . .

HARE: When do you inspect items—as they come in?

MARCELLE: No, I inspect the hot items first.

HARE: Which are hot items?

MARCELLE: Well, those that are critically needed or the production line will stop. At any one time there may be several items, though.

HARE: Do different people in the organization differ as to what they think is important?

MARCELLE: Yes, definitely. Each project engineer believes that his job is the most important. They are all after me to do their job ahead of the others.

HARE: What do you do when this happens?

MARCELLE: What do you do? Well, I do what my boss says. If there is a dispute between several people on what should be done, I let him decide. It's very difficult for me to try to deal with all these engineers plus the purchasing agent myself. I wish we had an expediter or coordinator around here that would be able to establish priorities on all of these incoming shipments so we would know what to do.

HARE: Do you frequently reject incoming material?

MARCELLE: Yes, very often. We are very strict about our specifications and drawings. If the incoming material doesn't meet them, we send it back to the vendor. He then will either have to rework the materials to make them acceptable or do the order over. However, if the order is critical enough we might check each item in the shipment separately instead of using sampling. In that way we usually get enough items to keep production going.

HARE: When personnel allocates staff to your unit, do they consider this extra work you do in inspecting each item on an individual basis instead of using sampling?

MARCELLE: No, they don't and that's something that also causes me to get behind schedule. My technicians and inspectors have to do extra work like that. If we have a shipment of 500 items and we take a 10 percent sample and find more than 5 percent of the sample defective, we have a lot of extra work if that item is critical. We have to check 450 individual items one at a time.

HARE: What if the deviation from the specs is slight? Do you accept this?

☐ APPLIED CHEMISTRY . . .

MARCELLE: Not unless the QC manager and the ordering engineer agree to it and sign off on the MRB form. This is the materials review board slip. I don't allow any deviations myself. The drawing is my Bible. I must reject something if it's not exactly in line with the drawing. I'm pressured a lot to lower standards, but I won't do it. We can't do it.

HARE: Have you always worked here? How long have you been here?

MARCELLE: I came here twenty years ago. I worked for two big companies before I took this job. I like this company much better. I'm important here. Everybody knows me and knows what I do. I like that. Last summer I got an offer for $10,000 more a year and I turned it down. Money isn't everything. There are just too many other benefits from working in this kind of company.

Hare then visited the company's purchasing agent, Chuck Holmes. He headed a group of six buyers and clerks. Holmes had been with the company for only one year.

HOLMES: What's my most difficult problem? Getting people in this company to give us the information and drawings we need to order components, materials, and tools from suppliers. People give us incomplete information. I have to nag them to be specific. The vendors must have precise information. I think we have too much emphasis on oral communications in this company. We need more written communications so we can document things.

Another big problem is that everybody wants their order ASAP. We can't rush a vendor. He has a production schedule, too. He must have sufficient lead time to schedule in an order from us. Some guys around here say they need something immediately and then, when you bust your butt to get it for them, it just sits around on the floor for six months. Some guys have cried "wolf" just too many times for me to get excited anymore.

HARE: Any other problems?

HOLMES: Just the difficulty of being a purchasing agent in this company compared to my last job. This is a job shop. We have dozens of projects going on all of the time with many different project managers to deal with. It's not easy to keep track of all of them. We also are a growing company with purchasing orders increasing by leaps and bounds every year. We don't have enough space now and the stuff is put all over the place and sometimes gets lost. Also, you have to know the whole manufacturing process for each type of battery to do your job. This makes it tough.

Another problem is that some of the inspectors are just too fussy. They reject an order whenever there is the slightest deviation from specs. They are not being realistic. I'm the one who has to hold the vendor responsible for what are really minor problems.

HARE: How do you get along with everybody?

HOLMES: Pretty well. What I like about this place is that everybody is really open. Around here we are very informal and you go right over to talk directly to the person you may have a problem with. People speak their minds around here, and I like that. You don't have to spend all your time figuring what it is they really want, like in my old job. However, the people in the company don't really understand the outside environment. The world is changing today. Many materials are hard to get now, especially from other countries. People here don't understand the environmental concerns. They don't know many things are made from oil. They don't understand that many of our vendors use a lot of oil in their manufacturing process to heat materials. We are going to be facing some difficulties in the future that our managers don't realize. They just look inward. One other thing. Nobody around here ever shows any gratitude when you do a good job. They just get after you when something is late.

Hare talked next to Jeffrey Higgs, the Quality Assurance Manager of the pacemaker battery division.

HARE: What does quality assurance mean as compared to quality control?

HIGGS: What is quality assurance? Well, it's broader than quality control, which is just a matter of policing the production line. It means a guarantee of quality—there are a number of means of getting quality assurance other than to police actions. You can motivate the work force, for example, to emphasize quality.

HARE: Do your workers have a quality consciousness?

HIGGS: Yes, they do. I think it's because of the product we make. It's a pacemaker and our workers know somebody's life depends on this device. They think they do important work.

HARE: What are your biggest problems?

☐ APPLIED CHEMISTRY . . .

HIGGS: My biggest problems? Getting along with other managers, I guess. When we reject a production run, the production manager is naturally hostile. He thinks it's a reflection on him. That's not so, of course. There are many reasons why a sample may fail. The basic components or materials may be faulty when we get them. It's impossible for any product to have zero defects. The group I have the most trouble with, though, is the marketing group. They scream at me when an order is rejected and will not get to the customer on time. They say it's my fault as I should have done my inspections earlier in the process. They say I wait too long to test. But I only have so many people. I must use my inspectors in an optimum manner. They don't understand the production process. One marketing manager said once that my behavior was criminal. That really bothered me for a while. But I've gotten used to this sort of thing now.

HARE: So your biggest difficulty is with marketing?

HIGGS: That's right. I think the fact they are located in another building down the road contributes to the difficulties I have with them. Also, they are just too optimistic when dealing with customers. They tell the customers that we don't have quality problems.

HARE: Any other problems?

HIGGS: Well, keeping the production workers motivated is a problem. The work is routine. It's boring. Yet we need good quality.

Also, we sometimes have quality problems because the customers want changes in the product. They want the product put in a smaller package, or they want more capacity in the same package. They want more reliability. We have to modify the product all the time to keep up with customer demands. This change can create quality problems.

QUESTIONS

1. Analyze the problems at Applied Chemical Research Corporation in terms of the interdependence between organizational units.
2. Are there any ways to redesign the organization which would alleviate some of these problems? Would your suggested change result in different, but equally difficult problems?

REFERENCES

1. Blauner, R. *Alienation and freedom*. Chicago: University of Chicago Press, 1964.

2. Burns, T.G., and Stalker, G.M. *The management of innovation*. London: Tavistock Institute, 1961.

3. Child, J.C. Organizational structure and strategies: A replication of the Aston studies. *Administrative Science Quarterly*, 1972, 17, 163-76.

4. Clark, K.B. and Fujimoto, T. Heavyweight product managers. *The McKinsey Quarterly*, Winter 1991, 1, 42-60.

5. Filley, A.C. *The compleat manager; What works when*. Champaign, IL: Research Press, 1978.

6. Galbraith, J. *Organization design*. Reading, MA: Addison-Wesley, 1977.

7. Hall, R.H. *Organizations: Structures, processes and outcomes*, New Jersey: Prentice Hall, 1991.

8. Katz, D., and Kahn, R. *The social psychology of organizations*. New York: John Wiley, 1978.

9. Khandwalla, P. *The design of organizations*. New York: Harcourt, Brace, Jovanovich, 1977.

10. Kilbridge, M.D. Reduced costs through job enlargement: A case study. *Journal of Business*, 1960, 33, 357-62.

11. Kornhauser, A. *Mental health of the industrial worker*. New York: John Wiley, 1965.

12. Lawrence, P.R., and Lorsch, J.W. *Organization and environment: Managing differentiation and integration*. Homewood, IL: Richard D. Irwin, 1969.

13. Presthus, R. *The organizational society*. New York: St. Martin's Press, 1978.

14. Roy, D.F. Banana time: Job satisfaction and informal interactions. *Human Organization*, 1960, 18, 378-95.

15. Thompson, J.D. *Organizations in action*. New York: McGraw-Hill, 1967.

16. Thompson, V. *Modern organization*. New York: Knopf, 1967.

17. Tosi, H. *The environment/organization/person contingency model: A meso approach to the study of organizations*. Greenwich, CT: JAI Press, Inc., 1992.

18. Wheelwright, S.C. & Clark, K.B. Organizing and leading "heavyweight" development teams. *California Management Review*, 1992, 34(3), 20-29.

19. Wyatt, S., and Marriott, R. *A study of attitudes to factory work*. London: Medical Research Council, 1956.

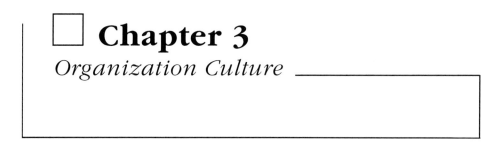

Chapter 3
Organization Culture

Two brothers, Larry and Karl, chose to attend different, small liberal arts colleges in Ohio. The geographical distance between the colleges is only 100 miles; the cultural distance is immense. At Larry's college, the students dressed very informally, usually in jeans and a T-shirt, often in sandals. The course requirements were flexible, permitting the students a great deal of freedom of choice. Professors are called "mister" and students are addressed by their first names. At Karl's college, dress is casual but not as informal. Women tend to wear skirts and blouses, men wear long sleeve shirts and slacks. The curriculum for each major is well defined. Professors are addressed as "Professor" or "Doctor" and it is the students who are called Mister or Miss. One summer, after deciding they wanted to spend time together, Larry decided to attend Karl's college for the summer term. He had a difficult problem adapting. He thought the students were arrogant, the professors stuffy, and classes too formal and constraining. Karl's friends liked Larry, but thought he was out of place. Larry, too, felt uncomfortable.

This example illustrates an important point about behavior in organizations: The difference in these two organizations is not what they do (they are both colleges). It is the difference in the cultural contexts in which the students, faculty, and staff work.

Culture works in organizations in two ways. First, the values and beliefs of members emerge from the social context, or the national culture, within which the organization exists. These values determine what they think is right or wrong as well as their preferences about work and the way they want to be managed. This broad concept of culture is discussed in more detail in Chapter 18. Second, organizations have unique configurations of values, or cultures, of their own. Organization culture manifests itself as a set of rituals, myths, and symbols that come to embody and convey important information to the members. In this chapter we focus on this latter concept, the organization culture.

The **organization culture** is the patterned way of thinking, feeling, and reacting that exists in an organization or its subsectors. It is the unique "mental programming" of that organization, which is a reflection of its **modal organization personality** [11]. The modal organization personality is the degree of homogeneity and the strength of a particular personality orientation in an organization. It results from four factors. First, people develop values during socialization in order to accommodate to the types of organizations in the society. Second, selection processes screen out many who might not "fit," and organization socialization changes those who do join so that some level of personality homogeneity develops in every organization [8]. Third, the rewards in organizations selectively reinforce some behaviors and attitudes and not others. Fourth, promotion decisions usually take into account both performance *and* personality of candidates.

SOURCES OF ORGANIZATIONAL CULTURE

The organization's culture is affected by three general factors: broad external influences, societal values, and organization-specific factors (see Figure 3.1). *Broad external influences* are factors over which the organization has little or no control such as the natural environment and historical events which have shaped the society.

☐ **FIGURE 3.1**   *Organization Culture: Sources and Manifestations*

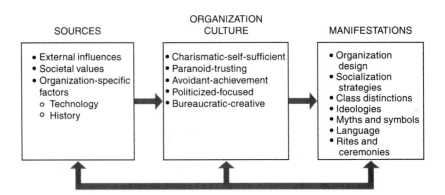

The second factor is *societal values and national culture*, for example, the dominant beliefs and values of the broader society — values such as individual freedom, beliefs about the goodness of humanity, orientations toward action, power distance norms, and so forth. For example, societies differ in time orientation. In a study of six countries which assessed three indicators of a time orientation, it was found that Japan has the strongest time consciousness, the United States is second, and Indonesia is last (see Table 3.1). Difference in time orientation within the broad society will be reflected in the cultures of organizations. In southern Europe, for example, the workday does not begin until 8:30 or 9:00 A.M., and it usually ends well after 6:00 P.M. This is very dif-

☐ **TABLE 3.1**   Pace of Life in Six Countries

	Accuracy of Bank Clocks	**Walking Speed**	**Post Office Speed**
Japan	1[a]	1	1
United States	2	3	2
England	4	2	3
Italy	5	4	6
Taiwan	3	5	4
Indonesia	6	6	5

Source: R. Levine and E. Wolff, "Social Time: The Heartbeat of Culture," *Psychology Today*, 1985, 19, 28-35 [15].
[a]Numbers (1 is the top value) indicate the comparative rankings of each country for each indicator of time sense.

ferent from the workday in the United States and is often quite uncomfortable for a person accustomed to working from 8:00 A.M. to 5:00 P.M.

Organization-specific elements are a third set of factors affecting the organizational culture. We have already discussed how the volatility of the technological environments will affect the organization's skill requirements. This could have a number of different effects on the organization's culture. In more volatile contexts, it is likely that there will be more educated employees who come with strong professional values developed through occupational socialization. This could create fragmented occupational subcultures, such as, groups with different ideologies and values which may make it quite difficult to develop a strong, single culture. Environmental volatility will also affect the organization's power structure, as we have discussed in the previous chapter for the mixed-type organizations. Those groups which interact with the more volatile environment will have more power and, therefore, become the dominant coalition, whose values will drive the culture.

Another organization-specific source of culture is the nature of the industry. Firms in the same industry share the same competitive environment, customer requirements, and legal and social expectations [10]. For example, there is a very distinctive culture of indirect selling organizations such as Mary Kay Cosmetics, Amway, and Tupperware. These firms do not "have well-defined criteria for recruitment, they discourage competition among distributors, have few rules and managers, spawn charismatic rather than rational leadership . . . and encourage employees to involve spouses and children in their selling activities" [25, p. 51].

Significant people and events in the organization's own history are also important. The effects of founders or significant managers such as Henry Ford of Ford Motor Company, Thomas Watson of IBM, Mary Kay of Mary Kay Cosmetics, and Ross Perot of EDS on the cultures of their organizations are well documented. Boeker showed, for example, the durability of the influence of

71

the dominant coalition which builds up around the founder in the firm's early years [3]. The durability of power of the dominant coalition was directly related to the length of time the founder remained with the firm.

Critical events may also become part of the folklore of the organization and are a reference point for members' values and beliefs. For example, when Apple Computers was experiencing serious competitive problems with IBM and having internal organizational and technical difficulties, Steven Jobs made a powerful speech, animated with a screen descending from the ceiling, at the 1984 sales conference. He challenged IBM in ways which openly excited employees and distributors. There were no changes in financial position, market position, or technology, only changes in "the organization, and how its employees (and competitors and potential customers) felt about it. That was all; that was enough" [19, p. 287].

A MULTI-LEVEL MODEL OF ORGANIZATIONAL CULTURE

A model developed by Gagliardi illustrates the multidimensional, multilevel nature of organizational culture and how it is affected by, and affects, selection, socialization, and reward practices (see Figure 3.2) [9]. To the extent that the organization's environment is relatively constant, these processes will work to stabilize the culture, sometimes making it difficult to change.

 **FIGURE 3.2** *A Multilevel Model of Organization Culture*

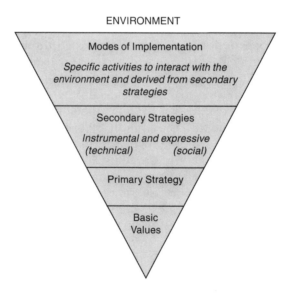

ENVIRONMENT

Modes of Implementation

Specific activities to interact with the environment and derived from secondary strategies

Secondary Strategies

Instrumental and expressive
(technical)   (social)

Primary Strategy

Basic Values

Basic Values of the Dominant Coalition. The source of organization culture is the basic values of the **dominant coalition**, the group which wields the most control and power. These values may have originated with the firm's founder and reflect his or her fundamental beliefs about what should be done, how it should be done, who should do it, and the way that members are treated.

The values that form the basis for organization culture represent the **organization's culture profile**. They tend to be broad and general criteria for judging whether actions, ideas, and attitudes of members are right or wrong. One set of values was identified by O'Reilly, Chatman, and Caldwell [17]. A profile of these values could be used to characterize and compare the culture of different firms.

1. *Innovation and Risk Taking.* Seeking new opportunities, taking risks, experimenting, and being unconstrained by formal policies and practices.

2. *Stability and Security.* Valuing predictability, security, and the use of rules to govern behavior.

3. *Respect for People.* Showing tolerance, fairness, and respect for others.

4. *Outcome Orientation.* Having concern and high expectations about results, achievement, and action.

5. *Team Orientation and Collaboration.* Working together in coordinated and collaborative ways.

6. *Aggressiveness and Competition.* Taking strong actions in markets in dealing with competitors.

The Primary Strategy.   According to Gagliardi the **primary strategy** of the dominant coalition is the maintenance of its cultural identity [9]. It does this by perpetuating their dominant values. To the extent that this strategy is successful, the dominant coalition will be able to maintain its position of power and control because these values are the rationalization and justification for crucial organizational policies, practices, and decisions such as key promotions, choices of products or services, and the selection of strategic niches. The recent history of several important firms in the United States is an illustration of what can happen when the top management is able to perpetuate its values in the face of significant environmental changes. The dominant coalitions in both IBM and General Motors were able to remain in power for years by implementing marketing and technology strategies which protected them. As long as IBM was able to remain in the mainframe business, in spite of the technological changes in personal computers, the managerial power structure remained somewhat stable and intact. After some severe losses, John Akers was replaced by Louis Gerstner. He was charged with turning IBM around. The aim literally is to change the way people in IBM think and do business and change the values which dominate the firm because the old set no longer works. The same thing happened at General Motors. During the 1980s, under the direction of Roger Smith, GM lost a large percentage of its market share to foreign manufacturers. Smith remained in the top position until he was replaced by Robert Stempel. Stempel, however, was part of the same dominant coalition as Smith and while he made some important changes, he was unable to have any substantive effect on GM, though admittedly his tenure was too short for any visible effects to be noticed. He was replaced when the board of directors finally made the decision to intervene and appoint a CEO with a different orientation from that of previous CEOs.

Secondary Strategies. The primary strategy is implemented by the translation of the values of the dominant coalition into organizational practices, policies, and products or services. Those which are more general and can be thought of as policies, practices, and guides which focus on areas such as the choices of markets, methods of competition, orientation of personnel, and philosophy about control are called **secondary strategies** [9]. Some of these secondary strategies were described by Hofstede, Neuijen, Ohayv, and Sanders in a study of differences in organizational cultures of ten organizations in Denmark and the Netherlands [11]. Below we discuss how some general practices or orientations are related to the values which constitute the organizational culture profile.

1. *Innovation and Risk Taking.* Innovation and risk-taking are reflected by a *process-orientation vs. results-orientation* [11]. In organizations with a process orientation, the primary focus tends to be on how things are done, on the individual task itself, with the belief that the results will take care of themselves. In the results-oriented organization, the focus is on the results obtained, with less regard for the means of achieving them.

2. *Stability and Security.* A *loose-control vs. tight control orientation* will result from the values for predictability, stability, and security. Tight control organizations have formal policies and practices which broadly restrict member behavior at work, perhaps even to the extent of having a dress code. Loose control organizational practices permit more freedom of action [11].

3. *Respect for People.* Tolerance, fairness, and respect for others depends upon whether the organization's practices are governed by an *employee-orientation vs. a job-orientation* [11]. This reflects whether the policies and practices of the organization tends to place more value on the people or the work. In employee oriented organizations, individuals are valued and important. They make decisions in a decentralized environment. The opposite is the case in job-oriented organizations.

4. *Outcome Orientation.* The concern with and expectations about results, achievement, and action will be reflected in the *achievement vs. avoidant orientation.* Achievement oriented practices and policies reflect high expectations, high levels of attainment, and supportive policies and actions. Avoidant orientations represent "safe" and relatively passive practices.

5. *Team Orientation and Collaboration.* Working together in coordinated and collaborative ways is facilitated by the degree to which communications are based on an *open-communication orientation vs. closed-communication orientation.* There is greater sharing of information among organization members in open systems than in closed systems [11].

6. *Aggressiveness and Competition.* The *customer orientation vs. internal orientation* affects the strength of actions in markets in dealing with competitors. In firms with practices that reflect the customer orientation, policies and practices make the firms market driven—close to the customer. When an internal orientation is dominant, organization units "perceive their task toward the outside as the implementation of inviolable rules" [11, p. 304].

There are two types of secondary strategies, instrumental and expressive. **Instrumental strategies** are the ways that values and beliefs are reflected in what the organization can do and how it does it. They broadly and generally define such objectives as the nature of the products or services, the markets that will be served, the philosophy of product quality levels, the orientation toward personnel within the firm, the nature of work relationships with the organization, and the general orientation of the organization to its constituencies.

Expressive strategies "operate in the symbolic field and seek to protect stability . . . . They enable the group to maintain its collective identity and offer a recognizable identity to the outside world" [9]. Expressive strategies involve the creation of symbols that have important meanings to the members and are easily identified by others as being associated with that organization. For example, in some firms there are very specific ways of dressing or referring to superiors. In one large firm, members always refer to anyone at a higher level as *Mr.*, *Mrs.*, or *Ms.*, as appropriate. In another firm in the same industry, it is quite common to use first names.

Modes of Implementation. When outsiders interact with an organization in any capacity, such as clients, customers, or suppliers, it is through specific **modes of implementation**. These implementation modes are the link between the values of the dominant coalition and the external environment. Such things as designs for products and services, approaches to managing human resources, the formal structure and control systems and technologies, can be traced back to the basic values of the dominant coalition. For example, in IBM, the top management's strong desire to protect its core values of stability and security resulted in the decision to remain in the mainframe business instead of developing personal computers and software. In Walmart, Sam Walton's paternalistic orientation toward employees can be seen by the presence of a greeter at the door of every Walmart store, and his competitive and aggressive market strategy is apparent in competitive pricing policies [14].

TYPES OF ORGANIZATION CULTURE

The modal personality of the dominant power group in the organization, usually key managers at top levels, will be the major determinant of the organization culture. This group makes the important decisions about the strategies and modes of implementation such as market strategy, organization design, the nature of the reward system, and who is advanced into this group.

One approach to characterizing the organization culture in terms of modal personality is suggested by Kets de Vries and Miller in *The Neurotic Organization* [12]. Neurotic people exhibit extreme psychological tendencies and

☐ COST CUTTING AT MERCEDES?

The embedded nature of organizational culture can be seen in the case of Mercedes-Benz. Its "mode of implementation" was the high priced, high quality luxury automobile completely manufactured in Germany. The "secondary strategies" reflected an internal orientation of designing and manufacturing the Mercedes to exacting engineering and production standards. This was reflected in a simple pricing strategy: determine the costs to produce the Mercedes this way, then add the profit margin. This, of course, reflected the long tradition and values of the company and the German people.

The entry of the Lexus and the Infiniti, cars of comparable quality but with a lower price, has had a significant effect on the comfortable market position that Mercedes held. To meet this challenge, Helmut Werner, the head of Mercedes, is trying to make changes in the company which cut against long standing tradition. For example, the work force has been reduced by over 13,000. He is attempting to cut manufacturing costs, which flies against the engineering dominated culture of Mercedes. For the first time in its history, Mercedes has assembly operations outside Germany, in South Korea, Mexico and one to come in Spain. Finally, in one of the most serious breaks from the past traditions, Mercedes is entering the lower priced end of the automobile market, introducing a model with many luxury features which will sell for less than $25,000. Werner insists now that the practice must be to "build to price." Of course, he is finding a great deal of resistance in Mercedes.

Adapted from John Templeton, "Mercedes is Downsizing—And that Includes the Sticker," *Business Week.* February 8, 1993, p. 38.

behaviors, leading to problems that affect them and others. These problems, however, are not so severe as to justify taking them out of society. The idea of the neurotic organization is similar. These are organizations in trouble, but still operating, and headed by executives or groups of executives with neurotic tendencies. When organizations are highly centralized and the dominant coalition is very powerful, the visions, beliefs, and actions of the neurotic managers are translated through managerial decisions into the secondary strategies and modes of implementation that reflect the organization's culture.

Kets de Vries and Miller have related five types of neurotic personalities to organization cultures (see Table 3.2) [12]. The *dramatic* executive personality leads to a *charismatic* organization culture. A *suspicious* personality is linked to a *paranoid* culture. A *depressive* orientation is related to an *avoidant* culture and a *detached* personality is associated with a *politicized* organization culture. *Bureaucratic* cultures are related to *compulsive* personalities. Sometimes the casualty is not from the manager's personality to the culture, but in the other direction. The organization situation could lead a manager to become a neu-

☐ **TABLE 3.2** Organization Cultures and Personality Types

Neurotic Organization Culture	Extreme Personality Type	Healthy Organization Culture
Charismatic	Dramatic	Self-sufficient
Paranoid	Suspicious	Trusting
Avoidant	Depressive	Achievement
Politicized	Detached	Focused
Bureaucratic	Compulsive	Creative

rotic. For example, a failing organization may induce a relatively normal person to become depressed.

A healthy organization will have a mixture of personality types, none of which will be both dominant and extreme [13]. So why study these extreme types of cultures? Because it helps in understanding the culture of "normal" companies. Extreme cultures are different from normal ones only by a matter of degree. Further, the processes that lead to neurotic organizations are not qualitatively different from those that lead to less extreme cultures—they are simply more extreme and intense.

The five types of neurotic organization cultures and the related styles of the managers who lead them are described below. Each is contrasted with a healthy culture that has a less extreme level of the same characteristics.

Charismatic vs. Self-Sufficient Cultures. A **charismatic organization culture** is associated with a dramatic managerial personality. Dramatic managers have feelings of grandiosity, have a strong need for attention from others, and act in ways to draw attention to themselves. They tend to be exhibitionists, seeking excitement and stimulation. However, they often lack self-discipline, cannot focus their attention for long periods of time, and tend to be charming but superficial. They frequently exploit others and often attract subordinates with high dependency needs.

In charismatic organization cultures, this emphasis on individualism is exaggerated, particularly at the top level. The executives have a high need for visibility and recognition outside the firm. The goal of the firm is to grow rapidly. Decision making is based on intuition, guesses, and hunches without careful analysis of the environment or the capabilities of the organization. Often the organization structure and human resources are inadequate to handle the desired growth.

Such managers exploit others, and power is concentrated at the top of the organization. This does two things: the top executive keeps close control and at the same time remains the center of attention.

The centralized control is facilitated by the characteristics of subordinates attracted to such organizations. They tend to have high needs for dependence, prefer to be directed, and overlook the weaknesses of the leaders. For the subordinates, everything revolves around the top manager or group of top managers. The subordinates have a great deal of trust that those who lead the organization can do no wrong.

Firms with a **self-sufficient culture** emphasize independence, individual initiative, and achievement. Members believe that the success of the firm is related to how well individuals, as individuals, succeed. In these firms, managers have opportunities to develop and advance at their own rates. Achievement and self-discipline are recognized and rewarded.

Paranoid vs. Trusting Cultures.   The **paranoid culture** results from a suspicious personality style. The suspicious manager feels persecuted by others and doesn't trust them and so behaves in guarded and secret ways, believing that subordinates are lazy, incompetent, and secretly wish to "get" him or her. He or she feels hostile toward others, particularly peers and subordinates, and acts aggressively toward them.

In paranoid cultures there is a strong sense of distrust and suspicion [12]. This often results from significant external events that threatened the firm, such as the effects of the oil crisis of the 1970s and the tremendous competitive pressures from the Japanese on the U.S. auto industry.

The top managers in paranoid firms are not proactive. The fear and suspicion that dominates the organization reduces its ability to respond quickly and spontaneously to important strategic opportunities. Managements are constantly searching for information about what is going in their environments. It is acquired through elaborate control systems that provide information the top management believes is required to cope with the external crises that they fear are coming. The information, however, tends to be highly distorted to confirm the suspicions of threat that are the basis for the paranoid organizations. The decision makers look for deeper, hidden reasons for the events that occur around them.

The members do not easily share important information with others because of fear that it could cost them some advantage. In paranoid cultures, the members tend to act passively and do not actively participate in important organization matters. This results in either organization paralysis or directive action by the top management in order to initiate events.

In a **trusting culture** this unrealistic fear is not present. There is a sense of trust, fairness, and openness toward others. Managers are self-confident, and they believe that other managers, professionals, and workers in the firm have the competence and motivation to succeed. This could result in active searches for new strategic niches in which the firm can gain some competitive advantage if such ventures are undertaken.

Avoidant vs. Achievement Cultures.   The depressive personality orientation leads to an **avoidant culture**. Depressive tendencies arise out of feelings of helplessness and dependence on others. The depressive person has strong needs for affection and support from others and feels unable to act on and change the course of events. These feelings of inadequacy are related to very passive behavior and inaction. Depressives often seek justification of their actions from other significant actors; in the case of managers, these might be experts and consultants.

A feature of organizations with avoidant cultures is that the dominant coalition seeks to avoid change. They are passive and purposeless. Managers avoid making decisions. Change is resisted because it may threaten the current organization values and power structure; appropriate action is avoided. The relative low level of external changes and the desire of the management to retain control results in little activity, low self-confidence, high anxiety, and an extremely conservative culture.

Such organizations are often in stable market and technological environments, with many of the structural properties of the mechanistic organization (discussed in Chapter 2). Managers are more concerned with maintaining the position of the firm in the present environment than with innovation.

Eventually, procedures, rules, and policies are overemphasized, and they often become ends in themselves. In other words, managerial energy goes into ensuring rule compliance, not into seeing that the organization performs effectively.

In an **achievement culture**, members of the top executive group value logical analysis and rational processes. They seek to understand the strengths and weaknesses of the firm relative to its competitors. Those managers recognize a need to change and feel confident that changes can be made. Having information about the availability of opportunities, managers are willing to make decision and take action to take advantage of them.

Politicized vs. Focused Cultures. **Politicized cultures** occur in organizations when the modal organizational personality is a detached orientation. Those with this orientation have a strong sense of detachment from others and of not being connected to the environment. They believe that interaction with others will lead to harm and avoid emotional relationships because they fear they will be demeaned by others. Aloofness and coldness characterizes their relationships. They are socially and psychologically isolated and do not care about it.

In politicized organization cultures there is no clear direction. The chief executive is not strong, but detached from the organization. Lacking leadership, managers at lower levels try to influence the direction of the firm. There are often several individuals or coalitions competing for power because of the lack of leadership. Managers are involved in these divisive power struggles to enhance their own position and status, and there is only minimal concern with the success of the organization.

In a **focused culture**, members share similar perspectives about the organization's sense of direction. This flows from the clear direction set by the top executives, and there is member commitment and enthusiasm toward these objectives.

Bureaucratic vs. Creative Cultures. The bureaucratic culture is a result of a compulsive modal organization personality. Compulsive people have a very strong need to control the environment. Such people view things in terms of domination and submission. They behave in meticulous ways and focus on very specific but often trivial details. Compulsive managers are devoted to their work and tend to show deference toward those at levels above them and act in autocratic ways toward subordinates. They have strong preferences for well-ordered systems and processes.

In the **bureaucratic culture** the concern is more with how things look rather than with how things work. Managers focus more on the rules of working together than on the purpose of those rules—achieving good organization performance. There are specific, detailed, formalized control systems, and they are used to monitor the behavior of the members. These control elements are derived from specific objectives, which have been broken down into very detailed, often trivial, plans of action [12]. These plans and derivative performance indicators then become the criteria against which performance is measured.

Such tight constraints arise out of the needs of top management to be in control. Careful planning and control processes provide a sense of security. This is enhanced when the managers find that careful planning also makes it easy to control the actions of those at lower levels.

The high control needs of managers are reflected in the ways that the authority structure is implemented and executed. Rank and position are important, and hierarchical deference is the norm. Ritualistic, deferential behavior toward superiors is expected from subordinates.

In the **creative culture**, members are more self-disciplined. They can work together as a team without excessive reliance on rules and procedures. They are knowledgeable about the work of others and the task interdependencies. Coordination among members is a somewhat intuitive process that develops from experiences of working together and being successful. The members know that cooperation is basic for success.

MANIFESTATIONS OF ORGANIZATION CULTURE

The important concepts, meanings, and messages that reflect culture are embedded in organization practices such as (1) organization design, (2) socialization strategies, (3) class distinctions, (4) ideology, (5) myths and symbols, (6) language, and (7) rites and ceremonials [25].

Each of these practices has instrumental manifestations and expressive manifestations. Instrumental manifestations are the ways in which the organization pursues its publicly stated goals. Expressive manifestations are the psychological and sociological effects on the members. For example, when Robert Horton became the chief operating officer of British Petroleum in the early 1990s, the company was in trouble. His predecessor, in the mid 1980s, had made some major strategic decisions which did not work out [6]. BP had greatly expanded its American refining and marketing operations, spending more than $7.7 billion to take over Standard Oil. Later, BP began making substantial investments in the North Sea, the Gulf of Mexico, and Colombia. Horton's strategy for turning the company around was to reduce costs, reduce managerial layers, and change the culture. To reduce costs, BP eliminated 8,000 employees from the work force. He attempted to foster a culture which emphasized teamwork and collaboration, empowering the work force, reducing the bureaucracy, and increasing the focus on globalization. The instrumental manifestations of these changes were reduced costs and a more streamlined organization, exactly the results intended. The expressive manifestations were quite different. The workers were resentful because they felt that the culture changes had been unilaterally imposed. There was a feeling among many that the cultural change was more of a public relations effort than a serious attempt to change BP's values. Instead of feelings of empowerment because they had more responsibility due to the reduction of layers of management, they felt overburdened with more work and that BP was still a top-down managed company.

Organization Design.   The modal personality of the executive group affects organization design in the following way. We said in Chapter 2 that the environment determines the generic form of organization and relationship of the organization subsystems. But there are still many decisions to be made about specific matters. For instance, if the organization culture is a self-sufficient one, in which individual achievement and independence are valued, the firm will probably be organized along product lines because that way it is simpler to allocate responsibility and costs to individuals. In this form, managers of product divisions have more control and therefore can be held more accountable. If the modal personality is suspicious, the functional form of departmentation is more likely. Since more cross-function coordination is needed, the top management group retains greater control.

Selection and Socialization Strategies.   Organizations will develop ways to select and indoctrinate members with values consistent with the culture. In one company, which was trying to develop a self-sufficient culture emphasizing teamwork, commitment, and cooperation, job candidates were asked whether or not they had worked in volunteer fire departments. The justification for such a question was that this type of job requires teamwork and a willingness to contribute, both of which were values desired in the firm. In the same firm, the first groups of employees were socialized and trained in groups, with very little individualized training, in order to increase the level of cohesiveness of the members. Selecting and socializing members so that their values are congruent with the organization culture increases job satisfaction and commitment to the organization and lowers turnover [17].

Class Distinctions.   **Class distinctions** refer to accepted power and status relations between subgroups. They are one basis for legitimizing influence relationships between subgroups. The most obvious class distinctions in an organization are hierarchical. These are consistent with the ordering of organizational levels and delegating the responsibility and authority associated with levels.

Other types of class distinctions develop. In some organizations, certain positions have higher status than others even though they are presumably at the same organizational level. In universities, there are often status distinctions between professors, such as a professor of medicine and a professor of education. High-status groups will have more power and find it easier to get resources.

Another class distinction could be among occupational groups. This will occur especially when groups of trained professionals work with less trained groups or other groups with different professional training and socialization.

Ideologies. The culture of any organization is built around a shared ideology [24]. The **ideology** of an organization is "the relatively coherent set of beliefs that bind some people together and explain their worlds [to them] in cause-effect relations" [2]. Ideology helps members make sense of decisions. For example, the major U.S. auto firms in the mid-1970s did not respond to the small-car import growth and the oil crisis. They believed deeply that it was unnecessary to move aggressively into small cars because their technical and managerial superiority would, in the long run, win in the marketplace. They felt no need for further justification than these beliefs, even in the face of contradictory evidence.

Myths and Symbols. A **myth** is "a dramatic narrative of imagined events, usually to explain origins or transformations of something. [It is also] an unquestioned belief about the practical benefits of certain techniques and behavior that is not supported by demonstrated fact" [24]. Myths are one of a subset of historical descriptions such as sagas, legends, stories, and folktales that have different degrees of accuracy. They all represent important events or circumstances that are passed on from one organization generation to another and become a basis for action. For example, Lee Iacocca has a reputation as an effective, tough-minded manager who can deliver results. This image began in the 1960s during his days at Ford. There were many stories at Ford about him. Several of these described his personal role in the development of the first Mustang, which was a very successful product in the 1960s. Others described his no-nonsense decision-making style. There were stories that he would summarily fire a person, right in a meeting, when he thought the person had done a poor job. Incidentally, during his early period at Ford, these stories were told with the intention of conveying his tough-minded management style in the company. When he was released by Henry Ford, some of these same events became part of the evidence used to justify the action. How much truth and how much fiction are in the myths and stories that arise from the organization's culture is not important. What matters is whether they transmit core organization values to others, and serve as a basis of control.

Symbols are objects to which organizational meaning has become attached.

> Symbols include things such as titles, special parking places, special eating facilities, automobiles, airplanes, office size, placement, and furnishings and other perquisites of position and power. [They are most] likely to be used to distinguish between vertical levels of power within the organization [18].

In any organization, the collection of symbols and signs will be unique and related to the shared perspective of members. One plant manager attempted to convey the concept of egalitarianism in the plant by installing a round table, as a symbol, in the conference room. The idea was that there were no "heads"; everyone should expect to contribute equally. However, another symbol carried a more powerful image. There was only one reserved place in the parking lot—it belonged to the plant manager.

Symbols can also distinguish status and power between individuals and groups at the same level. For example, in almost every company, it is simple to know which of the vice presidents (all presumably at the same organizational level) is most important by the location and size of office and pay differentials. In fact, it causes some consternation in an organization when a person wishes to have an office location and size that are different from others with similar status. Likewise, it can also cause problems when a lower-status person acquires symbols that are more appropriate to a higher-level position.

Language. In every organization, a unique specialized language exists. Like the mother tongue of a country, the organization's language is best used and understood by its members. Using it properly is, in fact, a way for individuals to be identified as a member. The organization's language is made up of jargon, slang, gestures, signals, signs, jokes, humor and metaphors, all of which allow members to convey very specific and clear meaning to other members [25]. For example, the ideology, which is drawn from the organization value orientation, will find its way into the language used to justify actions [18]. When the "right" language is used to explain an act, it is accepted because it reflects the culture. For example, a very effective president of a company was summarily fired by the chairman of the board. Even though the firm is among the largest in the United States, it is still under close family control, and those who work there know it. When the ex-president asked the chairman why he had been fired, the chairman replied, "Because I don't like you." When this story circulated among employees, everyone in the firm understood. In this company, personal loyalty is very important. The language was very consistent with the ideology.

Rites and Ceremonials. **Rites** are "relatively elaborate, dramatic, planned sets of activities that consolidate various forms of cultural expressions into one event, which are carried out through social interactions, usually for the benefit of an audience. [A *ceremonial* is] a system of several rites connected with an occasion or event" [24]. Like symbols and myths, rites and ceremonials convey

☐ **MINE'S BIGGER THAN YOURS— THE IMPORTANCE OF SYMBOLS** _____

In the reorganization of Dunnock Aircraft, Donald James was, effectively, demoted. He had been vice president of economic planning for 10 years, and his division had been instrumental in the company's success by producing accurate economic forecasts. In the new reorganization, he would still retain the title, vice president, but now he would be reporting to Louis Nicholas, who was in the newly created position of executive vice president of strategic planning.

▢ MINE'S BIGGER THAN YOURS . . .

When the reorganization was being planned, the CEO of Dunnock spoke with each key subordinate about it and tried to facilitate the change. In general, he wanted to assure them that they were still important and he would be relying on them as before. He promised them that they would stay at the same salary level and made several concessions to each of them, where it seemed possible. Donald James wanted one thing, he said, and that was to keep his office. This didn't seem to be such an extreme request to the CEO. He agreed.

The problem arose when Nicholas finally arrived at Dunnock. When he saw his office, he was unhappy. It was a large, older office with wood panels and a deep blue carpet. However, it was some distance from most of the staff. Donald's office was much more centrally located, much more modern, and equally attractive. Nichols went to the CEO and asked if it would be possible to exchange offices with James. "After all," he told the CEO, "Don works for me now. His office is the one that most people associate with the head of the economics group."

The CEO was concerned because of the commitment he had made to Don James, but he felt he had to support his new executive VP. He asked Don to come to his office for a meeting, and in the meeting he told him about Nicholas's request.

Donald James became extremely angry. "Is this the way you keep commitments?" he asked. "It's bad enough to be demoted, but now I am demeaned. Everyone at Dunnock knows about the commitment you made to me."

"Let me suggest something," the CEO answered. "You move down to Louis's space and you can remodel it any way you want. I'll give you a $50,000 renovation budget."

James agreed. He hired an interior designer, who planned an attractive, modern office. One feature of the design was some very elegant wooden cabinets and shelves. Instead of buying these from the budget, James had them made, at no cost, in the model shop, which employed craftsmen who made wooden models of aircraft parts in the early design stage. The head of the shop was an old friend who had come to Dunnock at the same time as Don and fished with him. By the time the office was finished, more than $70,000 worth of work had been done, though the actual outlay was only $50,000.

When Nicholas saw the completed project, he was angry. Now James's office was far more attractive than his. He was, he felt, the executive vice president, and it did not seem right that a manager who reported to him should have a better office.

☐ **MINE'S BIGGER THAN YOURS . . .**

> Nicholas went immediately to the CEO. After a heated discussion about the situation, the CEO agreed to give Nicholas a renovation budget of $100,000 to redo his office. When the work was done, Nicholas's office was larger and much more elegant than Donald's. However, it was not quite as attractive as the CEO's office.

important cultural meanings, by actions and interactions. Trice and Beyer have identified several organizational rites [24].

Rites of Passage. Rites of passage are intended to bring a person into an organization or to facilitate separation from it. When bringing one into an organization, they convey norms and values. They may be very elaborate, such as military basic training, or very simple, such as when a personnel assistant explains the company rules and policies to a new employee on the first workday. A rite used in one firm to communicate the level of expected commitment was to have the spouses of married prospective employees present when the job offer was made. During this discussion, both the good points and the bad points of the job were accurately described to both.

Separation rites help persons make clean breaks with the organization. Retirement parties signal the end of a career, and going-away dinners separate a person from one organization on the way to another. These rites often involve elaborate dinners, drinking, and discussions about past life in the organization.

Rites of degradation. These surround the act of removing someone from a position or from the organization. The reasons for removal may be that the person has not performed well or does not have values consistent with the organizational culture. In most organizations, these rites are less formal, but they nevertheless exist. In one large entertainment and publishing firm in the United States, releasing a top manager began with a rite of degradation. The chief executive would begin to point out that a manager was becoming a problem because "he couldn't handle the women." The firm was noted for having many attractive women executives and workers, and it was well known that many men and women had open relationships, regardless of their marital status. But when the president wished to remove a manager, the degradation rite started this way. Later, some "objective" performance deficiency would be identified, and the person would resign or be fired.

Rites of enhancement. These increase the status or position of a person after he or she is in the organization. Awarding recognition through the use of symbols and announcement of promotions are examples. Sometimes these are informal. In one firm the enhancement rite that later leads to promotion begins when the chief executive officer asks junior executives to join him on special public occasions.

Rites of renewal.   These have the goal of strengthening and improving the current social structure [24]. These rites often take the form of different types of training and development programs. These programs are usually quite conspicuous in organizations because time is set aside during which those in the organization must attend classes and because these programs usually employ a set of new symbols and language.

Rites of conflict reduction.   Conflict avoidance or reduction is desired in most organizations; yet the nature of organization itself gives rise to conflict. To resolve conflict, organizations use rites such as collective bargaining, the grievance process, the "open-door policy" where each manager's door will always be open to hear subordinates' problems, committees in which divergent views can be aired, and ombudsmen who are supposed to represent workers' interests impartially.

Rites of integration.   These are intended to increase the interaction of the organization's members, presumably to make working together easier. In integration rites, according to Trice and Beyer [24], official titles and organizational differences are eliminated for a short time so that people meet others as people. An example of an integration rite is the "dining in" tradition in the United States Air Force.

☐ INTEGRATION RITES— THE AIR FORCE'S "DINING IN" _____

The "Dining In" is a formal social event in the U.S. Air Force. It draws on an old tradition of military dinners, some think dating back to ancient military feasts. Its purpose is to bring officers and enlisted personnel together in a setting where they can interact socially, have the opportunity to know each other better, and develop closer bonds.

The "Dining In" has a very well-prescribed set of norms that are part of the formal dinner program. These norms reinforce many of the behaviors expected of military members in other settings. For example, some of the traditionally prescribed "rules of the mess" are

Thou shalt arrive within ten minutes of the appointed hour.

Thou should make every effort to meet all guests.

Thou shalt always use the appropriate toasting procedure.

Thou shalt enjoy thyself to the fullest.

There are sanctions, though far from serious, for violating these norms. On observing a violation, a member of the mess asks to be recognized by

☐ **INTEGRATION RITES . . .**

the presiding officer. The member then outlines in a formal manner the violator and the nature of the violation. If the violation is deemed serious, the violator is penalized, usually by being required to "go to the grog bowl" and endure the "punishment" of a drink.

The "Dining In" includes much good-natured bantering and roasting within and across ranks, but the effect, it is believed, is a more highly cohesive group.

MANAGING ORGANIZATION CULTURE

Managers are increasingly recognizing the power and effects of culture on the behavior of people in organizations. They are becoming interested in trying to manage it as a way to contribute to the effectiveness of the firm. However, while there is agreement that cultures exist in every organization and that they do change, there is disagreement over the degree to which they can be managed. Certainly in new organizations it is possible to try to shape the culture through carefully designed selection programs, socialization strategies, and the consistent use of symbols and language. Very quickly, though, the members of the organization modify the values intended by management, and the culture emerges.

It is more difficult to affect the culture of an existing organization, especially when an embedded management attempts to change it by using consultants and formal change programs. The reason that this is difficult is illustrated in Figure 3.3 Usually, attempts to modify culture center around revision of activities and practices, that is, modes of implementation and secondary instrumental strategies. Suppose, for example, a firm was headed by a compulsive chief executive who thought that productivity might be increased through some of the currently popular high worker involvement approaches. He might decide to move from a bureaucratic to a creative culture. Trainers and consultants, who use a set of team-building development approaches that give managers experience in working together, might be retained. There might be some organization redesign to facilitate activities among groups by creating new interdependencies. However, because the basic values of the dominant managerial group are not consistent with these practices, the change effort would fail. The modes of implementation and the secondary strategies required for a creative culture are not consistent with the primary strategy of maintaining values consistent with a compulsive personality.

☐ **FIGURE 3.3** *Why Culture Change Fails*

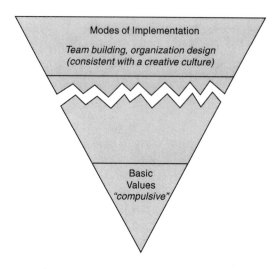

Cultural shifts occur when top management changes or when there is a significant change in the firm's environment to which it must adapt in order to survive. Figure 3.4 illustrates the case in which an environmental shift could require a modification of the organization's culture. Suppose that at one time (t_1) a company is operating effectively in the environment as shown bracketed by *A*. This means that the modes of implementation and the values (basic values *A*) from which they are derived are congruent. Suppose, however, that over time the external environment changes and at t_2 the environment now is

☐ **FIGURE 3.4** *Changes in Organization Culture as the Environment Changes*

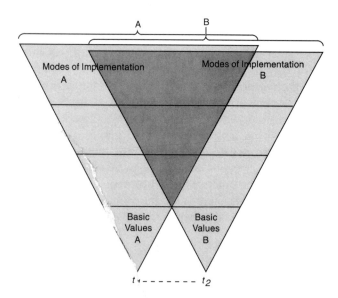

shown bracketed by *B*. This would require different modes of implementation, along with value set *B*, to operate effectively in it. In many ways, the modes of implementation for the new environment may be similar to those required by the old one, shown by the area of overlap in Figure 3.4. However, the problem of adjustment occurs in those areas where there is no overlap with the previous secondary strategies and modes of implementation. An example of this situation is the business of publishing college textbooks. In many respects, neither the target market for textbooks (students) nor the means of finding authors has changed much over the years. What has changed is the channel of distribution for used books, which is now so well organized that it has significant effects on the way publishers must now do their marketing. Now there are "used book" companies that buy large quantities of textbooks and sell them to the bookstores. The original publisher does not control these sales. While traditional publishers believe that the actions of the used book company are unethical and unprofessional, they are entirely legal. Publishers must change the way they do business, perhaps entering the used book market themselves. However, such a business approach (a new mode of implementation) is inconsistent with traditional publishing values, which the managers of these firms wish to maintain.

Three companies which have been affected by a changing environment are Ford, AT&T and Gillette. The environment for Ford changed with the advent of foreign competition beginning in the late 1960s. However, the environment did not shift sharply and severely in a short time period. Foreign manufacturers kept increasing market share gradually through a strategy of introducing high quality and very competitively priced cars into the U.S. market. The American manufacturers made some design changes, but did little to alter their processes to increase product quality. Further, many in this industry were convinced that eventually American consumers would prefer larger, traditional automobiles. Finally, after a long period of resistance, Ford began a serious and successful effort to improve its product quality, going through an extreme culture change. The success of this effort was finally realized in 1992, when the Ford Taurus replaced the Honda as the leader in U.S. auto sales.

The case of AT&T is different. The important environmental change it faced was from regulation to deregulation and the break up into the "baby Bells." This occurred over a rather short time. It created the problem of how to shift the culture from one which had accommodated to a protected and regulated environment to a culture consistent with operating in a deregulated competitive context. It seems to have successfully made the shift, operating the long distance telephone system in markets in which there is strong competition from MCI and Sprint as well as innovatively launching a subsidiary which markets the AT&T Universal MasterCard.

The story of Gillette is one of an old successful company that lost its market leadership in razors and razor blades to a new product, disposable razors [7]. In the mid 80s, disposal razors accounted for about half of the market after being introduced ten years earlier. In response, Gillette developed a revolutionary, high-priced, high-tech shaving instrument, called the Sensor. Instead of introducing the Sensor slowly into selected markets to gauge consumer reaction, a strategy consistent with its previous culture, Gillette decided on a bold approach. The product was introduced into the United States and Europe with a single, dramatic marketing campaign. The Sensor has been so successful that Gillette is unable to keep up with the demand.

IMPLEMENTING A CULTURE IN A NEW ORGANIZATION

When starting a new organization, many managers attempt to implement a self-sufficient culture that supports high performance. This has some important advantages: costs may be lower because less direct supervision is needed, worker morale and satisfaction are higher, and absenteeism and turnover may be reduced.

Creating such a culture is difficult, often because the basic values and assumptions of the managerial group conflicts with the modes of implementation required to support such an environment. This happened in the start-up of a new plant in which the management team wanted to create a self-sufficient culture. One element of their secondary strategy was to build a highly participative, self-managed work force. They wanted to create values that supported teamwork, active participation of the work force in decision making, high product quality, commitment, and a sense of trust (see Figure 3.5).

☐ **FIGURE 3.5**   *Attempting to Implement a Self-Sufficient Culture in an Organization Headed by a Dramatic Manager*

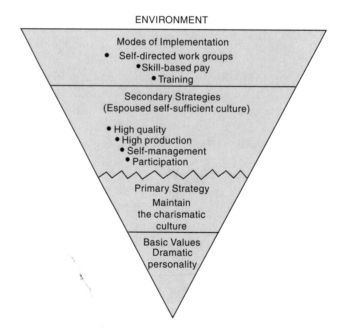

They sought to implement this in several ways. They were very careful in screening employees. They sought a work force willing to participate in decision making, without previous union experience, with high skill levels, and with a willingness to perform several different tasks. The pay system was to be based on the skills of the employees, not the tasks that they performed. This was to facilitate the workers' flexibility and willingness to work on different machines.

During the initial phases of the start-up, there was a great deal of worker enthusiasm, involvement, and trust. However, over time it became clear that many of the things that management wanted to instill in the culture were only verbalized values, not implemented practices. For instance, the plant management continually articulated the importance of high product quality. At the same time, the superintendents regularly shipped marginally acceptable products to customers.

There were also problems with the espoused value of participation. Initially, workers were told that they could bring any production problem to the attention of any manager in the plant. It soon became apparent that there were certain issues about the equipment that the plant manager did not wish to discuss. Soon the level of participation decreased to almost nothing.

One reason for the failure to implement the self-sufficient culture was that it was inconsistent with the personality orientation of the plant manager. As Figure 3.5 shows, he had a dramatic personality and his primary strategy, according to the Gagliardi model, was to maintain a culture that would support such values and beliefs [9]. In fact, the only reason that the self-sufficient culture was wanted in the first place was that the president of the firm strongly advocated it. The plant manager went along. However, when the president left the company, the plant manager was given more latitude in managing the plant and implementing his own philosophy. In the end, his dramatic personality prevailed.

This example demonstrates one of the serious difficulties of trying to create a particular brand of organization culture. There is often a serious gap between what managers say they want and the kinds of member behavior that are supported by the organizational culture.

ORGANIZATION CULTURE AND MERGERS

Problems arise when the cultures of two firms involved in a merger are incongruent. Such a situation is illustrated in Figure 3.6. This is what appears to have happened in the acquisition of Kidder, Peabody by General Electric (GE) [22]. Kidder, Peabody was a very profitable financial securities firm with a very entrepreneurial culture, in which individuals had a lot of free rein in operating. GE, on the other hand, had a more traditional structure with managers imbued with the GE philosophy as a result of its extensive management development efforts. As the GE philosophy and strategy were implemented in the Kidder, Peabody group the top performers there became dissatisfied. Many of them left, hurting the profitability of the Kidder unit. As performance dropped, GE began to take more control, which is exactly the opposite of what a free spirited entrepreneur wants.

◻ **FIGURE 3.6** *Incongruent Cultures of Two Firms in a Merger*

ENVIRONMENT

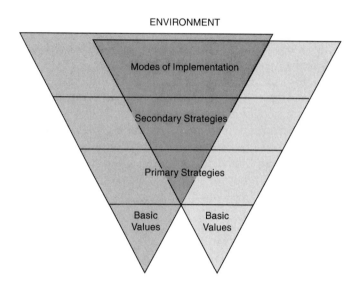

Modes of Implementation

Secondary Strategies

Primary Strategies

Basic
Values

Basic
Values

ORGANIZATIONAL SUBCULTURES

Most large organizations do not have a homogeneous culture. Instead, there are *organizational subcultures*, which are

> distinctive clusters of ideologies, cultural forms, and other practices that identifiable groups of people in an organization exhibit. They differ noticeably from the overall culture . . . and from each other [25, p. 174].

There can be different types of organizational subcultures, consisting of the various groups, either within or outside the organization, with which members identify [21]. This identification, as we will discuss in Chapter 10, arises because people (1) share similar attitudes, values and beliefs, (2) have common goals, (3) are able to be more influential with others instead of alone, (4) interact frequently and (5) find their needs satisfied from others who share the same subculture [16, 20]. The stronger these factors, the greater the identification with the particular subculture.

Hierarchical subcultures. Hierarchical subcultures exist at different organizational levels and may be seen in the differences, symbols, status, authority, and power between managers and workers. Hierarchical subcultures are probably most clearly visible and strongest in mechanistic organizations in which there is clear, strong stratification between levels. This occurs when the work at lower levels has been highly task-specialized so that minimal skills are required to do it. This weakens the power of lower levels and results in centralization of control and decision making. It also is facilitated when promotion to the managerial levels requires both competence and values congruent with those of the dominant coalition. The result is a management group with strong homogeneous values that are different from those of the work force in general.

Occupational/task subcultures. Members are likely to have strong identification with the others who have similar skills when these skills are very important to organizational success and the skills have been developed through intensive training during which there is strong occupational socialization (see Chapters 4 and 6). Then others who share the same occupation or task, inside and outside the organization, will be an important reference group. Mixed organization types and organic organizations are most likely to have strong occupational subcultures.

"Culturally diverse" subcultures. Many organizations are experiencing the same phenomena as Digital Equipment and US West. In one Digital plant with 350 workers there are 44 different countries represented, and they speak 19 different languages. US West's work force is composed of Caucasians, African-Americans, Hispanics, Asians, and Native Americans. Multi-culturalism in organizations has increased as these groups have entered the work force in more significant numbers and as companies have made serious efforts to reduce discrimination in selection and promotion practices (see Chapter 6). The result has been that there are organization subcultures based on values and beliefs of these groups that may differ in many ways from the dominant organization culture. It is also possible that the subcultures differ from each other and may, in fact, clash.

Diversity can provide the potential for higher productivity because a wider range of human talents contribute to creativity and there is less chance of "groupthink" [1]. On the other hand, it can lead to conflict and may make it difficult to develop cohesion. Which outcome occurs depends on how diversity is managed. Some firms have adopted "pluralism" as part of their corporate philosophy, promoting a "culture that promotes mutual respect, acceptance, teamwork, and productivity among people who are diverse in work background, experience, education, age, gender, race, ethnic origin, physical abilities, religious belief, sexual affectional orientation, and other perceived differences" [5].

To implement such a philosophy, firms inevitably turn to training and education. For these to be effective, they must, above all, have the strong support of the dominant coalition and be reflected in the primary and secondary culture strategies. Only then will training and education for multi-cultural, multi-ethnic integration work. When properly conducted (see Chapter 17), such programs can reduce the use of stereotypes, increase the ability of individuals to see things from the point of view of different cultures or groups, reduce the anxiety of being in the presence of others who are different, and reduce the frequency of non-culturally relative judgments [4].

SUMMARY

The fundamental values in a society are strong forces that affect the behavior of those in organizations. Culture is the patterned way of thinking, feeling, and reacting that is characteristic of human groups and that accounts for important differences between them. Values are ideas about what is right or wrong and good or bad that are the basis of much human action. Culture is transmitted through socialization.

The organization culture is, of course, significantly affected by the broader society in which the organization exists. However, decisions by key managers, particularly the CEO, give it a more specific form: it will reflect their dominant values.

Organization cultures can be categorized in different ways. In the approach we use in this book there are five different orientations, each of which may be thought of as a continuum: (1) charismatic/self-sufficient, (2) paranoid-trusting, (3) avoidant-achievement, (4) politicized-focused, and (5) bureaucratic-creative. For each of these cultures, there seems to be a distinctive pattern of top management activity and a particular set of policies that emerge in the organization.

The culture of an organization contributes to what it is and what it will be. There will be an effort to maintain the culture since it supports the current power structure in the organization. Therefore, it should be expected that the organization design, socialization strategies, and so forth will strengthen the current organization value orientations and systems. Likewise, those in organizations may do many things to ensure that the sources of culture do not change in such a way as to require changes in the organizational value systems. Many U.S. firms that have strong capitalistic and individualistic cultures support outside groups and foundations that attempt to strengthen the free-enterprise system. A good example is the extensive business support of the U.S. Chamber of Commerce. These firms also present their own economic and political philosophies directly to the public at large.

Even when there are strong external pressures that necessitate internal cultural modifications, the organization will resist. For example, even though there are social pressures and laws that protect women and minorities from discrimination, they still may have problems in work organizations because the culture usually reflects white, male, middle-class, Anglo-Saxon values in the ideologies, socialization strategies, and so forth. Those in organizations are sometimes slow to change and, in fact, some resisted when the laws were enacted requiring equal opportunity and access. Many managers resisted those laws because it was obvious that the culture and, consequently, the power structure would change.

☐ KEY CONCEPTS

Achievement culture	Ideology	Organization culture
Avoidant culture	Instrumental strategies	Organizational culture profile
Bureaucratic culture	Manifestations of culture	Paranoid culture
Ceremonials	Modal organization personality	Politicized culture
Charismatic culture		Primary strategy
Class distinctions		Rites
Creative culture		Secondary strategies
Dominant Coalition	Modes of implementation	Self-sufficient culture
Expressive Strategies		Symbols
Focused culture	Myth	Trusting culture

☐ STUDY QUESTIONS

1. Discuss the relationship between the culture of a society and an organization's culture.
2. How does the history of an organization affect its culture? Does it make a difference whether the organization is large or small?
3. What is the advantage of thinking of organization culture as a multi-level concept?
4. What are the instrumental effects of primary and secondary strategies? What are their expressive effects? What is it about these that make organization culture difficult to change?
5. What is meant by the organization culture profile? What are some dimensions that have been found to be useful representations of such a profile?
6. What are the concepts "modal personality" and "dominant coalition"? How do they relate to organization culture?
7. What is the reason for studying neurotic organization cultures? Do you think most organizations have these extreme types of culture?
8. Select one of the particular types of neurotic organizational cultures that you have experienced in your own work or read about in the popular press. Describe how this culture is manifested in organization policies, practices, and rituals.
9. What are the consequences of organizational culture? How do these serve to make the culture resistant to change?
10. Select a large well-known organization that you are familiar with and that has a culture you think restricts its ability to become more effective. What would you do to change the culture?

CASE

☐ HARRISON ELECTRONICS AND SARAH CUNNINGHAM

Harrison Electronics is a large, profitable, hi-tech firm located in New Jersey. It designs and produces advanced electronics products mostly for the space program or for specialized industry applications. The nature of the work is very advanced and important to national security, so the top management group is not too concerned about recent reductions in defense spending. The president of Harrison is John Dowd. He was a professor of electrical engineering at an important state university before he took a job at Harrison and moved quickly to the top. Dowd is a tough, hard-nosed manager who expects results. His philosophy is to make tough demands and to reward high performers. If he has one fault, it is that he is quick to call someone on the carpet. When he believes a person didn't do the job, he lets him or her know, in clear terms.

☐ HARRISON ELECTRONICS . . .

The major units in Harrison are the production division and the research group. There is a very small government contracts division. The research division is Dowd's pride and joy. Most of the staff are highly trained physical scientists. Dowd boasts that Harrison will always be a growth company as long as they have strong technical personnel. In fact, Harrison does have a good growth record, and there are always opportunities for advancement for those executives Dowd thinks are good. In addition, the best technical people are very well treated. They have the most advanced laboratory facilities and their offices are always well located and well appointed.

Recently Harrison had a government contract to develop some specialized computers. As a result, several people in the company, especially Dowd, thought the product had potential as a pocket notebook. Dowd set his research group to the task of developing the hardware and software necessary for the new product line. He and his staff put together a very ambitious schedule to complete product development and get the pocket notebook on the market.

Harrison added a vice president of marketing, Sarah Cunningham, who was hired from one of the leaders in the retailing industry. Sarah was a successful top manager in the appliance division, located in California, before coming to Harrison. Sarah is 35 years old, single, and had lived on the West Coast all her life. Sarah hired a top flight marketing staff and began to develop a plan to sell the new notebook.

But soon Sarah began running into problems. Her first surprise was the facilities and where they were located. The marketing group's offices were located in an office building three miles away from the main offices. Offices were neat, with the most modern technology, but smaller than those of executives at the same level. Then she couldn't get Dowd's ear to discuss marketing problems. He and other top people were, it seemed, more concerned with the technical matters. Sarah had to get most of her programs approved by the executive group, consisting of all engineers except her. It became difficult to get anything done. Soon the project began to run into scheduling difficulties. The best engineer assigned to her project was pulled off by Dowd to work on a new government contract. It became known around the company that the project was in serious difficulty, and there were rumors that it would soon be dumped.

John Dowd called a meeting of the group responsible for the project. He was very angry about the progress, and he told them, "I don't know why you people can't make this thing work. You've got the resources of the best technical staff in the country. I've spent a lot of money on the project. If it fails, it's your fault. I am holding you all personally responsible."

☐ HARRISON ELECTRONICS . . .

Sarah became concerned. She thought the criticism was unfair. She asked Dowd, "Don't you think that judgment is a little harsh? After all, we've had serious technical problems and our best engineer has been pulled from the project."

Dowd looked at her and glared. "Sarah," he said, "I don't know what you did in that damned department store where you used to work. Here we deal with hardware, not with fashion. We get results. That's what I want. If you can't get them, maybe you should look for something else to do." Then he turned and walked out of the room.

Sarah didn't know what to do or say. John Rice, an old Harrison hand, leaned over to her and said quietly, "Sarah, don't worry. The old man is going through one of his phases. This happens every time something gets behind schedule. He'll be okay, and so will you."

Sarah wasn't so sure.

QUESTIONS

1. Describe the organizational culture at Harrison Electronics.
2. What are some ways in which this culture is manifested?
3. What are the main sources of Harrison's culture?

REFERENCES

1. Adler, N.J. *International dimensions of organizational behavior.* Boston: PWS-KENT Publishing Company, 1991.
2. Beyer, J.M. Ideologies, values and decision making in organizations. In P. Nystrom and W. Starbuck, eds. *Handbook of Organizational Design.* vol 2. London: Oxford University Press, 1981, 166-97.
3. Boeker, W. The development and institutionalization of subunit power in organizations. *Administrative Science Quarterly*, 1990, 34, 388-410.
4. Brislin, R. *Understanding culture's influence on behavior.* Fort Worth: Harcourt Brace Jovanovich, 1993
5. Caudron, S. US West finds strength in diversity. *Personnel Journal*, 1992, March, 40-44.
6. *The Economist*, BP after Horton. July 4, 1992, 324, 59.
7. *The Economist*, Management brief: The best a plan can get. August 15, 1992, 324, 59-60.
8. Etzioni, A. *Modern organizations*, New York: Prentice-Hall, 1963.
9. Gagliardi, P. The creation and change of organizations: A conceptual framework. *Organization Studies*, 1986, 118-33.

10. Gordon, G.G. Industry determinants of organizational culture. *Academy of Management Review*, April 1991, 16, 396-415.

11. Hofstede, G., Neuijen, B., Ohayv, D. and Sanders, G. Measuring organizational cultures: A qualitative and quantitative study across twenty cases. *Administrative Science Quarterly*, 1990, 35, 286-316.

12. Kets de Vries, M.F.R., and Miller, D. *The neurotic organization*. San Francisco: Jossey-Bass, 1984.

13. Kets de Vries, M.F.R., and Miller, D. Personality, culture, and organization. *Academy of Management Review*, 1986, 11(2), 266-79.

14. Kotter, J.P., and Heskett, J.L. *Corporate culture and performance*. New York: The Free Press, 1992.

15. Levine, R., and Wolff, E. Social time: The heartbeat of a culture. *Psychology Today*, 1985, 19, 28-35.

16. March, G., and Simon, H. *Organizations*. New York: John Wiley, 1958.

17. O'Reilly, C.A., Chatman, J., and Caldwell, D.F. People and organizational culture: A profile comparison approach to assessing person-organization fit. *The Academy of Management Journal*, September 1991, 34, 487-516.

18. Pfeffer, J. *Power in organizations*. Boston: Pitman Publishing, 1981.

19. Pfeffer, J. *Managing With Power*. Boston, Massachusetts: Harvard Business School Press, 1992.

20. Rentsch, J.R. Climate and culture: Interaction and qualitative differences in organizational meanings. *Journal of Applied Psychology*, December 1990, 75, 668-681.

21. Sackmann, S.A. Culture and subcultures: An analysis of organizational knowledge. *Administrative Science Quarterly*, March 1992, 37, 140-161.

22. Schwartz, F.N. Management women and the new facts of life. *Harvard Business Review*, January-February 1989, 67, 65-76.

23. Templeton, J. Mercedes is downsizing—and that includes the sticker. *Business Week*, February 8, 1993, 38.

24. Trice, H.M., and Beyer, J.M. Studying organization culture through rites and ceremonials. *Academy of Management Review*, 1984, 9, 653-69.

25. Trice, H.M., and Beyer, J.M. *The Cultures of work organizations*. Englewood Cliffs, New Jersey: Prentice Hall, 1993.

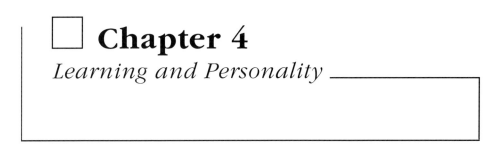

Chapter 4
Learning and Personality

Consultant Peter Senge says that many organizations have learning disabilities that inhibit them from becoming fully effective [44]. The disabilities are reflected in thought patterns, how things are perceived, and how people talk to each other. Senge argues that organizational improvement begins at the individual and group levels, where employees need to learn new patterns of thinking and interacting. Such changes lead in the direction of creating a "learning organization," one that constantly expands its capacity to create its future and can do what it was unable to do before.

What must an organization do to become a learning organization? First people need to identify what they care about to energize passion and commitment. Then they need to develop disciplines, or paths of development, and continued learning. One discipline is systems thinking: Seeing and acting on wholes and on the relationships between its parts rather than react to single events. A second discipline is personal mastery wherein individuals deepen their own skill, focus, and perception. Third, people need to share and alter their mental models to improve what is perceived and how it is interpreted. A fourth discipline is the development of a shared vision to provide a common identity and purpose. Finally, team learning is necessary to make the group smarter than the sum of its parts, and to keep the team effective as the vital learning unit.

Senge's focus on individuals and on their thinking and interactions is well founded. Individual behavior is a key building block of organizational effectiveness. Employee values, attitudes, personality, and perceptions are all decisive in shaping the quality of work. And learning is at the heart of behavior because it explains how people develop and how they might change or improve. If you believe that people can make or break an organization, then it is critical to know something about human behavior. Such knowledge is useful in many facets of managing people such as in selecting and training employees, affecting motivation, improving decision making, reducing stress, and enhancing teamwork. A manager cannot be a professional psychologist, but needs to know enough to manage from sound principles rather than from myths and guesswork. In this chapter, we present some basics about behavior and then discuss the relevance of learning and personality to life at work. In the next chapter, we explore attitudes, perception, and judgment tendencies.

SOME BASICS ABOUT BEHAVIOR

Figure 4.1 is a simplified model of human behavior that depicts four basic elements: the environment, the person, actual behavior, and the consequences of behavior. The environment contains the many elements that exist in the world outside an individual, which are stimuli or causes of behavior. The stimulus environment accounts for a good deal of human behavior. It interacts with the attributes of the person. These attributes also explain and govern behavior. A few important attributes are listed in Figure 4.1, but there are many more. To understand these attributes, we must infer what goes on inside a person or rely on what he or she tells us.

FIGURE 4.1 *Basic Model of Individual Behavior*

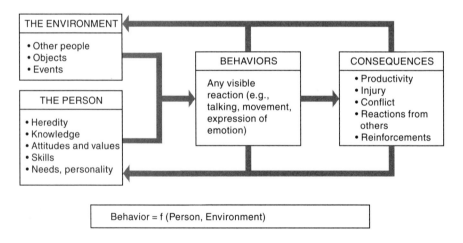

Behavior in the model refers to an overt act of the person that can be observed and measured, but observation of behavior may tell us little about why it occurred. Observable behavior can never be a complete or accurate representation of what goes on inside people, but such behavior does serve as a window to it.

Behavior has consequences; it has an impact on the world and accomplishes something beyond itself. It has intended and unintended effects; for example, behavior at work can produce products for sale, cause an injury, lead to conflict, or trigger reactions in others. Also, behavior has reinforcing consequences that affect the probability of its recurrence. Pleasurable consequences will have a different effect than painful ones.

Finally, the arrows in Figure 4.1 show that behavior, and its consequences serve as feedback mechanisms. People can learn from their behavior and from its effects. Also, behavior can change the environment, such as when we turn down the volume on a loud stereo to make it less annoying. We will discuss a few generalizations that can be made from the model and how these can be of value in managing people.

THE PERSON AND THE ENVIRONMENT

How a person behaves is determined by the person's characteristics interacting with the elements in his or her environment. The formula in Figure 4.1, states that behavior is a function of the person and the environment ($\mathbf{B=f(P,E)}$). Obviously, much of what we do in our conscious life is affected by events in the world around us. But *how* and *why* we respond are also likely to be a function of our internal state and characteristics.

A manager must understand this interaction between the person and the environment, because to overemphasize one in favor of the other risks misinterpretation of human behavior: it can lead to a wrong conclusion about a problem, and then to an inappropriate reaction. A supervisor may decide that an unproductive worker is lazy or inattentive (personal attributes) when actually the worker was behaving in response to pressure from peers or faulty equipment (environmental forces).

CAUSATION AND OVERDETERMINATION

Behavior may result from one or more causes. When there is more than one cause, behavior is overdetermined, especially if only one cause was sufficient to set the behavior in motion.

Multiple causation and **overdetermination** are extremely useful concepts for a manager because they help avoid misinterpreting behavior. Suppose an employee gets very upset over a request to perform an easy assignment. If the manager believes that the request is the only cause of the employee's reaction, he or she might conclude that this is just another case of an uncooperative or resistant employee. Suppose, however, that the manager assumes that there are multiple causes, any one of which might explain the employee's refusal to accept the assignment. The manager might discover, for instance, that the employee is behind in a previous assignment and also feels unfairly treated because co-workers were not willing to carry their share of the load.

SELF-EXPLANATIONS FOR BEHAVIOR

A person may not be able to accurately and fully explain his own reaction [31]. The employee who refused an assignment might say, "It's not my turn" or "I don't feel very well today." But these statements do not explain the cause of the resistance. Because of the difficulties in interpreting what people say, it becomes necessary to seek other information to help understand the behavior.

INDIVIDUAL DIFFERENCES

People are alike in many ways. But at a more specific level, the commonalities between people tend to disappear. People act, feel, and think differently—for practically every human attribute, there are individual differences. If we measure the motivation to succeed, we find that some people are high in this motivation, some are low, and the rest fall in between.

Similarities allow us to generalize about people, to simplify and order our world. Some generalizations are relatively safe (for example, people dislike being embarrassed), whereas others are more questionable or even dangerous (for example, punishment will reduce employee behaviors that cause work accidents).

On the other hand, knowing that people are different can cause complications because we might try to treat every person as unique. When dealing with others, it is probably best to err on the side of appreciating individual differences. This, at least, can help prevent poor generalizations.

STABILITY OF BEHAVIOR

In many ways people are stable and predictable. We often see behavior patterns that persist over time. There is some truth to the statement that past behavior is the best predictor of a person's future behavior. It is fairly safe for a manager to assume that what a worker has done in the past is quite likely to be repeated unless something significant changes.

Stability of behavior, however, does not mean that people do not change. Some aspects of our personality can change, and given the right circumstances, we might even change long-held values. It is, however, easier to change the knowledge, skills, or attitudes of people. We discuss the different issues and processes of change in Chapter 17.

APPROACHES TO LEARNING

Although people inherit certain characteristics and tendencies, much of what we are and do can only be explained in terms of a lifelong learning and socialization process. **Learning** takes place when a relatively permanent change in behavior, or potential for behavior, occurs that is traceable to a person's experience or to practice [10]. **Socialization** is the process by which a person learns and acquires the values, attitudes, beliefs, and accepted behaviors of a culture, society, organization, or group. As a result of these processes, similarities and differences arise between individuals and the cultures they live in.

Learning and socialization are basic to understanding how people acquire knowledge, attitudes, and skills. They explain how people develop their unique personalities, and they are central to interpreting how people perceive and make judgments about the world they live in.

Learning takes place within the individual. We don't see it happen; we can only infer whether learning occurred when we observe a behavior that is different from past behavior given the same stimulus. Learning and behavior are not the same thing. In other words, (1) behavior doesn't always ensure that a person has learned or changed in a significant or permanent way, and (2) learning doesn't ensure that behavior changes will always occur. Suppose an employee does poor-quality work. He may already have the skill and knowledge to perform better; therefore, learning is not necessary to improve performance. Other factors, such as illness, interruptions, or lack of motivation, might account for the poor performance. Also, a worker who learns new ways to improve quality may not apply what he or she has learned.

CLASSICAL CONDITIONING

The **classical conditioning** model of learning is based on the work of Pavlov [37]. In his most famous study, Pavlov conditioned a dog to salivate at the sound of a bell, just as it would if food were presented. Classical conditioning requires the presence of an existing and reflexive stimulus-response pattern such as withdrawing one's hand from a hot object or blinking an eye in response to a puff of air. When such a reflexive pattern exists, it is possible to pair the original stimulus (for example, the puff of air) with a new, different stimulus by presenting the two close together in space or time. Eventually the new stimulus will elicit the same response as the original one. The new stimulus is called a *conditioned stimulus*. For example, suppose a bell is rung just as the air hits your eye. After repeated pairings, the bell alone will cause the eye-blinking response. Figure 4.2 shows how this works.

FIGURE 4.2   *Classical Model of Learning*

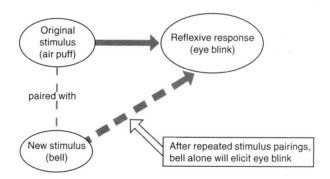

Classical conditioning does not explain how we acquire complex skills such as verbal behavior or skiing, but it does account for a lot of human learning. Many emotional responses can be understood in terms of the classical conditioning model. The fear and anxiety that you once experienced during an auto accident might well recur by hearing screeching tires that you heard at the time of the accident.

Classical conditioning can occur at work, but it often is difficult to know when it is taking place. Usually we can't identify or control conditioned stimuli that explain an employee's reaction. Previous classical conditioning may explain why a person reacts with fear or withdrawal, for example, when someone else makes an innocent remark. The classical conditioning model may help a manager understand such responses.

REINFORCEMENT THEORIES

Reinforcement theories of learning are used to describe situations where behavior is affected by its consequences [45]. This approach is shown in Figure 4.3. It is also called **instrumental learning**. For example, praise by a supervisor can be instrumental in sustaining good performance. This is different from classical conditioning because it is not necessary to have a reflexive stimulus-response pattern for learning to occur. The reinforcement approach accounts for a wide range of learning, from the simplest to the most complex behaviors. It applies to many aspects of behavior in the workplace, just as it does in everyday life. For example, employees may work late for recognition, or they may hide a mistake to avoid reprimand. Learning and reinforcement are central to many topics in this book such as culture and socialization, attitude formation and perception, career choices, motivation and training.

☐ **FIGURE 4.3**   *Reinforcement or Instrumental Model of Learning*

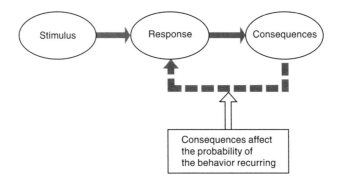

Behavior is viewed as having causes, or antecedents, that act as stimuli. But reinforcement theory focuses more on consequences of the response than on the stimuli that begin the behavioral sequence. Stimuli can trigger behavior, such as when we smell food and feel hungry or react to the ring of a telephone. But the particular response to the stimulus is going to be shaped by the consequence of reacting to it.

Sometimes the consequences of our behavior are within our control, such as when we take a part-time job to earn money to buy a car. The car is our goal, and earning money is instrumental in getting it. Many consequences, however, are beyond our control. They occur as side effects of our behavior, or they are controlled by others who react to what we do. For instance, taking the part-time job may require that you work evenings. This could cause a friend to become angry because you are less available. We can be very aware of some consequences but not as aware of others. However, consequences that we are less aware of can still affect our behavior, and therefore they affect the types of things we learn. Suppose your boss acts more pleasant whenever you do extra work. You might not be aware that she is rewarding a particular behavior, but it can affect you quite significantly.

Types of Consequences. Consequences always follow from behaviors. Some consequences have very little effect, but others can make a difference. They affect the probability of a behavior recurring. Consequences may be *positive (desired)* or they may be *negative (undesired)*. Pay and recognition are examples of positive consequences, and physical abuse and firing are examples of negative ones. The consequences of behavior are positive reinforcement, negative reinforcement (avoidance), punishment, and non-reinforcement (extinction). Figure 4.4 shows the nature of each type of consequence and its effects on the probability of a behavior recurring.

 **FIGURE 4.4**   *Types of Consequences and Their Effects*

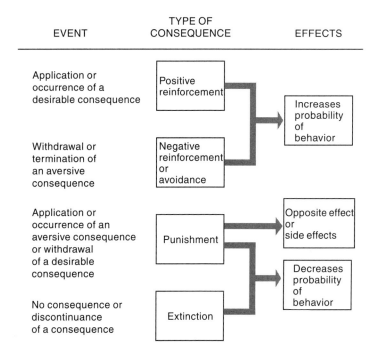

Positive reinforcement is the application or association of desirable consequences with a behavior. When a positive reinforcer is linked to a behavior, it increases the likelihood that the behavior will recur. Figure 4.5(a) shows an example of positive reinforcement at work. Suppose we wish to improve the quality of a secretary's work, meaning a reduction of typing errors. When the secretary types a letter with fewer errors, the supervisor could provide positive reinforcement through praise ("You did great"). If this continues, the stimulus ("Do good work") will eventually lead to lower error rates. Positive reinforcement can be very effective in improving work performance, but we need to follow some rules if rewards are to serve as positive reinforcers. We will discuss these in later chapters on motivation.

FIGURE 4.5   *Examples of Consequences in a Work Setting*

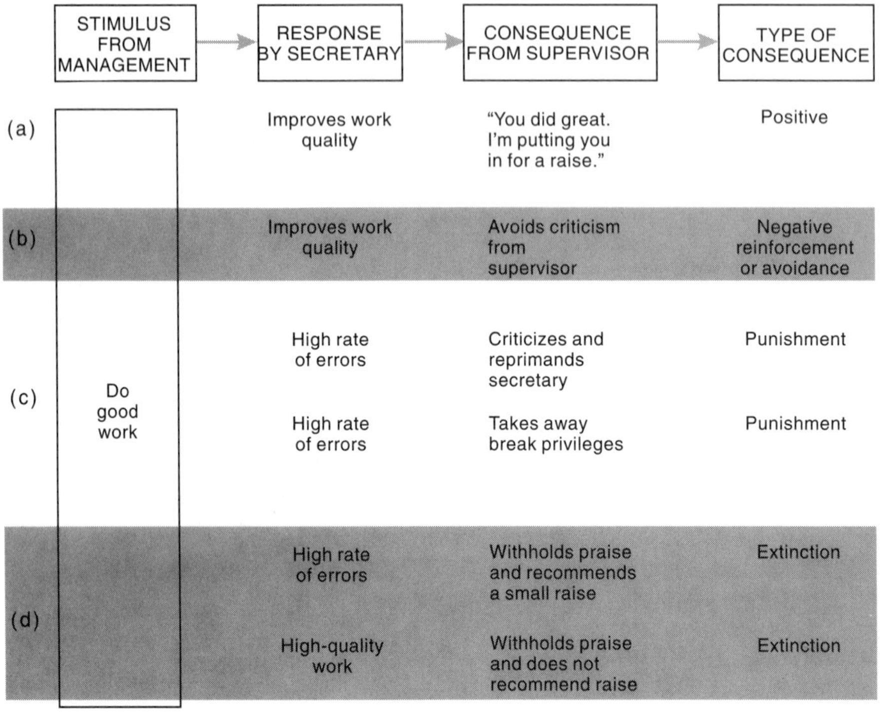

STIMULUS FROM MANAGEMENT	RESPONSE BY SECRETARY	CONSEQUENCE FROM SUPERVISOR	TYPE OF CONSEQUENCE
(a)	Improves work quality	"You did great. I'm putting you in for a raise."	Positive
(b)	Improves work quality	Avoids criticism from supervisor	Negative reinforcement or avoidance
(c) Do good work	High rate of errors	Criticizes and reprimands secretary	Punishment
	High rate of errors	Takes away break privileges	Punishment
(d)	High rate of errors	Withholds praise and recommends a small raise	Extinction
	High-quality work	Withholds praise and does not recommend raise	Extinction

Negative reinforcement occurs when an undesirable consequence is removed. It also increases the likelihood that the behavior will occur again. A worker in a plant with a high noise level finds that wearing earplugs will reduce the discomfort she gets from the noise. This should lead her to associate noise (in the plant) and the use of earplugs. The removal of the noise is a negative reinforcer—it strengthens the association between the stimulus (working in high noise . . .) and the response (wearing the earplugs) [40]. This is also called **avoidance learning**. We engage in the response to avoid a negative effect. Just as a person stops at a red light to avoid a ticket and fine, so a person at work may work hard to meet job standards to avoid negative consequences. Figure 4.5(b) shows how the secretary might improve work quality to avoid criticism from the supervisor.

Negative reinforcement governs a good deal of our behavior. Some think that this is a reasonable way to manage people at work; that is, employees who engage in undesirable behavior should expect something to happen to them. But there can be some difficulties with this approach. First, it creates a tense environment—it is difficult to work day after day where the main motivation is to prevent unpleasant outcomes. Second, relationships often deteriorate when another person, such as the boss, represents a constant threat to be avoided. Negative reinforcement is particularly problematic when it dominates the workplace in the absence of any positive reinforcement.

☐ A CASE OF AVOIDANCE LEARNING

Terry Harbor is a foreman in a plant that manufactures plastic containers. He has a daily production quota that requires a lot of hard work and some luck to meet—everything has to go just right. If a machine breaks down or a worker is absent, the quota may not be met.

An analysis of Terry's performance shows something interesting. He makes quota more often when he is on night shift. He explains this by saying that the front office people aren't around at night to interrupt his work, and his crew can get more done. But Terry does something else too, something that would anger the Plant Manager if he found out about it. Once in a while, when things are particularly bad, Terry "steals" some production from a "Delay for Quality Inspection" (DQI) inventory. The DQI is production that inspectors have set aside because some minor flaws need to be checked out further to see if a batch has to be destroyed or can be shipped. Terry knows from experience that 75 percent of the time these batches are acceptable for shipment, and he can sometimes tell which batches are the best ones.

Because the DQI is not closely managed, Terry can take production from it on nights when it is clear his unit will not be able to meet their production quota. He can even ship DQI stock produced by other crews, so that if a customer complains, his crew is safe.

What prompts Terry into this kind of behavior? One visit to a staff meeting with the Plant Manager, George Roberts, and the answer becomes apparent. Roberts uses these meetings very often to discuss quotas, and he presses his foremen very hard to meet them. More than once a foreman has been publicly chewed out at a staff meeting. Terry has simply figured out one way to keep the Plant Manager off his neck and to protect his crew and maybe his job.

Punishment can take two forms. Negative consequences (undesirable things) can be applied to a response or positive consequences (desirable things) can actively be taken away. Figure 4.5(c) shows how the secretary could be punished when there are high error rates. The manager may be very critical and reprimand the secretary. Figure 4.5(c) also shows how punishment can be applied by withdrawing positive consequences. Here the contingent result of low-quality work is taking away the secretary's extra break privileges. In both instances the response "high error rates" should be decreased.

There is an important distinction between punishment and negative reinforcement. In the instance of punishment, we learn to prevent negative consequences by withholding behaviors. For example, we don't criticize our boss if he treats us unfairly because we are afraid we might be fired. In negative reinforcement we *learn to do things* (perform responses) that stop the occurrence of a negative consequence. We might learn to avoid certain situations at work where we might be made angry by our boss [7].

To be effective, punishment needs to be carefully handled. It cannot be too mild, nor too severe—its magnitude should "fit the crime." It should be linked to the undesirable behavior and applied as close in time as possible. Punishment is more effective if it encourages an incompatible response or a desirable substitute response. Finally, it shouldn't be linked to a positive reinforcer like sympathy [27]. For example, after calling attention to a worker's error, it is not wise to show sympathy and affection because the worker appears saddened or upset.

Problems with the Use of Punishment. While punishment can affect behavior, there are serious problems with using it. First, it can have an opposite effect and actually become a positive reinforcer. A subordinate who is supposedly punished may in fact feel rewarded by having gotten his boss angry or by getting the attention and support of fellow workers.

The second difficulty is that punishment can have undesirable side effects. For instance, punishment can reduce the frequency of desirable behaviors. It contributes to a fearful environment in which people may stop taking initiative or trying new things, or they might cut back on bringing problems to their boss's attention. Punishment can deteriorate the superior-subordinate relationship. Punishment can lead to aggression; subordinates can always find ways to retaliate. Another problem is that punishment may be addressing a symptom and not the cause of the undesirable behavior. If the cause persists, the behavior will probably persist.

Finally, the manager can't control how other employees interpret the punishment. It is often the punished employee who controls the information that other employees receive about it. They return to the workplace and give their own interpretation of the situation. If they lack accuracy and completeness in their tale or if they distort their report to save face, the punishment will not serve as an example to others. This is ironic, because managers often punish to set an example but may end up at the mercy of misinformation and rumor.

Punishment at work should be a last resort. Reprimands and firing may have to occur, but it is best to try to correct the behavior first. Positive reinforcement is a much better alternative, and many examples exist of its effective use in improving performance and attendance (21, 30). It is more constructive to hold counseling discussions with an employee. Such discussions can uncover causes and lead to solutions that are more likely to succeed in eliminating undesirable behavior. They should focus on getting a commitment to change [28].

Interesting problems have arisen recently with the increasing number of employees that work at computer terminals. The opportunity for management to monitor performance can be handled in either a destructive or constructive way [20]. If employees feel watchdogged, pressured, or are punished as a result of monitoring, they may well learn the wrong things. Confusion, mistrust, and tension may lead them to hide mistakes rather than learn from them. Monitoring might not have the bad name it now has if it were used to improve methods of doing the work and increasing the quality of performance.

Extinction is another way to change behavior. **Extinction** involves the cessation of a previously established reinforcer that is maintaining a behavior. Either a positive or aversive consequence may be discontinued. Managers may extinguish a response of a worker by *not* reinforcing it for an extended period of time; the response then becomes less frequent and eventually stops. Figure 4.5(d) shows two examples of extinguishing behavior. In one case, the supervisor withholds both praise and punishment for the secretary when there are high error rates. In the other, praise and rewards are withheld when good performance occurs. In both cases the response rates may decrease, but one is desirable behavior and the other one isn't.

Extinction is important and quite common. For instance, when there is no distinction between rewards for average performance and outstanding performance, employees soon learn that high levels of performance don't pay off. In short, they have been extinguished from doing more than average or minimal performance. Another interesting case of extinction is when an employee seeks feedback on his or her performance. He or she might get a reply such as, "I thought you knew you were doing well; I haven't been on your back have I?" A boss who manages by saying little or nothing to the good employee might well be fostering mediocre work performance.

Extinction, then, can diminish undesirable or desirable responses. Managers should be very sensitive to the wide array of possibilities of extinction in the workplace. Employees shouldn't learn that good behaviors have little or no consequence.

Reinforcement Schedules. The consequences of behavior can occur in different patterns that affect how quickly a behavior is learned and how resistant it is to change or extinction. These patterns of consequences are called **reinforcement schedules**. The five reinforcement schedules shown in Figure 4.6 are (1) continuous, (2) fixed interval, (3) variable interval, (4) fixed ratio, and (5) variable ratio.

1. In **continuous schedules** a response is reinforced (or punished) each time it occurs. For example, when learning a new job, an instructor may be constantly present to respond in a reinforcing manner each time a worker does the right thing. Continuous reinforcement is also used in programmed instruction in a training setting. In this case, the trainee answers questions after having studied a portion of the training material and then receives reinforcement by looking up the answer.

It is not easy to apply a continuous schedule in interpersonal situations, because it requires the constant presence of another person. This level of attention is unusual at work. Supervisors cannot use continuous reinforcement or punishment schedules unless they monitor subordinates closely. Such monitoring is probably not advisable, except for short periods where a supervisor is coaching or training an employee on a specific task. Close monitoring can create an unfavorable climate if subordinates feel they are constantly watched. This form of "close supervision" has been shown to have undesirable effects on the satisfaction and productivity of work groups [26].

☐ **FIGURE 4.6**   *Schedules of Reinforcement and Their Effects on Learning and Extinction*

CONTINOUS SCHEDULE

Every Response Reinforced; Rapid Learning and Extinction

	FIXED	**VARIABLE**
INTERVAL (Time)	FIXED INTERVAL Reinforcement at fixed times. Learning fairly slow and connected to time. Moderately resistant to extinction	VARIABLE INTERVAL Reinforcement at varied, perhaps unpredictable times. Learning is slow and activity high. Very resistant to extinction.
RATIO (Responses)	FIXED RATIO Reinforcement after a fixed number of responses. Learning slow, activity high, and pauses after reinforcement. Moderately resistant to extinction.	VARIABLE RATIO Reinforcement after a varying number of responses. Learning slow, respone rule steady and very high. Very resistant to extinction.

2. In **fixed-interval schedules,** a response is reinforced after a fixed amount of time has elapsed. Fixed-interval schedules produce irregular performance rates, with behavior at its highest rate closer in time to when the reinforcement occurs. When performance appraisals are scheduled every six months, employees are likely to work harder as the time for appraisal nears. Pay is another example. It is generally given at a regular time of the week or month. It is difficult to say exactly what pay reinforces, but it is unlikely that paychecks reinforce performance because pay is often not a function of performance. The most probable effect of a regular paycheck is to reinforce attendance (if pay is reduced for lateness) or to keep people from quitting.

3. **Variable-interval schedules** are those in which the period of time between reinforcements is not constant. Variable-interval schedules are

common in work settings. Supervisors often visit workplaces at irregular intervals. Consider the example of a security guard who doesn't dare leave his post because he doesn't know when the post might be checked by a supervisor.

The problem with variable-interval schedules is that they might also effect the wrong behavior. If subordinates are rewarded by a visit from the boss, the visit might inadvertently reinforce an undesirable act. Suppose the boss makes an unscheduled visit and tells an employee what a good job she is doing, but arrives on the job site just after the employee has returned late from a work break. The employee may feel herself to be the victim of inconsistent signals or may feel some resentment (e.g., "Why wasn't she here when I did so well the other day?").

4. In **fixed-ratio schedules**, a certain number of responses must occur before a reinforcement follows. An example of a fixed-ratio schedule at work is a piece-rate payment system in which the employee is credited with additional pay for increments of productivity. Additional wages are received for each dozen cartons packed, each ten subscriptions sold or every four assemblies completed. Fixed-ratio schedules can produce high rates of response and can continue to do so as long as the reinforcement remains powerful.

5. **Variable-ratio schedules** are when the number of behaviors necessary for a reinforcement varies. A person might be reinforced after one response or after several, and the number of required behaviors changes. This schedule produces a very high and steady rate of response, typically without predictable pauses or bursts of behavior. Gambling and fishing are good examples of variable-ratio schedules. The payoff occurs at unpredictable times and sustains behavior over long periods. Hundreds of lottery tickets might be bought before that winning ticket comes along. It may take many casts before a fish is hooked.

Variable-ratio schedules exist at work when managers reward irregularly, either by accident or design. Some companies have tried to implement them formally by using lotteries to affect attendance. Employees with good attendance records are eligible for a drawing in which prizes are given, but unless the reinforcement occurs or its perceived likelihood remains, it won't affect behavior. Extinction would take place if the employee attends regularly but never wins a prize. Some organizations have tried "poker" games to affect attendance, with disastrous results. Beginning on Monday, employees receive one poker card a day if they attend work. The best hand wins a prize on the fifth (Friday) card each week. Employees with poor hands "drop out of the game," so to speak, because they have no chance to win. Attendance would then be at its worst on Friday.

Reinforcement, Extinction, and Shaping. The strength of a learned behavior or how resistant it is to change is a function of the reinforcement schedule (see

☐ **Investment in Human Capital** _____

The Donnelly Corporation in Holland, Michigan is a successful auto parts manufacturer. It sells its auto mirrors to every U.S. and Asian auto maker in business in North America. It controls 95 percent of the inside rearview mirror market in the United States, 60 percent in Europe and 50 percent in Japan. Donnelly attributes much of its success to its treatment of employees. It has been a highly participative organization for many years, and continual learning has been at the heart of its practices. The philosophy is that as employee skills grow, so does their capacity to assume responsibility for the success of the firm. Expectations, time, and money all aim at employee training and development. Donnelly agrees with many analysts, however, that training efforts must become more coordinated, focused and timely to have a maximum effect on their organization's continued success.

Figure 4.6). Continuous schedules lead to more rapid learning, but they also lead to rapid extinction of learned behaviors. When steady reinforcement is followed by withholding of reinforcement (extinction), the response rates quickly decrease.

Intermittent or partial reinforcement schedules result in slower learning, on the other hand, but they also slow down extinction. Once behavior is learned with partial schedules, it is very resistant to change. In part, a reason for this is that the behavior when there is no reinforcement has consequences similar to when the reinforcement was operating; that is, the person may continue to anticipate a reinforcement. If the behavior developed as a result of a fixed schedule, the person might anticipate the possibility that a new interval or different ratio of reinforcement is being put into effect. If the behavior developed as a result of a variable schedule, the person might simply assume that reinforcement is bound to occur again, sooner or later. But even without these conscious thought processes, intermittent learning schedules produce very resistant and durable behavior patterns. This is why people persist in some activities even when the odds are against them. In fact, most of what we learn is a result of partial schedules, not continuous ones. Most of these schedules are quite variable, not fixed. This creates a problem when managers try to use the most effective reinforcement schedules to induce new behaviors. They are up against difficult conditions when they try to extinguish old behaviors that were learned on partial schedules.

An alternative approach to changing behavior is to require, encourage, and reinforce *substitute behaviors* to replace undesirable ones. An effective way to do this is called **behavior shaping**, which involves reinforcing small increments of behavior that are in the direction of desired behavior until a final desired result is achieved. Behavior shaping may be used in all kinds of learning, not just when we are trying to extinguish or overcome old habits. Shaping requires that we break down a desired response into components and think of the desired behavior as a sequence of the components. Then if we can encourage a part of the behavior at the beginning or elsewhere in the sequence (whichever may be easier to do), it can be reinforced. This continues until the complete behavior is learned. For example, suppose that a manager in your department has been resisting the use of personal computers in his unit. You believe that the reason for his resistance is simply that he is afraid he will not be able to use them easily. Some ways that you can begin shaping his behavior so that he will eventually introduce personal computers are:

1. Take him to the office of another manager who has successfully introduced computers so that he can see the benefits that her department gained.

2. Assign him a simple task that requires the use of a computer on which he works with a supportive and helpful computer user.

3. Ask him to prepare a brief report on the costs, benefits, and user-friendliness of different computer brands.

Throughout this process, you would encourage and positively reinforce any behaviors consistent with your overall goal of introducing computers.

VICARIOUS LEARNING

People can also learn by observing other people and imitating or **modeling** themselves after what other people do [6]. This is called **vicarious learning**. From this perspective, individuals are viewed as thinkers who draw conclusions and make decisions about what they observe [50]. One stage of vicarious learning involves observing and thinking. Another stage occurs when the individual actively engages in new behaviors.

Several conditions are involved in vicarious learning [7, 48]. These are:

1. The learner must have a reason to pay attention to the model or stimulus. Anything that attracts attention, such as expertise or status, will contribute to attention.

2. The learner needs to retain sufficient information to pattern behavior after the model.

3. The person must have enough ability to engage in the model's behavior. Most of us cannot model ourselves after a great athlete or Nobel Prize winner in physics.

4. There must be a motivational or reinforcement element. The person must perceive the probability of rewards and eventually receive reinforcement for imitation. There must be some incentive and encouragement involved.

These conditions show that vicarious learning involves more than just reinforcing behavior. It is part of what is called **social learning theory** [6, 29]. This learning involves thinking, including intentions, goal setting, reasoning, and decision making in addition to reinforcements. Learning can take place by reading books, watching television, or interacting with people. Social or vicarious learning occurs quite naturally at work. For example, one key to a manager's success is to have a mentor to emulate [25]. Vicarious learning has been used effectively in management training programs in which supervisors observed, practiced, got feedback, and were reinforced for modeling effective supervisor behavior [23].

☐ A NATIONAL LEARNING PROBLEM

Among the many problems facing the United States, the need for an appropriately-educated work force is critical. According to *Business Week* the U.S. work force needs help; it trails rivals such as Germany and Japan in many measures of human capital [38]. One measure is worker training, which is said to be a key to raising productivity and wealth. Unless some changes are made, U.S. workers will lack the knowledge, skill, and attitudes necessary for organizations to remain competitive in a global economy. Thus, learning becomes a major force in organizations.

Many schools, programs, and training attempts in the United States are outstanding, but there is no overall system to focus efforts or to coordinate them in a meaningful way. A job training system would have mechanisms by which employers and schools could cooperate more. Vocational instruction and adult education would be widely available and relevant. Employee training priorities would be more reflective of pressing needs. For example, public schools which produce 56 percent of U.S. workers need to keep pace with job requirements including the improvement of math, verbal, and science skills. Well-designed apprenticeship programs could help attract workers into occupations where employees are needed. The American Society for Training and Development (ASTD) says that most of the $30 billion spent on training by Corporate America is accounted for by less than 10 percent of all companies. And a disproportionate amount goes to professionals and managers who have the most skill to begin with. An ASTD economist argues that 50 million nonprofessional U.S. workers need another $30 billion more for technical and other training to perform at peak efficiency. This calls for companies to budget 1.5 percent of their payrolls. Is this too much? In Germany and Japan 3 to 4 percent is the norm.

TRANSFER OF LEARNING

Transfer of learning occurs when behavior learned in one situation occurs in another situation. Sometimes the transfer is appropriate, but sometimes it is not. Suppose you take a job in a company in which there are relaxed standards of dress. So long as you are productive and dress neatly, you can succeed. If you change jobs and join another firm, your dress may no longer be acceptable, and you could suffer the consequences despite your good work. What you learned in the first company transferred negatively to the second.

For learning to transfer, it is necessary to have similar stimulus conditions to those that existed when the behavior was learned. For example, the use of similar or identical equipment at work that one used in training aids the transfer. It also helps to maintain the reinforcements and feedback that took place in training to the extent that they are necessary.

PERSONALITY

Personality is the relatively stable organization of all a person's characteristics, an enduring pattern of attributes that define the uniqueness of a person. Personality implies predispositions as well as patterns of overt behaviors, because attitudes and values are part of the pattern. There is no single theory that integrates all we know about personality; each theory and approach has its own way of characterizing it. For example, some approaches see personality as a set of predispositions to behave in similar ways across a variety of situations. These approaches emphasize people's traits, and their attitudes and needs that drive behavior [2, 11, 33, 35]. There are learning theories of personality, such as social learning theory discussed earlier, in which people are viewed as the sum total of all they have learned. Other approaches stress personality dynamics in terms of the perceptions, thoughts, and judgments people engage in as they cope and mature in the world around them [41]. The self concept grows out of an attempt to express oneself and use one's capacities. Finally, some theories look at the tensions that exist inside a person, and see personality as the consequence of internal conflicts and how they are resolved. You are probably familiar with the work of Freud who dramatized the struggle between our inner impulses and our moral conscience [15].

SOME BASICS ABOUT PERSONALITY

Even though behavior is the product of both the person and the situation, personality-driven behavior can show a good deal of consistency across different situations [13]. This is especially true if a broad disposition such as need for achievement is operating. A specific trait such as honesty may vary more with the situation. But even specific traits will effect behavior when conditions are appropriate [17]. For example, friendliness is more apt to emerge in the presence of other people.

It is also likely that personality will help determine the kinds of situations that people enter. Shy persons will avoid social situations. Once in these situations, the trait may still emerge, such as when the shy person's tension is apparent to others at a party. In some settings, however, personality attributes may be squelched. Sociability may be impossible to express in a hostile or threatening environment.

Under what conditions is personality likely to manifest itself or be a cause of behavior? It seems that personality effects are less apparent and less powerful in structured situations [34, 49]. In structured situations, rules, task demands, and other constraints act to limit behavior. Rewards and tight standards and expectations can add to the limits, making personality even less likely to emerge. In ambiguous situations that are loosely structured, personality characteristics are more likely to manifest themselves. Personality becomes a

115

stronger cause and explanation of behavior. One would therefore expect personalities to operate more actively in organic organizations and in matrix structures, as compared to bureaucratic or mechanistic settings [47]. Therefore, if one wants to understand behavior in personality terms, it is best to observe people when structure is loose or has broken down. Also, if you want personality to operate more fully in order to capitalize on personality differences, it is necessary to loosen controls and expectations, and otherwise permit more situational freedom. This may be helpful when creativity or adaptation to a novel problem is needed.

Schneider [43] has shed some additional light on the relative contribution of personality and situation on behavior. He refers to the "attraction-selection-attrition" cycle in organizational settings. The cycle says that people select the situation they prefer to enter. They are attracted to organizations they enter, and upon entry they make the situation what it is. As similar people become attracted, and as dissimilar people leave, the situation gets more homogeneous. In this manner, the people who make up the environment define it by establishing norms and maintaining the culture. So while the situation may effect behavior, it is the people in that situation that define it. Homogeneity of personalities may become a threat to the organization's survival. If one wants to change such a situation, it is necessary to change the mix of people and to select new people so as to add variability.

PERSONALITY IN THE ORGANIZATION SETTING

Personality is a useful concept for interpreting and managing in many organizational situations. For example, personality measures have long been used successfully as a way to select and place applicants for jobs [46]. Throughout this book, reference is made to personality in explaining a variety of topics. Dominant personalities are seen as central to defining an organization's culture. Personality is treated as a key factor in understanding adjustment to work and career, coping with stress, and problem solving and decision making behavior. Personality is also viewed as central to the dynamics of motivation, and interpersonal conflict and politics.

In the remainder of this chapter, we will present some personality concepts that have been studied particularly in the organizational setting.

FIVE IMPORTANT DIMENSIONS OF PERSONALITY

Over the years, many personality concepts have been discussed and measures developed for them. Analyses of these concepts has led to a grouping of them into five dimensions of personality. Concepts within these dimensions appear repeatedly in research and theory:

1. **Extroversion:** sociable, gregarious, ambitious

2. **Emotional Stability:** anxiety, depression, worry, insecurity

3. **Agreeableness:** friendly, cooperative, conforming, tolerant, trusting, good natured

4. **Conscientiousness:** dependable, responsible, achieving, persevering

5. **Openness to Experience:** imaginative, curious, cultured, broad minded

Barrick and Mount examined many studies that used these dimensions to predict success on the job and success in training for different types of workers [8]. Conscientiousness predicted success on the job and in training for all of the groups studied: managers, professionals, salespeople, police, and skilled/semi-skilled workers. Extroversion predicted job success for managers and salespeople. Extroversion and Openness to Experience did the best in predicting success in training settings.

ACCOMMODATIONS TO ORGANIZATIONAL LIFE

Individuals adapt to organizations and organizations adapt to individuals. Anyone who stays in an organization has to resolve conflicts between work and outside interests, establish work relationships, and achieve a minimal level of competence [14]. Socialization and personality play a role in the ways a person adjusts to work life and the level of satisfaction of the accommodation they eventually make. Regardless of how successfully they adjust, there are three basic types of accommodations. According to Presthus, they are the *organizationalist*, the *professional*, and the *indifferent* [39].

The **organizationalist** is a person with a strong commitment to the place of work. A person with this orientation exhibits the following tendencies:

1. Has strong identification with the organization and has a self-concept that is tied to it

2. Seeks organization rewards and advancement because they represent an important measure of success and organizational status

3. Has high morale and job satisfaction

4. Has low tolerance for ambiguity about work goals and assignments.

5. Identifies with superiors and shows deference toward them

6. Rationalizes organization pressures for conformity and compliance because of a desire to advance

7. Emphasizes organizational goals of efficiency and effectiveness

8. Has high status anxiety reflected by a concern with threats to organizational success

9. Avoids controversy

10. Maintains the "chain of command"

From early socialization experiences, the organizationlist develops an early respect for authority figures, realizing that they have the power to dispense rewards and/or sanctions. Compliance and respect for authority are viewed as the ways to success. Organizationalists are success oriented, and seek it in the organization context. They learn how to avoid failure experiences that grow out of being a "troublemaker." The organizationalist often comes from a family in which rewards are applied primarily by the father [39].

The **professional** is a person who is *job centered*, not organizational centered, and who tends to view organization demands as pressure or a nuisance and seeks to avoid them. But that is impossible since the professional must have an organization in which to work. At work, professionals experience more role conflict and are more alienated [19]. A professor who values teaching and research may not be very loyal to the university. If she were, she would be an organizationalist. But she must be in some university to teach and conduct research. This is a very conflicting role for the professional. Professionals exhibit the following tendencies:

1. Experience occupational socialization that instills high standards of performance in the chosen field

2. See organizational authority as nonrational when there is pressure to act in ways that are not "professionally" acceptable

3. Are highly ideological about work values

4. Tend to feel that their skills are not fully utilized in organizations. Self-esteem may be threatened when the professional feels that he or she does not have the opportunity to do those things for which he or she has been trained

5. Refuse to play the organizational status game except as it reflects their worth relative to others in the organization

6. Seek recognition from other professionals outside the organization

In early socialization, the professional learns that successful performance, not compliance with authority, gets more reinforcement. Many professionally oriented people come from the middle class and have become successful through a higher level of education or by other efforts to increase personal competence [39]. A professional is likely to have a strong "ideological" orientation and to be extremely concerned with doing well in his or her chosen field. Success for the professional is usually defined in terms of personal achievement, more than likely by recognition from external colleagues rather than by the rewards received internally in the organization. Organizational rewards are not without value, however, since they may reflect the professional's importance relative to others in the system. The recognition may be extremely fulfilling for the professional working in an organization, especially when he or she is accorded higher status and pay than those in other work groups.

The **indifferents** are people who work for pay, and work is not a critical part of their life structure. They may do their work well, but they are not highly committed to their job or the organization. The following are some characteristics of indifferents:

1. Seek higher-order need satisfaction outside work and the work organization

2. Are more oriented toward leisure, not the "work ethic"; they separate work from more meaningful aspects of life

3. Reject status symbols in organizations

4. Tend to be alienated from work and are not committed to the organization; indifferents are more alienated than either organizationalists or professionals [19]

5. Withdraw psychologically from work and organizations when possible

Indifferents often come from the lower middle class [39]. With a limited education, indifferents often work in routine jobs with few advancement opportunities. Research indicates that commitment is lower when jobs have narrow scope and more stress [16]. We must not assume, however, that only lower-level personnel are indifferents. Certainly we would expect to find fewer of them at higher levels, but they are not uncommon there. Often a person refocuses his or her life on other things. Employees who were once fiercely loyal may no longer follow orders without question. For example, early in a working career a manager may be extremely committed to the organization. He or she may seek its rewards and want to advance. However, in middle age and in later career life, the person may have been passed over several times for promotion or had other disappointments. When this happens, the person seeks reinforcement elsewhere. Thus, it is possible that through their promotion practices, organizations may turn highly committed organizationalists into indifferents.

AUTHORITARIAN PERSONALITY

Perhaps you have worked for someone who was punitive and rigid and who didn't respect you or was trying to demean or control you. You sensed he or she wanted you to be submissive and seemed intolerant of weakness. A person like this is an **authoritarian personality** [1]. Those who have an authoritarian personality believe in obedience and respect for authority and that the strong should lead the weak. They have an excessive concern for power based on their prejudices about people—they feel that some people are superior and should lead others.

Because of their beliefs in hierarchical order, authoritarians make good followers if they respect and accept a superior. Normally, however, it is not easy to relate to them. Maslow says that true authoritarians will take advantage of others, and the best way to deal with them is to assert your own authority if possible [32]. Extreme authoritarians are not overly common, but some people have such tendencies. This personality type is unlikely to fare well in a company trying to use more democratic or participative techniques that try to involve employees in decision making.

BUREAUCRATIC PERSONALITY

Gordon has postulated that a person's beliefs or values might dispose him or her toward a preference for rules, regulations, and order as a way of running organizations [18]. He called this a bureaucratic orientation but did not believe that it was based on prejudice as the authoritarian personality is. Yet the per-

☐ THE ABRASIVE PERSONALITY

Harry Levinson, a psychologist who has studied and written widely on behavior in organizations, has identified what he calls the *abrasive personality*. Such a person can be very difficult to deal with at work and contributes to tensions in relating to peers, superiors, and subordinates. The abrasive personality "has a knack for jabbing others in an irritating, often painful way. . . ." He or she criticizes brutally in a condescending manner, is impatient with others, won't delegate or trust, and makes others feel inadequate. This person acts in a privileged way, with self-admiration, confidence, and self-assurance. Unable to compromise, he or she is stubborn, inflexible, and lacks a sense of humor. In short, the abrasive personality is self-centered, isolated, perfectionist, and demeans or threatens others.

Levinson says that this extreme behavior is really an attempt to escape from a set of opposite feelings. The intense striving of the abrasive personality, at the expense of others, is actually based on an underlying sense of inadequacy and helplessness. A low self-image leads to a striving for perfection that will help make this person feel less vulnerable. In relations with others, the abrasive personality will over control them, act all-powerful, and push for an unattainable level of personal security and self-worth. This only adds to feelings of inadequacy and failure, which fuels the tendency to take feelings out on co-workers.

Source: H. Levinson, The abrasive personality at the office, *Psychology Today*, May 1978 [24].

son with a **bureaucratic personality** values hierarchy, rule conformity, and impersonal and formal relationships. He or she believes that employees should identify with the organization and defer to more experienced members, people at higher levels should have the prerogative to make important decisions, and people who work in an organization should subordinate their individual preferences to the needs of the organization. Those with a strong bureaucratic personality adapt well to military organizations and are more satisfied in organizations that have more rules, procedures, and regulations [18].

This approach to personality might be useful as a way to select and place people so that their personalities fit better with the demands and design of an organization. Work that is routine, repetitive, and proceduralized might be better supervised by a manager with a bureaucratic orientation.

MACHIAVELLIANISM

Another personality dimension called **Machiavellianism** has interpersonal and leadership implications for the workplace [12]. People who are high in this characteristic *(high Machs)* have high self-esteem and self-confidence and behave in their own self-interest. They are seen as cool and calculating, attempt to take advantage of others, and seek to form alliances with people in power to help serve their own goals. High Machs might lie, deceive, or compromise morality, believing that ends justify means. Truly high-Mach people would not even experience guilt—they somehow detach themselves from the consequences of their actions.

A high Mach also has a tendency to use false or exaggerated praise to manipulate others. They take care not to be swayed by considerations of loyalty, friendship, and trust. A high Mach might give lip service to such things, but when the chips are down, he or she will not let them stand in the way of personal gain. This gives them a big advantage over those who value friendship and act on trust.

Those with a Machiavellian personality are able to select situations where their tactics will work: face-to-face, emotional, unstructured, and ambiguous conditions. Not distracted by emotions, they are able to calmly exert control in power vacuums or novel situations. Machiavellianism is not rare in today's society. Studies show that there are many people with moderate to high Mach orientations.

LOCUS OF CONTROL

People can be characterized according to whether they believe what happens to them is externally controlled or whether it is controlled internally by their own effort [42]. A person who believes that important outcomes are controlled by others has an external **locus of control**. Belief in self-control of one's outcomes means an internal locus of control exists. An internal locus of control is correlated with needs for independence. For example, internal people want to participate in decisions that affect them. Internal control is also correlated with better adjustment to work in terms of satisfaction, coping with stress, job involvement, and promotability [3]. Internals also show fewer absences and more involvement at work [9].

Locus of control has implications for selecting, training, and placing people for leadership and other demanding situations. There is even some speculation that if locus of control in a society shifts from internal toward external, interest in work could be affected. As interest in work declines, so might productivity [7].

Rules, policies, and other management controls can interact with locus of control to affect motivation. Internal locus of control employees might experience frustration and respond with hostility or leave the organization. A variety of responses are possible when one's orientation toward control is inconsistent with the environment. Externals might react negatively to tasks or jobs that call for independent action. Thus, they might resist efforts such as job enrichment and quality of work life that add autonomy and decision-making responsibility to jobs.

PERSONALITY AND WORK-STYLE PREFERENCES

An early theory of personality [22] forms the basis for classifying people according to the kinds of jobs and interactions they prefer and the ways they approach problems [36]. Four dimensions, called **Myers-Briggs dimensions**, are used to describe the personality underlying these preferences. Each dimension forms a continuum that people fall along.

1. *Sensation-intuition dimension.* Sensation-oriented people like structured situations, established routine, realism, and precise and uncomplicated details and enjoy using skills already learned. Intuitive people prefer new problems, dislike repetition, and are impatient with routine. They enjoy learning new skills, follow their inspirations, jump to conclusions, and make errors of fact.

2. *Thinking-feeling dimension.* Thinking individuals are unemotional, and often unknowingly they hurt people's feelings. They like to analyze and put things in logical order. They seem impersonal and hard-hearted, and relate best to other thinking types. Feeling types are more aware of other people and enjoy pleasing them. They like harmony and are influenced by other people's needs and desires. They are sympathetic and relate well to most people.

3. *Introversion-extroversion dimension.* Introverts prefer quiet concentration and think a lot before acting. They work well alone and can stay with one project a long time. Much thought precedes action, sometimes without action. Introverts dislike interruptions, forget names, and can have problems communicating. Extroverts show impatience with long, slow jobs and like to work fast, uncomplicated by procedures. They prefer variety and action to contemplation. They are good with people and like them around, and usually communicate quite well.

4. *Perceptive-judgment dimension.* Perceptive people adapt to change and welcome new ideas. They can leave things open and unsolved and delay decisions without grave concern. They may start too many new projects, postpone unpleasant ones, and leave things unfinished. Judgment types prefer to plan work and follow the plan. They get things settled on just the essentials and are satisfied with conclusions. They decide too quickly and dislike switching off a project in progress.

These dimensions can be combined in a variety of ways. One basic combination is a mixture of the sensation-intuition and thinking-feeling dimensions. This particular configuration is shown in Figure 4.7. Each cell describes how the person prefers to deal with information and people and gives some examples as to the kind of occupations each type might be attracted to.

The sensing-intuition dimension and the introversion-extroversion dimension can be combined as shown in Figure 4.8, which also contains short descriptions of resulting styles in each cell.

FIGURE 4.7 *One Combination Possibility from the Myers-Briggs Theory*

	SENSING	**INTUITION**
FEELING	**Sensing and Feeling** • Sociable, friendly • Approach facts with human concern • Believe in orderly organizations to meet people's needs • Like human contact jobs such as teaching, welfare, customer relations	**Intuition and Feeling** • Enthusiastic, insightful • Like new projects, broad themes • Interest in human welfare • Prefer decentralized, loose organizations • Like jobs that affect people such as teachng, public relations, writing, research, personnel
THINKING	**Sensing and Thinking** • Practical, matter-of-fact • Logical, decisive • Lack interpersonal skills • Prefer bureaucratic organizations • Like technical, analytical job such as accounting, computer work, production	**Intuition and Thinking** • Logical, ingenious • Like changes, new possibilities, abstract thinking • Prefer theoretical, technical problems • Like impersonal, conceptual organizations • Like jobs that permit design and analysis like research, engineering, law, science

FIGURE 4.8 *Myers-Briggs Types Using Introversion-Extroversion vs. Sensing-Intuition*

	SENSING	**INTUITION**
INTROVERT	**INTROVERT/SENSING** Knowledge is important to establish the truth "Careful compilers"	**INTROVERT/INTUITION** Knowledge is important for its own sake "Academics"
EXTROVERT	**EXTROVERT/SENSING** Knowledge is important for practical use "Pragmatists"	**EXTROVERT/INTUITION** Knowledge is important for innovation "Innovators"

These concepts can be used to improve decision making. People can be taught when it is best to exert their sensing, intuition, thinking, or feeling modes. They can also learn when it is best to pair with each other to improve decision making. This is referred to as the mutual **usefulness of opposites**, and it works as follows:

1. *The sensing type needs an intuitive* to generate possibilities, supply ingenuity, deal with complexity, and furnish new ideas. Intuitives add a long-range perspective and spark things that seem impossible.

2. *The intuitive needs a sensing type* to bring up facts, to inspect, attend to detail, inject patience, and notice what needs attention.

3. *The thinker needs a feeling type* to persuade and conciliate feelings, to arouse enthusiasm and sell or advertise, and to teach and forecast if necessary.

4. *The feeling type needs a thinker* to analyze and organize, predict flaws in advance, introduce fact and logic, hold to a policy, and stand firm against opposition.

Frustrating the Mature Personality

Argyris' theory [4, 5] states that there is often a fundamental incongruence between the mature personality and the demands that many organizations place on employees. As people mature, they go from being passive to active, develop from a state of dependence to independence, and go from a simple behavioral repertoire to a complex one. Maturity also moves people toward deeper and varied interests, from a short to a longer time perspective, from subordinancy to equal or superordinate roles, and to higher stakes of self-awareness and self-control.

Argyris thinks that many organizational and managerial practices are inconsistent with the mature personality. Jobs are frequently highly specialized, consisting only of a few simple tasks. Managers, not workers, make most of the decisions and do most of the things that involve judgment and maturity. This makes employees feel dependent, externally controlled, and pressured to be passive rather than active at work. In short, they feel frustrated because they cannot act as mature human beings at work. A sense of failure develops because they cannot pursue meaningful goals. They experience inner conflict, and this will be strongest among those with the most mature personalities. The conflict is also more severe at lower organizational levels, where more directive controls are likely.

An employee can escape these conditions by quitting or by getting promoted, but these are not always possible. A more likely set of reactions are **defense mechanisms** such as daydreaming, aggression, regression, or becoming apathetic and disinterested in work or the organization. Employees might also form cliques or unions to protect themselves, and these groups can develop norms to withhold productivity, hide errors, and demand increased pay and benefits. At home, frustrated employees might teach their children not to expect much from work or their employers.

Frustrating conditions at work often get worse, not better. As employees react defensively, managers might become more directive, tighten controls even further, or try programs that fail because they are not based on the needs of a mature personality. Thus the situation feeds on itself.

SUMMARY

Managers need to learn all they can about human behavior because people are critical to organization success. The knowledge and skills a manager uses in dealing with people should be based on sound behavioral science models and principles. A complete model would include what is known about the person, the environment of behavior, the behavior itself and its effects. Key principles are that all behavior is caused and overdetermined, much behavior is learned, and the behavior is both stable and changeable.

Learning is a lifelong process. It takes place in a number of ways, such as through classical conditioning, reinforcement, and modeling. Learning theories explain how people acquire knowledge, attitudes, and skills. They are also central to understanding socialization and personality development. The reinforcement approach is a very useful one to managers, because they often control the consequences that follow an employee's behavior. These consequences include positive and negative reinforcement, extinction, and punishment. Each type of consequence has different implications. Schedules of reinforcement are also important—the timing and frequency of reinforcements makes a difference in how quickly something is learned and how resistant it is to extinction.

Personality is another way to characterize people. Many theories and concepts of personality exist. It is a useful way to understand and predict success at work and accommodations to organizational life. Personality is central to understanding many aspects of work ranging from culture to motivation. For example, the authoritarian, bureaucratic, and Machiavellian personality types are of interest in interpreting interpersonal and hierarchical relationships. Internal or external locus of control may be related to a person's leadership ability and promotability. Clearly, personality can also affect how people approach and solve problems.

☐ KEY CONCEPTS

Agreeableness	Fixed-interval	Overdetermination
Argyris's theory	schedules	Personality
Authoritarian	Indifferent	Positive
personality	Instrumental	reinforcement
Avoidance learning	learning	Professional
B = f(P,E)	Learning	Punishment
Behavior shaping	Locus of control	Reinforcement theories
Bureaucratic	Machiavellianism	Reinforcement schedules
personality	Modeling	Social learning theory
Classical conditioning	Multiple causation	Socialization
Continuous schedules	Myers-Briggs	Transfer of learning
Conscientiousness	dimensions	Usefulness of opposites
Defense mechanisms	Negative	Variable-interval
Emotional stability	reinforcement	schedules
Extinction	Openness to	Variable-ratio schedules
Extroversion	experience	Vicarious learning
Fixed-ratio schedules	Organizationalist	

☐ STUDY QUESTIONS

1. Think of a recent job you have held. Explain how the stimulus environment made a difference in how well you performed and how satisfied you were with the job.
2. Recall a fellow employee who did things on the job that you either liked or disliked. What do you think caused his or her behavior? Was the behavior overdetermined? Explain.
3. How does learning take place in classical conditioning? What use is this theory to a manager?
4. What is the central proposition of reinforcement, theory or instrumental, of learning? Why is this theory so useful to management?
5. Cite the types of consequences of behavior that affect learning under reinforcement theory. Which type is generally best to use? Which is most problematic? Explain.
6. What are the major schedules of reinforcement? Which ones are most common? How can managers use schedules better?
7. Define vicarious learning and the social learning theory elements. Explain the usefulness of these to managing behavior at work.
8. What is transfer of learning, and why is it important?
9. How do personality and situation interact to affect both behavior and the situation itself?
10. Can you define the three types of accommodations people make to organizational life?
11. How would you manage a subordinate with internal locus of control differently from one with external locus of control?

STUDY . . .

12. Have you ever met or worked with an authoritarian or bureaucratic personality? How did the experience affect you?

13. Refer to the two figures in the chapter that classify people using the Myers-Briggs types. Put yourself into one of the four cells in both figures. See if another person who knows you agrees with how you perceive your style.

14. Have you ever worked in an organization where managers behaved in the way Argyris's theory would suggest? What impact did it have on you?

CASE

CARL LOPEZ

In September of 1992, Carl Lopez, a student at the University of Kansas came to see Dr. Mary Evans, a professor of management. Carl Lopez had completed a summer course with Professor Evans the previous term.

Lopez:	Do you have a few minutes, Dr. Evans? I want to talk to you about the possibility of entering graduate school in the College of Business. I will finish my undergraduate degree this summer, and going to graduate school is starting to appeal to me.
Evans:	That's good, Carl. Good grades and good test scores are necessary, and, with more applicants each year, it is getting more and more difficult to get in.
Lopez:	In my last sixty credits I have received all As, with just one B. I usually score quite high on standardized tests, and I have some industrial experience as a supervisor.
Evans:	That all helps in being admitted. What company did you work for?
Lopez:	I worked for SOLARSYSTEMS for two years. I actually started there in an entry level position. I then became a working supervisor as I gained experience. I supervised my fellow workers and also did much of the more complicated work myself. I then became the unit supervisor and did not work with my hands anymore. I left, however, after about six months as a supervisor.
Evans:	Why did you quit? It sounds as if you were doing well.
Lopez:	Actually, I had a lot of trouble with my boss. I liked my old production manager, but he quit. We hired another

☐ CARL . . .

production manager with experience in a manufacturing company. Right away we had a disagreement. I had trained my workers to perform several jobs rather than just one and rotated them around various work stations during the day. My new boss did not like this and told me that each worker should have only one specialized job and should stick to it all the time. I felt that they would be bored if they worked on the same job all day. Besides we needed our people to have flexible skills, but he disagreed.

Evans: Is that all?

Lopez: No. A few months later all supervisors were asked to submit recommendations for pay increases for their employees. My boss, the production manager, said about a 5% raise on the average would receive a fair hearing. My group was working very hard and were excellent employees. So I submitted a much higher round of raise requests. Some were as high as 15% and several others 10%. I thought they deserved it.

My boss got angry, but I wouldn't budge. I continued on as usual, but nothing happened. After two months, no pay increases were given to my workers. They protested strongly about this at one of the weekly meetings I held with them. As we discussed the problem, I saw the personnel manager come onto the floor, and he was listening to what I was saying. I told my workers that they had legitimate grievances. I thought the company owed them a greater pay increase than they were willing to give. After my meeting, the personnel manager called me to his office. He told me I was not a professional manager and was nothing but an instigator of discontent. He said I was no manager. I told him, "You're right, I'm not suited for this place."

Evans: Then what?

Lopez: I quit that afternoon and looked around for spare jobs. I did some roofing and carpentry for awhile and other odd jobs. I was pretty unhappy at this time and started to go to a local church. There I met this wonderful man and his son who owned a real estate business. They also talked to me about my problems and steered a lot of remodeling business my way and persuaded me to study for a real estate license. I did that and started to straighten myself out. I stopped drinking and going out to night clubs and bars. I studied a lot. Several months later I passed my real estate examination and started selling houses.

☐ CARL . . .

Evans:	Were you successful?
Lopez:	Not at first. Actually, it was a bad market for real estate at the time. I did not make a commission for six months. But then I started to do very well and was able to put together quite a nest egg. That's when I decided to go back to school and work part-time in real estate. I have been doing that for the past two years, although typically I work about forty to fifty hours a week.
Evans:	You work that much! How can you do that and still get all As?
Lopez:	I have good discipline. I get up at 4:30 a.m. I run; then I study before classes. I arrange all my classes in the mornings, then I work in the afternoon. I usually meet clients and visit neighborhoods distributing my circulars. I usually work until 9:30 P.M. or so. Then I have dinner and maybe study a little before bed. Weekends I have to spend most of my time selling real estate. I only started dating this past spring. I met a girl at a wedding at which I was the best man. I liked her. The wedding took so much of my time, though, that I did not have time to study for a test and got my only B since I've been back in school. Since I had set a goal of obtaining all A's, I was pretty upset with the B, but then I realized that there are more important things in life than a B, such as the love I have for my friend, the groom.
Evans:	You said that you returned to school. What did you study the first time you went to school? Business? Why did you leave?
Lopez:	At first I was a pre-med student. My father has a Ph.D. in physics, and my mother is a school teacher. They encouraged me to be a physician. I did real well in school as a freshmen, but then I found out that girls liked me, and I started to party all the time. In high school, I was very shy and didn't date much. I looked different then, also. I was skinny and small. Anyway, my grades went down and I decided I didn't want to be a physician. I realized that I didn't want the life and death responsibility that comes with being a doctor. I didn't know what to do, so I quit. I went west to Oregon and got a job as a roofer. While doing that I put in some solar paneling in a few houses and really thought I would like to get into the solar energy field. I went to the library and found a list of companies in the field and wrote to them for a job. SOLARSYSTEMS wrote back a positive letter, and so I traveled back here to take the job I told you about. I still

☐ CARL . . .

would like to work in the solar energy field or some exciting field like that though. But, I do like real estate.

Evans: So you don't know now if you want to go to graduate school or not, or what aspect of business to major in. Marketing? Finance? Personnel? What?

Lopez: That's right. I want to use my abilities to the utmost. I want to be doing work that's exciting and interesting. I also want to do important work that is of benefit to mankind and the nation.

Evans: And do you think that management has these possibilities?

Lopez: Yes. I think business is good. It employs people. It helps to increase their standard of living. Although I am religious, I don't see anything bad in making lots of money. In fact, you can do more to help people if you have lots of money.

Evans: What do you think you are good at? What are your strengths?

Lopez: I'm a self starter. When I wasn't doing well in real estate, I went to the library and read all sorts of books on salesmanship; books by Dale Carnegie and others. But I don't do what others think, either. I make up my own mind about things. Also, I think I am very hard working compared to most other people I know. I am good at finding out things. One of my fellow supervisors at SOLARSYSTEMS said that I was a brownie because I used to carry in a cup of coffee to my old boss, the first production manager, that I liked. Then I would talk to him about all sorts of things. But I was just trying to learn about things and about myself. He knew lots more than I did.

Evans: Can you be dominant in a social situation? Can you tell people what to do? That's what you need to be well adjusted and effective in line management.

Lopez: Sure, in the real estate business I organize things for my clients. I know I wasn't a very good supervisor at SOLARSYSTEMS, but that was when I was just learning. I've learned a lot more about dealing with people since then. I have no doubts about my abilities. I know I can do anything I set my mind to. What I would like from you is just the information. I want to find out what you think are the best fields of business to go into in the future. I'm sort of leaning toward finance. It's quite an interesting field. But production, marketing, and general management are interesting as well.

☐ CARL . . .

QUESTIONS

1. How would you characterize Carl's personality?
2. What does Carl's personality suggest regarding the types of work and work situations he would be most satisfied and productive in?
3. What were some of the key learning experiences in Carl's life? Which theories of learning best describe these key experiences?

REFERENCES

1. Adorno, T., Frenkel-Brunswick, E., Levinson, D., and Sanford, R.N. *The authoritarian personality*. New York: Harper, 1950.
2. Allport, G.W. *Pattern and growth in personality*. New York: Holt, Rinehart and Winson, 1961.
3. Anderson, C.R. Locus of control, coping behaviors and performance in a stress setting: A longitudinal study. *Journal of Applied Psychology*, 1977, 62, 446-51.
4. Argyris, C. *Integrating the individual and the organization*. New York: John Wiley, 1964.
5. Argyris, C. *Personality and organization: The conflict between the system and the individual*. New York: Harper & Row, 1957.
6. Bandura, A. *Social learning theory*. Englewood Cliffs, NJ: Prentice-Hall, 1977.
7. Baron, R.A. *Behavior in organization: Understanding and managing the human side of work*. Boston: Allyn & Bacon, 1983.
8. Barrick, M.R. and Mount, M.K. The big five personality dimensions and job performance: A meta-analysis. *Personnel Psychology*, 1991, 44, 1-26.
9. Blau, G.T. Locus of control as a potential moderator of the turnover process. *Journal of Occupational Psychology*, 1987 (Fall), 21-29.
10. Bourne, L.E., and Ekstrand, B.R. *Psychology: Its principles and meanings*. New York: Holt, Rinehart and Winston, 1982.
11. Cattell, R.B. *Personality: A systematic, theoretical and factual study*. New York: McGraw-Hill, 1950.
12. Christie, R., and Geis, F., eds. *Studies in machiavellianism*. New York: Academic Press, 1970.
13. Epstein, S. and O'Brien, E.J. The person-situation debate in historical and current perspective. *Psychological Bulletin*, 1985, 98(3), 513-537.
14. Feldman, D.C., and Arnold, H.J. *Managing individual and group behavior in organizations*. New York: McGraw-Hill, 1983.
15. Freud, S. *New introductory lectures on psychoanalysis*. New York: Norton, 1933.
16. Fukami, C.V., and Larson, E.W. Commitment to company and union: Parallel models. *Journal of Applied Psychology*, 1984, 69, 367-71.
17. Funder, D.C. Global traits: A neo-Allportean approach to personality. *Psychological Science*, 1991, 2(1), 31-39.

18. Gordon, L.V. Measurement of bureaucratic orientation. *Personnel Psychology*, 1970, 23, 1-11.

19. Greene, C.N. Identification modes of professionals: Relationship with formalization, role strain and alienation. *Academy of Management Journal*, 1978, 21, 486-92.

20. Griffith, T.L. Teaching big brother to be a team player: Computer monitoring and quality. *Academy of Management Executive*, 1993, 7(1), 73-80.

21. Hamner, W.C., and Hamner, E.P. Behavior modification on the bottom line. *Organization Dynamics*, 1976, 4, 8-21.

22. Jung, C.G. *The integration of the personality.* New York: Farrow and Rinehart, 1939.

23. Latham, G., and Saari, L.M. Application of social-learning theory to training supervisors through behavioral modeling. *Journal of Applied Psychology.* 1979, 64, 239-46.

24. Levinson, H. The abrasive personality at the office. *Psychology Today*, 1978, May.

25. Levinson, D., Barrow, C.H., Klein, E.B., Levinson, M.H., and McGee, B. *Season's of a man's life.* New York: Ballantine Books, 1978.

26. Likert, R. *New patterns of management.* New York: McGraw-Hill, 1961.

27. Logan, F. *Fundamentals of learning and motivation.* Dubuque, IA: Brown, 1970.

28. Lussier, R.H. A discipline model for increasing performance. *Supervisory Management*, 1990 (August), 6-7.

29. Luthans, F., and Kreitner, R. *Organizational behavior modification.* Glenview, IL: Scott, Foresman, 1975.

30. Luthans, F., and Schweizer, J. How behavior modification can improve organization performance. *Management Review*, 1979, 68, 43-50.

31. Maier, N.R.F. *Psychology in industrial organizations.* 4th ed. Boston: Houghton Mifflin, 1973.

32. Maslow, A.H. *Eupsychian management.* Homewood, IL: Richard D. Irwin, 1965.

33. Maslow, A.H. *Motivation and personality.* New York: Harper & Row, 1970.

34. Mischel, W. The interaction of personality and situation. In D. Magnusson and N.S. Endler (Eds). *Personality at the crossroads: Current issues in interactional psychology.* Hillsdale, NJ: Erlbaum, 1977.

35. Murray, H.A. *Explorations in personality.* New York: Science Editions, 1962.

36. Myers, I.B., and Briggs, K.C. *Myers-Briggs type indicator.* Princeton, NJ: Educational Testing Service, 1962.

37. Pavlov, I.V. *Conditioned reflexes.* New York: Oxford University Press, 1927.

38. Pennar, K. Reinventing America. *Business Week*, October 23,1992, 10-14.

39. Presthus, R. *The organizational society.* New York: St. Martin's Press, 1978.

40. Reitz, H.J. *Behavior in organizations.* Homewood, IL:Richard D. Irwin, 1981.

41. Rogers, C.R. *Counseling and psychotherapy.* Boston: Houghton Mifflin, 1942.

42. Rotter, J. Generalized expectancies for internal vs. external control of reinforcement. *Psychological Monographs*, 1966, 80 whole no. 609.

43. Schneider, B. People make the place. *Personnel Psychology*, 1987, 40, 437-453.

44. Senge, P. *The fifth discipline: The art and practice of the learning organization.* N.Y.: Doubleday/Currency, 1990.

45. Skinner, B.F. *The behavior of organisms.* New York: Appleton-Century- Crofts, 1938.

46. Tett, R.P., Jackson, D.N., and Rothstein, M. Personality measures as predictors of job performance: A meta-analytic review. *Personnel Psychology,* 1991, 44, 703-742.

47. Tosi, H. *The environment/organization/person contingency model: A meso approach to the study of organizations.* Greenwich, CT: JAI Press, Inc., 1992.

48. Weiss, H.M. Subordinate imitation of supervisory behavior: The role of modeling in organizational socialization. *Organizational behavior and human performance,* 1977, 19, 89-105.

49. Weiss, H.M., and Adler, S. Personality and organizational behavior. In B.M. Staw and L.L. Cummings, eds. *Research in Organizational Behavior,* 6. Greenwich, CT: JAI Press, 1984, 1-50.

50. Wood, R. & Bandura, A. Social cognitive theory of organizational management. *Academy of Management Review,* 1989, 14, 361-384.

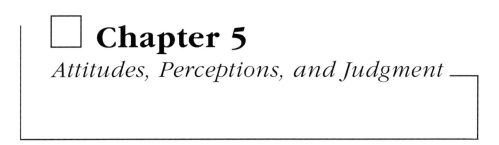

Chapter 5
Attitudes, Perceptions, and Judgment

Consider the following situations:

1. Last year your company laid off some of its workers in an attempt to reduce costs and stay competitive. Now things look even worse than they did before. Since the layoff, some of your best employees resigned for more secure employment. Your internal program for increasing quality of performance seems to be getting nowhere. Attempted improvements have run into responses ranging from indifference to active resistance. Your costs and competitive position have not improved significantly.

2. The state Civil Rights Commission informs your company that five complaints have been filed. Two complaints are from women who feel they have been unjustly denied a job, allegedly because they lack sufficient physical strength. Two employees claim unfair treatment over denial of training opportunities and promotions. The fifth is charging discrimination in his discharge, citing a biased performance appraisal.

3. An emergency arose in your St. Louis warehouse when heavy rains and floodwaters threatened to damage expensive inventory. If that inventory couldn't be delivered on time, key customers would suffer heavy business losses. Your employees contacted each other by phone and word of mouth. Some came in off vacation, and others canceled plans to pitch in. The inventory was saved by early deliveries and relocation to drier facilities.

In each of these circumstances, some combination of attitudes, perceptions, and judgments operated to explain the conditions described. In one case, employee attitudes were worsening over staffing practices, while in another they saved the day. Human perception and judgment were at the heart of refusing to hire, train, or promote some employees. Attitudes certainly played a role in handling the emergency situation. In this chapter, we look at how attitudes form and how they function. Perception and perceptual errors are viewed as products of learning and are related to personality and attitudes. We conclude with a review of the tendencies and biases that people exhibit in understanding and judging others' behavior.

THE NATURE OF ATTITUDES

It makes sense to understand people in terms of their attitudes, because strong attitudes are very likely to affect behavior [20]. In the world of work, we are concerned with attitudes toward supervision, top management, pay, benefits, promotion, or any event that might trigger positive or negative reactions. Employee satisfaction and attitudes represent one of the key areas for measuring organizational effectiveness.

A MODEL OF ATTITUDES

Attitudes reflect a person's likes and dislikes, their affinities and aversions toward any identifiable object in their environment [1]. **Attitudes** are predispositions to react in a favorable or unfavorable way to almost anything in the world around us. They reflect what people feel is good or bad and are thus evaluative in nature. The concept of attitude is complex. Attitudes should be viewed in terms of their components and their dynamics. Figure 5.1 indicates that attitudes are linked to values and beliefs, and they precede intentions to behave and actual behavior. Figure 5.2 shows the complexity of factors that might affect attitudes toward work.

☐ **FIGURE 5.1** *A Model of Attitudes*

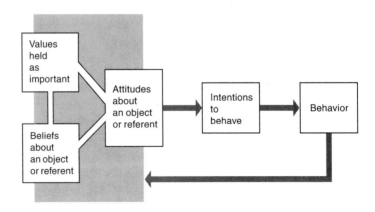

The Object of Attitudes. Attitudes always refer to some identifiable object. People have attitudes about something or someone: for example, toward the federal government, their supervisor, their job, or seat belts. It is not accurate simply to say someone has a "good attitude" or a "bad attitude." There must be some referent.

☐ **FIGURE 5.2** *Example of the Learning and Expression of Attitudes Toward Work and Career*

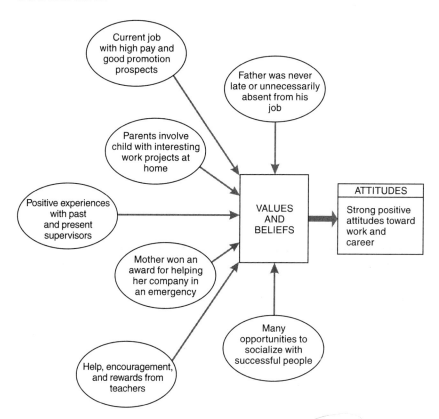

Values. One major component of attitudes is emotional. This is the *feeling component* of attitudes. The intensity of this feeling affects the likelihood and types of behavior that follow from an attitude. An intense attitude is more likely to result in behavior than when the feeling is weak.

Emotional responses are learned throughout the process of socialization. From very early infancy, people learn to like some things and dislike others. Through conditioning and reinforcement, they develop a whole range of general and specific feelings about objects. All this early learning lays the foundation for later attitudes.

This learning process also leads to the development of **values**. Values are more general than attitudes, and they need not have an identifiable object. Values form the underpinnings of attitudes and are usually consistent with them. For example, if someone values loyalty, then he or she will have positive attitudes for company practices that reward loyalty. By the same token, that person will have unfavorable attitudes toward practices or people who demean loyalty.

137

Values reflect a sense of right and wrong. They define the good life and identify goals worthy of our aspiration [17]. Values are expressed in statements such as "equal rights for all," and "hard work is the road to success." Values explain why people choose occupations and hobbies, why they volunteer their time to causes, why they form groups, and in many cases why different groups form battle lines against each other.

Beliefs. **Beliefs** are thoughts and ideas about objects and the conclusions people draw about them. Beliefs represent information about objects or events. Beliefs are the thinking component of attitudes. They do not refer to favorable or unfavorable reactions but only convey a sense of "what is" to the person.

Beliefs link characteristics to an object. Some examples of beliefs are: "A satisfied worker will be productive," or "Nuclear power plants are safe." Beliefs are not necessarily factual. However, they represent truth for the person. Beliefs can be quite absolute, such that a person thinks something is always true. Other beliefs are more like probability statements. One might believe that nuclear power plants are safe, or that satisfied workers are productive, but really mean that these are true most of the time.

Beliefs often persist for long periods, and they combine to help form our attitudes. Our knowledge, as reflected in our beliefs, helps to determine our feelings. We can determine people's attitudes by knowing their beliefs and values [7]. Suppose we believe our employer is fair and generous, but he or she never delegates decision making. If we value fairness and generosity but place less value on delegation, we would have positive attitudes toward our employer. If we value delegation and want to be involved in decision making, we could have a neutral or even negative attitude toward our employer.

Attitude and Intentions. Taking the previous example a bit further, our attitude toward our company might encourage us to take some action. Suppose our attitude toward the firm is negative because, despite fairness and generosity, we are frustrated by the decision-making practices. This could lead to the intention to seek work elsewhere or try to be promoted into positions where decisions are made.

Intentions to act have probabilities, too. It may be more likely that we will look for another job rather than try to change the system or get promoted. Our choice among different intentions is governed by many factors, including our estimates of which ones are most likely to succeed.

Attitudes and Overt Behavior. Attitudes often lead to overt behaviors. Except for behavior, all other aspects of attitudes are internal to the person and not observable. The behavioral component of attitudes is important because we draw inferences about attitudes, beliefs, values, and intentions from observing what people say and what they do.

☐ **EXECUTIVE PAY:**
VALUE ISSUES GALORE _____

How much business executives should be paid is a complex question. Recently, reactions to executive pay have come in from all quarters of society. Stockholders, unions, boards of directors, and even legislators have grappled with the issues. According to *Business Week* the average CEO of a big U.S. corporation earned a record $3,842,247 in total pay in 1992 [2]. The top 20 CEO's ranged from $11.2 million to $127 million. Moreover, executive pay in the United States has increased in a dramatic way. That is, in 1960 the average CEO earned 41 times an average factory worker and 19 times what an engineer made. In 1992, these figures are at 157 times the factory worker and 66 times the engineer. By way of contrast, the 1991 figures find executives of the 50 largest Japanese companies averaging $872,646, about one fourth of the U.S. average. These Japanese CEO's make less than 32 times the average factory worker there.

What are these CEO's worth? What should it take to attract them to these positions? What are the effects of higher or lower pay levels? These are clearly value questions. But some say we can make better judgments about pay by using more objective criteria. This can be partly accomplished by tying pay more closely to performance, but anyone who thinks this will remove the value judgments is kidding themselves.

SOURCES OF BELIEFS, VALUES, AND ATTITUDES

Through socialization, we are exposed to countless personal experiences. Some are direct, such as when we interact with someone. Others are less direct, such as when we learn about things from other people or from books and television. The following are some examples of sources of beliefs, values, and attitudes.

Direct Personal Experiences. Positive or negative experiences we have with an object or person contribute strongly to what we believe and feel about it or them. We learn firsthand that candy tastes good or that it is wrong to be late for work.

Association. The human mind has the capacity to link common events or to generalize across them. Thus, our first work experience might result in attitudes we hold about work for a long time to come. These associations may also result from very remote experiences. For example, having a bad experience with an employee from the personnel department could affect our attitude toward other staff departments or toward the personnel profession in general.

Interaction with People. Parents, brothers and sisters, teachers, friends, and many others are critical in shaping our attitudes. Other people provide reinforcements; they act as models that we emulate, and they serve as sources of information. We identify with specific groups of people and come to think of ourselves as part of these groups.

Mass Media. Mass media transmit information that shape our beliefs. The effects of this exposure can be quite subtle. Zajonc [27] hypothesizes that repeated, simple exposure can cause us to like something; it does not even require the development of a belief or a value. Television has been a particular focus of attention because of its supposed impact on children. By the time children get to high school, they spend as much time watching TV as doing schoolwork [18].

THE FUNCTIONS OF ATTITUDES

Attitudes serve many purposes for people. The functions they perform are shown in Figure 5.3 and described below.

☐ **FIGURE 5.3**   *What Functions Attitudes Serve*

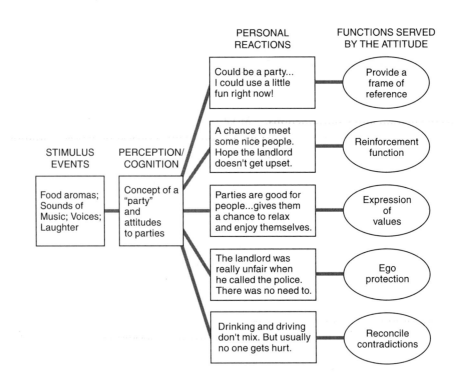

Provide a Frame of Reference. Attitudes help us to make sense of the world by giving us a frame of reference from which to view the world or interpret a particular situation.

In selecting and organizing facts, we extract only part of the total information available. We are likely to select those facts that are consistent with our attitudes and ignore or discount those that aren't. This gives meaning to what we perceive. If our attitude toward an organization is positive, we might interpret what it does in a positive way and ignore practices that are inconsistent with our attitude. Recently a large United States university was severely penalized by the NCAA for violations of rules. Even though there was undisputed proof, many strong alumni supporters refused to believe that the school should have been punished or even that it was guilty.

Reinforcement Function. Attitudes can serve as means to an end. If we have a cooperative attitude at work, we might be rewarded by recognition or favorable treatment. We learn that a negative attitude toward cooperation might hurt our chances for promotion. Or suppose a person has threatened us in some way. A negative attitude toward such a person can help us be on guard when we are around them.

Expression of Values. Expressed attitudes demonstrate our values and allow us to share them with others and affect the world we live in [10]. Strong democratic values at work might be expressed through the way that decisions are made, how staff meetings are conducted, or whether employees are consulted in solving problems.

Ego Protection. Attitudes help us maintain our self-image and self-respect. For example, a supervisor might have feelings of superiority or dominance over subordinates. An attitude that subordinates are lazy and not trustworthy or that they are not trained well enough to do their jobs well tends to enhance the supervisor's feelings of superiority.

Reconciliation and Contradictions. Most people have contradictory attitudes or beliefs that don't always add up to an internally consistent whole. Attitudes help us put our thoughts in separate compartments and thereby reconcile contradictions [16]. Suppose a person feels people should be promptly corrected if they do the wrong thing. At the same time, he might accuse his superior of unfairness when she calls attention to an error. How is the contradiction reconciled? It might be that one belief (prompt correction of errors) is part of an attitude toward subordinates or irresponsible people. The other belief (feeling unfairly treated) is connected to an attitude about one's own independence or competence.

EMPLOYEE ATTITUDES AND SATISFACTION

As indicated in Chapter 1, employee attitudes and satisfaction represent one of the major areas where organizational effectiveness should be measured. How employees feel about their job situation and their commitment to the organization are among the most critical consequences that managers can strive to improve. For example, employee attitudes about their pay and benefits, their co-workers and supervisor, and work hours and conditions are among the many factors that both managers and researchers have considered important to examine.

Attitudes and satisfactions are not just outcomes or consequences of managerial strategies. They can also impact on other outcomes in important ways. For example, there is ample evidence that employee satisfaction is correlated with lateness, attendance, and turnover. Organizations suffer significant direct and indirect costs when workers miss work. When they quit, the costs of recruitment, selection, and getting the new employee to full productivity can be considerable.

☐ EMPLOYEE ATTITUDE SURVEYS

Organizations have many reasons for measuring employee attitudes. Some do it routinely, perhaps once a year. Others survey attitudes as part of a special effort or research project, such as in preparation for a management development program or in connection with a reorganization. Some surveys are specific, such as assessing reactions to a new benefit plan, whereas others cover dozens of aspects of work. Questionnaires are frequently used that ask employees to rate how satisfied or dissatisfied or how favorably or unfavorably they feel toward things such as:

The chance to try out my ideas
The variety of work I do
The cooperation of my fellow workers
The pay I receive for my job

and so on through as many as a hundred items. Responses are usually anonymous, but data can be collected so that analyses can be made by department, organizational level, age groups, and the like. Doing so permits data comparisons and feedback to particular groups. Departments, for example, can learn where they stand relative to others.

It takes a lot of know-how to design a good survey and collect, analyze, interpret, and feed back the data. Inexperienced organizations can get help to do it right. But skill and experience are not enough; it takes a commitment to act on the survey results. Unless management is willing to do something about what the survey reveals, it might be better not to do one in the first place.

However, job satisfaction does not necessarily mean high performance. Many employees, regardless of whether their work performance is high or low, may be quite satisfied with many aspects of their employment. One might conclude from this that there is no connection between satisfaction and job performance. Much to the contrary, one of the key goals in managing behavior in organizations is to create linkages between employee performance and their satisfaction. Many managerial strategies discussed throughout this book are aimed at strengthening this linkage. For example, as indicated in Chapter 2, organization structure and task design decisions can have powerful implications for employee feelings. Later, in Chapters 7 and 8, several important motivation theories and strategies are presented that focus on creating a work environment and designing job assignments that allow employees to derive satisfaction from having done a good job.

A person's values and attitudes can be quite stable, and perhaps affect their general dispositions to like or dislike work or their employers. This may limit how much managers can succeed altering the way employees feel and act. But particular attitudes and satisfactions at work can and do change, sometimes quickly, as events change [23]. An employee who is happy and working hard one day, can become dissatisfied and resentful the next day as a consequence of some managerial action. Many organizations therefore pay close attention to attitudes by conducting periodic **attitude surveys** of employees, and by seeking feedback in other ways.

COGNITIVE CONSISTENCY AND DISSONANCE

Cognitive dissonance is based on the idea that people need to experience consistency, or consonance, between their behavior and attitudes, beliefs, or thoughts (cognitions) [6]. When there is dissonance (inconsistency), we are motivated to reduce it because we experience discomfort. Another basic idea of this theory is that we are motivated to explain, or justify, our behavior, thoughts, or feelings. In short, cognitions themselves must be consistent, but they must also coincide with behavior. If not, we experience discomfort and feel pressure to change somehow. Suppose you like foreign cars but think that failure to "buy American" is unpatriotic and damaging to U.S. workers. One way to reduce the dissonance is to justify your preference for foreign cars by changing your attitude toward American cars. You might characterize them as poorly designed. You might express an attitude toward the American automobile industry by calling it irresponsible, or you could even argue that the more competition it faces, the faster the industry will shape up.

Another dissonant condition is **insufficient justification** to act *against* one's beliefs and attitudes. Suppose you reprimand a subordinate, a behavior that you find somewhat unpleasant and perhaps unnecessary. If you were ordered to do so, you may have no dissonance because your boss has given you **sufficient justification** (a direct and clear-cut order) to do it. But if your boss only hinted at a reprimand, the justification may be insufficient. You would therefore need more justification than your boss provided. You might justify the reprimand by reevaluating the employee and deciding that what he did really deserved a reprimand or by concluding that your boss's hint was really an order.

Dissonance, and the change in our attitudes that follow from it, can be reduced *before* we take action, as a way to justify planned action. This is called **decisional dissonance**. It can also be reduced *after* we act to justify the action that we took. This is called **postdecisional dissonance**. In this case, you actually perform the act that produces or worsens dissonance. Following the act, the dissonance may remain strong and the motivation to reduce it persists. Imagine

143

that you reprimand the employee when you still felt it was wrong and were still opposed to it. If the employee has a hostile reaction to the reprimand, the employee's negative reaction can be used to confirm that he deserved the reprimand, reducing your dissonance.

Another dissonance condition arises with **disconfirmed expectations.** If we find that the product our firm produces is unreliable, dissonance arises because we face a situation that we did not expect. Here again, dissonance can be reduced by developing a belief that rationalizes, or explains, the condition. We might think that the unreliability is due to the customers' failure to follow directions.

Dissonance is more acute, of course, when we are personally involved—if our own personal decision led to a result we did not expect. There is a paradox here. Often people do not admit they made a bad decision. Dissonance theory predicts that people will persist in the original decision and repeat it as a way of justifying it. Thus, people often compound their errors rather than continue to face the dissonant feeling of having been wrong in the first place [25, 26]. This was clearly demonstrated in a study by Staw [24]. He had students play a business game in which they allocated funds to different projects. Those students who allocated funds to unsuccessful projects made subsequent further investments in the same project. This was especially the case for students who felt responsible for the bad decision.

PERCEPTION

Perception is the process of creating an internal representation of the external world. It is a process of interpreting what our senses provide in order to give meaning to the environment we are in. The resulting interpretation is the perceiver's reality, and it can vary widely from person to person. Perception is a dynamic process, a search for the best interpretation of available data [8].

In this section, we will focus on the feeling and thinking aspects in perception, with emphasis on just two sensory modes: what we see and what we hear. Then we examine how our perceptions affect behavior. We will discuss the perceiver, the event or object being perceived, and the situational context in which the perception occurs. Figure 5.4 illustrates these components and shows that they interact to determine both the interpretation and the action that takes place.

THE PERCEIVER

The way we perceive is learned, just as attitudes, skills, and personality are learned. Also, what we learn affects our perception. For example, Eskimos have no concept that corresponds to what we call "snow." They actually perceive snow in different ways, depending on its particular characteristics and potential uses.

Physical and emotional states can shape and determine our reality. When a person is hungry, sights and sounds that point to food will be salient. Emotional states are particularly relevant when eyewitnesses observe a crime. Eyewitness perceptions may be so inaccurate and variable that one must wonder why they are relied on so often [15]. Some report things that never happened, and overlook small details as well as significant and glaring stimuli. For example, some may fail to see a bright red shirt or hear an important statement made by a criminal.

☐ **FIGURE 5.4** *A Perceptual Model*

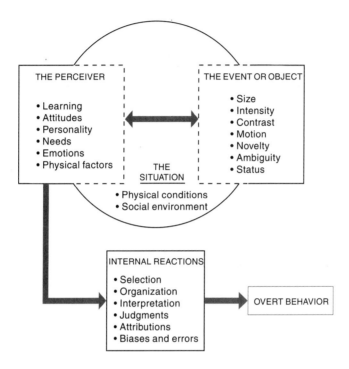

THE PERCEIVER
- Learning
- Attitudes
- Personality
- Needs
- Emotions
- Physical factors

THE EVENT OR OBJECT
- Size
- Intensity
- Contrast
- Motion
- Novelty
- Ambiguity
- Status

THE SITUATION
- Physical conditions
- Social environment

INTERNAL REACTIONS
- Selection
- Organization
- Interpretation
- Judgments
- Attributions
- Biases and errors

OVERT BEHAVIOR

THE EVENT OR OBJECT

Certain attributes of events and objects affect whether they are perceived and how they are perceived. *Size* has an effect: larger objects are more likely to be seen than smaller ones. The *intensity* of the object or event enhances its noticeability: particularly loud noises are likely to be heard, and bright or shining objects will likely be seen. *Contrast* also affects perception. Anything that stands out by virtue of its color, its relationship to its background, or any other factor that differentiates it is more likely to be attended to. *Motion* also facilitates perception: a moving object draws attention in a stationary environment or background. *Novelty* helps to enhance perceptibility. New, unusual, or unexpected stimuli attract our attention. Experts in advertising creatively utilize these characteristics of stimuli and apply them to magazine and newspaper advertisements, to billboards, and to radio and television commercials.

The *ambiguity* of an event or object also has an impact on perceptions. Something that is ambiguous, or incomplete, is actually more subject to personal interpretation. Because ambiguity is discomforting, people add meaning to the stimuli or attribute motives to a person associated with the stimuli. For example, after interviewers talk to an applicant for a job, they often draw conclusions that are not justified by the applicant's behavior. They often fill in gaps about the applicant's past experience, and do it in a way that confirms their good feelings or negative suspicions.

Finally, *characteristics of other people* affect perception. One excellent example of this is how the status of a person affects perception. Higher-status people are more likely to be noticed, and they usually are perceived to be more knowledgeable, accurate, and believable.

☐ IBM: NEW PERCEPTIONS ON AN INTERNATIONAL SCALE

For many decades, IBM was universally perceived as an invulnerable giant of the computer industry. Its employees enjoyed good pay, excellent benefits, and above all, job security. These perceptions of IBM have become a thing of the past in the 1990s. Gone are its dominance in computers, its company songs and clubs, and its no-layoff practices. In Poughkeepsie, N.Y., the original home and heart of IBM, employees and townspeople alike are suffering the effects of the downturn in certain sectors of IBM's business [22]. The work force dropped from 10,000 in 1990 to near 8,000 in 1993 and is expected to drop to 6,000 in the future. The "family" is breaking up in Poughkeepsie. Even in IBM Europe, the company is restructuring into 200 autonomous business units to help deal with dropping profits and to meet the competition better. Some 10,000 jobs may be gone within a year in a sink or swim effort to compete [14]. The once loyal IBM employee is bitter about the situation and how the company is handling it. Morale is at an all-time low. The principle of "respect for the individual" as espoused by IBM's founder Thomas J. Watson, Sr. is fading while IBM tries to rebound in the computer world.

SITUATIONAL FACTORS

The same event under two different conditions results in different perceptions of it. Imagine a person holding a knife in a kitchen in which food is being prepared for a meal. Imagine the same person holding the same knife the same way in the midst of a public demonstration. The knife is often unnoticed in the kitchen setting but would be prominent in the demonstration. Furthermore, the observer's predictions about what might happen would probably be different for each situation.

Perceptions can also be affected by the presence of another person. Suppose we are criticized by our boss in the presence of a higher-level manager. Our interpretation might be that our boss is seeking favor or support from the higher manager. Were we alone with our boss during the criticism, we are less likely to draw such a conclusion. In short, perceptions occur in a context, which predisposes us to expect certain events and lends an additional ingredient to how we interpret, judge, and react to stimuli.

PERCEPTUAL TEASERS

Distortion and errors in perception occur even when we look at simple figures such as the ones below. Imagine how many more errors one might make in complex situations, especially those in which one is emotionally involved.

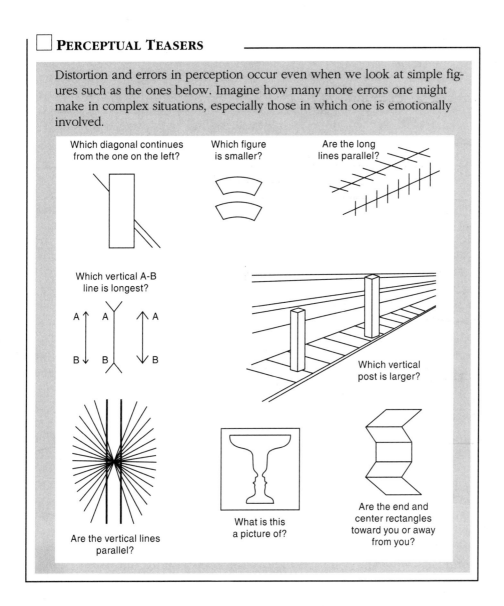

Which diagonal continues from the one on the left?

Which figure is smaller?

Are the long lines parallel?

Which vertical A-B line is longest?

Which vertical post is larger?

Are the vertical lines parallel?

What is this a picture of?

Are the end and center rectangles toward you or away from you?

PERCEPTUAL SELECTION AND ORGANIZATION

A great deal of **selection** takes place as we engage in perception. Out of the many stimuli that bombard people only a few actually penetrate and become part of their experience. The remainder are excluded. **Selective perception** is at the heart of the perceptual process, and we have seen how selection of stimuli is affected by our personal characteristics, attributes of the object itself, and the situation in which perception takes place.

In managing people at work, it is essential to begin with the premise that each individual lives in a slightly different world. Sometimes the differences are vast and sometimes they are slight. The selectivity principle urges managers to exercise care in drawing conclusions about another person's perceptions.

Perception involves another powerful mechanism: **organization**. People tend to group stimuli into patterns so that they become meaningful wholes rather than fragmented parts. An example is the words that you are now reading—the separate letters are ignored in favor of the whole word. Another example is the inclination to see physical patterns. It takes only three dots for us to "see" a triangle and four to "see" a rectangle or square.

We also organize more complex events. Suppose one of your subordinates is late for work and is working slowly, producing below par. You are going to "organize" these facts in a way that makes sense to you. You may classify all the behaviors as rooted in laziness. You would also be affected by the consistency that surrounds events. For example, you might see the worker's lateness, slowness, and low productivity as consistent. This would be reinforced if there was union trouble in the plant and you believed the worker was behaving under union pressure. However, if there were no union problems and you believed the worker was a loyal employee, it would be more consistent to believe his behavior was due to a temporary condition such as illness.

Varied perceptions and interpretations lead us to make judgments about others. Of particular interest are judgments that distort or misrepresent the facts or that disagree with the perceptions of others. Such distortion and disagreement are at the root of a host of problems in managing people.

JUDGMENT TENDENCIES

Several human tendencies lead to inaccurate or unreliable judgments about the things we perceive. Optical illusions are a good example of how the actual characteristics of an event are not the same as what we perceive.

But for managers, the most important perceptual biases are those that arise in relationships with other people. There are many such situations at work—performance review and appraisal, selection interviewing, group meetings, customer relations, and so on. Perceptual biases can be triggered by things such as speech characteristics or clothing [19]. These biases create distortions that are particularly crucial to understand. Once understood, it becomes possible to overcome judgment errors. Although some people are much less prone to them than others, Figure 5.5 shows various ways we might react to others and the types of errors that occur.

FIRST IMPRESSIONS

Impressions of others are often formed very early in a relationship. This tendency is a particular problem because first impressions are often lasting ones. Usually first interactions are of a relatively short duration, so it follows that these early impressions are based on limited information. In other words, we use only a few cues when judging others, then continue to maintain the judgment.

☐ **FIGURE 5.5** *Judgment Tendencies*

HALO: EMPHASIS ON A SINGLE CHARACTERISTIC

Many people have a particular thing that they like or dislike strongly in others. For example, if clothing is an important concern for a person, it can become a dominant basis to make biased judgments about others. Should another person dress poorly, the result may be a negative overall image. This tendency is referred to as the **halo effect.** This means that one or a few characteristics of an individual affect the evaluation of other characteristics.

Halo is also likely to be related to our own self-image. We will have very positive evaluations of those who possess characteristics we believe we have. A manager who is always on time for work is likely to be favorably disposed toward subordinates who are punctual and negatively disposed toward those who come in late.

PROJECTION

Projection is a form of defense mechanism by which people protect themselves against undesirable characteristics that they themselves possess but do not recognize having. In essence, we see traits in others that we ourselves have. For example, we might blame a co-worker's mistake on sloppiness when sloppiness is really a trait we dislike in ourselves. Projection is bound to create misperception. If others do not possess what we project onto them, the false impression we created will govern our behavior, and further misperceptions will likely follow.

Implicit Personality Theory

Practically everyone is an amateur psychologist and has ideas about personality. People have a human tendency to link characteristics of others into a pattern, or to form an **implicit personality theory**. This causes us to draw conclusions that we assume to be true about the personalities of others. For example, statements such as, "honest people are also hard working," "late sleepers are lazy," or "quiet people are devious," all link one characteristic of a person to another. Any of the linkages could be wrong. Hard work and honesty need not go together. The late sleeper might not be a poor worker. The quiet person might simply be shy or fearful. Engaging in implicit personality theory is amateur psychology at its worst. A safer way to draw conclusions about people is to link two characteristics together only if there is evidence of both characteristics on repeated occasions.

☐ GENDER JUDGMENTS IN GOLF

Discrimination on the basis of gender still draws attention in many spheres of work life. Continuing problems exist for females as they attempt to achieve fair treatment in climbing the corporate ladder, serving on a par with men in the military, or otherwise trying to enter male-dominated territory. Lesly and Bongiorno report that in sports, women professional golfers find it nearly impossible to land jobs as country club professionals [13]. There are only 191 women who are head pros or directors of golf courses compared to 7,779 men. Women are in demand as assistant pros, often at less than one third the head pro salary. Kerry Graham, president of Ladies Professional Golfers Association's teaching and club professionals, says that top clubs hire only males. One woman who is a head pro says, "You always have to prove yourself . . .". Women do not feel welcome in the male pro ranks and some are striking out on their own by opening private golf schools.

Stereotyping

In implicit personality theory, we link two or more characteristics together. **Stereotyping** is another form of linking, but it involves connecting characteristics of people to characteristics of the group we place them into. If we discover someone is Italian, we might think he is emotional. If he is Irish, we might conclude he drinks whiskey. Other groups we can use to stereotype are ethnic groups, old people, men, women, professors, used-car salesmen, newspaper reporters, supervisors, or just about any other group that has any meaning to a person.

Members of groups, especially cohesive groups, share certain values and beliefs, and they might even share traits or behaviors. In some cases, therefore, we are quite safe in drawing conclusions about people based on their group membership. It is likely that we are likely correct in concluding that professional athletes are healthy, or that the average weight that women can lift is less than the average men can lift. Such generalizations require qualification and have to be carefully stated. For example, there are women who can outperform men in lifting weights.

Often stereotyping is nothing more than a perpetuation of old myths and prejudices. Careful inquiry might show that very few if any members of a given group possess the characteristic they are said to have. Yet stereotyping is a common and widespread phenomenon. Stereotypes persist because they are useful, and they help us organize the world around us. They are fed by ambiguity and sometimes fear or threat and reinforced in many ways. Stereotypes are so embedded in society that they are difficult to change. Think of how women are portrayed in many television commercials and movies. Women's rights organizations spend much time and energy fighting and trying to change stereotypes. Stereotypes are also reinforced by our language, such as in the noun "chairman."

ATTRIBUTION THEORY: MAKING CAUSAL INFERENCES

Underlying our perceptions and judgments is the desire to know why things happen. It is fundamental to human nature to want to explain the causes of our own and others' behavior. The question "Why?" is a search to explain, organize, and justify our experience. For example, inability to explain the causes of an event can leave us in a state of dissonance. As stated earlier, dissonance motivates us to explain the situation in order to reduce the dissonance. Also, if we know why something happened, we can predict future events better.

Our conclusions about causes also help us decide how to react to an event. Suppose our boss gives us an undesirable assignment. We can blame her for being unfair and resist the assignment, or we can see her as having no choice but to do so, and therefore accept the duty.

Attribution theory explains why and how we make causal attributions. *Causal attributions* are mediators between our perceptions of events and our responses to these events. They are judgments that affect our behavior, our feelings, and the conclusions we draw about events that we experience (see Figure 5.6). Casual attributions often involve judgment errors. Wrong inferences about causation will create problems similar to those created by errors that grow out of other perceptual tendencies.

Judging Other People's Behavior.   The basic psychological model in the previous chapter is based on the idea that behavior is determined by the person and the environment. Attribution theory research reveals, however, that we do not give equal weight to both the person and the environment in judging oth-

151

ers. Rather, there is a very common tendency to attribute causes of behavior to the internal characteristics of the person. Ross called this the **fundamental attribution error** [21]. Thus if we see people cheat or steal, we are more likely to characterize them as dishonest than we are to conclude that the situation caused them to act that way. We have a tendency to underestimate the situation as a cause even when we are told the person was forced or instructed to behave as he or she did [9].

☐ **FIGURE 5.6**   *A Model of Attribution Theory*

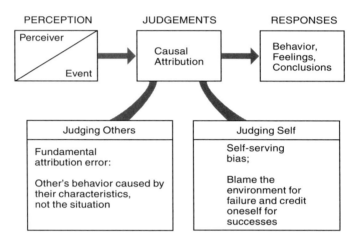

For instance, if we observe a debate in which participants are assigned a position to defend, we will most likely attribute their arguments to their beliefs rather than to the debating rules they are following. Somehow, what people say or do, even under instruction or other situational pressures, leads us to conclude more about them than about the situation. Perhaps this is because we see the situational influences as operating through people and not independent of them.

Several conditions cause the fundamental attribution error. First, if we believe that the other has free choice in the situation, we are more likely to attribute causality to him or her personally. This makes sense, for we can conclude that the person was free to do otherwise, but chose to act as he or she did.

Second, we are more likely to attribute internal motives to people when they take action we view as important, and especially when those actions affect us personally. Suppose someone dents our car in a parking lot but left the scene before we appeared. We are likely to brand the person as dishonest for failing even to leave a note or call a police officer. If, however, we make an external or situational attribution, we might conclude that he or she had to leave the scene because of an emergency at home.

There are several other factors that affect our attributions about others [11]:

1. *Consistency.* If a person behaves the same way in similar situations, we are more likely to see the behavior as internally motivated. Sup-

pose a worker is absent on a critical and important workday. We are more likely to attribute her absence to internal motivation if she had been absent a lot in the past.

2. *Distinctiveness.* Distinctive behaviors are those that are relatively unique to a situation. If a behavior is less distinctive, we are more likely to make internal attributions. Continuing the example above, we are even more likely to attribute the absence to internal motivation if the worker is usually absent on critical workdays.

3. *Consensus.* This factor deals with how others behave in the situation. When the person we are judging acts differently than others act in the situation, we are more likely to think of that person's behavior as internally motivated.

4. *Privacy of the act.* Actions that are taken in the absence of other people are more likely to be judged as internally motivated. When others are present, we might attribute the action to social pressure. When people are alone, we attribute the action to them.

5. *Status.* In general, higher-status people are seen to be more personally responsible for their actions. They are thought to have more control over their own actions and decisions and doing things because they choose to, not because they have to.

To be less prone to the fundamental attribution error, it is necessary to pause and reflect on the situation as well as the person and thus identify situational forces that account for behavior. It certainly would lead to searching for more data to explain the event. While this can complicate and delay matters, it may lead to a more accurate and less biased judgment.

Judging Our Own Behavior. People also make attributions about what causes their own behavior. This attribution is affected by a **self-serving bias**, a tendency to perceive oneself favorably. People credit themselves when they succeed but blame external factors when they fail [28]. Success is usually attributed to hard work, ability, and good judgment. Failure, on the other hand, is attributed to bad luck, unfair conditions, or impossible odds. Car drivers often report bizarre explanations which deny personal responsibility for accidents. "An invisible car came out of nowhere, struck my car, and vanished." "As I reached an intersection, a hedge sprang up, obscuring my vision. . . ." "A pedestrian hit me and went under my car."

The self-serving bias operates in game situations that call for skill but involve chance. We believe we win games because of skill but lose them because of bad breaks. However, the self-serving bias extends far beyond game situations and into everyday occurrences. When we deal with others, we often see our own actions as externally justified, but attribute others' actions to their internal disposition. You get angry because you are provoked. Your antagonist's anger, however, is attributed to his or her personality. The objective truth hardly matters, and the self-serving attributions persist, often in the face of contrary evidence.

People tend to overrate themselves on nearly any factor that is subjective and socially desirable [5]. They see themselves as better than average. These tendencies extend to our feelings about our own intelligence, leadership ability, health, life expectancy, interpersonal skill, and so on. Self-serving attributions and self-congratulatory comparisons operate in many ways [17]. We believe flattery more readily than we believe criticism. We overestimate how well we would act in a given situation and the accuracy of our judgments.

People don't always externalize fault when they fail, and they sometimes attribute their success to luck. Yet the self-serving bias is quite common. Interestingly, it seems to be strong among people with high self-respect and self-esteem. People with low self-esteem are more self-depreciating and engage in self-blame rather than blame external events for failure. They are less likely to exhibit the self-serving bias. On the other hand, when low-self-esteem people have a strong need for respect, they could be more likely than the average person to exhibit the self-serving bias. This is why some people constantly refer to their own activities, exploits, and successes. The self-serving bias acts as a boastful cover for their feelings of inferiority and is an attempt to gain recognition in order to enhance self-esteem.

Some Organizational Implications of Attribution Biases. Biased assessments of others and of ourselves can occur in many ways in organizational situations. A work group is likely to blame other groups or departments when failures occur on the job. Here, the self-serving bias is not very conducive to cooperation between groups or to behavior that tries to find the true causes of failure. Performance appraisal is another situation where attribution biases operate. The attribution errors can create serious disagreements between raters and ratees about why they performed well or poorly. It is even more critical a problem when ethnic or sex differences are added to the situation. Feldman-Summers and Kiesler found that there is a tendency to attribute female successes to hard work or luck rather than to ability [4]. Such sexually biased attributions place women at a disadvantage because they would receive less credit than males for their accomplishments. From a female's perspective, it is better if their successes are attributed to their ability, rather than to external or situational conditions. Males, on the other hand, are more protected from adverse evaluations. Their successes usually are attributed to competence, and their failures to bad luck. Interestingly, both males and females make these biased attributions. With the influx of females into full-time employment and into managerial ranks in recent years, these biases represent a serious problem.

Some research shows that we look at both effort and ability in evaluating performance but give more weight to effort [12]. Effort is weighted higher for both good and poor performance. Good performance is rated higher and poor performance lower when effort is seen as the cause rather than ability. Thus we are evaluated more on how hard someone thinks we are trying. If our boss feels we put in a lot of effort, we will be appraised higher when we succeed. If we are perceived as not trying very hard, we will be rated more poorly when we fail. *Such as Fran Smith situation in the Walltown Supermarket.*

SUMMARY

Attitudes, perceptions, and judgment tendencies have widespread and important implications in the world of work. Employee attitudes can make a huge difference in the effectiveness of an organization. They affect such things as attendance, retention, work commitments, and interpersonal relations. Perceptions and judgments are critical because they enter into so many work situations: selecting applicants, making assignments, appraising performance, giving feedback, solving problems, and so on.

Attitudes refer to what people like and dislike and predispose people to act favorably or unfavorably toward an object or event. They function in several ways to help people adapt to their world. Attitudes are related to beliefs and values. All three are acquired from infancy through our experiences and associations with people, events, and the media. Specific attitudes can be learned at any time and apply to any experience. Employee attitudes about various aspects of their job are often studied by employers, because it is known that attitudes affect satisfaction, performance and constructive voluntary contributions to organizational success.

The study of perception is central to understanding how people react. Each of us has certain perceptual tendencies that define the world from our own personal point of view. Values, emotional states, needs, and personality all come into play. Characteristics of the object and situation also affect what we select, how we organize what we perceive, and how we make interpretations. Most critical are the errors in judgment we make about the world around us. A particularly interesting tendency is how we make causal inferences about what we perceive. We tend to attribute other people's behavior to their personality rather than to situational forces. When judging ourselves, however, we are more likely to have a self-serving bias. We also attribute our successes not to external forces, but to our own skills and abilities.

☐ KEY CONCEPTS

Attitudes	Fundamental	Perceptual
Attitude surveys	attribution error	organization
Attribution theory	Halo effect	Post-decisional
Beliefs	Implicit	dissonance
Cognitive dissonance	personality	Projection
Decisional dissonance	theory	Selective perception
Disconfirmed	Insufficient	Self-serving bias
expectations	justification	Stereotyping
First impressions	Perception	Sufficient justification
	Perceptual bias	Values

STUDY QUESTIONS

1. Define and differentiate between attitudes, values, and beliefs. How are these three concepts linked together to help explain behavior?
2. What are the various ways that attitudes, values, and beliefs are formed?
3. What functions do attitudes serve for people?
4. List five people, objects, or events about which you have strong attitudes, positive and negative. In what ways might these attitudes affect your behavior as a manager? How will subordinates react to such behavior?
5. What kinds of new attitudes do you think you might learn as you advance upward in management?
6. What is the purpose of employee attitude surveys? What cautions should be taken in their use?
7. Define cognitive consistency and dissonance. Cite several factors that help to cause dissonance.
8. What characteristics of an event or object are likely to affect how it is perceived?
9. Define five major judgment tendencies or errors that people commonly commit.
10. Describe three work situations that show how a particular judgment error might damage the relationship between a superior and a subordinate.
11. According to attribution theory, what are the two basic judgment errors people commit? Cite several organizational implications of attribution errors.
12. List the ways in which an applicant for a job can behave in order to affect or control the judgment tendencies of the interviewer.

CASE

FREEMAN INSURANCE COMPANY

Steve Chalmers and Jack Girard were psychologists who worked in the Human Resources Division at Freeman Insurance Company Headquarters. They were involved in a project to design new organizational systems for the insurance company. One facet of the project was an attitude survey of the data entry clerks to be used as a pilot study for a later survey of all employees. The data entry clerks were chosen to be the first group studied because of a high absenteeism and turnover rate in this department.

In the next few weeks, Chalmers and Girard collected data from past and present data entry clerks with interviews and questionnaires. They analyzed the results and a report was sent to the top management of Freeman Insurance. They presented an oral report to the top management,

☐ FREEMAN . . .

then set up a meeting to discuss the results with George Green (Controller), Tom Andrews (Assistant to the President), James Patrick (Superintendent of data processing in charge of data entry clerks, computer programmers, and systems analysts), Phyllis Birk (a temporary data entry supervisor), and Betty Johnson (Personnel Manager). The direct supervisor of the data entry clerks, Ruth Malone, was absent because of illness.

Andrews started the conversation:

Andrews:	Well, George, do you want to start off this discussion?
George:	Not really.
Andrews:	How about Steve Chalmers? It's his report. Before you begin Steve, maybe I should tell you what happened last week, since you may not have heard. Late last Tuesday afternoon the data entry clerks marched in and asked if they could see Jim Patrick. He agreed, and then they gave him a long list of complaints.
Patrick:	Yes, they said they disliked their supervisor, Ruth Malone. They didn't like her method of assigning them work, of evaluating their performance, and so on. I told them I wanted a chance to discuss these issues with Ruth when she came back to work, so they are still waiting for an answer.
Green:	Have they complained to Ruth herself?
Patrick:	Yes, and, listen to this, she told them that they could not complain to anyone higher, or they would be fired.
Johnson:	It would have disturbed me more if they had complained when she was there.
Andrews:	No! It disturbs me that they felt they had to wait until she was not there. This shows real fear of her.
Chalmers:	I think that this action shows great discontent. It's very hard to get enough courage to complain about your supervisor to higher management.

(Period of silence.)

Chalmers:	I hadn't heard about this. I must say, though, I'm not very surprised because this validates the data we collected and summarized in the report. I assume you have all read it?
Wilson:	Actually, I did not get the report to them until late yesterday afternoon, so they might not have had a chance to read it.
Andrews:	I started to read it last night but I got so sleepy that I had to go to bed.

☐ FREEMAN . . .

Chalmers:	Maybe that's an indication about how dull my writing is.
Andrews:	Not at all. The report seemed quite interesting except for all the numbers. I'm not used to interpreting means and standard deviations.
Chalmers:	Well, then let me emphasize some of the more important things. First, about one half of the data entry operators do not understand the method used to evaluate their work. (A somewhat complex grading system assigning points to operators on the quantity of their work and errors made had been introduced about six months previous by an industrial engineering consulting firm).
Patrick:	(Loudly) Damn! I don't understand that. The system was explained to them! The consultant himself took a lot of time to explain it to them! I don't think anybody could explain something to that group!

(Silence.)

Chalmers:	(Somewhat taken aback) The report also indicated that, by and large, they feel that higher management is not interested in them.
Patrick:	(Loudly) What do they mean by higher management? Is it me or the president? I don't think it is me. They see me all the time. I talk to them all the time.
Chalmers:	I assume they meant the top men in the company when they responded to the term higher management. Actually we didn't define the term in the questionnaire.
Andrews:	I'm not sure. I think they might mean you, Jim, higher management in the department.

(Silence)

Chalmers:	They also indicate that there is favoritism here.
Patrick:	What's that mean?
Chalmers:	For example, from the interviews, we found there is an attractive woman on the first shift who they believe is being favored.
Patrick:	Doris! She's our best worker. When the consultant trained the operators, Doris was the only one the consultant said didn't need training. I suppose that's why they are saying she's favored. Shouldn't the best employee be favored?
Johnson:	But she shouldn't have been left out of the training.

☐ FREEMAN . . .

Chalmers:	Female employees are often quite sensitive about better treatment for more attractive employees. But look here, the results also show some negative feelings about the supervision they receive.
Johnson:	Well, what happened certainly bears that out.
Chalmers:	Some of the comments in the open-ended section at the end of the questionnaire also are worth mentioning. They bring up things that the questionnaires did not cover. For example, there were several complaints about not receiving any breaks.
Peary:	Don't you give these employees breaks?
Patrick:	Sometimes we do and sometimes we don't. We look at the workload and if it's high that day we skip the breaks.
Wilson:	If I were a data entry operator, I would think my productivity would be higher if I had breaks.
Chalmers:	Research shows definitely that breaks contribute to higher productivity.
Peary:	I don't believe it, Patrick. No breaks in your group. What else?
Chalmers:	They also don't like their overtime assignments.
Green:	How are overtime assignments made now?
Patrick:	I just assign overtime on a rotating basis.
Andrews:	Why not have them volunteer?
Patrick:	I used to do that, but most of them won't volunteer. The same ones volunteered all the time. It's fairer when everybody gets about the same amount.
Peary:	It's obvious that most of them don't like to work more than the scheduled hours. How often do they work overtime?
Patrick:	About three days a week.
Peary:	The same three days each week?
Patrick:	Yes.
Peary:	Well, if it is predictable, why don't you use part-time employees on those days?
Patrick:	(Sarcastically) That's a brilliant idea. How do you find them?
Chalmers:	Here's another reaction: "They should stop treating us like children."

☐ FREEMAN . . .

Patrick: Listen, a supervisor of that group has to act like a kinder-garten teacher. They are just like children.

(Long silence)

Andrews: Damn it, Patrick! I was going to let that go by, but I won't. With an attitude like yours it's no wonder we have problems.

Green: Come on, people, let's get back to the main issues. What are we going to do about the Ruth Malone problem? What are we going to tell her? Who's going to tell her? What advice do we give her when she comes back? By the way, Phyllis, have they ever talked to you about Ruth?

Birk: Yes. I told them that Ruth is just moody, the way they are some days. They said that she's not like them.

Birk: Another thing. They are worried about getting fired over this incident. They want something done soon.

Johnson: I don't know why they are worried. They can get another job anytime.

Patrick: Well, I'll tell all of you right now. If it comes to choosing between Ruth Malone and those operators I'll stick with Ruth and let all of them go. At least I'd let the agitators go. When I brought up this problem with my consultant, he said that I should fire the agitators.

Chalmers: I might also mention here that according to a recent National Labor Relations Board ruling, a concerted action by a group of nonunionized employees can bring them the protection of the labor laws.

Johnson: Is that so? We must be sure that we are not put in a position of seeming to reward group action. That could cause trouble.

Peary: What do we do now? If some of their gripes are legitimate, what changes can be made in their situation?

Patrick: I still do not think that most of the employees are unhappy. They are being stirred up by a number of agitators, and I know who they are.

Andrews: On the positive side, how about some supervisory training for Ruth and the others?

Patrick: Ruth is the only one of our supervisors to have taken supervisory training.

Johnson: We have got to find a way to communicate with them without building up resentment. How about an annual performance review?

☐ FREEMAN . . .

Patrick: The average operator would never have one. Most of them don't last a year.

Birk: We ought to have periods set aside in which all supervisors can listen to grievances.

Green: Don't ever use the word grievance in this company. Use complaints or better yet employee concerns.

Patrick: Well, in all of this, I hope you remember that, unlike the rest of this place, I have a production operation here. We must have speed, tight schedules, and so on. These aren't like most white-collar jobs.

Chalmers: Any other questions about the report? I'm sorry, but I really have to go. I have an appointment in an hour, and it's some distance from here.

Andrews: So do I. Let's adjourn for now. I don't think we're getting anywhere.

(The meeting breaks up.)

QUESTIONS

1. What does this case illustrate about employee attitudes and perceptions?
2. Why did the data entry employees take the action they did?
3. Evaluate Patrick's behaviors and attitudes and their effects on employee attitudes.

REFERENCES

1. Bem, D.J. *Beliefs, attitudes, and human affairs.* Belmont, CA: Brooks-Cole, 1970.
2. *Business Week,* Executive pay: The party ain't over yet. April 26, 1993, 56-63.
3. Cardy, R.L., and Kehoe, J.F. Rater selective attention, ability, and appraisal effectiveness: The effect of a cognitive style on the accuracy of differentiation among ratees. *Journal of Applied Psychology,* 1984, 69, 589-94.
4. Feldman-Summers, S., and Kiesler, S.B. Those who are number two try harder. The effect of sex on the attribution of causality. *Journal of Personality and Social Psychology,* 1974, 30, 846-55.
5. Felson, R.B. Ambiguity and bias in the self-concept. *Social Psychology Quarterly,* 1981, 44, 64-69.
6. Festinger, L. *A theory of cognitive dissonance.* Evanston, IL: Row, Peterson, 1957.
7. Fishbein, M., and Ajzen, I. *Belief, attitude, intention and behavior: An introduction to theory and research.* Reading, MA: Addison-Wesley, 1975.

8. Gregory, R. *Eye and brain: The psychology of seeing.* 3d ed. London: Weidenfeld & Nicholson, 1977.

9. Jones, E.E., and Harris, V.A. The attribution of attitudes. *Journal of Experimental and Social Psychology,* 1967, 3, 2-24.

10. Katz, D. The functional approach to the study of attitude change. *Public Opinion Quarterly,* 1960, 24, 163-204.

11. Kelly, H.H. The process of causal attribution. *American Psychologist,* 1973, 28, 107-28.

12. Knowlton, W.A., Jr., and Mitchell, T.R. Effects of causal attributions on a supervisor's evaluation of subordinate performance. *Journal of Applied Psychology,* 1980, 65, 459-66.

13. Lesly, E. and Bongiorno, L. Women golfers have a handicap, all right. *Business Week,* 1993 (April 19), 94.

14. Levine, J.B. For IBM Europe, this is the year of truth. *Business Week,* April 19, 1993, 45-46.

15. Loftus, E. F. Eyewitnesses: Essential but unreliable. *Psychology Today,* February 1984, 22-26.

16. Maier, N.R.F. *Psychology in industrial organizations.* 4th ed. Boston: Houghton Mifflin, 1973.

17. Myers, D.G. *Social psychology.* New York: McGraw-Hill, 1983.

18. Oskamp, S. *Attitudes and opinions.* Englewood Cliffs, NJ: Prentice-Hall, 1977.

19. Parsons, C.K., and Liden, R.C. Interviewer perceptions of applicant qualifications: A multivariate study of demographic characteristics and nonverbal cues. *Journal of Applied Psychology,* 1984, 69, 557-68.

20. Perlman, D., and Cozby, P.C. *Social psychology.* New York: Holt, Rinehart and Winston, 1983.

21. Ross, L.D. The intuitive psychologist and his shortcomings: Distortions in the attribution process. In. L. Berkowitz, ed. *Advances in experimental social psychology,* 10. New York: Academic Press, 1977.

22. Schwartz, E. I. In Poughkeepsie, a bitter family breakup. *Business Week,* 1993 (April 5), 23.

23. Sellars, C.L. and Frew, D.R. A longitudinal investigation of job satisfaction. Milwaukee, WI: *Midwest Academy of Management Proceedings,* 1990, 222-227.

24. Staw, B. M. Knee-deep in the big muddy: A study of escalating commitment to a chosen course of action. *Organizational Behavior and Human Performance,* 1976, 16, 27-44.

25. Staw, B.M. and Ross, J. Knowing when to pull the plug, *Harvard Business Review,* 1987 (March-April), 68-74.

26. Staw, B.M., and Ross, J. Behavior in escalation situations: Antecedents, prototypes, and solutions. In L.L. Cummings and B.M. Staw, eds. *Research in organizational behavior,* 9, Greenwich, CT: JAI Press, 1987.

27. Zajonc, R.B. Attitudinal effects of mere exposure. *Journal of Personality and Social Psychology Monograph Supplement,* 1968, 9, 1-27.

28. Zuckerman, M. Attribution of success and failure revisited, or the motivational bias is alive and well in attribution theory. *Journal of Personality,* 1979, 47, 247-87.

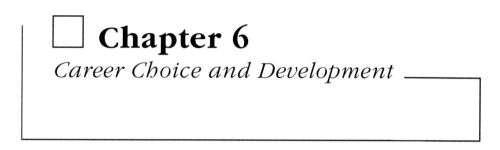

Chapter 6
Career Choice and Development

Jennifer Thomas is in the last semester of law school at State University. Her performance at law school has been outstanding. She is a member of the Law Review and in the top 5 percent of her class. Because of this record, she is being sought by many law firms in the state.

After considering all her opportunities, she arrived at two alternatives. One possibility is a large, prestigious firm, Smith, Finch, and Krupinski, located in Capital City. Her uncle has been a senior partner there for many years. The other alternative is to practice law in her father's smaller firm, also located in the state capital.

She has considered almost all the factors that she thinks are important in the choice. First, she wishes to live in Capital City because she was born there and her family is in that area. Second, after long conversations with her uncle and her father, she has concluded that there would be no substantial long-term financial advantage working for either firm. Her father's income and her uncle's income are almost equal and have been throughout their law careers. Third, there are some advantages to working in the large firm, but there are other, different advantages in the small firm. For example, in large law firms there are good legal libraries and support staff, but at the same time office politics can be very vicious. In her father's firm, the office politics are minimal, but the legal facilities aren't the same as in the larger firms. However, a good legal library is available at the state capital library, if she needs it.

Her choice seems to have come down to what kind of law she will practice. In Smith, Finch, and Krupinski, Jennifer will specialize in one area of law. During her first two years as an associate of the firm, she will have a chance to work in different areas such as public utility regulation, environmental law, tax, labor law, and trusts. In her third year, with the counseling of senior partners, she will select an area of specialization. When she becomes a partner, most of her time will be spent working in the area in which she has specialized.

In her father's firm, Thomas and Associates, she will be a member of a firm that has a general practice. They do some corporate work, but mostly for small local firms. They work in real estate and small trusts and do some criminal work, divorces, and so forth. Jennifer knows that if she works in Thomas and Associates she will do many different things.

When she began thinking about these two alternatives, she was initially inclined to go to Smith, Finch, and Krupinski, primarily because she felt it would not be a good idea for her to go to work in "Dad's firm," as she called it. However, her father plans to retire in six years, so Jennifer would be on her own. It would be Thomas and Associates, but the "Thomas" would be Jennifer, not her father.

In this chapter, we address the types of problems Jennifer faces in her choice of where to work. We focus, first, on the concept of a career and the stages of career development. Second, organization socialization is discussed, and the focus turns to the development of individual orientations to work and the workplace. Finally, we suggest some things one can do to manage a career.

CAREERS

A **career** is more than just the job or sequence of jobs a person holds over a lifetime. A career is the individually perceived sequence of attitudes and behaviors associated with work-related experiences and activities over a person's life [20, 30]. This definition implies several things:

1. A career refers to the different jobs a person holds over his or her lifetime.

2. The processes and activities that prepare one for a job are part of the career.

3. Job-related attitudes, values, and beliefs are an aspect of a career.

4. The relationship of a person's self-identity to work is a dimension of a career.

CAREER SUCCESS

It is fairly conventional to judge a person's career success by the organizational level achieved, the pay or income earned, or the standing in a profession. Career experts, however, argue that this is too simple a conception, that career success should be judged on several dimensions: (1) career performance, (2) career attitudes, (3) career identity, and (4) career adaptability [30].

Career Performance.   Career performance can be judged by the level of objective success and the level of psychological success. **Objective success** is usually reflected by the achievement of the most common measures of success, such as pay and the attainment of reputation or high office in an organization. For example, a person who earns $75,000 each year is more successful than one who makes $50,000, or the company president is thought to be more successful than a vice president.

Attaining objective success depends on how well you perform your job *and* the extent to which it is valued by others in the firm. But while it is generally true that the best performers are the most successful, this is by no means always the case. Sometimes a person who is a very good performer gets passed over for another who is not quite so effective. Or two people may be equally capable, but their careers might progress at different rates because they work for different firms. For instance, there are greater advancement opportunities in the electronics industry than in, say, the steel industry.

Objective career success may also be attained by individuals who work outside organizations. Artists can become famous working alone. Success may also be measured by the reputation one has with colleagues. To some, to be recognized as a "leader" in a field may be a more important indicator of career success than money.

The second measure of career performance, **psychological success**, occurs when the person's self-esteem increases. Self-esteem is the value one places on one's self [30]. Psychological success may be linked to objective success. It may increase when a person advances in pay and status at work. It may decrease as one experiences job disappointment and failure. But self-esteem may also increase as one begins to sense personal worth in other ways, say through family involvement or by developing confidence and competence in a particular field. Objective career success may then become secondary in a person's life. This sometimes happens after one has achieved some degree of economic security, enough to be certain that personal and family commitments can be met. The achievement of psychological success explains why some people who had been advancing rapidly but then slowed down can be quite happy with their life.

Career Attitudes.   **Career attitudes** are those specific individual attitudes related to work. These are attitudes about the work itself, the place of work, the level of achievement, and the relationship between work and other parts of a person's life. Career attitudes begin to be formed early in life, before a person has a job, and they continue to be shaped by the person's work experiences.

Career Identity.   Individual identity is the unique way that a person believes he or she fits into the world. Work, career, and a place in an organization will have an effect on identity. **Career identity** is that particular facet of a person's identity related to occupational activities.

There are other components of identity: subidentities that center around family, social relationships, and other parts of a person's life. An example is shown in Figure 6.1 [30]. A woman who is married, with children and a career has subidentities that overlap and, taken together, represent the way she views herself.

At any one time, one of these subidentities may be more important than others, but the importance can change over time. For example, in early career stages, the work identity may be very important, but later the emphasis may shift to the family. Also, the importance of subidentities of different persons in the same career stage may not be the same. One person may identify more strongly with family and children while another may have greater identification with work.

☐ **FIGURE 6.1**   *Different Subidentities*

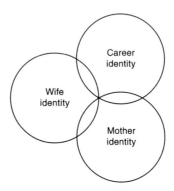

Career Adaptability.   **Career adaptability** is the individual's willingness and capacity to change occupations and/or the work setting in order to maintain his or her standards of career progress. The level of career adaptability has important implications for managers, professionals, and persons who aspire to career advancement. Those interested in advancing to higher levels must be able to handle different jobs and to make frequent moves.

Career adaptability has taken on added significance even for those who do not have advancement interests but rather wish to continue to protect themselves against corporate downsizing, which affects workers at all levels. For example, since 1980, while employment in Fortune 500 firms in the United States dropped from over 12 million employees to around 9 million in 1991, there was also a significant shift in the composition of jobs [78]. In 1979, there were around 20 million employees in manufacturing (23 percent of the nonfarm employment) but in 1991, that number had dwindled to around 18 million (17 percent of the nonfarm employment), about a 15 percent loss in jobs. During the same period, service sector employment increased from 17 million to 29 million, a very significant increase. The difficulty is, however, that the average wage in the service sector was $330 per week compared to $455 in manufacturing. These changes have implications for blue collar workers who must often take lower paying positions as they move from manufacturing to service jobs, or retraining implications for those who wish to continue to earn high incomes.

Such retrenchment adjustment is also very common among managerial and professional ranks. Many firms have made very significant reductions in both the number of managers and have slowed down the rate of increase in managerial compensation.

CAREERS AND LIFE STRUCTURE

Work is a key component of the life structure. At any one time, "one or two components have a central place in the life structure . . . occupation and marriage-family are usually the most central" [44]. The **life structure** is the basic pattern of the relationship between these factors at any one time.

As a person goes through life, the life structure changes. This may occur because of a change in any one of the components or because of a change in the relationship between components. For instance, a person may emphasize work in the early years and neglect his or her spouse. Both husband and wife might develop effective, stable ways of coping with family-work relationships. Suppose after that adjustment has been made, the person experiences serious illness and decides to devote more time and effort to family, less to work. This means that the family component must now change, as well as the work component. These changes can be quite disturbing. There will probably be a very unsettling transition period until the life structure achieves some balance again. This is illustrated in Figure 6.2. Work is the dominant element at time 1. Between time 1 and time 2 there is a transition period during which the people involved must settle important issues about their relationships. At time 2, the life structure has become stable again, but this time the family is the dominant factor.

◻ **FIGURE 6.2**   *Life Structure Changes*

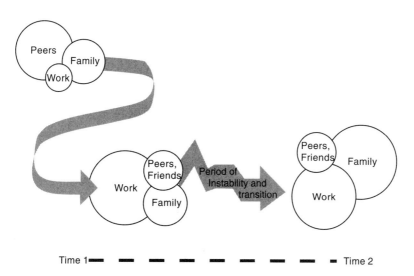

Levinson and his colleagues believe that life structure changes at particular, regular times [44]. They divide a person's life into eras, or 20- to 25-year cycles. These eras are:

1. Childhood and adolescence (ages 0-22)

2. Early adulthood (ages 17-45)

3. Middle adulthood (ages 40-65)

4. Late adulthood (ages 65 and above)

Each era is distinct from the other, and during each one, a stable and settled life structure develops. Between each era is a *transition period*, a "boundary zone," when the outgoing era ends and the new one begins. In moving from one period to another, the person has to work at certain tasks that will determine the quality of life: building and changing the life structure, developing an identity that links the person to the rest of the world, and working on the single components of the life structure [44].

CAREER STAGES

A person moves through a series of **career stages**. There are four active career stages, which correspond approximately to the eras described by Levinson and his colleagues [14, 30, 44, 64]. In Table 6.1 we show these four stages and several different dimensions of careers and the career cycle. First, we show the major tasks which must be resolved during each period. The resolution of these tasks affect the life structure in subsequent stages. Second, we indicate changes in the role of the person in the occupation and the organization over time. Third, we define changing individual needs. Finally, we point out some of the pressing work issues that a person faces in early, middle, and late parts of each stage.

Transition periods overlap the end of one career stage and the beginning of another. Transition periods are "frequently times of crisis—of profound inner conflict, of feeling in a state of suspended animation" [44]. For example, the first major transition period occurs between 17 and 22 years of age, during the time a person is moving from adolescence to becoming an adult. Work, family, and other components of the life structure undergo major changes during these transition periods. Relationships of the earlier period are changed, terminated, or perhaps strengthened. The person may be looking toward the future with a great deal of uncertainty.

The Exploration Stage. The **exploration stage** extends from birth into the early 20s. During this time values, attitudes, and beliefs are developed that remain important throughout life. One learns to deal with parents and other authority figures and has early exposure to work and career. The major role is that of a child and a student. A person begins to acquire the foundation on which later skills and work values are built. Pulakos and Schmitt found that high school students' expectations of job satisfaction were related to job attitudes in later life [58]. Another study found that job attitudes as adults were correlated with those held in early life [68].

Toward the end of this period, the person begins to separate from family and early friends and takes steps toward independence and into the adult world. Preliminary organizational and career choices are made, and a person usually makes some commitment to training of some kind. Those who attend college pick a major, some join the military, others go into vocational training, or take entry-level work positions.

TABLE 6.1   Career Stages

General Career Stage—Age	Exploration	17	Novice	33	Establishment	45	Late Career	65
Era (Levinson et al., 1978)	Childhood and Adolescence		Early Adulthood				Middle Adulthood	
Major Tasks	Develop basic values Separate from family Take preliminary steps into adulthood		Form dreams and aspirations Form occupation Form mentor relationships Form love, marriage, family relationships		Establish a niche in society Work toward advancement		Make crucial choices about work, love, and peer relationships Give choices meaning and commitment Build life structure around these choices	
Work/Occupational Role	Child, Student		Apprentice, Learner		Contributor and full member of the organization in the area of technical competence		Mentoring Senior, experienced person	
Individual Needs	Move from lower order to higher order need		Stability, roots, membership		Become independent Be affirmed by society		Esteem Autonomy Self-actualization	
Issues (Schein, 1970) Early Stage	Movement from lower order to higher order needs		Develop first life structure Develop competence Learn ropes		Begin to establish identity within the organization		Accept and cope with career progress Come to terms with organization	
Midstage			Begin to make commitment to a career Make choices about love, family relationships		Advancement at same or different rate than peers		In still advancing career, use broad general management skills In plateaued career, train others, maintain skills and value to organization	
Late Stage	Make first organization choice Make early steps in career		Work out flaws of first life structure Make or reaffirm choices Enter managerial ranks		Assess and evaluate career progress Begin to mentor others		Learn to manage a life less dominated by work Learn to accept new work roles based on declining motivation and competence	

The Novice Stage.   During the **novice stage**, from age 17 to about 33, the person's work role changes and so do the major life tasks. The center of a person's life must now shift from family to his or her own world. The person becomes immersed in career and in an organization, but as an apprentice, a novice, a beginner. As a novice, a person learns the relevant skills, competence, attitudes, and values for the culture of a specific organization and a specific job. It takes years to become competent in an occupation and to learn the ropes [44]. Simon, for instance, has pointed out that even great artists and chess players do not achieve prominence until they have worked at their craft for at least 10 years [65]. By the end of this stage, however, the person becomes competent to the point where he or she can be a full contributor to an organization.

The major tasks during the novice period are to crystallize aspirations and dreams, begin forming an occupational identity, begin establishing a mentor relationship, and start marriage-family-love relationships. A person's needs for stability and for membership with others become dominate in the novice phase.

A critical period occurs around age 30, which is a time of questioning whether or not the choices and commitments that were made earlier were the right ones. Some will make different choices about spouses, relationships, jobs, and careers. For work, particularly, these choices are affected in part by the level of organizational commitment. Organizational commitment is more strongly and negatively related to turnover in this career stage than in later career [12].

The Establishment Stage.   From the early 30s to the mid-40s, a person becomes established in a career. The two major tasks of this **establishment stage** are (1) trying to establish a place in society and (2) working toward advancement and improvement in the various components of the life structure. These tasks reflect the person's need for independence and for recognition from those who are important in his or her life.

In the early part of the establishment stage, the person has "junior" status, even though he or she has developed organizationally relevant skills. A senior person, a mentor, may be very helpful in showing the person how to operate effectively in the organization during this period. Managers who had a career mentor experienced more rapid promotion and were more satisfied with their compensation [18, 83].

During the establishment stage, some may begin to slow down in their rate of advancement. Others may continue to advance more rapidly. They will begin to outpace their peers and start to encroach into the areas of more senior personnel. They may be seen by some as being too "aggressive."

Toward the end of this stage, the nature of the career is fairly well set. The person becomes a senior member of the organization. Levinson and his colleagues [44], who studied the adult development of men, call this "becoming one's own man. The major . . . tasks of this phase are to accomplish the [early] goals, to become a senior member in one's world, to speak more strongly with one's own voice, and to have a greater measure of authority."

Between the ages of 35 and 45, another critical transition period occurs that spans the boundary of the establishment stage and the late career stage. This is the "midlife" or "midcareer" crisis. It is another period during which the life structure that has recently stabilized is subjected again to serious evaluation. Questioning centers around what the person has done with life, family, children, and career. By now the status at work is well defined. One is either still advancing, has stabilized, or is in a period of decline. The person must evaluate the present and future career status and come to terms with it. Judgments will be made about relationships with spouses, children, and the other elements of the life structure. In some instances, the person's judgment is positive and the outlook for the future may be quite good. In other instances, the person may have a sense of futility about the past and feel powerless to act about the future.

Often the midcareer-midlife crisis is resolved after a marker event, a significant change in some element of the life structure, such as a serious illness, divorce, or job change. A marker event serves to sever or change old relationships and signal the beginning of new ones.

Late Career.   The **late career** period from age 45 until retirement is a time when the person's work role is coaching others and being a senior, experienced contributor. If his or her career has advanced, the person will be in general management rather than in the management of technical functions. If the career path has slowed, the person will be in a mid-level to upper-level managerial position, probably still a productive member of the firm. However, peers and even younger people will begin to pass the person on the promotion ladder.

A declining career is a problem for both the person and the organization. There is some research on the effects of organizational commitment in this stage [12]. The effects of lower commitment on turnover are significant in this stage. Lower levels of commitment are also related to absenteeism, which is one way to show dissatisfaction without leaving the firm. Cohen also found that for those in this career stage, the more highly committed members were also the highest performers [12].

The main tasks during this late stage are to make critical choices about the components of the life structure, to make commitments to those choices, and to build a new life structure around them. Toward the end of this stage, the person must prepare to disengage from the organization. Retirement is imminent and will mean a major change in the person's life. Work, which has always been an important and time-consuming component of the life structure, will no longer hold a central place.

A Comment on "Stage Models."   Stage models have been criticized because of the way they were developed. Schein's career-stage model was based on studies of MBAs and his consulting experiences. The Levinson study was based on interviews with 40 men from four occupational classes who were born in the 1930s and was done during the late 1960s and early 1970s. Both studies are male biased and reflect the life stages of white men from that particular time in history or from those particular groups. Growing up in a different social context may not result in the same "life stages" or "career stages" as we have outlined here. Further, it could well be that the experiences had by these men are not at all similar to those that women and minorities would have had, or will have.

ORGANIZATION SOCIALIZATION: LEARNING HOW TO ADAPT TO WORK

Learning to work and how to adapt to work organizations begins long before a person actually takes a job. In Chapter 3, we discussed how cultural values are transmitted through socialization, and in Chapter 4 how learning and socialization are related to the individual's personality. As we pointed out, many of these experiences result in an orientation toward work and the workplace. Here we build on this previous material to show the role and effects of socialization on a person's work life.

We focus on three distinct phases of socialization (see Figure 6.3). The early socialization period refers to the experiences and circumstances that occur in the formative years of life, the exploration stage. Parents, socioeconomic factors, personality, and cultural-social factors are important. Preliminary work socialization occurs before one starts work, but it is a set of experiences that shape more work-specific attitudes, values, and beliefs. This happens as one experiences occupational socialization, develops competence, and makes choices about work organizations. Organizational socialization begins when one enters the organization and begins to modify previously developed attitudes and beliefs to the culture of the organization.

FIGURE 6.3 *Socialization and Work*

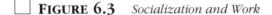

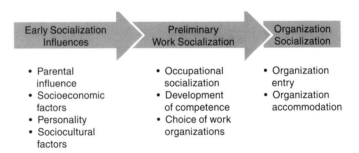

EARLY SOCIALIZATION INFLUENCES

Most experts emphasize the importance of childhood experiences in personality formation; that is, adult psychological and behavioral patterns reflect the experiences one had as a child. In very early years, the child starts learning how to adapt to organizations when learning how to respond to authority and authority figures such as parents and teachers. Authority figures have power, can give rewards or withhold them, and can administer punishment or refrain from its use. The response to authority figures learned at home becomes further developed and reinforced in churches, schools, and other organizations.

Such **early socialization** experiences set the stage for the development of work values. The important factors that affect a person's work values, attitudes,

☐ **THE BRITISH CEO** _____

Cox and Cooper studied the careers of 45 British CEOs of companies with more than 1,000 employees [13]. The CEOs were assertive, outgoing, innovative-minded, had high needs for institutionalized power but felt that goals had to be achieved through people. They were highly committed to their work and their firm. This commitment was reflected by a workweek which was usually 6 days and long hours (12 hour days were not unusual). When asked why they did this, some of the replies were "I simply love my work.", "I never look at the time.", "There is never a dull moment."

These CEOs developed a sense of self-sufficiency and ability to cope with the world at a very early age, often due to the loss of a parent, usually the father. They reported, however, that their childhood was happy and normal.

In their early work experiences, they reported they had much responsibility. As they moved through their careers, they tended to work in a wide range of business functions such as marketing, finance, and production. They also experienced high career mobility: Most had worked in several companies and only six had spent their whole career in one company.

Charles J. Cox and Cary L. Cooper, The Making of the British CEO: childhood, work experience, personality and managerial style. *The Academy of Management Executive*, 1989, Vol. 3, No. 3, pp. 241-245 [13].

choice of work, and choice of occupation are parental influence, socioeconomic background, personality, and sociocultural factors.

Parental Influence.   Children learn much from their parents about work. According to one theory, the type of parent-child relationships affects a person's career choice [60, 61]. Three forms of parent-child relationships affect work attitudes (see Figure 6.4).

In the *child centered approach* parents direct much attention to the child. Parents are primarily concerned with satisfying basic needs of the child such as food, shelter, and a secure environment, which can be done rather quickly. They are not as quick in reinforcing behaviors to satisfy a child's higher-order needs, such as social and emotional support. Child-centered parents may be (1) overprotective or (2) overdemanding. The overprotective parent reinforces socially desirable behavior. According to Roe, the child becomes dependent and learns conformity [60]. The overdemanding parent reinforces higher-order needs when a child exhibits achievement-oriented behavior.

☐ **FIGURE 6.4** *Childrearing Practices, Orientation, and Career According to Roe [60]*

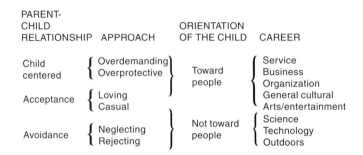

Acceptance of the child is the second type of child rearing. Acceptance may be of a casual, somewhat indifferent nature. Or it may be very loving where the parent is concerned with meeting the child's needs at all levels. As an adult, a person raised by such parents is concerned with satisfying needs at all levels.

The third parental style is *avoidance.* Parents may simply not provide the basic physical requirements, or they may reject the child. This leads to an orientation by the child not toward the parent, but more inward.

These child rearing practices lead to adult orientations that are either "toward people" or "not toward people." The relationship of childrearing practices, orientations, and careers is shown in Figure 6.4.

> People in service occupations are primarily oriented toward people and probably come from a home that generated a loving, over-protective environment, while scientists tend not to be oriented toward people and come from a home atmosphere where rejection and avoidance of the child predominated [53].

Socioeconomic Factors. Socioeconomic factors include social class (upper, middle, lower), family income, occupational status, education levels, and so forth. A good deal of research demonstrates the importance of socioeconomic factors on work orientations. For example, Tinto has shown that highly educated, well-to-do parents can contribute to their children's achievements in a way that less well-to-do parents cannot [74]. Studies have also shown that a larger proportion of children from higher social classes aspire to careers in business or in the professions while a larger proportion of children from lower-class groups believe that they will work in service trades. Several studies show that career choices are related to the occupations of fathers, grandfathers, and mothers [2, 29, 53]. These studies generally demonstrate that children initially aspire to a career similar to that of the father and other family members and are likely to end up in one that resembles it. For example, if fathers are teachers, the offspring will often aspire to go into teaching and may end up there or in a similar career. The sons of individuals in higher-level occupations tend to end up in higher-level occupations themselves, and the offspring of those in lower-level occupations tend to take jobs similar to those of their parents. This, of course, is determined to some extent by the educational opportunities available, which are most often dependent on family income.

Also, those in higher social classes have different work values for themselves and their children than those in lower classes and pass them to the children [42]. Fathers from upper classes tend to place higher value on self-direction and less value on conformity, while the opposite is true for fathers from lower classes. One way that this is reflected is in the ways that young managers from higher socioeconomic status reacted to career mentoring at work. Those from higher socioeconomic backgrounds who had good career mentoring had higher promotion rates and pay than those from lower socioeconomic backgrounds. This suggests that they may have been able to capitalize at work on what they learned in early years from their family experience [83].

Personality. Super [73], Holland [36], and Osipow [53], argue that career choices are an extension of personality, an effort by a person to implement broad personal behavior styles in the context of work. Super believes that occupational choice is the result of a long developmental process, during which individuals are learning about themselves and developing a self-concept [73]. In the earlier years (before age 25), they are attempting to find out what kind of human being they are and what are their strengths and weaknesses. The self concept that is formed then becomes an important determinant of occupational choice.

Holland grouped occupations into a set of six **work environments** [36]. *Realistic* work environments contain jobs such as military officer, electrician, printer, and farming. *Investigative* work environments are characterized by jobs such as a mathematician, professor, chemist, or biologist. Social work and teaching are jobs in the *social* environment. Accountants, phone operators, and bank tellers are in the *conventional* work environment. The *enterprising* work environment is made up of careers in law, sales, and politics. Finally, musicians and artists are in an *artistic* environment.

Different behaviors, skills, and attitudes are effective for each environment. There are six **personality orientations**, with the same descriptive names of the environment with which they are associated (see Table 6.2):

1. *Realistic orientation.* These people tend to be aggressive and oriented toward activities that require physical coordination, skill, and strength. They prefer concrete rather than abstract problems and seek to avoid activities in which interpersonal and verbal skills are important.

2. *Investigative orientation.* These people tend to focus on thinking, analysis, and organization rather than doing, persuading, and dominating. They generally avoid close interpersonal contact, being somewhat withdrawn.

3. *Social orientation.* Those with a social orientation seek and excel at close interpersonal relationships. They avoid intellectual problem solving and situations in which extensive physical skills are required.

☐ **TABLE 6.2** Work Environments, Sample Occupations, and Personality Orientations

Work Environment	Sample Occupations	Characteristics of Personality Orientation
Realistic	Military officer Electrician Printer Farmer	Aggressive Prefers activities requiring coordination, skill Concrete—not abstract
Investigative	Mathematician Professor Chemist Biologist	Focus on thinking Prefers action Avoids close personal contact
Social	Social worker Arbitrator Home economist	Seeks close personal contact Avoids intellectual problem solving
Conventional	Accounting Phone operator Bank teller	Seeks well-defined situations Self-controlled Complies with rules
Enterprising	Lawyer Salesperson Politician	Seeks personal power and status Uses verbal and interpersonal skills to dominate others
Artistic	Musician Painter Sculptor	High self-expression Low self-control Dislikes structure Expressed feelings

Source. Adapted from Holland, J.L., *Making vocational choices: A theory of careers*. Englewood Cliffs, N.J.: Prentice-Hall, 1973 [36].

4. *Conventional orientation.* These people prefer well-defined, structured situations. They need to be self-controlled and often subordinate their personal needs. They comply with rules and identify strongly with others who have power and status.

5. *Enterprising orientation.* Enterprisers use their verbal and interpersonal skills to manipulate and dominate others. They seek power and status for themselves.

6. *Artistic orientation.* These people tend to be self-expressive through artistic means. They show little self-control, express feelings easily, and tend to dislike structure.

In an examination of Holland's model of career selection, Hill and Collins-Eaglin compared a group of 30 technical professionals to more than 100 managers [34]. The technical professionals were very high on the "investigative" and the "realistic" dimensions but were lower on the "social," "enterprising," and "conventional" dimensions than were the managers. There is also some evidence that managers who are in work environments congruent with their primary personality orientations are more satisfied with their work than those in an incongruent setting. Mount and Muchinsky [51] studied 548 managers and assessed person-environment congruence. Overall job satisfaction was significantly greater for those in a congruent state than for those who were not.

Cultural-Social Factors.   Culture obviously affects work values. For example, preferred work situations of Dutch university students differ in a significant way from American university students [35]. Pay, advancement, good working relationships, and job security were more important for American students than for Dutch students. The Dutch students placed more importance on participation, freedom of action, development opportunities, and contributing to the organization and to others. These differences, according to Hofstede, can be linked to historical roots in the countries' cultures [35]. The Netherlands have a long tradition of careful balancing of diverse political interests arrived at by reaching a consensus, while the American values may be affected by an orientation to the resolution of problems by "market" mechanisms.

PRELIMINARY WORK SOCIALIZATION

The second stage of the development of work attitudes and values shown in Figure 6.3 is **preliminary work socialization**. A person begins to develop more specific orientations toward a certain career or orientations relevant to a particular type of organization before beginning a career in a work organization. There are three aspects of preliminary work socialization: (1) the development of competence, (2) occupational socialization, and (3) the choice of a work organization.

Development of Competence.   During preliminary work socialization a person usually begins to develop specific career and **occupational competence** by acquiring knowledge and skills in one area rather than another. People do some things better than others and are encouraged in selected directions. The young person who thinks about a career in business may go to college and major in accounting, finance, or economics. Another who has had early success in mathematics may choose an engineering program or computer science.

Specialized training has important effects. First, the person learns certain things (say, accounting) and doesn't learn others (such as, engineering). This limits initial career opportunities to the chosen field. Second, the person discovers how someone in the chosen area attacks problems and thinks. He or she learns to act like someone who is an accountant before ever working as one. The person also forms relatively specific expectations about work and work organizations, usually long before spending a day on the job.

Occupational Socialization.   When specialized training is required, educational experience is a form of **occupational socialization**. For some, this begins in professional school, where the would-be professional is first exposed to the perspectives, values, and ways of thinking characteristic to the chosen field. Students in clinical psychology or architecture, for example, not only learn technical aspects of their field but also learn how to act like psychologists and architects.

Occupational socialization occurs under very controlled conditions in medical schools, seminaries, convents, and military academies. The person is separated from other parts of society and is submerged in the organization culture as well as learning the tasks of the profession. Professional values are fostered by participation in student groups, by taking courses, and through interaction with teachers. The person begins to act like a "professional" without thinking about it. Reinforcements from teachers are especially influential in shaping the new professional, since in many professions the teacher has much to do with the initial placement of students. The process of developing a *professional self-image* is a slow one, however, and the student probably does not have a professional self-image until treated as one by those who have achieved that recognition. After successful completion of this training, the person is admitted to the field and is commissioned, ordained, or passes through some other acceptance ritual. By this time, organizational and occupational values are deeply embedded.

Other preliminary work socialization is less formal, as in secondary schools, universities, and colleges and sometimes while a person holds a part-time job during his or her early years. Apprenticeships in the trades, for instance, have strong effects on later work values. These less formal and less controlled forms of occupational socialization do not have as strong effects, but they still shape later work experiences. For example, it has been shown that there was closer alignment of individual and organizational values for those entry level accountants who attended firm-sponsored recreational and social activities as students before joining the firm than for those students who did not participate in such activities [11].

The Choice of Work Organizations.   People pursue an "ideal job" [66]. What constitutes this concept of the ideal job is self-perception [43], personality [61], beliefs about being successful [4], and the information one has about the company [26]. Students, for example, formed their image of a firm from the general reputation of the company and the information presented in recruitment information [26]. The more information and the frequent exposure to it, the more positive the corporate image.

This positive image, or ideal work setting, is the basis for evaluating job opportunities. Soelberg [66] found that job alternatives were considered in parallel. The students would follow some leads, but not others. When a student had several job alternatives, they were not compared on similar criteria; each alternative was considered against different standards. A "favorite" job was usually selected early and was the one that was closest to the person's job goals. This choice was made *before* other job alternatives were ranked against each other. The ranking of other alternatives was done *after* the "favorite" job was chosen. The purpose of the ranking was to confirm the person's "favorite." Job search continued even after a person had a number of acceptable jobs.

This was a lengthy process during which the person resolved the uncertainties and problems with the "favorite" job and at the same time arrived at a way to justify the "favorite" choice as rational. Perceptual distortion occurred to make the "favorite" appear to be a much better choice than the other job possibilities.

The research we have just discussed and the conclusions drawn from it are based on the premise that someone has a choice of jobs and organizations in which to work. This is generally true for college graduates or those who have skills that are in demand and are from higher social classes. However, chance, luck, and economic factors may play an important role in taking jobs at all occupational levels, but they may be especially important at lower ones. A person with limited skills and few work alternatives may have to take a job where one is available, just to earn a living.

☐ BAD LUCK AND CAREER CHOICES

Patricia Barron, born in Oxford, England, broke her leg, and it changed her life. She was a dancer and a teacher of dance when it happened. Not being able to stay in dance, she went off to Harvard and got an MBA, with the idea that she would combine graduate training in business with her previous skill and have a career in arts management. Instead she took a job at McKinsey and was shipped off to a consulting engagement in Tanzania. Later she went to Xerox and opened their offices in China. This put her on the "fast track," and she began to move rapidly up the managerial ranks. On the way, she acquired experience in marketing, information systems, and international management. By the time she was 50 years old, she was named president of Xerox's Office Documents Products Division, the unit which is responsible for the fax and office copier business.

Adapted from Resa W. King, "Patricia Barron," *1993 Business Week 1000*, 1993 [41].

ORGANIZATION SOCIALIZATION

Throughout **organizational socialization**, a person learns to adapt to the specific work setting. It begins when someone enters the organization and continues throughout working life.

Every organization has a unique culture, and a person who wants to do well must come to terms with it (see Chapter 3). Organization cultures differ even though organizations may produce similar products and have similar structures. Generally the cultural differences have to do with organization expectations with respect to norms of performance and norms of involvement.

Norms of performance specify the type and level of work behavior expected from someone. **Norms of involvement** are those expectations that an organization has about the way its members show commitment and loyalty.

Some norms are more important than others. Schein calls the most important norms—those that must be accepted by organizational members—*pivotal norms* [63]. *Peripheral norms* are less important. They may be desired in a member, but it is not essential that the person accept them.

These norms and expectations are reflected in the psychological contract. The **psychological contract** refers to the mutual expectations between an organization and its members. Schein states the concept of the psychological contract this way: "The individual has a variety of expectations of the organization and the organization a variety of expectations of him. These expectations not only cover how much work is to be performed for how much pay but also involve the whole pattern of rights, privileges, and obligation between the worker and organization" [63].

The psychological contract between an organization and an individual is informally and continuously negotiated throughout the organization socialization process. New members learn preferred values and ways of doing things. The learning may be direct, as when a new employee is told about performance standards and rules, or it may be learned through "behavioral modeling," in which the employee imitates others in the organization. Future behavior will also be influenced by the person's dominant reference group. A new production employee may be far more concerned with approval from fellow workers than from a supervisor.

There are two phases of organizational socialization. The first is **organization entry**, the time after a person joins the organization and has his or her first experiences as a member. It is a transition period when one becomes aware of what differences exist between personal values and the requirements of the organization. The second phase, **organization accommodation**, occurs when the person comes to terms with the organization.

Organization Entry. Joining an organization can be a disrupting experience. A person faces changes, contrasts, and surprises and has to make some sense out of them and somehow adapt to them. These are different stages to organization entry, and they are related to how the individual is integrated into the organization [46].

Change is the first stage. Many things about a new job will be different from the old experiences. The most important difference may be the change in role requirements. For example, in the first job, a student must make the transition from the role of a learner to that of an employee. The degree of change can be critical. A personnel executive who transfers to another personnel position in the same company will experience less change than if he or she moves to a different firm or into new responsibilities.

Contrast is the second phase of organization entry. The newcomer begins to notice what is different from past experiences. Individuals become aware of the contrasts, and these form a basis for defining and responding to the new situation.

Surprise is the difference between the "individual's anticipations and subsequent experiences in a new setting" [46]. A new job may be surprising in a number of different ways, including:

1. Expectations of the job may have been too high.

2. Personal expectations are not met by the job.

3. Certain features of the job weren't anticipated.

4. Personal job feelings were incorrectly forecasted.

Sense making is attributing meaning to experience [46]. An individual will form a concept about what should be done in the organization and whether or not it can be done, then act on those decisions. A person may find that he or she can work effectively and continue the individual-organizational relationship. On the other hand, the person may become disenchanted and leave.

Organization entry is affected by a number of factors. One is the person-organization fit, the congruence between patterns of organizational values and individual values. For new accountants during their first year of work, Chatman found that those whose values matched those of the hiring firm were more satisfied and indicated stronger intentions to say [11].

A second factor involves the expectations a new person brings to the job. Before starting the job, one tends to have positive but often inaccurate expectations about the company, working conditions, co-workers and opportunities for advancement. These expectations arise very often from what one hears in the recruitment and selection process when interviewers try to create a positive image of the company. The effects of unmet expectations are costly. They are related to lower job satisfaction, lower organization commitment, higher intentions to leave, lower organization tenure, and lower performance [81].

The **organization socialization** process itself is a third factor which affects organization entry. Van Manen has suggested several different ways that organizations socialize members [79]. Some of the more important ways are:

1. *Formal/Informal Socialization.* In formalized processes, which usually occur upon initial entry, the setting in which the socialization occurs is separated from the work place and the activities of the newcomer are specifically defined. The informal process is of the "sink or swim" variety, in which the person must work through initial experiences without much guidance and direction.

2. *Individual/Group Socialization.* Individuals may begin their work experience alone or in groups. Group socialization is often used when large numbers of recruits are brought into an organization at one time, as is the case for firms which have management training programs to socialize large numbers of college graduates who come into the firm following spring graduation.

One study which examined the effects of some of these different organization socialization practices on members was conducted during the startup of a new plant in which some employees were exposed to formalized group socialization and others to informal individual socialization [84]. Those who entered in the formal group process experienced higher job satisfaction and lower conflict between job and family roles.

Organization Accommodation. The adjustment and change which takes place during organization entry that new members have:

1. Demonstrated at least a minimally acceptable level of competence.

2. Resolved conflicts between work and outside interests.

3. Established work relationships [21].

It does not necessarily mean that the adjustment is reflected by high job satisfaction, high organizational commitment, high work effort, and a peaceful accommodation between work and home interests. Rather, there are different patterns of psychological and behavioral accommodation. Psychological accommodation can be understood of organizational personality orientations such as the organizationalist, the professional, and the indifferent, as discussed in Chapter 4 [57]. Behavioral accommodation may be understood in terms of willingness to meet work requirements and organizational citizenship behavior, discussed later [52].

CAREERS AND WORK FORCE DIVERSITY

Much of what has been written on careers is based on studies of white males because, during the time that the research was done, they constituted the bulk of the work force and held virtually every important management position. Now that has changed. Today, the work force of U.S. companies is far more diverse. In fact, white males in the work force, for example, are now a minority of the work force, a far different situation than has existed for more than several hundred years of our industrial history. This has occurred as more women and racial and ethnic minorities have entered the work force, making it much more culturally diverse than just one decade ago. Some of the management issues of dealing with this diversity are discussed in this section.

WOMEN AND CAREERS

From 1900 to 1980, the percentage of women in the work force increased from less than 20 percent to over 50 percent [31, 62]. It is estimated that by the year 2000, 65 percent of the entrants in the work force will be women [55]. This growth is not confined to traditional female-dominated occupations such as nursing and teaching. Women are seen in increasing numbers in professional programs which had historically been segregated, such as law schools, medical schools, engineering programs, and business schools which prepare participants for higher-level occupations. An analysis of data from the 1970 and 1980 U.S. censuses concluded gender segregation declined and there were wage improvements for women both in occupations and in industry groupings [23]. Women are now 42 percent of those in managerial or administrative positions, 53 percent of the professionals (includes scientists, engineers, lawyers, nurses, teachers, etc.) and 48 percent of all technicians [55].

Performance at Work. It is clear that women have, as a group, not achieved the same level of pay or organizational attainment as men. It is equally clear that these differences cannot be justified on the basis of performance alone. There are no meaningful differences in ability between men and women [77].

Women can manage as well as men. When studies do show differences in men and women managers, they are usually executed in laboratory settings. When research is conducted in field settings, the gender of the leader (or manager) is neither related to the way the leader behaves nor to the performance and satisfaction of subordinates. The different findings indicate that in actual work settings, when women have the opportunity to actually perform a job, they perform equally as well as men [16]. In field studies, women's performance is likely to be judged on the results they achieve, whereas in laboratory studies, the traditional female stereotype is more likely to operate [59, 75].

Pay and Promotion.   If women can perform as well as men and if pay and promotion systems are merit based, pay and promotion should be identical. Yet compensation differs. In 1986, the median income of women was $16,843, or 65 percent of the income of males, which was $25,894 [6]. This earnings gap has been decreasing, though. It is a result of the increasing trend for women to enter higher paying occupations and advance in them. Fields and Wolff found that between 1970 and 1980 gender segregation decreased and women experienced wage improvements relative to men [23]. In a study of male and female managers, Jacobs [38] found that women were less likely to be in managerial positions and that the gender gap in earnings between male and female members narrowed between 1970 and 1988. Stroh, Brett, and Reilly examined the career and pay history of over 1,000 men and women managers who were transferred to other jobs in 1987 or 1988 by Fortune 500 companies [71]. They found that women in their study were experiencing similar promotion rates as men, but that they still lagged behind in salary progression.

There are several reasons which account for such a pay discrepancy. First, women are paid less than men for jobs of similar difficulty. One study compared the pay of men and women who performed similar work. Jobs were rated for relative comparability using the job description and analysis in the *Dictionary of Occupational Titles*. In the majority of work-similar situations studied, earnings discrimination unfavorable to women was found [40]. Gerhart suggests that one of the important factors contributing to this could be differences in starting salaries paid to men and women for similar jobs [27]. He studied, in one firm, salary histories of men and women and found gender-based pay discrepancies for both starting salaries in 1976 and current salaries in 1986. Over the 10 year working history of those studied, the salary gap, which was large in the beginning, diminished. He concluded that the major portion of the discrepancy that remained in 1986 could be attributed to the lower initial starting salaries for women ten years before. One important determinant of the difference in starting salary was the college major of the women and the men. If this is so, then since the number of women entering traditionally male fields is increasing, it should be expected that the starting pay gap should narrow.

Second, women are overrepresented in low-paying industries. Ward and Mueller [82] studied the effects of industrial sector and organizational level on wages of men and women [82]. Women are found in disproportionate numbers in service industries in which there are low profit margins, undeveloped internal labor markets, low job skill needs, and lower wage rates. Even in those industries in which women tend to be over represented, they are more likely than men to be in lower authority positions, and men are more likely to receive higher compensation than women. A clear example of this can be seen in nursing. This is a "traditionally female" occupation — over 90 percent of nursing jobs are held by women. Yet female salaries are 95 percent of male salaries. There are greater percentages of men in industries such as transportation, manufacturing, and electronics. These industries have high market concentrations, product diversification, high profit margins, sophisticated internal labor markets, high wage rates, and low employee turnover. Women in these industries received lower earnings than men. Similar discrepancies exist in the professions of engineering and law.

Third, in some organizations women may be in jobs doing less complex work and/or at lower organizational levels. These jobs have lower pay rates. In a study of work assignments in manufacturing plants. Form and McMillen found that women were more frequently assigned to simple repetitive tasks in which they used hand tools, whereas men were assigned to work on machines that required higher skill and on which they had more autonomy [24].

Fourth, a portion of the discrepancy can be attributed to different rates of pay and promotion at lower and higher organizational levels. Women do well at lower levels of the organization, where their promotion rates and salary progression equals or exceeds that of men [28, 49, 69, 76]. These salary progression rates change at higher levels. The women studied by Stroh and her colleagues advanced at similar rates as men, but they experienced less geographical mobility and had lower rates of pay progression [71].

One explanation of these changes in pay and promotion rates could be that many women leave the workplace to raise children during the critical establishment stage of a career. This stage, from the early 30s to the mid 40s, is one during which individuals in a career cohort begin to advance at different rates. Some begin to outpace others. Being out of the organization during this period could cause one to lose valuable experience, which extracts its price later in the form of lower salaries relative to others in the cohort.

Much of the research cited above has been done during a period of significant change in the roles and number of women in the work force. There has been progress, and it is likely to continue as the women who have entered the managerial and professional labor force at lower organizational levels advance their careers.

Occupational Status. Women are not generally accorded the same occupational or organizational status as men. Women in traditionally "male" occupations, such as engineering or law, are not seen as having a high status and prestige as men in the same occupations [56]. This could be because they haven't yet reached higher level positions. Jacobs found that women are less likely than men to be in higher level management positions [38]. When they enter the labor force in positions with the same status as men, working women's occupational prestige does not increase as much over the career cycle [48].

Status discrepancies between men and women may not affect women's level of performance, but it seems to be related to attitudes and perceptions.

Deaux found that men and women who worked in relatively similar management jobs experienced similar levels of job satisfaction [15]. However, the men tended to rate themselves as better performers than the women, attributing their high performance to skills and ability more than women did. Male managers also reported better relationships with their supervisors than did the female managers with their supervisors. When there are large occupational status discrepancies between men and women, women tend to have more liberal political attitudes than when the status discrepancies are small [1].

Work Expectations.   Historically, women have had different expectations about work and careers than men. Fottler and Bain found that women high school seniors had lower occupational aspirations than their male counterparts [25]. They also have different expectations than men about what they want from jobs (see Figure 6.5). More women than men beginning new jobs wanted more interesting work, but women expected fewer promotion opportunities and lower salaries. This poses a problem because job candidates with higher pay expectations are offered higher salaries than those with lower pay expectations [47]. Such a result is, in fact, shown in Gerhart's finding that the largest contributing factor to lower female salaries after 10 years of work in one firm was their lower starting salaries [27]. Women were also more likely to prefer personnel and other staff positions, which tend to be lower-paying jobs, than higher-paying positions such as finance and marketing.

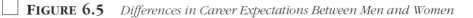 **FIGURE 6.5**   *Differences in Career Expectations Between Men and Women*

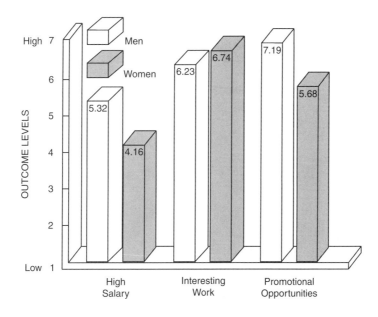

Marriage and Careers.   Marital status is related to several different aspects of a career. Having a wife is related to higher wages for men [33, 38, 54] and, while the evidence is less consistent, it seems that married women are penalized to some extent. Jacobs found that marriage had a positive effect on male salaries but a negative effect on female salaries [38]. For example, a National Bureau of Economic Research report indicates that married women in their 40s earn 15 percent less per hour than comparable single women.

When both spouses have careers (**dual-career** couples), it creates strain on both wives and husbands. Working married women reported higher levels of physical and mental well-being than housewives [7]; however, they may experience higher levels of work stress than single women. A study that compared married and unmarried flight attendants found that the married flight attendants experienced more role conflict, stress, and dissatisfaction than did the single ones [45]. Husbands experience stresses when they have a working wife. Men in dual-career marriages experienced more role conflict and role ambiguity than those in single-career marriages [39, 67].

Generally, dual-career couples suffer more job stress and poorer mental health than single-career couples [67, 72], which is exacerbated as interests of females shift from the home to work and interests of men shift from work to home. There is greater role conflict both at work and within the family for dual-career spouses with high job involvement and high work expectations [32]. They are also likely to experience greater strain between work and family demands. The effects of these role strains are lower quality of work life and lower quality of family life.

These effects stem from the many problems that working couples face. First, finding two desirable jobs in the same geographic region may be difficult. If the couple must work in separate, distant locations, this will create strain in the relationship. Second, the separate careers may advance at different rates. If a wife's career advancement is more rapid, this could lead to strains since it is inconsistent with the traditional model in which the male holds the primary occupation in a family. Ross and her colleagues [62] found that both working spouses were less depressed when the wife's employment status was congruent with the expectations of both the husband and the wife. Third, children add complications to the lives of dual-career couples. The responsibility of raising children must be added to the other tasks necessary to make a successful life. Bryson, Bryson, and Johnson found that the number of children in dual-career families was *not* related to the job performance of either spouse, but it did affect the allocation of responsibilities at home [5]. As the number of children increased, the burden for child care fell disproportionately on the wife. This seems to be related to female earnings, which were lower when their share of work at home was higher [8]. When the husband shares tasks at home, however, wives are less depressed. Incidentally, helping at home is *not* related to level of depression of the husband [5].

RACIAL AND ETHNIC DIVERSITY

The work force in the United States is far more multi-cultural than ever. For example, Digital Electronics Corporation has a plant that employs 350 workers who are from 44 different countries and speak 19 different languages [19]. US West, a telecommunications company in Denver, has a work force in which 13 percent of the managerial force are African Americans, Hispanics, Asians, or

American Indians. They select women for management jobs 50 percent of the time [10]. Their objective is to have a work force in each location which mirrors the racial, gender, and ethnic distribution of the regional work force.

The proportions of these racial and ethnic subgroups in the population and in the work force have changed in recent times. For example, Hispanic Americans increased their numbers in the United States by 30 percent in just seven years in the 1980s. There have been large increases in Asian Americans in society and in the work force as well [22].

In spite of these increasing numbers, the percentage of Hispanic Americans, Asian Americans, and African Americans in management is still very small. They experience a similar "glass ceiling" as women which restricts their advancement [17]. While some very slow progress has been made in promoting women through the glass ceiling, the progress for African Americans, Hispanics, and other minorities of color is almost non-existent [22].

There is very strong evidence of bias in hiring and advancing minorities. After examining the research on selection procedures and performance evaluation, Martocchio and Whitener concluded that minorities scored lower on cognitive ability tests and were rated lower by supervisors [50]. Hiring biases are also affected by other factors such as gender (Latino women minorities suffer less hiring discrimination than men), the source of recruitment (private employment agencies are more discriminatory), the type of job (there was more discrimination for jobs not requiring college degrees), and location of the job (there was greater bias when selecting for inner city jobs) [3]. However, the bias issue does not exist only in the dominant white male group. For example, a survey of males, females, African Americans, Asian Americans, Native Americans, and Hispanic Americans reveals that bias and stereotyping exists in all groups [22]. There were also differences among white men (49 percent), white women (17 percent), black respondents (88 percent), and Hispanic respondents (79 percent) about the desirability of using timetables and hiring and promotion goals as remedies for discrimination.

MANAGING CAREERS

The concept of career is undergoing a change which requires more active personal strategies to manage one's work life. Most of the theory and research on which this chapter is based was developed during a period in which the U.S. economy was expanding and employees, both workers and managers, might spend their whole career in a single firm. For example, in 1981 the average job tenure in U.S. firms was 12 years but by the end of 1992 was under 7 years [9]. Much of this change is due to global competitive pressures which forced firms to become more efficient. Much of this efficiency was sought by reducing the work force at all levels. The numbers of lost jobs are dramatic (a loss of almost 6 million jobs between 1987 and 1991) and the firms which have experienced large job cuts are among the largest, most important in the United States (for example, Black and Decker, General Motors, AT&T, Eastman, CBS, ABC, and Amoco). Cascio says ". . . our views of organizational life, managing as a career, hard work rewards, and loyalty will never be the same" [9]

Thus, a person is well-advised to be active in self-career management. Rather than waiting for fortune, good or bad, to strike, a person can try to develop the skills required for success and to create opportunities for it. Some of the more important things one can do are:

1. **Have a Career Goal.** A **career goal** is a logical part of one of the major life tasks, forming and modifying a dream. This suggests something very important about career goals. They are not meant to be static. One should set specific goals but change them as one learns more about oneself and the situation. For example, a student may enter college with the goal of becoming a journalist but find that a marketing career is much more attractive. Very few people end their work career in the occupational areas in which they began. A goal, however, provides some anchor and some basis for direction.

2. **Develop Competence.** A person must develop two types of competence: career and occupational competence. **Career competence** includes those skills that contribute to a person's career maturity. Being able to appraise one's strengths and weaknesses, having and using information about job and career opportunities, and planning how one can achieve goals are career competence skills [38].

   Job-related skills, activities, and attitudes constitute **occupational competence.** There are two different strategies to develop occupational competence early in a career. One strategy is to be narrow—to learn some job-specific skills in college, vocational school, or an apprenticeship program. For example, the student who studies engineering or bricklaying is ready to work in an organization immediately after training is completed. The second approach is a broad one—to learn a general set of skills that would be applicable in different jobs. A person can take courses in mathematics or liberal arts and become skilled enough to work in a bank or a manufacturing plant. A person who takes this broad approach may start a job in a firm at a lower salary than one who has followed a more narrow approach, but most studies show that on average, salary and advancement at work generally even out in the long run.

3. **Assess the Work Setting.** Two important things about the work setting are (1) the organization in which you work and (2) the specific job that you have. Knowledge about the organization is important for several reasons. First, rates of promotion may be much slower in firms in more traditional industries. Second, some career paths are more promising than others.

   What are the promotion rates? This will give you some idea of how quickly people get promoted. You will find higher promotion rates in growing firms than in more stable ones.

   What is the nature of careers in the organization? Some firms seem to keep their employees until retirement, whereas in other firms, people "burn out and bail out." One major U.S. firm is noted for hiring young managers and paying them very well, but using them up. An ex-manager from the firm said, "No one ever retires from there. You quit. You can't stand the strain."

☐ WHY MANAGERS FAIL

The *Wall Street Journal* carried a report of a study about why managers fail. The research, conducted at the Center for Creative Leadership, found some of the reasons why managers are passed over for promotion or may even be fired. Interestingly, these reasons did not have anything to do with performance deficiencies. The main reasons managers fail are:

1. *Inability to get along.* Managers who fail tend to be poor listeners and lack good interpersonal skills. They do not give or take criticism very well, and they often create a work environment from which subordinates want to escape.

2. *Failure to adapt.* Many failures, particularly for those who at one time were on a fast track, are due to the manager's unwillingness or inability to adapt to change. This is often a problem when the firm is undergoing a serious external threat or during restructuring resulting from mergers and acquisitions.

3. *The "me only" syndrome.* Some managers want to take all the credit for the success of a unit, even when it is owed to the work of others. This selfishness can quickly alienate people, particularly subordinates who did important work or colleagues with whom the manager is competing for advancement. These managers are "narcissists who eventually run aground."

4. *Fear of action.* Some managers are unwilling to act because they have high-failure avoidance needs. This restricts their ability and willingness to put themselves on the line.

5. *Inability to rebound.* Every manager has a setback now and then, sometimes severe. Those managers who cannot rebound tend to become defensive about failure and blame others for it. Successful managers have the capacity to handle failures in a constructive way.

It is interesting to note that the factors outlined in the *Wall Street Journal* report are all indicators of personal values. They are quite consistent with the Good Enough Theory of Promotion. Managers often fail because they don't have the right orientation for the organization.

Source: C. Hymowitz, "Five Main Reasons Why Managers Fail," *Wall Street Journal,* May 2, 1988 [37].

Where do managers go? It is particularly helpful to know the promotion ladders in an organization. This is the chain of jobs held by those who are rapidly promoted within the firm. It is also useful to know where people go when they quit or are hired away. This will tell you something about how others value the experiences offered by the firm.

Find out what your specific job entails. Some jobs are dead-end positions with little or no opportunity to move out of them. For instance, in one manufacturing plant, all plant superintendents and plant managers have been promoted from production management positions. No one has been promoted to plant manager from jobs in personnel, production control, accounting, or quality control. In this organization, these jobs are dead ends. If you want to be a plant manager, you must avoid them. If you take one of these dead-end jobs for experience, work your way out of it later, back into the promotion track.

Is the job challenging? Job challenge gives you a chance to stretch your skills. Succeeding in a challenging job will be noticed by those who make promotion decisions.

How successful were others who held this job? There is more to being successful than just having the right attitude and a lot of ability. Sometimes the job itself can be a critical factor. One way to assess the impact that a job may have on your career is to find out how successful previous incumbents were. A study done in the U.S. Navy showed that it is possible to predict the success of a person as well if you know how successful the previous jobholder was as you can if you know something about the person who is taking the job [70]. Any job requires a certain set of behaviors and interaction with others, which do not change drastically when another person takes the job. If the job was a losing proposition for the person you are replacing, it could be the same for you.

4. **Work at Excellence.** Good performers are less often passed over for promotion. Performing well requires ability and motivation, but also an understanding of the criteria used to judge performance. Find out what people get rewarded for doing. Listen to what others tell you about the performance and involvement norms, and observe the behavior of those who have advanced.

While performance excellence is vital for advancement, it is usually not enough. A person's attitudes, values, and beliefs enter into advancement decisions, so if yours are consistent with those of the individual or group making the promotion decision, you have a better chance of advancing than if they are not. We call this the **Good Enough Theory of Promotion.** According to Good Enough Theory, it is not necessary to be the *best* candidate of those under consideration for promotion. It is only necessary to be judged to have *adequate* competence (in other words, to be good enough) to do the job. When there are several candidates for a position and each of them meets the minimum criteria, then the person whose values and commitments are most similar to those of the decision makers will be advanced. The Good Enough Theory is illustrated in Figure 6.6. Performance is shown on one axis. It is divided simply into "not good enough to be promoted" and "good enough." The other axis is divided into "organizationally appropriate" and "not organizationally appropriate" attitudes and values. Those who fall into the "yes-yes" cell are much more likely to be promoted than any other candidates. For most promotion decisions there are usually a large enough number of people in that category so that a person who falls into the "yes-ability/no-attitude" cell is usually passed over.

☐ **FIGURE 6.6**   *The Good Enough Theory of Promotion: Performance and Attitudinal Requirements for Advancement*

5.   **Develop Career Mobility. Career mobility** takes on added importance in a period of corporate downsizing. There are two types of career mobility *within* the current organization and moving to *outside* organizations. You may seek to change jobs within the firm when you are dissatisfied with either the content of the present job or its particular advancement opportunities. Of course, your opportunity to change jobs within the firm depends on position openings in other units. If your advancement rate is too slow in your present firm, you may wish to leave if you have the occupational competence that is needed by a different employer. But the demand for your skill in the market is related to economic factors. In a recession, it is more difficult to change jobs than in periods of growth.

It is often risky to go to another firm. A new person may have unrealistically high expectations about the position and the firm that he or she will be joining. If these expectations aren't met and the job doesn't work out, there could be significant economic and psychological costs. For example, a company recruited a person who was believed to be the "best quality control man in the industry." During the recruiting period, the company executives and the candidate were excited about future prospects. But he failed to consider some important differences between the job he left and the one that he took in the euphoria of evaluating the new job. Six months later, he was fired. What were the costs? He had moved his family from another part of the country. He still had an unsold home in the city from which he moved, and he was between jobs and with no immediate prospects.

6. **Consider the Effects of Career Choices on Others.** The quality control manager's career choices affected his family life. Because work and family are so interrelated, one is going to affect the other, and career choices must be made with the other components of the life structure in mind. How a job will affect a spouse and children and how it will change family life aren't the only problems. Today there are a growing number of dual-career families, in which both wife and husband have careers. Some of these problems have been discussed earlier in this chapter.

7. **Monitor Your Career.** It is useful to assess periodically whether or not you are moving in a way that is compatible with your aspirations. You will want to decide whether you are advancing as you thought you would. If not, what steps should you take? Should you revise your aspirations? Should you change jobs? Should you leave the organization? You will also want to make a judgment about the relationship of your career progress to the other components of the life structure.

SUMMARY

A career includes all the jobs that a person will hold in a lifetime, plus the training and preparation necessary to qualify for such jobs. A career is an important part of an individual's life but is by no means the only critical life component. Individuals must make adjustments among their various life roles, such as spouse, parent, and occupation.

Individuals move through different career stages. In an initial exploration stage some preliminary career choices are made, in the novice stage the individual learns the basic behavioral and attitudinal requirements of the career, and finally in the establishment stage the nature of the career is set. This is followed by a late-career stage. Each stage has its own unique demands and pressures, and individuals must learn to cope with them.

Different factors have been identified as important contributors to occupational choice decisions. Child-rearing practices that affect the individual's personality and self-concept influence occupational choice. The occupation of parents and the cultural values transmitted to the child also play a part in such decisions.

Work socialization follows occupational choice. Individuals must learn about the characteristics and culture of their work organization and of their chosen occupational field. In learning about the more important, or "pivotal," norms of their organization or occupation, individuals may be directly taught by others, may learn through the process of observing others, or may learn through the process of conditioning by behaving in certain ways and having such behaviors responded to in different ways by others.

In adjusting to organizations, new employees face changes, contrasts, and surprises that are difficult to absorb and understand. Individuals, of course, have expectations about their new jobs or organizations that may or may not be satisfied, and organizations also have expectations about their new members. Dissatisfaction and maladjustment occur when such expectations are not met.

Career decisions are important to both individuals and organizations. Job, organizational, or occupational maladjustment can negatively affect an individual's performance, morale, and health as well as those of others associated with that person, such as family members. Poor career adjustment has important consequences for the organization as well, since it may negatively affect employee performance, degree of involvement, and commitment to the organization.

A factor that complicates adjustment to work and organization is the changing nature and role of women in the work force. They are an increasing part of it and are moving into different types of work than in the past, such as professional and managerial. However, pay and opportunity discrepancies between men and women that do not seem to be related to capability still exist. Another issue is the dual career. These problems must be resolved in the future. The current interest in career and organizational adjustment can provide important dividends in lessening the dysfunctions that may result from poor career and organization choices.

☐ KEY CONCEPTS

Career	Late career	Organization
Career adaptability	Life structure	accommodation
Career attitudes	Norms of	Organization entry
Career competence	involvement	Organizational
Career goal	Norms of	socialization
Career identity	performance	Personality orientations
Career mobility	Novice stage	Preliminary work
Career stages	Objective success	socialization
Dual career	Occupational	Psychological contract
Early socialization	competence	Psychological success
Establishment stage	Occupational	Sense making
Exploration stage	socialization	Work environments
Good Enough		
Theory of		
Promotion		

☐ STUDY QUESTIONS

1. In what ways can psychological success and objective success be related? Can you have one without the other?
2. How does "career identity" relate to other subidentities? Can you describe a case where these identities could be in conflict? What are the subidentities that characterize your life right now?
3. What are the "eras" of the life cycle? How are they related to career stages?
4. What is the significance of the "transition period" between career stages?
5. What is the "midcareer" crisis? Can you suggest how it can be related to career development?
6. What are the phases of organizational socialization?
7. How can the behavior of parents affect job and career choices? How would you say your parents affected your career choice?
8. What is occupational socialization? Differentiate it from organizational socialization. Analyze to what extent you have experienced occupational socialization at this stage in your life.
9. Give some examples where there is strong occupational socialization before one actually assumes an occupational role.
10. Select two personality orientations discussed in Chapter 4. What are the implications of these types for management and control? Can you relate these personality types to people you know?

CASE

☐ HANK BATTLE

Hank Battle was born in New Orleans in 1942. After graduating from a small liberal arts college he became an officer in the United States Marine Corps and was sent to Vietnam in 1964. He was wounded twice in combat. After the second wound, he was sent back to the United States where he recovered and was discharged in 1967. In 1968 he enrolled in a graduate school of business at Southern State University and completed his MBA in 1970. His first job after graduate school was as a cost accountant in a shipyard near Boston, Massachusetts. He worked there for one and a half years, then quit to take a position as a supervisor with a container company located in a small city near Boston. He didn't last long there, being fired after only three and 1/2 months. During his job search, he found some help from a private employment agency where he was tested, and it was suggested that he was well suited for work in sales. He was placed in a large, national drug firm as a pharmaceutical salesman. He liked the work, calling on physicians in a territory in Massachusetts,

☐ HANK . . .

and worked there for eighteen months. Then he heard about an opportunity to do the same type of work at F&M, a better known drug company in the New England area. He applied for the job, was hired in 1974, and has been with F&M ever since. He is a pharmaceutical representative, the same position he started in back in 1974.

Hank has been married for 25 years. He met his wife, Alexandra, when he was in graduate school. She was an accounting student who he hired as a tutor when he was having problems in the cost accounting course. Over the last three years, their three daughters have finished college and started their own careers in other parts of the state. Alexandra, who had not worked when their daughters were young, returned to school recently and completed a masters degree in accounting. She just began working with a small, local CPA firm as an auditor and is very pleased to be back in a field which she enjoyed as an undergraduate.

With his daughters grown and on their own and his wife going back to work, Hank's life has changed a lot. He has also become a little more restless at work, feeling the pressures of some of the general economic problems that have hit the area. This led him, at the suggestion of his family physician, to have a series of appointments with Dr. Nicole De Blasis, a counseling psychologist, to work out some of his uneasiness. What follows is a report of one of his counseling sessions in which they talked about his work history.

Dr. De Blasis: You have had a succession of jobs. Is this because you did not know what you wanted to do after leaving high school?

Battle: Yes, that's right. One of my greatest difficulties in life has been in deciding what I wanted to do as a career. This has caused me a great deal of anguish over the years and even today, I still am not sure of what type of career or job would be best for me.

Dr. De Blasis: Well, take your first job after graduate school. You worked in the shipyard as a cost accountant. Why did you leave that job?

Battle: For one thing it was boring. I just don't like to work with figures all of the time. I'm just not cut out for that. Besides, I didn't think that the job was getting me anywhere. I was quite ambitious at the time. I wanted to reach the higher levels of management and to earn a bit of money.

☐ HANK . . .

Dr. De Blasis: So you then went to work for National Container Corporation.

Battle: Yes, that was a real supervisory position where I could prove myself to the company.

Dr. De Blasis: You ran into some difficulties, however, on that job.

Battle: I didn't fit into that type of organization. I supervised workers operating machines that made boxes. These workers were from the poorest section of the city and were difficult to supervise, at least for me. They did not have very positive attitudes about the company or their jobs. My boss, the superintendent, was constantly after me to get tougher with them. He was always pushing me to speed them up. To give you an idea of what he was like, I had an older woman, around fifty and petite, working on boxes for refrigerators. They were very large and she was having difficulty handling them. I could see, though, that she was giving this job all the effort she had. I saw the superintendent standing behind her with a stopwatch, yelling at her to work faster. I just don't go for that. I also didn't like all the shoe licking that went on. One time the boss took all of us supervisors out to lunch. It was really disgusting to me to see how some of my fellow supervisors were trying to butter up the superintendent. I thought to myself, "If that's what you have to do around here to get promoted, they can forget about it." A little while later the superintendent called me into his office and said I wasn't working out in that job. He thought I just wasn't pushy enough.

Dr. De Blasis: How did you react to that?

Battle: I was quite upset. At that point I didn't know what I should do. I wasn't sure about what I was qualified for; so I went to a testing agency.

Dr. De Blasis: So, what did they say about you?

Battle: They said that I wasn't suited for work as a production supervisor. The tests indicated that I would do best in sales. They found me a job with a pharmaceutical company which would require calling on physicians in the area south of Boston and telling them about the company's products. I was interviewed and hired. After two months of training, I was put out on my own. I found that I liked the work. I worked in that company for about 1 1/2 years and then went to my present job at F&M.

Dr. De Blasis: Why did you leave that job?

☐ HANK . . .

Battle: I wanted to get a promotion and nothing much was happening at Hone-Swenson, so when I heard about some openings at F&M, I went over there. I told them I wanted to stay in New England. There was one territory open in Massachusetts and another in Vermont. I applied for Massachusetts as my first choice and Vermont my second. I got my second choice up here in Vermont, but I am happy. I really like it up here now.

Dr. De Blasis: Hank, you have been with this company now for a long time so you must like it. How does it compare with the previous drug company you worked for?

Battle: It's products are much better than those at Hone-Swenson, and, of course, I like that. I don't like to ask physicians to use drugs that are not the best available on the market. Selling the best is very important to me. Also the physicians react positively to me because they know my products are of the highest quality. They, of course, want to use the most effective drugs possible. They have to answer to their patients.

Dr. De Blasis: You haven't been promoted, yet you are still working in a territory. Are you satisfied with this or do you plan to look for something else?

Battle: Well, I like the freedom, autonomy, and the opportunity to meet the variety of people that I do. Especially when they are very intelligent, like physicians. I learn a lot from the physicians that I talk to. Sometimes we don't have much time in their offices to talk, but we are together for longer times at conventions and at the demonstrations that I organize. I also take physicians out to dinner at times. I like working with a reputable company. We have the finest research department in the industry, and I know they are always going to give me great products to use. This company doesn't just make "me too" products which are copies of somebody else's. They try to be unique.

There are some things I don't like about my job. Often the company works up a sales or promotion campaign for a drug. Some of these programs are offensive to the physicians; so I don't like to use them. They don't like a hard sell, anything dishonest, or a program that emphasizes the package rather than performance. Actually the company doesn't want a hard seller either. They say it should be product quality and not pressure that sells our products. Some of the products they ask me to show physicians are things they already know about. I don't want to show them redundant products. I want to show them exciting

197

☐ HANK . . .

pharmaceuticals. I also don't like being held responsible for goals that I have no influence over. They always set goals for me. These generally specify a certain amount of particular drugs to be sold in my territory over a three month period of time. All sorts of things influence the attainment of those goals besides my effort. I also don't like the paper work much. I have to get the doctors to sign for all my drug samples and I have to file reports on what I do with my drug samples as well as reports on what I did each week. But I realize this tracking is necessary.

Dr. De Blasis: You didn't mention the problems in traveling and the lonely nights you have to put up with. Isn't that a negative factor?

Battle: It is, especially in the winter. But I do work in a beautiful location. I love to look at the scenery while I am driving. Also, I know people all over the state now. I talk to the physicians, I talk to their receptionists, talk to people I know who own or work in various restaurants, motels, and service stations.

Dr. De Blasis: You must be quite the extrovert. You don't feel uncomfortable talking to others?

Battle: I start a conversation with anybody I meet right away. I figure that I can learn from everybody. People tell me all about themselves. We trade views on marriage, child rearing, politics, sports, world affairs, anything. It all depends on what the other person wants to talk about. So I wouldn't say that I'm really lonely at all in the places that I go to. Now that's not to say I do anything that I shouldn't either. I'm a family man, a one woman man.

Dr. De Blasis: Anything else you'd like to tell me about your reactions to your job?

Battle: No, I think we covered everything. I like my job fairly well right now and don't know of any other job that I would want at the present time. As I told you, I would like more money, but I guess I don't want to make any sacrifices in my lifestyle that would be necessary to get more money. Ever since my duty in Vietnam, I realize how important it is to have a good life. It's just that I didn't know what a good life was for a long time, and now I think I do.

☐ HANK . . .

QUESTIONS

1. What type of a person is Hank Battle? His personality, his needs, etc.?
2. Given this, how well does his present and past jobs fit him as a person? What other jobs might be appropriate for him?
3. What career stage is Hank Battle in? What are the issues with which you expect he will have to deal in the future?

REFERENCES

1. Auster, C. The relationship between sex and occupational statuses: A neglected status discrepancy. *Sociology and Sociology Research, 1983*, 67, 421-38.
2. Beck, S.H. The role of other family members in intergenerational mobility. *The Sociological Quarterly*, Spring 1983, 24, 173-285.
3. Bendick, M., Jackson, C.W., Reinoso, V.A., & Hodges, L.E. Discrimination against Latino job applicants: A controlled experiment. *Human Resource Management*, 1991, 30(4), 469-484.
4. Blau, P.M., Gustad, J.W., Jessor, R., Parnes, H., and Wilcox., R.S. Occupational choice: A conceptual framework. *Industrial Labor Relations Review*, 1956, 9, 531-43.
5. Bryson, R.J., Bryson, B., and Johnson, M.F. Family size, satisfaction and productivity in dual career couples. *Psychology of Women Quarterly*, 1978, 3, 67-77.
6. Bureau of the Census, 1988. Chapter 7
7. Burke, R.J., and Weir, T. Relationships of wives' employment status to husband, wife and pair satisfaction, and performance. *Journal of Marriage and the Family*, 1979-38, 267-78.
8. Cannings, K. Family commitments and career success: Earnings of male and female managers. *Industrial Relations*. Winter of 1991, 64(1), 141-146.
9. Cascio, W. Downsizing: What do we know? What have we learned? *Academy of Management Executive*, 1993, 7(1). 95-104.
10. Caudron, S. US West finds strength in diversity. *Personnel Journal*, March 1992, 40-44.
11. Chatman, J. Matching people and organizations: Selection and socialization in public accounting firms. *Administrative Science Quarterly*, 1991, 36, 469-484.
12. Cohen, A. Career stage as a moderator of the relationships between organizational commitment and its outcomes: A meta-analysis. *Journal of Occupational Psychology*, 1991, 64, 253-268.
13. Cox, C.J. & Cooper, C.L. The making of the British CEO: Childhood, work experience, personality, and management style. *The Academy of Management Executive*, 1989, 3(3), 241-245.
14. Dalton, G.W., Thompson, P.H., and Price, R. Career stages: A model of professional careers in organizations. *Organization Dynamics*, 1977, 5, 19-42.

15. Deaux, K. Self-evaluations of male and female managers. *Sex Roles*, 1979, (5) 581-80.

16. Dobbins, G.H. & Platz, S.J. Sex differences in leadership: How real are they? *Academy of Management Review*, 1986, 11(1), 118-127.

17. Domingues, C.M. Executive forum: The glass ceiling. Paradox and promises. *Human Resource Management*, 1992, 31(4), 385-392.

18. Dreher, G., F. and Ash, R.A. A comparative study of mentoring among men and women in managerial, professional, and technical positions. *Journal of Applied Psychology*, October 1990, (75):5, 539-546.

19. Dreyfus, J. Get ready for the new work force; if demographics are destiny, companies that aggressively hire, train, and promote women and minorities—the growing segments of the U.S. labor market—will succeed. *Fortune*, April 23, 1990, 21(9), 165-170.

20. Feldman, D.C. *Managing careers in organizations*. Glenview, IL: Scott, Foresman, 1988.

21. Feldman, D.C., and Arnold, H.J. *Managing individual and group behavior in organizations*. New York: McGraw-Hill, 1983.

22. Fernandez, J.P. *Managing a diverse work force*. Lexington, Mass.: Lexington Books, 1991.

23. Fields, J. and Wolff, E.N. The decline of sex segregation and the wage gap: 1970-1980. *Journal of Human Resources*, Fall 1991, 26(4), 608-622.

24. Form, W., and McMillen, D. Women, men and machines. *Work and Occupations*, 1983, 10, 147-77.

25. Fottler, M.D., and Bain, T. Sex differences in occupational aspirations. *Academy of Management Journal*, 1980, 23:(1), 144-49.

26. Gatewood, R.D., Gowan, M.A. & Lautenschlager, G.J. Corporate image, recruitment image, and initial job choice decisions. *The Academy of Management Journal*, 1993, 36(2), 319-348.

27. Gerhart, B.A. Gender differences in current and starting salaries: The role of performance, college major and job title. *Industrial and Labor Relations Review*, April 1990, 43:(4), 418-433.

28. Gerhart, B.A., and Milkovich, G.T. Salaries, salary growth, and promotions of men and women in large, private firm. Working paper, Center for Advanced Human Resource Studies, New York School of Industrial and Labor Relations. Ithaca, NY: Cornell University, 1987.

29. Goodale, J., and Hall, D.T. Inheriting a career: The influence of sex, values and parents. *Journal of Vocational Behavior*, 1976, 8, 19-30.

30. Hall, D.T. *Careers in organizations*. Pacific Palisades, CA: Goodyear Publishing Company, 1976.

31. Hall, R.H. *Dimensions of work*. Beverly Hills, CA: Sage Publications, 1986.

32. Higgins, C., Duxbury, L., and Irving R., Work-family conflict in the dual career family. *Organizational Behavior and Human Decision Processes*, 1992, 51(1), 51-75.

33. Hill, M.S. The wage effects of marital status and children. *Journal of Human Resources*, 1979, 14, 579-93

34. Hill, R.E., and Collins-Eaglin, J. Technical professionals, technical managers and the integration of vocational consciousness. *Human Resource Management*, Summer 1985, 24:(2), 177-89.

35. Hofstede, G. Cultural constraints in management theories. *Academy of Management Executive*, 1993, 7:(1), 81-94.

36. Holland, J.L. *Making vocational choices: A theory of careers.* Englewood Cliffs, NJ: Prentice-Hall, 1973.

37. Hymowitz, C. Five main reasons why managers fail. *Wall Street Journal*, May 2, 1988.

38. Jacobs, J. Women's entry into management: Trends in earnings, authority, and values among salaried managers. *Administrative Science Quarterly*, 1992, 37, 282-301.

39. Keith, P., and Schafer, R. Employment characteristics of both spouses and depression in two-job families. *Journal of Marriage and the Family*, 1983, 45: (4), 877-84.

40. Kemp. A., and Beck, E.M. Equal work, unequal pay. *Work and Occupations*, 1986, 13, 324-46.

41. King, R.W. Patricia Barron. *1993 Business Week 1000*, 1993.

42. Kohn, M.L., and Schooler, C. Class, occupation, and orientation. *American Sociological Review*, 1969, 34, 659-78.

43. Korman, A. Toward a hypothesis of work behavior. *Journal of Applied Psychology*, 1970, 54, 31-41.

44. Levinson, D., Barrow, C.H., Klein, E.B., Levinson, M.H., and McGee, B. *Seasons of a man's life*, New York: Ballantine Books, 1978.

45. Levy, D. Work and family interaction: The dual-career family of the flight attendant. *Humboldt Journal of Social Relations*, 1984, 11(2), 67-86.

46. Louis, M.R. Surprise and sense making: What newcomers experience in entering unfamiliar organization settings. *Administrative Science Quarterly*, 1980, 25, 226-51.

47. Major, B., and Konar, E. An investigation of sex differences in pay expectations and their possible causes. *Academy of Management Journal*, 1984, 27, 777-92.

48. Marini, M.M. Sex differences in the process of occupational attainment: A closer look. *Social Science Research*, 1980, 9, 307-61.

49. Markham, W., South, S., Bonjean, C., and Corder, J. Gender and opportunity in the federal bureaucracy. *American Journal of Sociology*, 1985, 91, 129-51

50. Martocchio, J.J. & Whitener, E.M. Fairness in personnel selection: A meta-analysis and policy implications. *Human Relations*, 1992, 45(5), 489-497.

51. Mount, M.K., and Muchinsky, P.M. Person-environment congruence and employee job satisfaction: A test of Holland's theory. *Journal of Vocational Behavior*, 1978, 13, 84-100.

52. Organ, D.W. *Organizational citizenship behavior: The good soldier syndrome.* Lexington, MA: Lexington Books, 1988.

53. Osipow, S.H. *Theories of career development.* 2nd ed. New York Appleton-Century-Crofts, 1973.

54. Pfeffer, J., and Ross, J. The effects of marriage and a working wife on occupational wage attainment. *Administrative Science Quarterly*, 1982, 27, 66-80.

55. Powell, G. *Women & men in management*, 2nd ed. Newbury Park, CA: Sage, 1983.

56. Powell, G., and Jacobs, J.A. The prestige gap: Differential evaluations of male and female workers. *Work and Occupations*, August 1984, 11, 283-308.

57. Presthus, R. *The organization society.* New York: St. Martin's Press, 1978.

58. Pulakos, E.D., and Schmitt, N. A longitudinal study of a valence model for the prediction of job satisfaction of new employees. *Journal of Applied Psychology,* 1983, 68, 307-12.

59. Renwick, P.A. & Tosi, H.L. The effects of sex, marital status, and educational background on selection decisions, *Academy of Management Journal,* 1978, 21, 91-103.

60. Roe, A. Early determinants of occupational choice. *Journal of Counseling Psychology,* 1957, 4, 212-17.

61. Roe, A., and Seigelman, M. *The origin of interests.* The SPGS Inquiry Series, No. 1, Washington, D.C. American Personnel and Guidance Association, 1964.

62. Ross, C., Mirowsky, J., and Huber, J. Dividing work, sharing work, and in between: Marriage patterns and depression. *American Sociological Review,* 1983, 48:(6), 809-23.

63. Schein, E.A. *Organizational psychology.* New York: Prentice-Hall, 1970.

64. Schein, E.A. *Career dynamics.* Reading, MA: Addison-Wesley, 1978.

65. Simon, H.A. Solving problems and expertise. Symposium. University of Florida, 1982.

66. Soelberg P. *Unprogrammed decision making.* Proceedings of the Academy of Management, 1966, 3-16.

67. Srivastava, K., and Srivastava, A. Job stress, marital adjustment, social relations and mental health of dual-career and traditional couples: A comparative study. *Perspectives in Psychological Researches,* 1985, 8(1), 28-33.

68. Staw, B.M., Bell, N.E., and Clausen, J.A. The dispositional approach to job attitudes: A lifetime longitudinal test. *Administrative Science Quarterly,* March 1986, 31(1), 56-77.

69. Stewart, L.P., and Gudykunst, W.B. Differential factors influencing the hierarchical level and number of promotions of males and females within an organization. *Academy of Management Journal,* 1982, 25(3), 586-97.

70. Stogdill, R., Shartle, C., Scott, E.L. Coons, A., and Jaynes, W.E. *A predictive study of administrative work patterns.* Columbus, OH: Bureau of Business Research, Ohio State University, 1956.

71. Stroh, L.K., Brett, J.M. and Reilly, A.H. All the right stuff: A comparison of female and male managers' career progression. *Journal of Applied Psychology,* 1992, 77(3), 251-260.

72. Sund, K., and Ostwald, S. Dual earner families' stress levels and personal lifestyle related variables. *Nursing Research,* 1985, 34(6), 357-61.

73. Super, D.E. *The psychology of careers.* New York: Harper & Row, 1957.

74. Tinto, V. Patterns of educational sponsorship to work. *Work and Occupation,* August 1984, 11(3), 309-30.

75. Tosi, H.L., and Einbender, S.E. The effects of the type and amount of information in sex discrimination research: A meta-analysis. *Academy of Management Journal,* 1985, 28, 712-23.

76. Tsui, A.S., and Gutek, B.A. A role set analysis of gender differences in performance, affective relationships and the career success of industrial middle managers. *Academy of Management Journal,* 1984, 27(3), 613-35.

77. Tyler, L. *The psychology of individual differences,* rev. ed. New York: Appleton-Century-Crofts, 1965.

78. Uchitelle, Louis. Stanching the loss of good jobs. *The New York Times*, January 1993, Sec. 3, 1.

79. Van Maanen, J. People processing: Strategies of organizational socialization. *Organizational Dynamics*, Summer 1978, 64-82.

80. Wanous, J. Organizational entry: Newcomers moving from outside to inside. *Psychological Bulletin*, 1977, (84), 601-18.

81. Wanous, J.P., Poland, T.D., Premack, S.L. and Davis, K. Shannon. The effects of met expectations on newcomer attitudes and behaviors: A review and meta-analysis. *Journal of Applied Psychology*, June 1992, 7(3), 822-296.

82. Ward, K.B., and Mueller, C.M. Sex differences in earnings: The influence of industrial sector, authority hierarchy, and human capital variables. *Work and Occupations*, November 1985, 12(4), 437-63.

83. Whitely, W., Daughterty, T.W. and Dreher, G.F. Relationship of career mentoring and socioeconomic origin to managers' and professionals' early career progress. *Academy of Management Journal*, 1991, 34(2), 331-350.

84. Zahrly, J. and Tosi, H. The differential effect of organizational induction process on early work role adjustment. *Journal of Organizational Behavior*, 1989, 10, 59-74.

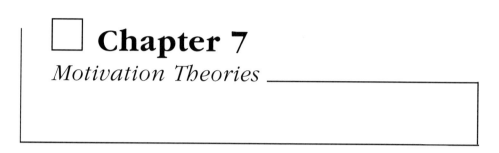

Chapter 7
Motivation Theories _____

John Spooner was a Canadian engineer working in South East Asia as the general manager of an engineering company in Brunei (North Brunei). One of the greatest problems he encountered was determining what employees really meant in relationship to what they said. The situation was complicated by the mixture of diverse nationalities, e.g. Bruneian, Malaysian, Chinese, and Indian; religions, e.g. Muslim, Buddhist, Hindu and Christian; and languages, e.g. Malay, various Chinese and Indian dialects, and English.

The company was small enough (120 employees) that, after a while, he was able to recognize and track the activities of individuals, as well as follow technological and financial progress.

After having established himself and getting to know the competence of his staff, one of the more perplexing and previously unseen problems surfaced. Langi, one of the better employees, came to him and said, "I want to quit. I have some personal problems at home."

After experiencing a few "Langis" he came to realize only after much questioning and the particular coercion of the local personnel manager, that what Langi really meant was that he wanted a salary increase.

It is unlikely that this would have been discovered if he had not become familiar with the employees' records and been alarmed that so many of the "good" employees were leaving. The company was dynamic and awarded remuneration adjustments and benefits according to overall progress. However, Langi, like his predecessors, felt the company's good fortune was more directly related to his individual efforts and thus should be rewarded accordingly. Asian "politeness" precluded direct requests for what is believed to be a genuinely deserved increase [22].

If you were to ask a group of managers to describe their biggest concern, they would probably answer just as John Spooner would, "To keep a highly productive and motivated work force." For most managers, the terms *productivity* and *motivation* go together.

Motivation is a seductive subject for managers and they believe in it for many reasons, some right and some wrong:

1. *Work motivation is an important value in Western society.* In Western society in general, and particularly in the United States, there has been a historical stress on the "work ethic." The work ethic is the belief that work is good and that it should be valued. This belief is so strongly ingrained in some that if they do not have an opportunity to work, they have psychological and social problems. Health statistics from areas experiencing long and extensive layoffs show increases in anxiety, depression, and often suicide.

2. *Many managers believe the improved performance resulting from motivation is free.* Imagine that you hire a worker for $10 per hour who produces five units per hour. The unit labor cost is $2. If the worker has the potential to produce 10 units each hour and does so without buying new equipment, the unit labor costs drops to $1. To get such a gain with improved equipment would cost money.

   Still, it is wrong to think that it is possible that improvements can be made through "motivation" without cost. A highly motivated work force only comes with good selection, sound compensation practices, training, and the use of good human resource management practices.

3. *Motivation explains why some organizations are more productive than others.* Suppose you take a tour of two breweries and there are no identification signs to inform you whether you are in a Schlitz brewery or one owned by Anheuser-Busch. The equipment looks very similar. The two buildings look alike. If there are any differences in productivity and the equipment is the same, it is only logical to conclude that these differences arise because of the people involved.

This is exactly the conclusion that many reached about the decline in market share of the U.S. automobile industry and the increased share of the Japanese manufacturers over the last 20 years. Many believed that the Japanese workers were more motivated and that the problem in U.S. firms was a result of strident unions and unwilling workers. It took several years for the U.S. firms to believe, first, that there was a market for smaller cars and, second, to change their approach not only to the manufacturing process but also their approach to managing the work force. The recent successes of GM's Saturn and Ford's Taurus suggest that the industry may have learned how to deal with at least some of their problems.

MOTIVATION: TWO DEFINITIONS

The term **motivation** has at least two connotations in the field of organizational behavior. First, it is viewed as a *management* strategy. Used this way, motivation is seen as management activity, something that managers do to induce others to act in a way to produce results desired by the organization or, perhaps, by the manager. In this context, we might say, "The role of every manager is to motivate employees to work harder or do better."

Second, as a *psychological concept*, motivation refers to the internal mental state of a person, which relates to the initiation, direction, persistence, intensity, and termination of behavior [25]. In this chapter, we discuss motivation as a psychological concept and some of the important motivation theories in organizational behavior. In the next chapter, we focus on motivation as a management strategy.

CLASSES OF MOTIVATION THEORIES

Any motivation theory attempts to account for the *reasons* people behave as they do and the *processes* that cause the behavior. Those which focus on "what" motivates behavior are called **content theories**. Those which focus on "how" behavior is motivated are called **process theories**.

We use this distinction between content and process theories of motivation because it highlights the main orientation of a particular formulation about motivation. However, content theories have some process orientation and process theories usually have some content dimensions. For example, content theories usually focus on a human need of some type. The strength of that need and the specific way that a person wishes to satisfy it are usually learned through socialization, a process that can be understood in reinforcement theory terms. As you study the theories in this chapter, you will see that these two orientations, content and process, are present in each of them.

THE MOTIVATION/RESULTS MODEL

Consider the following situation. Lance Roberts has a burning desire to be a good tennis player. He spends hours practicing, reads all the instructional magazines, regularly takes lessons, and plays a match every day. Blaine Davis is one of Roberts's regular weekly matches. Every Wednesday afternoon they play tennis and Davis usually wins. It is especially frustrating to Roberts because Davis hardly practices and plays only twice, at the most three times, each week.

This example shows that performance (or results) is a function of *both* motivation and ability. This is the basis of a very fundamental relationship for understanding human performance in organizations.

$$\text{Performance} = f(\text{Ability } 5 \text{ Motivation})$$

Figure 7.1 shows how these three factors are related. On one axis is performance; on the other, motivation. The lines in the figure represent the abilities of both men. They show that Roberts has less tennis ability than Davis. Therefore, if both are equally motivated (say at point X), then Davis will always win. Lance will only win when he has high motivation (at point Y) and Blaine is not highly motivated to perform (near point Z).

Our approach in this book to managing performance is built on the **motivation/results model** (M/R model) shown in Figure 7.2. In the motivation/results model, performance, ability, and motivation are treated in a more complex form. There are three basic components in the M/R model. The *outputs*, or results, consist of work performance and individual satisfaction. The *inputs* that produce the results are human factors and organizational factors. The moderating element between the inputs and the outputs is *managerial motivation strategy*.

☐ **FIGURE 7.1**   *Relationship Between Performance, Motivation, and Ability*

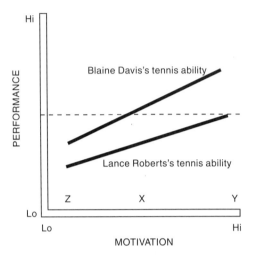

☐ **FIGURE 7.2**   *The Motivation-Results Model*

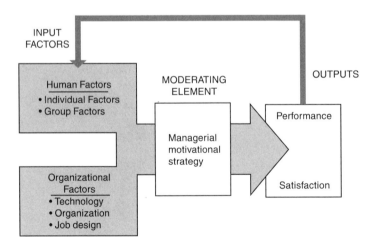

OUTPUTS IN THE M/R MODEL: PERFORMANCE AND SATISFACTION

The motivation/results model deals with two outcomes from work effort. One is performance, and the other is some level of individual satisfaction. **Performance** is the result of the application of mental or physical effort. Performance levels can be stated in different ways, in terms of quantity or quality, and may reflect some subjective judgment by a manager. A particular level of performance may be judged as "high" for one person, but the same level may be only "satisfactory," or perhaps "unsatisfactory," for another.

Satisfaction is another important result of performance. It is a function of the extent to which the task provides a person's desired levels of both intrinsic and extrinsic outcomes.

PERFORMANCE—A MULTIDIMENSIONAL VIEW

Any job has several parts. The different parts of a job are called performance components. A **performance component** is a relative discrete subtask for which the requisite ability is different from other abilities. Suppose, for example, that a plant superintendent must manage production and quality levels, prepare work schedules, order supplies, deal with subordinates, and run departmental meetings. This job has six components, each of which requires a different ability (see Table 7.1). Knowledge of the work force is required to prepare good schedules while problem-solving skills are necessary for running departmental meetings.

TABLE 7.1   Performance Components of a Superintendent's Job

Plant Manager's Priorities	Performance Component =	Required Ability	X	Motivation to Perform the Component
	(Performance =	f[ability	X	Motivation])
High	Manage production levels	Knowledge/ capacity to use technical processes		High
High	Manage quality levels	Competence in statistical quality control		Moderate
Low	Prepare work schedules	Knowledge of the work force		Low
High	Deal with workers	Interpersonal skills		Moderate
High	Run meetings	Problem-solving and definition skills		Low
Low	Order materials	Product/technical specifications: usage rates and demand		High

☐ PERFORMANCE COMPONENTS: WHAT IS A PROFESSOR'S JOB?

Take a minute or two to think about the professor for this class. Is he or she "good"? The answer depends on many things. What do you, a student, evaluate? More than likely you are going to rate a professor by performance in the classroom. Perhaps you will consider something about whether or not he or she keeps conventional office hours and has treated you with some courtesy during class and office visits. If you think the professor is good, it's normal for you to believe that he or she should be rewarded accordingly. If you think the professor is a poor teacher, you probably believe that he or she is overpaid.

But there is more to the professor's job than what you see. Professors in most colleges and universities are expected to do more than teach and advise students. There are many other performance components. At some universities, a professor's job would include at least the following performance components:

1. Teaching undergraduate students
2. Teaching graduate students
3. Advising and counseling
4. Directing theses and dissertations
5. Serving on committees in the university
6. Conducting research
7. Professional publication
8. External professional service
9. External community service

When a student rates a professor, it is usually on teaching and advising. When a professional colleague rates the same professor, it is usually on research and publication. The dean or chair of the department may use yet different combinations.

This is why it very often happens that you feel a professor is not fairly paid. Suppose you learn that your professor in this course makes $3000 less than the average for professors in the college. You may be surprised, especially if he or she is a brilliant teacher. How can you explain it? Easily, especially if the dean places a higher value on research and publication than on teaching for pay and promotion. You may not think it's right (after all, you consume the teaching), but the dean may be following a strategy of trying to improve the professional standing of the school.

What you will find if you go to other schools is that these same performance components might make up the job of professor, but the factors may take on different weights between schools.

Now put yourself in the shoes of your professor. If you are a great teacher and do not like to do research, in what kind of school would you like to teach? Or suppose you preferred research over teaching?

There are several important things to learn when viewing performance in this way. First, specific and different abilities are required for the various parts of a job. A person may be more talented in one performance component and less in another. A quarterback for a football team may be an excellent passer but a very poor runner. Second, a person may be more motivated (willing to put forth more effort) for one performance component than others; for example, the superintendent might rather manage production and quality. Third, for some performance components, significant levels of technology may be required to achieve results. For example, required production levels cannot be achieved unless the appropriate equipment is operating effectively. Technology is not critical, however, in running a meeting; for this, human skill is most crucial. Thus, a different technology-skill mix may be required for the different performance components. Some may be technology dominated, as would be the case for ordering supplies if the inventory is maintained in computer files. Other performance components, such as problem solving, are human skill-dominated.

SATISFACTION

Feelings of satisfaction or dissatisfaction may also develop as a result of task-oriented work and performance. A person may feel good after performing a task, especially if he or she is highly involved with it. Feelings of self-esteem may be enhanced when a person is doing something he or she believes worthwhile. Work activity may also lead to rewards such as pay, promotion, and higher status. Factors other than an employee's performance such as vacation policies and trust in management also affect satisfaction.

When work is rewarding, job satisfaction will increase. When it is not, dissatisfaction may increase. Satisfaction follows performance when the performance leads to outcomes valued by the person. Therefore, in Figure 7.2 we show that satisfaction resulting from work has an influence on the human factor, especially individual needs. For example, a worker high in achievement needs who is successful is likely not only to be satisfied but also to develop higher achievement orientation. The reverse may also be true. When performance is low, a person experiences a need deficiency that may not be possible to satisfy, perhaps requiring more effective managerial motivation efforts to restore performance.

INPUTS IN THE MOTIVATION/RESULTS MODEL

In this section we discuss two inputs to the M/R model, *human factors* and *organizational factors*. The people, the technology, and the organizational context within work all affect performance. Individuals bring personalities and abilities to an organization and fellow workers affect them. The technology and the organization structure will also affect what people are capable of producing and the satisfaction they got from it.

☐ RESPONSES TO JOB DISSATISFACTION: EXIT, VOICE, LOYALTY, AND NEGLECT

Job dissatisfaction is a common outcome of mismanagement of rewards and other elements of the motivation process. An interesting study applied Albert Hinchman's *Exit, Voice, and Loyalty: Responses to Decline in Firms, Organizations, and States* to work organizations [12]. He found that employee turnover, transfers, complaints, suggestions, toughing-it-out, absenteeism, and lateness actually form a set of options as responses to job dissatisfaction. These responses have been characterized as: exit, voice, loyalty, and neglect.

A later study showed that employees respond differently depending on several characteristics. Dissatisfied employees with more stake in the company (such as length of service or specialized training) respond to dissatisfaction constructively [13]. They do so by making suggestions or speaking up about dissatisfaction (voice) or by being steadfast and waiting for favorable change (loyalty). But employees with lesser stakes leave (exit) or become neglectful. Dissatisfied employees who have good job alternatives select active solutions—either exit or voice.

For the practicing manager dissatisfied employees present a real challenge. Good-performing, successful employees, the ones needed to accomplish goals, will be among those making forceful suggestions and complaints, and if the costs are not large, they will be among the employees most likely to leave.

Sources: D. Farrell, Exit, voice, loyalty, and neglect as responses to job dissatisfaction: a multidimensional scaling study, *Academy of Management Journal*, 1983, 26, 596-607 [12].

D. Farrell and C.E. Rusbult, Understanding the retention function: A model of the causes of exit, voice, loyalty, and neglect, *Personnel Administrator*, April 1985, vol. 30, no. 4, pp. 129-34 [13].

HUMAN FACTORS

The M/R model includes two human factors: (1) individual characteristics and (2) group forces. Individual characteristics such as needs interact with other factors in the workplace. Individual need patterns vary, and so does the way people satisfy similar needs. This is the basic idea underlying the importance of people's organization orientations (discussed in Chapter 4 and 6). The organizationalist may satisfy achievement needs by becoming successful within the firm. The professional may seek recognition and achievement within a group of colleagues who are also specialists. The indifferent may find achievement needs satisfied in social organizations outside the work setting.

An important individual factor is ability. **Ability** is the capacity to carry out a set of interrelated behavioral or mental sequences to produce a result. For example, to play the piano requires that one be able to read music, understand chord structures, and have the manual dexterity to finger the keyboard.

Generally it is easy to see ability differences between two individuals; it is often apparent among individuals who perform similar jobs. It is also important to remember that individuals have different abilities. A person may be a highly skilled architect but have very low communication skills. Since most job performance is multidimensional, it follows that the person who is assigned to do the job must have adequate ability for each different performance component. For example, the production superintendent's job involves scheduling work, dealing with subordinates (handling grievances, supervision, etc.), and running departmental meetings. Each of these separate activities requires different skills and a person can be good in some and poor in others.

Group forces also affect performance and satisfaction. Groups develop production norms and they exert pressure to ensure that members conform to these norms. Groups may inhibit or facilitate a person's performance. In addition, groups can affect perceptions and attitudes as well as behavior. Individuals, however, differ in their susceptibility to group pressures. Individual compliance is greatest when values and attitudes are congruent with the group's and when the individual places a high value on group acceptance [18].

ORGANIZATIONAL FACTORS

Technology and organization design are important elements of the motivation/results model. **Technology** refers to the methods, tools, facilities, and equipment a person uses in performing a task. Auto workers "use" a complex production system with highly independent activities to manufacture a car. An artist's technology may be a drawing board, paint, and a brush. The technological structure can vary tremendously from one organization to another—as, say, between a steel mill and an advertising agency. It also varies across jobs such as when one group of employees must use computers while another group simply uses pencils and paper in their work.

Technology interacts with ability to affect performance, but in different ways. In general, most work performance components involve the use of some technology. For some performance components, technology is very important. For example, the production line is critical for the performance component "managing production levels" of the superintendent. For other performance components, the impact of technology is very weak and human skill is important, as for the performance component "dealing with subordinates."

Because of these different types of interaction between skill and technology, we differentiate skill-dominated and technology-dominated work. In **skill-dominated work** individual skill is the most important factor. A clothing designer's job is an example of skill-dominated work. Giving a designer better equipment is likely to have only a marginal effect on performance. Giving Davis and Lance, the tennis players discussed earlier, better equipment will probably not improve their game, because this is a skill-dominated task.

Contrast this with assembly-line work, an example of technology-dominated work. Only limited human skills are required in the job. Technology is the most important factor. Figure 7.3 shows how technology can affect performance. Here the person has to have enough motivation and ability to perform at a minimum level, for instance, to get the machine running. From there on, the equipment determines how well the job gets done. The lower and upper limits of performance are set by the technology. When technology sets such limits, one cannot expect performance to increase simply because one obtains competent or more motivated people.

☐ **FIGURE 7.3**   *Technology-Dominated Work*

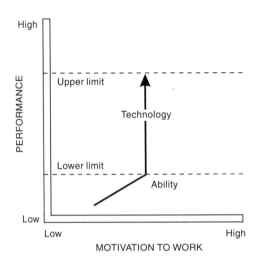

Technology and human skill may be interchangeable. When technology is substituted for human skill, it often leads to more predictable and dependable performance. Consider a task so simple as making coffee. Until the introduction of coffee machines, brewing a good cup of coffee required skill. Since the invention of home coffee makers, however, anyone who can read and follow instructions can make a good cup of coffee. An example of the substitution of technology for human skill is the use of "robotic" eyes for parts inspections on assembly lines. This advanced technology yields much higher accuracy rates and inspection speeds than those that could be achieved with traditional quality control methods.

The distinction between technology-dominated and skill-dominated work is a useful one for managers because it provides guidance about critical factors in achieving the desired performance results. For technology-dominated work, the most effective way to obtain improved performance is to make substantial improvements in the technology and the way it is used. This usually means experimenting with new methods or more investment in capital equipment and is often rather expensive, but necessary. For skill-dominated work, improvements can occur only when increased human competence is applied. This can be achieved (1) if workers have the necessary ability and are willing to put forth the effort required, (2) if workers do not have the competence but are trained, (3) if those without competence in the job are replaced by others with the requisite skill, or (4) if performance components are reassigned to others.

Organization structure and job design affect performance in two ways. First, they determine what abilities are required at work. When a job is narrowly defined, only a limited number of skills may be used. More broadly defined jobs, which would probably be the kind of jobs in organic organizations, call for a wider range of abilities for good performance.

Second, the characteristics of organization and job design can affect individual needs. A study of 200 telephone company employees found that those with higher order needs in more complex jobs experienced higher motivation, satisfaction, and quality of performance [14]. Spector analyzed the results of 20 studies which showed that employees with higher growth need strength tended to respond more positively to complex, enriched jobs than did those with low growth need strength [36].

MANAGERIAL MOTIVATION STRATEGIES

Managerial motivation strategies are attempts to act on the human input factors in the motivation/results model, within the technological constraints of the situation; in other words, to increase the person's motivation to perform so that they exert more effort and achieve a higher level of performance. Figure 7.4 shows how managerial motivation strategies fit into the motivation/results model. Figure 7.4 represents the relationship between motivation, ability, and performance for two football teams about to play each other. For simplification, we assume that the teams are equal in personal motivation (at level 2).

FIGURE 7.4 *Role of Managerial Motivation Strategies*

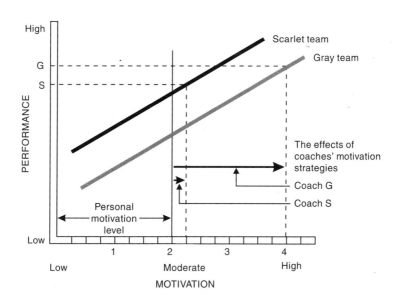

Suppose the coach of the Scarlets (Figure 7.4) takes the game between the teams lightly because of the Scarlets' superior ability. He gives the team only a little boost to level 2.25. But the coach of the Grays inspires them to put forth a great deal more effort. If the coach of the Grays can move the players to a high level of motivation (to level 4.0), they will win the game despite having less average ability. In the next chapter we present a variety of strategies for actively managing motivation.

CONTENT THEORIES OF MOTIVATION

Content theories of motivation emphasize the reasons for motivated behavior; that is, "what" causes it. A content theory would explain behavioral aspects in terms of specific human needs or specific factors that "drive" behavior. For example, it might be said that "Joan is motivated to work for higher *pay*" or "John did that because he has a high *need* for power." In this chapter, we discuss four content theories: The need theory, Herzberg's two-factor theory, the job design approach, and McCelland's achievement/power theory.

NEED THEORIES

Need theory approaches to motivation assume that people engage in particular behaviors to satisfy their needs; that is, unsatisfied needs dominate an individual's thinking and energize them to act. A **need** (or a motive) is aroused when the person senses that there is some difference between the present (or, perhaps, a future) condition and some desired state. When a "need" is aroused, the person, feeling some tension, acts to reduce the need. Such a sequence is shown in Figure 7.5. Suppose a manager tells her work group about a vacancy at a higher organizational level and that the position will be filled by the most productive worker in the group. The information may be a stimulus for some, arousing the workers' desire for advancement, achievement, or more pay. If the need is aroused, then those in the group might search for ways to satisfy it. They might work harder, the response desired by the manager. If the harder work leads to a promotion for one of the group, then that person's need is satisfied. If it does not, the desire for promotion may be suppressed and lead to frustration or the person might seek a job elsewhere.

☐ **FIGURE 7.5**   *A Needs Approach to Motivation*

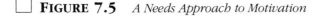
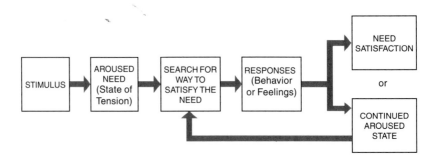

Maslow's Need Theory. In organizational behavior, the most popular need theory of motivation by far was developed by Abraham Maslow [31]. He outlined an approach that included the following concepts:

1. **There are five basic need categories.** These are physiological, safety, belonging, esteem, and self-actualization needs.

   Physiological needs are the basic requirements for survival. Humans must have food in order to live, and shelter is necessary. Physical well-being must be provided for before anything else can assume importance for a person.

   Safety needs reflect a desire for protection against loss of shelter, food, and other basic requirements for survival. Security needs also involve the desire to live in a stable and predictable environment. It may involve a preference for order and structure.

   Belonging needs reflect the person's desire for love, affection, and belonging. The need to interact with others and have some social acceptance and approval is generally shared by most people. For some, this need may be satisfied by joining groups. Others may find sufficient affection from their family members or other individuals.

   Esteem needs are those human desires to be respected by others and for a positive self-image. Individuals strive to increase their status in the eyes of others, to attain a good reputation or a high ranking in a group. Self-confidence is increased when self-esteem needs are satisfied. When self-esteem needs are thwarted, feelings of inferiority or weakness often result.

   Self-actualization needs are the individual's desire to do what he or she has the potential of doing. The desire for self-actualization is called the "highest-order need."

2. **The basic needs are arranged in a hierarchy.** An individual's needs form a hierarchy. Maslow claims that the higher-order needs (belonging, esteem, and self-actualization) are not considered important by an individual until the primary, or lower-order needs (safety and physiological) are at least partially satisfied. Maslow also feels that a person is not motivated by a need that is satisfied. Once a need is satisfied, the person is concerned with the next level of the need hierarchy.

A person seeks to move up the **hierarchy of needs**, generally striving to satisfy the need deficiency at the next-highest level. Maslow hypothesized that unsatisfied needs dominate the individual's thoughts and are reflected in what the person is concerned about.

ERG Theory. **ERG theory** is similar to Maslow's approach, though there are important differences. In ERG theory there are three, not five, basic need categories [2]. They are *existence needs, relatedness needs,* and *growth needs* (hence the label ERG). Existence needs encompass Maslow's physiological and security needs for material things. Relatedness needs include security needs for interpersonal matters, love and belonging needs, and needs of an interpersonal nature. Growth needs focus on the need to confirm personal esteem and self-actualization.

Like Maslow's theory, ERG theory states that unsatisfied needs will dominate behavior and that once a need is satisfied, higher-order needs are desired. For example, the less existence needs are satisfied, the more their satisfaction is desired. As they become satisfied, relatedness needs become more desired. Growth needs continue to be desired even as they are satisfied. But unlike Maslow's theory, ERG theory states:

1. The less relatedness needs are fulfilled, the more existence needs will be desired.

2. The less growth needs are fulfilled, the more relatedness needs will be desired [34].

This implies that if a person is deprived of a higher-order need or does not have the potential to satisfy it, he or she will focus on *lower*-order needs. In other words, he or she will *regress* on the hierarchy.

Need theory is elegant in its simplicity and appeal. If, as the theory suggests, people are concerned with lower-order needs first, then if an organization provides adequate wages, benefits, and security, the person will be motivated by higher-order needs and seek self-actualization. Yet this is not so easy to translate into practice for a very simple reason. A particular need may be satisfied in many ways. For instance, one person's esteem needs may be satisfied by being recognized as the best worker in a department. Another may find this need satisfied by others' recognition of his or her dress style—being acknowledged as the sharpest dresser in the group.

Ways to satisfy needs are learned through socialization, and so people differ with respect to the needs that are important to them. We learn through experience that some situations are more rewarding than others and seek these out; other situations we try to avoid.

TWO-FACTOR THEORY

The application of need theory to motivate people posed problems for manager, because it is difficult to translate "needs" into management strategies. Research by Herzberg, Mausner, and Snyderman provided some guidance for managers in solving this problem [19]. Their study challenged a long-held assumption about how a person's work satisfaction affected performance and motivation. Before, it was assumed that if a person was dissatisfied with part of the job (for example, pay), all that had to be done was to improve the factor (increase pay). This would lead to higher satisfaction, greater motivation, and higher performance. But Herzberg and his co-workers concluded that there are two sets of factors (hence the name *two-factor theory*) that affect people in the workplace, each of which worked in different ways. These were hygiene factors and motivating factors.

Hygiene factors create dissatisfaction if they are not present. If they are present in a job setting, dissatisfaction will be lower, but satisfaction will not be high. Hygiene factors are associated with the *context* of a job. They include working conditions, status, and company policy. A complete list is given in

Table 7.2. Therefore, according to the two-factor theory, providing fringe benefits, nice offices, and good vacation plans serve mainly to minimize dissatisfaction and to keep people in the organization; it does not lead to higher motivation or better performance.

Motivators are related to high satisfaction and willingness to work harder. When they are present, these job factors may induce more effort, but if they are absent, it will not produce dissatisfaction in most people. Motivators are associated with the *content* of the job. They are factors such as responsibility and achievement (see Table 7.2). Therefore, a person in a challenging job is likely to be satisfied and motivated to perform better. But the lack of challenging work does not cause dissatisfaction, merely the absence of satisfaction. A person who is well paid will not be dissatisfied; however, high pay will not lead to motivation.

☐ **TABLE 7.2**   Basic Elements of Two-Factor Theory

Hygiene Factors	Motivators
1. Technical supervision	1. Responsibility
2. Interpersonal relations—Peers	2. Achievement
3. Salary	3. Advancement
4. Working conditions	4. The work itself
5. Status	5. Recognition
6. Company policy	6. Possibility of growth
7. Job security	
8. Interpersonal relations—Supervisor	

This theory became popular with managers because it gave them a direction in managing motivation. For instance, if worker dissatisfaction is seen as the major problem, then the hygiene factors must be improved. But to improve performance the manager must work on the motivators, and this means changing the nature of the work to make it more challenging and intrinsically rewarding.

Herzberg's work has been the subject of much research and controversy. First, the results may be a consequence of *method bias*. He used the "incident recall" method, an approach in which subjects are asked, "Think of a good work experience," or "Think of a bad work experience." With this method there is a tendency for the person to attribute good experiences to themselves, as when *they* did a good job, and bad experiences to others or to the context, as when *their supervisor* prevented them from doing a good job. This could account for why the particular hygiene and motivating factors were discovered. Studies which used other methods, such as questionnaires, reached different conclusions [21]. Second, *individual differences are not considered.* For example, self confidence and skill both may affect whether or not a job is seen as challenging. A highly skilled systems analyst may find it challenging to design the information system for a new plant while an equally intelligent person with less computer competence may find the same assignment frustrating.

Even with these problems, the two-factor theory is an important contribution. It did provide some guidance to those who design jobs, and it was widely used by practicing managers. Of more importance, though, is that Herzberg's research directed attention in a very dramatic way to the role of the work itself as a factor that affects worker motivation and performance. This is a fundamental premise of several managerial motivational strategies discussed in the next chapter.

THE JOB DESIGN APPROACH

Working from Herzberg's idea that the work itself is an important motivating factor, Hackman and Lawler set out the first structure of the **Job Characteristics Model**, which is the basis of the job design approach to motivation. If specific job characteristics are present ". . . employees will experience a positive, self-generated response when they perform well and that this internal kick will provide an incentive for continued efforts toward good performance" [16]. Later, Hackman and Oldham refined the approach, including four general groups of variables [15] (see Figure 7.6). These are

1. Personal and work outcomes

2. Critical psychological states

3. Core job dimensions

4. Growth need strength.

FIGURE 7.6   *The Job Characteristic's Model: The Relationships Among Core Job Dimensions, Critical Psychological States, and Work Outcomes*

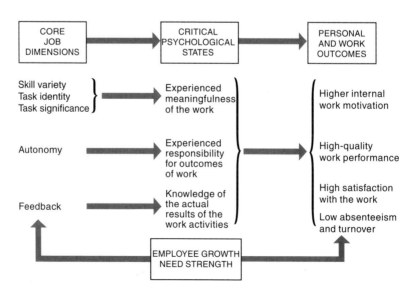

Work Outcomes.   There are four work outcomes in the job characteristics model. *Internal work motivation* is the extent to which the person doing a job is motivated by the work itself—how the task rather than external factors such as pay and supervision affect the person's willingness to put forth more work effort.

Quality of work performance is another outcome. In meaningful jobs, individuals will produce fewer errors, lower numbers of rejected parts, and lower scrap rates. The job characteristics approach does *not* predict that people will produce more. Productivity, though, may increase if an output level is maintained, and work quality is improved.

Job satisfaction is a third outcome that is affected by the characteristics of work. Job satisfaction is the person's attitude toward work in general, or to specific facets of the work.

Absenteeism and turnover are the final set of outcomes in the job characteristics model. Both absenteeism and turnover can be quite expensive for firms when they are high and out of control.

Critical Psychological States.   The work outcomes in the job characteristics model are affected by three **critical psychological states** that exist when a person is performing well in a job. They give the person a kick out of the work.

Experienced meaningfulness of the work occurs when the person believes that it counts for something, and generally that something is important either to the person or to someone else. For instance, most Peace Corps volunteers feel that their work is "the toughest job you will ever love." This feeling exists even though a volunteer's work assignment may be a very ordinary task, at a very low pay level, and in very undesirable working conditions. Most volunteers believe that their work makes an important difference, however small, to someone. It certainly made a difference to the volunteer.

Experienced responsibility for outcomes of work occurs when a person believes that he or she is personally accountable for the results of work. This is also the case for Peace Corp volunteers. Usually volunteers are working alone or with only a few others. They know that they are responsible for the success or failure of projects.

Knowledge of results is when a person is able to make an assessment about the adequacy of inadequacy of work performance. In many instances, getting knowledge of results is not as simple as it may appear. An engineer who designed the telemetry for deep space probes could not know whether the work was done right until months or years have passed—the engineer will know the results only when the telemetry equipment begins transmitting information from the prescribed location in space, for example, Mars and beyond.

Core Job Dimensions.   High levels of meaningfulness, responsibility, and knowledge of results exist when certain core job characteristics are present. The **core job dimensions** are (1) skill variety, (2) task identity, (3) task significance, (4) autonomy, and (5) feedback.

Skill variety is the number of different abilities and capacities that are required to perform. A clerk in a clerical pool who only types outgoing letters has a job that is of a low skill variety. A personal secretary to the chief executive officer may use a wide range of different skills such as typing and dealing with different people from both inside and outside the organization.

Task identity is the extent to which a person is responsible for the whole job, from beginning to end.

Task significance is the effect that work has on others, either in their work or in their lives. This occurs when the person can link his or her task to some value created for the customer.

Autonomy is the degree of freedom that a person has in the job. High autonomy exists when an individual has freedom to determine when, how, and where a job is to be done. When autonomy is high, so are perceived feelings of responsibility.

Feedback is the amount of information that a person gets about the results of the job. One way to get feedback is from other workers or supervisors. Another form of feedback may be from the job itself—a basketball player gets immediate feedback when a shot goes through the hoop or it doesn't.

Different core job characteristics contribute to different psychological states. Work meaningfulness is affected by skill variety, task identity, and task significance. Experienced responsibility is a function of autonomy. Knowledge of results is determined by feedback.

Growth Need Strength.   The job characteristics model stresses the importance of individual differences as moderators of the effects of task characteristics on workers. Hackman and his colleagues believe that growth need strength is the important individual factor. **Growth need strength** is the extent to which a person desires to advance, to be in a challenging position, and, generally, to achieve. When people with high growth strength are doing a job high in core dimensions, they are more likely to experience high internal motivation, high satisfaction, high work quality, and low turnover and absenteeism than are those with low growth need strength [36].

ACHIEVEMENT/POWER THEORY

The Achievement/Power Theory was developed from the work of McClelland and his associates [4, 32]. This approach has generally been called *achievement theory* because of McClelland's original focus on the need for achievement. More recently the power motive has received a good deal of attention; therefore we call this approach **achievement/power theory**.

The foundations of this theory are the concepts of *motive* and the *force of motives* on behavior. Motives are "effectively toned associated networks arranged in a hierarchy of strength and importance" within a person [32]. They are clusters of *expectancies* growing up around cues (reinforcements and other consequences) that are emotional experiences for the person. They are learned, not innate. Motives are an aspect of the personality, and they develop as the personality emerges.

The Achievement Motive.   The **achievement motive** is an internal drive state of the individual that reflects the extent to which success is important and valued by a person. The strength of the achievement motive is related to one's socialization experiences [17]. If a person's early success experiences were very rewarding, we would expect the person to have high achievement motivation. If these success experiences were not rewarding, another motive (say, power) may have a more dominant place in the motive cluster. Reinforced success in school may lead to high academic achievement motives while reinforced success in a part-time job might lead to work achievement motives. One person's achievement motive may differ from another's in terms of level and area of focus. For instance, the organizationalist may be driven by this motive to be successful in the firm, whereas a professional may be driven to be successful in an area of technical expertise and not seek organization success. When the achievement motive is generalized, a person wants to succeed in everything.

> For such a person, achievement is directed toward the top of the motive hierarchy; it takes only minimal achievement cues to activate the expectation of pleasure and thus increase the likelihood of achievement striving [34].

Those with high achievement motives tend to prefer certain types of conditions which activate the achievement need. These conditions are:

1. Success must be attained by the person's own efforts, not those of others or luck. Basically, high achievers wish to take responsibility for success and not have it attributed to other factors.

2. The situation must be challenging, but not impossible. McClelland calls this an "intermediate" risk level [32]. The risk of success cannot be so high that success is impossible, otherwise the high achiever will avoid it. Neither can it be so low that the task is easy, because it would represent no challenge.

3. There must be concrete feedback about success for the person [32]. High achievers want to keep track of how well they are doing. They avoid situations where there can be any doubt about their achievement.

There is evidence that the level of achievement motive is correlated with entrepreneurial success. This is because those high in achievement motives play a "one man game that need not involve other people" [33]. The entrepreneurial situation in business has most of the characteristics of one in which the achievement motive would be aroused. Entrepreneurs know that if they win or lose, they are responsible, accountable, and in charge.

The opposite side of achievement motivation is the *motivation to avoid failure*. For some, the achievement motive may be more dominant than the motive to avoid failure, as shown in Figure 7.7(a). In others, the motive to avoid failure may be strongest. When the motive to avoid failure is stronger than the achievement motive (Figure 7.7(b)), individuals seeks to *avoid* circumstances in which they are likely to fail rather than seeking situations in which they can be successful. Failure avoidance, rather than achievement, is their driving motive. For example, when setting personal performance goals, they tend to set them at such a low level that they cannot fail or at such a high level that no one expects the goals to be achieved.

FIGURE 7.7 *Relationship Between Achievement Motive and Motive to Avoid Failure*

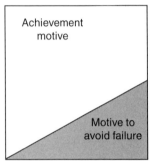

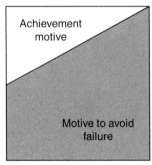

(a) HIGH ACHIEVEMENT/ LOW FAILURE AVOIDANCE

Achievement motive

Motive to avoid failure

(b) HIGH FAILURE AVOIDANCE/ LOW ACHIEVEMENT

Achievement motive

Motive to avoid failure

The Power Motive.   McClelland's interest in the power motive and its relationship to management came about because of his work in achievement motivation. Initially, he thought that successful managers would be very high in achievement motivation and that a "man with a high need to achieve does better work, gets promoted faster, and ultimately ends up as president of the company" [33]. He found many top-level executives, however, did not have high achievement motivation. He speculated that power motivation may be an important attribute of leadership and managerial effectiveness.

The **power motive** is the person's need to have an impact on others, to establish, maintain, or restore his or her prestige or power [33]. This motive can be manifested in three different ways. First, a person may take *strong actions* such as assault and aggression, giving help or assistance, controlling others, influencing or persuading others, or trying to impress someone. Second, a person may act in a way that *results in strong emotions by others*, regardless of

ACHIEVEMENT MOTIVES AND POWER MOTIVES—THE RIGHT MOTIVATION FOR THE RIGHT JOB

BTA is a large, very diversified firm that has divisions in the service industry, manufacturing, and distribution. The corporate strategy of BTA is to grow internally and by acquisition. It has some large, steady, very profitable divisions and also some small, growing units with high potential. An interesting aspect of BTA, from the viewpoint of motivation theory, is how Angela Fortune, Vice-president of Human Resources, uses concepts of achievement motivation and power motivation in the selection of managers for the different divisions.

When she is evaluating a candidate to head one of the divisions, her first concern is to decide whether the division is a stable one or if it is one of

☐ ACHIEVEMENT MOTIVES . . .

the growing divisions. If it is a growing division, she tries to find a person high in achievement motivation. This is because she believes growth, success, and personal achievement are entrepreneurial motives and she wants to place an entrepreneurial-oriented person in these divisions.

For the more stable divisions, she will seek a manager high in power motivation, because she believes, like McClelland, that a person motivated by power will be more effective in managing a "going" concern.

Fortune is very familiar with McClelland's theory, and she knows that there is not much research support for these ideas. However, the theory is quite logical and consistent to her and, in addition, her own experience at BTA is enough evidence for her. Over the years, she has seen entrepreneurial managers take very productive, but stable, units and try to make them grow, leading to some very unprofitable outcomes. Likewise, she knows of several instances where high power motivation managers given the responsibility for growing divisions were ineffective.

Her selection strategy seems to have worked so far. Since she has begun using these ideas in her selection decisions, BTA has experienced a high rate of growth and profitability. Of course, many other things have contributed to this, but it is certain that the right manager in the right job can never hurt.

whether or not the act itself seems to be strong. Third, this motive is often reflected by a *concern for one's reputation* and, perhaps, taking actions that would enhance or preserve it.

McClelland reports that men high in the power motive are more likely to read "sporty" magazines such as *Playboy* and *Sports Illustrated*, and they may drink more liquor and accumulate prestige possessions [33]. Men with high power motivation tend to prefer sports in which they actively compete with others, such as basketball or football, and not those where they compete against a clock or other similar standard, such as track and golf. Finally, these men are more likely to belong to several organizations and to hold office in many of them.

Women and men are similar in how the power motive is manifested. Winter examined several studies in which the power motives of men and women were compared [44]. Like men, women with high power motivation held organization offices, preferred jobs in power-oriented careers (such as business, teaching, and journalism), preferred to be highly visible in their organizations, and tended to acquire prestige possessions. An important difference was that women tended not to drink as heavily as men.

The power motive may take one of two different forms. One is personalized power and the other is socialized power. **Personalized power** is adversarial. Those with a personalized power orientation prefer person-to-person competition in which they can dominate. Life to them is a "zero-sum game . . . the law of the jungle ruled; the fittest survive by destroying their adversaries" [33]. They tend to drink somewhat heavily and gain considerable satisfaction from power fantasies while under the influence of alcohol. These persons are high in the power motive but low in inhibition, or self-control.

Socialized power tends to be manifested in a more impersonal way. A person with a socialized power orientation believes that he or she exercises power for the good of others, tends to be careful about the use of personal power, plans carefully for conflict with others, and knows that someone's win is another person's loss. Such people have high power needs but tend to be high in inhibition. They appear to prefer a more disciplined expression of their power motivation than those who have a personal power orientation.

People with strong socialized power motives, low affiliation needs, and high inhibition are said to have a configuration of motives called the "leader motive pattern" [33].

PROCESS THEORIES OF MOTIVATION

Theories which focus on how behavior change occurs, or how a person comes to act in a different way are called process theories. There is less emphasis on the specific factors (or "content") that causes behavior. For example, a content theory would contain hypotheses about behavior such as, "Increases in pay can improve satisfaction and performance," while a process theory explains, one way or another, how that happens. Four process theories are discussed in this chapter: reinforcement theory, expectancy theory, equity theory, and goal-setting theory.

REINFORCEMENT THEORY

Reinforcement theory, one of the learning approaches discussed in Chapter 4, is an important motivation theory. The various types of reinforcing consequences, schedules of reinforcement, and shaping that were discussed in relation to the formation of personality also operate in work organizations and, as we will show in the next chapter, may be applied as a managerial motivation strategy. Reinforcement theory also applies to other theories of motivation discussed in this chapter, such as expectancy theory and goal-setting theory, as managers attempt to reward successful performance or goal achievement.

Much research supports reinforcement theory. The most consistent results are those studies that are done under highly controlled conditions. When animals are taught to run mazes or to press a bar for food pellets, the effects of rewards and reinforcement schedules are very consistent with reinforcement theory basic propositions. Studies of human behavior in which there are similar experimental controls also show the impact of contingent rewards. Research on the behavior of students in a classroom or patients in a mental hospital shows clear effects when rewards can be made contingent on performance of a desired behavior. For instance, a study of the effects of reinforcement on the behavior of psychotic patients showed that the patients exhibited the desired responses when the reinforcement contingencies were applied. When the contingencies were withdrawn, the performance dropped; it increased later when the reinforcements were made contingent again. In this study, the conditions were under the control of the researchers. They could observe the patients and reinforce them as they behaved in the preferred way [3].

There are just too many factors that get in the way of tying consequences to behavior at work so that the effects are as clear as they are in other, more controlled studies. The work world is not so controlled and contrived as the laboratory. It is more difficult to observe subordinates frequently, and it is very difficult to find powerful enough consequences that can be made contingent on performance. For example, it is almost impossible to make pay an effective consequence in the sense implied by reinforcement theory. Paychecks are received, generally, on a fixed-interval schedule. Pay increases are given infrequently. It is also often very difficult to develop a good performance measure for some activities. Suppose you are an engineer working on a project that won't be finished for three years. Would you be willing to wait that long to be rewarded?

Effects of Extrinsic Rewards on Intrinsic Motivation.   Reinforcement theory is based on the application of **extrinsic rewards** to behavior. When a person performs well, rewards such as pay, benefits, or praise and recognition are given. Some question has been raised about the effects of the extrinsic reward applications on people's intrinsic motivation. **Intrinsic motivation** is the drive to perform that results from a person's internalized values and beliefs that the task is rewarding in and of itself. This means that the rewards for someone with high intrinsic task motivation are "self-administered"—the positive feelings one has when the task is completed. These include experiencing a sense of autonomy, personal growth, and task accomplishment when the job is well done.

Some believe that the use of extrinsic rewards might have a negative effect on intrinsic motivation [9, 38]. According to this argument, if a person receives extrinsic rewards for performing an intrinsically motivating task, then the intrinsic task motivation will decrease. Suppose you play golf for the university team. You practice hard and play your best because of the challenge of winning and the competition of the game. This is intrinsic motivation because your reward comes from within yourself. There are low extrinsic rewards. After college, you become a professional player and begin winning large sums of money in tournaments. Your motivation (the cause of your effort) changes from intrinsic to extrinsic. Now you do it for the money. The reason for this, according to Staw [37], is the way a person attributes causality to his or her actions:

> If external pressures on an individual are so high that they would ordinarily cause him to perform a given task . . . then the individual might infer he is extrinsically motivated. . . . In contrast . . . if the external rewards are extremely low or non-salient, the individual might then infer that his behavior is intrinsically motivated.

A study to test this idea was conducted by Deci [9]. College students worked on a series of puzzles that were designed to be intrinsically interesting. After the students had worked for a while on the puzzles, one group was told that they were to be paid for the task and a second group was told nothing. If extrinsic rewards did decrease intrinsic motivation, then those who would receive pay would react differently than those who did not. To test this, Deci assessed what the students did with their free time during the experiment. He reasoned that those students who were intrinsically motivated would spend their free time solving puzzles, but those who were not intrinsically motivated would do other things. Sure enough, the students who were to be paid for solving the puzzles spent less time working with them on breaks—they were more likely to read magazines. Those who were not paid spent more time, on average, solving puzzles during breaks.

Such a result suggests that there could be negative effects of extrinsic rewards, if used according to reinforcement theory. However, later studies have been more helpful in understanding the results of Deci's studies and how they may be used in work settings. First, the negative effect of extrinsic rewards on intrinsic motivation seems to operate for interesting jobs and not for uninteresting ones. Therefore, if we assume that most work in organizations is not highly interesting, then there is no problem. Certainly most work on plant floors and in offices is not very interesting, and most people wouldn't do them without pay (an extrinsic reward) [37].

Second, in any work organization, pay serves more purposes than just a contingent reward. There are strong norms about the importance and meaning of pay. It is a way for people to keep score of how they compare to others and how they are valued by the organization. As Staw points out, in industrial organizations where "extrinsic reinforcement is the norm . . . tasks may often be perceived to be more interesting when they lead to greater extrinsic rewards" [37].

EXPECTANCY THEORY

The basic premise of **expectancy theory** is that individuals will put forth effort to do those things that will lead to the results (outcomes) that they desire; it is a rational approach to motivation. It implies that people make an assessment of the costs or benefits of the different alternatives that they have and then select the one with the best payoffs [42]. The following example illustrates some key concepts in expectancy theory [20]. Suppose a car salesman has two different ways to approach work. He might (1) spend a lot of time calling prospective buyers or (2) wait until customers come into the store. What the salesperson does depends on the preference for certain outcomes and the expectations about those outcomes. Figure 7.8 shows how such a problem might be set up if the two possible outcomes are "$100 bonus" at the end of the month or "no bonus." Figure 7.8 also shows the expectancy for each of these outcomes for the different sales efforts. Suppose the salesman estimates that calling customers has a probability (an expectation) of .8 that the bonus will be earned and an expectation of only .2 of earning the bonus if he waits for the customers. The motivation to call customers is much higher. According to expectancy theory, the salesman would choose the work behavior, calling customers. The figure shows how this is calculated. The expected value of "calling customers" is $80, i.e., ([.8 × $100] + [.2 × $0]), while the expected value of "waiting in the showroom" is $20, i.e., ([.2 × $100] + [.8 × $0]).

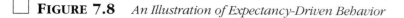

FIGURE 7.8 *An Illustration of Expectancy-Driven Behavior*

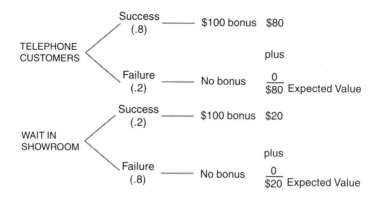

We must know some other things about the salesman before his behavior can be predicted with expectancy theory. For instance, we assumed that the salesman values the bonus and that he feels he can succeed if he tries to sell. In addition, there are other results, or outcomes, associated with both success and failure. For example, failure or success will affect opportunities for advancement, personal satisfaction with work, and, perhaps, relationships with other members of the sales staff. Finally, there is the question of ability. A person with high selling ability will be more successful than one with lesser skills, given similar levels of motivation. These elements of expectancy theory are shown in Figure 7.9.

FIGURE 7.9 *Some Key Concepts in Expectancy Theory*

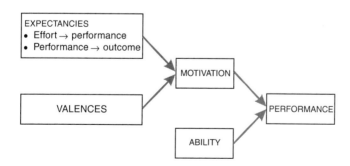

Expectancy. An **expectancy** is an individual's estimate, or judgment, of the likelihood that some outcome (or event) will occur. It is a probability estimate and can range from 0 to 1.0. If the salesman believes it is necessary to show cars to five buyers in order to sell one, the expectancy is .20.

There are two kinds of expectancies (see Figure 7.10). The first, called the **effort-performance expectancy** (E → P), is the person's belief about the level of effort put forth and the resulting performance that it will lead to. In Figure 7.10, the effort-performance expectancy is shown as the relationship between "How hard I work to sell cars" and "How many cars I sell." The effort-performance expectancy is .2. The salesman would have a low E → P if he thought extra effort would not yield more sales.

☐ **FIGURE 7.10**   *Effort-Performance and Performance-Outcome Expectancies*

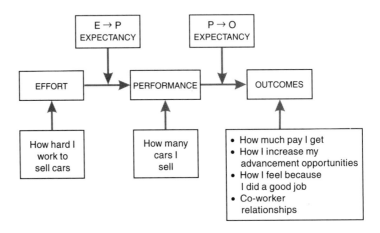

The second type of expectancy, **performance-outcomeexpectancy** (P → O), is the expectation about the relationship between a particular level of performance and attaining and certain outcomes. In Figure 7.10 the performance-outcome expectancy is shown as the linkage between "How many cars I sell" and "How much pay I get."

Figure 7.10 shows there may be several different outcomes for a particular performance. It shows four outcomes for the performance. "How many cars I sell." These outcomes are (1) "How much pay I get," (2) "How I increase my advancement opportunities," (3) "How I feel because I did a good job," and (4) co-worker relationships. All these outcomes affect the level of motivation. As an illustration, a salesperson may feel that if he or she puts forth a great deal of effort, high performance (E → P) will result. This level of performance may have a high probability of increasing income and self-esteem, but a low probability of advancement can lead to resentful co-workers. These several outcomes of performance (pay, advancement, self-esteem, and co-worker relations) are all P → O expectations.

High P → O expectancies, particularly with respect to attaining rewards, are necessary for high performance. This is called the performance-reward linkage, and if it isn't made, then we shouldn't expect a person to put forth effort.

Valences.   Not all outcomes are equally valued by a person. The salesman in the example above may have a strong desire for some outcomes but care less for others. He may, for example, wish to have the pay increase and the advancement but avoid antagonizing co-workers. In expectancy theory these preferences are called **valences**, which are anticipated satisfactions (or dissatisfactions) that result from outcomes and are the individual's estimate of the pleasantness—or unpleasantness—of outcomes.

When an outcome has a low positive valence, a person will not exert much force to attain it. Take the case of a regional staff manager for a brokerage firm. Her current work is in southern California. She grew up there, married, and has children. Her family and her husband's family live there. She is happy and does not want to move. She is very successful, and always listed as one of the top five managers in the entire country. Her supervisor informs her that there will be an opening in New York and she is the leading candidate for the job. However, she has to "prove herself" by improving performance for the next three months. The advancement opportunity has little valence for her. We shouldn't expect her to put forth much effort to get the promotion [39].

EQUITY THEORY

Suppose that Alan Jones is one of four production supervisors in a manufacturing plant. Of the four supervisors, he has the most experience and believes he has at least as good a production record as any of the others. However, his annual salary is $40,000 a year while the other supervisors earn $50,000. According to equity theory, he will perceive himself as inequitably paid. This will cause him to be upset and will lead him to do something to reduce the inequity. According to equity theory, the other supervisors may feel there is inequity too. They may also act to bring about a state of equity.

In **equity theory** people are motivated to maintain "fair relationships with others and to rectify unfair relationships by making them fair" [5]. A fundamental premise is that individuals want their efforts and achievements to be judged fairly relative to others. Unlike other theories that explain motivation by *intra*personal comparisons (e.g., "what I have now" compared to "what I would like to have"), equity theory explains motivation by *inter*personal comparisons (what I have now compared to what others have).

Three key factors used in explaining and understanding motivation in equity theory are: (1) inputs, (2) outcomes, and (3) referents [1].

1. *Inputs.* Inputs are what a person brings to the job, such as age, experience, skill, and seniority, and contributions to the organization or group. They can be anything that he or she believes relevant to the job and that should be recognized by others.

2. *Outcomes.* These are things that the person perceives to be received as a result of work. Outcomes may be positively valued factors such as pay, recognition, promotion, status symbols, and fringe benefits. They may also be negative: unsafe working conditions, pressure from management, and monotony.

3. *Referents.* In equity theory, a referent is the focus of comparison for the person, either other individuals or other groups. For example,

Alan Jones may compare himself to one of the other supervisors, say Paula Dawkins, or to the whole group of production supervisors.

Inequity (or equity) is based on the comparison of two *ratios* of outcomes to inputs. A state of **equity** means that the ratios of outcomes to inputs for the person (Alan) and the referent (Paula) are equal, as shown in the following equation.

$$\frac{\text{Outcomes (Alan)}}{\text{Inputs (Alan)}} = \frac{\text{Outcomes (Paula)}}{\text{Inputs (Paula)}}$$

In other words, Alan Jones would not think it inequitable if his pay is $40,000 and Paula Dawkins's is $50,000, but only if he thought Paula made greater inputs to work. What causes inequity perceptions is when he believes that his inputs are at least equal to Paula's but his outcomes are not. Suppose that the inputs to work (everything that Alan and Paula contribute to work) could be hypothetically valued at $60,000. The equity relationship can be seen in the following equation.

$$\frac{\text{Outcomes (Alan)}}{\text{Inputs (Alan)}} < \frac{\text{Outcomes (Paula)}}{\text{Inputs (Paula)}}$$

$$\frac{\$40,000}{\$60,000} < \frac{\$50,000}{\$60,000}$$

or

$$.66 \quad < \quad .83$$

For Alan this is **underpayment inequity**. He gets less out of the job than does Paula, relative to what they both contribute. According to equity theory, this underpayment results in dissatisfaction that stems from anger at being underrewarded. According to Kanfer, the research shows that those who believe they are underpaid relative to others reduce the quality of their work [23]. Cowherd and Levine found this effect in their study of pay differentials between hourly workers and lower level managers [8]. The greater the pay differential, the lower was the quality of the product.

There is also **overpayment inequity**. If Paula assesses her outcomes and inputs relative to Alan's as shown in the equations above, she experiences overpayment inequity (her .83 is greater than Alan's .66). Overpayment inequity means that the person believes he or she gets more out of the job relative to the inputs than the referent. Overpayment inequity leads to dissatisfaction, just as does underpayment inequity, but in this case the dissatisfaction results from feelings of guilt that the person (in this case, Paula) develops. The dissatisfaction, whether it arises from guilt or anger, will cause the person who experiences it to do something to bring the situation into a state of equity.

The effects of overpayment inequity are illustrated in a study of how layoffs affected those who continued working [6]. When co-workers were terminated because of low performance, those remaining thought that they had performed more favorably on the assignment than those terminated. When co-workers were terminated on a random basis, the remaining workers worked harder, increasing their inputs, as equity theory predicts.

Restoring Equity.   When inequity is perceived, action is taken to restore it. Certainly judgments about what constitutes inequity and ways to restore it are affected by individual differences. For example, an interesting study by Vecchio [41] found that people who were morally mature (i.e., had a strong conscience and high ethical standards) were more likely to respond to inequitable situations. Some of the ways that equity might be restored are

1. *Modify inputs.* For Alan, the inequity can be reduced if he reduces his inputs. For instance, he might lower his commitment to the organization, put in fewer hours, and not be as concerned with quality as he had been in the past. If Paula experiences overpayment inequity, she could increase her inputs. She might try to raise the quality of her work or increase her effort.

2. *Change outcomes.* One way for Alan to decrease his feelings of inequity would be to get more out of his work. He may seek a pay raise, try to increase his power, or seek more privileges. Paula might alter her outcomes by refusing a pay increase (unlikely) or by taking on less intrinsically satisfying work.

3. *Rationalize the inputs and outputs.* It is possible to reduce inequity by psychological distortion. Alan could increase his outcome by a process called *task enhancement* [43]. That is, he could rationalize that his job has higher status or is more important than he earlier believed. He could psychologically distort inputs by changing his judgment to believe that he puts less effort into the job. Paula might also "convince" herself that her job is more important than Alan's.

    Psychological distortion of the other person's outcomes and inputs is also possible. Alan may rationalize that Paula's actual contributions aren't as great as his but that she has done so well because she had the advantage of being a woman during a time when the company was under pressure to move women into management. This would make her inputs seem greater and bring the ratios into balance.

4. *Leave the field.* Alan may get another job. Then in the new setting he escapes inequity and finds a fairer situation.

5. *Act against the other person.* One way to bring about equity is to modify the ratio of the other person behaviorally and psychologically. Alan might convince Paula to put forth more effort, thus increasing her inputs. Or he may be able to decrease her outcomes by a political strategy in which he undermines the confidence others have in her so that she leaves the company.

6. *Change the referent.* Alan may find it easier not to compare himself to Paula. If he can find another person in the plant who seems to have a similar ratio of outcomes to inputs with whom he compares himself, he will reinstate a sense of equity, his satisfaction will increase, and his anger will decrease.

GOAL-SETTING THEORY

Goal-setting theory is based on a simple premise: performance is caused by a person's intention to perform [29]. Goals are "what a person is trying to accomplish" or intends to do, and according to this theory, people will do what they are trying to do [28]. What follows from this is quite clear. First, a person with higher goals will do better than someone with lower ones. Second, if someone knows precisely what he or she wants to do, or is supposed to do, that person will do better than someone whose goals or intentions are vague. These are the basic ideas that underlie the following propositions.

1. *There is a general positive relationship between goal difficulty and performance.* This, however, does not hold for extremely difficult goals beyond one's ability. Difficult goals lead to better results than easy goals. This has been shown time after time in very different research settings. Laboratory experiments on goal difficulty have been done using all sorts of different tasks—subjects have proofread manuscripts, worked on word puzzles, and solved math problems [30, 40].

   When the same problem is studied in the world of work, the results are the same: difficult goals lead to better results [40]. For example, logging crews that had hard goals did better than those with easy goals and software engineers who had difficult work goals put forth more work effort and had higher performance [27, 30, 35].

2. *Specific goals lead to higher performance than general goals.* This is a particularly important point to remember because managers have a tendency to set goals that are too general for their subordinates [7]. The support for this proposition from both laboratory studies and field experiments is very impressive. A large number of laboratory studies show the superiority of specific goals [40]. In laboratory studies, typically two groups of subjects are given the same task to perform. The members of one group are told that they should "do their best." The other group is given specific quantitative goals, such as "solve 15 problems."

   The results of field experiments with keypunch operators, marketing personnel, production workers, and laboratory personnel are also very positive. These studies show that

   > individuals given specific, challenging goals either out performed those trying "to do their best," or surpassed their own previous performance when they were not trying for specific goals [30].

   One study by Latham and Baldes was conducted on logging crews [26]. The job of the logger was to cut trees, load them onto trucks,

234

and haul them to the sawmill. An analysis of the work showed that initially the loggers did not load the trucks near their maximum allowable weights—the average load was about 60 percent of the maximum (see Figure 7.11). Before any specific goals for the loggers were set, the loggers were given the general goal "Do your best." During that period, the trucks continued to carry 60 percent of their allowable capacity. Then specific goals were set for the workers—they were told to load their trucks to 94 percent of the legal weight. Figure 7.11 shows that after the specific goal was set, the loads increased rather dramatically.

FIGURE 7.11   *Effects of Specific vs. General Goals for Log-Truck Loading*

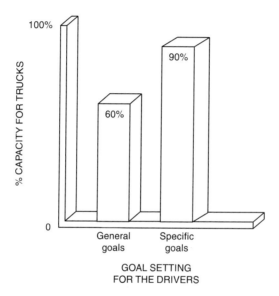

3. *Participation is related to performance through goal acceptance and commitment.* Initially, goal setting theorists thought that participation in setting goals was not related to performance unless it led to a person's setting more difficult or specific goals. This was a controversial proposition for two reasons. First, since the late 1950s, when Peter Drucker popularized the theory of management by objectives, participation in goal setting has been a keystone of many managerial philosophies. Second, since the early 1970s, the growing quality of work life movement in American industry has systematically increased worker involvement and influence over working conditions. Erez, Early, and Hulin have clarified the role of participation [11]. It seems that participation does not directly affect performance but operates through commitment to goals. In the study, workers in an animal laboratory were divided into two groups. In the participative group, the members jointly devised a method for observing the animals daily in a laboratory. When they finished determining how the task should be

done, they then decided by consensus the goal for the task. Another group performed the same task, but the same goals were assigned by a supervisor. Those in the participative group were more committed to, or accepted, the goals more than those in the group to which the goals and tasks were assigned. In addition, the level of individual goal acceptance was related to the level of performance.

Participation probably contributes to commitment and, ultimately, to performance when the person has some real choices about the way to achieve a goal as well as information about the goal and the task. Early found that there was an interaction between information about goals and having a choice about how to achieve a goal which affected performance: "Choice was only beneficial to performance when higher information was provided. Information was a potent enhancer of goal acceptance and performance" [10].

These findings indicate that participation is a complex process. It cannot be limited only to narrow areas in which superiors want to have subordinates set goals but must be more broadly based [7]. It must also be realistic participation, in the sense that subordinates have some choices about ways to perform the task, the goal levels, and what information they would like to have to perform the task.

4. *Feedback about performance with respect to goals is necessary.* Both clear goals and feedback about performance are necessary for higher performance [30]. A person must know whether or not the desired level of performance has been achieved. Tubbs' meta-analysis of both laboratory and field studies on goal setting confirmed the feedback effect [40]. He found that when there was specific feedback, difficult goals had very strong effects on performance. When there was no feedback, difficult goals had weaker effects. In a study of Michigan Bell service personnel, Kim and Hamner compared the performance of two groups of workers [24]. One group had goals but did not get feedback about whether or not the goals were being achieved. Another work group had goals set and also received feedback about their results. The group that had goals *and* received feedback performed better than the group that only had goals. The goals-feedback group had lower costs and a better safety record.

Other Considerations in Goal-Setting Theory. Goal-setting theory appears to be a neat, orderly approach to motivation and performance. But it does not account for two important factors, individual differences and goal complexity. As Locke and his colleagues point out, limited assessment has been made of the effects of *individual differences* in goal setting [30]. It seems logical that some personality differences should affect goal acceptance and willingness to put forth effort to achieve goals. One factor, self-esteem, has been found to be an important personality factor that may interact with goals to affect performance. Carroll and Tosi found that managers with high self-esteem reported that they worked harder toward performance goals than those managers who had low self-esteem [7].

Goal complexity is another problem. In all the laboratory studies, goals were set for simple tasks. Even many of the field experiments generally studied relatively low-level, simple tasks such as typing or loading trucks. Work goals for managers and professionals are much more complicated. Consider, for example, how one would set goals for the plant superintendent, discussed earlier in the chapter, with six or more performance components. We simply do not know from Goal Setting Theory, for instance, how the superintendent sets priorities and makes choices between tasks for which goals have been set that are likely to differ in specificity and difficulty. Further, it does not appear that the role of ability is addressed in the theory. Some research which addressed these issues is reported by Wood, Mento, and Locke [45]. They found that goal specificity and goal difficulty had weaker effects for more complex tasks than for simple tasks. This implies that there is likely an upper limit for the impact of goals on managerial and professional work.

A CONCLUDING COMMENT

The various theories of motivation that we have discussed all focus on causes of human behavior. Each approach uses different psychological concepts, however, to explain behavior. For example, the concepts used in reinforcement theory include positive reinforcement, punishment, and reinforcement schedules. Expectancy theory is built around such ideas as valences, expectancies, and outcomes. Since these different theories have psychological bases and concern the same variable, human behavior, it is only logical that they can be related to one another. Expectancies, for example, develop as a result of previous learning experiences. Learning theory may also explain the development of particular motives. Strong achievement needs may result from the positive reinforcement of success experiences in early life. In fact, this is exactly the point we make in Chapter 4 in the discussion of learning and personality.

It is also important to note that various theories have boundaries. There is no one best theory of motivation, and some seem better suited to deal with certain topics than others. Landy and Becker point out that need theories are most widely used to study satisfaction and work effort [25]. Reinforcement theory focuses on effort, performance, and absenteeism and turnover. Expectancy theory can be used to predict job and organization choices and withdrawal behavior. Goal-setting theory has been related to choice behavior and performance.

In the final analysis, understanding each of these different approaches is useful because it gives the manager several ways to look at problems. As a result, he or she may arrive at better solutions more quickly and effectively.

SUMMARY

Several motivation theories were discussed in this chapter. Need theories, a class of content theories, suggest *what* motivates people. They give clues to managers about what they can change so that increased employee performance and satisfaction as well as organizational effectiveness can result. Maslow's need hierarchy approach, ERG theory, and achievement/power theory are all examples of need theories. The job design approach describes ways that work itself can be modified to build in more motivational power. They suggest a number of strategies designed to activate and satisfy the needs of employees at all levels. The two-factor theory, for example, argues that there are critical differences between hygiene factors and motivators. Each one has very different implications for management action. To affect performance and higher-order need satisfaction, it is the motivators that require attention. The job design approach broadens this idea, outlining specific facets of work which affect motivation.

The remaining approaches to motivation emphasize the process of motivation—how it occurs. Reinforcement theory, also discussed in Chapter 4, explains behavior and its persistence in terms of consequences associated with the behavior. Expectancy theory is based on the premise that a person will put forth effort toward behavior that leads to desirable results. It is a rational approach that suggests people seek to enhance their payoffs. Expectancy theory calls for the management of factors to get performance and ways to reward it. Equity theory argues that people are motivated to maintain fair relationships with others and to rectify unfair ones. A number of conditions can trigger feelings of inequity at work, and these trigger reactions such as withholding performance, seeking better payoffs, or leaving the field. Goal-setting theory predicts how well people perform based on the characteristics of goals they have. Difficult and specific goals and feedback have been consistently associated with high performance.

It is important to remember that in all these theories the same factor is considered: human motivation underlying behavior. The theories examine it from different perspectives and with different concepts, but relationships exist among the various models.

☐ KEY CONCEPTS

Ability	Goal-setting theory	Performance
Achievement	Growth need	Performance
power theory	strength	component
Achievement motive	Hierarchy of needs	Performance-
Autonomy	Hygiene factors	outcome
Content theories	Intrinsic	expectancy
Core job dimensions	motivation	Personalized
Critical psychological	Job characteristics	power
states	model	Power motive
Effort-performance	Knowledge	Process theories
expectancy	of results	Reinforcement theory
Equity	Managerial	Satisfaction
Equity theory	motivation	Skill-dominant work
ERG theory	strategies	Skill variety
Expectancy	Motivation/Results	Socialized power
Expectancy theory	model	Task identity
Experienced	Motivation	Task significance
responsibility	Motivators	Technology
Experienced	Need	Technology-dominant
meaningfulness	Need theory	work
Extrinsic rewards	Overpayment	Underpayment inequity
Feedback	inequity	Valence

☐ STUDY QUESTIONS

1. Why are managers so deeply interested in motivation? Why are the different definitions of motivation important for managers to know?
2. Differentiate between content theories and process theories of motivation. Why are "need" theories of motivation "culture bound"? How are process theories affected by cultural influences?
3. Compare and contrast the approaches of Maslow, Alderfer, and McClelland.
4. Discuss the key elements of the job characteristics approach to motivation. Analyze the motivational character of a job you have had in terms of the approach.
5. What are the characteristics of a person high in achievement motivation? Power motivation? What is the difference between personalized power motivation and socialized power motivation?
6. Explain the relationship between motivation, ability, and performance.
7. What are the key concepts of expectancy theory? Describe the relationship between the concepts of expectancy theory. What is the theory seeking to predict?
8. What are the concepts in goal-setting theory? What is the relationship between participation in goal setting and goal success? Do you agree with this? Explain.

STUDY . . .

9. Distinguish between the different consequences of behavior in reinforcement theory.
10. How is it that extrinsic rewards can decrease intrinsic motivation? Why would this idea appeal to a manager? Or would it?

CASE

GREEN SPRING BEDDING COMPANY

The Green Spring Bedding Company, located in western South Carolina, produces a well-known brand of mattresses which are sold in department stores. At one time, the work force numbered 75 workers, but now, in Spring 1993, there was a slowdown in the industry so there were 35 production workers, both male and female, on the assembly line. The women did the lighter jobs. The men were primarily from various minority groups. The supervisors were almost all Anglo-Saxon males.

The mattresses were produced on two assembly lines, which were operated based on orders for mattresses. On some days the lines would make different size mattresses. Each worker performed a specialized task such as cutting the material for the mattress covers, assembling the springs, sewing on the mattress covers, packaging the mattress, and so on. When a worker completed his or her task, the mattress was pushed on rollers to the next work station.

There was pretty tight control at Green Springs Bedding. The supervisors' office was glass enclosed, on a level above the production floor, so that they could observe the assembly line quite easily. There were also TV monitors throughout the building which constantly displayed various parts of the production operation. There were performance standards for each task. These were set with data from time studies and industry standards. Workers were paid a bonus for reaching the standard.

Because of the downturn in sales, Carl Hines, the plant manager, wanted to do something to increase productivity without spending money, which was very tight, on new manufacturing equipment. He thought that it might be possible to increase the motivation levels of the work force. Hines called several consulting firms and was shocked at the cost of a study. One night at dinner with friends he met Max Pilati, a professor of management at the nearby state university. He told Professor Pilati about his problem and the fact that he had no way to get a budget to support this study. "One way that I could help you with this," Pilati said to Hines, "is to send out Jennifer Werner, one of my graduate students, who is looking for a site to do her dissertation research. You will only have to pay the expenses, but there is no fee and you will get some useful information." How could Carl refuse such a good offer?

☐ GREEN SPRING . . .

The next week, Jennifer showed up at the Green Springs plant. She interviewed all the workers and had them complete some questionnaires used frequently to assess worker attitudes, as well as some individual differences, such as locus of control and the priority of their psychological needs.

When she analyzed the data from the interviews, she found some consistency in the workers responses. For example, typical responses to a question about how happy they were with their jobs were:

It's okay. I've worked in worse places. The pay is okay.

Why do you want to know? Has this anything to do with the company's attitude toward the union?

It depends on the day. Some days are good and some are not. What are the worst days? Oh, I don't know. I don't like it when king sized mattresses are scheduled. They are difficult to deal with.

What changes would I like to see? Well, more money of course. Also, as a woman I don't like the men staring at me all the time while I operate my sewing machine. Maybe they could separate the women from the men with a wall or something.

I don't like the location of this place. I worked for this company when it was in the city and it was easy to get to work. Now I have to drive and it takes me a longer time to get to work. Other than that it's an okay place to work. The president has always been fair to me and he's a pretty good guy, a much better person than most of the foremen to tell you the truth.

She found the following typical responses to a question about how often they reach performance standards:

Not usually. They're pretty hard to reach.

Not too often but I get pretty close and I'm satisfied with that.

I usually make them. I'm a good worker and everybody around here knows that.

There were a series of other questions about the performance standards. She thought the following replies were representative of what other workers told her:

Q: Why did you reach standard last week but not the previous three weeks?

☐ GREEN SPRING . . .

A: Simple—the rent was due last week.

Q: Would reaching standard consistently improve your paycheck?

A: Sure. I would get more money but to tell you the truth it really isn't worth it. I owe so much that whatever I earn goes to bills.

Q: Would the other workers make comments if you reached standard all the time?

A: Sure.

Q: Would it bother you to have the others get on your case for reaching standard?

A: Yes, it would.

Q: Would a pat on the back from the foremen please you?

A: Not really.

Q: Would you feel good about yourself for reaching standard?

A: No—I don't relate to this job that much.

Q: What else would happen if you reached standard every day?

A: I'd be damned tired!

Q: How much would it help your promotion prospects to make standard consistently?

A: Very little, I think. Somebody like me isn't going to be promoted.

Q: Would making standard regularly make it less likely you would be laid off?

A: Sure. They keep the best workers. But I'm already one of the best so I don't worry about it.

Werner also evaluated the results of the questionnaires which she administered. From the job satisfaction questionnaire it appeared that the workers were about average on satisfaction with pay, satisfaction with the work group, satisfaction with the company, satisfaction with the job itself, but significantly below average on satisfaction with supervision.

There was also a relatively consistent pattern of responses to the measure of locus of control (the belief that you control your life versus your life is controlled by forces outside of yourself). Most of the workers were internals—they believed their own efforts controlled their destiny. On a questionnaire used to measure the priority of their psychological needs, the workers scored highest on the higher order needs (i.e. the needs for achievement, promotion, growth, etc.).

☐ GREEN SPRING . . .

Jennifer Werner gave Carl Hines a short report in which she summarized her results. After he read it, he called her and Professor Pilati and asked if they could come up with a set of recommendations to help him have a more stable and motivated workforce.

QUESTIONS

1. What does this case show about the work concerns and motivations of ordinary rank and file employees?
2. Which motivational theory best explains the behavior of the workers in this case?
3. What other theories of motivation are helpful in understanding the responses of the workers at Green Springs?

REFERENCES

1. Adams, J.S. Inequity in social exchange. In L. Berkowitz, ed. Advances in experimental social psychology. Vol. 2, New York: Academic Press, 1965, 267-99.
2. Alderfer, C. *Existence, relatedness, and growth: Human needs in organizational settings.* New York: Free Press, 1972.
3. Allyon, T., and Azrin, N. The measurement and reinforcement of behavior of psychotics. *Journal of the Experimental Analysis of Behavior*, 1965, 8, 357-83.
4. Atkinson, J.W. and Feather, N.T. *A theory of achievement motivation.* New York: John Wiley, 1966.
5. Baron, R.A. *Behavior in organization: Understanding and managing the human side of work.* Boston: Allyn & Bacon, 1983.
6. Brockner, J., Greenberg, J., Brockner, A., Bortz, J., Davy, J., and Carter, C. Layoffs, equity theory, and work performance: Further evidence of the impact of survivor guilt. *Academy of Management Journal*, 1986, 29(2), 373-84.
7. Carroll, S.J., and Tosi H.L. *Management by Objectives: Applications and research.* New York: Macmillan, 1973.
8. Cowherd, D. M., and Levine, D. I. Product quality and pay equity between lower-level employees and top management: An investigation of distributive justice theory. *Administrative Science Quarterly*, 1992, 37(2), 302-320.
9. Deci, E.L. The effects of externally mediated rewards on intrinsic motivation. *Journal of Personality and Social Psychology*, 1971, 18, 105-15.
10. Early, P.C. Influence of information, choice and task complexity upon goal acceptance, performance and personal goals. *Journal of Applied Psychology*, 1985, 70:3, 481-91.
11. Erez, M., Early, P.C., and Hulin, C. The impact of participation on goal acceptance and participation. *The Academy of Management Journal*, 1985, 28(1), 50-66.
12. Farrell, D. Exit, voice, loyalty, and neglect as responses to job dissatisfaction: A multidimensional scaling study. *Academy of Management Journal*, 1983, 26, 596-607.

13. Farrel, D. and Rusbult, C.E. Understanding the retention function: A model of the causes of exit, voice, loyalty, and neglect. *Personnel Administrator*, 1985, 30(4), 129-134.

14. Hackman, J.R., and Lawler, E.E. Employee reactions to job characteristics. *Journal of Applied Psychology Monograph*, 1971, 55, 259-86.

15. Hackman, J.R., and Oldham, G.R. Motivation through the design of work: Test of a theory. *Organizational Behavior and Human Performance*, 1976, 16, 250-79.

16. Hackman, J.R., and Suttle, J.L., eds. *Improving life at work: Behavioral science approaches to organizational change.* Santa Monica, CA: Goodyear Publishing, 1977.

17. Heckhausen, H. *The anatomy of achievement motivation.* New York: Academic Press, 1967.

18. Helmrich, R., Bakeman, R., and Sherwitz, L. The study of small groups. *Annual Review of Psychology*, 1973, 24, 337-54.

19. Herzberg, F.A., Mausner, B., and Snyderman, B. *The motivation to work.* New York: John Wiley, 1959.

20. House, R.J., and Wahba, M. Expectancy theory in managerial motivation: An integrated model. In H. Tosi, R.J. House, and M.D. Dunnette, eds. *Managerial motivation and compensation.* East Lansing, MI: Michigan State University, Division of Research, College of Business Administration, 1972.

21. House, R.J., and Wigdor, L. Herzberg's dual factor theory of job satisfaction and motivation: A review of the evidence and criticism. *Personnel Psychology*, 1967, 20, 369-89.

22. Inzerilli, G. *Critical incidents in international management.* Unpublished manuscript: Erasmus University, Rotterdam School of Management, Rotterdam, The Netherlands, 1991.

23. Kanfer, R. Motivation theory and industrial and organizational psychology. In M. D. Dunnette and L. Hough (eds.), *Handbook of Industrial and Organizational Psychology*, Palo Alto: Consulting Psychologists Press, 1990, 75-170.

24. Kim, J., and Hamner, W.C. Effect of performance feedback and goal setting in productivity and satisfaction in an organizational setting. *Journal of Applied Psychology*, 1976, 61, 48-57.

25. Landy, F.J., and Becker, W.S. Motivation theory reconsidered. In L.L. Cummings and B.M. Staw (eds.), *Research in organizational behavior.* Greenwich, CT: JAI Press, 9, 1987, 1-38.

26. Latham, G., and Baldes, J. The practical significance of Locke's theory of goal setting. *Journal of Applied Psychology*, 1975, 60, 122-24.

27. Latham, G., and Locke, E.A. Increasing productivity with decreasing time limits: A field test of Parkinson's law. *Journal of Applied Psychology*, 1975, 60, 524-26.

28. Locke, E.A. Toward a theory of task motivation and incentives. *Organization Behavior and Human Performance*, 1968, 3, 152-89.

29. Locke, E. A., and Latham, G. P. *A theory of goal setting and task performance.* New Jersey: Prentice Hall Inc., 1990.

30. Locke, E.A., Shaw, K., Saari, L.M., and Latham, G.P. Goal setting and task performance: 1969-1980. *Psychological Bulletin*, 1981, 90, 125-52.

31. Maslow, A.H. A theory of human motivation. *Psychological Review*, 1943, 50, 370-96.

32. McClelland, D.A. Toward a theory of motive acquisition. *American Psychologist*, 1965, 20, 321-23.

33. McClelland, D.A. *Power: The inner experience.* New York: Irvington, 1975.

34. Miner, J.B. *Theories of organizational behavior.* New York: Macmillan, 1980.

35. Rasch, R. H., and Tosi, H. L. Factors affecting software developers' performance: An integrated approach. *Management Information Systems Quarterly*, 1992, 16(3), 405.

36. Spector, P.E. Higher-order need strength as a moderator of the job scope-employee outcome relationship: A meta-analysis. *Journal of Occupational Psychology*, 1985, 58, 119-27.

37. Staw, B.M. *Intrinsic and extrinsic motivation.* Morristown, NJ: General Learning Press, 1976.

38. Staw, B.M. Knee-deep in the big muddy. A study of escalating commitment to a chosen course of action. *Organizational Behavior and Human Performance*, 1976, 16, 27-44.

39. Tosi, H.L., and Young, J.W. *Management: Experiences and demonstrations.* Homewood, IL: Richard D. Irwin, 1982.

40. Tubbs, M.E. Goal setting: A meta-analytic examination of the empirical evidence. *Journal of Applied Psychology*, 1986, 71(3), 474-483.

41. Vecchio, R. An individual difference interpretation of the conflicting predictions generated by equity theory and expectancy theory. *Journal of Applied Psychology*, 1981, 66, 470-81.

42. Vroom, V.H. *Work and motivation.* New York: John Wiley, 1964.

43. Weick, K.E. Reduction of cognitive dissonance through task enhancement and effort expenditure. *Journal of Abnormal and Social Psychology*, 1964, 66, 533-39.

44. Winter, D.G. The power motive in men and women. *Journal of Personality and Social Psychology*, 1988, 54(3), 510-19.

45. Wood, R.E., Mento, A.J. and Locke, E.A. Task complexity as a moderator of goal effects: A meta-analysis. *Journal of Applied Psychology*, 1987, 72, 416-425.

Chapter 8
Applications of Motivation Theories

The board of directors of CONCO approved a $20 million capital expenditure for a new manufacturing plant. They based the decision on very aggressive forecasts of return on investment and worker productivity that were prepared by the office of the vice president of production. Technologically, the plant was to be different from others in CONCO. It would have the most advanced production technology with a rated capacity 20 percent above earlier production processes. The approach to managing the work force was also to be different from the way other plants in CONCO and in the industry were managed. The typical plant was characterized by a hard-driving, directive style of supervision. Plants were heavily unionized, and there were adversarial relationships between the work force and the managers.

Even though they were under strong pressures for high productivity and profitability, the executive group responsible for the new plant decided to use a different management approach. The VP of production, the new plant manager, and the director of human resources wanted to have a work climate that would lead to high productivity as well as one that would be a positive place to work. They believed that it would be possible to achieve this combination of high performance and high satisfaction if employees (1) were highly involved in decision making, (2) worked in self-directed work groups, (3) had the skills and the opportunity to work at several different jobs, and (4) were paid on the basis of the skills they possessed and not the actual tasks they performed.

The management of CONCO wished to create a High Involvement Organization (HIO), only one of several different ways to manage the performance of organization members by attempting to create a "motivating" environment. In this chapter, we discuss a number of different managerial motivation strategies, the central element in the Motivation/Results Model developed in the previous chapter. The objective of these strategies is to raise the level of member motivation so that members will exert more effort in the direction of its goals while at the same time positively affecting member satisfaction. In general, a manager can:

1. *Define work goals so that they are clear and challenging.* The manager should ensure that subordinates know what level of performance is expected in some measurable, quantifiable terms if possible. These goals must be attainable. Unattainable goals have an E→P expectancy of zero, and very difficult goals have low E→P expectancies.

2. *Clarify what is appropriate performance.* There are often several ways to achieve a goal. For example, cost reduction for the manager of the new CONCO plant might be achieved by effective control of all costs or by omitting preventive maintenance programs. He or she should know what is considered the preferred way to achieve reduced costs. Clarifying such expectations for subordinates is an important aspect of the coaching role of the manager.

3. *Remove barriers to performance.* By providing adequate resources, training workers, or removing unnecessary bureaucratic constraints, the E→P expectancy can be increased.

4. *Know what employees value.* A group of employees may have a wide range of preferences. If a manager knows what individual preferences are, then he or she may be able to tailor some rewards to the specific values of employees.

5. *Reward performance.* Extrinsically rewarding good performance can modify the P→O expectancy of a person. To the extent that high rewards follow good performance, one can expect an employee to engage in that performance more frequently.

6. *Create an intrinsically rewarding work environment.* This can be accomplished by making the job more challenging and interesting while at the same time increasing the autonomy and responsibility of workers.

☐ MOTIVATION AND YOUNGER JAPANESE MANAGERS

Japanese workers and managers have a long standing reputation for being hard working and highly motivated. A recent study by the Hakuhodo Institute of Life and Living in Japan discovered an important difference in attitudes and motivation between younger and older white-collar workers. The older managers are still extremely loyal to the firm, are somewhat passive, do not change jobs often, and they put in 12 hour days.

☐ **MOTIVATION AND YOUNGER . . .**

> The cohort immediately behind them, in their mid 40s, is more assertive; they are more competitive, value consensus less, and prefer individual, not group challenges. They expect more leisure time than the older workers.
>
> The 30 year olds are different from both the other groups. They do not seem to be as fiercely loyal and willing to accept assignments that they are given. They want work which utilizes their skills. When they have the choice, they select jobs which demand less overtime work. They separate their work life from their private life. Finally, they are not as resourceful as their older colleagues. The report indicates that they need more direction and help from others in solving problems.
>
> *Source: The Economist.* "The Lure of Leisure." May 2, 1992, p. 81 [7].

These strategies are embodied in the many organization-wide approaches to managing performance and satisfaction. In the following sections, we will discuss some of the more widely used managerial motivation strategies which are based on the theories in the previous chapter.

HIGH INVOLVEMENT ORGANIZATIONS

The **High Involvement Organization (HIO)** is an increasingly used approach to creating an organization that promotes the motivation of employees in the work place and improves the effectiveness of the organization. Its roots are in the **Quality of Work Life (QWL)** movement which began in the 1970s. Both QWL and the HIO attempt to change the adversarial relationship between workers and managers that dominates many firms and replace it with a cooperative approach. High Involvement Organizations may use a number of different management practices, all discussed elsewhere in this book. These practices include, but are not limited to, participative decision making, self-directed work groups, job design programs to enrich work, total quality management (TQM), improved safety and working conditions, innovative compensation plans to emphasize gainsharing and skill development, the elimination of organization levels, and minimization of bureaucratic processes and practices. A survey of 1600 organizational units found that, in 1987, more than 50% used some aspect of HIO practices (see Table 8.1). In this section, we discuss some of the more common and more important aspects of HIOs: job enrichment, self-directed work groups, compensation practices, and lean organization structures.

JOB ENRICHMENT

The design of work in HIOs, usually based on the Job Characteristics Model [12], is aimed at increasing (1) skill variety, (2) task identity, (3) task significance, (4) autonomy and (5) feedback so that workers will have more meaningful jobs, a greater sense of responsibility, and more feedback. There are five basic strategies for designing jobs to increase their motivating potential [12]. Figure 8.1 shows these strategies and how they are related to the core job dimensions, critical psychological states, and personal and work outcomes.

☐ **TABLE 8.1**   Experiences with Employment Involvement Practices in Selected Firms

Involvement Practice	Firms Using (Percent)	Mean Years in Use
Small problem-solving groups	23	6.8
Quality circles	22	3.7
Team or group suggestions	21	7.9
Cross-functional employee task forces	20	7.0
Other employee involvement efforts	12	6.4
Labor/management participation teams	10	7.0
Quality of work life programs	8	5.1
Self-directed, self-managed, or autonomous work teams	8	9.4
Total using at least one employee involvement practice	50	

Source: J.C. Hoen, "Bigger Pay for Better Work," *Psychology Today,* July 1987, 57 [15].

☐ **FIGURE 8.1**   *Strategies for Implementing Job Redesign and Their Relationships to Job Characteristics*

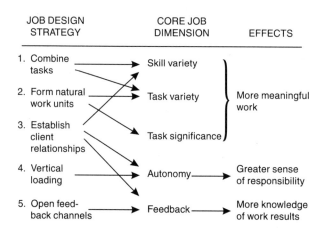

1. *Combining tasks.* Small tasks, especially those that are "fractional-ized," should be combined into larger, more complex tasks. If the new task is too large for one person, it may be assigned to a self-directed team. Combining tasks may increase *skill variety* and *task identity.*

2. *Forming natural work units.* Tasks should be grouped into units so that as much of the work as possible can be performed in the same unit. This leads to a sense of ownership of the job, increasing *task identity* and *task significance.*

3. *Establishing client relationships.* If possible, it is desirable to link the worker with the purchaser of the product or the service. Since the worker cannot often interact directly with a customer, it may be possi-ble to devise ways that the customer can give the worker feedback. If client relationships can be established, *skill variety, autonomy,* and *feedback* should improve.

4. *Vertical loading.* The job should be enriched by vertical loading, such as, adding responsibilities from higher organization levels as opposed to horizontal loading or adding more tasks from the same level. Verti-cal loading gives the person more responsibility for work. The greater amount of control will lead to an increase in the level of *perceived job autonomy.*

5. *Opening feedback channels.* There are two ways to provide feedback. *Job-provided feedback* occurs when the person knows how to judge performance from the job itself. *Management feedback* comes from the supervisor or from reports such a budgets and quality reports. Removing obstacles to increase job-related feedback will improve per-formance.

SELF-DIRECTED WORK GROUPS

While well-designed jobs can increase the sense of responsibility, the develop-ment of **self-directed work groups** places even more responsibility on the indi-viduals who make up the team. These groups, typically referred to as teams, usually have responsibility for some decisions once reserved for management. Teams may be headed by a person from the managerial ranks or may have a member of the team designated as "team leader." The team leader is usually one of the more highly skilled members, but team leadership may rotate from person to person.

Groups are encouraged to work together as a unit, identify problems and look for solutions to them, help and train each other while maintaining high quality production. Often they have responsibility for controlling other mem-bers of the team through self-regulating activities such as recommending disci-plinary action if necessary, making individual work assignments, and sometimes deciding on member pay increases [34].

THE "CRANK" TEAM: A CASE OF A SELF-DIRECTED WORK GROUP

An example of a self-directed work group is the "crank" team that was created by a plant manager to solve a very critical technical problem. The problem developed when the crankshafts in the plant's six presses began having problems. This was unusual because these presses had a history of very dependable performance in other plants. They were regarded as the best in the industry, and their reputation was built largely on this dependability. However, these presses were a new design. The old design had been modified to provide increased speed and accuracy. In this respect, the presses were different from previous models.

The plant manager and the production staff were surprised when the crankshafts started to develop cracks. One supervisor with over 16 years of experience in this industry said that he had *never* seen a crankshaft break. Engineers were consulted from the company's office headquarters of the company and from the equipment supplier. The plant manager was dissatisfied, getting little help from them, and so he took a rather bold step. He formed the "crank" team.

The "crank" team was a group of six of the best, most technically qualified workers in the plant. They were all excellent machinists, electricians, or mechanics. They had been trained by the manufacturer to perform regular maintenance on the equipment and how to run it, but they had not had any instruction beyond that. None of them was a college-trained engineer. They were just bright and competent. They had all been working in the plant since it began operations three years ago and had been involved in the installation of the equipment.

The plant manager thought the "crank" team was a good idea because he believed that his work force actually knew more about the equipment than the equipment designers. After all, it was prototype equipment and his plant was the first to be running it. In addition, he had a lot of confidence in the quality of the work force and particularly in those he put on the "crank" team.

The "crank" team members were taken from their regular work crew and assigned to the project. They were given a great deal of latitude about working schedules and design parameters. Their basic charge was to "get the presses running right." Within two months they had the problem solved. The plant manager was certain that it would have taken longer if the headquarter's engineers or the equipment manufacturer had worked on the problem. Even the equipment manufacturer agreed with him.

JOB ROTATION AND CROSS-TRAINING

HIOs invest heavily in training to achieve work force flexibility because permanent work assignments are often discouraged and **job rotation** by team members is encouraged. For example, the initial group of employees at the GM Saturn Plant received as much as 700 hours of training in the early stages of the Saturn startup [35].

To achieve this work force flexibility, HIOs use skills cross-training, problem solving training, and interpersonal training. In **cross-training**, workers are taught the various skills necessary to perform the required tasks of the group. Training also becomes an instrument of worker socialization, an important element in the screening process to be discussed below.

NEW COMPENSATION APPROACHES

To complement cross-training and job rotation, HIOs often use compensation strategies which seek to support higher productivity and performance as well as provide motivation for workers to increase their skill and competence. One such pay strategy is a **skill-based pay** system. In a skill-based pay, workers are paid for the skills they possess, not for the job on which they are working, as in more traditional pay systems. The idea is that a more versatile worker is more valuable to the organization [33]. For example, a large beverage company opened a new HIO plant in which one of the key elements was skill-based pay. At first, many managers were skeptical whether the HIO strategy would even work and felt that it would be even more difficult in an industry characterized by "hard nosed" union relationships. Instead, they found that the workers accepted the skill-based pay system, that productivity and profitability were very high. Surprisingly, there was much more management flexibility since workers were willing to move to different jobs as needed since they would not suffer any wage rate change that might occur under a more traditional wage system.

Also, HIO firms often develop profit-sharing or gainsharing compensation programs. These are designed to share increases in profitability and productivity with the workers. Some plans, like the Scanlon Plan (detailed later in this chapter), share cost savings that result from worker suggested improvements. Productivity-sharing plans distribute the gains achieved by increased productivity.

LEANER MANAGEMENT STRUCTURES

When the nature of the compensation system and the design of the jobs themselves create increased motivation, a greater sense of responsibility, and more self-direction on the part of workers, there is less need for supervision. To put it another way, if workers are able to monitor their own job performance because accurate task feedback is available about a challenging job for which there are performance incentives, there is less need to have a supervisor looking over the workers' shoulders. After successful implementation of HIO philosophy and practice, it is often the case that at least one level of management is eliminated from the organization. In the beverage plant described above, the use of the self-directed work groups, skill-based pay, and higher worker participation resulted in one less layer of management than similar plants in the industry. This meant that there were three to five fewer managers, a saving of between $180,000 and $270,000 each year.

TOTAL QUALITY MANAGEMENT (TQM)

A sharply focused effort on the improvement of product or service quality may be a part of the HIO philosophy and process, often with some sort of **Total Quality Management (TQM)** program [5]. The guiding principle is to create a system of processes embedded in an organization climate that are totally dedicated to the customer. The goals are to create highly loyal customers, minimize the time required to respond to problems, develop a culture that supports teamwork, design work systems that increase motivation and lead to more satisfying and meaningful work, and maintain a focus on continuous improvement [5].

There is no single method for organizations to achieve these goals, though there seem to be some techniques common to most approaches to TQM. For example, statistical quality control methods are used to identify causes of quality problems and to measure improvements that take place, close relationships are developed with suppliers (such as Just-In-Time (JIT) inventory systems) to minimize inventory expenses, and benchmarking is used to identify other organizations to be used as a base for comparison to the firm's activities. TQM also uses some approaches from other applied motivational strategies such as Management by Objectives and Organizational Behavior Modification, as we will show later in this chapter.

MINIMIZING WORKER/MANAGEMENT STATUS DIFFERENTIALS

The lean management structure, along with the use of self-directed work groups, has another implication for managers. Instead of the traditional managerial role of direction and supervision, managers must take more facilitating roles, place more trust in the workers, and take a hands-off approach. At the same time, workers must believe that managers will not violate the integrity of those areas in which the group has been delegated the responsibility for self-direction. Some companies, such as NCR, Domino's Pizza, and Donnelly Mirrors refer to employees as "stakeholders" or "associates" to reinforce the more cooperative and trusting culture which they are trying to develop.

This trust relationship can only develop when the work force is well informed and feels secure that management is not hiding anything, and after some history develops that management does, in fact, trust the work groups. Managers must therefore give up hierarchical control and must necessarily act as team leaders, coaches, and facilitators.

NON-TRADITIONAL SELECTION AND SOCIALIZATION PRACTICES

The HIO, obviously, requires an organization culture which is different from the more hierarchical, traditional models of management to which many employees are accustomed. This means that the person-organization fit will be of a different type than in those traditional firms. Bringing people into HIOs often is done with an approach that is specifically designed to bring "a 'whole' person who will fit well into the organization's culture" [2]. They tend to use relatively "thick" screening procedures and carefully designed socialization processes, especially when the HIO is a startup organization.

This **thick screening process**, for example, will include the assessment of technical knowledge, skills, and abilities using written tests or performance tests. Personality tests, which assess the capacity to work in teams, to act independently, to accept responsibility, and to tolerate ambiguity can also be used. Usually applicants face a series of interviews both with managers and members of the team on which they might work. Finally, there are strong socialization processes such as training or other "rites of passage" which applicants experience [2].

The thickness of the screening process may vary, depending upon the desire to ensure that members fit well with the culture. For example, in one startup organization, the selection screen was very thick. First, every applicant for non-managerial jobs was required to attend, without pay, a pre-employment course in which basic manufacturing skills were taught. The course was designed by the company and covered such areas as blueprint reading, mathematics, safety, and mechanical design and repair. There was competence testing during the course, and individual scores were among the factors used in selection. Second, the applicants were interviewed by at least seven managers, including team supervisors. These interviews were intended to assess technical skills, interpersonal skills, and potential for working within the HIO culture. Interviewers looked for initiative, good communication skills, the ability to work without supervision, and a high achievement orientation. Third, employment offers were made by the plant manager to the successful applicants in the presence of spouses or significant others.

IMPLEMENTING THE *HIO* CONCEPT

It is much easier to design a High Involvement Organization philosophy and structure for a new organizational unit, such as a new manufacturing plant. Then these different elements can be in place when the managers and workers begin operating it. There will be no need to change an existing culture. The greater challenge is to be successful in creating an HIO to replace the management philosophy and approach of an existing organization. In either case, however, the implementation efforts must be widely supported in spirit by the effort of the management. There is often resistance to HIO concepts from both the worker side and the management side which must be overcome. Resistance arises because changes are not well understood by some workers and by some managers, and such problems may have implications for the redistribution of power [2]. In some instances, supervisors lose power and feel threatened. Also, unions have not always supported such efforts because they believe that changes in jobs should be a subject of contract negotiation.

Some guidelines for implementing these concepts come from an analysis of the differences between successful and unsuccessful job design programs [11]:

1. *Diagnose the work system.* Some jobs cannot be easily changed because the technology limits much modification. To try to change these tasks may end in failure. A diagnosis will point to those jobs that show greatest potential for improvement and will highlight problems that need to be solved before any job design is implemented.

2. *Focus on job changes.* Jobs must be modified and not just talked about. In many cases, attempts to change jobs are planned by managers and staff. Announcements are made about the program, but nothing happens to the work.

3. *Anticipate problems.* When there is a major change in jobs, other effects must be anticipated. Changing one job will have effects on other jobs.

4. *Deal with difficult problems early.* Some important matters must be resolved before these complex programs are implemented. These must be discussed openly and consensus reached early. Some of the more difficult issues are:

   a. How strong is the commitment of the worker, the management, and the union, if there is one?

   b. What standards will be used to evaluate the success of the HIO effort?

   c. How will problems that are uncovered be solved?

5. *Ensure that the organization's culture is consistent with HIO practices and procedures.* Often managers are attracted to the HIO concept because of its potential for improving organization effectiveness without understanding that managerial practice and the organizational culture must be HIO compatible. For example, an authoritarian culture which fosters status differentials between managers and workers will be a disastrous context for an HIO organization. Therefore, early in the implementation process, the culture should be analyzed to determine this fit, and appropriate organizational development methods should be undertaken, if necessary.

THE EFFECTIVENESS OF HIGH INVOLVEMENT ORGANIZATIONS

There are many well documented instances of firms, large and small, which have successfully created High Involvement Organizations. Perhaps the most famous and earliest case is that of Volvo [29]. In Sweden, Volvo changed the process of auto manufacturing from an assembly-line process to a work team system. Work teams were responsible for different components and for the assembly itself. It one plant, the workers were organized with 30 teams of 15 to 20 workers. These teams not only worked on the assembly process but also met with management to discuss problems and recommend ways to improve performance. In this plant, turnover was drastically reduced and down time was cut. There were some cost increases, but these were thought to be short-

☐ DIFFICULTIES WITH HIOS

Even in cases that are thought to be successful, the High Involvement Organization concept can be difficult. General Motors' Saturn plant, which was built upon the HIO philosophy, began to experience some problems after a few years of operation. When opened in the late 1980s, the work force was almost completely supportive of a non-union plant, but recently about 30 percent voted to return to the more traditional labor-management style of an arm's length relationship instead of the cooperation necessary in HIOs.

The company, because of production pressures, has had to make some changes in its approach to managing the work force. Whereas in the beginning workers received many hours of training, it is now necessary to reduce the amount of worker training. In addition, Saturn is now beginning to hire a large number of new employees who, not being part of the initial training and indoctrination into HIOs, may prove to be less committed. There has also been pressure that is a result of the increase in the work week from 40 to 50 hours to meet demand. All these problems are making it more difficult to maintain the cooperative spirit that the Saturn plant was noted when it opened.

Source: David Woodruff, Saturn: Labor's love lost? *Business Week*, February 9, 1993, pp. 122-123 [35].

run problems. Other successful experiments have been conducted at Indiana Bell, General Foods, and the General Motors Saturn Plant.

There is even stronger support than the anecdotal case study provides. Three meta-analyses of job enrichment show that enriched jobs are associated with higher performance and higher job satisfaction [8, 10, 30]. Guzzo and his colleagues concluded that job enrichment had some of the strongest effects on worker productivity than any type of intervention [10]. Fried and Farris found that more enriched jobs were related to higher performances [8]. However, the effects were not large. One reason for the modest effects may be seen from the following studies, both generally supportive of job enrichment strategies. The first is an analysis of the effects of quality circles (QCs), a common element of HIO efforts [21]. It showed that workers who participated in QCs were more satisfied with participation in decision making, the opportunity to make suggestions, organizational communication, and opportunity for advancement than the workers who were not involved in quality circles. Figure 8.2 shows the changes in rates of productivity achieved. There were also some differences between the two groups in terms of performance. Over a 30-month period, the quality circle groups had greater increases than the nonparticipants in the percentage of time spent on production, efficiency, and productivity. The QC group also lowered its absenteeism rate more rapidly than the nonparticipants.

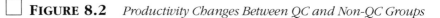

□ FIGURE 8.2 *Productivity Changes Between QC and Non-QC Groups*

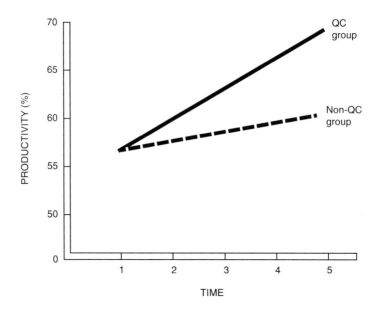

Another study of QCs found that there were improvements in job satisfaction, organization commitment, and performance when quality circles were introduced into manufacturing plants of a medium-size electronics plant [9]. These gains continued for an 18-month period, then began to deteriorate, eventually returning to their original levels. Still, the management of the firm generally believed that there were other long-term gains that would continue to benefit the company.

These results suggest that job design approaches have effects similar to those found with other types of managerial motivation approaches in organizations: there is often an initial gain when implemented, but then some regression toward previous performance levels. This occurs because the "new" approach just gets old to the organization members, and/or the management commitment to it diminishes. In Chapter 17, we will suggest some ways that may be used to improve the long-term effectiveness of programs such as this.

MANAGEMENT BY OBJECTIVES (MBO)

Management by Objectives (MBO) is probably the most popular and most widely implemented approach to managerial motivation over the past 30 years. Many of the largest firms in the United States and Europe, among them companies such as Purex, Black & Decker, ARA Services, and Tenneco have made systematic efforts to build MBO into their management philosophy. It has not always been successful because it is not easy to implement.

MBO is a process in which the individual members of an organization work with one another to identify common goals and coordinate their efforts in reaching them. The positive effects of MBO in organizations can be explained by goal-setting theory, but it had been advocated and implemented long before goal-setting theory was developed [17]. Peter Drucker, Douglas McGregor, and George Odiorne were advocating MBO in the late 1950s and early 1960s [6, 22, 25].

Two things must be done to use MBO effectively. First, it is necessary to implement it organization-wide. Second, each manager and subordinate must be willing and able to work with goal setting. A superior and a subordinate attempt to reach a consensus on (1) what goals the subordinate will attempt to achieve in a given time period, (2) the means by which the subordinate will attempt to accomplish the goals, and (3) how and when progress toward goals will be assessed. After there is agreement, the superior will periodically review performance, possibly quarterly, along with a final performance review at the end of the year. It is complicated to use MBO because it is no simple matter to set specific goals and measure them in the world of managing.

ORGANIZATIONAL IMPLEMENTATION OF MBO

The major problem with using MBO occurs when it is not strongly supported by management throughout an organization [27]. If some managers use it and others do not, then the positive effects aren't likely to occur [4]. These are the reasons for cases in which MBO fails in organizations rather than for any theoretical weaknesses.

The responsibility for developing overall organizational goals is typically top management's—usually the chief executive's—in conjunction with the board of directors or a group of vice presidents. Once these goals are developed, subunit goals (marketing, production, etc.) are stated, usually in the form of general plans. When these have been developed, they are communicated to the next-lower levels. This can be done by a series of cascading meetings between superiors and their subordinates and work groups, continuing from the top management level to the lowest point of supervision.

THE EFFECTIVENESS OF MANAGEMENT BY OBJECTIVES

When management is strongly committed to building an objectives-oriented approach into its organizational culture and philosophy, the payoffs can be very high. A meta-analysis of the effects of MBO in companies that attempted to implement it showed that in those organizations with "high commitment" to the implementation of MBO, the average gain in the productivity was 56 percent. The productivity increase in companies with "low commitment" to implementation was only 6 percent, a dramatic difference [27]. In addition, analysis of the effects of MBO on job satisfaction showed that satisfaction increased with the implementation of MBO, regardless of the degree of organizational commitment *or* the increase in productivity. These results seem especially persuasive for two reasons. First, these are evaluations of actual organizations in which MBO was implemented [27]. The findings of these studies in the world of work nicely confirm those in the laboratory, which formed the basis for goal-setting theory [18]. Second, these studies used managers as subjects, not clerks, students, or workers. They give strong support to the use of MBO as an applied managerial motivation strategy.

One final point that is useful to note, total quality management (TQM) programs have the goal setting dimension of MBO. They focus very sharply on quality as an organization objective.

POSITIVE-REINFORCEMENT/OB MOD PROGRAMS

Reinforcement theory is the basis of positive-reinforcement programs and **organizational behavior modification (OB Mod)** programs. The basic premise of these programs is that to improve performance (change behavior) it is necessary to change the stimulus (antecedents) and the consequences (reinforcers, punishments, and so on).

Figure 8.3 illustrates the steps in a positive-reinforcement program [14]. The first step is to identify the specific behaviors that are to be changed; they must be accurately and reliably observed and then recorded. The behavior should be observable and measurable. Behaviors are observed and usually recorded on a chart of some sort to establish a baseline rate, the basis against which behavior change is measured. Suppose that we wish to improve the quality of secretarial work. In the first stage of a positive-reinforcement program, we would record the error rates of each secretary in the office.

☐ **FIGURE 8.3**   *Positive Reinforcement Program Components*

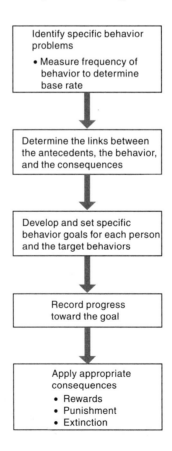

The second step is to determine the links between the target behavior, its consequences, and its stimuli. Suppose this sequence can be diagrammed as shown in Figure 8.4. The analysis shows that there are no negative consequences for low performance nor are there positive consequences for high performance.

FIGURE 8.4   *Behavioral Diagnosis in Positive Reinforcement*

The next step shown in Figure 8.3 is to develop a specific goal for the secretary for the target behavior, reducing error rates. These goals should be stated in the same way as the behavior was defined in the first step. We might, for example, start with a goal of reducing typing errors by 30 percent.

Recording progress toward the goal is the next step. Generally it is best for the person to maintain his or her own personal record to measure progress.

> This process of self-feedback maintains a continuous schedule of reinforcement for the worker and helps . . . obtain intrinsic reinforcement from the task. Where employees can total their own results, they can see whether they are meeting their goals and whether they are improving over their previous performance levels [14].

The final step is to ensure that the consequences of behavior are the ones that are likely to lead to the desired result. Basically, the supervisor must make every effort to positively reinforce the desired behavior when it occurs. This can be done by observing the charted record. When the employee makes performance changes in the desired direction, the manager must apply the positive consequence.

Reinforcers can take many different forms. One of the strongest is praise and recognition for good work. Others are money (when it is a consequence of good performance), some autonomy in choosing work assignments, opportunities to improve one's status and self-esteem, and, lastly, power to influence co-workers and management. Table 8.2 is a list of some rewards that managers believe they can use for reinforcers. Many more could be added to such a list.

THE EFFECTIVENESS OF POSITIVE-REINFORCEMENT PROGRAMS

These programs have been widely used in some of the largest and best-managed U.S. organizations. Major improvements in productivity, reductions in turnover, and improved safety have resulted when such programs are properly implemented. When performance-contingent rewards were given to salesclerks, performance increased [20]. Orpen found higher performance and higher satisfaction were linked to performance-contingent rewards [26]. Hamner and Hamner analyzed the results of "positive reinforcement" programs in

☐ **TABLE 8.2**   Classifications of On-the-Job Rewards

Consumables	Manipulatables	Visual and Auditory	Tokens	Social
Coffee-break treats	Desk accessories	Office with a window	Money	Friendly greetings
Free lunches	Personal computer	Piped-in music	Stocks	Informal recognition
Food baskets	Wall plaques	Redecoration of work environment	Stock options	Formal acknowl-edgement of achievement
Easter hams	Company car		Movie passes	
Christmas turkeys	Watches		Trading stamps (green stamps)	
Dinners for the family on the company	Trophies	Company literature	Paid-up insurance policies	Feedback about performance
	Recommend-ations	Private office		Solicitations of suggestions
Company picnics	Rings/tie pins	Popular speakers or lecturers	Dinner/theater/sports tickets	Solicitations of advice
After-work wine and cheese parties	Appliances and furniture for the home	Book club discussions	Vacation trips	Compliment on work progress
	Home shop tools		Coupons redeemable at local stores	Recognition in house organ
	Garden tools		Profit sharing	Pat on the back
	Clothing			Smile
	Club privileges			Verbal or nonverbal recognition or praise

Source: From F. Luthans and R. Kreitner, *Organizational Behavior Modification and Beyond* (Glenview, Ill.: Scott, Foresman, 1985), 127. Reprinted with permission [19].

Michigan Bell, Connecticut General Life Insurance, General Electric, and B.F. Goodrich [14]. These companies used praise, recognition, and other nondirect compensation (time off or freedom to choose activities) as reinforcers for production workers. These reinforcers were quite effective in bringing about improvements in attendance and increased performance. Praising supervisors has reduced hazardous conditions in departments [31]. Some companies are also designing reward systems to encourage managers to pay more attention to long-run, rather than short-run, interests of the organization [32].

The requirements for effective implementation of positive reinforcement programs are: [14]

1. *Reward people with what they value.* Unless someone values a reward, it is not likely to affect their behavior. There are several ways to discover what people value. One is to use consequences that are widely valued, such as praise, a smile, or recognition. Another is to ask people. A third is to observe how a person uses free time on and off the job to find out what they like or dislike.

2. *Link the reward to the behavior.* This can be accomplished by first clarifying what might constitute outstanding performance. The connection can also be made by rewarding very soon after performance or by verbally explaining why the employee is being rewarded.

3. *Fit the magnitude of the reward to the magnitude of the behavior.* A small reward such as a brief word of praise is insufficient for a rather substantial contribution by an employee. It is also possible to overact to performance, such as putting a story about the employee in the company newspaper and throwing a party when the performance was not sustained or outstanding. This rule requires some judgment.

4. *Better performers should be rewarded more than average performers.* Who complains when every employee gets the same reward treatment? The best performers do, and there is not much that can be said to the best employees when they have *not* been differentially recognized. Who complains when the best employees are rewarded better? The poorer performers are more likely to make inquiries. Thus, when using such discrimination in rewards, the manager needs to prepare for questions raised by the poorer employees and attempt to improve their performance.

5. *Reward more often.* Many managers are stingy with rewards either because they are embarrassed to give them or because they fear the employee might become "spoiled." Good rewarding does not mean giving employees whatever they want whenever they want it. Good rewarding is based on the existence of performance standards, and if the reward is linked to performance, it need not lead to the spoiling effect.

6. *Reward after performance.* Avoid rewarding before the behavior takes place. For example, suppose a supervisor grants a merit raise to an employee and explains to the employee that the raise is an act of good faith and that the employee will improve on unacceptable performance in the future. This might work on the rare occasion that the employee agrees he or she needs to shape up and really respects the supervisor. Usually, however, the reward will act as a reinforcement for past behavior. The employee might conclude that his or her behavior couldn't have been *that* bad, or the boss would never have granted the merit pay.

Positive reinforcement is good rewards management. It shifts the emphasis and energy of the manager toward a larger number of employees, rather than focus all the attention and time mainly on poorer employees. It can be handled in a way that makes all but the worst employees feel that the organization recognizes and appreciates their effort and contributions.

PRODUCTIVITY GAIN-SHARING APPROACHES/THE SCANLON PLAN

Gainsharing plans provide bonuses to employees based on profit improvement, cost savings, or productivity increases achieved as a result of the employees' contribution of ideas or more productive work effort [28]. The *Rucker Plan* is based on the value added to the product. This is assessed by measuring the difference between the market value of the product and the costs of materials, supplies, and services used in the production process. As this value added to the product increases, workers receive a percentage of the increase. The *Improshare Plan* pays a bonus to both production and non-production workers for improvements in productivity based on assessment of base productivity measures.

The **Scanlon Plan** is one of the more widely known and oldest of the gainsharing approaches. It was developed as a way to integrate the interests of the work force with the interests of the company so that there would be a strong spirit of cooperation between labor and management. In the Scanlon Plan, this is achieved by creating an environment in which the employees have a good deal of information about the company's situation, both problems and successes, and an opportunity to contribute to the solution of the problems. A key element of this play is that the employees benefit, through pay, from the problems that they help to solve [23].

The Scanlon Plan is a participatory philosophy of management that involves using a pay incentive system and a suggestion system [23]. It is not simply a method of incentive payment, such as a sales commission plan or a piece-rate system. It is much broader than that because in the Scanlon Plan the work force must be involved in many different ways. It requires not only a commitment to **participative decision making** and joint problem solving but also an organization structure and management style that is congruent with participative decision making and joint problem solving [16].

The core of the Scanlon Plan is (1) a system of committees for intergroup cooperation between labor and management in which efforts are made to find ways to reduce costs and (2) a formula for determining and sharing the cost savings. These cost savings are shared by the workers and by the company [1].

HOW THE SCANLON PLAN WORKS.

Figure 8.5 shows how the Scanlon process operates. There is an organizational climate characterized by high levels of trust between the workers and management. Workers and management are both willing to take responsibility for their actions and to share the responsibility of decision making. The climate also is conducive to participative decision making. This leads to the second step, the participative opportunity. Workers and management together seek ways to improve the operation so that productivity increases. Productivity increases result in a bonus to the workers when the workers are responsible for them. This leads to a sense of equity that results from the belief that workers share in gains that they help to generate. Finally, the effects should be improved levels of job satisfaction and organizational commitment.

Figure 8.5 shows three feedback loops that are critical to the success of the Scanlon Plan [24]. First, there must be mechanisms that communicate how well the participation system is working. For the climate to remain supportive, both workers and management must continually work together. Second, productivity and pay information must be shared in order for the climate to stay supportive. Finally, when workers and managers perceive that pay is equitable and there is high commitment, the climate is further strengthened.

☐ **FIGURE 8.5** *Scanlon Plan Components*

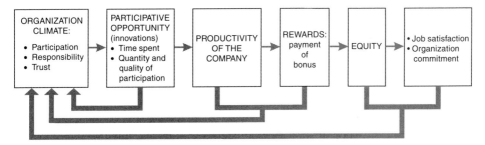

There are two types of committees that operate in the Scanlon Plan: *production committees* and *screening committees* [1]. Production committees are spread throughout the organization. There are members of management and labor on these committees, but the committee usually is dominated by the workers. These committees meet regularly (usually monthly) to find ways to operate better. When a suggestion for improvement is agreed on by the production committee in a department, it is implemented. If there is disagreement or if the proposal requires the cooperation of other units, then the proposal goes to the screening committee.

The screening committee is a plant-wide group with equal representation from the workers and the management. The committee has

> three major tasks: (1) to determine the bonus for the month, (2) to hear reports from management about any factors that might influence future operations of the plant, and (3) to act upon any material that has come to them from the various production committees. Management reserves the right to accept or reject suggestions, but . . . the acceptance rate under this system is high [1].

The formula for calculating cost savings that are the basis for the bonus paid to the workers is an important element in the Scanlon Plan. These formulas are usually quite complex and often take several years to work out so that they are "right." A base cost point is selected against which current costs and cost savings can be compared, and the cost savings are split between the company and the workers [23]. The savings must be a result of the worker suggestions, since capital improvements arising out of technological improvements are not part of the Scanlon Plan savings for distribution to workers. Obviously complicated accounting matters enter into this calculation, sometimes making it questionable. This is, of course, one of the reasons why it is necessary for a climate of trust and mutual cooperation to exist between labor and management.

REQUIREMENTS FOR EFFECTIVE GAINSHARING PLAN.

From a meta-analysis of 33 case studies of gainsharing plans, Bullock and Tubbs have shown that when they are implemented well, they can have very positive effects on firm performance regardless of factors such as organization size, the presence of a union, technology differences, or the firm's environment [3]. Among the important factors are:

1. Employee involvement in the design of the plan.

2. Employee favorability toward gainsharing.

3. The existence of formal involvement structures, such as the production committees and the screening committees.

4. A participative management style in the organization.

5. The use of outside consultants in the design and implementation of gainsharing.

SUMMARY

Managerial motivation strategies are a key element in the Motivation/Results Model discussed in the previous chapter. These are attempts to act on human factors, within technological constraints, to increase a person's drive to conform. We considered several ways that organizations attempt to develop company-wide approaches to motivation of members.

The High Involvement Organization (HIO) is an approach that has been growing in popularity in the United States. The goals are to increase productivity, quality, and satisfaction of the work force. There are many variations in the elements that make up High Involvement programs. Self-directed work groups, worker participation, leaner management structures, total quality management, and job enrichment are some of the more frequently used elements.

Management by Objectives (MBO) is the organization application of goal-setting theory. In MBO, managers at all organizational levels set goals with subordinates. This goal setting, if done right, coordinates activities within the firm as well as providing specific and difficult targets. The goals set also provide a useful basis for performance appraisal.

Reinforcement theory is the underlying basis of organizational behavior modification programs. They focus on changing the antecedents (stimuli) and consequences of behavior (reinforcers, punishments, and so on) to improve performance. This approach can be quite effective when the conditions are such that desired behaviors can be identified and rewards associated with them.

Productivity gainsharing is an attempt to increase the involvement of workers and management more directly in the performance of the organization by giving them a greater stake in the firm's profitability. In all gainsharing programs, workers and/or managers make income above regular wages and salaries if profitability can be increased through their contributions. These increases may be a share of increased earnings or a share of increased savings.

All of these managerial motivation strategies are complex and difficult to implement effectively in organizations. They demand a great deal of managerial knowledge and persistence but have potential to bring about improvements in performance.

☐ KEY CONCEPTS

Cross-training	Managerial	Quality of work life
Gainsharing	motivation	Scanlon Plan
High involvement	strategies	Self-directed work
organizations	Organizational	group
Job enrichment	behavior	Skill-based pay
Job rotation	modification	Thick screening process
Management	Participative	Total Quality
by Objectives	decision making	Management

☐ STUDY QUESTIONS

1. What is Management by Objectives? Relate it to goal-setting theory. What are some differences that you can see between goal-setting theory and the practice of MBO?

2. Do an analysis of your own study habits using the positive-reinforcement/OB Mod approach discussed in the chapter.

3. Why is it difficult to link reinforcements to performance at work? For what type of work can this be done most easily?

4. What is the Scanlon Plan? Why does it work? Under what conditions can it work best?

5. Reflecting on other relevant chapters in this book, what does it take to create effective self-directed work groups?

6. What are the strengths and weaknesses of skill-based pay? Based on your knowledge of reinforcement theory, what behaviors should increase? Decrease?

7. Analyze the total quality management concept from the perspective of goal setting theory and reinforcement theory. How does it differ from organizational behavior modification?

8. The HIO movement is growing in the United States. Why do you think so? What are some implications for the work force?

9. What are the key implementing concepts for job design?

10. What is the effect of organization culture on any one of the managerial motivation strategies discussed in this chapter?

CASE

☐ INTERNATIONAL LID COMPANY

The International Lid Company makes lids for aluminum beverage cans. The company is about to open a new plant, which increases their capacity by 25 percent. This will make International the largest lid producer in the world.

The lid that they will produce in this plant will be used on beverage cans, beer, and soft drinks. It is a lid with an attached opening tab, which allows the consumer to open the can, but the lid stays attached. This means that opening tabs are not separate from the lid, making it very attractive from an ecological point of view.

The lid is somewhat complicated to produce (see the figure below). Large aluminum coils are fed into the lid press, which stamps out round lid shells with a curled edge. The press discharges these shells on both sides, as shown in Figure 1. The shells then go to the liner, where an adhesive is applied. This adhesive is important in sealing the can when it is filled at the brewery or at the soft drink plant.

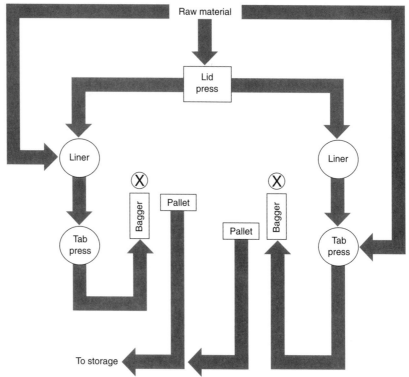

THE BASIC PRODUCTION SYSTEM

☐ INTERNATIONAL LID . . .

From the liner, the shell goes to the tab press where the opening tabs are attached. A narrow strip of aluminum is fed into the tab press, and the tab is formed and attached to the round shell. This machine works with very tight tolerances because there are several critical operations. First a light score (cut) must be cut into the lid so that the tab will open when pressure is applied. This score must be deep enough so that the lid is easy to open but not so deep that the lid will leak under pressure. Attaching the tab is also a very difficult process because of the way the metal is stressed.

From the tab press, the lids are conveyed to a bagging station. Here they are placed in long paper sleeves, the date and time of production are noted, and they are stacked on a pallet. When the pallet is full, it is then transported to the finished goods inventory storage area.

On each line, there are only two tasks that require the constant presence of a worker (as long as the lines are running smoothly). These are the bagging tasks, which are shown in Figure 1 with an X. The remainder of the equipment requires monitoring to ensure that production meets specifications and to maintain the raw-material inputs. Minor maintenance must also be done during regular operations and, if there are serious problems, major maintenance.

The new plant will have three production lines. The general layout is shown in the following figure. There will be adequate inventory areas, a quality control room, and a machine shop. The plant's equipment will be the most modern in the industry, and it is expected that the equipment will run in a very predictable, dependable way.

The management team has been selected for the plant by the executives of International Lid. They have chosen three top manufacturing managers. Ronald Gary has had 10 years of production experience at other International plants, Joe Bonn has been a supervisor and assistant plant manager for many years at another can company, and John Zerley is a bright young engineer from the home office. Together they are going to determine how the plant will be run.

They have a manufacturing manpower budget of 20 persons on each work team. A work team operates the plant during a shift. Gary, Bonn, and Zerley believe that it will be necessary to have the following work assignments set for certain of the 20 workers. There must be at least 6 baggers, 4 workers in quality control, and 2 workers to move raw materials to the lines and to transport goods to inventory. For the remaining staff, they believe it will be necessary to have at least one man-day committed to maintenance and one man-day to a utility worker. They are now trying to decide how to assign the remaining workers.

☐ **International Lid . . .**

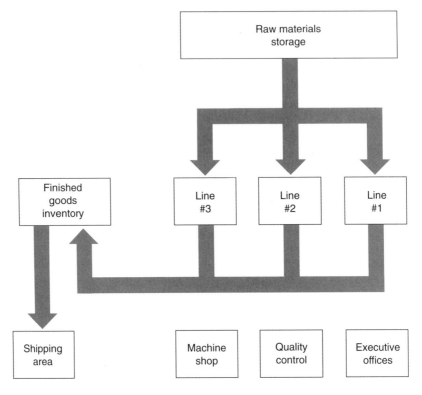

Questions

1. What has to be done to make International Lids a "High-Involvement" organization?
2. How could the concepts of OB Modification be used in the design of the work system?
3. What are the implications for the top management group (Gary, Bonn, and Zerley)?

References

1. Alderfer, C. Group and intergroup relations. In J.R. Hackman and J.L. Suttle, eds. *Improving life at work: Behavioral science approaches to organizational change.* Santa Monica, CA: Goodyear Publishing, 1977.
2. Bowen, D. E., Ledford, G. E., and Nathan, B. R. Hiring for the organization, not the job. *Academy of Management Executive,* 1991, 5(4), 35-51.
3. Bullock, R.J. & Tubbs, M.E. A case meta-analysis of gainsharing plans as organization development interventions. *The Journal of Applied Behavioral Science,* 1990, 26(3), 383-404.
4. Carroll, S.J., and Tosi H.L. *Management by Objectives: Applications and research.* New York: Macmillan, 1973.

5. Ciampa, D. *Total Quality: A User's Guide for Implementation*. Massachusetts: Addison-Wesley Publishing Company, 1992.

6. Drucker, P. *The practice of management*. New York: Harper, 1954.

7. *The Economist*, The lure of leisure, May 2, 1992, 81.

8. Fried, Y., and Farris, G. The validity of the job characteristics approach: A review and meta-analysis. *Personnel Psychology*, 1987, 40, 287-322.

9. Griffin, R. Consequences of quality circles in an industrial setting: A longitudinal assessment. *Academy of Management Journal*, 1988, 30:2, 338-58.

10. Guzzo, R., Jenne, R.D., and Katzell, R. The effects of psychologically based intervention programs on worker productivity: A meta-analysis. *Personnel Psychology*. 1985, 38, 275-91.

11. Hackman, J.R. Work design. In J.R. Hackman and J.L. Suttle, eds. *Improving life at work: Behavioral science approaches to organizational change*. Santa Monica, CA: Goodyear Publishing, 1977, 96-162.

12. Hackman, J.R., Oldham, G.R., Janson, R., and Purdy, K. A new strategy for job enrichment. *California Management Review*, 1975, 17, 57-71.

13. Hackman, J.R., and Oldham, G.R. Motivation through the design of work: Test of a theory. *Organizational Behavior and Human Performance*, 1976, 16, 250-79.

14. Hamner, W.C., and Hamner, E.P. Behavior modification on the bottom line. *Organization Dynamics*, 1976, 4, 8-21.

15. Hoen, J.C. Bigger pay for better work. *Psychology Today*, July 1987, 57.

16. Lawler, E.E. New approaches to pay: Innovations that work. *Personnel*, 1976, 53, 11-24.

17. Locke, E.A. Toward a theory of task motivation and incentives. *Organization Behavior and Human Performance*, 1968, 3, 152-89.

18. Locke, E.A., and Latham, G.P. *A Theory of Goal Setting and Task Performance*. New Jersey: Prentice Hall Inc., 1990.

19. Luthans, F., and Kreitner, R. *Organizational behavior modification and beyond: An operant and social learning approach*, 2nd ed. Glenview, IL: Scott, Foresman, 1985.

20. Luthans, F., Paul, R., and Baker, D. An experimental analysis of the impact of contingent reinforcement on salespersons' performance behavior. *Journal of Applied Psychology*, 1981, 66(3), 314-23.

21. Marks, M.L., Hackett, E.J., Mirvis, P.H., and Grady, J.F. Employee participation in a quality circle program: Impact on quality of work life, productivity and absenteeism. *Journal of Applied Psychology*, 1986, 71(1), 61-69.

22. McGregor, D. An uneasy look at performance appraisal. *Harvard Business Review*, 1957, 35, 89-94.

23. Milkovich, G.T., and Newman, J.M. *Compensation*. Plano, TX: Business Publications, Inc., 1987.

24. Monge, P., Farace, V., Frost, C., and Greenwood, W. Relationship of the Scanlon participative management program to organizational innovation, productivity, and interorganizational innovation transfer. Paper. Michigan State University, 1982.

25. Odiorne, G.S. *Management by Objectives*. Los Angeles: Pitman, 1965.

26. Orpen, C. The effects of contingent and noncontingent rewards on employee satisfaction and performance. *Journal of Psychology*, January 1982, 110(1), 145-50.

27. Rodgers, R., and Hunter, J.E. Impact of management by objectives on organizational productivity. *Journal of Applied Psychology*, 1991, 76(2), 322-336.

28. Scarpello, V., and Ledvinka, J. *Personnel/human resource management.* Boston, MA: PWS-Kent, 1988.

29. Schleicher, W.F. Volvo: New directions in work technology. *Machine Tool Blue Book.* Wheaton, IL:Hitchcock Publications, 1977, 74- 85.

30. Stone, E.F. Job scope-job satisfaction and job scope-job performance relationships. In E.A. Locke, *Generalizing from laboratory to field settings.* Lexington, MA: Lexington Book Company, 1986.

31. Sulzer-Azaroff, B., and DeSantamaria, M.C. Industrial safety hazard reduction through performance feedback. *Journal of Applied Behavioral Analysis*, 1980, 13, 287-95.

32. Tosi, H.L. & Gomez-Mejia, L. The decoupling of CEO pay and performance: an agency theory perspective. *Administrative Science Quarterly*, 1989, 34, 169-189.

33. Tosi, H.L., and Tosi, L.A. What managers need to know about knowledge-based pay. *Organizational Dynamics.* Fall, 1986, 52-64.

34. Tosi, H.L., Zahrly, J., and Vaverek, K. The Relationship of worker adaptation and productivity to new technology and management practices: A study of the emergence of a sociotechnical system. Organization Studies Center, Graduate School of Business Administration, University of Florida, 1990.

35. Woodruff, D. Saturn: Labor's love lost? *Business Week*, February 8, 1993.

☐ **Chapter 9**

Stress

Sam Allen was admitted to the hospital with a bad case of hives. Large red welts had broken out all over his body causing such serious pain that his physician, John Gibbs, put him in the hospital. Sam didn't like—and he didn't believe—John Gibbs' explanation of why he had the hives. John told Sam that it was his new job as Director of Marketing that caused the problem.

Sam had time to think about that explanation. When Arnie Heston had told him that he was going to be the new director of marketing, Sam was pleased. For the past six years, he had put in long, hard hours in his job as a sales engineer, and it had paid off.

After he moved into the director of marketing's office, he was struck by how different the job was from his old one as sales engineer. As a sales engineer, Sam set his own schedule. He was away from the office most of the time because he was calling on his customers. He had a lot of control over when and where he worked. He worked hard, but he worked on his own schedule. And another part of his old job he liked was that he always knew how well he was doing by simply getting his current sales figures.

The new job was different. Sam had more status, a nicer office, a better car, and a secretary. But the things that began to get to him, he thought, were those that were out of his control. For instance, his appointment calendar was always full. Usually these appointments were made by someone other than Sam. Now he reported to Bryan Kraft, the vice president of marketing. Kraft was a high producer, but he was difficult to work for. For example, at least once a week he would, on short notice, call a meeting at 4:30 that would last until 7:30 or 8:00 P.M. Bryan always apologized for "cutting into family time," but after the meeting he would want everyone to come out for dinner and drinks with him. It was his way of making up for the imposition. Most of the staff went because they thought Bryan wanted them to go along. For Sam that meant he would get home at midnight. He missed putting his children to bed and his wife Adrienne, a lawyer, wasn't particularly pleased with the late hours.

Sam also began to feel uneasy about the fact that now he didn't have control over his own success. Instead of producing his own sales, now the people who worked on his staff had his future in their hands. This was the first time he had ever been in such a position.

Sam tried to meet all his new commitments. He went out of his way to spend more time, and better time, with Adrienne and the children. He tried to leave a little unscheduled time in his calendar for some projects that he wanted to start. He started to get less sleep and he was tired. Sam started to smoke again, after being off cigarettes for 10 years. One night, Adrienne told him that she thought he was drinking a little more than he had in the past.

Sam knew he was under pressure, but that was part of the job, he thought. When Sam broke out with hives, he didn't think that went along with it.

Sam Allen's reaction to the strain of his new job is not uncommon. People often experience symptoms such as hives, migraine headaches, depression, and back pain when stressed. Other, more serious physiological effects can be caused by stress, such as ulcers, hypertension, and coronary heart disease. Some symptoms of stress, perhaps those that are most conventionally associated with it, are psychological. People who work in stressful work settings are more likely to have a sense of futility and lower self-esteem, which may lead to lower levels of mental health and physical well-being [10]. Blue-collar workers have disproportionately high levels of mental health problems [46]. Stress can lead to divorce, broken friendships, and frustration. Also, physical or psychological illness is often thought to be a sign of weakness by the person.

☐ THE GLOBALIZATION OF STRESS

For many years, concern about work place stress was an important issue in the United States and Britain. The International Labor Organization (ILO) estimates that turnover, absenteeism, lower productivity, and health care costs make the price of stress in the United States about $200 billion each year. It is estimated at 10 percent of Britain's economic output. Now, the ILO reports, Canada, Japan, Sweden, and France are among the countries in which there is a growing sense of the need to attack stress. What has pushed this concern? It has become an issue for companies because they have assessed the financial damage that it has caused to their profitability. The result is that, worldwide, many organizations have made stress prevention an important element in their human resource management strategy.

Source: Frank Swoboda, "Employers Recognizing What Stress Costs Them, U.N. Report Suggests." *The Washington Post.* March 28, 1991, p. H2 [48].

Organizations pay a high cost for employee stress. First, critical levels of stress can lower work performance. There are also very high direct costs due to stress-related lawsuits, workers' compensation, and healthcare premiums. For example, in California 99 percent of the claims for psychological and stress-related problems are litigated at a cost of around $11,000 each [47].

In this chapter we focus on stress in work organizations. We examine the meaning of stress, its causes, how it is manifested by individuals, some personality factors that seem critical, and how it can be managed. Generally, the focus is on work-related stress, but we discuss some extra-work considerations because we believe that stress may emanate from many sources and has effects beyond the workplace.

A MODEL OF STRESS AND COPING

Figure 9.1 shows a way to conceptualize stress. The person is constantly interacting with the environment, objective and psychological, in which there are stressors. Stress may be manifested in physiological, psychological or behavioral responses. The nature of the response depends upon individual differences. Some are more sensitive to the presence of stressors. Some use more effective coping mechanisms.

FIGURE 9.1   *A Model of Stress*

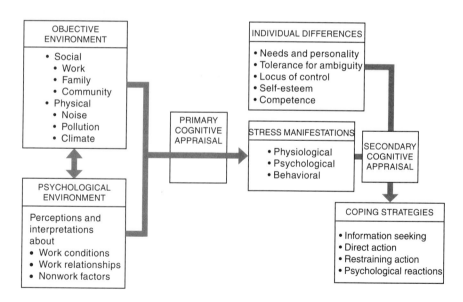

Stress is a non-specifically induced psychological state of an individual that develops because the individual is faced with situations that "tax or exceed available resources (internal or external), as appraised by the person involved" [26]. It is a dynamic condition in which the person is confronted with (1) an opportunity, (2) a constraint, or (3) a demand for which resolution is both uncertain and important [44]. Its effects are not always negative, as was the case for Sam Allen. Each of us has experienced a stress-inducing situation that was a positive learning experience. For instance, preparing to take your first examinations in college might have induced stress. As the time came closer you become more tense, worried about the exams, and studied harder. When you walked into the classroom and took your seat, butterflies were in your stomach, and your palms were sweaty. If you were well prepared, these reactions disappeared when you started on the exam and found you could solve the problems or answer the questions. You learned that you were able to perform well on examinations, and as a result, later exams were not as stress inducing as the first.

Even performing poorly could be a positive developmental experience if you learned where you went wrong, what your limits are, and how to do better next time. You became stronger, and the next time you faced the examination situation, you knew what to do. Over time, exams could become less and less stress inducing.

A positive, healthful, and developmental stress response is called **eustress** [45]. Just as tension causes muscles to strengthen, some level of stress may lead to better performance and a more adjusted personality. **Distress** includes those stress responses that weaken a person's physical and psychological capacity to cope with environmental stressors. As one becomes less resistant to stress, he or she may perceive a larger number of more severe stressors in the environment. This may make it more difficult to cope, leading to more serious physiological and psychological problems.

These different responses to stress are shown in Figure 9.2. A moderate level of stress is likely to result in higher performance (see Figure 9.2). Under low levels of stress, the person experiences little stimulation. There is no challenge, and boredom sets in because mental and/or physical skills are underutilized. When a person experiences high stress, personal resources are strained—a person is stretched beyond physical and mental limits. Under moderate stress levels performance is high because physical and mental capacities are challenged. The person is motivated but not anxious, and mental attention is focused on the task at hand.

 **FIGURE 9.2**   *Relationships Between Levels of Stress and Performance*

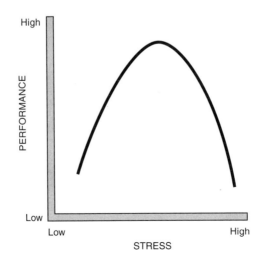

Stress is nonspecifically induced, which means that it develops from many different environmental factors, and the separate effects of each are difficult to isolate. These factors are called **stressors**, and they exist in both an objective and a psychological environment.

OBJECTIVE ENVIRONMENT

The **objective environment** contains those conditions in which the individual is embedded and that may affect him or her. Working conditions, other people, noise, and heat are all examples of possible stressors in the work environment. Nonwork elements such as social pressures, demands from spouses and children, and community problems may also induce stress, and they can certainly affect what happens on the job. These are important pressures because, as we have pointed out in Chapter 6, the relationship between work and family and other critical aspects of a person's life must be resolved to develop a stable life structure.

PSYCHOLOGICAL ENVIRONMENT

The **psychological environment** is the way that a person experiences the objective environment. For instance, a person in a job that requires dealing with people outside the organization (a fact of the objective environment) tends to report more incompatible job demands or role conflict (an aspect of the psychological environment) than a person who works completely within the organization [23].

INDIVIDUAL DIFFERENCES

When a person experiences the objective environment, the way it is perceived and interpreted may be different from the way others would react when exposed to the same situation. This judgment occurs through a process called **cognitive appraisal**—the way the person assesses the significance of the various aspects of the environment [27, 31] (see Figure 9.3). In the case of Sam Allen, he could have judged the demands as (1) stressful, (2) positive, or (3) neutral. How they are actually judged depends on the person, so that one person could feel stressed while another feels neutral. This assessment, called a *primary cognitive appraisal*, determines the intensity and quality of the individual's emotional response [26]. When the primary cognitive appraisal is positive, the person will have reactions such as pleasure, joy, and relaxation. When the environment is appraised as stressful, the person's response will be anxiety, fear, and so forth. Suppose your boss states, "your project report was incomplete." You may appraise this event in at least two ways (see Figure 9.3). You might believe, "My boss called me incompetent. He shouldn't do that. I can't stand to be called incompetent." Such a cognitive appraisal may lead to feelings of job anxiety, low job satisfaction, and frustration because you are not sure how to improve your report-writing skills. Another, but positive, way to appraise the same event is, "I am a human being and I have some faults. I am not perfect. This is good feedback. I am going to strive to do better." This may lead to more constructive actions to deal with exactly the same event.

□ **FIGURE 9.3** *The Effects of Two Different Cognitive Appraisals of the Same Event*

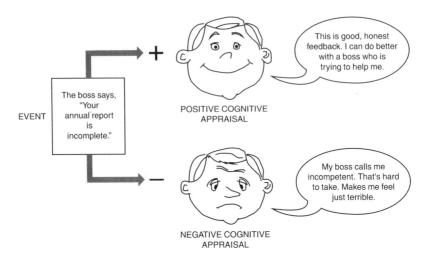

□ **THE SAME EVENT—
DIFFERENT COGNITIVE APPRAISALS**

Chris Steffen is recognized as a tough, no-nonsense chief financial officer with a record of being able to cut costs. He has done this in companies such as Eastman Kodak, Chrysler, Hyatt and Allied Tube and Conduit. However, his job-hopping career leads many to think that he has persistent problems being able to accommodate and fit in. The reason is that in at least two of these companies (Kodak and Allied Tube and Conduit), he left within three months after beginning the job and in some of the others there were reports of conflict with other managers.

Theodore Krengel, the chairman of Allied Tube, when interviewed about Steffen's leaving after only a short tenure, said Steffen left because the two clashed when the "new CFO began making changes without consultations and peppering board meetings with ideas he hadn't broached" with him.

Steffen had a different version of leaving. First, he claimed that he was not employed at Allied but was a consultant, though the Allied personnel records indicate that he was a full time manager there. Further, when he was told of Krengel's report, he said that there was "absolutely no problem between them" and that he remembered the story in a very different way.

Source: Mark Maremont. Is Chris Steffen too tough for his own good? *Business Week*. June 17, 1993, 1991, pp. 80-82 [29].

It is possible to alter the way one responds to the environment by reappraising it. The first reaction to feedback from your boss might cause you to feel quite stressed. However, if you reappraise the situation, you might conclude, after all, that you are not incompetent. You could, therefore, affect your stress level by what you think and tell yourself about the situation.

A person adapts to stressors which are perceived to be frequent and intense [45]. First, there is an **alarm reaction**. When a person experiences a stressor, physiological changes warn the body it is under pressure. Adrenalin flow increases; blood pressure rises, and muscles become tense. Next is the **resistance** stage, in which the body tries to restore its balance, expending physical and psychological energy to seek this equilibrium. Different physiological, psychological and biological responses may be ways that a person responds to stress. The final stage is exhaustion. If the resistance is not successful, the person simply wears out. Over time, the stressors may use up all the person's psychological and physiological energy. When a person reaches the **exhaustion stage**, both physical and mental illness may occur.

Stressors do not necessarily have the same effects on different individuals, but the outward appearance of individuals under stress is not necessarily related to their physiological response. In stressful situations, some have "hot reactions" and experience dramatic physical changes. Blood pressure shoots up, heart rate may increase or decrease, and blood vessels may become more or less resistant to blood flow. Other people are "cool reactors"—under stress their bodily functions change more or less at rates appropriate to the situation. At the same time, both the hot reactor and the cool reactor may appear to be very calm on the outside. The hot reaction may overstimulate the body's nervous system and lead to arterial spasms and other circulatory problems. It also causes the body to increase its production of adrenalin, potentially a serious problem because adrenalin stimulates both physical and mental activity, and the person may become addicted to it. That is, the person is able to operate best only under conditions of an adrenalin surge.

Some individual differences seem to be associated with stress and stress responses. Tolerance for ambiguity, locus of control, achievement needs, self-esteem, individual competence, and Type A/Type B personality have been related to how an individual copes with stress. These are discussed later in the chapter.

STRESS MANIFESTATIONS

When a person experiences stress, two things happen. First, there are responses to the stressors themselves. Physiological, psychological, or behavioral reactions that are triggered by the cognitive appraisal of the situation. These are called **stress manifestations**.

Physiological Responses.   Bodily functions change when one is stressed. These changes may be immediate or long-term reactions. When a stressor is recognized, an immediate biochemical bodily reaction initiated by the brain leads to an increased flow of adrenalin. In response to stressors, blood sugar increases, the heart beats faster, muscles tense, perspiration increases, and all senses become heightened.

The longer-term physical reactions are, perhaps, more of a problem. As one experiences stress over long periods, the body begins to show signs of wear and tear. Serious health problems such as coronary heart disease and cardiovascular illness have been associated with occupational and organizational stressors [10, 13, 22, 43]. Other specific illnesses associated with stress are ulcers, hypertension (high blood pressure), headaches, and migraine headaches. Some believe that even illnesses not normally associated with stress, such as cancer, may be affected by stress. This could be the case to the extent that stress leads to breakdowns in the body's immune system [11].

Psychological Responses. It is psychological manifestations that are conventionally associated with stress. Psychological responses are thoughts and feelings that may be work-specific or non-work-oriented. There are several work-specific responses to stress. For example, in a study of the effects of stress, Motowidlo, Packard, and Manning found that nurses who experienced more frequent and intense work stressors were more depressed, had greater work anxiety, and were more hostile toward coworkers [31]. Other work-specific responses are lower job satisfaction, lower confidence in the organization, anxiety about work and career, increased alienation, and lower commitment to work [31].

Non-work-oriented responses are either short-term or long-term changes in the individual's psychological state. When these effects persist, they may reflect a change in personality, which is in itself a coping response. Some of these non-work psychological responses are lower self-confidence (or self-esteem), denial of the situation, an increased sense of futility, neuroticism, tension, general anxiety, irritation, hostility, and depression [6, 31].

Behavioral Responses. People may act differently under stress. Increased use of alcohol, smoking, and changes in eating patterns are symptoms exhibited by experiences people stress. Stress has also been associated with increased absenteeism and lateness at work. Exposure to environmental stressors has also been related to poor performance at work [6, 9]. Motowidlo and his colleagues found that nurses under high stress had reduced work concentration, composure, perseverance and adaptability, and the quality of their patent care was lower [31].

Stressed individuals are less interpersonally effective. When exposure to stress resulted in higher depression in the nurses studied by Motowidlo and his colleagues [31], there was less tolerance with doctors and less warmth toward other nurses. Stressed individuals are more aggressive toward others, they are more competitive, and group cohesiveness is reduced [9]. Communication with others may also be reduced. All these responses may be part of a more general coping syndrome of withdrawal from others, avoiding contact, and rejecting influence attempts from those who may be exerting pressure.

COPING STRATEGIES

Coping is the way individuals handle either the stressors or themselves [26]. A person sensing a stressor, either consciously or unconsciously, chooses a way to respond to it. This occurs through a *secondary cognitive appraisal* process, which is different from the primary cognitive appraisal in which one becomes aware of the stressor.

There are two functions of coping [27]. The first is a problem-solving function; we may try to change the environmental stressor or our own behavior so that the stressor is less likely to occur or to be so severe. For instance, suppose we feel stress because we constantly receive negative feedback about our performance. If we are doing well, we might be able to change this feedback by making sure that our boss gets the correct information about how well we are doing. We may also change the feedback by improving our performance if we have not been up to par.

The second function of coping is to manage the physiological and emotional reactions to stress "so that they do not get out of hand and do not damage or destroy morale and social functioning" [27]. Basically, this means managing one's emotions.

Lazarus [26] suggests several different **coping strategies**: information seeking, direct action, restraining action, and psychological modes. **Information seeking** is trying to find out what the stressors are and what causes them. Because uncertainty is a property of stress, information seeking can be productive if the result is reduced uncertainty. However, it is possible that "ignorance is bliss." Sometimes the truth may be quite disruptive. Stress was found to be higher for employees who actively sought and obtained information about a major organizational change which might have had negative effects on them [3].

Direct action may take several forms. When experiencing job stressors, you may work harder, take pills, drink more, change jobs, or change the environment in some way. You might try to escape it by getting out of the immediate danger. Or you might choose to respond by taking direct or indirect actions to remove the stressors.

Another form of direct action is to seek and develop social support. Acceptance and help from others may buffer the effects of the stressors as well as help you find more constructive solutions. If you are experiencing stress because of conflicting demands from your boss, you might seek out an older colleague (perhaps a mentor) with whom you can discuss the problem and come up with a solution that helps.

Restraining action is another way to cope with stress. There are times when the best way to deal with stress is not to act, especially when taking action might lead to other, less desirable outcomes. For example, acting on an immediate impulse to a problem at work might lead to a person becoming so angry when another person is promoted that he or she might resign in haste. This could result in serious upheaval to family, a significant change in a person's career, and other undesirable results. Waiting before taking another course of action is probably a more effective way to cope with such stress.

Psychological coping reactions are quite common responses to stress. Emotions, and often subsequent behavior, are determined in part by what the person says to himself or herself about the situation. Denial of the existence of a problem, psychological withdrawal from the situation, and other defense mechanisms may change the perceptions of the objective environment so much that the perceived environment is one in which the person can operate more comfortably, at least in the short run.

When psychological coping modes distort reality and are used extensively, they may represent a poor adjustment to stress. For example, if a person who consistently has a difficult time performing a job but denies the failure or attributes it to wrong causes may continue to stay in an unsuccessful situation. In the long run, this may diminish self-esteem.

Coping and Personality. Because people will differ in their cognitive appraisal of the same situation, they will use different coping strategies, the choice of which is affected by personality. Personality effects on coping strategies were demonstrated in a study of a new plant start-up [52]. Workers who were impatient, aggressive, and precise about details (characteristics of a Type A orientation, discussed later in this chapter) chose direct action strategies of simply working harder at the new job. Those with low self-esteem reported that they psychologically withdrew from the jobs. For example, they were more likely to let their minds wander, take breaks, or go get something to eat or drink. Those who considered work a central element in their life structure tended to complain about the work situation and sought help in learning and doing the job.

SOURCES OF STRESS

Stress is a result of the transaction and interaction between the person and the environment. In this section, we discuss environmental stressors. Some are in the objective environment, most are part of the psychological environment. We distinguish between *work factors* and *nonwork factors* which are sources of stress.

WORK FACTORS

There are good reasons to attempt to minimize stressors which exist in the work context. From the personal perspective, work can be hazardous to your mental and physical health, an idea which is not consistent with the Western work ethic, such as, that work is rewarding and valued in and of itself. From the organization's point of view, work-induced health problems, both physical and mental, may create serious financial responsibilities. It has been estimated, for example, about 95 percent of workers' compensation claims resulting from mental stressors may be due to cumulative psychic workplace trauma, which is caused by employee abuse by managers [55]. In this section, five work-setting stressors are discussed.

1. Occupational factors

2. Role pressures

3. Participation opportunities

4. Responsibility for people

5. Organization factors

Occupational Factors.   Some jobs are more stressful than others. Blue-collar workers are more likely to be exposed to working conditions that lead to physical health problems because many of their jobs are more physically dangerous or they are exposed to more toxic substances [46]. Studies have shown that those who work in routine jobs have high levels of alienation from work and boredom, and that machine paced work was more strongly related to tension, anxiety, anger, depression and fatigue than non-paced work [19, 25].

The research of Karasek and his colleagues suggests what causes such high levels of **occupational stress** in some jobs and not others [22]. They found higher risk rates of coronary disease in some jobs and less in others and that the level of coronary risk is a function of two job factors: the *level of psychological demand* and the *level of decision control over work* (see Figure 9.4). High risk jobs make high psychological demands and provide low decision control. People in these jobs are constantly under pressure from others, say a customer, and they must respond in a way that the other person wishes, not in the way they would like to. Consider a waiter. When the customer is ready to order, the waiter must be there. Food can't be delivered until it is prepared by the cook. The waiter is in the middle between the cook and the customer and subjected to demands from both while having little control over the situation. High demand/low control jobs are shown in the lower right quadrant of Figure 9.4. Cooks, assembly line workers, fire fighters, and so on have higher coronary disease risks. Fox, Dwyer, and Ganster showed that nurses in a hospital work setting can also fall into the high risk quadrant [11]. Their findings help to validate the model, as nurses in that quadrant had less job satisfaction, higher blood pressure, and higher levels of salivary cortisol. Blood pressure is typically associated with coronary risk. Cortisol is associated with reduced immune reactions and depression. These nurses also carried stress reactions to their home settings after work hours, further increasing their chances for longer term health effects.

Role Pressures.   Robert Kahn and a group of researchers at the University of Michigan's Institute for Social Research examined the extent of role conflict and role ambiguity in organizations, their causes, how they relate to personal adjustment, and how personality might modify the effects of role strain [21]. This research is based on the premise that individuals are more effective at work roles when they are clear about what is expected of them and when they do not have severe conflicting demands.

Role conflict occurs when a person is in a situation where there are pressures to comply with different and inconsistent demands. If the person complies with one demand, it is difficult or impossible to comply with other demands. Suppose a student has a Tuesday evening history class in which the instructor schedules an exam, but then finds out that her statistics exam is to be given during the same Tuesday evening class period. She can't do both exams.

☐ **FIGURE 9.4** *Stress at Work*

The particular type of role conflict depends on the sources of the demands. An **intrasender role conflict** is inconsistent expectations from a single person. A manager, for instance, may expect subordinates to increase production but does not give them added resources. Often managers resort to this kind of demand when there are cost-cutting drives or other programs to increase efficiency.

Intersender role conflict occurs when two or more different individuals place incompatible demands on a person. For example, the quality control manager of a plant expects the production supervisor to reject more units of the product while the production manager wants increased production output and therefore fewer rejections.

Person-role conflict occurs when organizational demands are in conflict with one's values. An example of this is the behavior of "whistle-blowers." Whistleblowers call public attention to unethical or illegal actions by an organization, even though there can be great personal costs. They are often subject to much pressure from the organization and frequently are fired. In fact, a federal law is designed to protect the employment status of U.S. government employees who bring information to the attention of Congress about wasteful spending or other unethical practices of federal agencies. Whistleblowers often take these actions because they are motivated by personal beliefs about ethical responsibilities of government officials and the public trust with respect to spending.

In most organizations, person-role conflict is not likely to be a serious managerial problem, since individuals who have serious personal differences with organizational values would probably discover this early in their organization socialization and leave.

Role ambiguity is another type of role strain. It is the uncertainty about the expectations of others. One type of role ambiguity, **task ambiguity**, refers to uncertainty about the work requirements themselves. This is common, for example, when a person takes a new position and is trying to learn how to do the job. It also occurs when responsibilities are not clear because of vague job descriptions or unclear instructions from a manager. **Social-emotional ambiguity**, the second type, is uncertainty about how one is evaluated by another person. This happens when work standards are unclear and performance judgments are subjective. It is also a problem when someone does not receive feedback from others.

Role overload or role underload are also stressors. **Role overload** occurs when the work requirements are so excessive, they exceed the limits of time and/or ability. **Role underload** is when work does not make use of a person's abilities. In these jobs, such as security guards and receptionists, where a person is underutilized, the jobs require "few of the worker's skills and abilities (although they make heavy demands on those few)" [23]. Persons in such jobs characterize them as boring and monotonous. Such work is associated with higher levels of absenteeism, lower job satisfaction, alienation, and decreased maturation.

Role conflict and role ambiguity are both associated with a broad set of negative work reactions, including higher job tension and anxiety, lower job satisfaction, lower organization commitment, and a higher propensity to leave an organization [17, 20, 49]. A moderate negative relationship also exists between individual performance, role conflict, and ambiguity [20].

Participation Opportunities. Managers who report higher levels of participation in decision making feel much lower stress, job anxiety, and threat than those who report low participation [49, 50]. Participation is important for two reasons. First, it is related to other stressors. Participation is associated with low-role conflict and low-role ambiguity [21, 49]. Second, high participation gives a person the feeling of some control of the stressors in the environment, reducing the effect of stressors compared to when a person has no real or perceived control [9].

Responsibility for People. Responsibility for others may lead to stress at work [10]. As a manager, effectiveness depends on those who work for you. If for any reason you do not have confidence in them or in your ability to manage them, then you are likely to experience stress because you do not perceive control over the situation. In addition to that, responsibility for others calls for making decisions about pay, promotion opportunities and career paths of others, and exerting a good deal of influence over their lives.

Organizational Factors. The organization itself affects stress. For instance, many believe that the mechanistic form of organization is too restrictive and does not maximize human performance potential, whereas an organic structure is more likely to release human productive capacity [2, 38]. Four characteristics of organizations have been shown to be stressors:

1. *Organization level* may be related to stress. Executive work has a good deal of role overload, executives have responsibility for others, and a good deal of conflict and ambiguity is present in the job. Managers tend to have more time constraints and efficiency problems. The very characteristics of the managerial role, such as constant interruption, short times on any one activity, and so forth, make effective use of time difficult. Workers at lower levels are more likely to have role overload and role conflict due to conflicting demands from supervisors and lack of resources [35].

2. *Organization complexity* refers to the rules, requirements, and complicated networks that exist in large organizations. Role strain tends to become increasingly a problem as work becomes more specialized, more levels of supervision are introduced, and more complexity is added [21].

3. *Organization change* may be another important stressor. Organizations in volatile environments must constantly modify the jobs and responsibilities of employees as they must accommodate to different external pressures. Some changes reduce a person's job security, status, and power. Mergers, acquisitions, retrenchment, and downsizing will create uncertainty, job anxiety, and higher stress (50.

4. *Organizational boundary roles* are stressful because the role incumbent is subjected to role conflict which emanates from internal sources and external sources. For example, sales personnel must meet customer demands at the same time that they must satisfy company requirements.

There are many important differences among organizations that may translate into different types of stressors being more extreme than others. In mechanistic organizations, as the members learn to operate with the more clear and rigid lines of authority that are present, role conflict problems may become more serious when there is any pressure to deviate from these organization guidelines. But organic organizations are not so highly structured, perhaps leading to lower role conflict but higher role ambiguity.

Nonwork Factors

Suppose that two administrative assistants have been working for you for several years, that both have very similar work assignments, and that both are exposed to the same set of work stressors in their objective environment. They are likely to experience different levels of stress and will exhibit different stress responses. They may make different cognitive appraisals of the same objective environment. Personality differences may account for their different reactions. Another possibility is that one is experiencing stressors in the nonwork environment, such as divorce, the recent death of a parent, a very ill child, or marital difficulties. In this section we show the relationship of stress responses to some of these nonwork environmental factors such as (1) life structure changes, (2) social support, (3) locus of control, (4) Type A/Type B, (5) self-esteem, (6) flexibility/rigidity, and (7) ability.

Life Structure Changes.   Some of the natural flows of life can induce stress as a person goes through the transition periods of life and career stages. For instance, each of us will experience the death of a spouse or a close family member. Each of us faces the prospect of changing jobs. One approach to assessing the impact of such changes is the *Social Readjustment Rating Scale*, developed by Thomas Holmes and Richard Rahe [16]. They asked people to rate how long it would take to adjust to over 40 different stress-producing events, and how severe the adjustment to each of the events would be. From this, they developed a ranking and a weighting for each event. Basically, the idea is that if an individual accumulates a large number of stressor points in a relatively short period, he or she is more likely to exhibit a stress reaction. Table 9.1 shows some of these events with their weights. For example, the death of a spouse is very stressful; changing jobs less so. The nonwork events are more severe stressors than the work events.

TABLE 9.1   Relative Difficulty of Adjustment to Selected Life Changes

Nonwork		Work	
Event	**Weight**	**Event**	**Weight**
Death of spouse	100	Fired at work	47
Divorce	73	Retirement	45
Jail term	63	Business readjustment	39
Death in close family	63	Change in responsibilities	29
Marriage	50	Trouble with boss	23
Death of close friend	37	Change in hours/	
Wife begins/stops work	26	working conditions	20

Source: T.H. Holmes, and R.H. Rahe, "The Social Readjustment Rating Scale", *Journal of Psychosomatic Research* (Ireland: Pergammon Press, 1977), 213-218. [16]

High life stress is related to how individuals seek information to cope with stress-inducing events. Weiss, Ilgen, and Sharbaugh found that when faced with high life stress, individuals tended to seek help off the job [53]. They sought help from friends, took continuing education courses, or sought a new job. When faced with work stress, people tend to seek help from others at work, looking for help from workers and superiors.

Personality affects the way managers handle stressful life events. Over 800 executives in a large public utility were studied to find out if those who experience a high degree of stress without falling ill had a different personality structure from those who become sick under stress [24]. A life-stress measure was obtained for each of the managers using the Holmes and Rahe *Social Readjustment Rating Scale*. Recent illnesses of each executive were also assessed to determine how often and how severely each had been sick. Lastly, some personality factors thought to moderate effects of stress were measured. Those executives who experienced high stress but low levels of illness had different personality characteristics from those who experienced high stress and had high illness rates. These managers were more *hardy*. Hardy managers tended to feel more in control, were less alienated from themselves, and were more oriented toward challenge and adventure [24, 40].

Other studies support the idea that hardiness moderates the effects of stress [18, 33]. Interestingly, the level of hardiness of women in secretarial positions did not affect their reactions to stressful life events [43]. Perhaps the specific characteristics that make men "hardy" are different from those that make women more resistant. Another possible explanation could be that hardiness effects would appear in a sample of women more comparable to the white, middle-class executives studied by Kobasa [43].

☐ RESPONSES TO LOSING A JOB

Alan Morgan has recently been released from the hospital. He has just recovered from a case of severe depression that he and his therapist believe was a result of his work experiences over the last three years.

Alan is 45 years old. He has been married for 23 years and has three children in college. Several years ago, he was released from his job as a district manager for an auto parts firm. His annual salary was $55,000. He had been with the firm since he graduated from college.

He was released because sales had dropped drastically, not because he wasn't capable. As his boss said to him, "Alan, it's not your work. We've got to cut back and we're thinning out the management ranks. I could be next, the way things are going."

Alan was disappointed but felt that he would find a similar job reasonably quickly. His hopes were short-lived. He spent eight months looking for a comparable job without success. He quit looking for a while because he was so frustrated. Finally he found a job that was interesting, challenging, and with a future that looked promising. However, the salary was $40,000, much less than he had been making.

288

☐ RESPONSES TO LOSING . . .

Four months ago, the bottom fell out again. The new company merged with a larger one. There was a major reorganization, and Alan was out of work again. The reasons were the same. His performance was good, but it was necessary to thin out the management ranks.

This time his attempts to find work were feeble. He stayed around home and wouldn't associate with old friends. The family lived off their savings. He became more and more withdrawn and depressed. One day, he had extreme chest pains. "A heart attack!" he thought. Alan's wife rushed him to the hospital. The family doctor couldn't find anything wrong and suggested that Alan might be experiencing stress reactions. He referred him to a psychiatrist, who recommended that Alan needed hospital care.

Social Support. Losing a job is stressful, and it has been related to such effects as arthritic symptoms, cholesterol elevation, and escapist drinking [23]. However, these effects were reduced, or buffered, when a person had a social support system to help deal with the situation. Social support is the communication of positive feelings of liking, trust, respect, acceptance of one's beliefs, and, sometimes, assistance from others who are important people in one's life [23].

Social support is important because it affects a person's psychological environment. When a person has social support, events may seem less stress inducing because the resources that one draws on are greater—help from others—and therefore the demands of the environment can be met. It is perhaps as simple as the fact that you have some help in dealing with pressure.

Perceived Environmental Control. To have real or perceived control over stressors is related to reduced stress levels and active coping responses [9]. Specifically, the **locus of control** has been shown to moderate stress reactions. Persons with an *internal locus of control* believe that they can influence their environment, that what they do and how they do it determines what they attain. Those with an *external locus of control* believe that they have little influence over the environment and that what happens to them is a matter of luck, fate or due to the actions of others [42].

Internal's coping strategies are different than external's. Anderson demonstrated these differences in a study of entrepreneurs whose businesses were severely affected by a hurricane [1]. The storm resulted in severe flooding problems in Pennsylvania. In one community, 430 small businesses were extensively damaged. Over 100 of the owner-managers of these businesses were interviewed to determine how they adapted to this situation, which most would agree to be stress inducing. Internals perceived the situation as less stressful than the externals. Entrepreneurs who were external tended to be more defensive. Interestingly, the internals were more effective in bringing their businesses back from the disaster. When the internals faced a potentially stressful situation, they acted in a way to take control of events by engaging in more task-oriented coping behavior. This is more likely to solve the problem than resorting to more emotional defensive actions.

Not only do internals cope differently, it seems they also manifest stress in different ways from externals. Internals faced with a stressor are more likely to believe that they can have a significant effect on outcomes while externals are more likely to acquiesce, to be passive, and to see events as more stressful [54]. When faced with stressors, internals report lower stress levels and are less likely to become severely and frequently ill [3, 24, 54].

Type A Behavior Pattern.   Those who are hard-driving, highly competitive, impatient with others, irritated when they are in situations that they believe get in the way of achieving their goals, and strive to accomplish more and more in less and less time manifest a **Type A Behavior pattern**. The **Type B Behavior pattern** is the opposite. Those who exhibit this pattern tend to be less aggressive, less competitive, and more relaxed. Different responses to stress have been linked to the Type A Behavior pattern and the Type B Behavior pattern. Physiologically, Type A's tend to have more extreme bodily responses to stress and to recover more slowly than Type B individuals [15]. Those who are Type A are more likely to have a higher incidence of risk factors associated with cardiovascular disease as well as having a higher incidence of coronary disease itself [30]. They have higher pulse rates when faced with challenging tasks and also tend to have elevated blood pressure when their self-esteem is threatened [37]. In a study of a new plant start up, Type A workers reported a higher incidence of sexual dysfunction and increased frequency of headaches [56].

Behavioral responses to stress for Type A individuals may contribute to the more extreme physiological responses. Behaviorally they are less able to handle conflict through accommodation [4]. They smoke more and are more impatient, aggressive, and time pressured [39, 56].

Psychologically, Type A persons experience more subjective stress in their environment that is moderately uncontrollable or uncontrollable. Exposed to stressors they are more angry, time pressured, and impatient [15, 39, 40]. They also respond more cognitively to stressful situations: they are more likely to use denial and suppression than those who are Type B.

One explanation of these different reactions is that the Type A may internalize stress and, perhaps, failure. When they fail, they try again and again to solve the problem. If they are not successful, they feel that they did not try hard enough, leading to greater frustration and annoyance. They feel ineffective and attribute the failure to themselves. The cost of their exposure to stressors and coping with them is very high [7].

Self-Esteem.   Self-esteem is the way a person perceives and evaluates him- or herself. An individual's self concept can have an effect on job performance and response to stressors. Those who have a positive and a reasonably accurate concept of "self" have high self-esteem. They tend to have confidence in themselves—not that they charge headlong into unknown situations with adventurous disregard, but that they know their capacities and potential and act accordingly.

Self-esteem seems to moderate how a person responds to stressors. In one study, workers with low self-esteem withdrew psychologically from the stress of starting a new job in a new plant [52]. People with low self-confidence tend to have more intense reactions to high stress than those with high self-confidence [21]. In her study of life stressors and illness,s Kobasa found that the self concept made the difference [24]. Those executives who had a complex set of personal characteristics such as a clear sense of personal values, goals, and capabilities tended to have lower rates of illness than those who did not have such a self concept. She gives this example of how an executive with a strong self concept might respond to a job change:

> The hardy executive does more than passively acquiesce to the job transfer. Rather, he throws himself actively into a new situation, utilizing his inner resources to make it his own . . . [He has] an unshakable sense of meaningfulness and ability to evaluate the impact of a transfer in terms of a general life plan with its established priorities [24].

Another study found that people with complex self perceptions responded differently to stressful events than those who had more simple self conceptions [28]. When they had higher reported exposure to stressful events, individuals who described themselves as having many different dimensions to their lives were less depressed, perceived lower stress, and had fewer incidents of flue and other illnesses than those with simple cognitive representations of themselves. Perhaps the impact of a negative event occurs to a smaller portion of their self-representation [28].

Flexibility/Rigidity.   Flexible people experience different stressors and have different stress reactions than rigid people [21]. Flexible people are relatively adaptive to change, somewhat free and open and responsive toward others. They may show some indecisiveness because they may struggle more with decisions. The flexible person does not have clear-cut rigid rules for handling situations.

The main stressors for flexible people are role overload and role conflict [21]. Their flexibility makes them susceptible and willing to respond to many pressures because they can be easily influenced. Perhaps this openness reflects "interest in variety and innovation, and their general expansiveness leads them to undertake many tasks that are not specifically required. . . . [They are] fall guys to work imposed by others; they tend to overload themselves. Their jobs continue to grow until they are overtaxed" [21]. Flexible people try to change their behavior as the situation demands in order to reduce pressures. They make performance promises, a commitment to get the job done. When the demands are high and the deadlines are near, a second strategy comes into play. The flexible person turns to peers and subordinates for help and collaboration.

The rigid person is closed-minded, generally somewhat dogmatic in orientation toward life. Rigid people have a preference for neatness and orderliness. They are also inconsiderate of others, tend to be critical in judging others, and not very tolerant of others' weakness. Rigid people respond differently to stressors. First, they tend to deny or reject the pressures; in other words, the rigid person simply may not react when experiencing role pressure, but will ignore them. Second, the rigid person sometimes pushes away those who are pressing too hard. Third, under pressure a rigid person may become increasingly dependent on his or her boss. This is a useful way to cope with any role strain because a superior can often protect a person from role conflict (by giving the person priorities for compliance), role ambiguity (by clarifying responsibilities), and role overload (by reducing work load requirements). Fourth, a rigid person responds to work stressors by working harder. He or she may spend more time and effort on the job trying to get more done and ignore other facets of his or her life. To the extent that results are achieved, the rigid person has accomplished two things: removing the stressor by completing the work and being seen as more valuable to the organization.

Ability. There is not much evidence to show how ability affects responses to stressful situations [6]. However, it is reasonable to think that it does. In times of crisis, experts are called in to solve problems. A physician trained in trauma medicine knows what to do in a serious automobile accident emergency, whereas a psychiatrist may not. Professional athletes are regularly involved in competition with severe time pressures and extreme performance demands. They know what to do and, perhaps more importantly, are able to focus intensely on relevant factors, not extraneous ones. Some research does indirectly support this—supervisors' experience is positively related to performance when stress is high [12, 32].

The high-ability person may perform better in stress-inducing situations for three reasons. First, it is less likely that he or she will experience role overload. The greater the ability, the more one can do. Second, high-ability persons tend to know their upper limits. They are, therefore, better able to assess their likelihood of success in stress-inducing situations. You will recall that stress occurs in situations that are uncertain and important. The high-ability person will probably face less uncertainty than the low-ability one. Third, high-ability people have more control over a situation than low-ability people, and situational control affects how a person responds to stressors.

Research on social facilitation suggests something about the effects of ability, performance, and stressors. Social facilitation refers to the effect of the presence of other people on performance. In the presence of others some people perform very well, whereas others do not. The difference in performance has to do with the person's ability: high-ability people tend to do better in the presence of others, whereas those with low ability seem to do worse [5].

STRESS MANAGEMENT

There are several ways to manage stress. It may be possible to change the objective environment to remove a stressor or to alter the psychological environment that the person experiences. Perhaps it is possible to alter the stress symptoms in some way so that they will not have debilitating long-run effects. All of these general approaches work, and the most effective way to manage stress may be a broad attack on several dimensions.

PERSONAL APPROACHES TO STRESS MANAGEMENT

Stress can be managed, at least in the sense that a person can avoid stressful conditions, change them, or learn to cope more effectively with them. There are so many ways to do this that an extensive discussion of each is beyond the scope of this chapter. However, some that are currently thought to be useful and seem particularly relevant to organizational stress are discussed here.

Psychological Strategies. Psychological approaches to managing stress attempt to do one or more of the following:

1. Change the environment in which the stressor exists.

2. Change the cognitive appraisal of the environment.

3. Change some activity or behavior to modify the environment.

Suppose you are experiencing high stress from work. One way to resolve the problem may be by changing jobs within the company or leaving the firm. Or you may change your cognitive appraisal of the situation. You may tell yourself that the situation is not as destructive as when you felt stress from it. You can also change your behavior at work, perhaps by performing your job in a different way.

Counseling and psychotherapy have long been used to solve stress-induced problems. A second party, trained in mental health intervention, works regularly with the person to determine the sources of stress, help modify his or her outlook, and develop alternative ways to cope. Often this is done by helping a person gain enough self-confidence and self-esteem to try a different way of coping with stress.

Therapists and counselors use many different approaches. These methods tend to be based on learning theory and the use of internal or external reinforcements. They are behavioral self-management tools to help a person monitor, facilitate, and modify his or her own behavior. The role of the therapist is to teach these methods to a person and then withdraw so that the person can use them independently [34].

Developing a social support base is another way of coping with stress. Close friends may provide a listening ear, a less-biased assessment of the situation, some help in working out of a stressful situation, and, finally, suggest ways to change your behavior so that it is more adaptive.

Managing your life can diminish stress and its symptoms. Many stress-inducing situations occur because of poor personal planning and time management. For example, students often have test anxiety because they do not believe they have enough time to prepare for tests. Here is a typical scenario. A student has two midterm examinations scheduled the following week. Because both exams cover a lot of material, the student begins to worry, especially if it is important to get good grades. She goes to one of her instructors to ask for permission to take a make-up exam. The reason given is, "I don't have time to prepare." In cases like this, the anxiety can easily be avoided or at least reduced by preparing earlier in the term, instead of waiting until the last minute.

Relaxation, meditation, and *biofeedback* are a few of the mind-clearing approaches that individuals may use to cope with stress. These approaches either detach the person from the stressor or help the person refocus on other, less-stressful situations. These approaches may also have important and positive effects on physiological stress symptoms. For example, relaxation approaches can reduce hypertension and heart rates.

Physiological Approaches.   Being in good physical condition will help one deal more effectively with stress. Proper exercise, a wise diet, and not smoking are likely to yield positive physiological effects for anyone. Heart rate decreases, blood pressure is generally reduced, and the body becomes more resistant to pressures.

ORGANIZATIONS APPROACHES TO STRESS MANAGEMENT

Organizations realize that if it is possible to reduce the number and intensity of stressors or to help employees cope more effectively with them, there should be increased performance, reduced turnover and absenteeism, and substantial reductions in costs. This problem can be attacked through the implementation of employee wellness programs and by management practices which modify the work environment.

Employee Wellness Programs.   Over the last 10 years an increasing number of organizations have instituted some type of employee wellness program. These programs, along with stress management, include health risk assessments, exercise facilities and programs, individual counseling when employees feel job or personal strain, and regular seminars and lectures.

Wellness programs are effective in reducing work stress [41]. They are also very cost-effective when they have the support of top management and are accessible to a large number of employees. For example, Adolph Coors Company saved an estimated $1.9 million over the last decade by reducing medical costs and sick leave and by increasing productivity [8].

Management Practices to Modify the Work Environment.   There   are   several ways that some work stressors can be ameliorated by good management practices. Among these practices are:

1. *Improving communication* with employees will reduce uncertainty. This is a way to lessen role ambiguity and may also have direct effects on role conflict if better communication clarifies lines of responsibility and authority.

2. *Effective performance appraisal and reward systems* reduce role conflict and role ambiguity. When rewards are clearly related to performance, the person knows what he or she is accountable for (reduced role conflict) and where he or she stands (reduced role ambiguity). When a good coaching relationship between a superior and a subordinate exists along with the performance appraisal system, the person may perceive more control over the work environment. He or she

may also sense some social support for the task of getting the job done well.

3. *Increasing participation* in decision making will give the person a greater sense of control over the work environment, a factor associated with less negative reactions to stress. There is a strong relationship between participation and job satisfaction, role conflict and role ambiguity. Increasing participation requires decentralization of decision making to more people and delegation of responsibility to those who are already accountable for work performance.

4. *Job enrichment* gives the person more responsibility, more meaningful work, more control, more feedback. Uncertainty will be reduced, greater control over the work environment will be perceived, and there will be more variety. Job enrichment increases motivation and encourages higher work quality, especially among those with high growth needs.

5. *An improved match of skills, personality, and work* is also a way to manage stress at work. There is nothing so frustrating as being placed in a job that you can't handle and do not have the potential to perform well [31]. Similarly, in some jobs there is a good deal of natural stress because the work that has to be done is just set up that way [22]. For these tasks, organizations should seek highly skilled and competent persons with personalities that help them cope effectively.

SUMMARY

Stress is a major determinant of health problems—both physical and mental; and much stress comes from the work setting. Since stress depends on the relationship of a person to the environment and what is happening in that environment, one must look for the causes of stress in the person as well as environmental forces. The objective environment is the actual context of a person's job. The psychological environment is the way the person experiences the objective environment. The same job conditions might be experienced in quite different ways by different people because individuals have different needs, concerns, and personalities and therefore appraise the situation differently.

We now recognize that an individual can experience too much stress or too little stress. Too much stress may cause poor health, absenteeism, emotional breakdowns, and other dysfunctional behaviors. If there is too little, the motivation of the individual will be inadequate. The organization can manage stress in a situation by careful selection of personnel and by the manner in which the work of individuals is arranged or designed. The selection approach—selecting "internals" rather than "externals," those with high self-confidence, those who are flexible rather than rigid people, and high-ability people—can reduce the amount of stress experienced by individuals in the organization. In designing work, it appears that stress may be lower if employee decision control over work is higher, if there is less ambiguity about what is to be done on the job, and if a person does not have to comply with different and inconsistent demands. In addition, the total amount of work to be done is also a determinant of the amount of stress experienced as well as the amount of responsibility that one has for others.

There is some emphasis on teaching individuals how to cope better with stress both on and off the job. Various relaxation methods appear to help individuals to cope with stress. Maintaining good nutrition, personal habits, and general health are also useful in reducing stress. Learning to organize one's work and life and to delegate some activities to others may also be helpful in certain situations.

☐ KEY CONCEPTS

Alarm reaction	Objective	Role conflict
Cognitive appraisal	environment	Role overload
Coping strategies	Occupational	Role underload
Direct action	stress	Social-emotional
Distress	Person-role	ambiguity
Eustress	conflict	Stress
Exhaustion stage	Psychological	Stress manifestations
Information seeking	environment	Stressors
Intersender role conflict	Resistance stage	Task ambiguity
Intrasender role conflict	Restraining action	Type A Behavior pattern
Locus of control	Role ambiguity	Type B Behavior pattern

☐ STUDY QUESTIONS

1. What are the key elements in the stress and coping model?
2. What is meant by the statement that stress is "nonspecifically induced"?
3. How is the psychological environment related to the subjective environment in the stress model?
4. What is a "cognitive appraisal"?
5. Distinguish between coping responses and stress manifestations. What are some ways to cope with stress? Apply these concepts to a stressful situation you personally experienced.
6. How can stress have positive effects?
7. What key characteristics about a job seem to be related to stress?
8. What is role conflict? Role ambiguity? What are some other types of role strain? Show how you experienced each of these on a job.
9. How can the work setting itself contribute to stress? Interview a manager or visit a company and document sources of stress.
10. How are "life events" related to the effects of stress?

CASE

☐ OCEAN VIEW SEAFOOD RESTAURANT

Ocean View is a seaside resort town. It has only 2,500 residents but in the summer, from June 15 to Labor Day, the town fills with as many as 200,000 vacationers. Families traditionally return year after year to enjoy the simple pleasures of sun, surf, and boardwalk amusements. In addition, there are several thousand young people who spend the summer working in motels, restaurants, shops, bars, and on the beach.

One of the most famous restaurants in town is The Ocean View Seafood Restaurant. It was founded by its present owner and president, Jack Davis, in the 1950s, as a steamed crab, carry-out shack. Today the restaurant seats over one thousand people and is one of the largest seafood restaurants in the country. Its success over the years is because of its food, atmosphere, and prices. The restaurant employs 150 waitresses, 50 busboys, and 35 cooks. Because employment is available only during summer months, the majority of waitresses, busboys, and cooks are students.

The waitresses are all hired by Jean Davis, the president's wife. She places emphasis on attractiveness and youth. Experience is not particularly important because, she says, May and June are always slow periods so the waitresses can gain the experience necessary to keep up with the fast pace of July, August, and early September. However, she prefers to hire waitresses who had worked for her in the past. About 30 percent of the waitresses usually returned for a season. The result of her approach is that the average waitress is an attractive, middle-class, college sophomore. Waitress turnover during the season (June 15 to Labor Day) is estimated to be less than 10 percent.

The Head Busboy hires all the busboys. He claims to be able to judge whether or not an individual is likely to remain on the job. About 20 percent of the busboys return each season. Busboy turnover is about 25 percent during the season.

The Executive Chef hires all the cooks. His main selection criteria are (1) the likelihood of remaining on the job, (2) the willingness to work hard, and (3) the ability to withstand the high pressure and stress on the job. While experience as a cook is desirable, it's far down the list of selection criteria. Much more important is experience at The Ocean View Restaurant because almost all of the food is prepared in advance by a small preparation department made up of eight older employees and several senior cooks who set up the five different kitchens necessary to handle the large number of customers. As a result, cooks are frequently drawn from the ranks of the busboys. It is very rare for a cook to quit during the season. About 60 percent of all cooks return each season. The average cook tends to be a college junior, about 21 years old, and in his second year as a cook.

□ OCEAN VIEW SEAFOOD . . .

The salaries earned by the cooks at the restaurant are below average for Ocean View cooks, whereas the tips earned by the waitresses are above average. The busboys feel that they earn less than they could in other Ocean View jobs requiring the same amount of time and effort. Still, those who work there regard it as the "best place" to work in Ocean View.

The members of the three work groups are in frequent contact with each other on and off the job. The waitresses live together in groups of up to six, in summer cottages and apartments, and groups tend to congregate in the same cottage and apartment complexes. For example, in one apartment complex with ten units, six were filled by the restaurant's waitresses. These same patterns appear to be true of the busboys and the cooks, several of whom shared a large beach house. This made it easy for Ocean City Restaurant employees to party together. It was a rare night when there was no party at the beach house. Frequently as many as 50 people might spend some time at the beach house in a single night, most of them restaurant employees.

The work interaction is more prescribed. The busboys are responsible for placing a clean covering on the tables. Then waitresses place the silverware on the tables. When the hostess has seated customers, a waitress brings water and takes orders for drinks and appetizers. When the appetizers are served, orders are taken for the main course. The waitress then writes a kitchen check. A single kitchen check represents an average of five platters of food. Some parts of the order are prepared by the waitress. These include salads, cold side dishes, and steamed seafood. The kitchen prepares the hot food. When the food is ready the waitress calls a busboy to carry her tray to the dining room.

Each of the five kitchens carries out its operations in the same way. There are seven jobs and six workers in each kitchen. The jobs are pusher, set-up, fryer, broiler, flat-topper, and runner. The other job, kitchen head, is filled by the pusher. The pusher's job is the most difficult. It involves placing food on platters and coordinating the output and timing of the broiler, fryer, and flat-topper so that all the food on one kitchen order is filled at the same time. At busy times, on average, the pusher will prepare six platters, or one kitchen check, per minute. When the order is ready, the pusher calls the waitresses to pick it up. The cooks often trade jobs at times other than the rush hour to provide for a change of pace. This proves valuable in the kitchen since when someone is sick, or when a kitchen gets hit especially busy, the crew can adjust by changing jobs.

The delivery of cold or sloppy platters constitutes the major complaint of the waitresses against the kitchen personnel because they believe that the amount of the tip is significantly influenced by whether the main course delivery is properly timed and whether the food is hot. Thus, their earnings are dependent on their ability either to judge kitchen speed and/or to

☐ OCEAN VIEW SEAFOOD ...

"sweet-talk" the cooks and find a busboy to carry the food to the table. To determine how soon a kitchen check will be processed so she can serve the customer, the waitress estimates the work speed of the kitchen crew and the existing queue of kitchen checks. Waitresses also prefer kitchens that are the most consistent, whose cooks are most understanding and that turn out the nicest looking platters. These judgments are difficult and take some time to make for the inexperienced waitress because the waitresses are assigned to different kitchens on different days for reasons of fairness.

There is often a great variance in the number of kitchen checks for the different kitchens. One kitchen may have as many as 40 checks while another has fewer than five. In spite of this, the cooks frequently boast about the number of kitchen checks they have worked during the rush hour (4:30 P.M. to 9 P.M.). This could be more than 200 kitchen checks and, on occasion, a kitchen exceeds 300 kitchen checks. When a kitchen is this busy, those who work in it are given two cases of beer by Jack Davis.

The cooks rate the waitresses on their ability to pick up their food on time, to write neat checks and to refrain from complaining during very busy, stressful periods of the work day. Cooks have been known to tear up sloppy kitchen checks, to make waitresses rewrite them, or simply to make jokes about the hieroglyphics. Waitresses have also been banned from kitchens by some cooks because they consistently pick up their orders late. When food is cold, the cooks usually blame the waitresses for not pacing themselves properly. Other problems occur when platters that are exactly the same are left too long under the heat lamps waiting to be picked up. When platters are sloppy, the cooks simply point to the 40 or 50 kitchen checks in the queue and complain that the hostesses are not organizing the customers properly. One cook has even pushed platters off the heat table and onto the floor when a waitress was so late that the food was ruined.

The busboys rate the waitresses and the hostesses according to how they ask them to clear tables or carry trays of food, and since waitresses are required to give 10 percent of their tips to the busboys at the end of the day, on the generosity and honesty in reporting their tips. The busboys become very hostile and aggressive toward waitresses they suspect are cheating them.

The waitresses and the hostesses rate the busboys on their speed, availability, and cordiality. Waitresses often complain that it is difficult to find busboys to carry out the orders. It is not unusual for a busboy to help one waitress more than others, nor is it unusual for a waitress to give a particular busboy more than 10 percent of her tips. In general, younger busboys, are rated as more productive and enthusiastic than older ones.

☐ OCEAN VIEW SEAFOOD . . .

The waitresses are also subject to kidding and harassment by the kitchen crews. Under the pressures of both the kitchens and the customers in the dining room, it is not an unusual sight to see waitresses in tears being comforted by other waitresses, busboys, or cooks. In spite of their continual teasing of the waitresses, the cooks want to have a good reputation among the waitresses and frequently go out of their way to help a waitress in distress. The busboys and chefs are also under pressure, but they seem manifest it in more private ways. When they do express it, it usually takes the form of anger and yelling.

QUESTIONS

1. What are the various factors that would contribute to a stressful experience in this restaurant?
2. What organizational and personal factors help to alleviate or reduce the stress experienced here?

We express our appreciation to Stephen M. Doilney, who wrote the original version of this case, for permission to use it here.

REFERENCES

1. Anderson, C.R. Locus of control, coping behaviors and performance in a stress setting: A longitudinal study. *Journal of Applied Psychology*, 1977, 62, 446-51.
2. Argyris, C. *Integrating the individual and the organization*. New York: John Wiley, 1964.
3. Ashford, S. J. Individual strategies for coping with stress during organizational transitions. *Journal of Applied Behavioral Science*, February 1988, 24, 19-36.
4. Baron, R. A. Personality and organizational conflict: Effects of the Type A behavior pattern and self-monitoring. *Organizational Behavior and Human Decision Processes*, October 1989, 44, 281-296.
5. Baron, R.A., and Liebert, R.M. *Human social behavior: A contemporary view of experimental research*. Homewood, IL: Dorsey Press, 1971.
6. Beehr, T.A., and Newman, J.E. Job stress, employee health, and organizational effectiveness: A facet analysis, model, and literature review. *Personnel Psychology*, 1978, 30, 665-99.
7. Brunson, B.I., and Matthews, K.A. The Type A coronary-prone behavior pattern and reactions to uncontrollable stress: An analysis of performance strategies, affect, and attributions during failures. *Journal of Personality and Social Psychology*, 1981, 40, 906-18.
8. Caudron, S. The wellness payoff. *Personnel Journal*, July 1990, 69, 54-60.
9. Cohen, S. After-effects of stress on human performance and social behavior. *Psychological Bulletin*, 1980, 88, 82-108.

10. Cooper, C.L., and Marshall, J. Occupational sources of stress: A review of the literature relating to coronary heart disease and mental ill health. *Journal of Occupational Psychology*, 1976, 49, 11-28.

11. Fox, M.L., Dwyer, D.J. & Ganster, D.C. The effects of stressful job demands and control on physiological and altitudinal outcomes in a hospital setting. *Academy of Management Journal*, 1993, 36:2, 289-318.

12. Frost, D.E. Role perceptions and behavior of the immediate superior: Moderating effects on the prediction of leadership effectiveness. *Organizational Behavior and Human Decision Performance*, 1983, 31:1, 123-42.

13. Ganster, D. C, & Schaubroeck, J. Work stress and employee health. *Journal of Management*, June 1991, 17, 235-271.

14. Hamner, W.C., and Tosi, H.L. The relationships among various job involvement measures. *Journal of Applied Psychology*, 1974, 59, 497-99.

15. Hart, K. E., and Jamieson, J. L. Ph.D. Type A behavior and cardiovascular recovery from a psychosocial stressor. *Journal of Human Stress*, March 1983,

16. Holmes, T.H., and Rahe, R.H. The social readjustment rating scale. *Journal of Psychosomatic Research*, 1967, 11, 213-18.

17. House, R.J., and Rizzo, J.R. Role conflict and ambiguity as critical variables in a model of organizational behavior. *Organizational Behavior and Human Performance*, 1972, 7, 467-505.

18. Howard, J.H., Cunningham, D.A., and Rechnitzer, P.A. Personality (hardiness) as a moderator of job stress and coronary risk in Type A individuals: A longitudinal study. *Journal of Behavioral Medicine*, 1986, 9(3), 19-23.

19. Hurrell, J.J. Machine paced work and the Type A behavior pattern. *Journal of Occupational Psychology*. 1985, 58, 15-25.

20. Jackson, S.E., and Schuler, R.S. A meta-analysis of research on role ambiguity and role conflict in work settings. *Organizational Behavior and Human Decision Processes*, 1985, 36, 16-38.

21. Kahn, R.L., Wolfe, D.M., Quinn, R.P., Snoek, J.D., and Rosenthal, R.A. *Organizational stress: Studies in role conflict and ambiguity*. New York: John Wiley, 1964.

22. Karasek, R.A., Baker, D., Marxer, A., Ahlbom, A., and Theorell, T. Job decision latitude, job demands, and cardiovascular disease: A prospective study of Swedish men. *American Journal of Public Health*, July 1981, 71, 694-704.

23. Katz, D., and Kahn, R. *The social psychology of organizations*. New York: John Wiley, 1978.

24. Kobasa, S. Stressful life events, personality, and health: An inquiry in hardiness. *Journal of Personality and Social Psychology*, 1979, 37, 1-11.

25. Kornhauser, A. *Mental health of the industrial worker*. New York: John Wiley, 1965.

26. Lazarus, R.S. The stress and coping paradigm. In C. Eisdorfer, D. Cohen, and P. Maxin, eds. *Models for clinical psychopathology*. New York: Spectrum, 1980.

27. Lazarus, R.S. *The stress and coping paradigm*. Paper presented at the conference: Critical Evaluation of Behavioral Paradigms for Psychiatric Science, 1978.

28. Linville, P.W. Self-complexity as a cognitive buffer against stress-related illness and depression. *Journal of Personality and Social Psychology*, 1987, 52:4, 663-76.

29. Maremont, M. Is Chris Steffen too tough for his own good? *Business Week*, June 7, 1993.

30. Matteson, M.T., and Ivancevich, J.M. The coronary-prone behavior pattern: A review and appraisal. *Social Science and Medicine*, 1980, 14, 337-51.

31. Motowidlo, S.J., Packard, J.S., and Manning, M.R. Occupational stress: Its causes and consequences for job performance. *Journal of Applied Psychology*, 1986, 71:4, 618-29.

32. Murphy, S. E., Blyth, D., and Fiedler, F. E. Cognitive resources theory and the utilization of the leader's and group member's technical competence. *The Leadership Quarterly*, Fall 1992, 3, 237-254.

33. Nowack, K. Who are the hardy? *Training and Development Journal*, 1986, 40:5, 11-118.

34. Osipow, S.H., Walsh, W.B., and Tosi, D.J. *A survey of counseling methods.* Homewood, IL: Dorsey Press, 1980.

35. Parasuraman, S., and Alutto, J.A. An examination of the organizational antecedents of stressors at work. *Academy of Management Journal*, 1981, 24, 48-67.

36. Parkes, K.R. Locus of control, cognitive appraisal, and coping in stressful episodes. *Journal of Personality and Social Psychology*, 1984, 46:3, 655-68.

37. Pittner, M.S., and Houston, B. Response to stress, cognitive coping strategies and the Type A behavior pattern. *Journal of Personality and Social Psychology*, 1980, 39, 147-57.

38. Presthus, R. *The organizational society.* New York: St. Martin's Press, 1978.

39. Puffer, S. M., and Brakefield, J. T. The role of task complexity as a moderator of the stress and coping process. *Human Relations*, March 1989, 42, 199-217.

40. Rhodewalt, F., and Agustsdottir, S. On the relationship of hardiness to the Type A behavior pattern: Perception of life events versus coping with life events. *Journal of Research in Personality,* 1984, 18, 212-223.

41. Rose, R.L., and Veiga, J.F. Assessing the sustained effects of a stress management intervention on anxiety and locus of control. *Academy of Management Journal*, 1984, 27, 190-98.

42. Rotter, J. Generalized expectancies for internal vs. external control of reinforcement. *Psychological Monographs*, 1966, 80 whole no. 609.

43. Schmeid, L.A., and Lawler, K. A. Hardiness, Type A behavior, and the stress illness relationship in working women. *Journal of Personality and Social Psychology*, 1986, 51:6, 1218-23.

44. Schuler, R.S. Definition and conceptualization of stress in organizations. *Organizational Behavior and Human Performance*, 1980, 2, 184-215.

45. Selye, H. *The stress of life.* New York:McGraw-Hill, 1974.

46. Shostak, A.B. *Blue-collar stress.* Reading, MA: Addison-Wesley, 1980.

47. Stevens, H. J. Stress in California. *Risk Management*, July 1992, 39, 38-42.

48. Swoboda, F. Employers recognizing what stress costs them, U.N. report suggests. *The Washington Post*, March 28, 1993, H2.

49. Tosi, D.J., and Tosi, H.L. ABCD model of cognitive, affective and behavioral responses. Paper. University of Florida 1980.

50. Tosi, H.L. Organizational stress as a moderator of the relationship between influence and role response. *Academy of Management Journal*, 1971, 14, 7-22.

51. Tosi, H.L. The organizational control structure. *Journal of Business Research*, 1983, 1(3), 271-79.

52. Tosi, H.L., Vaverek, K.A., and Zahrly, J.H. Personality correlates of coping strategies on new jobs. Paper delivered at the annual meetings of the Academy of Management, 1986.

53. Weiss, H.M., Ilgen, D.A., and Sharbaugh, M.E. Effects of life and job stress on information search behaviors of organizational members. *Journal of Applied Psychology*, 1982, 67, 60-66.

54. Williams, J.M., and Stout, J.K. The effect of high and low assertiveness on locus of control and health problems. *The Journal of Psychology*, 1985, 119(2), 169-73.

55. Wilson, C. B. U. S. businesses suffer from workplace trauma. *Personnel Journal*, July 1991, 70, 47-50.

56. Zahrly, J., and Tosi, H.L. Antecedents of stress manifestations. Paper delivered at the annual meetings of the Academy of Management, 1987.

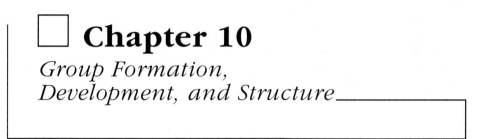

Chapter 10

Group Formation,
Development, and Structure

The organization of the microchip business in Motorola is complex. There are three product lines and three geographic divisions. The geographic divisions are judged on the basis of sales, profit, and market share. The product groups are evaluated on the basis of costs, quality, and timeliness of production. This is managed in a "messy" way. Twice each year, three representatives from the product group and three from the regional units meet and develop a strategy for the subsequent period. They have to reconcile the divergent interests of each of their units with that of the overall company [6].

Early 1993 also saw the turmoil in American corporate boardrooms as these groups attempted to revitalize the office of their CEOs and their top management teams. Powerful old-line leaders of companies such as American Express, Westinghouse Electric Corporation, Digital Equipment Corporation, and IBM found themselves replaced by younger CEOs. The boards were responding to a number of pressures: company performance, employee concerns and shareholder inputs. New CEOs were expected to break from the past, form a new management, and lead the organization into a new era. The need for a cohesive top corporate team has always been a major concern of boards. But even beyond this, the boards themselves are undergoing change. The trend is to use more outsiders in these groups, and to have the membership configured to contribute more to the operation of the company. Boards are seen as stronger sources of ideas and control, rather than as rubber stamps for CEO decisions.

At lower levels in countless organizations, teams and teamwork seem to hold a big part of the American strategy to become more productive and competitive. One can read about the use of teams at Citibank, the Girl Scouts of America, or Eli Lilly to name just a very few of the organizations relying on small groups [14]. Employees from different functional areas form into task or project teams to tackle any of a wide variety of problems. They may be guided by a fellow worker or facilitator who often has replaced a traditional supervisor in such settings. Teams are typically delegated a good deal of responsibility not only to identify and attack problems, but to take responsibility for each other's learning and development.

Needless to say, groups are important in the life of the modern employee. An increasing proportion of time is spent in work groups of all kinds. There are several reasons for this. First, more effort is being given by management to make the workplace more democratic. There is increasing use of representative committees, task forces, and project teams that cut across department lines and hierarchical levels. More employees participate in decisions that are often made in group meetings.

Second, fewer employees work in simple, highly structured firms with stable environments and routine technologies. Instead, they work in service, recreational, and government organizations whose work is variable and whose environments are volatile and complex. These conditions call for flexible and dynamic structures that use project teams and committees extensively in monitoring and adapting to change.

Third, many organizations are giving lower-level employees direct responsibility for making the organization effective, beyond just involving them in decision making. This often occurs when middle management levels are removed or when delegation is maximized. The consequence is that employees take more responsibility in improving quality, revising methods, monitoring operations, meeting customers, and the like. Groups of all kinds are also used when these practices are put in place.

For these and other reasons, managers need to know a lot about groups. In this chapter, we discuss the basic nature of groups, size effects, and how groups form, develop, and become effective. Attention is also given to key roles in groups, how norms and controls operate, and status effects.

WHAT IS A GROUP?

Shaw defines a **group** as two or more people who interact and influence one another [18]. Patients in a doctor's waiting room or passengers on a bus aren't a group unless they interact long enough for them to have some influence on each other. Without interaction and influence, several people in proximity to one another are referred to as a **collection**. People in collections are usually aware of one another, such as in a movie theater. Although there is not much interaction, and less influence than in an active group, there are some effects of being in a collection. Years ago, the television show "Candid Camera" filmed many such situations. A member of the show's cast, who had been sitting among the actual patients in a waiting room, stood up and held his arms out horizontally. It wasn't long before others in the waiting room were doing the same thing!

GROUP EFFECTIVENESS

In the remainder of this chapter, we will discuss some key structural properties of groups. Before proceeding, however, we need to think about what constitutes **group effectiveness**. The measures of effectiveness used throughout this book also apply to groups. In Chapter 1, several of these measures were identified and defined as results or consequences of activities. Among them were productivity, satisfaction and attitudes, attendance, retention, learning and adaptation, and physical and mental well-being. These are shown in Figure 10.1

☐ **FIGURE 10.1**   *Measures of Group Effectiveness*

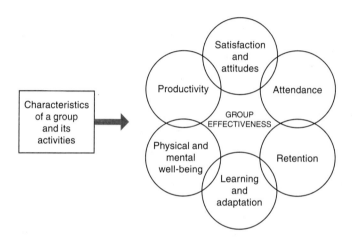

GROUP SIZE

Groups can vary widely in size, and size in turn affects member behavior. On the low side, groups of two or three are sufficiently unique that they deserve special attention. Larger groups show different effects.

DYADS: GROUPS OF TWO

In **dyads** no third person is available for an opinion or for help when a disagreement arises. As a result, tensions frequently arise between the two people because they have no outlet, and negative feelings tend to remain unresolved. People in dyads seem to sense this and tend to avoid giving strong opinions or acting in a way that might lead to disagreement. In dyads, opinions are sought more frequently than they are given. Dyads avoid disagreement because it can lead to failure, and this may foster consensus even when it doesn't exist.

Avoiding disagreement can be a mistake, especially when it affects the quality of the dyad's work. By facing disagreement, ideas are expressed freely in working together. If two people assigned to a dyad can't deal with disagreement or if the task will suffer from lack of it, dyads should probably be avoided.

TRIADS: GROUPS OF THREE

Triads pose other problems. Suppose Alan, Betty, and Cathy are on a project team assigned to solve a problem. Alan makes a suggestion. Betty agrees wholeheartedly, but Cathy disagrees. The instant Alan and Betty agree, Cathy faces difficulty: the odds are two against one, and Cathy hasn't even had a chance to think about it. What choices does Cathy now have? She can go along with Alan and Betty, hoping to have her way another time. But if she doesn't, Cathy must confront the other two or try to sway one or both of them.

Now suppose Betty disagrees with Alan, Cathy faces a new bind. Does she side with Alan or Betty? Does she assume the more difficult task of trying to resolve the disagreement, or does she simply withdraw and let the matter sit?

Events like this are a natural consequence of the triad. This is why people often leave triad meetings with considerable tension. Even when people are congenial, repeated imbalances in interactions occur. The triad has very high potential for power struggles, unplanned and planned coalitions, and general instability. Managers should probably avoid the use of triads, especially when the task calls for frequent interaction and influence opportunities.

THE "SMALL GROUP"

The "small group" concept is of interest because interacting work teams, special project teams, committees, or task forces are usually small groups. Usually a small group has at least four members. On the high side, the upper limit is perhaps as many as 15; if groups are larger, it is much more difficult for people to interact. Fewer than 10 people can conduct a discussion quite adequately. But when groups get large, individuals sense the interaction problems and may become less involved and withhold ideas. Students experience this in large classes, and avoid speaking up because they intuitively know everyone cannot do so.

There should be an odd number of members, as even-numbered groups are more likely to have deadlocks. Because of this groups of five, seven, or nine members are more effective.

EFFECTS OF SIZE

Some of the things that occur as group size increases are discussed below. They are shown in Figure 10.2 beginning with dyads and ranging to larger groups.

1. *There is less opportunity to participate.* In addition to the natural inhibitions that people experience in groups, the amount of time available to a person to talk is reduced as size increases.

2. *Group cohesion.* Group **cohesion** is the tendency to want to be in a group and the attractiveness and togetherness of its members. There are several reasons why cohesion is lower in larger groups [21]. One is that interaction decreases; another is that with more members, there are more differences in attitudes and interests, which diminishes cohesive potential. Third, in larger groups it is more difficult to get

agreement on goals. Group goal consensus is a prime source of cohesiveness.

3. *Satisfaction decreases.* People in smaller groups are generally more satisfied [9, 18]. What diminishes cohesion also reduces satisfaction; interaction, shared goals, and less conflict all contribute to satisfaction. In smaller groups, it is easier for members to feel they contributed to the group's success.

4. *Formality increases.* In order to manage a larger group, it must often be broken down into subgroups. This is a natural tendency as group size increases. Control also becomes a problem as groups get larger, so it is natural for norms and rules to develop. Larger groups even formalize communication by using written memos to supplement face-to-face discussion.

5. *The effects on performance depend on the task characteristics* [20]. If adding more people to a task helps rather than hinders effectiveness, then size is an asset to performance. If the people work independently, such as in a typing pool, more people means more productivity. Size can also be a benefit for some interdependently performed tasks. Consider a military unit that had to relocate to a new site. Entire 60-foot metal huts were moved, almost in one piece. Floor platforms were removed, and dozens of soldiers were able to use the cross beams of the floor inside to lift the hut onto large skids. They were then towed on skids by trucks to the new site.

   When the size of groups is increased, errors in problem solving can be reduced. A larger group can be beneficial because people can check work for possible errors.

   Sometimes task success is controlled by the weakest members of a group. For instance, on assembly lines the weakest members become a bottleneck for members who precede them, and their errors can prevent those ahead of them from performing well.

☐ **FIGURE 10.2**   *Effects of Group Size*

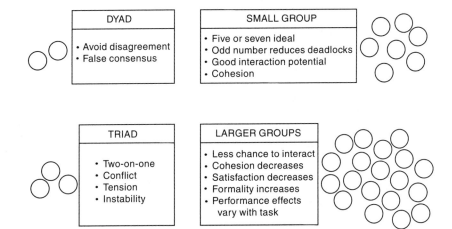

309

PROCESS LOSSES

Beyond a certain size, a group loses effectiveness. For example, a project team may be so large that people simply interfere with each other. Another problem lies in **process losses** [20]. As numbers increase, it is more difficult to coordinate action. If interaction is required, more problems arise. Subgroups or cliques may form and act on their own to the detriment of the task. Large numbers also affect feelings of responsibility: members may feel more free to do less or conclude that their lack of effort won't make much difference. Process losses also occur when productivity gets blocked; when one person's behavior prevents another person from performing [5]. For example, ideas are often lost in group discussions when some members cannot or do not speak up because others make it difficult for them to do so.

TYPES OF GROUPS

REFERENCE GROUPS

Reference groups, or primary groups, are important enough to people to shape their beliefs, values, and attitudes. They are a place where people can test their ideas and get feedback, guidance, or support. They serve as standards of comparison against which people can evaluate their behavior. A person facing a decision might draw on a reference group's values or talk with someone in that group before making a choice.

The family, for example, is an important reference group. The people we fish or hunt with, a local volunteer group, or a work team can also be reference groups. Reference groups are those people we identify with, even though we may not be a member. For example, you might identify with top managers as a group, even though you are not yet among them.

If we identify with a group, we are more prone to be influenced by it. Group pressure can lead us to restrict our productivity or go out on strike. A person's behavior is much more predictable once we learn his or her reference groups and the values the group espouses.

SOCIAL AND TASK GROUPS

Social groups exist primarily to provide recreational or relaxation outlets for members. Most bridge clubs, bowling groups, and gourmet clubs exist so that people can enjoy themselves in good company. Sometimes work goals could be involved, as might be the case for a company softball team or computer club. But the work is secondary to the social benefit. Social groups can exist in organizations: on and off the job, employees form friendships, lunch together, or socialize in other ways.

Task groups exist primarily to accomplish some sort of work: social benefits for members are secondary or may even be absent. Departments, committees, project teams, task forces, quality circles, and audit teams are all organizational task groups. They usually have a defined purpose and have deadlines, specific work assignments, and a reporting relationship in the organization. Some task groups are relatively permanent; others are temporary groups. In this and subsequent chapters, we focus on task groups because they are the ones of greatest concern to managers and to organization effectiveness.

FORMAL AND INFORMAL GROUPS

Some groups are created as part of the formal organization structure whereas others are not. The formal organization is the hierarchy and the various departments that exist in it. Formal organization is reflected in the goals, policies, rules, and procedures that are designed to accomplish the organization's tasks. Any group that is purposely designed into this configuration is a **formal group**.

Informal groups arise out of individual needs and the attraction of people to one another. Membership is usually voluntary and is based on common values and interests. Sometimes the origin of these groups is independent of the organization. For example, friends may eat together at work or socialize after work hours. On other occasions, an informal group develops in response to the organization, such as when workers band together to protest an unpopular management action. Informal groups are called cliques [3]. **Horizontal cliques** of people of similar rank and work area are among the most common. **Vertical cliques** consist of people of different organizational levels, such as when old-timers group around a common interest. **Random cliques** cut across vertical and horizontal lines and arise around any issue or interest. These groups may develop to bypass company rules or to enhance the members' power. They might consist of people who also like and trust each other and perhaps interact outside work in a church group or neighborhood.

Informal groups can be very effective and very powerful. This may explain why some managers view them with doubt and suspicion. They tend to see informal groups as disruptive and potentially harmful to the formal organization. Some managers seek ways to gain the support of informal groups and informal leaders to reduce their threat or to enhance some company purpose.

The power of informal groups can be channeled so that they contribute to, rather than subvert, organizational goals. Informal groups arise at work because many employees are concerned about their freedom at work, about control over their jobs, and about establishing good relationships with others [13]. In addition, employees have some free time at work that they can spend as they see fit. Employees also bring their outside culture into the work setting, so logically they may turn to each other when they become concerned about autonomy, when they need to get help from others, or when they just want to socialize. Informal groups serve basic needs and are just as important, enduring, and rewarding as the relationship that employees have with the formal organization. Autonomous self-expression of employees blends with task requirements to make up the totality of organizational interactions. Katz argues that managers should therefore view the informal organization as a stable and legitimate structure and accept it [13]. The informal group can become a problem when it conflicts with some formal purpose, but even this isn't necessarily bad. It may signal some error on management's part or be a symptom of a poor relationship with employees.

HOW GROUPS FORM

At one extreme, people are eager to become a member of a group. They sometimes pay high membership dues to join a country club or buy an airplane to join a flying club. People can also pay physical and psychological costs, as in the case of fraternity hazing or marine boot camp. At the other extreme, people may be forced into groups, much to their frustration or resentment. More than one employee has served on a committee rather than run the risk of angering a boss by refusing the assignment. The several factors that determine whether a group will form are shown in Figure 10.3. Some of these are personal characteristics, and others are situational.

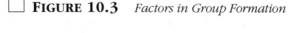 **FIGURE 10.3** *Factors in Group Formation*

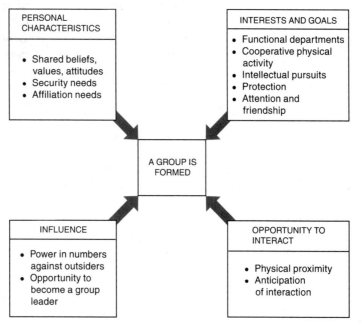

PERSONAL CHARACTERISTICS

People are more likely to form groups with those who share their beliefs, values, and attitudes. It is much easier to interact with those who share our attitudes: it permits us to confirm our beliefs, to converse with others with minimal conflict, and to express ourselves with less fear of contradiction. Birds of a feather do flock together [16]. Groups form around political philosophies and parties, ethnic and religious affiliations, or factors such as sex, age, or intelligence. A notion persists that "opposites attract", or that people with different attitudes compliment one another. The research evidence to support this idea, however, is not strong [16].

COMMON GOALS

Shared goals that require cooperation are a powerful force behind group formation. Managers organize employees around functions such as sales, production, accounting, or maintenance. If people in these groups also have similar characteristics, the basis for group formation and cohesion may even be strengthened.

Some goals require cooperative physical activity. For example, a group is obviously superior to an individual in moving large or heavy objects. Common goals can also exist for intellectual or recreational pursuits. Art appreciation groups and bridge or chess clubs are examples. Groups also form when there are benefits in getting other people's ideas, in testing our own ideas, or in talking about past experiences or planning new ones.

Interests and goals also grow out of emotional needs. Many people simply have strong needs to belong and affiliate. Safety and security needs are satisfied by groups. Groups also form readily in the face of threats or stress. An excellent example is the infantryman who depends on buddies for everything from emotional support to his life. Employees may be more prone to join a union if they perceive that the union has the ability to meet their needs and interests [25]. Positive feedback from others can make a person feel competent and proud.

POTENTIAL TO INFLUENCE

Many managers have been approached by a group of workers with a complaint or a request. The work group knows that a manager might be more prone to listen when their complaint is prefaced with a "we" instead of an "I." Co-worker support may be necessary to get attention and action.

Groups also provide opportunities for individual members to influence each other. In an informal organization, the role of informal leader can be very important to some employees. If an employee can gain acceptance as an informal leader, he or she can satisfy many personal needs and gain visibility that could even boost a career.

OPPORTUNITY FOR INTERACTION

Groups can form when physical proximity and interaction permit relationships to develop. Studies have consistently demonstrated how proximity and interaction lead to friendships and group formation in college dorms, apartment complexes, and work organizations [18].

Interaction and group formation can be influenced in an organization, for example, through the design of office space. Pathways and barriers can affect group membership and identification. People are more likely to form groups with others in their vicinity. Managers often cooperate with architects to design space in order to foster interactions. Employees who work closely together can be located near each other to increase interaction and allow the needed cooperation to take place.

Even the anticipation of interaction can foster liking of another person. People report liking someone they expect to meet more than someone they don't [4]. An anticipated meeting seems to provide a built-in incentive to view the relationship as pleasant and potentially rewarding; if so, the relationship is more likely to turn out that way eventually.

GROUP DEVELOPMENT

Groups go through certain stages of development [2, 12, 23], depicted in Figure 10.4. Early in the life of a group, members engage in behaviors useful for forming the group and orienting members. Often a period of conflict or "storming" follows, as the group struggles along. The next phase involves becoming better organized and cohesive, sometimes referred to as "norming." As the group continues to mature, it will still have relationship difficulties to resolve if it is to mature fully as a high-performing team.

Not all groups develop to full maturity. In some cases, the group may fail to arrive at common goals and dissolve early in its life. Other groups may struggle for a long time in tension and conflict and never become fully effective. Many factors that spell success or failure are within the group's control. Others are not, such as when members are replaced without group approval.

☐ **FIGURE 10.4**   *Stages in Group Development*

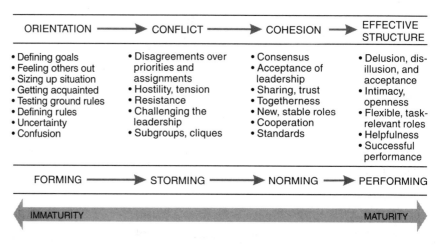

For a task group to succeed, it needs to become organized. Initially, there is an **orientation period**. Members seek to define the purposes of the group and begin to establish its activities and priorities. Much of the early conversation revolves around defining group goals and objectives, although it need not be confined to these topics. Members are also getting to know one another during this stage and are very likely to be seeking roles they might fill, as well as testing the ground rules for behavior.

This early stage can be chaotic and uncertain. When a formal leader exists, pressure is exerted on him or her to guide the group through this stage. In the absence of a formal leader, the group might select one or simply allow one to emerge.

In the early orientation stage, there is little to disagree about. But as goals and purposes emerge and as a leader exerts influence, a **conflict stage** usually emerges. The leader is usually put to a test, and challenges to leadership could arise. The group may divide over these issues and form two or more subgroups rather than attempt to restructure the group or change the leadership.

If a group successfully resolves these early conflicts, it is more likely that it will mature, moving into a **cohesive stage**. If consensus develops around goals and leadership and a sense of liking and trust develops, individuals begin to feel cohesive and express a readiness to move ahead.

☐ GROUP DEVELOPMENT: STUCK IN FIRST GEAR?

Empower America is a high-powered group set up in early 1993 by the defeated Republicans to chart new directions for the party and the country. Part of its agenda is to offer alternatives to "Clintonomics" and to promote government encouragement of entrepreneurialship and individual freedom [24]. Charter members of the leadership team consisted of some very prominent figures: Jack Kemp, former Housing and Urban Development Secretary; William J. Bennett, drug czar under the Bush administration; Vin Weber, former Minnesota Representative; and Jeanne J. Kirkpatrick, former U.N. Ambassador. But almost five months into the year, there was hardly any evidence that a group had formed, no less gotten through any stages of development. One GOP strategist defined the situation as ". . . a big wind-up, but we're still waiting for them to throw some pitches."

The group members seem to be following different roadmaps. Kemp is for supply side economics, Kirkpatrick is concerned about a new world order, and Weber is trying to keep things peaceful. An effort to create a grass roots lobby for progressive conservatives seems to be less than fully succeeding. Few other common goals are operating to pull the group and staff of 26 together. Empower America is dismissing the slow start. But how much time is enough to get a group rolling?

Some groups never make it through the conflict stage. Disagreements and resistance prevail. Energy goes into more conflict, or some people just leave. Others may stay but withdraw psychologically, exhibiting silence and lack of commitment.

If a group gets through orientation, conflict, and cohesion, its members then face problems that stem from *interpersonal/relationships*, such as intimacy and openness. These operate on at least two levels. One level is how well the group deals with emotional tensions that arise out of dissatisfaction of members. For example, do members feel free to say they are being unfairly treated? The other level is how idea generation is affected. Unless the participants can freely offer alternative definitions of a problem and differing solutions, problem solving and decisions will suffer.

Many groups settle the hierarchical and goal issues well but fail to resolve interpersonal issues. There are three phases in dealing with interpersonal difficulties: (1) delusion, (2) disillusion, and (3) acceptance [12]. Once power and authority issues are resolved, **delusion** may set in. The group has a leader, and goals and priorities take shape. But the group deludes itself into believing that everything is fine. Disagreements are not fully faced, and key interpersonal difficulties are ignored. Individuals may still be reluctant to express problems for fear that the group will be disrupted. If the problems are minor, little harm is done, but if they are severe, frustration will arise that eventually will seek outlets. Conflicting subgroups might arise out of these difficulties.

The awareness of differences and the polarization into subgroups cause **disillusion**. If not resolved, the group might still get its task accomplished, but cohesion will decrease as the group proceeds in a loosely knit fashion. Subgroups can remain, but the task alone is the main glue holding the group together.

If the group is successful in resolving these issues, a stage of **acceptance** is achieved. Subgroups become less prominent. Communication increases and the needs of individuals are more freely expressed. When the task and the emotional needs of group members are handled well, the group has achieved **maturity**. It takes considerable skill from both members and leaders to bring a group to full maturity. Mature groups (1) accept feelings in a nonevaluative way, (2) disagree over real and important issues, (3) make decisions rationally and encourage dissent, but don't force members or fake unanimity, (4) have an awareness of their process, and (5) members understand the nature of their involvement. Mature groups are not that common [2].

According to Gersick all task group stages do not always occur [8]. But the timing of certain kinds of events is very common. That is, groups very frequently tend to display two bursts of activities. One occurs about half-way toward the perceived deadline, when members reevaluate their task and change direction where necessary. Progress is renewed at this transition point. A second burst of activity occurs near the end of the task when group members race to meet the deadline. In between these bursts, inertia seems to prevail.

GROUP STRUCTURE

As groups develop and pursue their purposes, certain structural characteristics become evident. **Group structure** refers to the roles and relationships among the members and to the forces that maintain the group's organization. Structure is dynamic and changes over time.

The size of a group is a factor in group structure. Earlier in the chapter we showed how the size of a group affected the nature and pattern of member interactions, interactions in dyads and triads, how the structure changes as groups get larger, and the possible effects of odd versus even numbers of members.

FUNCTIONS AND ROLES

People in small task groups engage in certain key functions and assume individual roles. Functions are activities that occur in the group; for example, a project team requires functions such as library research, customer surveys, and data analysis. **Roles**, however, are defined in terms of expectations that members hold for each other's behavior. Groups expect each member to perform his or her role in a certain way. The key aspect of roles lies in the specific expectations that members communicate to each other. There are several different types of functions and roles in groups, and each has different implications [1].

Task Functions and Roles. Task groups need certain behaviors that contribute to task accomplishment. In general, members have to clarify goals, give and seek suggestions and opinions about the task, and help the group succeed. Specific **task functions and roles** grow out of the purposes of the group and the goals it sets. Groups with specific and difficult goals tend to perform better than groups with general or vague goals, mainly because it helps them to plan better how to achieve the goals [19]. The better the groups' goals are defined, the more adequately specific assignments can be made. Roles can be very specifically defined to include needed activities, deadlines, and standards of performance.

Many complications arise in role assignments. Poor planning of assignments causes gaps or duplications of effort, which later slow the group down or detract from effective performance.

When a task group becomes ready to make individual assignments, sometimes a member will quickly volunteer for what he or she feels is a choice assignment. Other members are then faced with less desirable work. Some members want to do work that is easy for them, while others want to learn a new skill. Figure 10.5 shows the complications that arise as members' desires and abilities come into play in assuming group roles. In the short run, it is probably impossible to please everyone in assigning tasks. In the long run, it might be possible to enhance productivity, learning, and satisfaction by careful and open consideration of the desires and the abilities of group members. Establishing task functions and roles is the basic activity of organization design, which we examined in an earlier chapter.

Socioemotional Functions and Roles. As the group works on the task and as members get to know one another, other functions come into play. People give and receive help. They reward or punish each other and give or receive feedback. Tensions develop that need releasing. Joking and laughter are not uncommon, nor are disagreements and arguments. People turn to each other for acceptance and understanding. All of these are examples of the **socioemotional functions and roles** of groups. Socioemotional needs of members are important, yet most groups do not deal adequately with them.

Task and socioemotional roles are not entirely independent, and they both affect all aspects of group effectiveness. Dissatisfied members may perform

FIGURE 10.5 *Dilemmas and Techniques in Making Task Role Assignments*

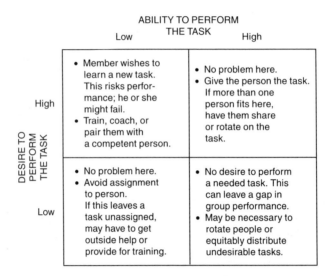

their assignments poorly, or they might quit the group or psychologically withdraw. These reactions also affect retention and cohesion.

Groups can be more effective if the socioemotional side of the group receives attention in the form of helping and rewarding. Actions that show support and acceptance of others contribute a great deal. Listening and showing understanding make people feel positively toward each other.

Roles and Leadership. The task and socioemotional functions are integral parts of understanding leadership. It is relatively rare to have both of these functions handled by one person. Some people are more skilled as *task leaders:* they are more concerned about work and exhibit a tendency to avoid or deny emotional factors. Other people are better *socioemotional leaders.* They put the feelings of the group ahead of task accomplishment. Their philosophy is, "If people are unhappy, we'll accomplish little. The job won't get done when folks are upset."

These **leadership roles** may be performed at different times by different people in the group. The role behaviors shift from time to time to another member. Generally, however, these roles are concentrated in only a few members. If we were to observe a group that formed without a designated leader and made a record of the actions and roles people took, the result might look like that shown in Figure 10.6. What can we conclude from Figure 10.6 about the functions and about leadership?

1. Carla is probably the group leader, based on her total of 50 recorded acts. She is also primarily responsible for task leadership.

2. John clearly has a preference for task functions. He may have aided or perhaps competed with Carla for task leadership.

3. Henry appears to be the socioemotional leader of the group, exceeding everyone in this category, including the active Carla.

4. While Sam and Stephanie contributed to important group functions, neither is likely to be viewed as a leader.

5. Most group members contributed something to one or both functions.

An ideal group would have (1) an appropriate distribution of task and socioemotional roles and (2) member roles that fulfill the leadership needs of the group. But this is not always the case in groups. For example, roles may be duplicated or not performed at all, or members might compete for key roles.

FIGURE 10.6   *Hypothetical Frequency of Behaviors in a Small Task Group*

GROUP MEMBER

	Carla	Sam	John	Stephanie	Henry
Task Behaviors	37	6	6	2	2
Socioemotional Behaviors	13	8	0	4	31
Totals	50	14	20	6	33

ROLE COMPLICATIONS

Groups face many problems that require constant attention, especially in the early stages of group development. Most groups adequately handle task issues, particularly if they make good individual assignments that match member desires and skills. On the other hand, most groups struggle when faced with role difficulties and when group members act disruptively.

Role Ambiguity and Conflict.   One complication arises when members experience **role ambiguity**, which occurs when people feel uncertain about what is expected of them or when they are not sure what behaviors will earn them acceptance or rejection. Group members can also experience **role conflict**, which results when a person feels difficulty in meeting conflicting demands. Role conflict can take several forms. A person can be a father, a manager, a friend, a husband, a fund-drive chairman, and a Little League coach all at one time. The demands of these roles compete with one another for time and commitment. Within a single role such as manager, conflict can arise from pressure to act in a way that conflicts with the person's values from pressure to meet the expectations of others whose requests conflict with one another. Role ambiguity and role conflict were discussed in Chapter 9 as an important cause of stress reactions.

Disruptive Actions and Roles.   Some groups are disrupted by acts of particular members that not only interfere with the task but can work to reduce satisfaction. Some members might force their ideas on others and refuse to see different points of view, often generating defensive or aggressive behavior in others.

It is not easy to cope with disruption or to correct it. Skillful leaders might take disruptive people aside and try to bring about a change. The entire group can confront a disruptive individual and appeal to his or her sense of fairness and goodwill. Groups sometimes threaten or ostracize the individual. If the disruptive behavior is rooted in the basic personality of an individual, it is more difficult to handle. Sometimes the group might just have to ignore or work around the difficult member. Another technique is to get help from outside the group, perhaps from a higher authority.

GROUP NORMS AND CONTROL

There are many ways that groups exert control over members (see Figure 10.7). For example, control is partially achieved if there is consensus on goals. It is further strengthened if members understand and accept their roles and assignments. Control is also operating when members reward or punish each other for certain behaviors. The need for control in groups is partly rooted in people's need for *predictability.* People are generally uncomfortable with chaos, ambiguity, and conflict.

☐ **FIGURE 10.7**   *Factors in Group Control and Predictability*

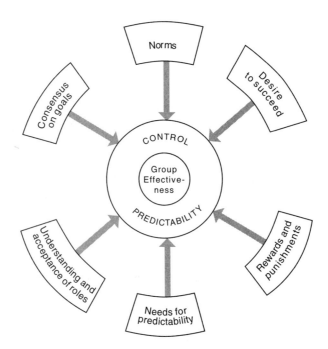

An important factor which affects control and predictability in a group is group norms. **Norms** are shared group expectations about behavior. They refer to how members ought to behave. Unlike role expectations, which apply to an individual, norms apply to all group members, but not always equally. For example, we might expect all members to be on time for a meeting but excuse one member under special circumstances.

FUNCTIONS AND DEVELOPMENT OF NORMS

The control and predictability provided by norms give members a sense of security and comfort. Norms are also ways to express values, attitudes, and beliefs because they are reflections of the "oughts" and "shoulds" of life. When we believe someone should do something, we are expressing what we feel is right, good, or useful.

Norms put boundaries on member behavior that may be narrow or wide. At a religious service, very little deviance from norms is tolerated. Some companies have very rigorous dress standards. For example, in one company a manager wore a blazer to work on Friday and his boss asked him if he was "starting the weekend early." Obviously a dress norm had been violated [10]. A wider boundary exists for how college students dress. Almost any clothing is acceptable for classroom attendance, as long as conventional standards of decency are met.

The more narrow the boundaries of a norm, the more control is exerted. Tight control can have positive or negative effects. It is usually very desirable to members in ideological or religious groups. For example, most Catholic nuns changed from wearing formal habits to wearing street clothes in the 1960s. When introduced, this change upset some nuns, particularly those who preferred stricter controls. Sometimes, however, tight group control threatens individual freedom too much and can produce such effects as resistance and rebellion. These can be damaging to a group that wants to hold itself together.

Norms benefit both individuals and groups. Even trivial norms, such as how we handle an eating utensil, serve a purpose. They make social interaction easy and convey a sense of sharing. They also add to one's self-identity and identification with a group or culture. In a small task group, people often enter with similar social norms, so that few problems will arise around such matters as eating or dress habits.

Important norms are more likely to emerge around values and behaviors that are central to the group. If attendance at meetings can affect the group's success, being on time and attending all meetings will surely become a norm. The more important the issue and the more it is shared, the more likely and quickly the norm will develop. Important norms are often reflected in bylaws, rules, and procedures that members are expected to follow. However, some values are not shared by all group members or not considered critical. In these cases, the norm is not central to the group, and deviations are tolerated more.

☐ PRODUCTIVITY: NEW THEMES AND OLD NORMS

One of the most common themes in American management in recent years is "productivity improvement" or "total quality management (TQM)." The main force behind this is the growth of foreign competition and the consequent devastating range of effects that penetrate all corners of American life. Thousands of American companies have attacked the productivity issue with old, tried-and-true techniques and with new programs galore. Productivity consultants appear in every city ready to help, government support and involvement thrives at all levels, universities provide research and service centers, and labor unions and management enter into unprecedented agreements. The media remind us every day of America's need to do better.

All this new attention to productivity runs headlong into some very old truths. First of all, it is widely accepted that workers do not produce all they can produce, and that managers do not expect them to. The result is an age-old question that reappears in all attempts to change productivity: "What is a fair day's work?" So does the question, "What is a fair day's pay?" In short, employees are sensitive to what they do for their pay. They also share certain expectations with one another, and these end up as work group norms. Experienced managers and consultants are aware of these norms too and know they cannot simply ask workers to "produce more" or "work harder." Managers can ask them to find or use improved methods or to "work smarter, not harder." Even here, workers' willingness to change is not unlimited.

NORMS: WIDESPREAD AND POWERFUL

Norms are so common that they often go unnoticed. Many of our habits, such as driving on the right side of the road or becoming silent when a theater curtain rises, are things that we do without thinking and probably learned through socialization. We become so accustomed to behaving in patterned ways that we lose sight of the fact that norms are operating. In other cases, norms are not so habitual. When we join a new group or take a new job, it would pay to be a bit cautious and look for clues about what is acceptable behavior.

The power of norms lies in two things. First, they sensitize us to expectations, real or potential. Second, the power of norms is a function of each individual's ability and willingness to act in a way that is consistent with them. A norm's power to control us depends on how we feel about the consequences of violating it. If we value our membership in a group, we can protect that membership by complying with norms. Some people also have higher needs to be accepted and approved by others, making them more susceptible to group norms.

Groups enforce norms in many ways. They can reward people who comply with social acceptance, higher status, and more influence. For those who deviate, sanctions can be imposed by the group; the group might warn an individual, withdraw privileges, impose a punishment, or expel or ostracize a member.

WORK GROUP NORMS

Many norms in organizations originate from management expectations or from work rules and procedures of the formal organization. They develop and operate in informal groups. A new employee's entry and socialization in an organization requires the learning of its varied norms. They form one basis on which employees are evaluated. Violation of norms can be personally costly. Occasionally those who deviate succeed, but they are the exception rather than the rule. When they do succeed, they usually are either highly competent and hard to replace or they have some political clout to withstand the consequences of ignoring norms.

Many central **work group norms** revolve around productivity. Employees can be such poor performers that they become a burden on their peers. Therefore, productivity norms often have a lower limit to prevent such problems. Norms also put upper limits on productivity. **Ratebuster** refers to an individual who performs above what the group will tolerate. Ratebusters can cause serious problems because workers in a group often have an idea of what constitutes a fair day's work. Controlling productivity not only spreads the work out to more people for a longer period but also prevents management from raising its expectations. Productivity norms operate even when workers are paid extra for more production, such as in piece-rate or bonus systems [17]. Norms might also put limits on how much workers should cooperate with superiors. Workers who exceed these levels may be viewed as "apple polishers."

On the more positive side, some organizational norms emphasize equality and equity of rewards [15]. Employees typically feel very strongly about equality of opportunity and fairness in rewarding people. An equity norm would require that people be rewarded according to their worth and their performance. Organizations try to be fair in their treatment of people but will also reward differently. Equality and equity are important work **fairness norms**, and the purpose of each is to avoid favoritism. Other work norms might involve loyalty or confidentiality. Commitment and trust are two powerful values underlying such norms. For example, a common norm in organizations is to avoid reporting fellow workers to a supervisor.

Reciprocity norms are also carried into organizational life. The idea of returning a favor or fulfilling an obligation is an important norm to foster cooperation as well as balance in social or work interdependencies. Employees will often pitch in and help each other out when the need arises. They will cover for someone who is absent or has to leave work early.

Another key organizational norm is social concern for employees [15]. This norm fosters taking care of people who need it or otherwise contributing to the quality of an employee's life at work. For example, if a death occurs in an employee's family, fellow workers will do all sorts of things to help out. Other examples include giving birthday cards and cakes, sharing rides to work, or bringing lunch to someone who is too busy to take a break.

Management can foster many norms that contribute to organizational success, such as norms effecting work quality, helpfulness, or customer relations. A norm of secrecy may be critical to keep competitors from stealing ideas. In one company this norm was strengthened by buttons worn by employees which read, "I know a lot but I can keep a secret" [26].

STATUS

Every organization exhibits some hierarchical differentiation between people. Hierarchy helps to bring order and control, and it is also a way for people to acknowledge and express status differences between each other.

Status is the relative position or standing of a person in a society or group. It is an index of rank or worth. Like norms, status is a common social force, and often it is habitually accepted. Status is quite apparent and easily identifiable. The following is a partial list of factors we might use to accord status to a person:

1. Title or position
2. Education, knowledge, or expertise
3. Awards or prizes earned
4. Income
5. Ownership of resources or property
6. Personal attributes such as appearance, size, dress, age, or sex
7. Behavioral clues such as work or recreational activities
8. Interpersonal clues such as communication patterns or reactions of others
9. Physical location in relation to others
10. Cultural identification or nationality
11. Physical surroundings such as home or office

From the list, we can see that status is accorded people on the basis of their accomplishments and characteristics, on the nature of their interactions with others, and on the conditions of the situation in which they work and play.

Status is rooted in what is culturally valued and results from the evaluation of others. The most common evaluation criteria probably are education, skill, level of responsibility, or accomplishments [11, 22]. Studies have examined the status of occupations. At the top of the lists are college professors, physicians, Supreme Court justices, scientists, architects, and the clergy. Various managers, some salespeople, nurses, actors, and musicians fall in the middle ranks. Lowest-ranked occupations include trash collectors, newsboys, waiters and waitresses, coal miners, and gas station attendants.

Power and influence also affect status. Jencks studied the characteristics that get a person to the top of the status list [11]. While personal characteristics and educational achievement account for entry into status occupations, it was family background that carried the most weight in the ranking. Parental income, occupation, education, and race were very important.

Achieving status is not a simple process. Some factors are within an individual's control, such as how hard he or she works, but some are obviously not controllable, such as family background. In a small task group, someone with more education, a respected title, or a fine reputation would probably be accorded high status immediately. But people can also earn status in a group through their contribution and relationships with others. They could become a respected member or even the group leader.

☐ GLOBAL MANAGERS: UNCLEAR STATUS?

According to a study by Feldman and Thompson many recent graduates in the field of international business are struggling to find out where they fit into the organizations they join [7]. The authors surveyed 459 male and female managers who graduated with a Master's Degree in International Business between 1977 and 1992. In addition to the stresses of the transition from school to a new job, graduates also suffered considerable culture shock from working in foreign countries or with joint ventures or subsidiaries. Graduates were not given sufficient opportunities to integrate themselves into a new culture or to adapt themselves to the international business environment. Assignments were often such that these managers were not able to fully use their international business and foreign language skills. The conditions for learning a new culture and foreign organizations were left to chance or mismanaged. There was little evidence of planning to effectively integrate and utilize these managers upon their return to a U.S. position. Some global managers felt they were left out of faster track opportunities for advancement while overseas.

To remedy these problems, the authors suggest that a global manager's job be better designed and allow for the learning and adjustment necessary for international situations. Chances must be provided for learning specific business and cultural practices as well as to hone more traditional technical areas such as finance or marketing. Stronger relationships with co-workers and mentors would serve to facilitate learning and acceptance of these new managers. Opportunities to work with and manage multicultural groups would help. Finally, companies have to anticipate and plan ahead for the day when these managers return to U.S. assignments, taking care not to block them from fast track opportunities.

STATUS CHANGES

Factors that determine status depend a great deal on the situation. A short person will have difficulty achieving status on a basketball team or any activity where height counts, but size need not prevent him or her from becoming a national hero or movie star. Status can also have very specific limits. A group of physicians might grant an architect status, but not for his or her knowledge of medicine. In a fair-minded society or group, people can improve their status and earn great respect by providing any valued activity. As long as there are opportunities for an individual to contribute, there is potential for status improvement.

Achieving status is much harder than losing it. It takes a good deal of effort to climb up a steep cliff, but not much to slip and fall to the bottom. Physicians get caught for drug dealing and professors are fired for falsifying research. Entire groups can lose their status. Americans' faith in some aspects of medicine, their evaluation of the law profession and politicians, and their views toward chemical companies have dimmed in recent years.

STATUS DISTRIBUTION

Status distribution in a group is usually uneven: those with high status have disproportionately more than those with low status. Status might be more evenly distributed if it were based on some combination of competence and contribution. Instead, status is usually derived from factors that often have little to do with competence or contribution. Furthermore, contributions or competence are quite differently valued. For example, many groups will value the writer of a group report more than the person who did skillful editorial work.

It may be reasonable that some contributions are more valuable than others, but if differences are overplayed, group cohesion and individual feelings can suffer considerably. These difficulties get worse when group members disagree on the value of contributions and on the status distribution across members. **Status incongruence** can occur when members get either more or less status than others feel they deserve.

OTHER EFFECTS OF STATUS

Some effects of status are beyond those discussed above. Extremely high-status people are treated with **deference**; that is, they are shown courtesy and respect. This is true even if one personally dislikes the high-status person.

Those with high status exert more influence over others with lower status because of what gave them status in the first place. High-status people do not necessarily put their energies into influencing others; for example, some artists work for art's sake, not to control others.

An analysis of the interaction patterns of a group would show that high-status people initiate and engage in more communication than those with lower status. In turn, status affects the nature of that communication. In another chapter we will show how location in a communication pattern and in an organizational hierarchy can affect communication frequency, direction, and accuracy. Communication is an active means of exerting influence.

A group often chooses its high-status member to represent it to an outside person or to another group. The group will put its most prestigious and skilled person forward. It is possible, however, that someone with less status within the group will be more influential with outsiders.

Finally, high-status members of a group can violate group norms more than low-status people. To earn high status, a member has to exemplify the values of the group and actually conform to its norms. But once it is achieved, a high-status person is more free to violate norms than others are, partly because they have "paid their dues." They are credited with such payment and permitted to deviate on occasion. Acceptance of deviation may be a way of rewarding high-status people or acknowledging their power. However, high-status people can't violate norms too often nor can they act to undermine an important norm. To do so is to risk losing the status they have earned.

SUMMARY

People spend enormous amounts of time in groups, and groups are becoming more common in work settings. Reference groups are powerful in shaping values, but people are influenced by many other social and task groups as well. In organizations, both formal and informal groups, as well as other interaction patterns, make up the fabric of the structure.

Groups vary in size, but typical small groups range from four to about a dozen people. The smaller dyads and triads have distinct and different characteristics. Larger groups have a tendency to organize into smaller subgroups to facilitate effectiveness.

Groups tend to form around people with similar attitudes and beliefs and who share interests and goals. Group formation is also facilitated when people need the power of numbers to influence others or to accomplish a task. However, even the opportunity to interact can cause a group to form. Patterns of group development can either lead to its failure or to group success and maturity, depending on how well the group members handle the stages of its development. Early in its life, a group has to establish goals as well as resolve the question of leadership and personal commitment. Conflict that surfaces must be resolved if the group is to become cohesive. Members must also deal with questions of intimacy and openness. Group members can delude themselves into feeling all is well, but when this is not the case, the members become disillusioned and struggle further before the group can mature.

Effective groups are productive, have satisfied members, and are able to attract and retain members. To remain effective, groups often have to provide learning and growth opportunities for their members.

The basic building blocks of group structure are the functions and roles assumed by its members. A balance of task and socioemotional roles tends to aid success. Disruptive individual roles can threaten the group at any time. One of the key problems is the success of the leadership roles members take.

Groups develop norms that define behavioral expectations and contribute to the control necessary for achieving effectiveness. No group can be understood without some knowledge of group norms, and group members cannot adequately operate in a group unless they are aware of norms and help enforce them. Another central aspect of a group life is the status accorded each of its members. Status can be a force that contributes to group success or it can create difficulties that prevent the group from developing into an effective unit.

☐ KEY CONCEPTS

Acceptance	Group structure	Role conflict
Cohesion	Horizontal cliques	Roles
Cohesive stage	Informal groups	Social groups
Collection	Leadership roles	Socioemotional
Conflict stage	Maturity	functions and roles
Deference	Norms	Status
Delusion	Orientation period	Status distribution
Disillusion	Process losses	Status incongruence
Dyads	Random cliques	Task functions and roles
Fairness norms	Ratebuster	Task groups
Formal groups	Reciprocity norms	Triads
Group	Reference groups	Vertical cliques
Group effectiveness	Role ambiguity	Work group norms

☐ STUDY QUESTIONS

1. What are the characteristics of dyads and triads that make them unique types of groups? What are some implications for management?
2. Give an example from your own experience that shows how a large group you are in suffers the effects of increasing size.
3. Which of the key values, beliefs, or attitudes you hold were shaped by a reference group? Describe events that were particularly influential.
4. What holds an informal work group together? What are some key norms that might operate in an informal group? How do relationships with management affect such groups?
5. Think of one group you like or want to be in and another you dislike or wouldn't join. What are the reasons you are attracted to one and repelled by the other?
6. What are the major stages of development in small groups? What is necessary for a group to achieve maturity?
7. How can the effectiveness of a group be measured?
8. For a task group you are in, analyze the task, socioemotional, and disruptive roles in the group. Is there one or more than one person in the group who you would call the leader? Explain.
9. Define role conflict and role ambiguity. Should these conditions be eliminated? If so, why?
10. What are the different factors that contribute to control and predictability in a group?

☐ STUDY . . .

11. What are norms? Under what conditions are norms likely to be powerful in affecting member behavior?
12. What is status? How can it be acquired?
13. Describe a situation, real or hypothetical, that demonstrates how status contributes to group effectiveness and detracts from it.

CASE

☐ WOODSIDE ACADEMY

Woodside Academy is a small (500 students), all-female, religious private high school located in the Woodside suburb of Chicago, Illinois. According to a recent new mission statement of the school's philosophy, Woodside strives to prepare average and above average students for college entrance with a college preparatory curriculum that includes rich and varied intellectual discovery and development. The teachers in the school are increasingly laypersons instead of teachers from the religious order. The new curriculum reflects the orientation of the lay teachers at Woodside. Both types of teachers have high teaching standards, especially the older teachers from the religious order.

To implement this teaching philosophy and system, Woodside adopted a flexible, modular schedule. This schedule consisted of a five-day cycle, with each day comprised of twenty modules, each one twenty minutes long. Each day included both structured time (class time) and unstructured time (which the students called "free time"). Almost all courses consisted of one large group lecture and two small group discussion sessions in each week. Classes were usually two modules (forty minutes) long.

At the beginning of each quarter, a student received the course syllabus which outlined course objectives, requirements, and the evaluation system. To obtain a grade of Very Good (A), Good (B), or Satisfactory (C) a student had to fulfill certain objectives. Objectives took the form of tests, projects, papers, book reviews, and in-depth studies. To pass a course all students had to fulfill the objectives for a Satisfactory (C). Those students desiring a grade of Good (B) or Very Good (A) had to meet other objectives. These additional objectives provided the opportunity to study a subject in more detail or to explore a related topic of interest that was covered in class. In this objectives system, grades of B or C required a 70 percent score on all tests and a grade of A required a score of 80 percent on all tests. One feature of the Woodside grading system was make-up tests. Tests that were failed could be retaken again until a satisfactory score of 70 percent was achieved.

☐ WOODSIDE . . .

If a student did not complete the work before the end of the quarter, she received a grade of Incomplete. As soon as the work was completed, an appropriate grade was issued. Extra work was expected to be turned in on the due date, but there was usually no penalty for late work. Most extra work was turned in during the last week of the quarter. As with extra work, make-up examinations were usually completed the last week of the quarter. This meant that the last week of each quarter was very hectic for both students and faculty, as students hurried to turn in required work, extra work, and to make up tests. For many, the first few weeks of the new quarter were equally hectic because carry over work from last quarter was being completed as work for the new quarter was starting.

The idea behind a flexible modular schedule was to provide students with unstructured time during the school day in which work on objectives could be completed. Each major department (English, Foreign Languages, Math, Science, Social Studies, and Religion) had its own media center where students could study in work groups, work independently, meet with teachers to discuss course work, or receive individual help. Each media center contained course tests, relevant books, reference materials, maps, models, filmstrips, and so on. In addition to these departmental media centers, there was a library with additional resources and reading material. The library was a good place to study because no talking was allowed and this rule was enforced, unlike the media centers which tended to become noisy and rowdy if no teacher was present.

Besides the library and the six media centers, there were only five other areas where students were allowed during the school day; the cafeteria, the gym, the students' lobby, classrooms not being used for structured classes, and outside the building on certain areas of the school grounds.

On a typical day at Woodside, what would a visitor to the school see? All of the students were dressed alike, wearing the same uniform to school each day. They tended to be quite close to each other. The students' lobby and the cafeteria were usually half full of students socializing, talking, playing cards, and so forth. The library and the media centers were typically only one-third full. Different media centers and sections of media centers became the meeting places for different groups of friends.

Lisa Kelly was almost always in the library during unstructured time. She was somewhat uncomfortable there because most of her best friends were to be found in the media centers. She was in the library because she was a very serious student. She knew that unless she did very well in school and was admitted to a good university, her parents, who she adored, would be very disappointed with her. Neither of them had attended college and they expected a great deal from her. She did make some new friends among the library crowd, but they were not the really close friends that she had before. She didn't know exactly how to act with them in the same way she did with her old friends.

☐ WOODSIDE . . .

After a while, Lisa noticed that most of the students at Woodside settled into a routine. The same few students were working toward As and Bs, but most of them were working toward Cs. In general, most students worked toward the grade they expected to receive for a course. Those that expected a C completed the work for a C and received a grade of C. Those that expected an A completed the work for an A and received a grade of A.

QUESTIONS

1. What kinds of groups have formed at Woodside, and what kind of influence do they likely have on group member's behavior?
2. What kinds of norms govern behavior at Woodside? How would you evaluate such norms?
3. What would you do if you were in charge of Woodside to use group forces to strengthen student performance?

We express our appreciation to Christina M. Giannantonio, who wrote the original version of this case, for permission to use it.

REFERENCES

1. Bales, R.F. *Interaction process analysis: A method for the study of small groups.* Reading, MA: Addison-Wesley, 1953.
2. Bennis, W.G., and Shepard, H.S. A theory of group development. *Human Relations*, 1965, 9, 415-57.
3. Dalton, M. *Men who manage.* New York: John Wiley, 1959.
4. Darley, J.M., and Berscheid, E. Increased liking as a result of the anticipation of personal contact. *Human Relations*, 1967, 20, 29-40.
5. Diehl, M. and Stroebe, W. Productivity loss in brainstorming groups: Toward the solution of a riddle. *Journal of Personality and Social Psychology*, 1987, 53, 497-509.
6. *The Economist*, Asia beckons. May 30, 1992, 324, 63-64.
7. Feldman, D.C. & Thompson, H.D. Entry shock, culture shock: Socializing the new breed of global managers. *Human Resource Management*, 1992, 31:4, 345-362.
8. Gersick, C.J.G. Making time: Predictable transitions in task groups. *Academy of Management Journal*, 1989, 3, 274-309.
9. Hare, A.P. *Handbook of small group research.* New York: Free Press, 1976.
10. Iacocca, L., and Novak, W. *Iacocca: An autobiography.* New York: Bantam Books, 1984.
11. Jencks, C. *Who gets ahead: The determinants of economic success in America.* New York: Basic Books, 1979.
12. Jewell, I.N., and Reitz, H.J. *Group effectiveness in organizations.* Glenview, IL: Scott, Foresman, 1981.
13. Katz, D. Explaining informal work groups in complex organizations: The case for autonomy in structure. *Administrative Science Quarterly*, 1965, 10, 204-21.

14. Katzenbach, J. R. and Smith, D. K. *The wisdom of teams: Creating the high-performance organization.* Boston; Harvard Business School, 1993.

15. Leventhal, G.S. The distribution of rewards and resources in groups and organizations. In L. Berkowitz and E. Walster, eds. *Advances in experimental social psychology*, 9. New York: Academic Press, 1976.

16. Myers, D.G. *Social psychology.* New York: McGraw-Hill, 1983.

17. Roy, D.F. Quota restriction and goldbricking in a machine shop. *American Journal of Sociology*, 1952, 57, 426-42.

18. Shaw, M.E. *Group dynamics: The psychology of small group behavior.* New York: McGraw-Hill, 1981.

19. Smith, K.G., Locke, E.A., and Berry, D. Goalsetting, planning and organizational performance: An experimental situation. *Organizational Behavior and Human Decision Processes*, 1990, 46, 118-34.

20. Steiner, I.D. *Group process and productivity.* New York: Academic Press, 1972.

21. Thomas, E.J., and Fink, C.J. The effects of group size. *Psychological Bulletin*, 1963, 60, 371-84.

22. Trieman, D.J. *Organizational prestige in comparative perspective.* New York: Academic Press, 1977.

23. Tuckman, B.W. Developmental sequence in small groups. *Psychological Bulletin*, 1965, 63, 384-99.

24. Ullmann, O. The right's new attack dog: Wimpy bark, no bite. *Business Week*, 1993 (May 24), 47.

25. Youngblood, S.A., DeNisi, A.S. Molleston, J.L., and Mobley, W.H. The impact of work environment instrumentality beliefs, perceived labor union image, and subjective norms on union voting intentions. *Academy of Management Journal*, 1984, 27, 576-90.

26. Zachary, G.P. At Apple Computer proper office attire includes a muzzle, *Wall Street Journal*, October 6, 1989, p.1.

Learning Resources
Centre

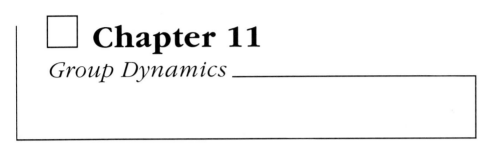

Chapter 11

Group Dynamics

Consultants often identify wide differences between organizations in how well groups are managed. Consider the following observations extracted from a consultant's report after studying two different medium-size hospitals.

> Observations of staff meetings at Liggett Memorial Hospital reveal open discussions and many instances of cooperative suggestions. Special project teams, consisting of employees from different levels and specialties, are taken seriously and often used to attack problems or implement programs. Interviews with employees and observations in the wards uncover many instances of cooperation, information sharing, and helpfulness. While some status tensions exist, good relationships are common between nurses, volunteers, technicians, custodians, and many other specialists. Most departments take pride in their work. Communications are sprinkled with humor and playful bragging, but not at the expense of other units. Absenteeism and lateness are uncommon. A survey of patients describes the staff as supportive, pleasant, and responsive. Patients also report satisfaction with how they were treated when admitted and discharged. . . .

> The quality of service at Coggins Community Hospital is declining as reported in interviews with personnel and in survey responses from patients. Patients complain about slow response and instances of inconsiderateness or indifference by staff. Staff members were observed arguing within earshot of patients. Observations of wards show little evidence of cooperation or mutual help, except in emergency situations with patients. Staff meetings in most departments are viewed as time wasted: important problems are not addressed. The few project teams that have been used were criticized for misrepresenting employees, and several key reports are still pending. Nurses and technicians are complaining of being treated in an unprofessional manner by administrators and physicians. Nurses have filed grievances over two recent promotions. Absences and lateness incidents are increasing. . . .

These excerpts point out sharp differences between Liggett and Coggins, some of which are easily traced to group and other interpersonal influences. For example, why are there differences in cooperation and helpfulness? What explains the behavior in, and attitudes toward, staff meetings and project teams? Clearly, too, the hospitals differ in how cohesive employees are, and how fairly they are treated and represented by others. These factors appear to be having a differential impact in employee behavior and patient treatment. Management can act to affect many of these group dimensions, which are the subject of this chapter.

INFLUENCE IN GROUPS

The process of *group influence* is one of the most widely studied subjects in the social sciences. **Influence** is a process by which the behavior or characteristics of people affect the behavior or characteristics of others. It operates in all types of human interaction and interdependency. Figure 11.1 shows the various influence forces that can affect social behavior. Our focus in this chapter will be on influence processes in small groups.

FIGURE 11.1 *Factors in Influence, Obedience, and Conformity*

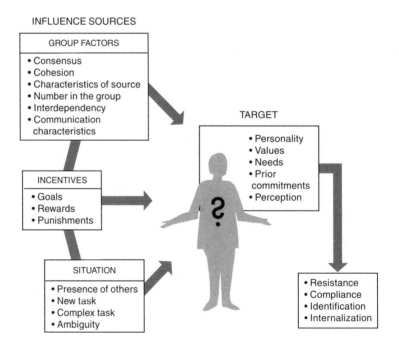

WHAT IS CONFORMITY?

Suppose you resist pressure from a friend to go fishing instead of to work. You justify your decision by saying you need the money. This example demonstrates the dynamics of conformity and influence. Are you resisting conformity by refusing to go fishing? Are you conforming by going to work? Obviously, you, the friend, and your work are exerting some influence over your behavior.

Conformity is not just doing what other people do. It involves more direct influence and requires that you would not act similarly when alone. Conformity is "a change in behavior or belief . . . as a result of a real or imagined group pressure" [20]. There is a negative connotation to conformity. It suggests a loss of individualism, a sacrifice of self-esteem, or a character weakness. Since Western society values individualism, self-respect, and strength of character, few people wish to be judged puppets, subject to the whims of others.

Does this make conformity bad? Not necessarily. It depends on at least two factors. One is whether the conformity results in what are agreed on as good or bad outcomes. If you go along with fellow managers in price fixing, our values tell us this result of conformity isn't very good. But if conformity causes cooperative effort to save a life or prevent an accident, we would agree that it is worthwhile. The second criterion we use to judge the goodness of conformity has to do with the nature of the change it involves. Consider the following three conditions, not all of which reflect conformity.

Compliance. **Compliance** is when people conform in spite of their own beliefs and preferences. The reasons for this can vary. A highly valued reward or feared punishment can tempt or force people to sway from their values. When someone acts this way, your reaction can range from sympathy to revulsion. It is easy to forgive a manager for obeying questionable orders from a superior. It is not as easy to accept it when a salesperson cheats a customer for personal gain. Compliance is the least attractive type of conformity, and it gives conformity its negative connotation even when it can be justified and understood.

Identification. In **identification** people conform when they respect or are attracted to others who support a particular action. Conformity is based on either trying to gain the favor of others or attempting to model others' behavior. Identification is much more voluntary than compliance, but its roots lie in the values and aspirations that we have. People are more vulnerable to influence when they identify with a source.

Internalization. When people accept requests or orders because they are consistent with their beliefs and values, and influence is successful because the desired behavior is intrinsically rewarding to them, it is called **internalization**. It is not conformity, because conforming behavior requires a change from how we would act alone.

Internalization can operate quite apart from identification. Suppose you don't identify with your superior, and your relationship is marked by dislike and distrust. You would still execute an order from him if the order called for a behavior or goal you personally valued. Internalization can explain why people behave according to group and societal norms. But unlike conformity, such behavior does *not* call for a change from what you would ordinarily do.

FACTORS BEHIND CONFORMITY

A number of classic studies show how a group can influence individuals to conform. In some famous experiments, Asch asked subjects in groups to compare the length of one line to three other lines and to match that line with the one of three closest in length [2, 3]. When alone, people made correct matches almost all the time. But when a subject was placed in a group, there were startling differences. Some of the group members were the experimenter's confederates, who gave an obviously wrong answer. About two-thirds of the time, people resisted the influence of the confederates and stuck to the correct answer. But more than one-third of the people agreed with the wrong answer. This was a simple judgment task with no explicit rewards or punishments for being right or wrong; there was no overt pressure to conform. Figure 11.2 shows the rate at which judgment errors increase as the number of confederate opponents of the subject increases.

☐ **FIGURE 11.2** *How Judgment Errors Increase as the Number of Opponent Confederates Changes*

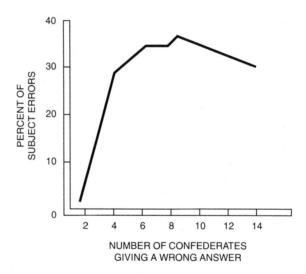

Sherif also used confederates to test conformity to others' judgments. In these experiments, the amount of movement of a pinpoint of light in a dark room was judged. The light appears to move even though it is stationary, because the eye moves somewhat [37]. This is called the **autokinetic effect.** Once a subject reported the amount of movement he or she saw, confederates would say that it moved a different distance and direction. In this study, a large percentage of people conformed to the group judgment. Other studies using the same light judgment will carry that false judgment into a future setting and use it in the presence of a new naive subject [16].

There is similar evidence of **suggestibility** in real life. Rumors can spread and people can be led to believe that invasions have occurred or that disaster may be imminent. Phillips found that car accidents, plane crashes, and suicides increase after suicides are widely publicized [33]. The proposition here is that publicized suicides may have an effect on people. The actual location of the publicity and the newsprint space it received predict the location and magnitude of the effect.

When you read about power, authority, and leadership later in this text, keep the problems of conformity in mind. People who achieve positions of authority and leadership should learn that followers will often comply because of the power of those to whom they report. In one case, a company president wrote a simple handwritten but ambiguous note on a company advertisement and sent it to a vice president. The vice president and others thought the president was angry about the contents of the ad. They reacted by almost canceling a contract with the company's advertising agency. Later, it was discovered that the note had been misinterpreted. People in the organization were obeying an "order" that was never intended.

Other Factors Influencing Conformity.   The presence of others who support **resistance to conformity** lowers the odds that a person will comply. Few people like to stand alone, and there is power in numbers. In some cases, only one other ally can help us to resist conforming.

The larger the number of people applying pressure, or the more people who seem to agree with each other, the more likely we are to give in to the pressure. But it only takes a few people to create a significant pressure to conform (see Figure 11.2). Adding more doesn't necessarily add equal increments to pressure. In fact, we are more influenced by several quite small groups than we are by a single larger group [42].

People conform more in public. When acting in private, such as in a voting booth, conformity is much less likely. Thus if a manager can get information anonymously, it will be more individualized and less socially biased.

Another factor affecting conformity suggested earlier is when a situation is ambiguous or unstructured. Susceptibility to conformity increases with uncertainty. The pinpoint of light in the studies using the autokinetic effect had somewhat greater effects on conformity than the lines of different lengths. The line-matching task was more clear-cut. Reliance on others increases when criteria for judgment and predictions are vague and uncertain.

Finally, a person's prior commitment affects conformity. We tend to hang on to earlier convictions even when faced with pressure to change. We can get people to resist conformity by having them state their position on an issue before subjecting them to the influence of others.

SOCIAL FACILITATION

For influence to take place, other people don't have to offer judgments, give orders, or otherwise exert direct pressure. **Social facilitation** means that the mere presence of others, without active involvement, can influence behavior. Whether the presence helps or hinders performance depends on the nature of the performance required, or what the person's **dominant response** is in the situation [45]. People perform better in the presence of others on easy or previously learned tasks. People do worse or make mistakes in the presence of others on new or complex tasks. This is an important principle for managers to understand. It suggests putting people together in view of each other when they do work at which they are capable and practiced, such as on a factory floor or in an open room of typists. Conversely, when a person is learning new tasks, the principle argues for giving employees a place to learn or practice alone, away from others.

How does social facilitation operate? People become apprehensive when they are observed and evaluated [10]. They also become distracted by the presence of others, and this would interfere with performance. Another explanation lies in individual differences. Some people are more affected by others regardless of the task. They are simply more aware of others, more concerned about others' reactions, and have a greater desire for social acceptance or approval. Social facilitation may also mean that the presence of others serves to arouse or sensitize people. Anxiety about evaluation need not be the only factor: performance can be influenced even on tasks where there is no right or wrong answer.

RISKY SHIFT AND POLARIZATION

An important issue is whether groups make riskier or less risky decisions than individuals. Much research gave rise to the surprising conclusion that groups are sometimes less cautious and will produce riskier conclusions than individuals [8, 40]. This effect, known as **risky shift**, was the opposite of the widely held belief that groups are conservative or cautious. Later studies showed that the riskier outcome does not always occur in groups, but together these studies give some insight into risk behavior.

What might cause a group to shift to a riskier decision, or a less risky one, compared to individuals? The answer lies in understanding the inclinations of members *before* they enter the group discussion. In general, group discussion tends to strengthen the members' first inclinations [28]. The group will enhance and strengthen the average of the members' prediscussion tendencies. That is, if individuals favor a particular decision before discussion, that decision will be strengthened.

Polarization occurs when group members solidify their agreement on an issue. Suppose the personnel department favors a new appraisal system for first-line supervisors, but these supervisors are predisposed against any change. Discussions within the personnel group will strengthen their inclinations favoring the new system. Discussion among supervisors will strengthen their biases against change. This would create an even larger gap between the two groups.

Polarization is one of the key factors in conflict, and there are several managerial solutions to minimize the problem. To reduce polarization, avoid premature meetings of subgroups for and against an issue. It is also helpful to mix membership in groups, or occasionally to invite outsiders or people with different ideas into meetings whenever feasible. Any action that calls for a focus on the total organization mission might reduce polarization.

LOWER STATUS AND MINORITY INFLUENCE

In general, high-status people exert more influence than lower-status people. Higher-status people usually control rewards and resources, and others tend to identify with high-status people. However, people with lower status can also exert influence in various ways.

One form of lower-status influence is to exhibit **helplessness** [6]. By appearing weak or showing need for assistance, low-status people can appeal to the humanity of higher-status people. This can be rewarding for some high-status people. Not only does it permit them to act generously, it perpetuates their sense of status and power. Low-status people cannot use helplessness excessively or they might become viewed as incompetent. Helplessness is not a particularly ideal characteristic for those employees who want to advance themselves, though on occasion it can be an effective way to exert considerable influence.

Ingratiation is another way for low-status people to exert influence by agreeing with or flattering another person. If done tactfully, this can earn "social credits." If the higher-status person sincerely accepts the flattery, he or she will be influenced by it. For example, a manager might comply with a request from a subordinate so as to not risk losing the flattery. Kipnis, in a study of a simulated business organization, showed that subjects who acted as managers rewarded ingratiation [21].

Ingratiation is not always received well by people of higher status. They don't want to be subject to the obligations that ingratiation can create. They may also see the behavior as insincere and manipulative. The ingratiating person risks disapproval from others.

Low-status people can also act in a deviant manner as a means to influence. Moscovici has shown that in a minority effect as few as two people can influence the judgment of a larger group [27]. Sometimes even a single group member can sway others toward his or her position. It depends on how the minority presents its point of view. Moscovici argues that the minority must show conviction, resist group counterpressure, act fairly, and present their position in a logical and rational way. These behaviors are not always successful, but they do give a minority a reasonable chance at being influential. Minorities must be perceived as sincere, courageous, and competent.

In a work organization, minority opinions often lose out to the majority. When this happens, dissatisfaction and resentment can be the result. Furthermore, the value of a minority opinion can be lost, which can damage problem solving and decision making. Management therefore has many reasons to be sensitive to minority and low-status positions.

GROUP COHESION

Cohesion, or cohesiveness, is the degree to which members of a group are attracted to one another and to group membership. Members of cohesive groups have a strong desire to stay in the group. Attractiveness is a key ingredient in cohesion, but it is possible for a person to want to keep membership and not be highly attracted to a group. Membership in a country club might be very useful to a person's career success, even though he or she doesn't particularly like some of the members. However, such motivation will not contribute much to group cohesion. Without attractiveness, cohesion will suffer.

Groups vary in cohesiveness, and cohesiveness can change over time, depending on the group's experience. Although cohesiveness is important, a group does not have to be highly cohesive in order to survive; a group can live and work together for a long time without becoming exceedingly cohesive. But they are not likely to pull together under pressure. Figure 11.3 depicts some causes and effects of cohesiveness.

☐ **FIGURE 11.3** *Causes and Effects of Cohesiveness*

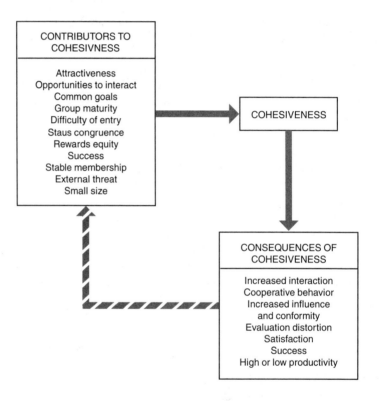

☐ **DIFFICULTIES IN
A QUALITY CIRCLE** _____

Many organizations have tried to increase employee participation by forming small groups of workers into *quality circles*. The main goal is to call on workers, especially those at lower levels, to identify problems and opportunities to improve methods, enhance quality, and reduce costs. Successes and failures of quality circles can often be traced to the dynamics early in a group's life. Quality circles have the same characteristics and difficulties as any small task team might face. Getting started on the right foot is not easy.

☐ DIFFICULTIES IN . . .

Imagine yourself assigned to a quality circle. You are a machine operator in a company that manufactures parts for the computer industry. You might consider how and why you were selected to join the quality circle. Are you being rewarded or punished? Is it because of your skill or knowledge? You've heard of quality circles, but you're not sure what they're supposed to do. For example, does the group merely suggest ideas, or is it also responsible for carrying them out?

At the first group meeting, you learn that the group is supposed to contribute to improved productivity and efficiency. But you are reluctant to reveal problems in your own department. Why hang out your dirty laundry when your department can settle its own difficulties by itself? In addition, are you representing your department in any way? What's the best way to keep your supervisor and fellow workers informed? Will you be able to bring their ideas and suggestions to a quality circle meeting?

You were able to keep quiet and just take it all in at the first meeting. However, as the group continued to meet, the pressure to say something built up. The group listed problems and opportunities, several of which came from you. Very often, though, you hesitated to speak up because there were two group members from the front office whom you weren't sure you could trust. But you know that if you don't pitch in to help on a problem, the group might not help you out when you need them.

There were many moments when the group seemed far from cooperative. Did others also fear open collaboration? You knew there were a few people who felt that they couldn't be blamed if the group failed—a friend of yours in the group admitted that much to you. While no member wanted to look bad, no one wanted to look like a jerk either. These dilemmas led to more than one unproductive meeting.

After five meetings, the group seemed to be going nowhere. There was little consensus on which problems the group should attack first. You knew that unless the group got its act together, the whole quality circle program might go down the tubes.

FORCES CONTRIBUTING TO COHESION

A number of factors foster group cohesion [17, 41]. Some were suggested in our earlier discussions and in the previous chapter. Other important conditions enhancing cohesion are discussed below.

Group Formation Factors. The conditions leading to group formation contribute to cohesion. When people are similar to one another and when they share

341

common goals and interests, the foundation for cohesion is laid. Recall, too, that similarity between people is a powerful basis for mutual attraction that is central to the definition of cohesiveness. The more important the goals are to each member, and the greater the perceived need for interdependence to accomplish goals, the higher the cohesiveness.

Difficulty of Entry.   Some groups are not easy to join. They carefully select members and may have elaborate rites of entry. The more difficult it is to enter a group, the more status the group is likely to have for someone desiring membership. A personal sense of status and accomplishment will result merely from being accepted into the group. An elitist feeling or attitude can develop that contributes to the spirit and cohesion of the group.

Status Congruence.   If the criteria for entry into a group are consistently applied, members can start out with similar, though not necessarily identical, status within the group. As members interact, their status can change, and a status hierarchy evolves. **Status congruence** results if there is consensus among members about this status hierarchy, and each behaves according to his or her status. Status congruence contributes to cohesion. *Incongruence* can lead to both frustration and resentment [15]. Incongruence can arise when work assignments are made or when status symbols are given. For instance, a group can be disrupted if a low-status member is assigned the best equipment.

Fair Rewards Allocation.   Cohesion is facilitated when rewards are allocated fairly or evenly. To be fair, rewards must be either equivalent to the contribution a person has made or consistent with a person's status level. Equal distribution of rewards can grow out of a group agreement to do so. Cohesion suffers when a member is given rewards inconsistent with what others feel he or she deserves.

Success.   When a group achieves a meaningful and shared goal, cohesion usually increases. Members experience a sense of accomplishment and pride. For example, strong feelings of cohesion are expressed by successful companies, combat units, or sports teams.

Stable Membership.   Stability of membership helps to keep cohesion at its level. New membership disrupts this. New members may not be accepted easily by the old members, and status struggles can emerge. Patterns of interaction can change, and norms might have to be enforced more actively. This is why it is often difficult for a new member to enter an already cohesive group, particularly if the new member is the leader. A manager who enters a highly cohesive group of subordinates has to tread softly until he or she learns group norms and relationships. The main task is to minimize disruption, particularly if the group is productive and respected.

External Threat.   Group cohesion can increase dramatically when an outside force is perceived as threatening to member goals and interests. Differences between members become less important as they pull together to protect themselves and resist the threat. The threatening party will feel less chance of success when faced with a unified response.

Small Group Size. Smaller groups tend to be more cohesive than larger ones. Larger groups tend to have interaction and organization problems. With increases in size, subgrouping and formalized procedures are established to prevent disorder. Cohesion is more likely to be stronger within the subgroups that emerge.

Small size contributes to cohesion in several ways. It permits more interaction and increases opportunity to participate. The informality of smaller groups also helps cohesion. Member satisfaction is likely to be higher, even for reasons other than cohesiveness.

SOME CONSEQUENCES OF COHESION

Cohesiveness affects the way members interact and exert influence, their perceptions, satisfaction, and productivity.

Interactions. There is more interaction and communication among members of cohesive groups. Members share needs and problems much more than they do in less cohesive groups. Similarity in interests, common goals, personal attractiveness, and size all contribute to these increased interactions.

Increased Influence and Conformity. A cohesive group can exert a great deal of power and influence over its members. They will respond more readily to demands than in a low cohesive group.

A leader who is respected by the group can even be quite directive [13], especially if the leader has the skill to organize the group against a threat. Directive leadership may also be acceptable when a group has a very important goal and there is some uncertainty in achieving it.

High susceptibility to influence can be a problem. If members cannot express opinions or feelings for fear of losing acceptance or membership, individualism and self-respect may be reduced. The group may lose the benefit of fresh ideas, and authenticity and honesty can suffer. In a later chapter we show how this can adversely affect group decision making.

But suppressive influence can be, on occasion, quite functional. A military combat leader in the field needs instant compliance in the midst of a dangerous mission. Democratic and shared influence under these conditions can cost team members their lives. The more appropriate time for individual expression and mutual influence is during planning sessions before the mission takes place, and after the mission is completed.

Evaluation Distortion. **Evaluation distortion** occurs when cohesive groups tend to overvalue their own behavior and accomplishments and to undervalue outside groups. A cohesive team in one plant may believe they are the best when another plant is performing more effectively. High self-evaluations reinforce the group's feelings of worth and togetherness.

Outsiders are evaluated lower for several reasons. First, the group's own status is enhanced by rating another group lower. Second, devaluing the other group is a form of defensiveness, in which the group denies its own weaknesses as a way to maintain togetherness. Stressing the positive may be unrealistic, but it preserves group spirit. Third, devaluing other groups can also give a sense of security.

Satisfaction.   Members of cohesive groups are more satisfied than members of less cohesive groups. The sources of satisfaction, already discussed, are friendliness, support, opportunity to interact, success, and protection against outsiders. Because cohesive groups can pull together against outside threats, satisfaction also grows out of a feeling of security.

Productivity: It Depends.   The relationship between cohesiveness and productivity is more complex. Stogdill examined a number of studies that correlated cohesiveness with group productivity [39]. In some, there was no relationship between cohesiveness and productivity. In others, cohesiveness was positively related to productivity, and in still others, more cohesive groups were among the least productive. These mixed results can be understood if we consider how cohesiveness is related to group goals. Seashore provided the clue in a study of industrial work groups [35]. He categorized several hundred of these groups into high or low cohesiveness. The *average* productivity of both groups was quite similar. But the productivity of low cohesive groups centered near the average. That is, low cohesive groups were less likely to have high or low productivity. In the high cohesive groups, however, productivity was not near the average but tended to be at the extremes, either highly productive or the least productive.

Figure 11.4 characterizes these results. When the cohesive groups had goals and norms that were consistent with organizational expectations, productivity was high. Keller also found that cohesiveness was the strongest predictor of project group performance in a research and development division [19]. When cohesive groups had goals and norms that were not consistent with

☐ **FIGURE 11.4**   *Productivity Between and Within High and Low Cohesive Groups*

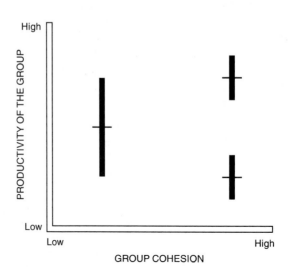

organizational expectations, productivity was low. Furthermore, Seashore found a greater resemblance of performance of members *within* the highly cohesive groups than among members of low cohesive groups [35]. This is consistent with the conclusion that cohesive groups influence their members more, regardless of their productivity level.

HELPING BEHAVIOR

Employees have many opportunities to exhibit helping behavior. They can assist a co-worker with a task or a personal problem, volunteer extra effort, or suggest improvements [14]. Constructive behavior and self-imposed standards of excellence are a form of positive self-leadership that can be very valuable to an organization [24]. In other words, how an employee feels and acts has powerful implications for productivity and satisfaction. Katz argued that such acts are essential if organizations are to excel, because success depends on employees going beyond formal role requirements [18]. Such patterns are referred to as prosocial or **organizational citizenship** behavior [7, 31]. It reflects the extent to which a person is willing to go beyond the norms of performance and involvement of his or her work role. Organization citizenship behaviors are actions that, in many ways, are not exaggerated, not extreme or heroic, and may seem even trivial and mundane. Still, they contribute in an important way to the effectiveness of the organization [30]. Among the behaviors that reflect organization citizenship are:

1. *Altruistic Behaviors.* Altruistic acts are those which help another specific person with a work problem. For example, much mentoring behavior by higher-level managers is altruistic when it is done simply because the senior manager believes it to be a personal responsibility to help younger managers learn the ropes.

2. *Conscientious Behavior.* Conscientious behavior is compliance with peripheral organizational norms, those which are desired but which need not necessarily be accepted. Thus, the conscientious person goes beyond the minimal work requirements by regular attendance, being on time for work, and generally showing respect for rules and policies.

3. *Sportsmanlike Behavior.* Inconvenience and frustration result from bureaucratic delays, thoughtlessness on the part of others, and inconsiderate actions by superiors. Sportsmanship is accepting these without complaint and without reacting by "making federal cases out of small potatoes" [30].

4. *Courtesy.* Courtesy is consideration for others who may be affected by one's decisions and actions, and is demonstrated by consulting with them and informing them how they may be affected.

5. *Civic Virtue.* This calls for active, serious, and responsible participation in the governance activities of the organization. It keeps one aware of what is going on, and continually contributing to the organization.

FACTORS RELATED TO HELPING BEHAVIOR

Some factors seem to foster or to hinder helping behavior (see Figure 11.5). Some are personal attributes, whereas others seem to be conditions of the situation [5, 28].

◻ **FIGURE 11.5** *Factors in Helping Behavior*

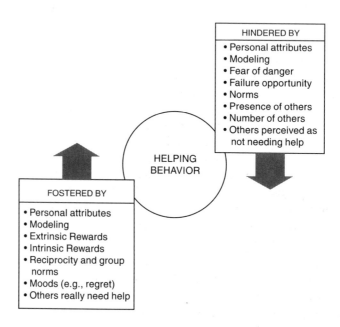

Personal Attributes. People differ in their willingness to help others, or **altruism**. Altruistic people seem to help others with no obvious benefit to themselves, with few expectations for personal gain. One personality characteristic, **empathic concern**, has been shown to be related to helping behavior. This is the capacity to internalize the feelings of another person. However, researchers have not been very successful in finding personality characteristics that reflect a consistent desire to be helpful [5].

Past and Present Modeling. Parents, other people, television, radio, and newspapers provide behavioral models. We can learn helping from our neighbors who organize to clean up the neighborhood or from fellow workers who help each other. Schwartz and Ames showed that even an aversive or repulsive model can affect helping [34]. If the aversive model disliked helping, others helped more. If that model appeared to enjoy helping, fewer people helped because they didn't want to act like a person they disliked.

Extrinsic Outcomes. People often help when they can obtain valued rewards. Someone might pay you to help them with a chore. Doing a good job can be a form of helping an organization to succeed. Many behaviors at work can be truly helpful to others, especially if they would flounder without such help.

Fears of *aversive outcomes*, conversely, can block helping. The risk of failing can frighten people away. Some physicians are reluctant to help in an emergency for fear that they may be sued for malpractice if something goes wrong. Good Samaritan laws exist in some states that protect professionals against aversive outcomes for helping others in distress.

Intrinsic Outcomes. Helping others can simply make people feel good. *Intrinsic rewards* provide a sense of having done the right thing or a feeling of pride in the action. Self-esteem and self-image are enhanced. Surely if you saved a child from drowning, you would feel quite good even if no extrinsic rewards were forthcoming. There is evidence that volunteers in clinics, libraries, and museums work only to help, since they are unpaid. They may experience higher satisfaction than paid co-workers [32]. Job satisfaction itself can also be a cause of helping behavior, further enhancing the pleasantness and productivity of a work environment [31].

An intrinsic reward may operate because we dislike a condition that exists, and helping provides us with a feeling of relief. Perhaps we feel responsible for the condition we are trying to alleviate and helping others relieves this.

THE INTERNATIONAL TRAINER

Training specialists gain a great deal of intrinsic satisfaction by helping employees at all levels in an organization. So they are particularly frustrated and disappointed when they fail in the classroom or other settings when they ply their trade. Such is the case where trainers with a history of success in the United States find themselves rendered ineffective, derailed so to speak, in an overseas assignment [25]. One trainer working with a group in Bankok, Thailand found it nearly impossible to break down the formality that trainees exhibited in the classroom. She had to cajole them to involve themselves in a role play exercise. She later found it even more difficult to get feedback and honest evaluations of her seminar because Thais are not culturally prone to criticize in the manner she had hoped for.

It turns out then, that a trainer's technical expertise is simply not enough to guarantee success in a foreign setting. Even curiosity and enthusiasm about a new culture, while essential, are insufficient. The training expert needs to have a healthy respect for the values and practices of a new culture, and a willingness to try new behaviors and avoid some old habits that could be offensive. Success in a new culture requires a tolerance for uncertainty and failure, and a professional dedication strong enough to persist through difficult conditions. A sense of humor helps, too. Above all, training professionals have to become good students themselves, and learn a host of things to become an effective source of help. Among these are learning the foreign culture and its language, and relating to key people who can serve as mentors and as sources of information. Trainers must manage their own learning, and exercise creative flexibility to adapt themselves and their training techniques to meet local demands.

Norms. Norms also affect helping. One widely recognized societal norm is **reciprocity**, based on the idea that helping fosters helping; it is also related to fairness and equity in human social exchange. This norm tells us to return the favor to those who help us. Reciprocity also causes people to expect help from those they have helped. For reciprocity to operate, a person must feel that help was really needed and that the other person gave it voluntarily, with good motives, and in a meaningful way. We are less likely to feel a need to reciprocate for trivial help or when the other person's motives were questionable.

Another norm that facilitates helping is **social responsibility**, which calls for helping others who are dependent on us. Individuals often give money and volunteer their time to worthwhile efforts. They vote for government programs for human services that help the sick, poor, or unemployed.

Mood or Preoccupation. Research shows that intrinsic rewards for helping may be greater when people are in a good mood [28]. Many things may effect mood. For example, people who feel fairly treated are more likely to feel better and show helpfulness more frequently [26].

Other moods also affect helping. When people have done something they regret, they are more likely to help. This may be a way to reduce guilty feelings or to restore feelings of self-esteem. But sadness, guilt, or other bad moods do not guarantee helping behavior, unless giving of help is seen as a way to eliminate the bad mood.

Another preoccupation that diminishes helping is when people are in a hurry, generally because getting somewhere fast is judged to be more important than offering help. Hurrying also makes people less likely to perceive an opportunity to help. Their attention is distracted from circumstances of the environment.

Presence of Others. The presence of others sometimes reduces the tendency to help. It can also reduce the amount of effort a person contributes to a task. For example, people may feel less pressure to volunteer when surrounded by others. Similarly, they might not exert as much effort when others are added to the task. This effect is called **social loafing**.

Social loafing occurs because with other people present, we assume that someone else will do what is needed and thus relieve us of the task. People seem willing to pass the buck even though nothing will get done if everyone loafs [4]. Social loafing helps to avoid becoming the patsy who contributes a lot while others get away with doing less. It also protects a person from failing, and it is difficult to fix responsibility or blame when other people are present. When people believe that their individual contribution can be evaluated, however, their degree of social loafing is sharply reduced [43]. Unproductive people do not enjoy being exposed. When an individual's contributions to a group are displayed, made public, he is less likely to loaf than when only the group performance is displayed. Individual visibility increases pressure to perform [29].

Social loafing can be a serious problem in work groups. Helping and individual effort might decline because of the presence of others. These effects can be overcome with norms and incentives to help and cooperate, with rewards for those behaviors, using similar groups and making individual contributions more visible, and fostering a culture where individualism and self-interest are supplanted by a spirit of commitment to group effort through collective cooperation [1].

The **bystander effect** occurs when people act uninvolved and are unwilling to help in certain settings such as emergencies. News stories often report of injured people left unaided or robbery victims whose cries for help went unanswered by bystanders. In a series of experiments, Latané and Darley found that as the number of bystanders increases, people who would otherwise help tended not to do so [23]. The presence of bystanders reduces the probability that someone will even notice the event or attend to it, especially if others don't. There may even be some subtle pressures not to react with alarm. Bystanders also seem to reduce the odds that the event will be interpreted as an emergency — if others don't treat the event as an emergency, people conclude that it probably is not one. Shotland states that if the situation is ambiguous or if helping is defined as interfering in a private relationship, intervention is less likely to occur [38].

Who Gets Help.   We are more likely to help some people than others. If we judge a person's needs as important, we are more willing to help [28]. Females get more help than males, especially those who are seen as attractive. People whom we like or perceive to be similar to ourselves are more likely to receive our help. Evidence on the question of race and help is mixed: a person's race sometimes enhances helping, sometimes inhibits it, or can make no difference at all.

FOSTERING HELPFUL BEHAVIOR

A number of steps can be taken to foster helping. One is to develop *cooperative norms*. This can be done through active attention to mutually supportive relationships. A manager can discuss with employees how they can help with a problem that arises in another work area. This tends to build a norm of responsibility for others and an orientation that goes beyond one's own department.

Appeals for cooperation can also be made. When help is needed, it can be called to the attention of people who are then asked for assistance. Face-to-face requests are often quite effective. They appeal to a person's self-image and may even trigger feelings of guilt over refusal. Appeals are also likely to be effective if they define the problem clearly, which aids the interpretation that help is indeed needed.

Rewards can also be used to foster helping behavior. Managers should watch for and recognize helpful individuals. When people help, they can be acknowledged in other ways; for example, exceptional instances can be publicized with a story in the company newspaper. The rewards system should not reinforce undue competitiveness, self-centeredness, and separateness. Frequently, high expectations for performance cause employees to try to produce at any price. In such situations, help can be the last thing to occur to anyone. It may even benefit employees to do subtle harm to others or ignore them rather than assist.

Employees can be taught in training programs the importance of helping and what factors enhance and inhibit it. Suppose employees are being trained to improve planning skills. Planning creates interdependencies between organizational units. Methods for managing independence can be taught that would include helping and cooperative behaviors.

COOPERATION AND COMPETITION

People in groups have choices about whether to cooperate or compete. In addition, situational forces in a group may foster either behavior. **Cooperation** means more than just helping. It means giving support to others, and contributing time and effort in situations where people jointly work together toward some end. Typically, the whole group can benefit from cooperation. Cooperation is often a natural consequence of social organization. Sometimes it occurs as a direct result of how tasks are designed. For example, a factory or an airplane cockpit can be designed for cooperative effort. Cooperation is also a common consequence of team activity; sports such as baseball or basketball are good examples. Teamwork is also necessary in military operations or to put out a forest fire.

Neither the opportunities to work cooperatively nor its benefits guarantees that cooperation will occur. It is quite possible for efforts to go uncoordinated or for competition to develop. In **competition**, people are more concerned with their own welfare, sometimes at the expense of others. Competition can cause harm to the competing parties, usually to the losing party. This often happens in sports, business, or street gangs.

Competition can also lead to some benefits. Salespeople can compete so that they gain and the company gains. If awards go to winners, the losers may suffer some, but the gain may more than offset it. Championship football games produce a loser, but the money paid to losers can be substantial, and there is also pride for having earned the right to compete. Therefore, whether competition is damaging or beneficial depends on the balance of benefits and cost that result.

Conditions Fostering Cooperation and Competition

Several factors can tilt individuals and groups toward either competition or cooperation. Some factors lie in the characteristics of individuals, some in the group composition and dynamics, and others in the nature of the task or environment of the group [17]. Figure 11.6 illustrates these factors and the conditions under which cooperation and competition are each beneficial.

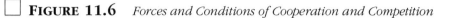 **FIGURE 11.6** *Forces and Conditions of Cooperation and Competition*

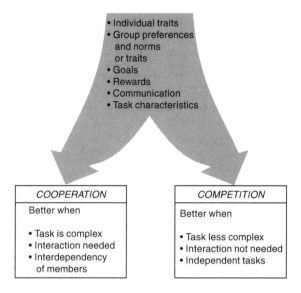

Individual Traits. Differences between people affect their tendencies toward cooperation or competition. There is wide variation in competitiveness for males and females, but on average males are more competitive. In addition to differences between people within a society, anthropologists have found cross-cultural differences in cooperativeness and competitiveness.

There are several ways to compete. Some people focus on their gains relative to others': winning over someone else is the primary motivation. Other competitors work primarily toward their own goals and have less interest in whether others gain or lose. They desire to excel against a personal standard, not an interpersonal one. The things they do to succeed may directly affect others.

Group Preferences and Norms. Because people are attracted to others who are similar to themselves, it follows that groups can form around preferences to cooperate or compete. For example, a task force leader might reject a competitive person because he or she could disrupt the group's coordination. A sales manager, on the other hand, might select a strong competitor in order to facilitate competition between salespeople to perform better.

These examples show that there is a distinction between norms that govern *within-group behavior* and those that govern *between-group behavior.*

351

There may be a norm of competitiveness within a group, particularly if this norm enhances group goals, but the dominant norm within a group will usually be cooperation. On many teams there is a need to cooperate during practice, such as when one player helps other team members to improve their game.

Norms governing relationships with another group can also be either cooperative or competitive. In some situations, competition is the norm, such as in sports or in the business world. Groups within organizations might compete for the same pool of resources. How to balance cooperation and competition in organization settings is a delicate and difficult issue.

Goals and Rewards.   These can be managed in a way to foster either cooperation or competition. Cooperation is more likely to occur where there are common goals that people understand, accept, and have the resources to achieve. It is also fostered by *shared rewards*. However, when an organization rewards only a few people or groups, competition is a probable result. Competition can reach destructive levels: people hoard resources, withhold information, refuse help, or engage in any behavior that gives them an advantage over others. Rewards can be managed so that they do not cause destructive competition. Competition can be held to acceptable levels if there are few incentives to win at the expense of others. Two divisions of a firm might compete for the introduction of their new products without harm if they both have adequate resources and if they work independently.

Cooperation is more easily achieved when employees perceive some chance of earning a valued reward. Within work groups, cooperation is maximized when members within the group share rewards equally. Group incentive plans have this attribute. Regardless of individual contributions, the group's product is assessed and rewarded. Group incentives, compared to individual incentives, encourage cooperation and sharing of ideas, and members are more willing to help and give each other feedback.

Communication.   Effective communication results in understanding, acceptance, or both between the people involved. But understanding and acceptance guarantee neither cooperation nor competition. For example, we can understand that other people are angry or hostile, and it might cause us to enter into competition with them. By the same token, communication can provide clear cues that the other person wishes to cooperate.

Communication is a necessary, though insufficient, prerequisite to cooperation. If people are to cooperate, communication cannot be held back, nor can it be distorted or misdirected. Good communication doesn't ensure cooperation, but poor communication will probably inhibit it.

Patterns of interaction can also affect cooperation. Studies of networks show that when communication must pass through a single person who is in a centralized and controlling position, communication is fast and accurate if the task is simple [36]. Where people are freer to talk to more group members, decentralized networks are more effective for success at complex tasks. Although the latter networks are slower, they place less burden on a single individual for group success. They also facilitate behavior more useful to success on complex tasks. The amount of communication and member satisfaction also increases in decentralized networks. If managers want effective cooperation on complicated tasks, they must provide opportunities for more complete interaction between group members.

Task Characteristics.   With complex tasks, people need to give and receive more information. Complex tasks have more elements than simple tasks. Less is known about how to perform them, and more problems can arise. Task complexity can also mean that it is difficult to give someone a clear job description. All this increases the need for interaction, because members are more independent in performing the task. Interpersonal cooperation and communication are both essential.

Compare a typing pool with a product development team. Typists can work alone in separate location, and interactions between them are not necessary to do the work. A product development team, however, has a complex task. Product feasibility, production issues, marketing questions, and technological problems are all woven together, and team members are highly interdependent at all stages of developing a new product. Each team member knows about the work of others so as to prevent duplication and wasted effort. When conditions change, members must keep each other informed. These teams hold frequent meetings and use a variety of communication methods to facilitate cooperation.

Some tasks benefit from competition. Typists can compete for quantity and accuracy. When tasks are performed independently, performance is enhanced with reasonable competition for rewards. Competition can be effective for independent tasks as long as there are few incentives to harm the other party, and if cooperation is fostered when necessary. For example, typists need to cooperate when helping each other to learn how to use new equipment.

EFFECTS OF COOPERATION AND COMPETITION

Cooperation and competition have different effects. Here we are most interested in how member interactions and perceptions affect their productivity and satisfaction.

Interaction Patterns and Perceptions.   Deutsch studied competing and cooperating groups and found that members of each type of group held perceptions consistent with whether the group was cooperative or competitive [11]. However, more positive expressions occurred in cooperative groups. Members of cooperative groups did more to relieve another group member of a task, and they exhibited greater helpfulness than members of competitive groups. They displayed more kinds of coordinative behavior such as attentiveness to others. There was high quality and understanding of discussions, more friendliness, greater diversity of contributions, and more orderliness than in competitive groups.

Cooperative group members also evaluate each other's efforts and contributions more favorably. One study of dyads examined how the two members made attributions after success and failure on a task [44]. When a prior established goal was exceeded, individuals in both cooperative and competitive dyads attributed success to themselves. This was not the case when they failed to meet goals. Cooperative pairs who failed to meet their goals attributed the failure to their partner. However, failure in competitive pairs was attributed to situational causes. Attributions of failure to others rather than to the situation may depend on the nature of the competition within a group. When working independently or competitively within a group, people may have a stronger tendency to blame the situation. When working on interdependent or cooperative tasks, the tendency is to blame others [17].

Productivity. Whether cooperative or competitive groups are more productive was partly answered in the previous discussion of task characteristics. Cooperation results in better performance for tasks that require interdependent action. For example, interaction and communication are critical to the success of a new-product development team because team members must share information, coordinate their plans and activities, and help each other. This is in contrast to the sales force that might be more productive under moderate competition. The productivity of salespeople is possible with minimal interaction with one another. Care must be taken, however, so that lack of cooperation is not damaging to groups such as sales forces. Competition might result in behaviors such as withholding critical information, which could damage the entire sales effort.

Deutsch showed that cooperative groups put more pressure on members to achieve the group goal [11]. In addition, they evaluate their group and its products more favorably. Cooperative groups were also more productive than competitive groups, perhaps because the tasks called for interdependent action. Kohn argues that performance suffers when the parties put more energy into defeating each other, and that suspicion and hostility are undesirable side effects of competition [22].

Satisfaction. It is not necessarily true that members of cooperative groups are more satisfied than members of competitive groups. Cherrington reviewed a number of studies and concluded that the major determinants of satisfaction lie in the members' expectations and the rewards they receive [9]. It is the rewards that cause satisfaction, and these are different in competing and cooperating groups. Cooperative groups reward members with friendliness, praise, mutual support, and perhaps sharing of bonuses or prizes. Competitive group members can be rewarded by winning, by getting feedback on their skill, or by praise from outsiders. Once again, individual differences operate here. Some people prefer competition and the rewards that it provides; others find cooperative activity more rewarding.

MAKING GROUPS REPRESENTATIVE

When groups initially form, their members are often supposed to act as a representative to an outside constituency. **Representation** of others is not a simple matter. Consider a university task force on planning. It allegedly had balanced representation. It consisted of a vice president, a clerical supervisor, a student, a faculty member, an athletic coach, a dean, and several others. One dean said, "If you please, deans do *not* represent deans on committees!" She argued that it was not her task to speak for other deans, but rather to speak for her own college. For example, the dean of a college of medicine wants to build a strong and prestigious medical school. Since deans compete for all sorts of resources, what one dean gets, another may lose. They coordinate some of their efforts, but on the whole they operate quite separately in getting students, facilitating research, and other matters.

The issue of representation is a complex and potentially explosive one. There are two key points about representation. First, when one represents others, it is almost never a complete and accurate representation. The second point is that it takes a lot of work to create conditions where adequate representation takes place.

The following are some things that can be done to improve representation:

1. *Have the larger constituency participate in the formation of the group.* If a committee is formed to address a company-wide issue, those who form the committee could seek a mix of members, each of whom works in departments that are most affected by the issue. Competence and experience would also serve as criteria. Affected units could select their own representative.

2. *Group members should meet with constituents between meetings.* As the work of the group progresses, representatives in the group can each meet with constituents. They can give progress reports and seek feedback and guidance from time to time.

3. *A representative can also delay a group action until it is possible to get constituents' opinions on an impending decision or vote.* This can be done with a formal motion to table an issue until a future date or with a request to postpone a decision until the member can get some approval to act.

4. *The group can involve constituents in its deliberations.* Groups can hold open meetings and invite specific people to appear at meetings and speak to the issue at hand. Another technique is to place non-members on subgroups that study issues and report findings and recommendations. In this manner, a committee of seven people could be temporarily expanded to 30 or 40 members, who extend participation even further by seeking inputs from the entire organization.

CHECKLIST: WORK TEAM EFFECTIVENESS

The purpose of this checklist is to serve as an informal guide for diagnosing the effectiveness of a work group. Both the leaders and group members should complete the checklist. The answers will serve as discussion points for improving teamwork and effectiveness. The larger the number of statements answered yes, the more likely the group is productive and the members are satisfied.

☐ Checklist . .

	Mostly Yes	Mostly No
1. The atmosphere is relaxed and comfortable.	———	———
2. Group discussion is frequent, and it is usually pertinent to the task at hand.	———	———
3. Group members understand what they are trying to accomplish.		
4. People listen to each other's suggestions and ideas.	———	———
5. Disagreements are tolerated and an attempt is made to resolve them.	———	———
6. There is general agreement on most courses of action taken.	———	———
7. The group welcomes frank criticism from inside and outside sources.	———	———
8. When the group takes action, clear assignments are made and accepted.	———	———
9. There is a well-established, relaxed working relationship among the members.	———	———
10. There is a high degree of trust and confidence among the leader and subordinates.	———	———
11. The group members strive hard to help the group achieve its goal.	———	———
12. Suggestions and criticisms are offered and received with a helpful spirit.	———	———
13. There is a cooperative rather than a competitive relationship among group members.	———	———
14. The group goals are set high but not so high as to create anxieties or fear of failure.	———	———
15. The leaders and members hold a high opinion of the group's capabilities.	———	———
16. Creativity is stimulated within the group.	———	———
17. There is ample communication within the group on topics relevant to getting the work accomplished.	———	———
18. Group members feel confident in making decisions.	———	———
19. People are kept busy but not overloaded.	———	———
20. The leader of the group is well suited for the job.	———	———

Reproduced with permission from A.J. Dubrin, *Contemporary Applied Management* (Plano, TX: Business Publications, Inc., 1982) [12].

ENCOURAGING IMPROVED WORK GROUPS

Managers can take a number of steps to foster group productivity, satisfaction, cohesion, and learning. Knowledge of group characteristics and dynamics can be put to use to increase effectiveness. Some specific ways this can be done follow.

1. *Employees should be viewed as social beings, subject to the influence of others.* Their behavior should be interpreted in light of the surrounding social forces. The manager must also understand and accept that the informal organization interacts with the formal organization structure.

2. *Care should be taken in establishing group size.* Unless there are strong reasons to do otherwise, groups of two and three should be avoided. Beyond this, odd-size groups of fewer than 10 members are best, particularly if interaction is required for effectiveness. If groups must be larger, they should be broken into subgroups as a means to facilitate interactive problem solving.

3. *Group members should select other members whenever possible.* Interpersonal attractiveness can create a strong force toward cohesion and cooperation. Likewise, replacements should be selected carefully so as to minimize disruption.

    If representation is important in a group, special steps have to be taken to help ensure it. This can be accomplished by open meetings, outside inputs, communication methods, and temporary expansion of group membership to include outsiders in the activities of the group.

4. *Help groups to develop and mature.* Leadership skills, training, or outside assistance can all help a group through its developmental difficulties. Group success depends on how well members resolve interpersonal tensions, status incongruencies, and other difficulties. Appropriate attention is needed to develop task and socioemotional roles and to control disruptive members. Groups should be allowed time and the place to interact so that development is not blocked.

5. *Encourage group productivity norms that are consistent with organizational goals.* The best-producing groups are cohesive ones with norms and goals that contribute to organization success. Some of the steps above will encourage development of such norms. Managers can also provide opportunities for groups to resolve productivity problems and use rewards that contribute to satisfaction. These actions can become a basis to make less cohesive groups more cohesive and more productive. Groups that are already cohesive and productive should be managed carefully so as not to turn them against the organization.

6. *Deal with group situations where cohesion is based on norms that are harmful to the organization.* Unproductive cohesive groups are a sign that something is wrong between employees and management. Employees may feel threatened or have little trust in the organization.

This is a difficult situation to deal with, but if the causes can be diagnosed, some sort of conflict resolution strategies can be undertaken (see Chapter 14).

7. *Take steps to combat the effects of social loafing.* This can be done partly by encouraging work teams to develop good productivity goals and by recognizing contributions of individual team members. Group rewards for productivity and for cooperative effort should be used.

8. *Exercise caution in using competition to encourage group productivity.* If the task requires little interdependence and opportunities for harmful competition of others are minimized, then competition can enhance productivity. Even under competitive circumstances, such as when sales personnel compete for awards, opportunities for cooperation and mutual helping should be encouraged. In all other situations, managers should encourage and develop norms of helping and cooperation that contribute to productivity, satisfaction, cohesion, and learning.

9. *Provide groups with as many opportunities for success as possible.* Participation in goal formation, special assignments, and other methods can give groups a sense of involvement. Successful achievement has a powerful impact on all aspects of group effectiveness. Opportunities for success are especially useful for newly forming groups: success helps keep them on a track toward maturity as opposed to dissolution.

10. *Empower teams to be more responsible, more self-sufficient and self managing.* Expect teams to identify, select, and solve problems as much on their own as possible, and to evaluate the quality of their own work. Help the group to cross-train members, and to share and rotate leadership. Minimize supervisory interventions.

SUMMARY

The process of influence and conformity in groups is one of the most important aspects of group dynamics. Wide differences exist between people in their susceptibility to pressures.

Cohesive groups exert strong influence on their members. Cohesiveness makes group members pull together toward a common goal. A team spirit usually accompanies cohesion. The effects of cohesion can be quite positive. It can also have a negative effect such as in group decision making or when cohesive groups defy management. From a manager's perspective a cohesive group that works toward the organization's goals is far better than cohesive groups that withhold productivity.

Helping behavior can be very critical to the success of a group or organization. But helping does not occur automatically: some conditions facilitate it, whereas others reduce its likelihood. These same conclusions hold true for cooperative and competitive behavior. A variety of conditions can affect the amount of helping, cooperation, or competition that occurs. These behaviors can be influenced by managers: steps can be taken to encourage or discourage cooperation or competition, depending on the task demands.

Groups have to take special steps if their members are to adequately represent people outside the group itself. Good representation can foster acceptance of the group's work. It can be achieved through methods that involve the constituency in the group's decisions and deliberations.

A solid knowledge of the varied dynamics of groups can be valuable to a manager. Much can be done by the informed manager to encourage effective work groups.

☐ KEY CONCEPTS _____

Altruism	Evaluation	Polarization
Autokinetic effect	distortion	Reciprocity
Bystander effect	Helplessness	Representation
Cohesion	Identification	Resistance to conformity
Competition	Influence	Risky shift
Compliance	Ingratiation	Social facilitation
Conformity	Internalization	Social loafing
Cooperation	Organizational	Social responsibility
Dominant response	citizenship	
Empathic concern		

☐ STUDY QUESTIONS

1. Is conformity good or bad? Explain.
2. The next time you attend the theater or a sports event, make a list of behaviors that you feel are good examples of conformity. Then assess whether the conformity was generally harmful or helpful to the conformer and to others.
3. As a manager, would you rather have employees behave out of compliance, identification, or internalization? Why? Under what conditions would obedience be particularly helpful or harmful?
4. What is the importance of lower-status or minority influence to a manager?
5. What are the major factors that contribute to cohesion in groups?
6. Suppose as a manager you had a group of workers reporting to you whose cohesiveness was moderate to low. How would you increase cohesion to improve productivity and satisfaction?
7. For the same group described in Question 6, what might a manager do that would increase the group's cohesion but lower their productivity?
8. What is the best way to manage a cohesive and highly productive group? What can a manager do to change a cohesive but unproductive group?

□ STUDY . . .

9. How can a manager encourage and sustain helping behavior in a group?

10. Describe a work situation that would benefit from competition between groups. What kinds of things should be done to keep competition from getting destructive?

11. What can be done to help make groups more representative? What happens when groups succeed as opposed to fail to adequately represent outside constituents?

12. What are some key actions a manager can take to encourage improved work groups?

CASE

□ THE GUARNERI QUARTET

Dick Cahill watched the musicians come into the recital hall from the main entrance and make their way to the stage one by one. After attending their monthly open rehearsals for about eight years he knew what to expect. They would take their usual seats on the stage; first violin to left front, second violin to left side, cello to rear toward right side of stage, and viola to front stage right. They would tune their instruments and then wait for the concert manager to announce what they would be practicing and the date and time for next month's open rehearsal.

Before starting, they agreed where they would begin. After playing together for about six minutes, the first violin stopped and said that he thought the cello was coming in a little loud. The second violin gave his opinion and the cello asked what was on the musical scores of the others at that point in the composition. "Shall we begin at measure thirty?" said the first violin. They started to play. Again and again various players would stop and tell the others that something was being played too slow, or too loud, or would inquire about what was on the score of another musician. Almost always the tone of voice was soft and slow, with no touch of anger. They were very accommodating to each other, listening very seriously to what each other had to say. Typically, when they thought something sounded wrong they demonstrated it by playing their instruments instead of verbal explanations. Sometimes one of them would play his part of a composition so the others could hear. When the quartet completed a piece to their satisfaction they would try something else for awhile.

At some rehearsals they would sometimes play without interruption for 15 or 20 minutes. Dick liked those times best. Actually, he enjoyed it all; as did most of the other 100 or so individuals who usually attended. The audience was usually quiet, although at times new people in attendance would start talking to each other when the musicians paused to discuss how a particular passage should be played. Sometimes newcomers would speak loudly enough to disturb the quartet and would be admonished by the cellist.

Usually about ten minutes before the scheduled practice was to end, the quartet would turn to the audience and ask them if there were any questions. Since about half of the audience were music faculty or students, there were many questions, most reflecting a high degree of knowledge of the music and the composers. At times the questions focused on the relationship of the musicians to each other, their experiences while on tour (which consumed more than 200 days a year), and their view of certain critics, concert halls, and composers. Other questions were more general such as why older stringed instruments from Italy sounded the way they did.

In these question sessions, the quartet members were always in very good humor, relaxed and joking among themselves and with the audience. Quartet members often told stories as answers to questions. When asked if they played better in the recording studio than when in front of a live audience, they indicated performances were better with audiences. There was, one said, a time in London when they were recording and not getting anywhere to their satisfaction. Jacqueline DuPre (a famous cellist), who they were to dine with that evening came in and sat down. Under the stimulation of just that one person they played the piece beautifully for the first time.

On a night when Dick watched the group in actual concert, the quartet was very businesslike and seemed to take their work very seriously. There wasn't much talking, although they communicated with almost imperceptible looks and gestures from time to time. While their eyes were focused on their music stands, they also would dart glances at the others from time to time to check on what they were doing. They did not actually look at each others faces while playing. They looked at the fingers. They used their peripheral vision to see the bows and fingers, especially of the one player they must follow at a particular time.

The Guarneri quartet (Arnold Steinhardt and John Dalley, violins; Michael Tree, viola; and David Soyer, cello), was formed in 1964. It is considered by many to be the finest string quartet of the present time. Unlike many string quartets, their music has been described as a unit of different voices not one identical sound. Throughout the year the Quartet plays concerts all over the world and frequently these are broadcast. They have many recordings with famous artists. A movie about the group, *High Fidelity*, was recently in movie theaters in many cities as well as at musicians' conventions. Two books have been written about the quartet. The first of

☐ THE GUARNERI . . .

these was titled *String Quartet Playing* by I. Fink and C. Merriell (Paganini-ana Publications, 1985) and the other was *The Art of Quartet Playing* by D. Blum (Alfred Knopf, 1986). Both books contain extensive interviews with members of the quartet.

In one interview, Steinhardt, who typically plays first violin, was asked the role of the first violin in a string quartet, "Was he the leader and the others followers?" Steinhardt explained that historically that was true and is still true for many quartets. The traditional view was that leadership was needed from the first violin to initiate the general course of action of the quartet. More specifically the first violin would delineate the style, suggest the mood, and set up the rhythm. While some lay persons wonder why this might be necessary since the musicians do work from musical scores, experienced music lovers know that in reality compositions from the pens of composers as Mozart and Grieg can be played in a wide variety of styles, moods, and tempos. In the Guarneri, however, and some other well-known string quartets Steinhardt indicated, the first violin is not the leader or the captain. Instead there is a "republic of equals" because of the excellence of the musicians, their own independent natures, their high degrees of self confidence. "Leaders are only needed" said Steinhardt, "where there are weak links in a group."

When asked whether they discuss a piece extensively before they play it, to set an objective or devise a plan to attain a particular sound, Steinhardt said that is not what happens. They do decide what sounds are possible in a piece, but only after playing it and hearing it performed by each other. The playing reveals not only the underlying nature of the music itself, but the capabilities of each musician to do certain things with that composition. Then they talk about it to decide what they think the proper sound should be. Decisions are made on pragmatic grounds.

In response to a question about the role of the second violin, Michael Tree said that this role often involved keeping the ensemble together tightly when the first violin is playing, more or less freely, the melodic line. The second violin at times also leads while the others follow or provide support. Tree said, however, that in the quartet there is no difference in the importance of the various instruments: All play an indispensable role in creating the whole. All must take the lead at times, and at other times provide support for the instrument that is taking the lead.

At one public rehearsal, a member of the audience ask the quartet if they felt free to change the music of a composer so as to improve it or make it more appealing to the listener. The quartet quickly and strongly responded, "No." It was their duty they believed to pass on to new generations the masterpieces the past and, if anything, reveal what these composers had intended to create to uncover their vision so to speak. They also noted which audiences take their type of music seriously; important patrons, universities, and musical organizations and societies. They

☐ THE GUARNERI . . .

described the many tips and suggestions they had received over the years form various artists or conductors with whom they had performed. Some of these suggestions might appear minor, such as moving their position to face the audience in a slightly different way to change what the audience heard.

Some members of the quartet made frequent reference to their former teachers indicating that they felt a responsibility to live up to the expectations of these now departed individuals. They also felt obliged to help create a new generation of musicians in return for what they had received from their teachers and mentors, pointing out that each teacher or mentor taught them something different, thus contributing to their development in different ways. For example, David Soyer the cellist, one day said:

> I must confess that sometimes while we're playing, I have the very weird sensation that someone is looking over my shoulder. I'm a bit embarrassed to admit that. It's as if some presence is there watching me, or even watching the whole quartet. Sometimes I sense Casals standing by my shoulder; sometimes it's Frank Miller (his teachers).

Steinhardt, in commenting on this, said:

> Whether or not they visit as apparitions, it's interesting to consider how the spirits of our mentors live on and are reborn in the individual player. It's a kind of crystallization or filtering through you of all the things you have absorbed from others through the years—a mixture of ingredients that then takes on its own individuality. It's clear that we ourselves can't accept all the credit for whatever good things there may be in a performance. If we're well enough prepared instrumentally and open to the experience, we are, in a very true sense, only vessels through which the music passes; we have to acknowledge a force greater than ourselves.

Of course, the significance of their long tenure together is not lost on the quartet members. They described once how they had benefited from advice from the famous Budapest string quartet, who told them early in their career not to socialize together more than necessary and to retain independence in their outside life. This is advice they follow. They also indicated that they came to realize that any lifelong affiliation requires a deep commitment. As Michael Tree indicated:

> Being in a quartet is almost like being in a marriage, and in many respects it's harder than a marriage. I had played quartets on and off for many years but I never realized just how great the sense of commitment must be on the part of every player in a permanent ensemble. As a solo artist or an orchestra member it would certainly be easier to choose not to participate in a particular tour or to cancel a concern in the middle of a tour if one isn't feeling well. As a member of a quartet you come to realize that you're responsible for other people's reputations and livelihoods as well as your own. One begins to feel a deep personal commitment offstage as well as on.

☐ THE GUARNERI . . .

When asked about misunderstanding and the difficulty of resolving their differences Dalley indicated:

We usually manage to reconcile the various viewpoints, I'm happy to say, but there are occasions when we don't. Unfortunately, a quartet is composed of an even number of players, and two against two creates an impasse. Obviously one of the interpretations must then prevail; yet it's not as if it wins out for all time. It may seem to be the most reasonable or convincing for the moment but they may change later on; there's a constant working-out process.

QUESTIONS

1. What does this case illustrate or show about the factors that contribute to high group cohesiveness?
2. What does this case illustrate or show about the factors that contribute to high group performance?

REFERENCES

1. Albanese, R., and Van Fleet, D.D. Rational behavior in groups: The free-riding tendency. *Academy of Management Review*, 1985, 10, 244-55.
2. Asch, S.E. Opinions and social pressure. *Scientific American*, 1955, 193, 31-35.
3. Asch, S.E. Studies of independence and conformity: A minority of one against a unanimous majority. *Psychological Monographs*, 1956, 70 (whole no. 416).
4. Baron, R.A. *Behavior in organization: Understanding and managing the human side of work.* Boston: Allyn & Bacon, 1983.
5. Batson, C.D., and Vanderplas, M.S. Helping. In D. Perlman and P.C. Cozby. eds. *Social psychology.* New York: Holt, Rinehart and Winston, 1983.
6. Berkowitz, L., and Daniels, L. Responsibility and dependency. *Journal of Abnormal and Social Psychology*, 1963, 66, 429-36.
7. Brief, A.P. and Motowidlo, S.J. Prosocial organizational behaviors. *Academy of Management Review*, 1986, 11, 710-725.
8. Cartwright, D.E. Determinants of scientific progress: The case of research on the risky shift. *American Psychologist*, 1973, 28, 222-31.
9. Cherrington, D.J. Satisfaction in competitive conditions. *Organizational Behavior and Human Performance*, 1973, 10, 47-71.
10. Cottrell, N.B., Wack, D.L., Sekerak, G.J., and Rittle, R.M. Social facilitation of dominant responses by the presence of an audience and the mere presence of others. *Journal of Personality and Social Psychology*, 1968, 9, 245-50.
11. Deutsch, M. A theory of cooperation and competition. *Human Relations*, 1949, 2, 129-52.
12. Dubrin, A.J. *Contemporary applied management.* Plano, TX: Business Publications, Inc., 1982.

13. Fiedler, F.E., and Garcia, J.E. *New approaches to effective leadership: Cognitive resources and organization performance.* New York: John Wiley, 1987.

14. George, J.M. and Brief, A.P. Feeling good-doing good: A conceptual analysis of the mood at work—organizational spontaneity research. *Psychological Bulletin*, 1992, 112(2), 310-329.

15. Heslin, R., and Dunphy, D. Three dimensions of member satisfaction in small groups. *Human Relations*, 1964, 17, 99-102.

16. Jacobs, R.C., and Campbell, D.T. The perpetuation of an arbitrary tradition through several generations of a laboratory microculture. *Journal of Abnormal and Social Psychology*, 1961, 62, 649-58.

17. Jewell, I.N., and Reitz, H.J. *Group effectiveness in organizations.* Glenview, IL: Scott, Foresman, 1981.

18. Katz, D. The motivational basis of organizational behavior. *Behavioral Science*, 1964, 9, 131-146.

19. Keller, R.T. Predictors of the performance of project groups in R&D organizations. *Academy of Management Journal*, 1986, 29, 715- 26.

20. Kiesler, C.A., and Kiesler, C.B. *Conformity.* Reading, MA: Addison-Wesley, 1969.

21. Kipnis, D. The powerholder. In J.T. Tedeschi, ed. *Perspectives on social power.* Chicago: Aldine, 1974.

22. Kohn, A. *No contest: The case against competition.* Boston: Houghton Mifflin, 1986.

23. Latane, B., and Darley, J.M. *The unresponsive bystander: Why doesn't he help?* New York: Appleton-Century-Crofts, 1970.

24. Manz, C.C. and Neck, C.P. Inner leadership: Creating productive thought patterns. *Academy of Management Executive*, 1991, 5(3), 87-95.

25. Marquant, M. J. and Engel, D.W. HRD competencies for a shrinking world. *Training and Development*, 1993, 47:5, 59-65.

26. Moorman, R.H. Relationship between organizational justice and organizational citizenship behaviors: Do fairness perceptions influence employee citizenship? *Journal of Applied Psychology*, 1991, 76, 845-55.

27. Moscovici, S. *Social influence and social exchange.* London: Academic Press, 1976.

28. Myers, D.G. *Social psychology.* New York: McGraw-Hill, 1983.

29. Nordstrom, R., Lorenzi, P., and Hall R.V. A review of public posting of performance feedback in work settings. *Journal of Organizational Behavior Management*, 1990, 11, 101-123.

30. Organ, D.W. *Organizational citizenship behavior: The good soldier syndrome.* Lexington, MA: Lexington Books, 1988.

31. Organ, D.W. The motivational basis of organizational citizenship behavior. In B.M. Staw and L.L. Cummings (eds). *Research in Organizational Behavior*, Vol. 12, Greenwich, CT: JAI Press, 1990, 43-72.

32. Pearce, J.L. Job attitude and motivation differences between volunteers and employees from comparable organizations. *Journal of Applied Psychology*, 1983, 68, 646-52.

33. Phillips, D.P. Suicide, motor vehicle fatalities and the mass media: Evidence toward a theory of suggestion. *American Journal of Sociology*, 1979, 84, 1150-74.

34. Schwartz, S.H., and Ames, R.E. Positive and negative referent others as sources or influence: A case of helping. *Sociometry*, 1977, 40, 12-21.

35. Seashore, S.E. *Group cohesiveness and the industrial work group.* Ann Arbor, MI: Institute for Social Research, 1954.

36. Shaw, M.E. *Group dynamics: The psychology of small group behavior.* New York: McGraw-Hill, 1981.

37. Sherif, M. An experimental approach to the study of attitudes. *Sociometry*, 1937, 1, 90-98.

38. Shotland, R.L. When bystanders just stand by. *Psychology Today*, June 1985, 50-55.

39. Stogdill, R.M. Group productivity, drive, and cohesiveness. *Organizational Behavior and Human Performance*, 1972, 8, 26-43.

40. Stoner, J.A. F. Risky and cautious shifts in group decisions: The influence of widely held values. *Journal of Experimental Social Psychology*, 1968, 4, 442-59.

41. Wexley, K.N., and Yukl, G.A. *Organizational behavior and personnel psychology.* Homewood, IL: Richard D. Irwin, 1984.

42. Wilder, D.A. Perceptions of groups, size of opposition, and social influence. *Journal of Experimental Social Psychology*, 1977, 13, 253-68.

43. Williams, K., Harkins, S., and Latane, B. Identifiability as a deterrent to social loafing: Two cheering experiments. *Journal of Personality and Social Psychology*, 1981, 40, 303-11.

44. Wolosin, R.J., Sherman, S.J., and Till, A. Effects of cooperation and competition on responsibility by attribution after success and failure. *Journal of Experimental Social Psychology*, 1973, 9, 220-235.

45. Zajonc, R.B. Social facilitation. *Science*, 1965, 149, 269-74.

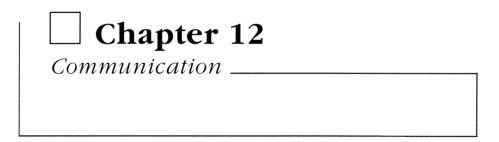

Chapter 12
Communication

The Crofton Company, a food-processing firm in the United States, is known to have a comprehensive communication program. From its beginning, the company has attempted to make every employee feel like an important part of the firm. It is a stated policy of the firm to utilize everybody's talents, mental as well as physical, to the highest degree possible. All new employees participate in an intensive employee-training program conducted by the company's human resource department. They receive extensive written materials and watch a video presentation on the company's history, products, employee policies, pay and benefits, and other aspects of the firm's operations. In addition, every unit of the company holds monthly meetings to disseminate information. In each plant, there are middle management teams of 12 to 20 members who meet every other week to study company products, production processes, and administrative procedures for the purpose of making suggestions to improve them. Putting these specialists together has facilitated communication and coordination among the units. The company invites a group of salespeople to the company headquarters each year to obtain information on customer needs and preferences as well as to keep these individuals informed about company plans and current problems.

The organization culture is conducive to good communication. Everybody, including the president, is on a first-name basis. The company conducts employee attitude surveys each year and uses employee focus groups to obtain employee opinions on impending changes. These reveal that employee morale is quite high compared to that of most other U.S. firms. Like many large U.S. firms, a Total Quality Management (TQM) approach has recently been implemented. TQM requires that units identify their inside customers — those that they were created to serve. To better serve such inside customers, each unit surveyed them to identify how services and products could be improved. The managers of Crofton recognize that good communication between the different levels of the organization can enhance morale and the willingness of lower-level groups to contribute. They also know the importance of good horizontal relationships among the specialized units in the organization and have facilitated this. They recognize the importance of the organization culture in fostering open communications, as shown by the first-name-basis policy among all organization members. Crofton also communicates with its customers through advertising and product-information manuals. Managers communicate to stockholders and investor groups with written reports and oral presentations. They must also communicate their needs to suppliers, to local community leaders, to representatives in local and national government, and to the general public through various public relations techniques.

PURPOSES OF INTERNAL COMMUNICATION SYSTEMS

Organizations are human communities in which the members are tied together in complex relationships. The nature of these relationships is influenced by the quality of communications among members, so it is not surprising that the effectiveness of organizational communication is related to that organization's success [50, 56, 58]. The basic purposes of communication in organizations are (1) to obtain a common focus or direction among organizational members, (2) to integrate the efforts of specialists, (3) to aid in making high-quality decisions, and (4) to build a community of employees with high morale and trust among themselves.

Communication within organizations takes place among individuals or among groups. It can be vertical (between different organizational levels) or horizontal (among members of the same level). Communication in organizations takes place not only through prescribed organizational channels, but also informally among organization members. People have a basic need to communicate with one another to express emotional states and to meet everyday needs. For a particular communication, it is probably impossible to fully separate out the personal from the official organizational purpose of the message.

COMMUNICATION AND PERSONAL NEEDS OF ORGANIZATIONAL MEMBERS

The personal needs served by communication are evidenced by the attention paid to the rumors spread through informal contacts—the so-called **grapevine**. Part of the grapevine's appeal is its usefulness for organizational sense-making; that is, stories and gossip help members understand something they may believe to have a great deal of ambiguity. Some of the anxiety experienced from this ambiguity can be resolved through hearing stories about people in the organization and what happens to them when they behave in different ways [32].

Official communications also affect how members perceive their organization. Communications help reality to be "enacted" or produced in their minds. What an organization or a job is like in an objective sense may be different from how it is subjectively perceived [27, 77]. Enacted reality is affected by the social influences of what top management, supervisors, and fellow employees say about the organization.

ORGANIZATIONS AS INFORMATION PROCESSORS

The way that organizations adapt to their environments depends upon how they make sense of developments in those environments. Environments present managers with ambiguity and uncertainty which must be handled or reduced through their deliberations. The outside environment, like all stimuli, is perceived and interpreted by members of the organization. They draw conclusions based on those perceptions, and these conclusions are then translated into decisions affecting organization strategies, policies, and practices.

The two essential jobs of an organization with respect to handling information are to interpret the outside world and to coordinate different subunits within the organization [15]. Information processing is easier if there is an appropriate structure to deal with environmental conditions.

COMMUNICATION EFFECTIVENESS IN ORGANIZATIONS

A dramatic example of communication failure in organizations is the explosion of the space shuttle Challenger. An investigation revealed that some engineers at Morton Thiokol, which built the shuttle rockets, had expressed serious technical reservations about a launch in cold weather. Their opinions, however, never reached the higher command levels of NASA, who gave the go-ahead for the flight.

Poor communications can cause many problems. They can be detrimental to innovation in an organization and cause delays in bringing new and needed products to markets. Communication deficiencies may keep work projects that should be initiated off a manager's personal task agenda. Some organization difficulties arise because problems are not reported to others; over time, they become crises and much more difficult to resolve. As a consequence, many decisions fail because they are not based on adequate information.

The evidence shows that widespread misunderstandings occur in organizations. For example, in many communication episodes between superiors and subordinates, Burns found that the superiors believed they were giving their subordinates instructions; but the subordinates viewed the same communications just as helpful information [9]. A number of studies found frequent misunderstandings between superiors and subordinates, especially with respect to knowledge of job problems [41]. Superiors also believe they communicate more with their subordinates than subordinates report [76].

There is also evidence that failures in upward communication are a serious problem in most organizations; many problems that should be forwarded up are in fact suppressed or very distorted [47]. Subordinates do not often communicate job problems upward to superiors, especially when the subordinates are strongly motivated to be promoted [57].

MANAGER COMMUNICATIONS SKILLS

Several studies of upward progression for managerial personnel show that communication skills are a major predictor of managerial success and upward mobility [22, 57]. Communication takes an enormous amount of any manager's time. Managers, depending on the organizational level, spend anywhere from between 50 to 80 percent of their average workday in communication activities of some type. Top managers especially spend a high percentage of their time in communication, mostly face-to-face [54].

Kotter analyzed the daily work of a group of top managers [34]. He found that all managers are constantly working on a **task agenda** during the workday. Figure 12.1 shows the types of items on these task agendas and how changes occur because the manager is constantly receiving new information from different organization members. The managerial job is done in a network of individuals both inside and outside the organization who provide the manager with information. This information may be input into planning processes, feedback on how well subordinates are doing on assigned projects, notification of new problems, or for social or personal uses [12].

☐ **FIGURE 12.1** *The Unit Manager's Task Agenda*

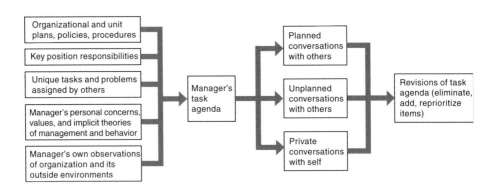

BASIC MODEL OF THE COMMUNICATION PROCESS

All communication involves sender(s), purpose(s), methods, receivers, message receipt, message understanding, message reactions, and feedback (see Figure 12.2). Communication effectiveness is the degree to which a message is received and understood and if the receiver's reactions to the message correspond to the sender's purposes in sending it.

Each person in a particular communication interaction may have personal objectives, which could be different from those of others in the interaction. For example, a subordinate may wish to (1) make the superior aware of a problem, (2) motivate the superior to do something quickly about it, (3) impress the superior with the subordinate's diligence and commitment to the organization's interest, and (4) persuade the superior to believe that one of the subordinate's peers is not very competent. The subordinate may achieve only the first objective and none of the others. Thus, from his or her perspective, the communication was only marginally successful.

FIGURE 12.2 *A Communications Model*

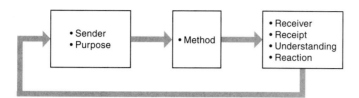

The superior's objectives for the same communication interaction may be (1) becoming aware of the unit's productivity problems, (2) establishing a good relationship with the subordinate, (3) learning more about the subordinate's attitudes, strengths, and weaknesses, (4) impressing the subordinate with the superior's competence, and (5) encouraging the subordinate to perform at a high level. All these objectives may or may not be achieved.

There are a number of factors which inhibit or facilitate the effectiveness of communications (see Figure 12.3). Some are individual characteristics of senders or receivers, such as emotional and perceptual limitations. Others include the forms of communication used, the characteristics of the organization and the unique or episodic characteristics surrounding the communication interaction itself.

FIGURE 12.3 *Specific Inhibiting or Facilitating Factors Affecting Communication Outcomes*

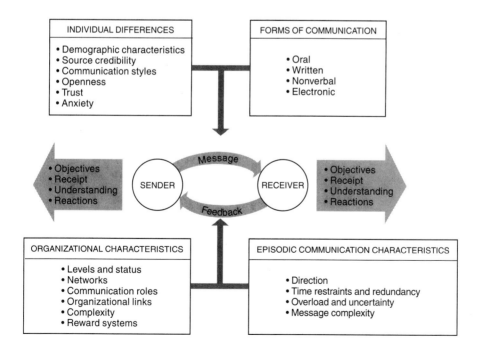

COMMUNICATION FORMS

Different forms of communication have advantages and disadvantages, and the appropriate form depends on the situation. The two most obvious **communication forms** are oral and written. Both may be one-way or interactive. For example, in one large university certain classes are televised in a large lecture hall, clearly a one-way oral communication process. Other classes use a discussion mode, with much interaction between the instructor and the students. Examples of one-way written communications are company letters, memos, employee handbooks, or company newspapers. Interactive written communications are letters or memos that invite a response and electronic media that organization members use to communicate via computer mail networks. Some forms provide for visual and audio communication, as when the sender of a message can be seen as well as heard. When this is the case, **nonverbal communication**, such as body language occurs. Sometimes it is unintentional.

ORAL VS. WRITTEN COMMUNICATION

Two-way communication is more satisfying than one-way communication and leads to greater accuracy and receptivity of messages [58]. It is a much richer medium [14]. But it can be time-consuming, inefficient, and unnecessary when the message is simple, easily understood, or acceptance of the message is not required. Two-way communication may be more critical when tasks are variable and complex or when there might be resistance to the message.

Managers show a marked preference for face-to-face communications probably because more meaning and information can be transmitted. Managers also prefer this form of communication because ideas can be expressed more tentatively than in a written communication and most of managers' communications involve a certain amount of selling and persuasion [12]. Pauses and voice inflections give emphasis to different words, stress different parts of the message, and communicate the sender's feelings about the subject. Oral communication, however, generates more pressure to please the other party but at the same time gives the parties an opportunity to strengthen their personal relationship, which may lead to greater interpersonal attraction [58].

There are also advantages to written communications. For example, comprehension may be greater because ideas and information can be expressed with more care and clarity and the message can be reread any number of times [54]. In addition, written communications may include more supporting information to strengthen a particular viewpoint.

NONVERBAL COMMUNICATION

Meaning goes beyond the words used in communication. The volume, rate and rhythm, pitch, pauses, sounds such as "ahs" and "ers," laughing, and sighing may convey meaning. Body gestures, posture, and facial expressions all transmit information [18]. Posture and gestures may imply status and social class. For example often upper social classes attempt to maintain an image of "dignity" which requires some control of emotion or, at least, control of gestures signifying an emotional state [7]. Facial expressions such as frowns, amount of eye contact, and other factors communicate feelings [25, 58]. For example, gazing is used to observe the reactions of others, to indicate the conclusion of a thought, to demand a response from another, to communicate a degree of arousal, or to attempt to suppress an anticipated response [58]. There is evidence that acts such as touching yourself rather than another, low levels of eye contact, and crossed arms and legs are related to feelings of conflict, a sense of distance, or dissatisfaction with another person [5].

Interpretation of body language may be difficult, however, since some individuals seem to communicate a different emotional state with their body than they are actually experiencing [5, 58]. When nonverbal and oral communications carry the same meaning, it is called **communication congruence**. When they are not congruent, nonverbal communication carries more meaning than verbal communication [25]. For example, people tend to be poor nonverbal liars [54]. The nonverbal messages are the more meaningful indicator of the sender's emotional state and feelings. A consistent discrepancy between a verbal and nonverbal language will lead to ambiguity, higher tension, and anxiety on the part of others.

Actions are another form of **nonverbal communication** that speak louder than words. What one does reflects intentions and feelings better than what one says. When what a manager says and does are inconsistent, individuals pay more attention to what is actually done. This can be seen in many of the failures to effectively implement Total Quality Management programs [53]. Without exception, these are introduced with enthusiasm by top management. There are development programs and systems put in place. However the real key to success is if quality is demanded by the decisions and actions of managers, not the rhetoric. Thus, for credibility, a policy must be followed by appropriate actions.

☐ UPWARD FEEDBACK HELPS MANAGERS WALK THE TALK

Many companies are installing programs designed to increase employee commitment to the organization through various empowerment practices. Such programs create employee expectations that managers will change their behaviors toward them. If such behavior changes do not occur, employee dissatisfactions rise, and employees will become discouraged. However, executives or managers may not be aware that their behaviors are not modeling those required by the new change programs their company is trying to implement.

Executives may inadvertently derail the very programs that they verbally support through the way they delegate tasks, make decisions, and provide

☐ **UPWARD FEEDBACK HELPS . .**

feedback to others. Using an empowerment rhetoric is not enough, they must "walk the talk" or recognize that the new company attitudes must permeate their own behavior.

Actual studies show that employees in companies do perceive that there is a gap between a company's quality talk and the actual actions of managers. In addition, there have been some decreases in recent years in the degree to which employees feel that their managers really seek their suggestions or even act on those they receive. In fact, one survey indicated that only 18 percent of hourly employees felt that their suggestions were not ignored.

One aid in getting managers to "walk the talk" is to use assessments of their behavior by others since they may be blind to their own attitudes. Such assessments can be gathered from peers, subordinates, customers, or superiors. Such assessments will not only help change managerial behaviors by providing managers with feedback about their behavior but will also create pressure to change behavior by the very fact that managers know that their behaviors are going to be monitored.

From Ludeman, K. (1993) "Upward Feedback Helps Managers Walk the Talk." *HR Magazine*, 38(5), 85-93 [40].

Non-verbal behavior can create difficulties in cross cultural communications. Some gestures are specific to a particular culture while certain facial expressions such as laughing, weeping, yawning, and blushing seem to be universal across many cultures and languages [7]. An inappropriate gesture could undermine a whole speech. Perhaps this is why in some cultures there is an attempt to control gestures because it could reveal too much about one's feelings at the moment.

ELECTRONIC TECHNOLOGY

In recent years, the use of electronic communication technology such as electronic mail and teleconferencing has skyrocketed. These new medias can make communication more efficient. For example, with electronic mail, messages are received and stored whether or not the recipient is present. Electronic networks allow several parties to communicate using their computers or directly by voice, as in teleconferencing which allows televised meetings among people separated geographically.

These new technologies lead to somewhat different behavioral outcomes than more traditional forms of communication. For example, communicating electronically rather than face-to-face produces more polarization, making it more difficult to obtain consensus on an issue [64]. This results, perhaps, because individuals feel psychologically closer to those in physical proximity and work harder to reach agreement with them. Electronic media also produces more uninhibited communication, such as swearing, probably because status differences among the parties are less obvious [64]. In addition, the new communication technologies, compared to face-to-face meetings, may result in a greater participation rate among those communicating but, maybe because of this, more difficulty in making a decision [63].

INDIVIDUAL DIFFERENCES AND COMMUNICATION

In organizations, personality differences and demographic characteristics such as gender, race, ethnicity, and age affect communication behavior. Communications will also be affected by amount and type of education, occupational experience, and organization experience.

DEMOGRAPHIC CHARACTERISTICS

There is evidence that communication can be affected by demographic characteristics. For example, a number of writers have concluded that men and women communicate differently in their relationships with others [27, 61, 68], though others argue that such differences may be exaggerated [20,72]. There is some research evidence which supports the idea of different gender-based communication patterns. Women are more sensitive than men to interpersonal communication skills, and they are more attracted to articulate people [51]. They talked differently than men to bosses, and peers believed that women may be more concerned about impressing bosses and peers [65]. Both women and minorities differ from white men in nonverbal behavior modes, which can cause misunderstandings in communication [28, 58].

Sex-related stereotypes may cause people to brand behavior as appropriate or inappropriate depending on whether it is exhibited by a man or a woman [26, 36]. For example, the idea that it is natural for males to dominate in mixed sex interpersonal situations and the stereotypes of the submissive females and aggressive and dominant males have been well documented [72]. Such stereotypes frequently cause communication problems between men and women. Male managers may have stereotypes about women that influence their opinion of female credibility [60], particularly when the male managers have limited information about women's qualifications [70].

Although communications may be intended to elicit particular reactions, other responses may occur simply because different groups put different meanings on identical words. Particular terms may evoke positive reaction whereas others generate negative or neutral reactions. For example, managers and labor leaders may react quite differently to such terms as "grievance," "arbitration," and "seniority." In one organization different management levels had quite different reactions to and perceptions of such terms as "incentives," "budgets," "conferences," and "cooperation" [33]. For example, a grievance may be viewed as a right and a protection by a union steward, but as disloyal or ungrateful act by a manager.

SOURCE CREDIBILITY

Source credibility is the belief that information is truthful and unbiased. The source is perceived by the receiver to be honest and impartial. Some personal factors associated with source credibility are perceived honesty, perceived competence, and open-mindedness (see Figure 12.4) [57]. The credibility of the source is also enhanced by the vitality of the presentation, such as when the message is articulated in a dynamic, energetic manner [59]. The effects of personal dynamism or vitality on source credibility were shown in the famous "Dr. Fox" studies [74]. In these studies, an actor, Michael Fox, was hired to present lectures to students. The content and the delivery style of the lectures varied. In some, factual information was presented in a very dry manner; in others, the lecturer presented nonsense material to the students but in a very energetic or interesting manner. When the lecturer presented material in a dynamic and entertaining manner, he was rated quite high by the students, even though the actual content of his lecture was nonsense. In addition, a person arguing for a position that appears to be opposite to his or her own best interests is seen as more credible than when arguing for his or her own actual interests [58, 73].

FIGURE 12.4 *Factors Related to Source Credibility*

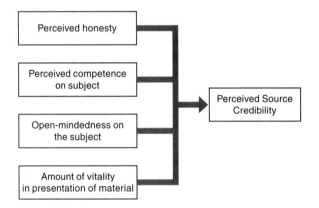

Credibility is especially important in the superior-subordinate relationship—it affects how they judge each other and relates to trust at work [44]. Higher credibility ratings of supervisors are also associated with higher worker satisfaction with supervisors, perhaps because the personal characteristics contributing to high credibility ratings are the same ones that are generally admired.

Managers do not have high credibility with their employees, especially on matters unrelated to technical expertise. The evidence also demonstrates, however, that nothing prohibits a superior from being perceived as trustworthy or credible by subordinates [56].

COMMUNICATION STYLES

There are different **communication styles**, and individuals react differently to them. A persuasive style is conciliatory in its approach. The sender tries to reason gently with the other person while maintaining respect for his or her opinion. In argumentative styles, the sender expresses vigorous dissent, followed by a rather blunt rejection of the other person's views. A person may use a neutral style, omitting any argument or evaluation. People tend to prefer the neutral style most, followed by the persuasive one. The argumentative style ranks lowest [55].

Listening styles are also important. Managers use different listening styles in relating to others. Some maintain a psychological distance from others and emphasize telling more than listening [4]. Others find listening easy but giving direct orders or commands difficult. These basic styles reflect the manager's personality and are not easily changed.

OPENNESS

Some evidence indicates that managers are typically "closed." In a study of 165 executives, Argyris found that most managers discouraged open expression of ideas and feelings by others as well as themselves [2]. **Openness** is the willingness to listen, to accept "bad" news, and to be tolerant of views divergent from one's own. Not dealing candidly with information can result in overlooking problems, inhibit creativity, and stifle innovation. Perceptions of openness are related to the actual behaviors of one person toward another. For example, one study showed that subordinate perceptions of openness of their supervisors were based on the nonverbal warmth of their boss (communicated through eye gaze, voice tones, and facial expressions) when interacting with them [69].

Openness about work-related problems affects performance and satisfaction. A study in a package delivery company found willingness to listen by supervisors related to higher performance in some departments [29]. Willits examined the communication pattern between the presidents and their immediate subordinates in 20 small shoemaking companies in New England [78]. Open communication of ideas by the executive group correlated with every measure of performance. In better-performing companies there is a freer, less guarded, upward flow of ideas and opinions than in poorer-performing companies. Quite a number of studies have shown the relationship of openness in communication to job satisfaction of workers and especially to satisfaction with their immediate supervisor [17].

TRUST IN OTHERS

Trust can refer either to one's feelings about the competence of another or to whether one thinks another person intends to pursue his or her best interests [57]. Trust is related to some aspects of a manager's behavior toward subordinates. A superior who trusts subordinates' competence allows them to have more influence in decision making [13]. A superior will not monitor the performance of a subordinate in whom he has trust as closely as that of one he

☐ CREATING A WORLD WIDE EMPLOYEE SATISFACTION MEASUREMENT SYSTEM

In the past, employers have attempted to bridge the communication gaps between management and lower levels of operative employees with employee satisfaction surveys. Since they are completed anonymously by random samples of employees, such surveys can bring to light dissatisfactions at a company's lower levels that are not revealed through normal every day operations. Xerox has used such surveys in the past to identify employee dissatisfactions with all aspects of their work environments including management practices, HRM program characteristics, and workload/resource issues. However, today many companies, such as Xerox, are worldwide companies with many diverse employees with perhaps quite different needs indicating perhaps the desirability of different types of needed organizational changes depending on the location of the employees involved.

The new Xerox international employee satisfaction program was designed through use of a pilot study and roundtable discussions with Xerox employees. Now 49 core questions make up the Employee Satisfaction Measurement Survey (ESMS) with 18 questions in the core designated as the overall satisfaction index. These core questions allow management to compare the levels of satisfaction and motivation on a country by country basis with those in other countries, and also responses are compared to available data on employees of other major international companies in those countries.

One outcome of these efforts has been to increase the amount and frequency of communications between managers and employees. Informal face-to-face dialogues between senior management and employees at a multitude of levels is taking place.

doesn't trust [11, 39]. A boss is likely to communicate information to subordinates who are highly trusted [58].

A supervisor's personality affects the level of trust. High authoritarians have less trust in others than those who are less authoritarian (see Chapter 4). Trust in others is probably also influenced by their actual behavior—their past performance, demonstrated competence, and whether they have harmed others' interests given an opportunity to do so. Organizations that lay off employees frequently find it difficult to create much trust between workers and management [52].

ANXIETY

Interpersonal anxiety is uneasiness or apprehension experienced subjectively when interacting with others. It affects the individual's feelings and beliefs that he or she may not be able to meet interpersonal demands of others. For example, a person may feel anxious because of fears that others will think he or she is stupid, dull, or inarticulate. Anxiety is a form of stress and can lead to such speech difficulties as repetition and tongue slips [43]. When these occur, they may increase interpersonal anxiety. If anxiety increases sufficiently, it may affect the person's ability to comprehend and objectively evaluate information. Significantly higher error rates result when a person is highly anxious [43]. In addition, the person's tense state may be very obvious to others, possibly raising their own tension levels which, in turn, will further inhibit communication.

ORGANIZATION CHARACTERISTICS AND COMMUNICATIONS

Organization design factors have an effect on the nature and flow of information. Here we discuss some effects of the following organization characteristics on communication:

1. Organizational level and status differences
2. Organization complexity
3. Reward systems
4. Communication networks
5. Communication roles
6. Communication links

ORGANIZATIONAL LEVEL AND STATUS DIFFERENCES

Level and status differences may significantly affect the quality of communications among organization members [47]. When individuals are socialized to defer to others of higher status and position, it takes the form of respect, submission, and acquiescence. Those with higher-status expect to control communication [58]. The person in control of a communication event does not necessarily do most of the talking. Besides talking, control can occur as well because of facial expressions, nods, body gestures, and other tactics.

Symbols may also communicate an individual's status. Symbols are guides about how to act with those who possess them. They are often deliberately manipulated to influence others. Office location, desks, furnishings, and organizational privileges may be status symbols. They create certain behavioral expectations about the appropriate amount of deference which should be shown to others.

There is good evidence that bosses are not aware of their subordinates' problems. In one study, 95 percent of foremen said they understood the problems of their subordinates, but only 34 percent of their subordinates actually thought that the foremen understood [38]. In another study, superiors and subordinates agreed fairly well on what the subordinates' jobs should be but did not agree very well on what subordinates' job problems and obstacles actually were [42].

379

Level differences may affect the feelings of those involved in communication, particularly the subordinates. Supervisors reported the most anxiety when talking to bosses, slightly less anxiety when talking to workers, and the least anxiety when talking with peers [31]. Managers place a higher value on communication contact with superiors than on those with subordinates and they listen more carefully when communicating with their bosses than with peers or subordinates [35]. Thus a manager may convey to subordinates, consciously or unconsciously, that the interaction with them is not valued.

Because organization level reflects status and power differences, communication distortion will occur [54]. The greater the stress differential, the more restricted the channels of communication, the more the tendency for information to flow from low- to high-status people, and the more distorted the content of the message. Distortion of upward communication is greatest when there is a large status differential between a superior and a subordinate and if the superior has the power to make or block promotions for the subordinate. **Communication distortion** occurs, in general, because individuals communicate what they perceive to be in their best interests [46]. Higher-level individuals want better performance from lower-level personnel, and lower-level personnel are trying to obtain as many rewards as possible. These different objectives make individuals selective in what they bring to the attention of others. For instance, pleasant matters are more likely to be communicated upward than unpleasant ones, and achievements are more likely to be passed upward than information about errors or difficulties encountered [55].

Adler pointed out that women may have special problems in communication because of perceived status differences [1]. She summarizes some research which indicates that high-status individuals tend to speak louder, more rapidly, point with their fingers, and maintain relatively frequent eye contact. At the same time, some research shows women tend to speak in a more tentative way in mixed-sex groups than they do in an all female group. These communication behaviors may cause women to be attributed lower status and receive lower ratings of their competence since this is not how high status competent individuals communicate [72]. When women do speak in an assertive way their ratings of competence from males go up, but their likeability goes down. When their communications are seen as more warm and friendly, they are not rated as high in competence but are more likable.

ORGANIZATIONAL COMPLEXITY

Organizations differ in structural complexity. Some consist of many different, specialized subunits, whereas others are smaller and simpler [21]. When there are a large number of specialized subunits, coordination is more difficult and both formal and informal communication increases [24]. Higher organizational complexity also leads to more formal, prescribed communications instead of the informal mutual adjustment processes used in simpler organization structures. When there are more specialized units, there are more committees established to facilitate communication among these units. This creates even more organizational linkages that exacerbate communication problems even more because the different subunits often have contradictory objectives, differences in perspectives and educational backgrounds, and their own specialized languages.

ORGANIZATIONAL REWARD SYSTEMS

Ample evidence indicates that individuals respond to the organization's reward systems (see Chapters 7 and 8). Given this, we could expect that organizational reward systems influence what information is transmitted. When a superior controls promotion or other potential rewards for subordinates, the subordinates will communicate the information to the superior that will enhance their own careers [47]. They may also distort information for the same reasons. Competition for rewards among individuals or groups causes information flow among such competitors to be reduced.

COMMUNICATION NETWORKS

Some experiments show how different communication structures affect performance and satisfaction. In the earliest of these experiments, individuals were placed in cubicles and allowed to pass each other messages through slots in the cubicle walls. The slots among the cubicles were opened and closed by the experimenter to create the various types of networks [18]. The location of people in different **communication networks** (see Figure 12.5) affects access to information.

☐ **FIGURE 12.5**   *Communication Networks*

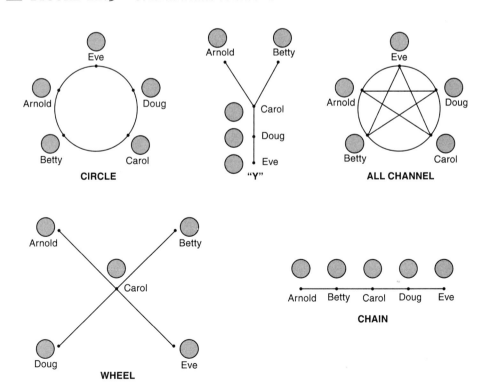

These experimental networks are like organizational networks. An organization's communication network is dominated by certain individuals (centrals) in key positions who have formal authority, power, or expertise [6]. Network effectiveness varies with the nature of the task. For example, a wheel-structured communication network is efficient for simple tasks, but the individuals at the end of the spokes, who simply take orders, are dissatisfied with their position. Performance on simple tasks is greatest in the Y structure, less in a chain, and least effective in a circle. However, the circle network, where each can communicate with all, seems to produce high performance and satisfaction for complex tasks, and it appears to be most effective when there are sudden and confusing changes in the task requirements [54].

Networks are not rigid. They change to fit the task. For example, in one study, individuals were initially organized so that each individual could contact all others in the group [19]. For simple problems, the group reorganized itself into the wheel structure. When more complex problems were introduced, the group shifted back to the all-channel structure because information requirements were too great for one individual to handle. Although there were initial problem-solving ability differences for individuals in the wheel or the circle, they eventually narrowed as individuals learned to cope with the problem-solving restraints imposed by the structure [8].

The networks described in Figure 12.5 are much less complicated than those in actual organizations. Nevertheless, these studies provide some guides to solving real communication problems. For example, the all-channel would be appropriate where a task is very complex, such as those patterns that require every individual to talk to all others. The wheel or the chain are probably sufficient when the task is simple and it is therefore unnecessary to obtain everyone's ideas [46].

COMMUNICATION ROLES

Individuals perform different **communication roles** in networks. Two important communication roles are the opinion leader and the liaison. **Opinion leaders** have high credibility with other members, especially in a particular subject area. Opinion leadership tends to be specific to certain topics or issues: the same person is not the opinion leader for several subjects, and anyone in a work group can be an opinion leader.

Liaison roles are performed by those who pass on information to others. Liasons connect two or more groups and may not be a member of any of them [18]. In the usual transmittal pattern one liaison passes information to several other managers. One of these may be another liaison person, who in turn passes it on. In a study of rank-and-file employees, 10 percent acted as liaisons, 57 percent were "dead-enders" who failed to pass on a message, and 33 percent were "isolates" who did not even receive a message [56].

Some liaisons in organization boundary spanning positions secure information from outside the organization and pass it to the inside. This is often information about the technological or market environment. In a study of research laboratories, only a few professionals acted as liaisons, transmitting scientific and technical information from the field, such as from scholarly journals, to other professionals in the research laboratory [56].

☐ A MULTICULTURAL WORKPLACE AT BRITISH PETROLEUM

When British Petroleum established a new finance center in Belgium, it was staffed with skilled managerial and technical personnel from 13 different countries. The management group of the new center believed that some multi-cultural training was needed if these individuals were to work together effectively.

In the training sessions the team members from the different countries explored their own cultures and then discussed what they had found with those from other nations. The team also worked to create a set of ground rules for communicating and interacting with each other and also a vision of the team for the future.

Certain cultural differences emerged quickly. The Germans wanted to establish proper procedures and to put them into operation quickly. The Dutch wanted to clarify their right to speak out when they wished. The Americans were astonished at the French custom of shaking hands with everyone in the work group each morning. The Germans did not expect to be called by their first names no matter how well they were known to others. The Dutch managers were unconcerned about authority issues and did not mind it when their subordinates took certain issues to the next higher level without telling them. The German managers were very concerned about this practice.

Participants from different countries also discovered they were not all paid similarly for similar work, and feelings of inequity arose. In communications, the Dutch were very direct but those from Belgium, the country nearest to Holland, were not very direct and tended to take a long time thinking about an issue before speaking out about it. The English did not mind working late and thought it appropriate, but the Scandinavians felt strongly about leaving by 5:30 at the latest and preferably by 4:30. Those who felt it was appropriate to go home early were stressed by those who wanted to work late. They felt that they would be put to a disadvantage by the late workers. Eventually the multicultural team proved to be successful, probably because it faced up to its adjustment problems very early.

COMMUNICATION LINKS

Changes, omissions, or distortions occur when a message is transmitted from one person to another [46]. As the number of communication links through which the message passes increases so do these problems. Individual change messages in various ways and for various reasons. Sometimes this is deliberate—as when a subordinate tries to simplify information to avoid communication overload for the supervisor. However, omissions and distortions occur for other reasons. The omission or distortion may correspond to the receiver's attitudes, may have been done to please the next person in the communication chain, or may have resulted from oversimplification.

EPISODIC COMMUNICATION CHARACTERISTICS

Episodic communication characteristics are associated with a particular communication event, and they affect understanding. So do the contextual factors in which it occurs, such as time constraints and noise. The amount of information that is being transmitted may also affect communication effectiveness, and finally, information complexity may make comprehension difficult.

DIRECTION OF COMMUNICATION

One-way communication occurs when information is transmitted from one source to another without feedback. Much organizational communication is one way, from higher levels to lower. For example, instructions, goals, and orders are often given without any feedback. One-way communication is especially likely when written communications are used and in situations where one individual must communicate to a large group.

Two-way communication is clearly more effective in problem solving as well as being more satisfying to participants, especially for complex problems. Where understanding is difficult, two-way communication may be necessary.

Two-way communication has a cost—it takes time. When communicators are skilled, it is possible that one-way communication can save time. In highly-structured organizations, where problems are routine and fairly simple, one-way communication may be more than adequate to achieve required task performance.

TIME CONSTRAINTS AND REDUNDANCY

If little time is spent in communicating or if noise interferes with receipt of the message, the communication may be missed entirely. **Redundancy** can reduce interference and noise and reduce the likelihood of missing a message. Redundancy may mean different things. To some people, it means repeating an idea several times in different ways in order to increase understanding. To others, redundancy is excessive explanation—using too many words to express an idea. The former feel redundancy is useful; the latter believe it is best to avoid it.

Benign redundancy, repetition with variation to increase understanding, can be helpful. Wason found that when two popular well-written essays were abstracted to one-fourth their original length, information recall was significantly less than with the originals [75]. Furthermore, to achieve a comparable degree of understanding, it took more time to read the abstract than the longer version. Why are there such problems with shorter versions of messages? In a brief summary, new information is presented at a much higher rate than in a longer version. This rate may exceed the reader's optimum information-processing capacities and the reader may require more time to comprehend the message.

Other studies show the positive effects of communication-channel redundancy. For example, presenting information in both oral and written form is more effective than either one alone [16, 37].

COMMUNICATION OVERLOAD AND UNCERTAINTY

Uncertainty is increasing for most organizations, and this trend is expected to continue. This is due to an increasingly unstable outside environment, the adoption of nonroutine technologies, organic organization structures, and increased interdependence of tasks [71, 81]. As uncertainty increases, the amount of information to be processed by the organization increases as well. This leads to information overload, which is one reason superiors try to limit communications from subordinates. Although increased communication between subordinates and superiors improves the subordinates' satisfaction, it also typically leads to overwork, more errors, neglect of important duties, increased frustration for the superior, and so on [4, 18].

Communication overload occurs when the amount of information exceeds the capacity of individuals to absorb and process it. This is especially likely at higher organizational levels, where the amount of time spent in communication is greatest. When a unit starts approaching communication overload, it simply cancels the lowest-priority messages, which are not sent at all. When individuals dealt with more than four alternatives, overload led to slowness in handling them [25].

MESSAGE COMPLEXITY

Message complexity can be too high [58]. The sender of a message may use words or concepts that are beyond the comprehension of receivers. Sometimes this is a matter of educational level and experience. For example, a financial analyst in an investment firm can easily understand a page of numbers that would bewilder a first-year accounting student.

IMPROVING COMMUNICATIONS IN ORGANIZATIONS

There are several things that can be done to make communications more effective and to improve understanding in organizations. Individuals can learn how to be more persuasive, organizations can be restructured, the architecture itself can be designed to facilitate interaction and upward communication channels may be opened.

A person is persuaded by communications only after a message has been received and understood, beliefs are modified and attitudes changed, and an intention to respond is formed [45]. Then the appropriate action will take place. This occurs, though, only for those situations in which the targeted individual is open to the message and only for topics that are important to the person [30]. When the person is less involved, other more elaborate approaches are necessary. Then source credibility, source likeability, the number of favorable arguments presented, and the use of attention getting devices such as humor or music are important.

Research points to some ways to make communication more persuasive. For example, arguments should be presented both for and against the proposal, especially if it is expected that the audience is in disagreement [3, 80]. Emotional appeals, as opposed to just discussing the merits of an issue in logical terms, can be effective in persuasion, especially when the audience is given explicit directions about how to act on the information [80]. Putting directions at the end of a message is especially important if immediate action is wanted [3]. Repetition of a message can be very helpful in these low involvement situations as well [3]. This may be because repetition builds familiarity and people prefer the familiar [30].

RESTRUCTURING ORGANIZATIONS

There are several ways to restructure organizations to improve communications. Greater decentralization, providing more latitude for organizational units, and creating self-contained units will improve their information-handling capacities. This should reduce information overload as well as other problems that arise out of the need to coordinate and control interdependent subunits.

ORGANIZATIONAL ARCHITECTURE

The open office is one in which employees are visible to each other from their work spaces. This concept is increasingly used in the physical design of buildings [66, 67]. Today about one third of all office workers in the United States do their job in the open office, or offices without walls. The innovative spatial arrangement has been studied to explore its effect on communications and employee satisfaction. Based on these studies, a number of conclusions can be made. First, some aspects of communication are improved because of easy access to colleagues. Lower-level employees seem to be more satisfied with working in open spaces than professionals and managers, but there is more noise intrusive speech from nearby workplaces and interference with mental concentration [48, 67, 79].

UPWARD COMMUNICATION FOR INNOVATION

Another approach to achieve better communications is the creation of ways for those at lower levels to communicate their ideas to those at upper levels. This is the reason underlying the origination of quality circles in Japan in 1961 by Kaoru Ishikawa. He suggested that small groups of workers be used by companies to address problems in their own work areas. A similar type of problem-solving approach for lower management levels is called multiple management; this is used in a number of U.S. companies. Groups made up of middle managers from different specialized functional areas provide ideas for improvement to higher management levels. They sometimes also serve as a communication link between rank-and-file workers and also between other lower-level managers and higher management levels [10].

SUMMARY

Communication is a way for those in organizations to make sense of their work environment. Communication skills are also critical for managerial success. Communication is effective when it results in the action intended by the sender. This means that the receivers must have access to the message, be receptive to it, have the ability to comprehend it, and be motivated to react in the desired way. A number of factors affect the success of communication. These include the form of communication used, individual differences of receivers, characteristics of the organization, and episodic characteristics of a particular message such as complexity and the use of feedback.

Dealing with such matters before a communication takes place might itself have a positive impact on communication effectiveness. There are several things that can be done to ensure that access, receptivity, comprehension, and motivation to react are improved.

KEY CONCEPTS

Communication congruence	Communication roles	Message complexity
Communication distortion	Communication styles	Non-verbal communication
Communication forms	Episodic communication characteristics	Openness
Communication networks		Opinion leaders
		Redundancy
Communication overload	Grapevine	Source credibility
	Liaison roles	Task agenda
		Trust

STUDY QUESTIONS

1. Assume that you wish to contact a company in order to obtain a job. In your opinion, which mode of communication would be most effective for you to use: writing the company a letter, calling on the telephone, or seeing someone in person? Why?

2. Suppose a company wants its supervisors to change to a more effective way of handling employee grievances. What would be a credible source of this type of information for the supervisors? Why?

3. What type of manager is likely to have the most diverse and lengthy task agenda in a given day—a manufacturing manager or a staff specialist? Why?

☐ STUDY . . .

4. Think of a time in the recent past when you met a person of higher status than you. Were you nervous or at ease? Why? What was there about that situation that caused you to feel this way?

5. Describe a situation in which openness in communication would be undesirable. Why would being open be bad in this situation?

6. In communication, liaisons play an important role. Think of our larger society. Which people play a liaison role in a societal sense? How do they perform this role?

7. Of the causes of poor communication described in this chapter, which are most prevalent in the typical college lecture course? What might be done to remove these barriers or to diminish their effect?

8. In designing a training program to improve managerial communication, what would the most important elements in such a program be? Why?

9. When would it be especially important for a company to use persuasive communication?

10. Of all the techniques discussed for improving communications, which appears to you to have especially high merit? Why?

CASE

☐ THE FIRST MARYLAND BANK

The First Maryland Bank was founded just outside of Baltimore, Maryland, in 1915. Since that time, it has grown to be the fourth largest bank in the state, with 41 branches in operation across the state. A few years ago, there were some serious problems in the proof department. The department employs 29 machine operators, six supervisors, three batch assemblers, a secretary, and a department head, Mr.Fish. The main function of the proof department is to post various items such as checks, deposits, and withdrawals against customer accounts as these items are received by the bank. It is essential that all items received by the bank during a given day are posted that same day. The items to be processed are sent to the proof department by messenger from the 41 branch banks and other administrative departments. They arrive at frequent intervals until about 3:30 P.M., when the last batches come in. When a batch arrives, it is broken by the three batch makers into small batches of approximately equal size and difficulty. These are then distributed into five baskets, which the supervisors pick up and distribute to machine operators. Supervisors do not have a posting machine and spend most of their time helping the operators who have problems. The actual posting operation is done on 27 machines. Each operator takes the stack of items placed on his machine

☐ THE FIRST MARYLAND . . .

by the supervisor and posts each one. The posting, itself, is extremely simple, clear-cut, and highly repetitive. It is not unusual for an operator to post 400,000 items on a busy day, though on a slow day 175,000 items may be posted.

The operator position has attracted only female applicants, most of them around 17 years old with a high school education. The average tenure of an operator was two years, and few operators stayed longer than four years. About 10 to 12 machine operators quit their jobs each year.

Mr. Fish, the supervisor, felt that one of his worst problems was the high rate of absenteeism among the department's machine operators. Of equal concern to him was the low output rates of the operators. He attributed his problems to three things: (1) the work was boring, (2) the operators were young, and (3) most operators were not the primary wage earners in their families.

From time to time, Mr. Fish talked to others about his problem. On one occasion he said:

> My two biggest headaches are the low productivity on the job and the high absenteeism. For example, last Monday we had nearly 50 percent of the operators absent from work. Even supervisors were absent. When the operators are here they just plod along at 500 to 600 items per hour, even on busy days. If they tried, they could triple their output. It seems that the operators don't realize that when one of them stays out on Monday or Friday it just makes it that much more difficult for the rest. You just can't hold customer items from day to day.

On another occasion, Mr. Fish talked about other problems of the proof department.

> The number of items varies quite a bit from one day to another. Mondays and Fridays are our bad days. There are often more than twice as many items to post on Monday than on Tuesday, Wednesday or Thursday. Friday is our second hardest day. On peak days, we have to get the most out of everybody if we are going to finish in eight hours. On other days, we can loaf a little   .   .   . Unfortunately, the operator's job here is very repetitive and monotonous and requires only a very low skill level. There really isn't much room for an operator to grow except to supervisor. We do make it a practice to promote from within. However, for the supervisor's position, we try to hire high school graduates when we can.

> The working hours for the proof department have always been 10 A.M. until we finish. On Mondays, we often do not leave until after 10 o'clock at night. The high absenteeism rates have been tolerated in the past because of the labor market around here. Every time we replace somebody, the replacement person is worse than the one who left.

☐ THE FIRST MARYLAND . . .

Under pressure from his boss, Mr. Fish began to work on the problems of absenteeism and productivity in his proof department. He devised a plan for improvement and presented it to Mr. Swab, his boss, and Mr. Schneier, the personnel manager. Mr. Fish began:

I feel that it is necessary to achieve higher levels of production from our employees. To do this, it is necessary to give them a reason for producing at higher levels. Integral to this would be reducing absenteeism. Thus, I have two immediate goals: (1) decrease absenteeism and (2) increase productivity rates.

Basically I have developed an incentive pay plan, along with providing the operators with regular feedback about their performance. The advantages are that it will favor the better workers, it will encourage higher performance, and it is a way of improving the overall department pay structure. All the details haven't been ironed out yet, but, generally this is how the program will work:

1. All new employees will start at the same rate.
2. These new employees will be called trainees and will remain trainees, at their starting salary, until they reach a certain minimum standard of output and errors.
3. All operators will have their production and error rates reviewed every 90 days in a personal interview with me.
4. Every 90 days the operators will be eligible for a salary increase. Whether she receives that increase will be determined by her output and error count.
5. The operator's output level will be determined by the average number of items of output per week, which have been maintained over the 90 day period.
6. Errors will be counted against an employee by classifying employees into one of three grades (A, B, or C) with respect to their error count. For example, an "A" grade employee may be allowed from 1 to 5 errors per 10,000 items of output. A "B" grade employee may be allowed 6 to 10 errors per 10,000 items of output, and so on. "A" grade employees will then be eligible for the greatest pay increase at the 90 day review period. "B" grade employees will be eligible for the second greatest pay increases, and so on.
7. All pay increases will be based entirely on production and error count.
8. The standards of output required for pay increases will be based on department's requirements.
9. The production figures and error count for each operator will be published on a large board in the proof room weekly.
10. When employees are absent, their weekly average is credited for that day by an amount equal to the output of the lowest day of the previous week.
11. Supervisors will receive straight pay which will never be lower than the pay of the highest operator.

12. Present employees will be given a period of 90 days at their current rate of pay during which time they may peg their production and error rates for the purposes of the incentive program.
13. For the first six months the program is in effect, employees will be reviewed monthly to help solve adjustment problems.

Three years after Mr. Fish's plan was accepted and implemented, he described to a colleague how he felt the plan had worked out. Absenteeism and turnover had fallen by one-third from the levels before the plan was initiated. Productivity had also improved, but it was not possible to know how much was a result of the incentive and feedback plan because new and faster proof machines had been introduced shortly after the plan was implemented. Nevertheless, Mr. Fish felt quite positive that productivity per hour had been improved as a result of the new plan.

A survey was done to get worker reactions to the plan, and interviews were conducted for a small sample of proof operators who had been with the organization for some time. The questions and responses are summarized in Table 1.

Although the employees' answers to these questions were often lengthy, they have been summarized in this fashion for purposes of brevity and insight. Both high and low performers, as well as old and new operators, were interviewed. The operators clearly seem quite favorable toward the system. These positive attitudes toward the system, however, may be also due to the fact that there are now shorter working hours about which the operators are very happy.

These shorter working hours are apparently the direct result of the incentive system, and thus the employees see the shorter days as a result of the incentives. Previously an operator who came to work all week could expect to work a 48 to 50 hour week. Since the installation of the incentive system, the average work week has declined to about 32 hours. A typical work week might be Monday 9:00 A.M. to 6:00 P.M., Tuesday, Wednesday, and Thursday 12:00 P.M. till 5:30 P.M. or 6:00 P.M. All the operators are still paid on the basis of a 40 hour work week, however. Thus, the faster the work is done, the quicker the operator's can go home.

QUESTIONS

1. How are communications between the operators and Mr. Fish different from before?
2. What are the main factors which have caused the changes?
3. If, as Mr. Fish, you had to implement this plan in your department, how would you do it?

☐ **Table 1**   Summary of responses to the Incentive Pay System
Questionnaire

1. How do you feel about the incentive system in this department?
   Very positive   2
   Positive   5

2. Does it treat all employees in the department fairly?
   Yes   7
   No   0

3. Does your pay check seem fairer to you under an incentive system as compared to a straight pay system?
   Yes   5
   Neutral   2

4. How do you like having your production made public?
   Okay, gives me a goal   3
   Neutral   3
   Negative   1

5. How do you feel about the departments top performers?
   Admire   5
   Neutral   2

6. Do you always get your fair share of the easier work to do?
   Yes   6
   No   1

7. Do you think you work harder under this incentive system than you would under a straight pay system?
   Much more   2
   Yes   4
   Neutral   1

8. (a) Do you feel the system puts a constant pressure on you to improve your performance? (b) On the department in general?
   a) Yes   4
      No   3
   b) Yes   0
      No   7

9. (a) Are there any problems with this type of system? (b) What are the advantages as far as you are concerned?
   a) Yes   0
      No   7
   b) Disadvantages
      1. Some new operators make more than some old operators
      2. There is an upper limit to your performance and pay.

☐ Table 1 . . .

10. What changes would you like to see occur in this system and/or in the department?
    None   6
    Don't know   1

11. In general, what do you like least about your job in this department?
    Monotony   2
    Nothing   5

12. What do you like most?
    Incentive pay system   2
    Short hours   4
    Running the machine   1

REFERENCES

1. Adler, N.J. *International dimensions of organizational behavior.* Boston: Kent Publishing, 1993.
2. Argyris, C. Interpersonal barriers to decision making. *Harvard Business Review,* 1966, 44, 84-97.
3. Aronson, E. *The social animal.* San Francisco: Freeman, 1976.
4. Baskin, O.W., and Aronoff, C.E. *Interpersonal communication in organization.* Santa Monica, CA: Goodyear Publishing, 1980.
5. Beier, E.G. Non-verbal communication: How we send emotional messages. *Psychology Today,* 1974, 8, 53-56.
6. Brass, D.J. Being in the right place: A structural analysis of individual influence in a organization. *Administrative Science Quarterly,* 1984, 29, 418-539.
7. Bremmer, J. & Rodenburg, H. *A cultural history of gesture.* Ithaca, New York: Cornell University Press, 1991.
8. Burgess, R.L. An experimental and mathematical analysis of group behavior within restricted networks. *Journal of Experimental Social Psychology,* 1968, 4, 338-49.
9. Burns, T. The directions of activity and communication in a departmental executive group. *Human Relations,* 1954, 7, 73-97.
10. Carroll, S.J. Obtaining product and process improvements: The multiple-management approach. In L.R. Gomez-Mejia and M. Lawless, eds. *Proceedings, High Technology Conference,* Boulder, CO, 1988, 300-304.
11. Carroll, S.J., Cintron, D., and Tosi, H.L. Factors related to how superiors set goals and review performance for their subordinates. *Proceedings of the American Psychological Association,* 1971, 497-98.
12. Carroll, S.J. and Gillen, D.J. Are the classical management functions useful in describing managerial work? *The Academy of Management Review,* 12(1), 1987, 38-51.

13. Carroll, S.J., and Tosi H.L. *Management by Objectives: Applications and research.* New York: Macmillan, 1973.

14. Daft, R.L. *Organization theory and design.* St. Paul, MN: West Publishing, 1983.

15. Daft, R. L. and Lengel, R.H. Information richness: A new approach to managerial behavior and organization design, in B. Staw and L. L. Cummings, eds. *Research in Organizational Behavior*, 6, Greenwich, Conn.: JAI Press, 191-233 (1984).

16. Dahle, T.L. An objective and comparative study of five methods of transmitting information to business and industrial employees. *Speech Monographs*, 1954, 21, 21-8.

17. Dansereau, F. & Markham, S. E. Superior-subordinate communication: Multiple levels of analysis. in F.M. Jablin, L.L. Putnam, K. H. Roberts, and L.W. Porter, eds. *Handbook of Organizational Communication*, Newbury Park: Calif.: Sage. 1987, 343-388.

18. Eisenberg, E.M. and Goodall, H.L. Jr. *Organizational communication.* New York: St. Martin's Press, 1993.

19. Faucheux, C., and MacKenzie, K.D. Task dependency of organizational centrality: Its behavioral consequences. *Journal of Experimental Sociology and Psychology*, 1966, 2, 361-75.

20. Fausto-Sterling A. *Myths of gender.* New York: Basic Books, 1985.

21. Filley, A.C. A theory of small business and divisional growth. Ph.D. dissertation, Ohio State University, 1962.

22. Finkle, R.B. Managerial assessment centers. In M.D. Dunnette, ed. *Handbook of industrial and organizational psychology.* Chicago: Rand McNally, 1976, 861-88.

23. Galbraith, J. *Organization design.* Reading, MA: Addison-Wesley, 1977.

24. Hage, J., Aiken, M. and Marrett, C.B. Organization structure and communications. *American Sociological Review*, 1971, 36, 860-71.

25. Hayes, M.A. Nonverbal communication: Expression without word. In R.C. Huseman, C.M. Logue, and D.L. Freshley, eds. *Readings in interpersonal and organizational communication.* Boston: Holbrook Press, 1973.

26. Heilman, M.E. Information as a deterrent against sex discrimination: The effects of applicant sex and information type on preliminary employment decisions. *Organizational Behavior and Human Performance*, 1984, 33, 174-186.

27. Helgesen, S. *The female advantage: Womens' ways of leadership.* New York: Doubleday, 1990.

28. Henley, N.M. *Body politics: Power, sex, and nonverbal communication.* Englewood Cliffs, NJ: Prentice-Hall, 1977.

29. Indik, B.P., Georgopoulos, B.S., and Seashore, S.E. Superior- subordinate relationships and performance. *Personnel Psychology*, 1961, 14, 357-74.

30. Jacoby, J., Hoyer, W. and Brief, A. Consumer psychology. In M.D. Dunnette, and L.M. Hough, eds. *Handbook of industrial and organizational psychology.* Palo Alto, California: Consulting Psychologists Press, 1992.

31. Kelly, C.M. *Actual listening behavior of industrial supervisors as related to listening ability, general mental ability, selected personality factors, and supervisory effectiveness.* Ph.D. dissertation. Lafayette, IN: Purdue University, 1962.

32. Kelly, J.W. Storytelling in high-tech organizations: A medium for sharing culture. *Journal of Applied Communication Research*, 1985, 13, 45-58.

33. Korman, A. A cause of communications failure. *Personnel Administration*, 1960, 23, 17-21.

34. Kotter, J.P. *The general managers.* New York: Free Press, 1982.

35. Lawler, E.E., Porter, L.W., and Tannenbaum, A. Manager's attitudes toward interaction episodes. *Journal of Applied Psychology*, 1968, 52, 432-39.

36. Laws, J.L. *The second X.* New York: Elsevier, 1979.

37. Lawshe, C.H., Holmes, W., and Turmail, G.M. An analysis of employee handbooks. *Personnel*, 1951, 27, 487-95.

38. Likert, R. Motivational approach to management development. *Harvard Business Review*, 1959, 37, 70.

39. Lowin, A., and Craig, J. The influence of level of performance on managerial style: An experimental object lesson on the ambiguity of correlational data. *Organizational Behavior and Human Performance*, 1968, 3, 440-58.

40. Ludeman, K. Upward feedback helps managers walk the talk. *HRMagazine*, 38(5), 85-93, 1993.

41. Maier, N.R.F., Hoffman, L., and Read, W.H. Superior-subordinate communication: The relative effectiveness of managers who held their subordinates' positions. *Personnel Psychology*, 1963, 16, 1-12.

42. Maier, N.R.F., Read, W.H., and Hooven, J. Breakdown in boss-subordinate communication. In *Communication in organizations.* Ann Arbor, MI: Foundation For Research on Human Behavior, 1959, 19-23.

43. Martin, B., and Sroufe, L.A. Anxiety. In C.C. Costello, ed. *Symptoms of psychopathology.* New York: John Wiley, 1970.

44. Martinko, M.J., and Gardner, W.L. The leader/member attribution process. *Academy of Management Review*, 1987, 12, 235-49.

45. Mcguire, W.J. *Attitudes and attitude change*, In G. Lindzey and E., eds. *Handbook of Social Psychology*, 3rd ed. Reading, MA: Addison-Wesley, 1985.

46. Monge, P. R. & Eisenberg, E.M. Emergent communication networks. in F.M. Jablin, L.L. Putnam, K. H. Roberts, and L.W. Porter, eds. *Handbook of Organizational Communication*, Newbury Park: California: Sage. 1987, 343-388.

47. O'Reilly, C.A., Chatman, J.A., and Anderson, J.C. Message flow and decision making. In F.M. Jablin, L.L. Putnam, K.H. Roberts, and L.W. Porter, eds. *Handbook of organizational communication.* Newbury Park, CA: Sage Publications, 1987.

48. O'Reilly, C. A., Chatman, J., and Caldwell, D. F. People and organizational culture: A profile comparison approach to assessing person-organization fit. *The Academy of Management Journal*, 1991, 34, 487-516.

49. O'Toole, J. *Vanguard management: Redesigning the corporate future.* Garden City, NY: Doubleday, 1985.

50. Oldham, G.R. and Brass, D.J. Employee reaction to an open-plan office: A naturally occurring quasi-experiment. *Administrative Science Quarterly*, 1979, 24, 167-184.

51. Olian, J.D., Carroll, S.J., Giannantonio, C.M., and Feren, D.B. What do proteges look for in a mentor? Results of three experimental studies. *Journal of Vocational Behavior*, 1988, 33, 15-37.

52. Ouchi, W. *Theory Z: How American business can meet the Japanese challenge.* Reading, MA: Addison-Wesley, 1981.

53. Port, O. & Smith G. Quality, small and midsize companies sieze the challenge-not a moment too soon. *Business Week*, November 30, 1992.

54. Porter, L.W., and Roberts, K.H. Communication in organizations. In M.D. Dunnette, ed. *Handbook of industrial and organizational psychology.* Chicago: Rand McNally, 1976.

55. Read, W.H. Upward communication in industrial hierarchies. *Human Relations*, 1962, 15, 3-15.

56. Redding, W.C. *Communication within the organization.* New York: Industrial Communication Council, 1972.

57. Richmond, V.P. & McCroskey, J.C. *Organizational communication for survival.* Englewood Cliffs, N.J. Prentice-Hall, 1992.

58. Roberts, K.H. *Communicating in organizations.* Chicago: Science Research Associates, 1984.

59. Roberts, K.H. and O'Reilly, C.A. Some correlates of communication roles in organizations. *Academy of Management Journal*, 1979, 22, 42-57.

60. Rosen, B. & Jerdee, T.H. The influence of sex-role stereotypes on evaluations of male and female supervisory behavior. *Journal of Applied Psychology*, 1973, 57(1), 44-48

61. Rosener, J.B. Ways women lead. *Harvard Business Review*, 1990, 119-125.

62. Salancik, G.R., and Pfeffer, J. An examination of need-satisfaction models and job attitudes. *Administrative Science Quarterly*, 1977, 2, 427-56.

63. Siegel, J., Dubrovsky, V., Kiesler, S., and McGuire, T.W. Group processes in computer mediated communication. *Organizational Behavior and Decision Processes*, 1986, 37, 157-87.

64. Sproull, L., and Kiesler, S. Reducing social context cues: The case of electronic mail. *Management Science*, 1986, 32, 1492-1512.

65. Steckler, N.A., and Rosenthal, R. Sex differences in nonverbal and verbal communication with bosses, peers, and subordinates. *Journal of Applied Psychology*, 1985, 70, 157-63.

66. Sundstrom, E. and Sundstrom, *M.G. Work places: The psychology of the physical environment in offices and factories.* Cambridge, England: Cambridge University Press, 1990.

67. Sundstrom, E., Herbert, R.K. and Brown, D.W. Privacy and communication in an open-plan office. *Environment and Behavior*, 1982, 14(3), 379-392.

68. Tannen, D. *You just don't understand: Talk between the sexes.* New York: Morrow, 1990.

69. Tjovsold, D. *Managing work relationships: Cooperation, conflict and power.* Lexington, MA: Lexington Books, 1986.

70. Tosi, H.L., and Einbender, S.E. The effects of the type and amount of information in sex discrimination research: A meta-analysis. *Academy of Management Journal*, 1985, 28, 712-23.

71. Tushman, M.I., and Nadler, D.A. Information processing as an integrating concept in organizational design. *Academy of Management Review*, 1978, 3, 613-24.

72. Unger, R.K. Imperfect reflections of reality. In R.T. Hare-Mustin and J. Marecek, eds. *Making a difference: Psychology constructs gender*, New Haven: Yale University Press, 1990.

73. Walster, E., Aronson, E., and Abraham, D. On increasing the persuasiveness of a low prestige communicator. *Journal of Experimental Psychology*, 1966, 2, 325-42.

74. Ware, J. Seduction in the classroom: The Doctor Fox effect. *Proceedings of Midwest Division of Academy of Management Conference*, 1975.

75. Wason, P.C. The retention of material presented through precis. *Journal of Communication Research*, 1962, 12, 36-43.

76. Weber, R.A. Perceptions of interactions between superiors and subordinates. *Human Relations*, 1970, 23, 235-48.

77. Weick, K.E. *The social psychology of organizing*. Reading, MA.: Addison-Wesley, 1969.

78. Willits, R.D. Company performance and interpersonal relations. *Industrial Management Review*, 1967, 7, 91-107.

79. Zalesny, M.D. & Farace, R.V. Traditional versus open offices: A comparison of sociotechnical, social relations, and symbolic meaning perspectives. *Academy of Management Journal*, 1987, 30(2), 240-259.

80. Zimbardo, P.G., Ebbesen, E.B., and Maslach, C. *Influencing attitudes and changing behavior*. Reading, MA: Addison-Wesley, 1977.

81. Zuboff, S. *In the age of the smart machine*, New York: Basic Books, 1988.

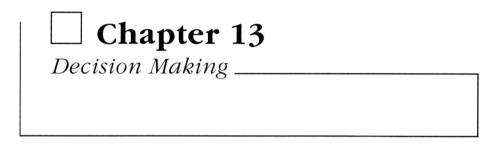

Chapter 13
Decision Making

The Tenerife air disaster demonstrates how very difficult it is to make effective decisions, especially when conditions are stressful [51]. A KLM 747 struck a PanAm 747 upon takeoff and 583 lives were lost. Both planes were originally diverted to Tenerife because of a bomb explosion at their intended destination in the Canary Islands. The accident occurred when the KLM plane took off down the runway before the PanAm flight had been cleared out of the way. The decisions that culminated in the accident were negatively affected by the interruption of normal events for both flight crews and for the ground controllers. The difficult conditions of maneuvering jumbo jets at a smaller airport was made even more stressful by time pressures felt by the KLM captain to minimize his delay at Tenerife. Communications were such that information was lost or not processed appropriately. Messages were unclear or misunderstood, and narrowed perceptions diminished the capacity to cope with unfamiliar conditions. There was also a breakdown in coordination within the various teams, in which, for example, subordinates did not challenge or confront openly when the fateful take-off started.

The Tenerife disaster is just one example of human decision-making situations with critical consequences. The consequences may effect many parties, including the decision makers themselves. Managers have even been held personally liable, and criminally charged for failure to meet social and legal responsibilities for worker safety [22]. Many decisions are not as complex or consequential. However, most decisions are far from easy, and usually not fully effective. For managers in particular, decision making is at the heart of their role. They make small and large decisions in every function they perform. Herbert Simon, Nobel Prize winner for his work on decision making, says that management and decision making are virtually the same thing [43].

In this chapter we present a model of problem solving and decision making. We describe characteristics of the process and explore individual and group decision making. Emphasis is given to the difficulties that arise and to methods for improving the process outlined in the model.

A MODEL OF DECISION MAKING

Figure 13.1 depicts a model that will guide our discussion of decision making. The terms "decision making" and "problem solving" will be used interchangeably throughout this chapter. The model applies to decision making at both the individual and the group level.

FIGURE 13.1 *A General Model of Decision Making or Problem Solving*

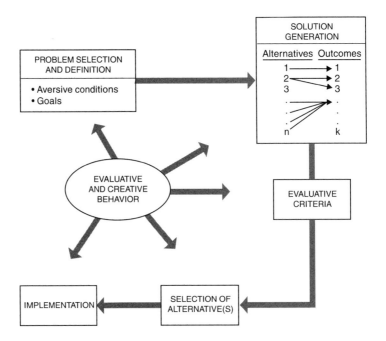

One key element in the model is the notion that evaluative behavior occurs at all points in the decision making process. People have a strong tendency to make judgments about what is good or bad or what is right or wrong. Perceptions, values, and attitudes come into play whether people are deciding alone or in a group. This tendency to evaluate often contributes to poor decision making. As we will see, decision making can be significantly improved by controlling when and how evaluations are made.

Similarly, creativity can be brought to bear throughout the process. Problems can be creatively defined. Creativity is particularly relevant in generating alternative solutions to a problem and in combining and implementing decisions. Although all people are not equally creative, they can learn to be more creative and benefit from using techniques that foster creativity.

Decision making begins with a judgment that a problem exists. Sometimes the problem is an uncomfortable or negative condition people want to elimi-

☐ IMPROVING YOUR CREATIVITY

Creativity is affected by many things, ranging from the personal characteristics of individuals to the organizational conditions that foster or hinder it [54]. Some companies such as 3M, for example, have a long history of emphasizing creativity. Over one quarter of their revenues come from products less than five years old, and 70 percent of their sales are attributed to ideas originating directly from their employees [10]. Creativity has several definitions. Some see it as rooted in hard-to-describe intuitions, feelings, insights, and impressions in contrast to more "rational" processes [4]. Others see it as a set of procedures and skills that can be learned and honed with practice [2, 3, 12]. Here, creativity is not mystical, nor is it confined within select people such as geniuses. Rather, the potential for creativity is in all our heads, in ideas which need only be unlocked through practice, encouragement, and high expectations. Some of the techniques one can use to improve creativity include the following:

1. Generate as many ideas as you can
2. Do not evaluate the ideas
3. Don't be logical
4. Challenge and question rules and habits
5. Ask, "What if . . ."
6. Don't be afraid to be foolish, crazy, or wrong
7. Relax physically
8. Believe that you can be creative
9. Let your mind wander off the problem
10. Use your ideas to suggest more ideas
11. Write each idea on a slip of paper or card
12. Arrange ideas into various combinations
13. Examine similarities and differences
14. Reverse ideas, explore opposites

nate, such as a stoppage on a production line. A problem can also exist when a person sets a goal, because a goal also represents a desire to improve on a current condition. A manager setting a sales goal considers the new sales level preferable to its present level. The problem is how to attain the new sales goal.

Once a problem is recognized and defined, alternatives are sought that could eliminate the negative condition or achieve the goal. Alternatives are activities that are believed will lead to a better state of affairs. When people generate alternatives, they make assumptions or predictions that certain outcomes will follow. The relationship between alternatives and their outcomes is not a simple one. One alternative can produce a single or several outcomes, or more than one alternative could be required to achieve a single desired outcome. Some outcomes are intended, while others are unintended side effects of the alternative. For example, a total effort to win a ball game can cause unintended injury to a player.

To choose among alternatives, people have to use criteria to evaluate them. Among the most common criteria used are feasibility, time, cost, and personal acceptability. Criteria will usually vary from person to person, and it is not always clear what criteria are being used.

Eventually, however, choices are made among alternatives. Once the choice is implemented, it becomes possible to evaluate once again. Here the evaluation can uncover faulty implementation or reveal that errors were made at an earlier stage of the decision process.

This brief overview greatly oversimplifies the decision process. The remainder of the chapter probes the model more deeply and suggests ways to improve decision making. First, though, we will examine a few points to help in understanding the process a bit more.

CHARACTERISTICS OF THE DECISION PROCESS

Decisions Within Decisions.   When a manager discovers that the machinery breakdown rate is excessively high, the overall problem may be how to reduce this difficulty to an acceptable level. But what happens as this problem is addressed? First a decision had to be made that the frequency or cost of breakdowns exceeds some tolerable standard. Decisions also must be made about the scope of the problem and what to include in defining it. For example, does a problem with one machine in a factory suggest that other machines are due to fail? People also decide which alternatives are to be generated and considered. In addition, decisions have to be made on criteria for evaluation: which ones to use and how they will be weighted. Decisions are made when it comes time for implementation and later evaluation. These **multiple subdecisions** are common, and any one of them can have an impact on the process.

Small Decisions Accumulate.   Many decisions we make are trivial and are made very quickly. Yet the consequences of a series of small decisions can accumulate into a serious problem. Picture an employee who postpones a call to a customer in order to get home on time. Another employee overlooks a detail on that customer's order because he has a headache. Later, a shipping clerk leaves the order off a truck rather than make an extra effort to load it. Taken together, these minor decisions can add up to the loss of a major account.

Decisions are Partial or Temporary Solutions.   It is almost impossible to prevent errors in decision making. Most decisions, therefore, never completely solve a problem. Even if they come close, the solution often contains seeds of new problems requiring attention. Since decisions are imperfect, they are partial solutions. This means that it is necessary to follow up on important decisions and to be prepared to modify them.

Stress Effects. Decision making can be a stressful process and cause considerable anxiety. Janis and Mann have said we are all "reluctant decision makers" [28]. They cite the words of Linus speaking to Charlie Brown in the Peanuts cartoon: "No problem is so big or so complicated that it can't be run away from!" Not surprisingly, people do not always deal systematically with an important decision. They might overreact and plunge headlong and headstrong into it. They might also show great resourcefulness in avoiding the decision. When facing complex and difficult choices, where the costs and benefits are high, emotion can dominate over reason.

Personal Factors in Decision Making. A person's values, attitudes, personality, and perception enter the decision process in all of its stages. They affect what one person perceives to be or not to be a problem. Beliefs and attitudes enter into the evaluation of alternatives and during implementation [9, 15]. Overall, decision making is an exercise of values. Human biases emerge as we define problems, set goals, and make choices. Group decision making often involves a clash of values and an attempt to resolve differing points of view.

DECISION EFFECTIVENESS

One can argue that the decision is effective if it solves the problem; that is, if an adverse condition is removed or if a desired goal is achieved. One can also look at costs of the decision, including its unintended side effects. In another approach, discussed later, a decision is considered effective if it has quality and is accepted by those affected by it. Finally, some argue that measures of effectiveness should focus on the decision-making process. In this approach it is recognized that decisions are rarely perfect. A good decision is one that results from the best-possible procedure, even if the outcome turns out not to be the best. The emphasis on process is characteristic of the ideal models discussed next.

IDEAL VS. ACTUAL DECISION MAKING

Attempts to show how people *should* make a decision are called **normative or ideal models.** Normative models are partly based on observation of the actual errors that decision makers tend to commit. Certain errors are very common, and in normative models an attempt is made to prevent or reduce them [28]. But it is easier to spot errors after the fact that to prevent them in the first place. The "Monday morning quarterback" has all the answers after the game but never had to decide during the heat of it.

Normative models are also called **rational or economic models** [16, 35, 43, 44]. Normative models have several characteristics [28]. A decision maker should adhere to them even though human abilities and the availability of information put limits on what can be done. The normative approach requires the decision maker to:

1. Explore a broad range of alternative courses of action
2. Survey all possible objectives sought and the values relevant to the choice to be made

3. Carefully evaluate the positive and negative consequences in terms of costs, risks, and benefits

4. Search further for new information to further evaluate alternatives

5. Account for new information and inputs, even when it might not support a preferred course of action

6. Reevaluate positive and negative consequences of all known alternatives, even those originally judged unacceptable, before making a final choice

7. Develop a detailed plan of implementation, including contingency plans to handle risks or new problems should they arise

For each phase of a normative model a number of techniques can be used, which are discussed later in this chapter.

Simon [42] and March and Simon [33] have questioned the normative models. Their argument is that decisions are made with **bounded rationality,** which means that decision makers are able to recognize only a limited number of alternatives and are aware of only a few consequences of each alternative. Human abilities are fallible and limited, information is never perfect, and money and time add limits as well. As a result, it is impossible to maximize benefits in decision making. Instead, people satisfice. **Satisficing** involves the selection of alternatives that meet some minimal criteria and causes a person to select the first acceptable alternative that arises. Suppose, for example, that a manger is dissatisfied with the quality of performance appraisals in her department. It would take considerable time and effort to uncover and define elements of this problem. It would also be a major effort to review alternative appraisal systems and thoroughly evaluate each one. Many complications would arise, and many questions would be unanswerable. This is a situation in which some information is unavailable. Alternatives are not easy to identify and difficult to select. Rationality becomes limited by these complexities, and decisions will be imperfect. In this situation there are many opportunities to satisfice, such as choosing a rating form that looks quite adequate rather than comparing the form to all possible alternatives.

ORGANIZATIONAL COMPLEXITIES

Many forces in organizations complicate the decision making process. For example, problems get redefined and decisions modified as different people become involved in the process over time. Even with normative approaches, organizational forces will have an effect. One approach to understanding organizational decisions is the **garbage can model,** or "organized anarchy" [7]. The garbage can decision process consists of four elements: (1) the participants with their various priorities, (2) problems to be solved, (3) solutions to be chosen and applied, and (4) decision opportunities.

The participants in complex organizations are the many decision makers with different goals and problems. They have limited time and energy and can't involve themselves in all decisions. So they get involved depending on their needs, goals, and availability.

Participants also have ideas they would like to see adopted. Sometimes these ideas are solutions in search of a problem, rather than a problem in search of a solution. For example, a manufacturing manager might want some new equipment he saw at a trade show. He will be sensitive to decision opportunities that will allow him to buy it. Thus, goals are established to justify decisions already made rather than the reverse.

Timing is also an important element in this model. The organization is viewed as a fluid structure in which people, problems, and solutions flow together and apart at different times. Decisions result from a disorderly convergence of these elements, heavily determined by patterns of timing and opportunities [34]. The garbage can model is most likely to operate when goals are ambiguous, methods for accomplishing goals are not well understood, and organizational units are scattered and loosely linked together. This model is also more likely to operate when an organization has many departments, committees, and task forces, each with vague or overlapping responsibilities.

☐ A GARBAGE CAN DECISION

Universities have many of the attributes in which the garbage can model flourishes. In one university, a decision was made to discontinue the music department and its programs. Students in the program were allowed to complete their studies, but no new ones were accepted. Faculty were urged to resign or seek administrative posts. On the surface, the decision to close the music department appeared orderly and rational. Enrollment was dropping, and costs were skyrocketing. The university was under legislative pressure to trim such operations to meet new funding levels for higher education in the state. It seemed reasonable that the music department be the first to be cut.

A closer examination revealed that the decision was much more complex. It resulted from the fluid interaction of many people and problems in the university over a four-year period. Different events and forces came into play that produced dozens of small decisions. Some favored the music department, but most eventually worked against it. For example, in the early stages of budget pressure, the music department was put on probation by a national accrediting association. Soon afterward, a new academic vice president called for a review of all programs on campus. In the midst of this, the chair of the music department retired and a search began for a replacement. The energy and time of the music faculty were eaten up preparing reports for the vice president's review and searching for a new chair. As a result, little time was left for improving themselves to get off their probationary accreditation status.

☐ A Garbage Can . . .

During the vice president's review, the search committee for a new chair was disbanded. It hadn't received good applications, and this provided the vice president with an excuse to discontinue the search rather than extend it. Throughout the process, other departments were competing for funds. Yet some faculty outside music joined with alumni and local citizens to support the music program. Student groups also got involved. Despite this support, the administration dragged its feet in replacing a key faculty member who took a job elsewhere.

Two years after its original visit, the accrediting association returned for a reevaluation. It recommended withdrawing accreditation because of lack of administrative backing for the music department. They cited failure to hire a chair and replace faculty. They also noted that other recommendations they had made two years earlier had not been implemented. Soon after the loss of accreditation, the university decided to close the music department.

The garbage can conditions are quite evident in this example. One interesting aspect is that loss of accreditation was used as a major reason to end the music program. It was the university itself that had made it difficult if not impossible to meet accreditation requirements.

INDIVIDUAL DECISION MAKING

In looking at individual decision making, we will describe how people typically behave, including the errors they make. Once we understand these behaviors, we can turn to ways to improve decision making. Thus both the actual and the normative are included in our discussion. Individual decision making concepts will be used later to discuss the process as it occurs in groups. In both cases, the basic model depicted in Figure 13.1 applies.

PROBLEM SELECTION AND DEFINITION

The choice of which problems to work on and the definition of a problem both provide a chance for errors in decision making. Some common errors in recognizing, choosing, and defining problems are

1. **Perceptual biases** make people aware of some problems and unaware of others. We block out or ignore problems based on our needs, values, and personalities.

2. Event sequences dictate what people select to work on. Problems are often dealt with in the order in which they arise.

3. Problems perceived as emergencies and problems perceived as solvable take priority over other problems.

4. People tend to be overly reactive. Given a choice between reflective planning and action taking, people will take action.

5. Problems are often poorly defined. Definitions may be inaccurate, incomplete, and not creative.

6. Problem definitions often contain built-in solutions that take the focus away from the problem itself.

7. People leap to solutions long before the problem is even moderately well defined.

8. Problem definitions are often stated in a way that provokes threat and anxiety in others.

Improving Problem Selection.   A number of steps can be taken to prevent **problem selection** from being dominated by our perceptions or by the order in which problems happen to arise. The first is to recognize that nothing is a problem until someone calls it that. A problem is nothing more than a personal, subjective conclusion that things aren't the way they ought to be. It might be wise, therefore, to check out our perceptions with others before concluding that a problem exists that is worth taking action upon.

Problem selection can also be improved if people make lists of problems and prioritize them. One technique for doing this is to periodically scan and monitor the environment for both problems and opportunities. For example, managers who engage in systematic planning begin with a thorough examination not only of what is, but of what is possible and desirable. They may identify conditions that need attention, such as failure to meet delivery dates or new product and market opportunities.

Value clarification is a process by which people can express and clarify the particular values they hold, especially those that bear on a decision at hand. This helps in problem selection and definition. For example, managers may consider introducing a new product but fail to discuss basic values they hold about product quality, market, or price. They might need to resolve whether innovation and new markets are more valued than reliability and reputation in existing markets. Value clarification can lead these managers in any number of directions. They can seek value consensus, or they might choose to exploit diverse values by working on both new and old markets.

Improving Problem Definition.   There is a big difference between problem selection and **problem definition.** Consider the following situations:

1. A manager discovers a 12 percent drop in second-quarter sales in Milwaukee.

2. A police chief is told burglaries increased 21 percent in the city in the past year.

3. A construction workers spots a small leak in a water pipe at a nuclear power plant construction site.

While these situations may be worthy of attention, they are not well-defined problems. Remember that we have habits that steer us away from defining problems and into trying to find solutions. Most people who read the list above think immediately about solutions, such as communicating with the sales force in Milwaukee, increasing police patrols, or replacing the leaky pipe.

Several things can improve problem definition. The first is to work toward a thorough definition. A second is to avoid the tendency to jump prematurely into solutions before the problem is completely defined. The third comes into play if you fail to do one of the first two. That is, if you have a solution in mind, ask yourself to link that solution back to some aspect of the problem. In other words, when a solution occurs to you, ask yourself how it relates to the problem at hand. This forces you to go back to the problem definition rather than develop the solution. Improving problem definition can help to get and use facts and information that is less ambiguous. Jackson and Dutton argue that when information is ambiguous, managers are more prone to react to threats and to ignore opportunities [25].

One way to better define a problem is to determine its causes. Investigate any events that might be related to the problem. Examine whether or not time of day could be a factor. Check to see whether the problem occurs elsewhere. Using the leaky water pipe as an example, one could ask: Is it faulty material? Was the pipe installed appropriately? Was it tampered with or damaged after installation? Without such questions, causes of the leak may never be known. Replacing the pipe is an action taken against a symptom: the leak itself. But if the causes remain (such as faulty material), the solution to replace the pipe will not be a lasting one. Each different cause could also require distinct and separate solutions.

Many problems can be creatively defined. There is a story that, years ago, the military was looking for ways to improve the efficiency of jet engines on aircraft. The problem was defined by the military as "how to burn a higher percentage of fuel in the combustion chamber so that less fuel passed through unburned." Supposedly, a teenager at an air show asked an official why they didn't recover the unburned fuel and ignite it rather than try to burn more of it in the first place. The problem was redefined. It became "how to catch unburned fuel and how to burn it." Jet engines soon had afterburners which dramatically increased their fuel efficiency.

GENERATING AND EVALUATING SOLUTIONS

The normative model tells us to generate, explore, and examine all possible solutions in a thorough and exhaustive manner, and to estimate the probabilities and values of all possible outcomes. Methods and criteria are established for evaluating and comparing alternative solutions.

Yet even when extensive efforts are made to do this, errors creep in:

1. Alternative solutions are evaluated prematurely. People tend to react positively or negatively to an idea as soon as it arises.

2. Because of premature evaluation, idea generation is curtailed. An incomplete set of possible solutions is generated because evaluation works against generation of alternatives. Satisficing is one result.

3. People do not use the definition of the problem as a source of additional solution ideas.

4. A variety of blocks interfere with exhaustive solution search [1]. Perceptual blocks put blinders on creative thinking, social and cultural values limit our thoughts, and patterns of thought keep us in mental ruts.

5. People fail to make their evaluation criteria explicit before using them to judge alternatives.

6. It is difficult for people to deal with both the value of a solution and the probabilities associated with it. Both are important, but we may ignore one or the other.

7. Emotions can lead to self-deception. People can mentally rationalize or justify an alternative they strongly prefer.

8. People rush into making a decision when there may be no need to do so. They fail to ask whether postponing a decision could have some benefits.

Improving Solution Generation. The way solutions and ideas are generated makes all the difference in the effectiveness of decisions. Let us examine some techniques to assist in the process.

One important practice is to separate idea generation from idea evaluation [30, 31, 39]. This suggestion is based on the premise that when we evaluate an idea, we cut off the generation of other ones. A positive evaluation is more harmful than a neutral or negative evaluation. If we are neutral toward, or dislike an alternative solution, we have an incentive to generate another one. But if we like an alternative, we might stop our search right there.

Brainstorming requires that we let our minds run free and avoid evaluating what we say or think [38]. All ideas are considered valuable. Using other people to generate additional ideas can often be well worth the effort. First of all, more ideas will result. But more importantly, perhaps, these additional people may not suffer the same perceptual or experience blocks as we. As a matter of fact, lack of experience with the problem may be an advantage. In decision making, experience can work for or against us. It is useful for evaluation, but it puts limits on our ability to see a problem from different perspectives.

Some techniques are designed to overcome particular blocks. We have just seen one way to overcome experience blocks: use inexperienced people. Another technique may be to mask the problem or hide its true nature before seeking solutions from others [23, 40]. As an illustration, picture an object about the size and dimensions of the one shown in Figure 13.2. The object is long and narrow and not much thicker than paper. Without revealing the true problem to you, we can ask you to think of all the ways you might separate the object into two pieces. How many can you list before reading any further?

Unknown to you, the object in Figure 13.2 is a blade of grass. The problem is one of searching for a new lawn-mowing concept. Was one of your solutions to whip a string through the center of the object? Cut it with a laser beam? Which one of your solutions has potential merit for lawn-cutting technology is a matter for further creativity, and for experts to decide eventually. Had you been told at the outset that lawn mowing was the problem, experience would have blocked your ability to think creatively.

☐ **FIGURE 13.2** *A Creative Challenge with a Masked Problem*

How many ways can
you separate the
object on the left
into two pieces
so that it looks
like the one on
the right?

Sometimes idea generation bogs down, and people can't seem to find a workable solution. One method to spur creativity then is to randomly locate a word in a dictionary [11]. This word is used as a stimulus for generating a new list of words through free association. The new list is then examined to see if it contains anything to help solve the problem. This **dictionary technique** is based on a sound principle. People often get into mental ruts. The use of a randomly selected word to foster new thinking is a useful way to break into new ideas and give direction to originality [40].

Another technique to generate solutions is to keep an interplay alive between the problem definition and the solutions. When a problem has been thoroughly and creatively defined, it will be broken down into a list of elements and causes. This list can be used as a basis to generate ideas by using the list entries as stimuli for generating ideas. In turn, when ideas are generated, they can be connected back to the problem definition and may even refine that definition. In this manner, an exhaustive and creative problem definition helps to foster an improved solution search [3].

Social and cultural blocks are also difficult to overcome. In fact, we may not wish to ignore values that put moral and ethical limits on our decisions. These limits, referred to as **bounded discretion**, operate in all of our decisions, directly and indirectly [41]. Robbery to solve a money problem or fraud to save a company might be alternative ways to solve a problem. Without bounded discretion, such decisions would reflect a breakdown in the social fabric.

Improving Solution Evaluation. Eventually every idea has to be tested. First it must pass our mental and emotional scrutiny. We can, in some cases, try ideas out before full commitment is made. These tests can take many forms, such as further discussions, computer simulations, or the full-scale construction of a test model, as is done with airplanes.

Another step can be taken to organize alternatives into different clusters before evaluating them. Suppose a manager is deciding how to reduce plant accidents. Alternatives might fall into distinct categories, such as machinery improvements, hours of work, employee training, and so forth. These clusters may then be evaluated for easier decision making.

Another important step, often overlooked, is to establish criteria to use for evaluating alternatives. Criteria are not easy to establish, but doing so and making them explicit can help decision making immeasurably [24]. Criteria can then be weighted by importance.

Eventually, of course, criteria must be applied to alternatives. This is a more complex process, but the heart of it is to see which solutions satisfy the most (or the most important) criteria. Suppose you were deciding among several job alternatives. Table 13.1 shows how a simple point system (1 to 7) could be used so that each job received points on each criterion. The job at CBS turns out to be the best of the five offers. To select any job except CBS suggests the use of criteria not originally considered.

Applying criteria to alternatives can be very complicated. For example, we can make some criteria "cutoff" factors. If a job is lacking in that criteria, it is eliminated; for example, jobs that fall below a certain salary level are taken out

TABLE 13.1 Evaluating Job Offers Across Several Criteria Using a Seven-Point Scale

Criteria	CBS	AT&T	Job Offers GE	GM	IBM
Salary	7	5	7	3	5
Location	7	7	2	3	3
Promotion	4	7	3	7	4
Benefits	5	5	3	5	6
Recreation	7	2	5	2	1
Type of work	7	7	3	4	2
Totals	37	33	23	24	21

regardless of their points on other criteria. Another complicating factor can be introduced by considering probabilities: lower-probability events would carry less weight. A number of decision-making techniques apply both probabilities and values. The application of both gives a **utility** to each decision alternative. This can be shown as follows:

$$\text{Utility of Alternative X} = \text{Sum of} \left(\begin{array}{c}\text{Outcomes of}\\ \text{Alt. X}\end{array}\right) \times \left(\begin{array}{c}\text{Probabilities of}\\ \text{These Outcomes}\end{array}\right)$$

If we calculate utilities for each alternative solution, we can select one with the highest utility score.

Solution evaluation is also improved if we know our personal tendencies. Some people take more risk and are more oriented toward seeking success. They are more likely to ignore what can be lost, and rather than protect themselves against losses, they will choose alternatives to maximize gain. Others will avoid the risks of maximum gain and will seek smaller but safer gains. Others may focus on losses rather than gains: their main motivation is to prevent losses, even if it means losing the chance at gaining something. This is a failure avoidance strategy and leads to conservative decision making.

Sometimes we deceive ourselves in choosing among alternatives. We select a choice we like and rationalize or make excuses for our choice. Soelberg, who studied the job selection process of college students, found some patterns of deciding that are quite interesting [45]. Students identify a favorite job early in their search process. Not fully aware of such a favorite, most students kept looking for a job even after receiving an offer from their favorite one. Soelberg believes that the search continued as a way to confirm the choice of original favorite: the search served to convince students of a choice that had already been made.

IMPLEMENTATION

Some decisions are implemented easily once we have decided what to do. Even a complex decision can have a simple implementation. For example, a company might consider many factors in deciding whether to buy from a particular supplier. Once one is selected, an order can be easily placed. Other decisions may require more in the implementation process. Consider the case of a company that decides to go ahead with a new product. The decision is just the beginning of a long process. Hundreds of new problems will have to be solved to get the new product ready. The long and detailed process from design to production, to sales and distribution of the product, will require much attention.

The ease of implementation will depend on how often we have implemented a decision in the past. If we have been through it many times, implementation can be a routine matter. But we are often in new territory when we carry out a decision, and when this is the case, we are always faced with new problems requiring new decisions.

Problems in Implementation.   **Postdecisional dissonance** can impede implementation of a solution [28]. After a decision has been made, people may waver and hesitate. As the decision is executed, anxiety can overcome good judgment. The decision maker can become extremely cautious and overly vigilant. Feelings of regret can set in. Minor setbacks can become signals of concern and evoke new uncertainties about the original decision.

Perceptual errors and *cognitive dissonance* can also follow a decision. If people are positively disposed toward a decision, they may ignore information that suggests the decision isn't working and interpret events to support their original choice. In terms of cognitive dissonance theory, people are motivated to reduce feelings of dissonance. Suppose you strongly favor a particular solution, but information that is unfavorable to your choice creates dissonance in your mind. It is likely to be ignored or distorted to support your original choice. The opposite can happen if you were opposed to a decision. Information favorable to that decision may be distorted.

People make decisions and sometimes stick to them over time, even if they are bad decisions. This is called **escalation of commitment** [5, 52]. People become trapped or locked into a course of action for several reasons [6, 46, 48]. They resist admitting they made an error in order to appear competent or consistent. They can save face by holding to their original position. They may feel that changing their position will be viewed as a sign of weakness and make them more vulnerable to criticism or exploitation. People may also feel that their original decision was a good one that will contribute to an improved situation. Escalation of commitment often occurs, such as when people pour money into a failing business or when they refuse to admit they are wrong in an argument. Escalation can be a potentially costly behavior if the person is wrong [47]. Escalation of commitment may decrease or be less likely when (1) the resources to stay with the decision are depleted, (2) the responsibility for the bad decision is shared or when people feel that more than one person was the cause, or (3) the evidence is strong that negative things will continue to happen [21, 53].

Improving Implementation and Evaluation.   One must first accept postdecisional conflict as natural, and not repress or ignore it. Such conflict is quite common because many decisions are complex and involve a good deal of risk or uncertainty. There are at least three ways to resolve postdecisional conflict [28]. One is to stick with the original decision, to *reaffirm* it. After weighting the evidence, we proceed as planned. Another strategy is to *modify* or *curtail implementation*. It might be possible to stay with the original decision but slow down a bit in implementing it. A third strategy is to *undo* the original decision. When the costs and risks of continuing outweigh the benefits of the original decision, it might be wise to drop or change the original choice rather than escalate commitment.

Decision makers can work diligently to seek information of all kinds. This posture of *active openness* can help overcome tendencies to pursue feedback selectivity during implementation. Another strategy is to give all information fair and thorough consideration, rather than deny it or rationalize it away. It takes considerable effort to actively seek pros and cons and to evaluate all sides of an issue.

Implementation is usually aided by a good plan, especially for complex projects. Recall our brief discussion of a company introducing a new product. This will require months of detailed planning. As the plan is drawn up, thought can be given to places where difficulty might occur. Then those responsible for implementation can anticipate problems and develop a *contingency plan* that would go into effect if problems occur.

It pays to *reflect back* on the entire decision process, whether one succeeds or fails. If all went well, it would be useful to know why. The same holds true of failure, of course. Learning why and where things went wrong helps to avoid those pitfalls the next time around.

Reflecting back on decisions is, unfortunately, not a common practice. One might expect failures to be more thoroughly examined than successes, but this may not be the case. After a failure, people might overreact and avoid making similar decisions. For example, the company who fails at introducing a new product might not attempt a new one for years. After a failure, people might also make the mistake of finding a simple but incomplete explanation. A person may be made a scapegoat for the failure, when there was really much more to it. These and other evaluative behaviors are not very useful. A more balanced, objective, and thorough analysis can come closer to the facts. As Figure 13.1 indicates, good evaluation can shed light on all phases of decision making, including the implementation itself.

GROUP DECISION MAKING

Organizations frequently use committees, task forces, project teams, and other types of groups in all stages of the decision process. This employee involvement or **participative management** philosophy is an attempt to get better decisions and more commitment by including employees in decisions that affect them, spreading responsibilities for decision making to all employees, not just managers.

Sometimes participation works well, and sometimes it doesn't. In order to succeed, the commitment to group decision making must be genuine. In addition, various skills are needed. First, managers must learn the steps and techniques of good decision making, discussed in the first part of this chapter. Knowledge of group dynamics is essential too. Managers need to know the benefits and disadvantages of groups over individuals working alone to decide whether to use a group and to what extent to involve it. Finally, leadership is needed to guide the process so that effective decisions have a chance of emerging.

BENEFITS AND DISADVANTAGES OF GROUPS

Groups have both assets and liabilities in decision making [32]. These are shown in Figure 13.3. To a large degree, success depends on the skill of the leader. Compared to individuals, groups have more knowledge and information. Groups also generate a great number of approaches to a problem, and members can knock each other out of ruts in their thinking. Group participation can increase understanding and acceptance of the decision and the commitment to execute it. Decisions of managers often fail because of faulty communication of the decision to those who must implement them. Employees often lack knowledge of rejected alternatives, obstacles, goals, and reasons behind the decision. They are overcome when a group is involved in the entire process.

A disadvantage of group decision making lies in social **pressure for conformity**. Good minority ideas can be suppressed by the majority, or a desire for consensus can silence disagreement. Some solutions, good and bad ones, accumulate a certain amount of support. Once support for a solution reaches a critical level, it has a high probability of being selected and other solutions are very likely to fail. Even a minority can build up support for a solution by actively asserting themselves. Thus, decisions can emerge from this support, rather than from their quality. Groups also can be dominated by members who are hard to control and who persuade, threaten, or persist in their point of view. A final disadvantage of groups occurs when it becomes more important to avoid disagreement or win an argument than to make a good evaluation of alternatives. Avoidance of disagreement and arguments prevents open and objective discussion.

 **FIGURE 13.3** *Benefits and Disadvantages of Group Decision Making*

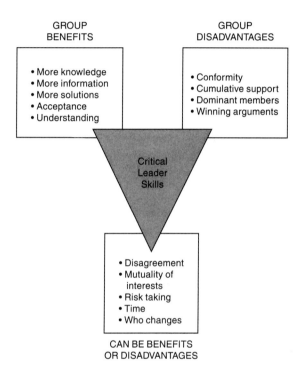

Some factors can be either benefits or disadvantages depending on the skill of the group leader [32]. If the leader suppresses disagreement or allows it to create hard feelings, it can damage the solution. But if the leader treats disagreement as acceptable, it can generate innovative solutions. The leader can also make a difference by emphasizing either conflicting or mutual interests. Mutual interests should be explored at all stages of decision making, beginning with the problem definition. Consensus begins in the process of seeking mutually acceptable solutions, but the leader has to work hard to probe areas of mutual concern. Unless he or she does so, conflict among members might lead to a poor solution. The leader can also affect the level of risk that a group takes: it can be guided toward a very safe and conservative decision or one that is riskier and more innovative.

Time can also be an asset or a liability. Groups generally take longer than individuals to make decisions. Even if both take an hour to decide, a group of five people has spent five work hours. Leaders who permit rushing to save time can risk acceptance and quality of decisions. A final factor that can help or hinder a decision is the question of who changes in the group. If the person with the worst ideas changes, the decision will benefit. But if the person with the best ideas is forced to change, the decision suffers.

Deciding When to Use a Group

Not every decision can or should be made by a group. Managers can make the decision alone or involve others in the decision process. They can assign the responsibility to an individual, a committee, or a task force. The question is, "Under what conditions is it best to use a group?"

Quality and Acceptance as Criteria. Quality and acceptance are useful in deciding whether to engage a group in decision making [31]. **Quality** refers to the feasibility and technical aspects of a problem and calls for the use of facts, analysis of data, and objectivity. **Acceptance**, on the other hand, deals with feelings, needs, and emotions and is subjective in nature.

Decisions can be classified into several types, depending on whether quality, acceptance, or both are important factors. Some decisions require attention mainly to quality, and not to acceptance. These problems are usually technical or scientific in nature, such as how to control pressure in a valve or devising a test to select among vendors' products. When quality is the main concern, employees are not likely to become emotionally involved in the outcome or decision, so the manager need only find experts with the knowledge and experience to find a quality solution. They can research, develop, and test technically feasible solutions. Facts and analysis will dominate decision making.

Some problems, however, involve mainly acceptance. For example, deciding who works overtime is an acceptance issue, assuming that the candidates for overtime are all able to do the work.

Other problems involve both quality and acceptance: deciding how to increase productivity, introducing new methods or equipment, reducing absenteeism, or developing new safety standards. Here quality solutions are essential, and employees affected by them will have strong feelings about them. The decision could fail unless employees accept it and can commit to its implementation.

The decision rule to use is, Whenever acceptance is critical, the manager must at least consider using a group for the decision process—unilateral decisions by the manager run the risk of being misunderstood or rejected. Even though shortage of time could argue against participation, group decision is a way to get acceptance.

Managers have a tendency to make unilateral decisions regardless of the type of decision [31]. Furthermore, they tend to emphasize quality, at least at the outset. When problems arise, many managers will naturally concern themselves with facts, data, feasibility, and other quality considerations. This tendency sets up a trap. Once the manager has thought about quality components, he or she becomes settled on a solution. Most managers are also sensitive to employee acceptance and they try to get it, but only after having considered quality. Because the solution is formulated before acceptance is achieved, the trap is set. Their problem now is how to get that acceptance. The most common approach they use is to persuade others to go along with the decision. Unfortunately, people tend to resist being told what they should like or dislike. Persuasion often leaves a residue of resentment and usually fails to deal adequately with feelings. Worse yet, if resistance continues, the manager might become frustrated and begin to force or coerce employees.

One way out of this trap is to try to get both quality and acceptance simultaneously, dealing with both together. The way to do this is by joint problem solving, through the use of group decision making.

☐ PROBLEM SOLVING JAPANESE STYLE

Japanese organizations have often been at the forefront of successfully involving their employees in problem solving and decision making. Many organizations around the world are making the same kinds of attempts to empower employees in this way. Success at this endeavor cannot be attributed to a technique or a program. The Japanese companies create a web of conditions in order to make involvement effective. At the most basic level of organizing, each employee is expected, as a normal part of his or her job, to evaluate how the work is done and to identify problems and opportunities for improvements. Coming up with new ideas and making suggestions are considered as part of a normal day's work. In some companies, over 90 percent of suggestions are implemented. The emphasis on problem finding is critical. Problems are treated as "golden eggs" to be sought, rather than as signs of failure or weakness. Managers who see or suspect problems are careful not to make claim to them. Rather, they skillfully attempt to get the employees to identify and define the problem so as to have them feel ownership and commitment to working on it. Thus, managers facilitate the process more than they take direct credit for problem solving. This requires them to also encourage discussions and meetings where employees can work on problems and devise solutions. Teamwork and cohesion are viewed as positive forces in such an organization culture.

The Vroom-Yetton Model. Another model for deciding whether to use a group has been developed by Vroom and Yetton [50]. They propose five different types of decision making, which vary according to the amount of subordinate influence. At one extreme is *unilateral decision making* by the manager. This is a quick and efficient way to make a decision. At the other extreme is *participative decision making*. The alternative styles are described below. As the decision approach moves from AI toward GII (A stands for autocratic, C for consultative, and G for group), the amount of subordinate influence over the final decision increases.

AI: The manager makes the decision with currently available data.

AII: Necessary information is obtained from subordinates, but the manager still decides alone. The role of the subordinates is input of data only; they have nothing to do with generating or evaluating alternatives.

CI: The manager discusses the problems with relevant subordinates individually. Then, without bringing them together, he makes a decision that may or may not reflect their input.

CII: The manager shares the problem with subordinates in a group meeting, gathering ideas and suggestions. He then makes the decision alone, which may or may not take the input of the group meeting into account.

GII: Problems are shared with the group. The manager functions in the "participative" style. His role is to provide information and help, facilitating the group's determination of its own solution rather than his.

The **Vroom-Yetton model** is aimed at helping the manager decide which of these five methods to use. The best style depends on the following characteristics of the situation in which the problem arises.

1. **Importance of Decision Quality**. How important is it to achieve a high-quality solution? If there is no quality requirement, then any acceptable alternative will be satisfactory to management, and the group can make the decision. For example, groups can decide how to accomplish or assign routine tasks where quality is not critical.

2. **Extent to Which the Decision Maker Has Necessary Information**. There are two kinds of information that make an effective decision: preferences of subordinates about alternatives, and whether or not there are rational grounds to judge the quality of alternatives.

    When the leader doesn't know subordinates' preferences, participation can reveal them. If the leader knows subordinate preferences, but the problem is such that an individual decision is more likely to produce a better solution than that of a group, then clearly the situation calls for the manager to make the decision alone.

    In what kind of situation is a group likely to make a better decision than an individual? Research indicates that an individual can do as well as a group when either (1) the problem has a highly verifiable solution or (2) the solution requires thinking through complicated interrelated stages, keeping in mind conclusions reached at earlier times. A group is superior when the problem is complex, has several parts, and the group members possess diverse but relevant talents and skills. Insight and originality can then be more likely obtained from a group than from an individual [29].

3. **Extent to Which Problem is Structured**. In structured problems, the alternatives or at least the means for generating them are known. Standard procedures used in most organizations give individuals all or most of the information they need. In an ill-structured problem, the

information may be widely dispersed through the organization. Different individuals will probably have to be brought together to solve the problem or to make a joint decision. For example, a machinist can figure out how to cut a new steel part given a blueprint but may need to consult with others if a new material is also involved.

4. **The Importance of Subordinates' Acceptance**. Acceptance by subordinates is not critical where a decision falls in the boundaries of the "psychological contract." In this case, carrying out the decision is a matter of simple compliance. The more commitment required from subordinates in the carrying out of a decision, of course, the more important subordinate acceptance becomes.

5. **Probability that an Autocratic Decision Will Be Accepted**. If a decision is viewed as within the legitimate authority of a manager, it will be accepted by subordinates without participation.

6. **Subordinate Motivation to Attain Organizational Goals**. Sometimes the objectives of superiors and their subordinates are incongruent. In such cases, participation in decision making may be more risky than in situations where the goals of the two are congruent. Thus, participative decision making works best where there is mutual interest in the problem.

7. **Subordinates Disagreement Over Solutions.** Subordinates may disagree among themselves over prospective alternatives. The method used to reach a decision must facilitate resolution of the disagreement, and thus group involvement is necessary.

All of these factors are presented in the form of questions in the Vroom-Yetton model, shown in Figure 13.4. The questions are answered on a yes-no basis. The decision tree format establishes the sequence of the questions to be answered by the manager. At the end of every path in the decision tree is one or more alternative approaches for making the decision.

An interesting analysis of this model was done by Field [17]. He carefully considered all the elements and concluded that there is a simple way to approach the choice of a decision strategy. If acceptance of a decision by subordinates is critical to effective implementation but the subordinates won't accept autocratic decision, then use the GII style. Otherwise, CII can be used.

A number of studies have been conducted to determine how much managers use particular decision-making approaches and whether the V-Y model is descriptive of such strategies. In one study of 385 managers from more than 100 firms, it was found that these managers used all five of the decision-making approaches. The most frequently used styles appeared to be CI and CII, in which the manager shares problems with subordinates and then makes the decision alone. In studies of actual problems solved by more than 600 managers in several different organizations, it was found that most of the problems did not have a pressing time constraint and that most involved some degree of both quality and acceptance [50]. Most managers felt they lacked some of the information needed to make a satisfactory decision. To solve these problems, the managers used approaches CI, CII, and GII in about equal proportions. Managers had a tendency to use participation more when (1) subordinates had necessary information, (2) a quality decision was important, (3) subordinates were trusted, and (4) acceptance was considered important. There was also more participation when it was unlikely that subordinates would accept an autocratic decision. Other studies show that participation is especially important in organizations in which individuals have become accustomed to it.

☐ **FIGURE 13.4**   *The Vroom-Yetton Decision Model*

   A. Is there a quality requirement such that one solution is likely to be more rational than another?
   B. Do I have sufficient information to make a high-quality decision?
   C. Is the problem structured?
   D. Is acceptance of decision by subordinates critical to effective implementation?
   E. If I were to make the decision by myself, is it reasonably certain that it would be accepted by my subordinates?
   F. Do subordinates share the organizational goals to be attained in solving the problem?
   G. Is conflict among subordinates likely in preferred solutions? (This question is irrelevant to individual problems.)

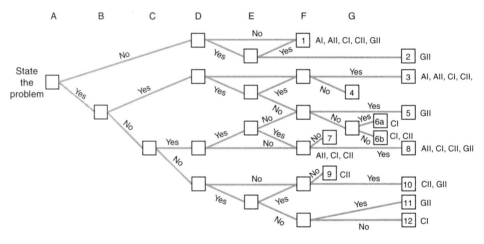

Vroom and Yetton also found that both the nature of the problem itself and the decision-making preferences of the managers influenced the degree to which participation was used [50]. Situational factors, however, were much more important than individual preferences in determining the choice of decision-making approach. The research also shows that middle and upper managers typically consult with their subordinates in decision making [26, 49, 50].

The Change Criterion.   The introduction of change in an organization is another reason to use group decision making to diagnose and plan the change effort. Countless changes are needed in running an organization or improving it, but change often triggers resistance, a common and quite human reaction. The aim is to deal with resistance and to help ensure that employees understand, accept, and commit to the needed changes. Change is often a difficult and ambiguous process. People are trying new things they are not used to doing, and many decisions have to be made in the face of uncertainty. Emotions, conflict, and acceptance all need to be dealt with. Employee involve-

☐ AN APPLICATION
OF THE VROOM-YETTON MODEL

Let us say that a manager wishes to change the work schedule so as to have at least one maintenance engineer on duty at all times between 9 A.M. and 9 P.M., six days a week, and that this represents a departure from previous work schedules. She has a number of alternative ways to make the decision. She starts with question A in Figure 13.4, "Is there a quality requirement?" She decides that there is none since a wide variety of different work schedules will be satisfactory so long as a maintenance engineer is on duty at all times between the hours of 9 A.M. and 6 P.M., six days a week. Because she answered no to question A, question D is next, "Is acceptance of decision by subordinates critical to effective implementation?" Suppose that the answer to question D is yes, since acceptance of the schedule is critical to its effective implementation. (If she had answered question D no, the decision tree shows a Type 1 problem situation, and any of the decision-making methods for dealing with a group listed earlier—AI, AII, CI, CII, GII—could be used to deal with the problem.) Because she answered yes to question D, she must next answer question E. Let us assume that she answers no to question E, "If I were to make the decision by myself, is it reasonably certain that it would be accepted by my subordinates?" A no answer to question E, according to the decision tree of Figure 13.4, presents a Type 2 problem situation. The recommended approach for making this type of decision is GII. A GII strategy requires the decision maker to share the problem with the group and to agree to accept any alternative that the group supports. A yes answer presents a Type 1 problem situation, and any method can be used to deal with the problem.

In problem types where many alternative decision-making approaches exist, as is the case for problem types 1, 3, 4, and 8, the decision maker may want to use the approach that requires the least time. But here it should be remembered that although a manager may be able to make a decision more quickly alone, it may take more time in the long run to communicate that decision to subordinates and to achieve an understanding of what is required than would a participative decision.

ment in the design, implementation, and evaluation of a change process can make all the difference in its success.

COMPUTER GROUP PROBLEM SOLVING

Some organizations are now putting personal computers to work in new ways [14, 18]. A computer can act as a decision support system by, for example, providing models and tools to attack problems. It can also be used as a training device to teach various methods of problem solving and decision making.

Computers can act in a networked system to create problem solving teams or to simply call upon employees to contribute at different stages of the problem solving process. **Computer brainstorming** allows members to enter and share ideas [20]. There is some evidence that more ideas are produced this way, and that employees feel better about their opportunity to participate.

GROUPTHINK

Groups can make poor decisions because they fall into a pattern called groupthink [27]. **Groupthink** occurs when a group collectively becomes defensive and avoids facing issues squarely and realistically. There are eight key symptoms of groupthink (see Figure 13.5):

FIGURE 13.5 *A Model of Groupthink*

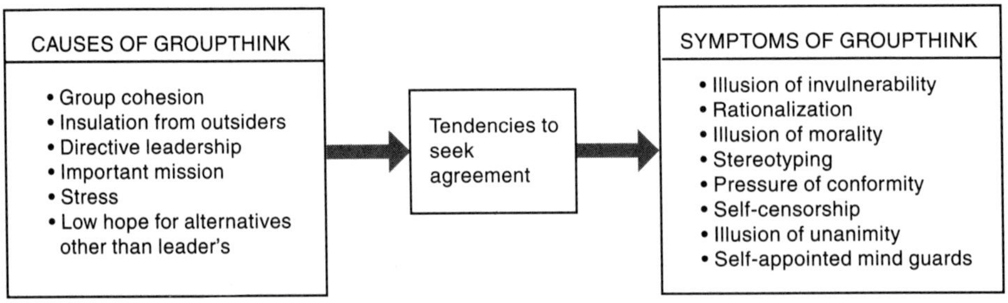

CAUSES OF GROUPTHINK		SYMPTOMS OF GROUPTHINK
• Group cohesion • Insulation from outsiders • Directive leadership • Important mission • Stress • Low hope for alternatives other than leader's	Tendencies to seek agreement	• Illusion of invulnerability • Rationalization • Illusion of morality • Stereotyping • Pressure of conformity • Self-censorship • Illusion of unanimity • Self-appointed mind guards

1. *Illusion of invulnerability.* The group acts as if it is protected from criticism. This gives members too much optimism and encourages extreme risk taking.

2. *Rationalization.* The group tends to explain away facts or ideas that press them to reconsider their position.

3. *Illusion of morality.* This is a belief that the group is acting in the name of goodness and causes inattention to ethical consequences.

4. *Stereotyping.* Rivals or enemies outside the group are treated as evil, too stupid to negotiate with, or too weak to harm the group.

5. *Pressure for conformity.* Group members are pressured to go along with the group's illusions and stereotypes. Dissent is suppressed as contrary to group expectations.

6. *Self-censorship.* Group members become inclined to minimize their own feelings of doubt or disagreement.

7. *Illusion of unanimity.* Silence comes to imply agreement. Perceptions develop that unanimity exists.

8. *Self-appointed mind guards.* Some members act to protect the group from adverse information.

Janis provides examples of groupthink in high-level government groups [27]. President Kennedy and his colleagues decided to invade Cuba at the Bay of Pigs, despite information that the attempt would fail and damage our relations with other countries. President Richard Nixon and his staff proceeded with the Watergate burglary of Democratic election headquarters and continued with its subsequent cover-up, despite its serious risks and implications. And negative information was ignored by decision makers in deciding to launch the space shuttle Challenger in 1986 [36]. Groupthink can occur in meetings in any organization, such as when managers meet under pressure to make an important decision.

Causes of Groupthink. Groupthink is often found in highly cohesive groups. Members' desire to remain in the group helps them to fall victim to one or more of groupthink's symptoms. If the group can insulate itself and has a strong, directive leader, groupthink is more likely. Stress helps too, such as when an important decision is needed but hope is low for finding a solution other than the one desired by the leader or other influential members. Such factors can combine to create disastrous conditions. Consider a situation where a plant manager and his subordinates are under pressure from headquarters to complete a rush order from a customer. They might easily convince themselves that machine breakdowns, employee fatigue, or union resistance won't be issues. Dissenting members of the team might be pressured to conform, and withhold their opinions.

Preventing Groupthink. A number of steps can be taken to counteract groupthink [27]. The leader must be impartial and unbiased so that group members feel free to openly discuss and explore issues. Members should be encouraged to be critical and express doubts and disagreements, and reinforced when they do so. Occasionally, members should be assigned the role of devil's advocate especially to challenge the majority position. It helps too if the group is broken into subgroups for part of its work and reconvened to address member differences. When the group nears consensus, the leader can schedule a "second chance" meeting where members are required to express all remaining doubts they have.

Groups can also use outsiders to counter groupthink. Fellow employees outside the group can be invited to meetings and asked to challenge the group's work. Between meetings, members should discuss the issues with people in their units and report their reactions. Management may also set up more than one group to attack all or part of the problem independently, and compare the results.

THE LEADERSHIP ROLE IN GROUP DECISION MAKING

Each group member can behave in a way that helps or hinders effective decision making. But the greatest responsibility is in the hands of the group leader, who is in a critical position to affect the quality and acceptance of a decision. Sometimes the leader is elected; sometimes he or she is appointed by a person in authority who formed the group to work on a problem. In organizations, the group leader is often someone in authority, such as when a manager holds a meeting with subordinates.

PROCESS VS. CONTENT

The leader of a decision-making group can be compared to an orchestra leader: he or she does not play an instrument, but rather conducts and guides the members [31]. The leader is at the hub of group activities, but plays a distinct and different role. The leader has to focus on the *process* of the group as well as on the actual *content* of the decision. The leader who focuses on process does things to urge members to define the problem well, helps them to generate alternative solutions, and so on. In focusing on process, the leader sees to it that members participate freely and that disagreements are handled appropriately. The leader can affect content by holding to high standards of quality and acceptance and by preventing the group from making unworkable decisions.

Many leaders become too involved in the content of a group decision. Leaders typically know a good deal about the problem at hand and have a natural tendency to offer their ideas and to contribute directly to the decision. Yet it is a mistake to do so, especially if process goes unattended. Shifting one's focus to process takes practice. Most people must unlearn past thinking habits and practice the acceptance of dissent and experimentation in decision making [37]. An effective training technique is role playing, which allows people to experiment with and practice behaviors that facilitate good process.

GUIDELINES FOR DECISION-MAKING LEADERSHIP

Leaders can do many things to facilitate good decisions. The guidelines presented below expand on the suggestions to improve decision making already discussed and apply to the group setting [31].

Getting the Problem Defined. To get a full and accurate definition of a problem, the leader of a group must overcome the tendency of people to define problems too quickly or simply. Group members must be asked how they view the problem, and what they feel caused it. The leader must probe the group and work toward a thorough definition. As the group members speak, the leader can record their ideas on a chalkboard or on flip charts. The group can be asked to differentiate symptoms from more basic, underlying causes. The leader can help by getting the problem stated in "how to" terms, such as "how to develop a work schedule that meets the needs of the customer and is feasible for the group." It is better to put the problem in situational rather than personal terms. For example, it is unwise to state the problem as "how to get Charley to work evenings." Depersonalizing helps members to respond to various aspects of the problem with more objectivity.

Keeping the Group on Problem Definition. Despite the leader's efforts to define a problem well, group members will still move off the problem too quickly. Some will begin to offer solutions too early. When this happens, the leader must turn the solution statement back into a problem definition and remind the group, "We are not ready for solutions yet," or say "How does the solution relate to the problem?" It has been shown that leaders who are merely instructed to focus on the problem get better solutions than leaders not so instructed. It is also true that later disagreements about solutions are often traceable back to disagreements about the nature of the problem, unless a leader works to get a thorough problem definition.

It is interesting that when groups are asked for a second solution to a problem, they do better the second time around. The reason is that the second time around, the problem gets more attention, and different solutions are examined.

Using the Problem to Generate Solutions. A full definition of a problem can be put to productive use by the group leader. Each element of the definition can be a source of solution possibilities. All the leader has to do is to keep the group working to generate ideas that respond to all of the problem elements. In this way, the leader not only encourages various solutions but helps to ensure thoroughness. Solutions are less likely to be incomplete if all the problem elements are attended to. In generating alternatives, the leader should call on any technique useful for doing so, including brainstorming and other techniques discussed earlier.

A special technique for idea generation in groups is known as the **nominal group technique**, shown in Figure 13.6 [13, 19]. The nominal group technique uses one or more small groups of people to generate and evaluate solution ideas and takes advantage of the principle of getting ideas from many parties. Note from Figure 13.6 that decision making is staged into steps to prevent people from jumping ahead too quickly. The technique is particularly powerful in preventing evaluation that blocks idea generation. It also takes advantage of social pressures in a positive way. Participants often work hard to generate ideas in the presence of others. The nominal group technique creates an atmosphere of creativity and expectations for good and creative solutions.

FIGURE 13.6 *A Method of Using the Nominal Group Technique*

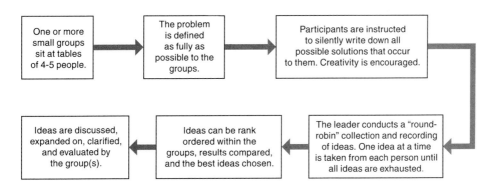

Preventing Premature Evaluation. The process of idea getting is blocked by idea evaluation. This is especially true when group members quickly agree on a solution and adopt the first acceptable solution that arises. The leader and members should see to it that evaluative statements are withheld until idea generation is at least adequate.

Gaining Consensus. Eventually, group members need to evaluate their ideas and arrive at a decision they can live with. The leader can help in several ways here. He or she can summarize the group's progress to help make sure the group is ready to make the decision. The leader can also get members to develop criteria to evaluate the alternatives they generated. Consensus can be directly tested by questioning where the group agrees or disagrees on any matter before them. The leader may have to organize and present a review of the group's work in order to adequately test and gain a true consensus.

Avoid Leader Solutions. A group leader, especially if it is a boss or other person in authority, should avoid offering solutions to the group. This is difficult for many leaders to do. They usually want to express their opinions in these situations. The problem is that a superior's idea is evaluated by group members on the basis of the source of the idea and not on its worth. Objective evaluation loses out to concern over how the boss will react if the idea is supported or challenged. It is rare that a boss is treated as a peer. A boss who offers solutions cuts off idea generation and objective evaluation. Maier has shown that leaders get better solutions from their groups when they are given no time to prepare or think about a problem [31]. When leaders prepare, they tend to think of solutions that they later find difficult to keep to themselves.

Dealing with Disagreement. There is more value in disagreement between people than in quick agreement. When group members agree, solution generation often comes to a close. If a disagreement occurs, however, solution generation is still alive. Leaders squelch disagreement when they say, "If we're going to argue, we'll never get this problem solved." Statement such as this, frustrated sighs, or other nonverbal cues soon tell group members to avoid disagreement. Ideas are accepted because no one wants to incur disfavor.

Disagreements can be made to pay off. This is done when the leader accepts and probes a disagreement. The leader can say, "Phyllis, your idea really contrasts with John's. Tell us what you have in mind, and then we can get John's point of view." This tells the group that it is acceptable to disagree, and no one will be punished for doing so. It also opens the door to new ideas. Often the disagreement can be traced to different definitions of the problem, or to goals that group had not earlier considered. Probing disagreement can prevent the "rubber stamping" or the avoiding of ideas. Managers should program disagreement into discussions with the use of devil's advocate roles or by asking for counter proposals [8].

Keeping in Touch with Reality. Groups have a tendency to waste time on obstacles that cannot be overcome. For example, they might suggest solutions that cost thousands of dollars when the money simply isn't there. Some facts, such as money constraints, have to be defined as conditions or limits within which the group must work. If, however, more money would be the only way to solve the problem, then the group can add that into the problem definition and seek ways to get it. But if it is a true and insurmountable constraint, the group must act accordingly.

As we suggested in discussing groupthink, the group must be sure to get and use relevant data. Time pressures often cause groups to ignore facts. They feel frustrated when they have to postpone a solution in order to gather more information. More data can often mean more complexity, which provides even more incentive to forge ahead without all the facts.

Using Visual Recording Techniques. Chalkboards, flip charts, or electronic devices should be used in group decision making. There are many advantages to doing so. If the leader is doing the writing, it helps keep him or her focused on process rather than content. When a leader records ideas, it serves as a rewarding recognition of a member. On the other hand, if an idea is not recorded, the person who offered it might feel ignored or punished.

Ideas on chalkboards and flip charts also allow the group to see and build on what was previously said. Once recorded, ideas are not lost, so members need not repeat their point of view. A written record exists of the group's deliberations.

Recording techniques can also be used by the leader to control a dominant or forceful group member who sometimes will repeatedly push a pet idea. If the group leader records the idea once it first arises and the dominant group member repeats his or her point, the leader can say, "Dan, the idea is written up here. Perhaps you have some others for us to consider."

SUMMARY

People are constantly making decisions, yet it is often an imperfect process that requires new decisions to compensate for prior decisions. The basic process includes defining the problem, generating and evaluating alternative solutions, choosing among solutions, and implementing the decision. Both evaluative and creative behavior are important in all stages of decision making. At each step in the process, a number of errors can be made that reduce the effectiveness of a decision. People frequently define problems too narrowly, or they fail to generate a sufficient number of alternatives. Premature and incomplete evaluation is also a common failure. Because of such errors, many ideal models and techniques for better decision making have been suggested. Ideal approaches can help decision making significantly but rarely produce perfect, lasting solutions.

Groups that make decisions commit many of the same errors that individuals make. Therefore, it would serve a group well to follow the suggestions offered by ideal models of decision making. One of the first steps consists of deciding when or whether to involve a group in decision making. It is generally argued that group decision making increases the opportunity to gain group acceptance and commitment to a decision, and that groups can have a larger reservoir of ideas. But it takes practice and skill to overcome the disadvantages of groups, such as pressures to conform. A skilled group leader can make a great difference in solution quality and acceptance not only by overcoming disadvantages but by bringing out the best that the group has to offer. Many useful techniques exist for doing so. Effective leaders can, for example, prevent the occurrence of groupthink. They can help the group to define problems, to avoid harmful evaluation, and to creatively generate solutions using methods such as nominal grouping. Computer networks may also be exploited as a device. Other leader behaviors call for the leader to focus on the group process and avoid offering solutions of his or her own. The leader can also assist in dealing constructively with disagreement and in testing consensus in the group.

KEY CONCEPTS

Acceptance	Multiple	Pressure for
Bounded discretion	subdecisions	conformity
Bounded rationality	Nominal group	Problem definition
Brainstorming	technique	Problem selection
Computer	Normative or	Quality
brainstorming	ideal models	Rational or economic
Dictionary technique	Participative	models
Escalation of	management	Satisficing
commitment	Perceptual biases	Utility
Garbage can model	Postdecisional	Value clarification
Groupthink	dissonance	Vroom-Yetton Model

STUDY QUESTIONS

1. Interview a manager or someone you know who recently made an important decision. Determine to what extent he or she followed the steps of an ideal or a normative model.
2. Evaluative behavior and creative behavior are critical at all stages of decision making. Show why this is true.
3. Define the elements of the normative approach to decision making.
4. What are the different ways to evaluate whether a decision or a solution to a problem was effective?
5. Working alone or with the help of a friend, identify a problem one of you has that will require a decision. Was the right problem selected? Can you improve on how the problem is defined?
6. Briefly describe as many techniques as you can that are useful for generating alternative solutions to a problem.
7. What are the advantages and disadvantages that groups have compared to individuals in decision making?
8. What criteria should a manager use to decide whether or not to use group participation in decision making? Are there different levels of group involvement? Explain.
9. Name some examples of management decisions where a group should probably not be used to make the decision. Then give examples where it might be best to use a group. Explain your choices.
10. What causes groupthink, and what are its symptoms? What can a leader do to prevent groupthink?

☐ STUDY . . .

11. Describe the nominal group technique and show why it contributes to improved decision making.
12. Make a list of statements a leader can say that (a) foster good problem definition, (b) help idea generation, (c) constructively deal with disagreement, and (d) prevent premature evaluation.
13. Investigate the various ways personal computers and networks are being used to facilitate employee involvement in problem solving and decision making.

CASE

☐ FRENCH METALS COMPANY

French Metals Manufacturing Company is a multinational joint venture between a French aluminum company (60%) and an American aluminum company (40%). The company had several plants located around the nation processing alumina into aluminum sheets and bars, including one in Bellville, West Virginia along the Ohio River. Both French and American managers and engineers work at Bellville. About two thirds were Americans and the other third was French. They generally got along well, although there were some differences. For example, the French tend to maintain a very formal relationship with their subordinates while the Americans have a lot of informal bantering and communication back and forth between levels. The Americans often feel that the French were too rule-oriented while the French sometimes have the opinion that the American way of management was too chaotic. There are virtually no differences in the way the two groups approach the technical issues in producing aluminum.

In 1990 the French plant manager of the Bellville plant, Emile Laurent, an engineer trained in France, invited Don Jennings to meet with him. Jennings worked for a consulting firm which specializes in decision making training. Laurent wanted him to train the plant's managers and engineers in problem solving techniques.

In preliminary meetings with Don Jennings, Laurent indicated that he was very dissatisfied with the level of performance in the plant as a whole. He wanted to improve it before he left for another assignment in about a year. Emile Laurent wanted Don Jennings to teach a problem solving course based on value engineering. He remembered, he said, a course in value engineering many years before and believed that the value engineering philosophy would be useful in Bellville. This approach, he went on, involved the constant questioning of every element of a product and process to ensure that each element made an important contribution to the whole. If not it would be eliminated or replaced with a better

☐ **French Metals . . .**

one, or one that cost less. Laurent wanted to have his managers and technical staff involved in a constant search to identify the purposes of everything that is done and ways of performing needed functions more efficiently and more reliably.

Don Jennings told him that he agreed, the plant's personnel were not paying any attention to identifying problems and solving them. On hearing that, Laurent gave an example of what he meant. Normally, he told Jennings, he arrived at the plant very early in the morning and toured the production facilities. He saw empty beer cans everywhere and, to him, that was a problem. Yet his production personnel seemed to do nothing after he told them about it. He was also disappointed that there are few suggestions for improvements in procedures and processes. In recounting these experiences, the French manager became very emotional and agitated.

Together, Jennings and Laurent worked out the agenda for the problem solving training, a modification of the standard program of the consulting firm. It would have two modules. The first would cover the problem solving process. The second would, because of Laurent's feelings about the present level of plant effectiveness, include diagnosing and brainstorming of current problems and a search for solutions to them. In these planning discussions, Jennings pointed out that one principle on which the consulting firm designed its training was that it is crucial to gain acceptance of solutions by those who have to implement them or are affected by them. Laurent told him he did not worry about this issue very much because if top management decided something needed to be done, most employees would do it.

The training sessions were conducted one afternoon a week for six weeks. In the first module, Jennings first discussed the issue of defining a problem. The notion of benchmarking or comparing your own practices with those of your best competitors or the best companies with respect to a practice was described. Then Jennings explained the value engineering concept and the fundamental elements underlying the industrial engineering approaches to management, both of which involve questioning a present situation in a systematic manner with a view toward improvement. Time was also spent explaining several approaches to diagnosis of the real causes of problems. This was followed by examining ways of generating problem solutions using various processes to foster creativity. The group also worked at how to develop criteria for choosing from among alternative solutions. Finally Jennings and the group discussed ways to gain acceptance for problem solutions in an organization.

The managers who attended these sessions seemed to find the training interesting and especially enjoyed the films, the role playing exercises, and the brainstorming exercises. Some, however, expressed reservations about its usefulness for their day-to-day work. During a coffee

☐ FRENCH METALS . . .

break, one manager said that while the training was interesting, most of them already knew about and used these techniques even though they did not know the technical terms for them. He was interrupted by one of his colleagues who said that he believed technically trained managers with long plant experience already knew how to solve technical problems in their primary area of responsibility. Another thought that the training was too "academic" and that it would have little practical value to an operating manager. Jennings replied that he hoped the manager was wrong.

When the first module was completed, the group moved on to the second; brainstorming current company problems. The people in the classroom seemed uneasy and reluctant to move into this phase. Jennings quickly found out why. Several times, Laurent pounded the table and yelled, trying to get the managers to admit there were problems. These outbursts surprised Jennings, even though he had recognized early that Laurent was a rather emotional person. After one of these sessions, Laurent told Jennings that the problems being identified were very petty and not very significant. For the last scheduled training class, Laurent appeared with three critical problems that he wanted solved and presented them to the group. He got these from talking to several of his key managers.

The first problem was excessive plant operating costs. After Laurent's presentation one of the American managers asked the financial manager, who was part of the group, how Bellville's costs compared to other plants. On each of several performance indicators, he told the group, the Bellville plant was typically around the average compared to the other aluminum plants of this company. For some measures they were a little higher and for other measures somewhat lower than the other plants. After hearing this, the production manager turned to Laurent, yelling at him in a very emotional way. "If our performance is okay, why are you wasting our time like this. I, for one, am not going to waste my time anymore. I am going back and do the job that I am paid to do by this company." At that point he stalked out angrily. After he left there appeared to be a very high level of tension. It was impossible for Jennings or Laurent to get those who remained to contribute any solutions to the problems that Laurent had brought to them.

QUESTIONS

1. What does this case illustrate about some of the basic difficulties in the process of problem solving in organizations?
2. How might the plant manager have better handled this in order to obtain better results?
3. Are there any special difficulties in this situation which may have contributed to the plant manager's problem improvement difficulties?

REFERENCES

1. Adams, J.L. *Conceptual blockbusting: A guide to better ideas.* San Francisco: Freeman, 1974.
2. Adams, J.L. *The care and feeding of ideas: A guide to encouraging creativity.* Reading, MA: Addison-Wesley, 1986.
3. Anderson, J.V. Weirder than fiction: The reality and myths of creativity. *Academy of Management Executive*, 1992, 6(4), 40-47.
4. Behling, O. and Eckel, N.L. Making sense out of intuition. *Academy of Management Executive*, 1991, 5(1), 46-54.
5. Bowen, M.G. The escalation phenomenon reconsidered: Decision dilemmas or decision errors? *Academy of Management Review*, 1987, 12, 52-66.
6. Brockner, J. The escalation of commitment to a failing course of action: Toward theoretical progress. *Academy of Management Review*, 1992, 17, 39-61.
7. Cohen, M.D., March, J.G., and Olsen, J.P. A garbage-can model of organizational choice. *Administrative Science Quarterly*, 1972, 17, 1-25.
8. Cosier, R.A. and Schwenk, C.R. Agreement and thinking alike: Ingredients for poor decisions. *Academy of Management Executive*, 1990 4:1, 69-74.
9. Cowan, D.A. Developing a process model of problem recognition. *Academy of Management Review*, 1986, 11, 768-69.
10. Curry, T., Gallagher, J.E., and McWhirter, W. Let's get crazy, *Time*, June 11, 1990, 41-42.
11. DeBono, E. *Lateral thinking for management.* London: American Management Association, 1971.
12. DeBono, E. *Lateral thinking: Creativity step by step.* New York: Perennial Library, 1990.
13. Delbecq, A.L., Van de Ven, A.H., and Gustafson, D.H. *Group techniques for programmed planning.* Glenview, IL: Scott, Foresman, 1975.
14. DeSanctis, G. and Gallupe, R.B. A foundation for the study of group decision support systems. *Management Science*, 1987 (May), 589-609.
15. Dutton, J.E., and Jackson, S.E. Categorizing strategic issues: Links to organizational action. *Academy of Management Review*, 1987, 12, 76-90.
16. Etzioni, A. Mixed scanning. A third approach to decision making. *Public Administration Review*, 1967, 27, 385-92.
17. Field, R.G. H. A critique of the Vroom-Yetton model of leadership behavior. *Academy of Management Review*, 1979, 4, 249-57.
18. Finley, M. Welcome to the electronic meeting. *Training*, 1991 (July), 28-32.
19. Fox, W.M. The improved nominal group technique (INGT), *Journal of Management Development*, 1989, 8(1), 20-27.
20. Gallupe, R.B., Bastianutti, L.M. and Cooper, W.H. Unblocking brainstorms. *Journal of Applied Psychology*, 1991 76:1, 137-142.
21. Garland, H. and Newport, S. Effects of absolute and relative sunk costs on the decision to persist with a course of action. *Organizational Behavior and Human Decision Processes*, 1991, 48, 55-69.
22. Garland, S.B. This safety ruling could be hazardous to employees' health. *Business Week*, February 12, 1990, 34.
23. Gordon, W.J. *Synectics.* New York: Collier Books, 1981.
24. Hogarth, R. *Judgment and choice.* New York: John Wiley, 1980.

25. Jackson, S.E. and Dutton, J.E. Discerning threats and opportunities. *Administrative Science Quarterly*, 1988, 33, 370-87.

26. Jago, A. *Hierarchical level determinants of participative leader behavior*. Ph.D. dissertation. New Haven: Yale University, 1977.

27. Janis, I.L. *Victims of groupthink*. Boston: Houghton Mifflin, 1972.

28. Janis, I.L., and Mann, L. *Decision making: A psychological analysis of conflict, choice and commitment*. New York: Free Press, 1977.

29. Kelley, H.H., and Thibault, J. Group problem solving. In G. Lindsey and E. Aronson, eds. *Handbook of social psychology*, 4. Reading, MA: Addison-Wesley, 1969.

30. Koberg, D., and Bagnall, J. *The universal traveler: A soft-systems guide to creativity problem solving and the process of reaching goals*. Los Altos, CA: William Kaufmann, 1976.

31. Maier, N.R.F. *Problem-solving discussions and conferences: Leadership methods and skills*. New York: McGraw-Hill, 1963.

32. Maier, N.R.F. Assets and liabilities in group problem solving: The need for an integrative function. *Psychological Review*, 1967, 74, 239-48.

33. March, J.G., and Simon, H. *Organizations*. New York: John Wiley, 1958.

34. March, J.G., and Weissinger-Baylon, R. *Ambiguity and command: Organizational perspectives on military decision making*. Marshfield, MA: Pitman Publishing, 1986.

35. Miller, D.W., and Starr, M.K. *The structure of human decisions*. Englewood Cliffs, NJ: Prentice-Hall, 1967.

36. Moorhead, G., Ference, R.K. and Neck, C.P. Group decision fiascos continue: Space shuttle challenger and a revised groupthink framework. *Human Relations*, 1991, 44, 539-550.

37. Nystrom, P.C., and Starbuck, W.H. To avoid organizational crises, unlearn. *Organizational Dynamics*, 1984, 12, 53-65.

38. Osborn, A. F. *Applied imagination*. New York: Charles Scribner's Sons, 1957.

39. Parnes, S.J. *Creative behavior guidebook*. New York: Charles Scribner's Sons, 1967.

40. Prince, G.M. *The practice of creativity*. New York: Harper & Row, 1970.

41. Shull, F.A., Delbecq, A.L., and Cummings, L.L. *Organizational decision making*. New York: McGraw-Hill, 1970.

42. Simon, H.A. *Models of man*. New York: John Wiley, 1957.

43. Simon, H.A. *Administrative behavior:A study of decision making processes in administrative organization*. 3d ed. New York: Free Press, 1976.

44. Simon, H.A. *The new science of management decisions* (2nd ed.) Englewood Cliffs, NJ: Prentice-Hall, 1977.

45. Soelberg, P. *Unprogrammed decision making*. Proceedings of the Academy of Management, 1966, 3-16.

46. Staw, B.M. The escalation of commitment to a course of action. *Academy of Management Review*, 1981, 6, 582.

47. Staw, B.M. and Ross, J. Knowing when to pull the plug. *Harvard Business Review*, 1987 (March-April), 68-74.

48. Staw, B.M., and Ross, J. Behavior in escalation situations: Antecedents, prototypes, and solutions. In L.L. Cummings and B.M. Staw, eds. *Research in organizational behavior*, 9, Greenwich, CT: JAI Press, 1987.

49. Vroom, V.H. and Jago, A.G. On the validity of the Vroom-Yetton model. *Journal of Applied Psychology*, 1978, 69, 151-62.

50. Vroom, V.H., and Yetton, P.W. *Leadership and decision making.* Pittsburgh: University of Pittsburgh Press, 1973.

51. Weick, K.E. The vulnerable system: An analysis of the Tenerife air disaster. In K.H. Roberts (Ed). *New challenges to understanding organizations.* N.Y.: MacMillan Publishing Co., 1993, 173-198.

52. Whyte, G. Escalating commitment to a course of action: A reinterpretation. *Academy of Management Review*, 1986, 11, 311-21.

53. Whyte, G. Diffusion of responsibility: Effects on the escalation tendency. *Journal of Applied Psychology*, 1991, 76, 408-415.

54. Woodman, R.W., Sawyer, J.E., and Griffin, R.W. Toward a theory of organizational creativity. *Academy of Management Review*, 1993, 18(2), 293-321.

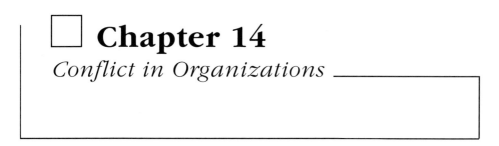

Chapter 14
Conflict in Organizations

The conflicts that break out in organizations almost never make the national news. But when they do, we have a chance to examine the interesting forms conflict can take. Such was the case with the *N.Y. Post* early in 1993. The paper had suffered financial difficulties, and a conflict arose over ownership of it. Abe Hirshfeld, with the support of the prior owner, won the right to buy the paper. A bankruptcy court judge ruled in his favor over Steven Hoffenberg, who had actually run the paper for several months. A second issue developed between the newspaper's employees and Hirshfeld. The staff was enraged over Hirshfeld's decision to fire 70 people (most all were soon reinstated) and in his lack of qualifications to run a paper. The staff wanted Hirshfeld to confine himself to the business end of the operation and leave the newspaper end to them. In an unprecedented move, the staff actually published an issue of the paper devoting a number of pages to criticizing their new boss! One article was titled, "Who is this nut?" Copies of the paper soon became collectors' items.

Disagreements and conflicts aren't always as dramatic as this, but countless disagreements do arise as people try to work together in most organizations. Opportunities are everywhere, and the actual occurrence of conflict is common. Labor unions and management dispute wages, work conditions, and layoffs. Parties take sides over the marketability of a new product idea, where to go on vacation, or on the accuracy of a referee's decision in a sporting event. Conflict is a common event, even though it doesn't always erupt into a raging battle. It can take many forms and have varied effects—not all of which are bad. The key lies in how it is viewed and the steps that the parties take to deal with it.

In this chapter, we discuss the conflict process and how conflict arises. Then various styles of reacting to conflict are explored. This is followed by a discussion of alternative ways to manage conflict and resolve it more effectively.

THE NATURE OF CONFLICT

Conflict can be a disagreement, the presence of tension, or some other difficulty between two or more parties. It may occur between individuals or between groups. Conflict is often related in interference or opposition between the parties involved. The parties in conflict usually see each other as frustrating, or about to frustrate, their needs or goals [18, 26]. Conflict can be public or private, formal or informal, or be approached rationally or irrationally [13].

CONFLICT AS A PROCESS

Conflict is not a static condition but a dynamic process that involves several stages. Parties can go through the process in many different ways, and they can go through it more than once. There are several approaches to describing the conflict process [6, 10, 24, 25, 29, 31]. A composite model integrating the different approaches is shown in Figure 14.1. This model will be the basis of our discussion in the remainder of this chapter.

Antecedent Conditions.   These are the conditions that cause or precede a conflict episode. Sometimes an aggressive act can start the conflict process. For instance, an employee might deliberately hide tools that other employees need to do their job, or one department may seek more resources than another department believes they should have. **Antecedents of conflict** can be subtle. For example, the pressures on a production department to keep costs down can frustrate sales managers who want to fill rush orders on short notice. But conflict may not develop because neither party holds steadfastly to its position. Then the conflicts remains **latent**.

☐ **FIGURE 14.1**   *Conflict Process*

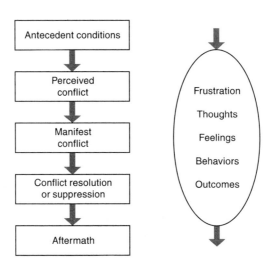

Perceived Conflict. For the conflict to progress, the parties must become aware that they have been threatened in some way. Without awareness, one party might act to the disadvantage of another but little else happens because the act is not perceived as a threat. Perceptions are closely linked to feelings. Thus, when people perceive actual or potential disagreement, frustration, anger, fear, or anxiety can increase. The parties start to question how much they can trust each other. They might feel unfairly treated or worry about their ability to cope with the difficulty. This stage of **perceived conflict** is critical because this is when the parties tend to define the issues. This sets a frame of mind and can affect a lot of what follows [23].

Manifest Conflict. Perceptions and feelings may cause people to react to the situation. A sales manager can try to pressure a production department to satisfy an important customer. Sales and production can independently (or jointly) appeal to their supervisors to intervene. A wide variety of other reactions is possible in this **manifest stage** of conflict: arguments, aggressive acts, appeals to goodwill, or constructive problem solving.

Conflict Resolution or Suppression. **Conflict resolution** can come about in several ways. The parties may agree about how to solve the conflict. They might take steps to prevent such conflict in the future. Conflict can also be resolved when one party defeats another. Sometimes there is **suppression** of the conflict. This happens when the parties avoid strong reactions or try to ignore each other when they disagree.

Conflict Aftermath. When conflict is resolved or suppressed, feelings remain. The **conflict aftermath** can be just as varied as the ways it is manifested or resolved. Sometimes good feelings and harmony result, as when a new policy or procedure is developed that clarifies the relationships between the parties and minimizes future conflicts. For example, the sales and production units can agree on rules to govern when orders will be rushed into production ahead of schedule. Then sales personnel can make appropriate promises to customers.

Conflict can also result in poorer working relationships. If hard feelings and resentment persist, these can trigger the next conflict episode. For example, poor solutions or losses by one party may reduce communication or prepare each party for bigger battles to come. The key question is whether the parties are drawn into more cooperation or driven further apart by the conflict.

PAST HISTORY OF THE PARTIES INVOLVED

Linkages between people and units of an organization persist over long periods of time. As a consequence, the parties develop a history of perceptions, attitudes, and behaviors toward each other. Party A's behavior toward B depends to a significant degree on Party B's past behavior toward A. If one party has historically been cooperative in its relationships toward another party, a single incident of noncooperation is not likely to have a significant effect. On the other hand, past behaviors that indicate noncooperation from Party A are likely to induce B to exhibit noncooperative behavior as well. In evaluating past behaviors, the parties are likely to put greatest weight on recent behaviors of the other.

DIFFERENT VIEWS OF CONFLICT

One view of conflict is that it is a *preventable* problem. It is assumed, for example, that conflict can be avoided simply by getting employees to change their attitudes and behavior so that cooperation can prosper. It is also assumed that conflict is preventable if managers develop positive working relationships, design plans, and implement policies and procedures that ensure mutual efforts toward common goals. This perspective has some merit. Some conflict in organizations is preventable, and some of it is a sign that something is wrong and can be corrected.

A second point of view is that conflict is *inevitable*—that there is no way to eliminate it entirely. This is true for many reasons, a number of which are described throughout this chapter. For example, organizations have multiple goals, not all of which are compatible. The goal of reducing costs is often in conflict with goals that call for innovation. Organization design also leads to conflict. Employees are grouped into departments of specialists, each with its own point of view. For example, conflicts arise between managers and auditors because the required work for each group actually creates problems for the other. Conflict can also arise because plans are incomplete or because policy is difficult to establish to cover all situations.

If some conflict is inevitable, then trying to prevent it may be more frustrating than the conflict itself. The best strategy is to accept the inevitability of certain kinds of conflict. Actions can then be taken to anticipate it. Employees can be trained to face disagreements and resolve them before they get out of hand. That way, conflict can be kept within tolerable limits and managed effectively.

A third point of view is that some degree of conflict is healthy for an organization [4]. When would this be the case? Suppose that sales, research, and production departments never exhibited any tensions or disagreements with each other. The relative peace between the departments may exist because each department is not doing its job effectively. For example, sales may not be sensitive and respond to new product or market opportunities. Hence, they rarely suggest changes that would create tensions with research and production.

Figure 14.2 suggests that there is probably some optimal level of conflict that should exist in most organizations. Too little conflict in an organization can be a threat to effectiveness. Employees may be avoiding each other instead of interacting to meet goals and seek improvements, such that new ideas are not being developed and shared.

Too much conflict can also hamper effectiveness. If individuals or groups disagree over too many issues or refuse to accommodate to the needs and problems of others, innovations may never come about, customers may be lost, and key issues may go unresolved. The organization will suffer considerably if conflicts are preventing cooperation and if members are consumed with winning internal battles.

☐ **FIGURE 14.2**   *Optimum Levels of Organizational Conflict*

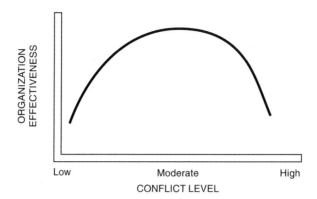

At an optimum level, quite different things happen. Each person and unit are doing their best. There are active attempts to improve quality and to introduce changes that might make the organization more competitive and more effective or efficient. Employees are stimulated, not bored and withdrawn. Different frames of reference and new insights that emerge may lead to new interactions and systems that improve organizational performance. Tensions and frustrations are channeled into productive, rather than destructive, efforts [36].

INTERGROUP CONFLICT

The parties in conflict can be either individuals or groups. When groups are in conflict, certain things similar to competition happen. Conflict encourages group members to work harder to accomplish the task, especially if task effort helps them to protect themselves, look better than the other group, or defeat it. The group becomes more cohesive and coordinates their efforts to put forth a united front. Internal divisiveness is viewed as making the group more vulnerable and weak. Groups are also more likely to accept directive or autocratic leadership if this is seen as helpful in the conflict.

Groups in conflict will tend to see the other party negatively, in threatening or hostile terms. Members will increase their alertness to the other group's actions, but communication with the other group decreases. A win-lose mentality sets in between groups. Distorted perceptions, such as stereotyping and projection, may increase.

These intergroup tendencies work against reaching a constructive outcome of the conflict. Several strategies for conflict resolution (discussed later in the chapter) include steps to deal with these tendencies.

ANTECEDENTS AND CAUSES OF CONFLICT

To manage conflict its causes must be understood and, if possible, changed. The causes of conflict are grouped into three major categories: characteristics of individuals, situational conditions that arise between people and groups, and the design and structure of organizations (see Figure 14.3).

☐ **FIGURE 14.3** *Antecedents and Causes of Conflict*

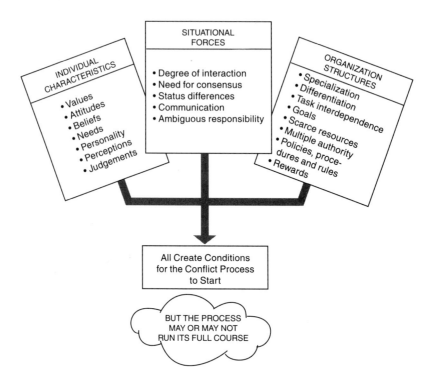

INDIVIDUAL CHARACTERISTICS

The following individual differences between people make some more likely than others to engage in conflict.

Values, Attitudes, and Beliefs. Our feelings about what is right and wrong, and our predispositions to behave positively or negatively toward an event can easily be a source of conflict. A worker who values autonomy and independence will probably react negatively when supervised too closely. There is also evidence of occupational maladjustment that causes people to leave some jobs and gravitate toward those that fit their values [20].

Values can create tensions between individuals and key groups in organizations. For example, union leaders are likely to have different values than managers. In one study, union leaders valued employee welfare and rated company profit maximization low in relative priority. Managers considered profit maximization as very important and rated employee welfare low. Equality was very important to union leaders but of minor importance to managers [5].

Values can be the reason people are drawn to certain kinds of organizations [17]. Figure 14.4 shows that people who work in stable structures differ from those in dynamic structures. People in stable organizational settings tend to be lower in tolerance for ambiguity, individualism, and professional values. They are less affected by reference groups outside the organizations. They have a lower preference for dealing with complex information and value hierarchical authority and power based on organizational position. Many organizations consist of a mix of stable structures and dynamic structures. For example, production divisions or accounting departments are typically stable and bureaucratically operated. On the other hand, research units or engineering groups are likely to be structured much more loosely. In mixed-organizations, these units have to interact and cooperate, but the value differences among members are the seeds of conflict.

☐ **FIGURE 14.4** *Value Differences in Mechanistic and Organic Organizational Structures*

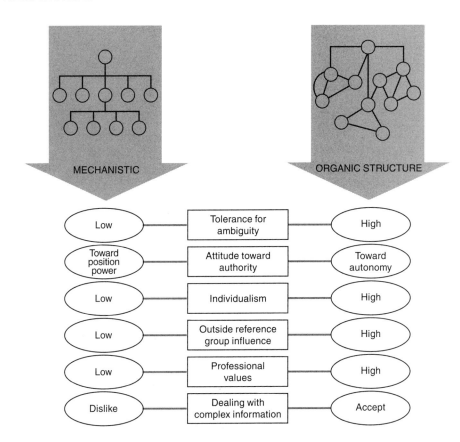

Needs and Personality. Personality and needs are related to propensities to enter conflict or explain clashes between people. Consider the following case in which people high in achievement needs were less willing to cooperate with others. This occurred in a chemical products company that had several plants making different products [16]. Some of the plants produced products for other plants in the company. The plant managers cooperated for a time with little difficulty. Then some of the older plant managers retired. The new managers hired from the outside had a different psychological makeup than those who retired. They were much more concerned about individual achievement and showed less cooperativeness. Disagreements arose, and performance in some of the plants deteriorated.

Perception and Judgment. If we perceive another person as a threat, we may act toward them in a way that increases the potential for conflict. Conflict can also arise if people make perceptual errors, such as stereotyping or the fundamental attribution error. One party might blame another for a problem and attribute the cause of the problem to the other person's motives. This would be a false attribution if the person who was blamed was forced to act as he did.

Perceptual differences operate strongly when the situation is ambiguous. Situational ambiguity allows perceptions and attitudes to come forcefully into

☐ CONFLICT ACROSS CULTURES

Given that individual characteristics are a product of socialization, we would naturally expect many cross-cultural differences on how people deal with conflict. Different styles of reacting to conflict are probably found more frequently in some cultures than others. When organizations have international operations and plants in many countries, they must be aware of such culture differences since a major aspect of culture is its tolerance of and reactions to conflict. In Japan, there is far less toleration of open conflict than in the United States, and people also react to others and attempt to gain control over their situation in different ways, a result of differences in child-rearing practices in the two cultures [12]. The Japanese attempt to deal with the issue of control over others with a style of accommodation, whereas the U.S. culture emphasizes the competing or direct confrontation style [39].

In a recent study, comparisons were made between the United States, Japan, China, Korea, and Taiwan [34]. The researchers examined similarities and differences in the values and behaviors relevant to how conflict is approached and resolved. Asian cultures are more likely to value group goals and responsibilities than they are to pursue individualistic needs. China, Korea, and Taiwan for example, showed highest concern for the self-esteem and self-image of the other party, and to avoid embarrassing or humiliating them. They gave others the opportunity to "save face" more so than in the United States, and are more likely to avoid conflict or be obliging when in it. In the United States, there is a stronger tendency to dominate the other party rather than avoid or oblige. In such individualistic cultures, people show more concern for preserving their own face which is the case for both the United States and Japan. Though more competitive, it is interesting that the individualistic emphasis tends also to foster more collaborative behavior. By comparison, Asian cultures are more likely to give in or accommodate to the other party.

play. Also, disagreement and conflict are likely when groups possess different knowledge and information that contribute to their opposing perceptions and judgments.

SITUATIONAL CONDITIONS

Situational conditions can encourage conflict when they define and affect how people interact with each other.

Interdependence and Need to Interact.   Conflict is less likely when people are physically separate and don't interact very often. As the association between parties increases, so does the probability of conflict. With active and complex interdependencies such as joint decision making, conflict potential increases even more.

Interdependencies are extremely common in organizations, but they need not result in conflict. Ancona has shown that more productive work groups are ones that actively interact with each other by asking questions, working jointly on projects, and sharing information and achievements [1]. Nelson says that in low-conflict organizations, ties between groups are strong and marked by frequent, productive interactions [22]. In high-conflict organizations, ties were strong within the groups but not between them.

Need for Consensus.   Conflict may be a function of whether or not agreements are needed between the parties. For example, a purchasing department acquires materials for other departments in a company. Many purchases will be routine and require little interaction or consensus among departments. But consensus might be an issue when purchasing furniture, computers, or buildings. Conflicts over quality, size, color, or location could occur when pressure for consensus exists.

Status Differences.   When people act in ways incongruent with their status, conflict can erupt. A classic analysis of status conflict was done in the restaurant industry [40]. For a variety of reasons, cooks believed they had higher status than waitresses. When waitresses communicated their customer orders to cooks, the cooks often reacted as if they were being personally ordered around by people of lower status. They often responded to the waitresses by delaying meals. In another study, engineers typically rejected innovative ideas from draftsmen because they felt it was the draftsmen's job to draw what they were asked to draw, not to be equal partners in the design process [15].

Communication.   Communication can lead to conflict because it is a double-edged sword. Barriers to communication can cause conflict, but so can the opportunity to communicate. We have seen how the need to interact can stimulate conflict. Information about another party can cause people to identify unfair conditions or differences in needs and values. This can start conflict that otherwise would have been avoided with less communication. In one study, conflict between departments was higher when departments were more knowledgeable about each other [38].

443

Ambiguous Responsibilities and Jurisdictions. People with clear-cut roles and responsibilities know what to expect from each other. When there is ambiguity about roles and responsibilities, the chances are that there will be **jurisdictional disputes**. In one organization, the sales department would actually locate and order materials when the production department claimed it didn't have them. Production would then accuse sales of overstepping its authority and violating procedures. Conflicts arose again and again. It resulted in late and defective orders, lost customers, and worker layoffs.

ADDITIONAL FACTORS IN COMPLEX ORGANIZATIONS

When large numbers of people join together in an organization, many things can lead to conflict. These are rooted in roles and responsibilities, interdependencies, goals, policies, and reward systems.

Specialization and Differentiation. Specialization can be at the root of conflict. Different groups of specialists usually need to coordinate their efforts. Unless the coordination is effective, problems will arise, such as lack of consensus, ambiguous responsibilities, or communication barriers. As the number of different specialities increases in an organization, conflict can also increase.

Organizations also create expectations which make cooperation difficult. This can be demonstrated by the example of the relationships between production, sales, and research units. Each unit has its own responsibilities and concerns. One study illustrates how each unit had different perspectives toward structure, interpersonal relations, and time, and each pursued different goals (see Figure 14.5) [14]. Sales concerned itself with customers and competition. Production sought cost reduction and efficiency. Research was focused on technical improvements and modifications with emphasis on scientific objectives. These factors sharply differentiated these units and were the basis for many disagreements.

FIGURE 14.5 *Orientation Differences in Organizations*

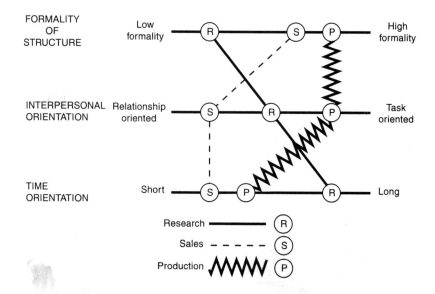

It's very appropriate for sales, production, and research to have different orientations. Research should be less formally structured, while production should be more routine. As stated earlier, some conflict is healthy, even though there may be difficulty in integrating such departments.

The distinction between line and staff departments is also a basis for conflict. Line departments are those that are directly involved in the major organization mission, such as sales and production departments. Staff units, which include personnel, accounting, purchasing, or legal departments, are indirectly involved and exist primarily to support, control, and assist the line units. They often engage in evaluating other units in the organization and develop new programs and procedures for them. Staff's evaluations may not be accepted by line people. Staff units also impose controls that line units may not understand or cannot accept. The problem is made worse because staff personnel, compared to line personnel, are frequently younger, better educated, and have fewer years of experience in the organization. Staff personnel may also use their own jargon, dress differently, and be situated at the top of the organization near the seats of power.

Task Interdependence.   Different degrees of interdependence can affect conflict [33]. When there is *pooled interdependence*, as when typists work alone to produce letters and reports, little chance for conflict exists. Conflict only arises on occasions where employees can give or deny each other help, where they can't agree on a complaint to management, or where there are personal problems. In *sequential interdependence*, the output of one person or unit becomes input to another, so that conflict can arise at points where people interface. The chances of conflict are even higher in *reciprocal interdependency*. A project leader, for example, might try to get a designer to give her project priority. If she gets her way, another project leader could suffer. The designer has difficulty deciding whom to please. It is not easy to play these demands ahead of time because projects develop at different rates.

Goal setting.   Clear goals can be an excellent source of direction and motivation in organizations, but they do not ensure that conflict is minimized or prevented. Disagreement can arise when top management is selecting among possible goals for the organization. Choices must be made and priorities established. Managers can seriously disagree over new products or services, whether to withdraw from certain markets, or when to build a new facility.

Goals can also cause conflict within a single unit of an organization. For example, within a production department, efficiency goals can be incompatible with safety and maintenance goals. A production manager might run equipment at excessive speeds and reduce maintenance as a way to increase productivity and reduce costs. These actions can increase accidents and also increase long-run costs because poor equipment maintenance causes them to break down sooner.

Scarce Resources.   If every unit in an organization had all the resources needed to do a job, they would be less interdependent and fewer conflicts would arise. When resources are scarce, however, both sharing and competition for resources create conflict.

Multiple Authority and Influence. Many organizations are designed so that each employee has only one superior. In management theory, this is known as the *principle of unity of command*. This principle is intended to prevent all sorts of problems such as keeping an employee from getting caught between conflicting demands from different higher-level managers and keeping bosses from squabbling over assignments to subordinates.

The unity of command principle is hard to maintain, because every employee is subject to many influences besides an immediate superior. A request from any high-level manager is hard for most employees to ignore. Peers can also pressure a fellow worker. These multiple sources of input can create conflict that can seriously affect a person's emotional state [27].

Policies, Procedures, and Rules. One purpose of policies, procedures, and rules is to reduce conflict by clarifying roles and responsibilities and smoothing the interaction between people. For example, a policy may state that machine maintenance is the responsibility of a particular person or department. If machine problems or failures arise, disagreements about who is to fix it are less likely to occur.

However, policies, rules, and procedures do not guarantee that conflict will be prevented because they cannot cover every situation. Exceptions to the rule will occur that may make it acceptable to break or bend it. People typically have to interpret rules every day. For example, supervisors often have to decide whether an absent employee deserves to get paid for the missed time. A decision to not pay could result in a grievance.

Policies, procedures, and rules can even contribute directly to conflict. These controls on behavior make people feel frustrated or sometimes insulted. Controls can restrict employees' freedom and autonomy which they value. They may feel a loss of trust and respect when controls are excessive.

Rewards. Reward systems contribute to conflict in several ways. They can lead to conflict between bosses and subordinates or reflect conflict between goals [11]. Suppose you work as a medical claims adjuster for an insurance company and are told to provide good service and award appropriate claims without overpaying. When customers call with questions, you take the time to respond to them. When a claim is unclear, you contact the physician or hospital involved. At the end of each month, however, your supervisor tells you you haven't processed enough claims. You realize that you can't continue to provide good service, reduce costs, and increase the number of completed claims. In addition to this conflict with your boss, you aren't sure whether the quantity or the quality of your work is more important.

CONFLICT REACTION STYLES

People deal with conflict in different ways. Some have an initial tendency to escape, and others are more prone to get involved. Once involved, people also vary in how they face the conflict. These styles of conflict behavior are discussed below.

A MODEL OF STYLES

Several important theories discuss styles of conflict behavior [3, 6, 9, 32]. Five different styles of reacting to conflict that are drawn from these theories are: *avoiding, accommodating, competing, compromising,* and *collaborating*. These five styles are set in a two-dimensional model shown in Figure 14.6. The horizontal dimension reflects the degree to which a person has concern for the *other* party's needs and goals. High concern toward the other party reflects cooperativeness and a desire to maintain the relationship. People who are low on this dimension are not interested in the other party's concerns, nor do they care much about preserving the relationship—they have an uncooperative attitude. The vertical dimension refers to how concerned a party is for his or her *own* needs and goals. People who are high on this dimension are assertive, and their main desire is to achieve their own goals. A low concern reflects unassertiveness and a willingness to sacrifice one's own needs and goals. The five styles of conflict resolution are combinations of these two dimensions. Each style has different characteristics and different uses [30, 32].

FIGURE 14.6 *A Model of Personal Stylistic Reactions to Conflict*

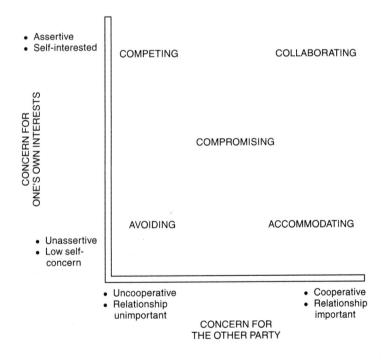

Avoiding.   Some are emotionally upset by the tensions and frustration of conflict; perhaps past conflicts hurt them somehow. Painful memories make them want to withdraw from disagreement. **Avoiding conflict** can also be based on a belief that conflict is evil, unnecessary, or undignified. People can physically withdraw by simply leaving the scene of a conflict. They can refuse to get involved by using silence or changing the topic of conversation. Psychologically, avoiders can also deny the existence of conflict or ignore it when it arises.

Avoiding conflict can be wise when issues are insignificant or when the costs of challenging someone outweigh the benefits. Avoidance may also be useful when there is little chance of success. For example, it's not easy to change another person's strong attitudes. Temporarily avoiding also buys time. This gives others a chance to cool down or to seek more information. Finally, it might be better to avoid conflict when others can resolve it more effectively or when it is over the wrong issue.

Accommodating. **Accommodating** means giving in to the wishes of another person. The accommodating person tries to preserve a relationship and fears doing things that drive people apart. Accommodators feel it is better to give up their own goals rather than risk alienating or upsetting others. Like avoiders, the value system of accommodators is a perspective that conflict is bad. But rather than avoid, they give in such a way that keeps or strengthens a relationship. This style can reflect generosity, humility, or obedience. An accommodator may also feel that selfishness, an undesirable trait, is what causes most conflict.

Accommodation may be a very good strategy when you are wrong; it permits the correct position to win and is a sign of reasonableness. It can be taken as a gesture of goodwill and help maintain a relationship. Giving in may be a good thing to do when the issue is much more important to the other party. Fighting is not very productive when the other party has a lot to lose and you have little to gain.

Another use of accommodation is to train subordinates. Suppose a manager lets a subordinate have his or her way in a disagreement. The subordinate can then execute his or her idea and, perhaps, learn from experience. Before a manager can give in, however, she must be sure that the potential errors are not terribly serious.

Competing. The **competing** style is one in which a person pursues his or her own wishes at the expense of the other party. Conflict is viewed as a game to be won. Competitors are both assertive and uncooperative. Winning means success and accomplishment. Losing means failure, weakness, and a loss of status. The competitor feels that there must be a winner and a loser when there is conflict, and he or she is not about to become the loser. Competitors will use many different tactics to win such as threat, argument, or persuasion.

A forceful position may be the best style in crises, when there is no time for disagreement and discussion. Managers may wish to use the style when unpopular but necessary decisions must be made. Suppose overtime work is needed in order to meet an order deadline for an important customer. If the issue is simply not debatable, the manager may have to deal with disagreement in a directive manner. Competition may also be a style to use when the other party has a tendency to take advantage of you. Competing serves as a way to protect yourself.

Compromising. **Compromising** is a give-and-take style based on the belief that people can't always have their way and have to find a middle ground they all can live with. Compromisers look for feasible solutions and will use techniques such as trading, bargaining, smoothing over differences, or voting. They feel that people should be more willing to set aside some of their wishes and to show sensitivity to the other person's will. Through compromise, relationships can endure if people hear each other's point of view and if they try to arrive at a fair agreement.

Compromise is a common way of dealing with conflict. It may be a particularly useful technique when two parties have relatively equal power and mutually exclusive goals. In situations like this, what one party gains, the other loses. The trick is to find an acceptable middle-ground solution. This is characteristic of many union-management bargaining situations, such as when pay increases, working conditions, and job security are at stake.

Compromise can be useful when there are time constraints. Time may not be available to solve problems that require a great deal of effort to sort out all the issues. Compromise can allow for a temporary solution until more time can be devoted to unravel and analyze the complexities. Finally, compromise may be useful when collaboration or competition fails to lead to a solution between the parties.

Collaborating. **Collaborating** is a willingness to accept the other party's needs, while asserting your own. In collaborating, it is assumed that there is some reasonable chance a solution can be found to satisfy both parties in the conflict. Such a solution might not be possible, but a collaborator believes that it is worth trying to find one.

For example, an organization planning to install a new computer system can use a collaborative approach. Different departments can join together to purchase the equipment or to design the system that meets various needs. Collaborative solutions cannot be found unless the parties express their needs and goals, which provides insights into what is causing the conflict. Collaboration also requires that the parties work diligently and creatively to generate all kinds of solutions. Collaboration, therefore, requires openness and trust, as well as hard work. It often follows the principles of good problem solving and decision making. Several collaborative approaches are discussed as confrontation techniques later in this chapter.

Collaboration is useful when each party is strongly committed to different goals and when compromise is potentially very costly. It is also useful when people agree on goals, but disagree on means to achieve them. Collaboration can lead to an appreciation of other people's point of view. Therefore, it can strengthen relationships if mutual respect is maintained. When collaboration is successful, the commitment to the solution is high.

How people behave in a conflict situation can affect the stability and the nature of a relationship. In one study, a subordinate, as part of an experiment, deliberately provoked a conflict with a superior. After the disagreement, the subordinate then responded in one of three ways: said nothing, offered a gift (a Life Saver) to the superior, or tried to elicit sympathy by saying that he was "uptight" because of his many deadlines that week. Figure 14.7 indicates that liking for the subordinate increased with the offer of a gift or by eliciting of sympathy. Thus, it helped when the subordinate took the initiative with a peace offering or a reasonable excuse. Furthermore, the study revealed that this higher rating of the subordinate was related to the boss's intention to use a compromise or collaboration style with that subordinate in the future, rather than an avoidance or competitive style.

FIGURE 14.7 *Superior Liking for Subordinates After Different Strategies for Conflict Reduction by Subordinates*

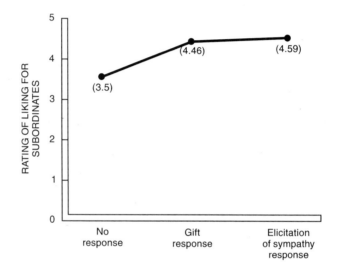

IS THERE A PARADOX?

Collaboration and conflict conjure up opposite feelings. To collaborate suggests cooperation, mutual support, and maybe even friendliness. Conflict, on the other hand, connotes fighting, disagreement, and antagonism. How then can collaboration be a way to deal with conflict? What can prompt people to collaborate when they are caught up in a conflict?

The first step, of course, is to accept collaboration as a way to approach conflict and then try to use it. This takes considerable practice and self-discipline. When we get into a conflict situation, it is necessary to control emotions and, maybe after a deep breath, take a stab at trying to find solutions that will benefit you and the other party.

Let us look at an example of collaborative conflict resolution. Envision a married couple disagreeing over where to go on a vacation. She wants to go where there are historical sights and museums. Her first choice is Boston. He wants to go to a resort where he can lie in the sun and relax. He's

☐ **IS THERE . . .**

got the Caribbean in mind. If each can state his or her needs and goals, the results could look something like this:

Wife's Goals	*Husband's Goals*
Learning	Relaxation
Guided tours	No alarm clock
Historical souvenirs	Suntan
Pictures of historical sites and artifacts	Golf
Good food	Good food
Swimming	Swimming

Given these goals, the couple can mutually generate vacation spots that might serve both their goals. They can first agree to get more information on different locations and what each has to offer. Certain vacation areas will offer things that will keep them both happy. Either Mexico or the Mediterranean could be a good choice. If they discuss when to go on vacation, it could be that Cape Cod near Boston would easily satisfy them both if they went in summer. They might even discover seaside resorts whose specialty is tours to historical sites. Collaboration doesn't always work, but mutually acceptable solutions are less often found using other styles.

STYLE FLEXIBILITY—OVERUSE AND UNDERUSE

Thomas and Kilmann indicate that there are harmful implications if any style is *overused* or *underused* [32]. Managers should be flexible enough to use a particular style when it best suits the situation. This would require a diagnosis of the conflict conditions, the selection of an appropriate style, and the ability and willingness to use different styles. Managers should be trained to diagnose and practice each style. Table 14.1 suggests that style flexibility would help to prevent the undesirable consequences of overuse and underuse.

CONFLICT MANAGEMENT STRATEGIES

By **conflict management**, we mean that a manager takes an active role in addressing conflict situations and intervenes if needed. A variety of actions are possible, ranging from preventing conflict to getting it resolved [28, 35]. Although avoiding conflict is a useful alternative, excessive avoidance can be very damaging to an organization [2]. Figure 14.8 depicts four classes of ways to manage conflict: (1) avoiding, accommodating, competing, compromising, and collaborating (2) confrontation techniques (3) improving organization practices, and (4) special roles and structures.

☐ **TABLE 14.1** Style Flexibility, Overuse, and Underuse of Conflict Reaction Styles

Style	Overuse: Using the Style Too Much	Underuse: Using the Style Too Little
AVOIDING	Subordinates deprived of help Disagreements persist Coordination suffers Subordinates decide Issues are not raised	Stirs unnecessary hostility Subordinates lose independence Nonavoider is overburdened Failure to set priorities
ACCOMMODATING	Lose self-respect/recognition Deprive others of ideas Seen as indecisive, weak Burdens others excessively Others feel manipulated into reciprocating later	Seen as rigid, unreasonable Prevents goodwill Ignores exceptions to rules False sense of losing face when opposite may be true
COMPETING	Others avoid competitor Makes others repeated losers Cuts off information from others Subordinate reluctance to fight Subordinates give in easily	Lose self-esteem Feel powerless, controlled by others Relinquish decision making Avoid/accommodate too much
COMPROMISING	Others tire of "deals" Gamesmanship atmosphere Game becomes more important than the issues Merits of issues can be lost	Seen as rigid, unreasonable Trapped into dealing and power struggles Lose opportunities to ease tensions
COLLABORATING	Some problems not worth it Unnecessary when stakes are low Can block accommodating Vulnerability to manipulation by others	Lose mutual-gain solutions Unduly pessimistic Lose chances for creativity Lose subordinate commitment Lose team cohesiveness

Source: K.W. Thomas and R.W. Kilmann, *Conflict Mode Instrument* (Tuxedo, NY: Xicom, 1974). [32]

☐ **FIGURE 14.8** *Conflict Management Strategies*

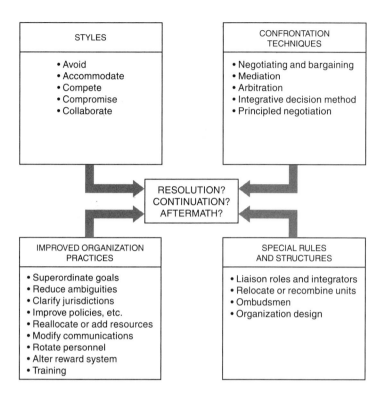

CONFRONTATION TECHNIQUES

STYLES
• Avoid
• Accommodate
• Compete
• Compromise
• Collaborate

CONFRONTATION TECHNIQUES
• Negotiating and bargaining
• Mediation
• Arbitration
• Integrative decision method
• Principled negotiation

RESOLUTION?
CONTINUATION?
AFTERMATH?

IMPROVED ORGANIZATION PRACTICES
• Superordinate goals
• Reduce ambiguities
• Clarify jurisdictions
• Improve policies, etc.
• Reallocate or add resources
• Modify communications
• Rotate personnel
• Alter reward system
• Training

SPECIAL RULES AND STRUCTURES
• Liaison roles and integrators
• Relocate or recombine units
• Ombudsmen
• Organization design

CONFRONTATION TECHNIQUES

Confrontation techniques require that parties in conflict decide to face each other on the issues, but do so constructively. The parties must be willing to work together to arrive at a **consensus decision**, one that both parties can accept. They do not try to avoid or give in. They may compete or compromise somewhat, but the major emphasis of confrontation techniques is *to find mutually acceptable and longer-lasting solutions*. An attempt is made to use the collaborative style as much as possible with some use of compromise. The aim is for both parties to satisfy their needs and goals to the greatest extent possible. Effective confrontation requires skill and experience and, above all, a positive and constructive attitude in which the parties are open to ideas and information.

Confrontation methods frequently use a third party. The outside parties can be consultants or mediators from government agencies that offer such services. Sometimes they come from within an organization, usually from the personnel department. Sometimes a trained manager or integrator can act as a third party in conflict resolution. A third party can see to it that certain steps are followed, be a source of help and advice, make sure all opinions are heard, and assist in many process decisions, such as when to have the parties work separately. In some instances, the third party may even make critical decisions that are binding on the parties.

Negotiating and Bargaining.   Bargaining is primarily a compromising style, but effective bargainers use a variety of techniques. They will occasionally act competitively and use force or threats. They will use accommodation, hoping that a concession on their part will stimulate the other party to concede a point in return. It is also possible for two parties to collaborate on some issues, jointly searching for a solution that is useful to both. One common business application of **negotiating and bargaining** is when labor unions negotiate contracts.

Bargaining can vary in the degree to which it is *distributive* or *integrative*. Distributive bargaining takes place when one party's gain is the other party's loss. Integrative bargaining occurs when the two parties work together to solve a problem to the benefit of both.

In many bargaining situations, the goal of each party is to obtain the most they can, often at the expense of the other party. How hard each party stresses to win is tempered by how willing they are to maintain a good relationship. If the relationship can be terminated without serious implications, people may drive a very hard bargain. You may bargain hard when buying a car, because you can usually buy elsewhere if the bargaining fails, but in a labor-management negotiation, bargaining might be less extreme because the parties must live together when it is over.

Bargainers use many different tactics. Bargaining will often begin with higher demands than the parties expect to get (or lower than they expect to give). Then concessions are made to work toward a mutually acceptable middle position. These concessions have to be made without appearing weak. Weakness can encourage the other party to demand more or offer less.

With many issues, bargaining gets more complex as concessions on one issue carry over to other issues. If management concedes to a salary increase to the union, they may be less willing to concede much on fringe benefits or working conditions. If the union concedes on new job descriptions, they may be less willing to give ground on sick-leave policy. Bargaining is even further complicated by time pressures, the past history of the parties, and longer-range considerations such as economic forecasts.

Mediation.   One common use of **mediation** is in labor-management negotiations. The parties can use third-party assistance to arrive at a solution. The Federal Mediation and Conciliation Service provides experienced mediators to help with the negotiation process. If both parties agree, a mediator is called in. Mediators are not empowered to make decisions or impose a solution, but they use many techniques to resolve differences. They may make suggestions and monitor the interaction of the parties. They may keep the parties apart, and bring them back together again. They can ease tensions with such methods and add objectivity to the bargaining. Mediators can be used in many other types of situations besides labor-management negotiations [8, 19, 21].

Arbitration.   **Arbitration** is another third-party approach to conflict resolution. Unlike mediators, arbitrators actually make decisions that bind both parties. Arbitrators are used in labor-management situations and less often in other situations. Arbitrations in labor-management relations are used in several kinds of situations. One is when contract negotiations have reached an impasse. Another is for grievances. The arbitrator hears both sides and may even follow a courtroom model. The offers and the points of view of both parties are heard. When the arbitrator feels he or she has heard enough, the arbitrator takes ample time to study the issues, then makes a decision binding on both parties.

Integrative Decision Method (IDM). The **integrative decision method (IDM)** is primarily a collaborative style that draws heavily on the problem-solving principles discussed in an earlier chapter [6]. In IDM, it is assumed that there may be a solution that is highly acceptable to both parties. The parties must work together to defeat the problem instead of each other. The six major elements in IDM are shown in Figure 14.9.

☐ **FIGURE 14.9** *The Integrative Decision Method*

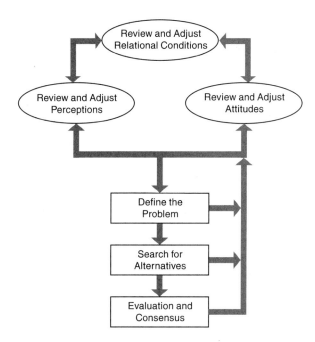

IDM requires that the conflict resolution process begin by adjusting the relationship between the parties. This is done before the actual problem is attacked, with the following steps:

1. *Review and adjust relational conditions.* Parties in conflict begin by creating an environment where problem solving and collaborative action can take place. This may call for a meeting in a neutral and relaxed setting. Ample time should be allowed, and the parties should agree to open and full communication. They can designate people in each group to help control the process and keep it on track.

2. *Review and adjust perceptions.* The parties must share the perception that a mutually agreeable solution is possible. Otherwise they are more likely to fight over two solutions, "your way or our way." Constructive perceptions open up communication and direct it toward solutions rather than have it defensively directed at the other party. For example, the parties should seek opinions by saying, "How did this problem start?" or "Who has a proposal?" They can avoid statements such as, "You know what we want. Why can't you agree?" or "You've heard our proposal. Is it yes or no?"

3. *Review and adjust attitudes.* The parties must discuss their feelings and beliefs so that they appreciate each other's position. Feelings of distrust and hostility can be reduced. Unless this is done, these feelings will emerge later and block any chance of agreement. Attitudes should be expressed in a depersonalized manner. Instead of saying, "Your actions were thoughtless. You got us into a lot of trouble," it is better to say, "When the report was submitted, our group felt we should have seen it first. We felt left out and worried about it." The latter statement shares feelings without attacking the other party.

   Other specific techniques may foster cooperation before problem solving begins [6]. Methods can be used to reduce stereotypes, share differences of opinion, improve communication, and remove threat. Eventually, the parties in conflict can proceed to work together for a collaborative solution. Three additional steps, performed in sequence, are needed in IDM.

4. *Define the problem.* The IDM process tries to define the problem in a manner that recognizes the existence of conflict. This is done by having each party explicitly state its needs and goals. One party might say, "What we want is to get these payments out to people when they need them, not a week or a month later." The other party says, "What we need is adequate lead time and accurate requests before we can issue the payments. Otherwise the whole system will break down. We can't violate agency procedures." Obviously, the first party has seen the second as slowing down payments. The second party sees the first as wanting rules broken and threatening the system. But instead of accusing each other, they express their needs and goals openly.

   Good problem definition requires that both parties avoid suggesting one-sided solutions. Problem definition is also improved if the parties jointly identify what causes the problem and what obstacles exist to solving it. For example, perhaps the payment problem is caused by failure to anticipate payment needs sooner. Agreement on causes and obstacles can draw both parties into jointly eliminating them.

5. *Search for alternatives.* In this step, the two parties work together to generate possible solutions using principles of effective problem solving. They should avoid evaluating solutions before an exhaustive list is generated. Outsiders can be used as sources of ideas. The parties

can use the nominal group technique, brainstorming, and other creativity techniques.

6. *Evaluation and consensus decision.* The list of possible solutions can now be evaluated. The major criteria used to evaluate the solutions are (1) acceptance: Will one or more of the alternatives meet each party's needs and goals? and (2) quality: Will the solution work? We have discussed these criteria in detail in Chapter 13 on decision making.

The integrative decision method is a demanding approach. It deals with both emotions and thinking, respecting the positions of both parties and trying to build on these in a unifying way. IDM may not always produce a feasible consensus decision, but it is a way of finding one if it exists.

Principled Negotiation. **Principled negotiation** is based on the same problem-solving orientation of the integrative decision method [7]. Table 14.2 outlines the elements of the technique and highlights its four major requirements. Principled negotiation is compared to "soft" and "hard" approaches to conflict resolution. The *soft approach* is similar to accommodating and overemphasizes giving in as a way to maintain a good relationship. The *hard approach* is similar to competing and overemphasizes one party winning at the expense of the other. Principled negotiation emphasizes the problem and tries to get the parties in conflict to work together toward mutual gain.

The four steps in principled negotiation are:

1. *Separate the people from the problem.* This reduces the effects of harmful emotions. The parties must avoid blaming each other. They must share their perceptions and needs, and put themselves in each other's shoes. They must allow each other to let off steam in an accepting way. Active listening is essential. The problem, however, must be stated in a way that doesn't contain accusations and doesn't deny the goals and values of the parties. It is better to say, "The problem is that we cannot agree on how to test the product," than "Your idea of a test is nonsense. It won't work!"

2. *Focus on interests, not positions.* Each party needs to state its interests and make its position explicit. For example, one party might say, "What I want is a product test that is thorough and realistic." The other party might say, "What I want is a product test that is feasible and done in one month." This requirement of principled negotiation legitimizes expression of needs without demeaning the other party. In a subtle way, the expression of interests also focuses the parties on the problem and on the future rather than on each other and past difficulties between them. Together they are being hard on the problem, but soft on each other.

3. *Invent options for mutual gain.* The parties jointly generate a number of possible solutions that might resolve their disagreement, without evaluating them. During this process, the parties can also uncover additional interests and differences in values or beliefs. They can

☐ **TABLE 14.2**   The Principled Negotiation Technique Compared to Soft and Hard Methods of Conflict Resolution

SOFT (relationship oriented)	**HARD** (goal oriented)	**PRINCIPLED NEGOTIATION** (problem-oriented)
Participants are friends	Participants are adversaries	Participants are problem solvers
The goal is agreement	The goal is victory	The goal is a wise agreement
Make concessions to cultivate the relationship	Demand concessions as a condition of the relationship	**SEPARATE THE PEOPLE FROM THE PROBLEM**
Be soft on the people and the problem	Be hard on the people and the problem	Be soft on people, hard on the problem
Trust others	Distrust others	Proceed independently of trust
Change your position easily	Dig in to your position	**FOCUS ON INTERESTS, NOT POSITIONS**
Make offers	Make threats	Explore interests
Disclose your bottom line	Mislead as to your bottom line	Avoid having a bottom line
Accept one-sided losses to reach agreement	Demand one-sided gains as the price of agreement	**INVENT OPTIONS FOR MUTUAL GAINS**
Search for the single answer: the one *they* will accept	Search for the single answer: the one *you* will accept	Develop multiple options to choose from; decide later
Insist on agreement	Insist on your position	**INSIST ON OBJECTIVE CRITERIA**
Try to avoid a contest of will	Try to win a contest of will	Try to reach a result based on standards independent of will
Yield to pressure	Apply pressure	Be reasonable; yield to principle, not pressure

Source: Fisher and W. Ury, *Getting to Yes.* Copyright © 1981 by R. Fisher and W. Ury. Reprinted by permission of Houghton Mifflin Company [7].

examine how much cost and risk they are willing to accept. Common interests can be identified as well. In this manner, options can be generated that grow out of mutual appreciation for each other's position. Conflict resolution is more likely if the options are sensitive to the other party's position.

4. *Insist on objective criteria.* Eventually, the parties should evaluate the options. Objective criteria consistent with principled negotiation include fairness, workability, and the durability of the solution. The parties should openly ask, "Which solutions do you consider to be fair?" or "Let's find solutions that will work and that will be lasting." Solutions should also satisfy each party's interests as much as is possible.

☐ DIRTY TRICKS

Suppose you are in conflict with another party who refuses to give in, compromise, or collaborate with you to find a solution. What if that person tries to deceive you, escalates demands, or uses dirty tricks to try to win? Fisher and Ury say that most people respond by either avoiding the other party if they can or with deceit and dirty tricks of their own.

These authors propose what they feel is a better strategy under these circumstances. To counter dirty tricks, Fisher and Ury say to use principled negotiation. That is, don't avoid or respond in kind. Instead, you should try to fix the process before getting back to the issues of the conflict itself.

There are three major steps in negotiating the rules of the game:

1. *Recognize the tactic.* Identify deception and other behaviors that bother you. Awareness of what the other party is doing helps you to deal with it.
2. *Raise it explicitly with the other party.* Tell the other party you feel or sense what he or she is doing and it's bothering you. This gives the other party something to think about, but more important, it opens the door to negotiating the process being used.
3. *Negotiate the tactics being used.* Question the legitimacy and desirability of the tactic. This takes the discussion off the conflict issue itself and focuses it on the process.

In executing the third step, you must use the tactics of principled negotiation. First, separate the people from the problem, and try not to be personal. Focus on the tactic. Second, focus on interests, not positions, by asking, for example, whether the other party is using the tactic for a particular reason. Third, invent alternative options by suggesting new tactics that lead to mutual gain. Finally, insist on objective criteria for fairness in process. For example, ask about where people sit, or how they might talk to each other.

☐ **DIRTY . . .**

Fisher and Ury also describe various dirty tactics such as using phony facts, communicating dubious intentions, partial disclosure, personal attacks, pressure tactics, and so on. They try to show how to deal with each tactic.

Source: R. Fisher and W. Ury, *Getting Past No: Negotiating with Difficult People.* (NY: Bantam Books, 1991) [7].

IMPROVING ORGANIZATION PRACTICES

Earlier in this chapter, we discussed a number of causes of conflict in the organization setting. A manager who knows and understands the causes of conflict can take steps to deal with it by changing the causal conditions.

Superordinate Goals.   Managers, especially those at the top, can set **superordinate goals** that draw units into collaborative efforts. The dean of the college of business administration can unite the accounting, finance, management, and marketing departments to work together in a fundraising campaign. If administrators, faculty, and students meet together to plan the campaign, they can decide on how to approach different donors. Goals can also be set concerning how the campaign money will be used. The good of the entire college can be integrated with the needs of each department, and behaviors that can lead departments into deep conflict can be prevented. Goals that are potentially incompatible or conflicting are more likely to be identified.

Reducing Ambiguities and Jurisdictional Disputes.   There are many ways to decrease ambiguities. The goal-setting process is one of these. Clear and non-conflicting goals clarify responsibilities. They can be devised so that each employee and unit doesn't interfere or compete with the work of the others. Good job descriptions can also clarify duties and expectations so there is little dispute about who is responsible for what. Reporting relationships can be clarified by preparing organization charts and discussing who has the authority to make certain decisions.

Improve Policies, Procedures, and Rules.   In many instances, an organization can establish policies, procedures, or rules to minimize ambiguities and reduce conflict. One such a case arose in the research division of a large equipment manufacturer. The scientists and engineers in this division often attended conventions and professional meetings to keep up to date, to present papers, and to work on problems they share with other scientists. Conflict repeatedly arose over attendance at these meetings. Some departments sent employees to as many as five meetings, others to only one. Complaints about fairness put many departments at odds with each other. A committee was established that prepared a fair policy to cover this situation. Costs were contained and conflicts over the issues reduced.

Reallocate or Add Resources.   When there is conflict in sequential interdependence, management can permit inventory to build up between departments so that one unit cannot blame another for holding them up. Better schedules can smooth and improve the balance of the work flow. Conflict also arises when employees have to get approvals for minor things such as office supplies. A budget for certain purchases can be allocated to each unit to solve such problems.

Resources can also be reallocated such that personnel and equipment are shifted into new organization structures. In one factory, a separate maintenance department serviced production machinery. There was constant conflict between the maintenance employees and the production supervisors over maintenance priorities. Favoritism and personalities dominated, and complaints were frequent. The vice president of production solved the problem by disbanding the maintenance department. Maintenance employees were placed within production units and now reported to their respective production supervisors. Each production supervisor was given maintenance responsibility and now had the personnel resources to do it. Conflict was virtually eliminated and production delays due to maintenance were drastically reduced.

Modify Communications.   Communications can be improved in a number of ways. One way is to eliminate the opportunity for it to occur. Recall the study of the restaurant industry cited earlier [40]. Cooks often found themselves "taking orders" from waitresses, whom they felt were of lower status, and resisted being told what to do by them. The problem was greatly reduced by requiring the waitresses to submit written customer orders and requests. Their orders were clipped to a rotating spindle from which cooks could select. The face-to-face interaction with the cooks was reduced, and so was conflict between them.

When two parties are interdependent, however, communication may need to be increased. Each party must keep the other informed and be able to anticipate difficulties that affect the relationship. For example, sales departments that interact with and understand production schedules can avoid unnecessary rush orders. They can also give production advance notice of possible changes in sales plans.

Rotation of Personnel.   Rotating personnel through different departments helps them to develop a fuller understanding of each unit's responsibilities and problems. Then, when the employee returns to his or her original unit, a basis for cooperation exists. Rotation is often used with new employees. It might be particularly useful when the organization is undergoing major changes. New projects, new products, reorganizations, and other changes can generate a host of issues that causes conflict.

Alter Reward Systems.   The way rewards are administered may decrease the chances of conflict erupting. Managers can be reinforced with positive feedback and good performance appraisals when they promote harmony. Even financial rewards such as bonuses can be consistent with conflict reduction. In

461

one factory where large conveyers were assembled, employees used to work independently on various tasks such as welding, bolting parts together, and wiring electrical circuits. They competed and argued over assignments, space, and tools. Many saw no benefit in helping each other. Management decided to create work teams. Each team was supplied with enough tools and also assigned with its own work area to eliminate the competition for space. To further prevent competition and conflict between the teams, a productivity and cost-savings bonus to be shared equally by the teams was introduced. In a short time, teams began to help their own team members and even offer assistance to other teams.

Training.   Many organizations conduct training programs in which employees learn to prevent, anticipate, and cope with conflict. They are given the chance to practice techniques of conflict resolution. They can assess their own conflict reaction style and learn how to use more than one style.

SPECIAL ROLES AND STRUCTURES

Additional steps must be taken in order to manage interdependences and to resolve disputes when they appear. Special organizational roles and some structural changes may have to be introduced to manage conflict.

Liaison Roles and Integrators.   If two or three units in an organization are often in conflict, we might expect that a higher-level manager would deal with it. For example, an executive vice president should be able to manage conflict among sales, production, and research divisions. Many companies have found this not to be the case and that additional roles called **liaison** or **integrator roles** are necessary [14]. Figure 14.10 shows these in a typical manufacturing firm. Sometimes a single individual can assume these roles, and sometimes it can be a committee.

People who fill these roles are expected to coordinate the groups and reduce conflict. They are responsible for holding meetings, supplying information, and seeing to it that employees keep in touch with each other when necessary. Sometimes liaisons and integrators have the authority to give orders or make decisions and tell the units what needs to be done. In other instances, they can only assist and advise.

Employees in these roles must have respect and credibility so they can influence the units they are coordinating. They must be knowledgeable about the needs and the technology of the units involved. They are more effective if they can lead discussions and help others to deal with disagreements. It is also useful if liaisons and integrators are not biased in any way. They cannot for example favor personnel over sales, or the machine shop over shipping. This helps them to act fairly and in an evenhanded way. They should also be oriented toward the good of the whole organization rather than only part of it.

☐ **FIGURE 14.10**   *Examples of Integrator and Liaison Roles in a Manufacturing Firm*

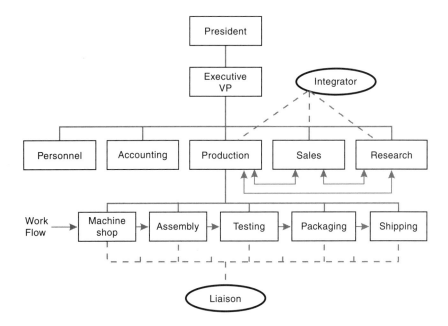

Relocate or Recombine Units.   Sometimes employees might be moved to new locations in the organization. In one company engineers were moved out of an engineering division into the manufacturing division. They were responsible for improving production methods and caused less conflict when they reported directly to production managers. Engineers also work directly with customers in some companies. For instance, a diesel engine manufacturer has field engineers work with truck manufacturers and owners who buy the diesel engines. A customer engineering unit can be located within the sales division instead of within the engineering division.

Relocation of personnel and units can reduce conflict considerably. Before the relocation, engineers were often caught between the production or sales managers and their own bosses in the engineering division. They often felt the dual influence in trying to follow their own superiors' requests while meeting the needs of managers in production or sales. The relocation eliminated the cross pressures and helped to prevent a good deal of conflict.

Ombudsman.   An **ombudsman** is a person who is assigned to hear complaints and mediate disputes between parties in an organization. The ombudsman must be a respected person with problem-solving and conflict resolution skills. Ombudsmen have been used increasingly in some business settings. They are frequently found in universities to deal with many problems such as the complaint of a student who feels unjustly treated by a professor. Meetings between the ombudsman and the parties involved can be used to try to reach a settlement or decide what to do if they cannot agree on a mutually acceptable solution.

463

Ombudsmen usually maintain a confidential relationship, just like a lawyer or minister, and never discuss or reveal the dispute without the consent of the parties involved. They might encourage the parties to involve others, but they will not do so unless approved by both parties.

Organization Design.   Conflict can be also managed through the effective design of the organization structure. Organization design was covered in Chapter 2. As we said, the structure that is chosen solves some problems but creates others.

SUMMARY

Since organizations involve so much interdependence between individuals and groups, conflict can easily arise and become a serious threat to organizational effectiveness. We do not assert that all conflict is bad, because conflict, if not at an excessive level, can be functional or useful to the organization. It can add to creativity, be a sign of health, and bring different points of view to the attention of decision makers.

Conflict is a dynamic process. It is first perceived and experienced. This may produce feelings of anger, inequity, or other emotional reactions in one or all parties involved. Then the conflict can become manifest and result in actions and reactions, at which point it may be suppressed or resolved. Finally, the aftermath can be either negative or positive. Conflict episodes set the stage for either higher levels of conflict or cooperation in the future.

A number of conditions are related to conflict and cooperation in organizations. Some of these have to do with individuals. For example, people may have values or personalities that clash, or differences in perceptions and needs. Situational forces are also triggers to conflict. Conflict is more likely when the parties need to interact and when they are interdependent with each other. Status differences, ambiguity in responsibility and authority, and specialization are also contributors.

Once conflict occurs, people can react in different ways. One party can accommodate the other, or the parties may compromise. Another style is to avoid and withdraw from the situation. Others prefer to pursue their own interests at the expense of another by engaging in competition. Finally, it is possible to collaborate, which involves trying to find a solution to the conflict that is mutually acceptable to both parties.

Confrontation techniques to resolve conflict have been suggested. These include integrative decision methods and principled negotiation, both collaborative strategies. Third parties can be used in these techniques, as is done in mediation and arbitration.

A number of approaches have been devised to reduce the incidence of conflict where it is possible and desirable to do so. One is to use superordinate goals. Another is to alter or remove conditions that cause unnecessary conflict. Changes can be made in procedures, resource allocations, assignments of personnel, rewards, and communications. Integrating and liaison roles can help. Units can be combined or relocated.

☐ KEY CONCEPTS _____

Accommodating	Confrontation	Manifest conflict
Antecedents of conflict	Consensus	Mediation
Arbitration	decision	Negotiating and
Avoiding	Integrative	bargaining
Collaborating	decision	Ombudsman
Competing	method (IDM)	Perceived conflict
Compromising	Jurisdictional	Principled negotiation
Conflict	disputes	Superordinate goals
Conflict aftermath	Latent conflict	Suppression
Conflict management	Liaison roles and	
Conflict resolution	integrators	

☐ STUDY QUESTIONS

1. Define and describe the various stages in the conflict process.
2. Describe a work situation you are familiar with in which you identify (a) preventable conflict conditions, (b) inevitable conflict conditions, and (c) conditions where conflict is a sign of organizational health and effectiveness.
3. Show how individual characteristics and situational factors operate as antecedents or causes of conflict.
4. Cite five organization structure characteristics and show how each one contributes to the likelihood of conflict.
5. Describe the five major styles of reacting to conflict. For each one, show how and where it is particularly useful.
6. Which is your preferred and backup style of conflict resolution? When do you switch from your preferred to your backup style?
7. What are the implications of overusing a particular style of conflict resolution?
8. Which style(s) do you rarely use in dealing with conflict? What are the risks or costs of not using the style(s) enough?
9. Define and differentiate between the roles of arbitrators and mediators.
10. Describe the major steps in the Integrative Decision Method and indicate why each step is useful.
11. What are the four major guidelines suggested by the principled negotiation technique? Give an example of how to use each guideline.
12. Describe five organizational practices that might help to prevent or reduce the severity of conflict.
13. Can you identify situations in which liaison roles or ombudsmen are good techniques for conflict management? Are there costs in using such roles, and are the costs worth it?

CASE

☐ DEDHAM GENERAL HOSPITAL

Dedham General Hospital is located in a medium-sized suburban community. It serves a large portion of the surrounding area and is usually operating at or beyond its capacity.

Each floor of the hospital has its own particular structure with regard to the nurses who staff it. The formal hierarchy runs from the supervisor (a registered nurse) to registered nurses (RNs) to licensed practical nurses (LPNs) to students and nurses' aides. Professionally, there are some duties that are supposed to be performed only by the RNs; these are spelled out in the hospital manual. In practice, however, the LPNs do much of the work that is supposed to be done only by RNs. The RNs are happy with this because they are very busy with other duties. Over a long period of time, the RNs and the LPNs have worked out how to get the required tasks done quite efficiently, without thinking of whose job it's supposed to be. The hospital is normally so crowded that, even with everyone performing all types of work, there never seems to be enough time or enough help.

A current sticky point in the hospital is vacation privileges. They are different for the various groups of nurses. RNs receive two weeks' vacation after nine months on the job while LPNs must work at Dedham for ten years before being eligible for the second week of vacation. The LPNs believe this is extremely unfair and have been trying to have the privileges somewhat more equalized. Their efforts have met with little cooperation and no success. The hospital administration has simply told them that the vacation privileges are those stated in the hospital manual and that they see no need to change them.

The Dedham Hospital Procedure Manual was developed in the 1950s. It has not been revised since. Everyone knows that it is outdated and there is little similarity between what is done now and the manual. Nearly everything has changed since it was written.

Some of the nurses at Dedham decided to take matters into their own hands. The LPNs on the fourth floor decided that if the manual was to be followed for vacation privileges, they would follow it in all phases, going strictly according to the book.

This is when the difficulties started. The RNs have more work than they can handle, and the LPNs are just as busy only doing their "prescribed" duties. Both are exerting as much effort as before, but less is being accomplished because of the need to jump around from place to place and job to job to work strictly according to the manual. An example of this is taking doctors' orders by telephone. When doctors phone in the type of treatment that a patient is to receive—medicines, times for dispensing such,

☐ DEDHAM GENERAL . . .

diet, and so forth—the manual prescribes that the order is to be taken by an RN. However, in practice whoever was nearest the phone would take the order. If an LPN took the order, she had it signed by the supervisor (stationed at the desk) as a safeguard. This saved the time and effort involved in getting an RN to the phone for every order. Now, however, since they are working according to the manual, the LPNs refuse to take the doctors' orders. They call for an RN when a doctor is on the phone. The RN has to leave the work she is doing, go to the phone, take the order, then go back to her unfinished work. This procedure wastes the time of the doctor, the RN, and the person who had to locate the RN. Going by the book has raised hostile feelings among both groups of nurses and among the doctors who work on the floor. Many believe this has led to a reduction in the high quality of patient care.

The conflict brought on by the vacation privileges controversy resulted in other complaints. In the manual, the categories described for vacation privileges are "supervisors," "RNs," "lab technicians," and "others." The LPNs resented being placed in the "others" category, believing that they deserved a separate listing because they have the same amount of training as other professionals, such as the lab technicians. Adding further fuel to the fire was the fact that the lab technicians got a second week of vacation after only one year at the hospital. Another problem was that RNs were allowed to sign themselves in on the job when they reported, whereas the LPNs were required to punch in. The LPNs' time was carefully monitored. They were docked in salary for any time missed.

The RNs complained to the hospital administration more vehemently than ever about being understaffed. They felt that there should be more RNs on every floor on every shift. The shortage was especially acute at nights when unfamiliarity with individual patients often led to mix-ups in the treatments.

The ill feelings led the nurses to argue among themselves. The LPNs felt that they were always doing more work than the RNs, that they spent more time with the patients because the RNs had more to do at the desk, and that they know more about treatments because they more often accompanied doctors on their rounds. They now voiced these opinions. The RNs argued that they were superior because of their longer and more extensive formal training.

All these factors combined to bring about a tremendous drop in morale and a marked decrease in efficiency, and the conflict was in danger of spreading to the other floors in the hospital.

☐ DEDHAM GENERAL . . .

QUESTIONS

1. Why is there such conflict between these groups?
2. What are the consequences of this conflict?
3. What might be done to alleviate the problem?

We express our appreciation to Thomas Kolakowski, who wrote the original version of this case, for permission to use it.

REFERENCES

1. Ancona, D.G. Outward bound strategies for team survival in an organization. *Academy of Management Journal,* 1990 33:2, 334-365.
2. Argyris, C. Skilled incompetence. *Harvard Business Review,* September- October 1986, 64, 74-79.
3. Blake, R.R., and Mouton, J.S. *Building a dynamic corporation through grid organization development.* Reading, MA: Addison-Wesley, 1969.
4. Cosier, R.A. and Dalton, D.R. Positive effects of conflict: A field assessment. *International Journal of Conflict Management,* 1990, 1, 81-92.
5. England, G.W., Agarwal, N.C., and Trerise, R.E. Union leaders and managers: A comparison of value systems. *Industrial Relations,* 1971, 10, 211-26.
6. Filley, A.C. Interpersonal conflict resolution. Glenview, IL: Scott, Foresman, 1975.
7. Fisher, R., and Ury, W. *Getting to yes: Negotiating agreement without giving in.* Boston:Houghton Mifflin, 1981.
8. Foldberg, J., and Taylor, A. Mediation: A comprehensive guide to resolving conflict without litigation. San Francisco: Jossey-Bass, Inc., 1985.
9. Hall, J. *Conflict management survey.* Houston, TX: Teleometrics, 1969.
10. Hickson, D.J., Hinings, C.R., Lee, C.A., Schneck, R., and Pennings, J.M. A strategic contingency theory of intraorganizational power. *Administrative Science Quarterly,* 1971, 16, 216-29.
11. Kerr, S. On the folly of rewarding A while hoping for B. *Academy of Management Journal,* 1975, 18, 769-83.
12. Kojima, H.A. Significant stride toward the comparative study of control. *American Psychologist,* 1984, 39, 972-73.
13. Kolb, D.M. and Bartinek, J.M. (Eds). *Hidden conflict in organizations,* Newbury Park, CA: Sage, 1992.
14. Lawrence, P.R., and Lorsch, J.W. *Organization and environment: Managing differentiation and integration.* Homewood, IL: Richard D. Irwin, 1969.
15. Lawrence, P.R., and Seiler, J.A. Experiments in structural design. In P.R. Lawrence and J.A. Seiler, eds. *Organizational behavior and administration.* Homewood, IL: Richard D. Irwin, 1965.
16. Lawrence, P.R., Barnes, L.B., and Lorsch, J.W., eds. *Organizational behavior and administration,* 3d ed. Homewood, IL: Richard D. Irwin, 1976.

17. Lorsch, J.W., and Morse, J. *Organizations and their members: A contingency approach.* New York: Harper & Row, 1974.

18. Mayer, R.J. *Conflict management: The courage to confront,* Columbus, OH: Battelle Press, 1990.

19. McGillicuddy, N.B., Welton, G.L., and Pruitt, D.G. Third-party intervention: A field experiment comparing three different models. *Journal of Personality and Social Psychology,* 1987, 53, 104-12.

20. Miner, J.B. *Studies in management education.* New York: Springer Publishing, 1965.

21. Moore, C. *The mediation process.* San Francisco: Jossey-Bass, 1986.

22. Nelson, R.E. The strength of strong ties: Social networks and intergroup conflict in organizations. Academy of Management Journal, 1989. Vol. 32, 377-401.

23. Pinkley, R.L. Dimensions of conflict frame: Disputant interpretations of conflict. *Journal of Applied Psychology,* 1990. Vol 75, 117-26.

24. Pondy, L.R. Organizational conflict: Concepts and models. *Administrative Science Quarterly,* 1967, 12, 296-320.

25. Pondy, L.R. Varieties of organizational conflict. *Administrative Science Quarterly,* 1969, 14, 499-506.

26. Rahim, M.A. A strategy for managing conflict in complex organizations. *Human Relations,* January 1985, 38, 81-89.

27. Rizzo, J.R., House, R.J., and Lirtzman, S.I. Role conflict and ambiguity in complex organizations: A review of the literature and development and validation of measurement scales. *Administrative Science Quarterly,* 1970, 15, 150-63.

28. Stulberg, J.B. *Taking charge/managing conflict.* Lexington, MA: Lexington Books, 1987.

29. Thomas, K.W. Conflict and conflict management. In M.D. Dunnette, ed. *Handbook of industrial and organizational psychology.* Chicago: Rand McNally, 1976, 889-935.

30. Thomas, K.W. Toward multidimensional values in teaching: The example of conflict behaviors. *Academy of Management Review,* 1977, 2, 484-90.

31. Thomas, K.W. Conflict and negotiation processes in organizations. In M.D. Dunnette, ed. *Handbook of industrial and organizational psychology* (2nd ed.), Palo Alto, CA: Consulting Psychologists Press, 1990.

32. Thomas, K.W., and Kilmann, R.H. *Conflict mode instrument.* Tuxedo, NY: Xicom, 1974.

33. Thompson, J.D. *Organizations in action.* New York: McGraw-Hill, 1967.

34. Ting-Toomey, S., Gao, G., Trubisky, P., Yang, Z., Kim, H.S., Lin, S.L., and Nishids, T. Culture, face maintenance and styles of handling interpersonal conflict: A study in five cultures. *International Journal of Conflict Management,* 1991, 2, 275-296.

35. Tjovsold, D. *Managing work relationships: Cooperation, conflict and power.* Lexington, MA: Lexington Books, 1986.

36. Tjosvold, D. *The conflict positive organization.* Reading, MA: Addison-Wesley, 1991.

37. Ury, W. *Getting past no: Negotiating with difficult people*, NY: Bantam Books, 1991.

38. Walton, R.E., Dutton, J.M., and Cafferty, T.P. Organizational context and inter-departmental conflict. *Administrative Science Quarterly*, 1969, 14, 522-42.

39. Weisz, J.R., Rothbaum, F.M., and Blackburn, T.C. Standing out and standing in: The psychology of control in America and Japan. *American Psychologist*, 1984, 39, 955-69.

40. Whyte, W.F. The social structure of the restaurant. *American Journal of Sociology*, 1949, 54, 302-10.

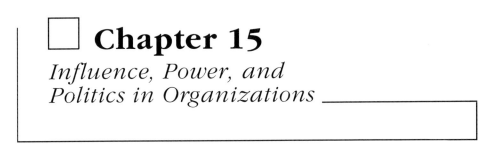

Chapter 15

Influence, Power, and
Politics in Organizations

It's 4:30 P.M. in the office of Canto and McConaughey, a CPA firm. The staff is starting to close the office for the weekend. An important client comes into the reception area and asks to see Sam Canto. She is shown into Sam's office. Fifteen minutes later she and Sam reappear. Sam is assuring her. "Don't worry," he says. "I'll put one of our best people on it. We'll have the work ready for you Monday at noon." The client smiles and thanks Sam. After she leaves, Sam picks up a phone and dials Gerry Pfaff, a young accountant who has been with Canto and McConaughey for four years and may become a partner next year.

"Gerry," Sam says, "I've got a problem. Pat Simmons has to have some work ready by Monday at noon. Since you do most of her work, can you get it done by then? It means work tonight and probably most of the weekend." As he listened to Gerry's answer, he nodded a few times and then smiled. "Thanks, Gerry," Sam Said, "I know this will take a lot of time. I hope it won't be too inconvenient for your family."

Why was Gerry Pfaff willing to work outside regular hours? Perhaps she needed the extra pay for overtime. Perhaps she owed Sam a favor, or maybe she was afraid she might not become a partner if she didn't work the weekend. Perhaps she did it because, as a professional, she felt it was her responsibility. What seems to be a very simple response to a simple request may have a complex explanation.

In this chapter and the next, we examine why and how people comply. In particular in this chapter, we will discuss the issues of influence, power, and politics, which arise in every organization. These processes bind people together in different ways. We will also discuss different types of power, how it is acquired, how it is used, how it is maintained, and how it is related to different types of organizations.

A MODEL OF INFLUENCE PROCESSES IN ORGANIZATIONS

In the example above, Sam has engaged in an influence attempt, and Gerry has engaged in an act of compliance. Influence attempts occur when legitimate authority or power is used. These relationships are shown in Figure 15.1. It shows that the bases for influence in organizations are the psychological contract, legitimate authority, and power. It also shows that influence attempts lead to results intended by the influence agent or to a modification of the relationship between the influence agent and the target.

☐ **FIGURE 15.1**   *The Bases of Influence in Organizations*

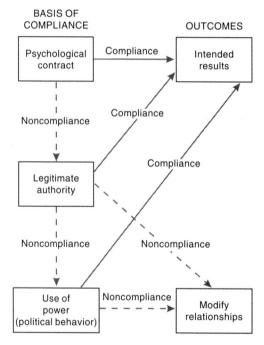

Influence is a process through which a person attempts to extract **compliance** with his or her intentions from others. For influence to exist, two parties (A and B) must be in an interactive and dependent relationship. This means that the actions of A can affect the actions of B, and vice versa. Influence occurs when one of the parties (A) induces the other (B) to respond in an intended way. For example, Gerry Pfaff may be dependent upon Sam Canto's CPA firm for a job and income. She will be less dependent if she has other employment opportunities. Likewise, the CPA firm is dependent upon her for the work she can do. It will be more dependent when there is a shortage of competent accountants and less dependent when there is not.

In an organization, there may be different motivational basis for a **dependence** [5]. In some cases, a person wants to join an organization or interact with another person because they share important values. This is usually the case for those who join political parties or religious organizations or become involved with ideological causes. The basis of these relationships is **commitment**, a strong, positive involvement in the dependence relationship. Zaleznick makes a very important point about this for managers: *a manager should not mistake compliance for commitment* [37]. Compliance can occur for other reasons, as we will see.

In other cases, a dependence relationship may be forced, as when a person is put in a jail or a mental institution. In this case, the person experiences **alienation** and wants to escape from the relationship. Then, dependence relationships must usually be maintained by force.

The third type of dependence relationship is **calculative involvement**, in which both parties assess the economic costs and benefits of maintaining the relationship. According to Etzioni, this is the type of dependence relationship that dominates most work organizations [5]. However, it is obvious that some levels of both commitment and alienation also occur frequently in work organizations.

The strength of influence one party has over another is a function of two factors. One is the *need to maintain the relationship*. When a person has a choice about whether or not to remain in a relationship, less influence can be exerted than when the relationship is necessary. A person with strong political beliefs who is a member of a party which espouses similar strong beliefs will be influenced much more by party leaders than another with weaker beliefs. The second factor, *power asymmetry*, is related to the first, but it is not necessarily the same thing. Power asymmetry means that one party (B) is more dependent upon the other, giving the other (A) more capacity to influence.

BASES OF INFLUENCES

The **psychological contract** is the basis for the distinction between legitimate authority and power which we use in this chapter. The **psychological contract** is the mutual set of expectations that exist between an organization and an individual. These expectations cover what pay the individual will receive as well as "the whole pattern of rights and privileges" of the person [28]. In return, the individual is expected to contribute both work and some commitment. As long as requests, commands, and directives fall within the boundaries of the psychological contract, the person will comply. Take the case of the accountant whose psychological contract is shown in Figure 15.2. In general, the accountant will do anything that falls within the boundary of the psychological contract.

However, there are two types of boundaries, *public* and *real*. The **public boundary** includes those activities that the person wants others, especially his or her superior, to believe are the elements of the psychological contract. In this example, the accountant wants the supervisor to believe that it is her job to work regular hours and to perform assigned auditing tasks.

In some instances, the accountant may be asked to do something that falls outside the public boundary, but inside the real boundary. The **real boundary** represents the "true" limits of the psychological contract. In our example, we show two activities that fall in this zone, working overtime and doing tax work. For obvious reasons, the accountant will want the supervisor to believe the psychological contract is constrained by the public boundaries because compliance with requests that fall between the real and public boundaries will make it appear that she is "doing a favor" for which there might be some quid pro quo—a favor in return for exceeding the requirements of the job.

☐ **FIGURE 15.2** *Boundaries of the Psychological Contract*

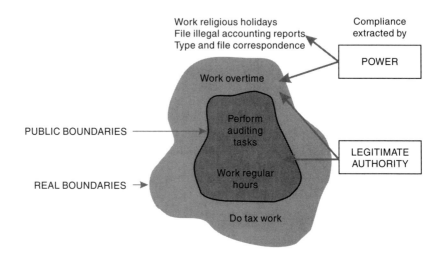

These boundaries are not static; they change. Sometimes they change by mutual consent, as when a person's job changes by promotion. Sometimes they change through the use of power exercised by another person.

We define all those requests from a superior which fall within the real boundary of the psychological contract and are accepted by the subordinate as legitimate authority. Power is used to extract compliance to requests which fall outside the real boundary, and sometimes it is used for directives which fall between the real and public boundaries.

Legitimate Authority. **Legitimate authority** is the right of decision and command that a person has over others. It is sanctioned, or approved, by those in the organization. Legitimate authority is embedded in the psychological contract and, through it, a superior can expect a subordinate to comply with organizationally sanctioned requests.

Legitimacy of authority refers to whether or not the person who is the subject of influence (B) believes that it is right and proper for another (A) to exert influence or attempt to exert it. Sam Canto would be exercising legitimate authority by requesting Gerry Pfaff to work overtime when it is part of the psychological contract. Sam Canto might fire Gerry Pfaff if she refuses to work overtime, and he could do so because the legitimate authority structure may contain those managerial rights for use in the case of noncompliance.

Legitimate authority is reflected in the organization's structure, which defines the general distribution of legitimate authority by position location. Higher-level positions have more legitimate authority than those at lower levels. Further, because legitimate authority accrues to a person as a function of their organization position, it is transferable from one person to another. This means that when a person leaves a position, he or she no longer has the authority associated with that position. It now is the right of the person who replaced the previous incumbent.

Different types of organizations will have different patterns of the distribution of legitimate authority [31]. For example, in mechanistic organizations there will be relatively highly centralized authority, policy, and decision making mechanisms. In addition, the distribution of legitimate authority will be somewhat stable over long periods of time because there are fewer external pressures to change it. On the other hand, in organic organizations, the legitimate authority structure is less stable and will change as the environment of the organization changes and the firm adapts to it. Authority will be less centralized and exist in closer proximity to the projects that are being done in the firm. There may also be instances of dual authority, as personnel are assigned to different projects or have both technical and functional supervisors, as would be the case in the matrix organization.

The organization culture will also reflect the legitimate authority structure. When large differences in authority exist between levels of managers, there will most likely be very significant differences in the symbols that represent status. Managers at the top level may have spacious, well-decorated offices set in very desirable locations in the headquarters building, whereas those at the next lower level may have smaller, less attractive offices.

The acceptance of legitimate authority stems from several sources. First, every culture has a concept of legitimate authority in which it is generally accepted that some forms of authority as well as relationships between superiors and subordinates are appropriate while other forms and relationships are not. For example, highly-centralized authority is culturally acceptable in some Latin countries (for example, Italy and Spain) whereas a more even distribution of authority across different organizational levels is preferred in Anglo-Saxon countries (the United Kingdom, Canada, and the United States) [9].

Second, when a person joins an organization, its culture is transmitted through organization socialization. An important theme in this process is to rationalize the authority structure of the organization so that members accept it as legitimate.

Third, the individual's organization orientation, initially developed by general socialization, affects legitimacy. The organizationalist usually has little trouble with most directives from higher levels. The professional may see many directives as less legitimate and respond more readily to influence attempts from colleagues. The indifferent responds primarily to reasonable job demands made during working hours and probably views everything else as nonlegitimate.

Power. **Power** is a force that can be used to extract compliance, but it differs from legitimate authority. Power is not sanctioned by the psychological contract, whereas legitimate authority is [24]. The use of power, in fact, distorts the boundaries of the psychological contract. This is possible because the boundaries of the psychological contract are flexible and can be modified, even though it may take considerable force to do so. The use of power in an organization is called **organization politics** by Pfeffer [24].

Power can be used to achieve organizationally sanctioned ends or the ends desired by the political actor. A person pressured to act in an organizationally unacceptable way may comply to avoid undesirable consequences. Suppose that Canto and McConaughey's culture supports ethical behavior in its practice. Gerry finds that the client is subject to a large penalty for failing to report a certain capital gain. When she reports this to Sam Canto, she is told that it would be best if she forgot about it. Gerry might act unethically, at great personal and psychological costs, because becoming a partner is important to her. Sam has exercised power, not legitimate authority.

People often respond to power even when they are not threatened with physical harm or with economic loss. People often comply when it is exercised by someone with legitimate authority who exerts influence beyond that limit. This has been shown dramatically in research by Milgram [21]. Subjects were asked to assist the experimenter in a study of the effects of punishment on learning. The subject was asked to be the teacher. The experimenter's confederate acted as the "learner." The confederate was taken to a separate room where he could be heard but not seen. The experimenter then showed the subject how to operate an alleged shock generator. The subject was instructed to apply shock whenever the "learner" gave a wrong answer, and to increase it when more wrong answers were given. Shock switches ranged from 15 to 450 volts and were labeled from "slight shock" through "danger: severe shock" to the highest two levels, which were simply marked "XXX." Although no shock was actually administered, the subject was led to believe that it was. When mildly shocked, the confederate groaned. As the shock levels increased, the reaction accelerated to shouts, screams, and cries to quit the experiment. After 330 volts, the confederate became silent. The experimenter prodded the subject to administer stronger shocks when the subject resisted. In one experiment, 63 percent of 40 male subjects, 20 to 50 years old, applied the maximum 450 volts. Milgram replicated these findings in over 20 experiments. Remarkably, over 75 percent of the subjects reported they were glad to have participated, while only 1 percent expressed regret, *despite the fact that many subjects exhibited stress symptoms while administering the shock.*

Milgram found that when the "learner" was brought into the same room, full obedience dropped 40 percent. When the experimenter delivered orders by phone, or when a lower-status person filled in for the experimenter, compliance dropped to about 20 percent. Nevertheless, all these percentages are very high. Such experiments make us question how far people will go in compliance to authority.

A person may possess different types of power [7]. The ability to reward or to coerce can extract compliance. So can being an expert or being charismatic.

1. **Reward Power. Reward power** is when one person has control over rewards desired by another. The more highly valued the rewards, the greater the power. Individuals in positions with high levels of legitimate authority have the right to make decisions about the allocation of rewards and promotions based on organizationally rationalized cri-

teria. When they use organizationally sanctioned criteria, it is the use of legitimate authority—not the use of reward power. However, reward power can be enacted through politics as a result of a person having legitimate authority. It could happen this way. Based on our Good Enough Theory of Promotion (see Chapter 6) a candidate for promotion doesn't have to be the most qualified person for a job but must be good enough to enter the selection pool. Usually these criterion are clearly specified and organizationally sanctioned. From that pool, a person is selected who, usually, has the "right" perspective as assessed by the judges. This is especially true when criteria and the judgments may reflect power enactment, not legitimate authority. In this sense, we can say that promotions in organizations are "political" decisions.

2. **Coercive Power. Coercive power** in an organization exists for the same reason that reward power does. The difference is that instead of rewarding another person, punishment is threatened or applied. Returning to the example of promotions, those who make decisions can exercise their judgment against individuals in punitive ways. For example, in one organization, a manager was removed from a position because her supervisor maintained that she wasn't performing well and wasn't a "team player." In several instances, she was late with reports and had experienced some problems working with other managers at her level. When the complete set of facts was analyzed, however, it was found that her unit was among the most productive, her subordinates among the best in the firm, and her customers the most satisfied. However, she had openly disagreed with her boss in meetings, and frequently she was right. She was replaced by another manager who was equally effective. The decision to remove her was justified on the basis that the managerial team would be able to work better together. The short-run effect on the organization was not significantly bad, but it was very clear to the other managers that more than competence was necessary to succeed in the firm.

3. **Expert Power.** We rely on and accept recommendations from accountants, lawyers, and physicians because we believe they have the knowledge to make better decisions in their specific area of competence. The same thing happens in work organizations. For instance, in designing and implementing a management information system, systems experts will design the system, specify equipment, and dictate how it should be used. **Expert power** usually takes time to develop; a person normally spends much time in formal training or developing skills on the job before this type of influence is acquired. Expert power is very task- and person-specific. For example, a systems expert may have a lot of influence in implementing computer information systems but no influence in the design of compensation plans for managers. Because of its specificity, expert power cannot easily be transferred from one person to another as legitimate

authority can. For instance, a new plant manager will have the same legitimate authority as the previous manager. He or she may even be able to extend it so as to develop reward and coercive power, as we discussed above. But expert power develops from demonstrating competence or having it "given" by others because the person has the appropriate education, certification, experience, and appearance. When a person with expert power leaves the organization, the replacement may *not* have the same amount of expert influence.

4. **Charismatic Power.** When individuals are susceptible to influence because they identify with another person, the type of power is called **charismatic power** [7]. It is based on the feeling of oneness that a person has with another, or the desire for that feeling. Charismatic power is based on personal attraction to be like the other. The stronger the attraction, the stronger the power. People who have charismatic power are called charismatic leaders. A person with charismatic power is

> set apart from "ordinary" [persons] and treated as endowed with supernatural or superhuman or, at least, specifically exceptional powers or qualities not accessible to the normal person. . . . What is important is how the individual is actually regarded by followers [34].

Some political leaders who have been called charismatic are Ronald Reagan, John F. Kennedy, Fidel Castro, and Mikhail Gorbachev. Ross Perot and Lee Iacocca are business leaders who fall into this category. Charismatic leaders engender

> unusually high trust in the correctness of the leader's beliefs, affection for the leader, willing obedience to the leader, identification with the leader, emotional involvement of the follower in the mission, heightened goals of the follower, and the feeling on the part of the follower that he or she will be able to accomplish the mission or contribute to its accomplishment [10].

Like expert power, charismatic power cannot be transferred from one person to another. However, it can become **institutionalized power** when charismatic power is transformed into legitimate authority [34]. An organization founded by a charismatic leader will attract followers and, as the number of followers increases, the beginnings of a hierarchy emerge. The charismatic leader appoints others to assist and delegates power to them to make some decisions. Others in the organization comply because they know that these persons are chosen by the leader. Eventually rules, policies, and procedures begin to develop in which the philosophy and practices of the leader are embedded. When the leader dies or leaves, the system of authority stays and becomes the structure of legitimate authority in an organization [6]. As time goes on, the members comply with influence attempts that, by now, have become reasonable and proper. When new members enter the organization, they experience socialization based on this system of legitimate authority [25].

Figure 15.1 shows that influence attempts lead to intended results or to a modification of the relationship between the influence agent and the target.

Intended Results. **Intended results** are the outcomes of influence attempts that are desired by the party that exerted the influence. From an organization's perspective, compliance should lead to organizationally valued results, such as high productivity and profitability.

In the case of Gerry Pfaff, there could be an organizational norm (or even a formal requirement) that when such emergencies arise, the staff member responsible for the account stays and works.

Results may also be intended because they are the wishes of a particular person but *are not* part of the organizational requirements for an employee. If, for example Gerry was not directly responsible to Sam Canto and not involved with the Simmons account, Canto might still exercise influence. He may have made Gerry aware that she would be evaluated for a partnership in the firm and that by working, she would be showing loyalty. In this case, the intended result is Sam's intention, but not the organization's.

Usually when legitimate authority, charismatic power, or expert power is used, the target person will react in a way intended by the power agent. The psychological response of the influence target is called **acceptance**. He or she will engage in the desired behavior, as well as rationalizing and justifying his or her compliance as being the right way to behave. In fact, that is exactly the response to legitimate authority by the personality type we have called the organizationalist (see Chapter 4).

Charismatic power and expert power also lead to acceptance. When charismatic power is accepted, the target's justification is ideological and normative. For expert power, the acceptance is rationalized by the belief that the competence of the expert is necessary to satisfy the target's needs.

There can be acceptance when reward or coercive power is used. This is particularly true when these types of power are the extension of legitimate authority; that is, when a person with legitimate authority exercises power in a political way. For acceptance under these conditions, the power agent must seek organizationally approved outcomes. When managers use their positions to force others to be more productive and efficient, these attempts are frequently accepted and may ultimately be rationalized.

Modification of Relationships. When a target of influence resists or fails to comply with the influence attempt, there is usually some modification of the relationship between the actors. Conventionally, the idea is usually that the influence agent, particularly when it is a manager, can take some action such as firing or disciplining the target, usually a subordinate. For instance, if Gerry Pfaff violates some organizational norm, Sam might fire or discipline her in some way. There are other ways a superior could act, such as assigning her to less desirable projects, not supporting her for promotion and pay increases, or changing their personal relationship at work.

There are also ways that the target of the influence can modify the relationship, which is most likely to occur when reward or coercive power are used. One way is by resistance, which could take several forms.

Appeals to reason is one resistance strategy. Minimal compliance with the influence attempt is another effective resistance strategy. This can be done by following the letter of the law and not the spirit. When air traffic controllers in the United States want to engage in protest, they often do so by slowing down landings at large airports such as Chicago and Atlanta by following the exact requirements to maintain the necessary distance between landing planes, which creates delays. Outright sabotage is another way to resist. This may be done by tactics from delaying the implementation of decisions to actually destroying information or damaging equipment.

Development of a counter force is another way to resist power. Influence targets who wish to resist power may try to develop their own power base, using approaches to acquiring power discussed in this chapter. They may develop coalitions, increase expertise, influence the environment, or acquire a sponsor. Success at any of these strategies will modify the balance of power.

Leaving the organization is perhaps the final act of resistance. An individual who cannot accommodate to the power structure or modify it may simply quit and find another better situation in which to live and work.

ORGANIZATIONAL AND PERSONAL BASES OF INFLUENCE

In some instances, the basis for influence is a function of being in some organizational position while in other instances influence is strictly due to some personal attribute, or set of attributes, of the influence agent.

Organizational-based Influence. Obviously a person in a higher-level position has more legitimate authority than another lower in the hierarchy, making legitimate authority a type of **organizationally based influence**. Further, the experiments by Milgram demonstrate that a person may have organizational based power, which is the capacity to influence others beyond the range of legitimate authority, as we have discussed earlier [21].

There are other types of position effects. Often a job description will give a person *control over information* desired by others. This is a source of power to the person in the position. Similarly, if a person *controls access to key people*, power accrues. Executive secretaries and high level staff assistants are likely to have influence because of this. Also, some people are in jobs where they seem to have some *perceived influence over the futures of others*, such as the personnel executive who handles transfers, assignments, and personnel reductions.

Personal-based Influence. **Personal-based influence** accrues to an individual who possesses attributes or skills desired by others. These attributes are usually independent of the organization's control. There are two types of personal-based influence. One is **expert power** which exists when a person has competence required by others. The other is **charismatic power**, when one person becomes psychologically dependent upon another.

ACQUIRING AND MAINTAINING ORGANIZATIONAL-BASED INFLUENCE

The pattern of power and influence relationships among units in an organization is called the **power structure**. For example, the marketing department may be more powerful than the human resource department and the finance group more powerful than both of them. However, the distribution of organizational power and influence is never what it appears to be on organization charts and in job descriptions. It is affected by a combination of situational factors and individual characteristics. For example, deans in a university do not have equal influence and power in the budgeting process. If they did, then budgets would be allocated to colleges on the basis of the number of students served and the cost of instruction. While these factors do count, a study by Pfeffer and Salancik shows that a department's or college's power also affects how much money it gets [26]. Some colleges are more important than others, and some deans have stronger predispositions to use influence and power than others.

In this section we will first consider situational factors that affect the power structure of an organization, accounting for some key differences in legitimate authority between subunits. Then we will examine individual characteristics related to the acquisition of legitimate authority and the propensity to extend it to become reward and punishment power. Finally, we will suggest how organization-based influence may be perpetuated.

SITUATIONAL DETERMINANTS OF ORGANIZATION-BASED INFLUENCE

Obviously, more important organization units have more power than those that are less important. But saying this is not enough—what is it about a subunit that makes it more important? The **strategic contingency theory** of organizational power explains power differences (see Figure 15.3) [8]. A subunit' power depends on whether or not, or how much, it controls strategic contingencies for the organization. "A contingency is a requirement of one subunit that is affected by the activities of another subunit" [8]. There are three conditions that make a contingency strategic.

1. **Coping with Volatility.** Organization subunits that interact with more volatile, threatening, and uncertain environments have more power than those that interact with stable ones. If a subunit can successfully interpret an unclear environment and help the organization cope effectively, it will be able to influence policy and strategy. This is why technical personnel will be influential in a technology-dominated mixed organization and marketing personnel powerful in the market-dominated mixed organization (see Chapter 2).

2. **Substitutability of Activities.** When there is no **substitutability of activities** of a subunit, that subunit will be very powerful. This is one reason why the research and development function in firms in stable environments is less powerful than when the technological environment is volatile. In the stable environment, routine research methods and analysis will be used and there are probably many people who could perform them, thus making it easy to find substitutes.

481

☐ **FIGURE 15.3**   *Factors Affecting Power from Strategic Contingency Theory*

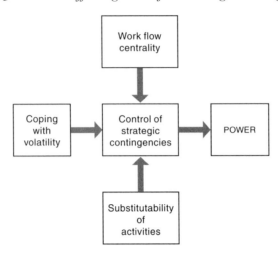

3. **Work Flow Centrality. Work flow centrality** has two aspects. The first is the extent to which departmental activities are directly linked to other units. Units with high work flow centrality are interconnected with many others. Most accounting departments have high work flow centrality because they obtain information from many units and provide it to other organization units. A unit with low work flow centrality would be a legal department, which may provide services to only a few other subunits.

The second aspect of centrality is **work flow immediacy**. This is the "speed and severity with which work flows of a subunit affect the final outputs of the organization" [8]. The higher the work flow immediacy, the greater the power. Suppose a firm has a policy of maintaining very small finished goods inventories. The production unit has a high work flow immediacy because if production stops, then goods do not flow to the customer.

Strategic contingency theory explains subunit power relationships very well. Crozier attributed the power of the maintenance department in a tobacco factory to the fact that this department controlled the primary uncertainty that affected production—machine breakdown [4]. In a study of channels of distribution, the power of a supplier was related to (1) whether or not there were alternate suppliers, (2) whether or not the resources controlled by the supplier were critical, and (3) the level of transactions between the supplier and the customer [1]. Boeker studied how a subunit's influence in semiconductor firms was related to the characteristics of the market at the time that a firm was founded [2]. In the early stage of the industry, when the primary market was the U.S. military and the defense industry, the research and development units were most dominant in semiconductor firms which began in that stage. Later the industry faced price competition and in firms founded during this stage, manufacturing units were the most influential. When the industry moved into a "custom application" stage, the newly founded firms were dominated by the marketing departments.

☐ STRATEGIC
CONTINGENCIES AT MACKSON _____

Today the Mackson Corporation (a fictitious name for a real company) manufactures and markets a very successful line of consumer products for use in the home. The line includes mixers, portable vacuum cleaners, and even some garden products. Recently they have had great success with a food processor. Mackson is an example of a firm in which the critical contingency is marketing and how coping with the market is related to subunit power.

Mackson's chief executive is Mike Kennelly. Mike started out in the marketing group in 1970 and has always had, he thinks, a sense of "what sells." Since he has become president there has been tremendous emphasis on marketing research, marketing strategy, and penetrating the home market. However, this was not always the case at Mackson. In the 1970s, Mackson was the premier designer-supplier of specialized industrial and commercial kitchen equipment. They had a reputation for producing a high-quality but moderately priced line of products. Their design group was, without question, the best in the industry. They set the design standard in both appearance *and* efficiency.

In the 70s, the company was run by the production people and the designers. The design group was powerful because of its excellence and performance. In fact, even though today the industrial products division is not the leader in terms of sales, the design group is still the best in the industry. The production group's influence stemmed from its ability to meet cost, time, and quality requirements.

The change at Mackson came when Mike Kennelly became president in 1985. He believed that Mackson could grow by entering new product lines and thought that it was a logical idea to enter the consumer product areas, but in lines in which Mackson had both capability and a reputation. He started into consumer products slowly, but by 1990 Mackson had a heavy commitment of money and people in this area of business.

There are many "old-timers" at Mackson who are unhappy with the change. They are, generally, veterans of the old days when production and design were emphasized. Now they think the company's products have lost the reputation they once had. One senior production executive recently said:

> Things aren't like they used to be. Before, we would send a designer out on a job and would produce first-rate equipment and be proud of it. Most of our installations, as a matter of fact, are still in place and they haven't been modified at all. Now we worry about whether or not we can come up with some new gadget that can be used in the house and if we can make it cheap and sell it fast. Our major discussion topic in executive committee meetings these days is whether or not we are going to spend our advertising money on soap opera slots or on the Super Bowl. That's not what this business is all about.

483

Another approach to power distribution is the **resource dependence perspective**, in which power is considered a function of whether or not a social actor controls the flow of money to organization units. Pfeffer argues that only a *very small* proportion of total funds must be controlled to exercise a great deal of power [25]. This is because most organizations operate with incremental budgets. This means that the current budget is made up from last year's budget—with an increment for growth. Controlling this increment is the key to power.

PERSONAL ATTRIBUTES AND ORGANIZATION-BASED INFLUENCE

People who seek, acquire, and use power and authority have strong predispositions to do so, and they compete with others who have similar predispositions [11]. In this section, we will discuss the personal characteristics of those who seek and acquire legitimate authority and reward and punishment power.

Legitimate Authority.   Because legitimate authority depends on the position a person holds in the organization, it follows that to increase it, a person must advance in the hierarchy, increase the amount of discretion in the current position, or move into subunits that are more powerful. Those who seek to do this are likely to have the following characteristics:

1. *Competence* is necessary. A person must be good enough at his or her job to be judged capable of performing at higher-level positions. Competence is usually demonstrated by past performance and achievement.

2. *Self-confidence* is the person's belief that he or she will be successful. Mowday found that people with high generalized self-confidence have stronger beliefs that their influence attempts will be successful [23].

3. An *organizational orientation* is also likely to be characteristic of one who seeks legitimate authority (see Chapter 4). A person with this perspective finds organizational achievement and advancement reinforcing, making high position a sought-after value for them. This orientation will also facilitate advancement because an organizationalist with an adequate level of competence usually has the right combination of factors to be successful, according to the Good Enough Theory of Promotion.

4. *Power needs* must be very strong. **Power needs** are a person's desire to have an impact on others, to establish, maintain, or restore the prestige of power. Power needs are one dimension of the leader motive pattern discussed in the next chapter, shown to be related to managerial success by McClelland and Boyatzis [20].

Reward and Punishment Power.   In organizations, reward and punishment power stems from the extension of legitimate authority because the person has some discretion in how it can be used. Therefore, the personal attributes discussed in the preceding section are necessary but not sufficient conditions to acquire reward and punishment power. In addition, the person must have a *political orientation.* A political orientation is the willingness or attempt to exert influence beyond the boundaries of legitimate authority [11]. The stronger the political orientation, the more reward and punishment power will be acquired. The following attributes are related to acquiring reward and punishment power [10].

1. **Machiavellians** (Chapter 4) have high self-confidence, high self-esteem, and behave in their own self-interest. High Machs are cool, are not distracted by emotion, and can exert control in power vacuums. They have a tendency to use false or exaggerated praise to manipulate others and are able to detach themselves from a situation.

2. **Personalized power motives** will be very strong in those who acquire reward and punishment power. People with a higher personalized power orientation have strong self-interest and exercise power in an interpersonal way with an adversary.

3. Cognitive complexity is the ability to make sense out of complicated and ambiguous situations. A person is able to find what patterns and relations exist in a situation even though they are embedded in noise and confusion. This is a necessary skill because the individual seeking power must be sensitive to subtle but complex situations in an organization in order to know when to exert influence [11]. Krackhardt demonstrated that accurate perceptions of the organization power structure were related to a person's power reputation [17]. He identified two types of networks, a friendship and a power network. Those who were attributed higher power by others had more accurate perceptions of the power network. The accuracy of perceptions of the social network was not related to reputational power.

4. Being articulate is another important skill. The articulate person will be able to present arguments logically, which should facilitate persuasion. He or she may be able to form coalitions easier and may be chosen by a group to represent them.

MAINTAINING ORGANIZATION-BASED INFLUENCE

Legitimate authority and organization-based power can be perpetuated and strengthened by maintaining the current structure of organizational relationships and the organization culture that support stable behavior patterns. This way the powerful subunit will maintain control over strategic contingencies, retain its centrality, and protect its level of nonsubstitutability. By perpetuating the organization culture, the norms and values that reinforce the power structure will not change. Figure 15.4 shows some things a subunit with institutionalized power can do to enhance it. A powerful subunit can (1) influence strategy, (2) obtain competent personnel, (3) affect the behavioral control systems, and (4) affect the redesign of the organization structure.

Influence over Strategy. Managers in powerful subunits can affect organization strategy by influencing whether or not an organization takes an aggressive or a passive approach toward its environment. Stronger subunits can also influence

485

strategic decisions about where the firm is located in the task environment itself. For example, several years ago a small electronics firm in California designed and manufactured advanced technological components for the defense department and NASA. It used a technology that has several consumer applications. A group from the small marketing department prepared an excellent proposal to develop a consumer products line. It was a well-conceived program that predicted substantial increases in revenue from the new product. The proposal was rejected by the top management group, which was composed mostly of engineers. They argued that the new product line would "change the nature of the firm and cause too much disruption." By remaining in the same market, the technically oriented top management retained its strong power position. It was not until recently, when there were substantial reductions in United States defense budgets, that the proposal was resurrected. This has, of course, implications for the power of the engineers in the firm.

Attracting Better Personnel.   Pfeffer gives an example of how a finance department in a firm perpetuated its power by attracting highly talented people [24]. The firm was experiencing financial control problems, and a large number of very highly talented people were hired in the finance department. Because this was a critical contingency and good personnel were attracted, it gave the subunit a greater capacity to deal with the environment. As the competence of the staff grew, so did the unit's power.

Influence over Behavioral Controls.   Selection, promotion, compensation, training, and socialization are types of behavior controls. If subunits can control and influence these activities, they will be able to perpetuate the power structure and their place in it. This occurs because the level of commitment and involvement of those who are selected and promoted to key positions will be affected by these processes. They will most likely accept the institutionalized power structure as legitimate.

☐ **FIGURE 15.4**   *Maintenance of Organizational-Based Power*

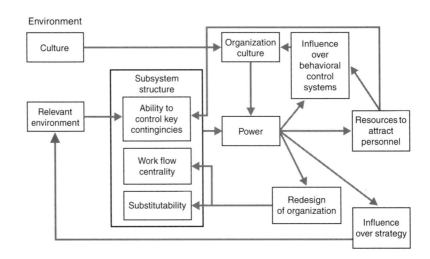

1. *Defining selection criteria.* Powerful subunits can affect both the skills mix and general value orientations of those who enter the organizations by influencing selection criteria. In Chapter 1, we noted that one of the important changes in management education since the 1960s was the development of quantitative skills. Since that time, in many colleges of business, those departments which teach quantitative subjects have developed a great deal of power. They are often successful in influencing other areas to select faculty who have these skills, even though they may not be particularly necessary to the teaching and research objectives.

2. *Affecting advancement criteria.* Although selection criteria are very important, control over advancement criteria is even more so. If an error is made in selection, it can be corrected by passing over for promotion those who fail to meet expectations. We have already pointed out the necessity to have both competence and the "right perspective" for advancement. By defining both the required competence and the right perspective, those who are in powerful positions can strengthen the existing culture, which reinforces the present power structure. This occurred when Lee Iacocca was fired from Ford Motor Company by Henry Ford II [13]. During his career at Ford, Iacocca was regarded by almost everyone in the company and in the automobile industry to be Henry Ford II's successor as CEO and Chairman of the Board. For reasons other than Iacocca's managerial performance, he was not promoted.

3. *Influencing compensation.* Because pay is important to status, the ability to influence pay criteria and decisions can perpetuate power. In one plant, the plant manager had a very strong interest in safety. When he took charge of the plant, he gave a great deal of legitimate authority to the safety engineering department. This group's power grew, and soon they became influential in most matters of plant engineering and design. They also had a significant effect on a very important compensation decision. The plant manager intended to implement an employee bonus based on achievement of production, quality, and safety goals. Because he wanted to emphasize the interdependence of all activities, it was to be a plant-wide bonus system. The safety group, however, believed that the bonus would have a greater impact on safety if the safety component of the bonus was based on departmental performance. This meant that safety goals would be set for each department, not the whole plant. In the end, the bonus system had a plant-wide component and the departmental safety component.

4. *Influencing training.* Because of their strategic position in organizations, powerful units are better able to define the subject of training. This is an important type of influence because in training much information is transmitted about the culture of the organization. For example, when key executives in one firm decided that it should have a

☐ PERPETUATING THE MILITARY POWER STRUCTURE

Two central concepts to the power structure of the military are (1) the sharp distinction between enlisted and officer personnel and (2) the structure of ranks within each group, particularly among the officers.

One of the most important elements in perpetuating the power structure is the institution of the military academy (West Point, Annapolis, and the Air Force Academy). First, the academies all have an opportunity to select excellent personnel. While it is true that there are many political recommendations for the academies, from this selection pool it is possible to choose cadets with the desired physical and mental characteristics, as well as the "right" attitudinal predispositions. Thus, the perpetuation of the power structure begins with the selection of cadets.

The military establishment also controls the specific experiences that students will have. Military officers define the academic curriculum. They set the rules for the academies. They design and prescribe the various ceremonies and practices of the academies. In fact, they also sanction the hazing practices that occur in the groups of cadets. These all reflect the norms and values of the military tradition, which support the current power structure.

Each cadet is required to go through these experiences. They shape the values that the cadet brought into the academy, forming a person who will be receptive to the culture. Acculturation happens in several ways. First, the cadet is separated from the outside world. He or she is, for example, required to wear a uniform to replace civilian clothes. The uniform not only differentiates the cadet from the rest of the society but identifies him or her with other cadets. Second, the cadet learns many subjects that are taught by officers. The teachers, very powerful socializing agents, also convey the norms and values of the military. Third, as the cadet moves through the years, he or she learns how to react to the authority structure (as a first-year cadet) and how to apply it (as a senior). Fourth, there are quite rigid rules that govern behavior. This, too, teaches the cadet something about authority. Finally, those cadets who cannot adapt or cope with this approach either leave voluntarily or are asked to leave.

By the end of four years, the cadets who graduate are inbred with the military tradition, which, of course, means that they can accept and perhaps even prefer the current power structure. Perpetuation of power is further enhanced as graduates of the military academy are favored for promotion to senior officer ranks and they become the ones who make policy, guide the curriculum, and determine the selection criteria for academy students of the future.

management-by-objectives philosophy of managing, they introduced it with a company-wide training program. Before the program was introduced, they were very careful to define what they meant by MBO. They developed very specific definitions of "goal," "tactic," "objective," and "action plan," which were made a basic part of the instructional program.

5. *Influencing organizational socialization.* The norms and values transmitted through organizational socialization reflect those of the dominant coalition. The effects of controlling socialization on an organization's culture are shown in a study by Zahrly [36]. In a new plant, the socialization of the work force was carried out by training that stressed teamwork, group projects that required teamwork, and discussions showing how teamwork was to be a foundation of the plant's management philosophy. Teams were formed and given a great deal of autonomy when they began working. Within 18 months, the teamwork norm was firmly embedded in the plant and transmitted to new employees.

Influencing Organization Redesign. Through organization design decisions, it is possible to retain control over key contingencies, to maintain work flow centrality, or to protect the nonsubstitutability of activities. The previous example of quantitative methods in colleges of business administration illustrates how this can occur. Because quantitative groups were very powerful, they were able to influence graduation requirements so that students in most areas must now take quantitative courses. This made the work of the quantitative groups very central to the instructional program. It also resulted in very large enrollments for these courses, justifying the addition of new faculty members in that area and, of course, with increased numbers there is usually increased power.

ENVIRONMENTAL DISCONTINUITIES AND POWER

The power structure of organizations tends to be relatively stable because those who hold power are reluctant to relinquish it. In semiconductor firms, Boeker found that the longer the founding entrepreneur stayed in the firm, the less likely it was that there was a shift in departmental power [2]. He concluded that the initially dominant departments were able to institutionalize their initial, strong power position.

Power structures are more likely to change in response to discontinuities, or changes, in the environment which "destroy the competence" of the dominant managerial coalition [33]. This occurs when markets or technologies change in ways that require different skills and competence. For example, replacement of James Robinson as chairman of American Express was due to the dramatic loss in profitability and market share. For years, the American Express card and other financial services provided by the company were unique and resulted in an enviable market niche. Then Visa and MasterCard entered the same market, providing more services in a slightly different, but very competitive package. American Express lost ground to them, in part because the market for financial services, especially the credit card had changed. The top management of American Express under Robinson was not, in Tushman and Romanelli's terms, competent to cope with the market discontinuities [33]. After some serious reorganization attempts, Robinson was replaced as chairman.

ACQUIRING AND MAINTAINING PERSONAL-BASED INFLUENCE

In some instances, the influence of one person over others is almost entirely a function of personal attributes. The expert adviser attracts a following because of the skills he or she possesses. The entrepreneur is often able to attract loyal subordinates because they believe in the message. These instances are examples of expert and charismatic power, both personal based and requiring a particular fit between the attributes of the power actor and the follower [25]. Personal-based power is also important to managers. If they can develop it, it can supplement legitimate power and be helpful in "motivating commitment to the tasks that require high effort, initiative, and persistence" [35].

It is more difficult to perpetuate personal-based power than organizational-based influence. Legitimate authority can be transferred from one person to another. Personal-based influence cannot. For example, whereas a new vice president will have the same legitimate authority as her predecessor, she will have to develop power.

ACQUIRING AND MAINTAINING CHARISMATIC POWER

Charismatic power results from the identification of one person with another. It is based on personal attraction which develops in certain contextual settings which interact with the personal attributes of those involved.

Charismatic Situations. It is generally thought that charismatic power develops in a crisis situation, when there are high levels of uncertainty and a group needs inspiration and direction. House, Spangler, and Woycke have shown how crises are related to charismatic behaviors of U.S. Presidents [12].

As long as the crisis continues, the charismatic leader will continue to have power. Martin Luther King became very influential during the turbulent period of the civil rights movement in the United States.

Organization start-ups are another situation in which charismatic influence can develop. In start-ups, members are usually seeking direction and support for their involvement in the new organization.

One explanation for the emergence of charisma in both crisis and start-ups is that the situational context is "weak." There are few cues from the environment, and the situation does not generate uniform expectancies for those in it [22]. When the situation is unstructured, those in it may not know how to respond. In this weak context, the charismatic person can provide psychological boundaries and direction by creating new meanings and beliefs for the followers. In the case of Chrysler, the economic future of many workers and executives was not clear. Iacocca defined a very clear vision for them as well as a way to achieve it.

Attributes of Charismatic Leaders. Some of the characteristics we have already discussed as personal attributes of people with the capacity to acquire legitimate authority are attributes of charismatic leaders. They are (1) need for power, (2) self-confidence, and (3) articulation skills.

In addition, two other attributes are present when charismatic power exists [11]. One is *nonverbal communication* skills. The charismatic person has the capacity to convey meaning to followers easily with body language, gestures, and symbols. The manipulation of symbols is very important. Revolutions all have slogans, symbols of unity, or other signs that identify the struggle and convey meaning to those involved in them. *Strong convictions about beliefs* are also an attribute of charismatic power. This belief is transmitted to the followers both verbally and nonverbally.

Perpetuating Charismatic Power.   Charismatic power develops when there are crises or high levels of uncertainty and a group needs inspiration and direction. As long as the crisis or uncertainty exists, the charismatic power will also probably remain. When the crisis ends or the problems are solved, charismatic power can be perpetuated only if it becomes institutionalized. Then the charismatic leader can remain in an influence position, at least as a figurehead, because of the symbolic meaning that he or she conveys to the group. In the late 1950s, Fidel Castro led a revolution in Cuba as a young, charismatic rebel. He remained head of the government and had charismatic power for many years. Perpetuating charisma can be done in several ways:

1. *Perpetuate the charismatic image.* By maintaining images that surrounded the leader during the period when charismatic power was the dominant model of influence and control, the perception of charisma can be retained. Castro still maintains the same appearance he had during the Cuban revolution. He keeps his beard and always appears in public in a fatigue-like uniform. Pictures of him appear everywhere. The way that the charismatic leader is seen by the group, after institutionalization, is usually very controlled so that the charismatic image is not destroyed.

2. *Control interaction with groups.* When the charismatic leader interacts with large groups, it is usually in controlled settings such as speeches, rites, or ceremonies. These can reinforce the organization culture as well as present the charismatic leader in a very positive light. When there is a small group with more interpersonal interaction between the leader and the members, these situations are usually very controlled. Usually the meetings are of a short duration. Normally, those who are in the meeting are carefully selected because they are loyal to the leader or to the organization. In most cases, they also appear to be representative of the larger group of followers.

3. *Evoke specific negative images of the past.* A charismatic leader can call to mind specific crises or times of uncertainty for group members. This reminds the group of "how bad it was" [3]. Revolutionary political leaders usually refer to very specific cases of tyranny and poverty under previous regimes. The charismatic business leader can evoke the difficult times when he or she was leading the firm

through the crisis. The charismatic union leader can bring to union members' minds the low wages, poor safety practices, and unfair working conditions of the past that gave rise to the need for a union.

4. *Speak in general, but positive, terms about the future.* [3]. This is the counterpart of the previous point. The charismatic leader can evoke images of "how good it will be" in the future. This is most effectively accomplished when the leader speaks in general terms. Avoiding specifics allows followers to project their own meaning into the leader's words. Because of the psychological link between the group and the leader, this will result in a strengthened bond between them.

ACQUIRING AND MAINTAINING EXPERT POWER

Expert power results from the possession of the ability to do things valued and needed by others.

The Context for Expert Power. Expert power can exist in situations in which specific skills are necessary in an organization and when the individuals who possess these skills are in limited supply. This often happens when the organization's environment is volatile. Then firms must import the newly required skills, and often there is little incentive to try to institutionalize them. Thus, the power remains with the individual.

Personal Attributes and Expert Power. To acquire expert power, a person must possess the necessary skills, whether they are physical, mental, or interpersonal, that can help others. It is difficult, however, to specify what personality factors might cluster around people with expert power because there are so many potential types of it. Expert power can be facilitated by the organization, however, or by other external institutions. Both of these can provide legitimacy by giving the expert the appropriate titles, licenses, or certification.

Perpetuating Expert Power. Three conditions are necessary to perpetuate expert power. First, the power holder must be able to maintain his or her skill level. In one large law firm, only one partner has expertise in environmental law. The "environmental expert" is important to the firm because he accounts for a large share of the firm's revenue. To maintain his expertise, he regularly reads, studies, and attends seminars on the topic. Frequently, he teaches a class in environmental law at a nearby university.

The second requirement is to ensure that the dependence relationship between the individual and the organization does not change in such a way as to weaken the expert's position. The law firm needs "environmental expertise" because it is a growing area of practice and an important share of the firm's revenue.

Third, the expert must maintain personal control of the expertise. This ensures that others cannot be substituted for him. If environmental law becomes a larger part of the firm's business, it may wish to add other experts in this area, threatening the expert's power. At this time, he controls this by a careful selection of clients so that new partners are not needed or by managing new experts who join the firm.

USING POWER IN ORGANIZATIONS

The use of legitimate authority is based on the psychological contract. The use of power is not. In organizations, power can be exercised in different ways. Suppose that a vice president of marketing is asked by the CEO to make a recommendation about which one of five new products a firm should develop. A nonpolitical evaluation process would subject each product to a rigorous assessment of costs and benefits. Suppose, however, that the marketing vice president prefers one of the products over the others. The vice president could influence the choice process by appointing a committee composed of people who are likely to favor the product. The VP could also define the criteria that will be used in the product evaluation process. In other words, the VP can "structure" the situation in a way that will lead to a favorable evaluation of the preferred alternative.

In organizations, power is not usually implemented by brute force and coercion, but rather in much more subtle ways. If force is used, those in opposition will probably try to use counter force. This will result in force against force, open conflict that organizations try to avoid because harmony is so highly valued. The subtle use of power allows the appearance of logic and rationality to be maintained. The power actor can have his or her way without overt pressure and force by using some of the approaches discussed here.

CONTEXTUAL CONTROL

The context can be structured so that the intended behaviors are likely to occur [15]. Influence strategies of this type are usually based on the legitimate authority structure of the organization. Legitimate authority can be extended in political ways because a position in an organization gives a person some degree of control over the allocation of resources, the distribution of rewards, and the implementation of sanctions. Managers can exert influence in many ways by careful **contextual control** of others' behavior and decisions.

Problem Definition. Managers, especially with subordinates, can often select or define the problem that is to be solved. This limits the range of solutions that can be considered. If the academic vice president of the university asks a committee to develop a program to "enhance the reputation of the university," the committee will attack the issue differently than they would if the problem is "How can the university enhance its reputation as a graduate institution?" People will have an opportunity to exercise some influence over the different ways that the problem is solved but not over the selection of the problem, which by definition was confined to graduate emphasis.

Subjective Use of Objective Criteria. An effective way to use political power is to influence the criteria used in decision making [24]. Suppose that the board of directors agree on the following criteria to use in the selection of a new president for a growing firm: (1) knowledge of the company, (2) knowledge of the industry, (3) successful performance in a similar job, (4) technical competence, (5) financial capability, and (6) interpersonal skills. All of these factors will not receive equal weighting in any decision. Political considerations will

493

determine which of them will be the most important in the selection. For example, much depends on whether there is an inside candidate favored for the job or an outside candidate is preferred. Figure 15.5 shows two ways to rank the criteria. Set A in Figure 15.5 would favor an internal candidate because company knowledge is highly ranked. Set B might favor an outside person because of the importance of industry knowledge.

☐ **FIGURE 15.5** *Two Possible Rankings of Criteria for the Selection of a President*

CRITERIA A	CRITERIA B
1. Successful past performance 2. Knowledge of the company 3. Technical competence 4. Financial capability 5. Interpersonal skills	1. Successful past performance 2. Knowledge of the industry 3. Financial capability 4. Interpersonal skills 5. Technical competence

A second but related political strategy is to discount objective criteria so that although one of the alternatives appears better than others, the rating of the alternative is lowered for subjective reasons. Suppose the board of directors agree that Criteria A are to be used for the evaluations of candidates and that two names appear on the final list of qualified applicants: one is from inside the firm and the second from outside. Further suppose that the outside candidate is now the president of a small but very profitable firm. Those who favor the inside candidate might argue that the success of the smaller firm is not due to the president but to other factors such as luck, lack of competition, or a special competitive advantage such as a patent. If they are successful in discounting the outside candidate's performance, then the insider will be selected.

Use of Outside Experts.   Political influence can be supported through the use of outside experts to justify and rationalize decisions [25]. This strategy combines legitimate power and expert power. It can be used in several ways. At one extreme, expert opinion can be brought in through research reports and published articles to support a position. At the other extreme, consultants or members at the board of directors can be used to make recommendations, to introduce changes, and to reinforce decisions [32].

Controlling Information.   A person can control when information is released, how much is released, and what others get. Suppose the board of directors, in the example above, favors an inside candidate for president. The number of outside candidates can be limited in several ways. One is by delaying the announcement of the position and setting an early date for the appointment. The board could also affect the selection by limited release of information. When prospective candidates inquire about the job, the board may provide general, not specific, information about salaries and benefits.

Controlling the agenda of meetings is another way to manage the flow and type of information [24]. Both the content of the agenda and the order in which items are considered can influence decisions. This is a common occurrence at stockholder meetings. The board of directors usually determines the agenda, with little time for shareholders interested in other matters to raise them. If such issues are raised, then the board can usually influence the decision because it controls the proxies.

Cooptation.   In a study of the Tennessee Valley Authority, Selznick described how the officials of the TVA successfully handled conflict with local groups [29]. They appointed representatives from them to governing roles, which reduced the resistance from these groups. The process of bringing representatives of other groups into the power structure is called **cooptation**. When individuals are brought into the power structure, they are likely to adopt attitudes and values similar to those already in power. A striking example of this was illustrated in a classic study by Lieberman that showed how the attitudes of employees changed after they became managers [19]. The study was done in a large public utility in which there was a very strong union. An attitude survey of the work force was conducted with a follow-up study one year later. During that year, several workers had changed jobs. Some had been promoted to supervisory positions and some were elected union stewards. The attitudes of both groups had changed from the previous year. Those who became supervisors now had attitudes like those of the management group. The union stewards shifted their attitudes to become more strongly oriented toward union values. Becoming a member of the different groups changed the values of these people. Lieberman found further support for the effects of cooptation when one year later, several of those who had been promoted or elected had gone back to the work force. Their attitudes had reverted back to those held by the rest of the work force.

Coalition Formation.   When two or more parties merge interests, power can be increased because the alliance has greater control over strategic contingencies or more resources. **Coalitions** can be formed with groups or individuals outside the organization, too. Suppliers, bankers, and large customers may be enlisted to increase power.

One way to develop coalitions is by promoting others with similar values or those who can be influenced into important positions. This practice could lead to the creation of groups of supporters, which can be useful when decisions that require some higher levels of consensus have to be made.

INFLUENCING BEHAVIORS AND STRATEGIES

As we have already noted, power is more effective when its use is subtle. Creating the contextual control conditions is usually done in ways that make it appear that force has not been used, though this is not always the case. There are several behavioral strategies which can be used in attempts to influence others [15].

Reason.   Reason is most frequently used as an influence tactic, especially for upward influence [14, 27]. It is an attempt to persuade another by providing them with information. The information is usually straightforward and presented in such a way that it results in the evaluation desired. For example, an engineering manager may propose a project reevaluation and provide her boss with an analysis of the costs and benefits of the project that she believes may not have been considered when the project was turned down.

Assertive Behavior.   Direct and forceful approaches toward another are often successful [16]. This usually entails a strong, aggressive effort to obtain compliance from others. In organizations, assertiveness often takes the form of direct orders to others. The "iron law of power" that states that the greater the discrepancy in power between the influencer and target, the higher the probability of assertive behavior [16]. Initially, however, managers do not usually attempt to influence others through assertive behaviors. They normally begin with simple requests and appeals to legitimate authority. If they meet with resistance, they are likely to become assertive.

Bargaining.   In bargaining, one person seeks to influence another through negotiation and the exchange of benefits or favors [16]. Whether bargaining is possible depends on several factors. First, each party must have something, a "good" desired by the other. Second, each must be able and willing to withhold their goods at a cost to the other. Third, both parties must be willing to negotiate.

If the engineering manager in the above example wanted to use a bargaining strategy in order to have her superior reconsider the rejected project, she might indicate her willingness to lead another difficult but perhaps undesirable project in the future. Thus, she would make a future commitment in exchange for the reevaluation.

Acquiring a Sponsor.   A sponsor is a person at a higher organizational level or in a powerful position who represents and advances the interests of another. Sponsorship provides influence in two ways. First, the sponsor may be an advocate for a person in a promotion decision. This could result in advancement for the person while at the same time creating a loyal subordinate for the sponsor. Second, the sponsor may advance ideas and projects that are developed by the person. If the projects and ideas are good, the sponsor may even be given some credit for bringing them to the attention of decision makers.

One way to acquire a sponsor is by **demonstrating competence**. A person who performs well on important tasks will usually come to the attention of someone at a higher-level position, who may be a willing sponsor. Another way to acquire a sponsor is through ingratiation. **Ingratiation** is an attempt by individuals to increase their attractiveness to others [18]. Ingratiation is usually accomplished through flattery and a display of commitment or potential commitment. Flattery positively reinforces the target. In one organization, a young engineer with high power needs successfully used ingratiation to acquire the sponsorship of a senior project engineer. The senior engineer had been assigned the task of improving the productivity of a plant that was having serious performance difficulties. He had very little support from the plant's staff because they feared that his changes would reduce their status. The young engineer, in a quiet and discreet way, began to let the senior engineer know that he believed the project could work. He gave the senior engineer a good deal of positive feedback about the plans that were being developed. He also made certain that the senior engineer believed that he too thought the resistance from the old staff was unwarranted. While he supported the change project, there was only one problem. Because he was new to the organization, he told the senior engineer that it did not seem wise to support the proposals publicly. Because there were no other supporters, the senior engineer began to confide in the younger person. He also started to sponsor him, recommending him for special assignments and early promotion.

Impression Management.   One way to develop power is by **impression management** to create the illusion that one has it. This is done by the control of information, or cues, imparted to others to manage their impressions [30]. Specialists practice impression management when they use jargon unique to their profession. The doctor's white coat and use of medical terms does nothing to increase technical competence, but it conveys important meanings to patients. A top executive may try to create the impression of power by high activity levels and demonstrations of organizational loyalty. This may be done by using symbols such as large offices, deep carpets, and special furniture. The executive may also remain aloof and apart from lower-level members to maintain status distinctions.

Those at lower levels can also try to manage impressions of them by superiors. They may seek to give the impression that they are loyal and to create the belief that they are competent in their job and always busy. Being a "good" subordinate may be a way to gain power because superiors may place trust in him or her. Then the subordinate may be able to expand the power from the current legitimate authority base.

Use of Sanctions.   Managers may influence others by threatening to impose sanctions or allocating rewards in punitive ways [15]. They can do this through the legitimate and formal authority of their position. For example, a common practice in some state and local government agencies is to solicit contributions for political campaigns from employees, even though such demands are illegal in most states. The incumbent politician makes it clear to workers that a "voluntary" campaign contribution is expected. The politician usually gets these contributions because the workers know that negative performance evaluations or undesirable work assignments might result if they are not on the list of contributors.

MANAGERIAL INFLUENCE PATTERNS

Studies have shown how managers use some of the influence strategies discussed above [14, 16]. Managers from the United States, England, and Australia were asked to indicate their preferred ways to influence both subordinates and superiors. In dealing with superiors, the managers ranked the influence tactics in the following order:

1. Reason
2. Coalition formation

3. Bargaining

4. Assertive behavior

5. Appeals to higher authority (sponsors)

With subordinates, the ranking of influence approaches was somewhat different. Reason was most preferred, but assertive behavior also ranked very high:

1. Reason

2. Assertive behavior

3. Coalition formation

4. Bargaining

5. Appeals to higher authority (sponsors)

6. Use of sanctions

Kipnis and his colleagues have identified three managerial influence profiles [16]. They grouped managers into clusters, depending on how often they used the influence tactics listed above. **Shotgun managers** used all the tactics with above-average frequency, apparently because they had many different problems to solve. They were also the least-experienced managers in the study. **Tactician managers** attempted to influence others through the use of reason and logic and were about average in their use of other tactics. This group tended to manage technically complex work groups, with skilled employees and work that required much planning. **Bystander managers** reported below-average use of all the influence tactics studied and seemed to exert relatively little influence on others. In general, they were in charge of relative routine work and supervised a large number of employees. They were also the managerial group in the study that was least satisfied with the effectiveness of their work.

SUMMARY

This chapter explained some of the most important and fascinating topics in organizational behavior: influence, power, politics, and compliance. They are at the heart of what managers do—get things done with and through others. A model of compliance processes was discussed. It showed that compliance, the degree to which a person acts in accordance with the wishes of another, can occur for several reasons. In some cases, individuals comply because of legitimate authority. In other instances, the use of power may lead to compliance.

There is a distinction between legitimate authority and power. Legitimate authority is the right of decision and command over others that is accepted as appropriate. Power is the use of force outside legitimate authority. Four types of power were discussed: reward power, coercive (punishment) power, expert power, and charismatic power.

Both legitimate authority and power accrue to individuals in certain situations. The characteristics of the situation and the individuals are related to the different types of influence that are exerted. The organizational context for power is related to the extent to which subunits interact with volatile environments, perform nonsubstitutable activities, or are central to organizational functioning.

We also showed how power can be maintained in organizations. Often maintaining power depends on a person's ability to perpetuate the settings in which power was originally developed. This can be done in different ways. In many instances, legitimate authority, reward power, and punishment power can be maintained because the power holders have control of organization processes, such as the choice of strategies, selection of personnel, and promotions.

The role of power and politics in organizations is important because they are ever present. Also, as you will see in the next chapter, the subject of leadership is quite closely linked to power.

KEY CONCEPTS

Acceptance	Influence	Power needs
Alienation	Ingratiation	Power structure
Bystander managers	Institutionalized power	Psychological contract
Calculative involvement	Intended results	Public boundary
Charismatic power	Legitimate authority	Real boundary
Coalitions	Machiavellianism	Resource dependence perspective
Coercive power	Manipulation	Reward power
Commitment	Organizational politics	Shotgun managers
Compliance	Organization-based influence	Strategic contingency theory
Contextual control	Personal-based influence	Substitutability of activities
Cooptation	Personalized power motive	Tactician managers
Dependence	Power	Work flow centrality
Demonstrating competence		Work flow immediacy
Expert power		
Impression management		

STUDY QUESTIONS

1. What is the importance of the concept of dependence in understanding power? How is dependence related to the level of the power that one person has over another?
2. There are three bases of compliance. What are they? Can you link them in any way to the types of organization that were discussed in Chapter 2 or to the organizational orientations discussed in Chapter 4?

499

☐ STUDY . . .

3. How is the psychological contract related to the use of power in organizations? Does the psychological contract mean that individuals will comply willingly with orders and directives?
4. In this chapter, we differentiated between power and legitimate authority. What is the difference?
5. What is meant by organizational politics?
6. What is the difficulty with relying on charismatic power as a basis for influence in organizations?
7. What is the basis of the strategic contingency theory of power?
8. List and define the organizational-based power strategies. Can you think of any situations in which you have been personally affected by one of these approaches? Where you have used one of them?
9. Why is impression management a way to develop and hold power? Give some examples of ways that you have seen it used.
10. Use the ideas in the section "Maintaining Organizationally Based Influence" to explain why it is difficult to bring about a significant change in organizations.

CASE

☐ THE BREWTON SCHOOL

When Boyd Denton was appointed superintendent of the Washington County school system in 1985, he was given the charge, by the school board, to improve the quality of student performance. His strategy for achieving this was to implement his philosophy of " competence and delegation." First, he would find very strong and very competent principals for each of the schools. Second, he would give each of them a great deal of autonomy. He allowed principals to make hiring decisions, to evaluate teachers, to make salary decisions, and to decide how to spend the budget allocated to each school.

From 1985 to 1990, the school system made significant gains in student achievement. However, there was one school, Brewton, that was a problem for Denton. The principal at Brewton was David Starr. Starr was one of the first principals that Denton hired, but now Denton believed that he had made a mistake.

At Brewton, the teachers did not seem to care about the students. They were, by any measure, mediocre. However, they were very loyal to Starr. He was well liked by them, and they supported him. The reason was that Starr never put any pressure on them for performance and did not really hold them accountable.

☐ THE BREWTON SCHOOL

When Denton became aware of this, he discussed it with Starr. Starr became angry and threatened to quit. He told Denton that the reason Brewton wasn't a good school was because Denton didn't give them enough resources to do the job right. Denton pointed out the opposite. In fact, by every budget measure, Starr and the Brewton school were well treated.

By 1990, Starr and Denton were on very bad terms. They argued often, and all the other principals saw Starr as a prima donna and uncooperative. In one of their arguments, Starr threatened to resign. Denton told him, "Bring me the letter, now." Starr left the office and returned 20 minutes later with a letter of resignation. Denton didn't hesitate. "I'll take it," he said.

Denton searched for a replacement and found Joe Melcan, a bright young assistant superintendent in a nearby district. When he hired Melcan, Denton told him:

> I want you to get Brewton straightened out, and I'll help you. The teachers are well paid, and you've got enough resources there, but the job does not get done.

> One of the main problems you will have is that most of the teachers are very loyal to Starr. They won't help you much, but I'll give you whatever help and support you need.

Melcan's approach was as straightforward one. He would let everyone know what was expected of them, make pay as contingent on performance as possible, and hire good, new teachers. He thought that in three or four years, there would be enough turnover that with subsequent replacement, he could make Brewton into a high-performance school.

Denton watched Melcan's progress and was pleased. Three new, young teachers were hired. Melcan instituted a different evaluation approach from Starr's. He started to give substantial recognition to good teachers and less to those who weren't so good. This was a major departure from the way Starr had managed, and many of the Starr loyalists were angry. Some complained to Denton, and some filed grievances. When Denton and the union investigated, they found that the charges were without foundation. It was true that things had changed—now the school was not managed in the style of Starr, but in a performance-oriented style by Melcan.

This was exactly what Denton thought had to be done. Between 1990 and 1992, student performance improved considerably. However, many of the teachers who were old Starr supporters were dissatisfied. They continued to complain and grumble. Each time they came to Denton, however, he supported Melcan.

☐ THE BREWTON . . .

In 1993, Denton left Washington County to become an assistant to the state superintendent of schools. He was replaced by Mitchell Kraut. Kraut had been an assistant superintendent for Denton for several years. Two things about Kraut were of concern to Melcan. First, Kraut had been a teacher at Brewton during the first years of Starr's time as principal. They had, in fact, become close friends. Second, Kraut had announced that he was going to centralize many activities that had been performed previously by the principals. No longer would the principals make budget decisions, evaluate personnel, or hire faculty. Joe Melcan was very worried.

QUESTION

1. What was the basis of Joe Melcan's power during his tenure?
2. What are the potential effects of the change to centralization on Melcan?
3. How do you think the supporters of Starr will react to the change? To Melcan?

REFERENCES

1. Bagnozzi, R. and Phillips, L. Representing and testing organizational theories: A holistic view. *Administrative Science Quarterly*, 1982, 77, 459-88.
2. Boeker, W. The development and institutionalization of subunit power in organizations. *Administrative Science Quarterly*, 1990, 34, 388-410.
3. Conger, J.A., and Kanungo, R. Toward a behavioral theory of charismatic leadership in organizational settings. *The Academy of Management Review*, 1987, 12(4), 637-47.
4. Crozier, M., *The bureaucratic phenomenon*. Chicago: University of Chicago Press, 1964.
5. Etzioni, A. *A comparative analysis of complex organizations*, New York: Free Press, 1961.
6. Etzioni, A. *Modern organizations*, New York: Prentice-Hall, 1963.
7. French, J.R.P., Jr., and Raven, B. The bases of social power. In D. Cartwright, ed. *Studies in social power*. Ann Arbor: University of Michigan Institute for Social Research, 1959, 150-67.
8. Hickson, D.J., Hinings, C.R., Lee, C.A., Schneck, R., and Pennings, J.M. A strategic contingency theory of intraorganizational power. *Administrative Science Quarterly*, 1971, 16, 216-29.
9. Hofstede, G. *Culture's consequences: International differences in work-related values*. Beverly Hills, CA: Sage Publications, 1980.
10. House, R.J. *Power in organizations: A social psychological perspective*, unpublished manuscript. Toronto: University of Toronto, 1984.
11. House, R.J. Power and personality in complex organizations. In B.J. Staw and L.L. Cummings, *Research in organizational behavior*, 1988, 10. Greenwich, CT: JAI Press, 305-357.

12. House, R. J., Spangler, W. D., and Woycke, J. Personality and charisma in the U. S. presidency: A psychological theory of leader effectiveness. *Administrative Science Quarterly*, September 1991, 36(3), 364-396.

13. Iacocca, L., and Novak, W. *Iacocca: An autobiography*. New York: Bantam Books, 1984.

14. Kipnis, D. The use of power in organizations and in interpersonal settings. *Applied Social Psychology Annual*, S. Oscamp, ed., 1984, 5, 179-210.

15. Kipnis, D. Psychology and behavioral technology. *American Psychologist*, January 1987, 42(1), 30-36.

16. Kipnis, D., Schmidt, S.M., Swaffin-Smith, C., and Wilkinson, I. Patterns of managerial influence: Shotgun managers, tacticians, and bystanders. *Organizational Dynamics*, Winter 1984, 12, 58-67.

17. Krackhardt, D. Assessing the political landscape: Structure, cognition, and power in organizations. *Administrative Science Quarterly*, 1990, 35, 342-369.

18. Liden, R.C. & Mitchell, T.R. Ingratiatory behaviors in organizational settings. *The Academy of Management Review*, 1988, 13(4), 572-614.

19. Lieberman, S. The effects of changes in roles on the attitudes of role occupants. *Human Relations*, 1956, 9, 385-402.

20. McClelland, D.A., and Boyatzis, R.E. Leadership motive pattern and long-term success in management. *Journal of Applied Psychology*, 1982, 67, 737-43.

21. Milgram, S., *Obedience to authority*. New York: Harper & Row, 1974.

22. Mischel, W. The interactions of person and situation. In D. Magnusson and N.S. Enders, eds. *Personality at the crossroads: Current issues in interactional psychology*. Hillsdale, NJ: Erlbaum, 1977.

23. Mowday, R. Leader characteristics, self-confidence and methods of upward influence in organization decision situations. *Academy of Management Journal*, 44, 1980, 709-24.

24. Pfeffer, J. *Power in organizations*. Boston: Pitman Publishing, 1981.

25. Pfeffer, J. *Managing with power* Boston, Massachusetts: Harvard Business School Press, 1992.

26. Pfeffer, J., and Salancik, G. Organizational decision making as a political process: The case of the university budget. *Administrative Science Quarterly*, 19, 1974, 135-51.

27. Porter, L.W., Allen, R.W., and Angle, H.L. The politics of upward influence in organizations. In L.L. Cummings and B.S. Staw, eds. *Research in Organizational Behavior*. Greenwich, CT: JAI Press, 1981.

28. Schein, E.A. *Organizational psychology*. New York: Prentice-Hall, 1970.

29. Selznick, P. *TVA and the grass roots*. Berkeley: University of California Press, 1949.

30. Thompson, V. *Modern organization*. New York: Knopf, 1967.

31. Tosi, H. *The environment/organization/person contingency model: A meso approach to the study of organizations*. Greenwich, CT: JAI Press, Inc., 1992.

32. Tosi, H.L. & Gomez-Mejia, L. The decoupling of CEO pay and performance: an agency theory perspective. *Administrative Science Quarterly*, 1989, 34, 169-189.

33. Tushman, M. L., and Romanelli, E. Organizational evolution: A metamorphosis model of convergence and reorientation. In L. L. Cummings and B. M. Staw, eds. *Research In Organizational Behavior*, Connecticut: Jai Press Inc., 1985, 7, 171-222.

34. Weber, M. *The theory of social and economic organization.* T. Parsons, trans. New York: Free Press, 1947.

35. Yukl, G. *Leadership in organizations.* Englewood Cliffs, NJ: Prentice-Hall, 1989.

36. Zahrly, J. An analysis of the source of an organization's culture. Paper delivered at the Midwest Business Administration Association Meetings, Chicago, IL, 1985.

37. Zaleznick, A. Power and politics in organizational life. In E.C. Bursk and T.B. Blodgett, eds. *Developing executive leaders.* Cambridge, MA: Harvard University Press, 1971.

Chapter 16
Leadership

What makes an effective manager? In an analysis of management in France, Barsoux and Lawrence say that French managers see their job as an intellectual activity that requires intensely analytical work [2]. They value and excel in quantitative analysis and strategic planning. Above all, those who head large firms must be clever. This emphasis on cleverness is manifested in their recruiting materials, which almost never mention motivation and drive as requisites for a managerial position. The French seem to prefer managers with an analytical mind, independence, and intellectual rigor. They have a strong bias for intellect, rather than action. Unlike the Anglo Saxon view of management, they do not place high emphasis on interpersonal skills and communications, so valued as managerial attributes in other countries.

Some have argued that this concern with what makes an effective leader in organization studies is overdone, and that leaders may not have such large and important effects on outcomes in organizations because:

1. Organizations exert strong forces that limit the types of behavior and characteristics of people in managerial and leadership roles.

2. Other members of the organization limit the behavior of leaders through norms and expectations that are powerful constraints on actions.

3. External environmental forces have significant effects on the success or failure of organizations.

The concern with leadership is based, it is argued, on the need to credit individuals with organization successes and failures. In one study, researchers tested the idea that the "relative prominence of the use of leadership in understanding complex, organized systems varies to a significant degree with the performance of the system" [41]. Meindl and his colleagues found that the emphasis on leadership in the popular press was greatest during periods of national prosperity, suggesting that the "romance" associated with the concept of leadership may be based on the belief that leaders actually influence, or should be able to influence, the direction of the organizations that they head [41].

This fascination with leadership affects how we interpret it in the popular press. This was demonstrated in a study of how Donald Burr, the founder of People Express Airline, was presented in the press [9]. During the initial founding phase, Burr was characterized as evangelistic, entrepreneurial, and charismatic when People Express broke into the airline industry with a new concept of low cost fares, even though they were losing money. In the second phase, as People Express began to make money, Burr was described as a maverick, a visionary, a whiz, and a competitor, an image consistent with the idea of an innovative and successful manager. Finally, in the period when the company began to lose money, he was represented still as preacher and visionary, but now a fighter. The failure of People Express was seen as not his fault. The point about this study is that, even though a firm went through a cycle of growth, success, and failure with the same CEO, there was little change in the way he was characterized in the media. Thus, Chen and Meindl conclude: "Whatever particular [constructions of leadership] emerge, their themes must not diminish the significance of leadership as a way of understanding performance" [9].

However, the empirical evidence, like common sense, demonstrates that leaders do have strong effects on organizations. For instance, changing CEOs can affect the evaluation of the firm by equity holders. One of the many studies on this issue demonstrated that an announcement of a change in CEOs increased the short term value of stocks of small firms when the new CEO is an outsider [46]. Smith and White have shown that CEOs affect the strategy of a firm [49]. More importantly, analyses by Wiener and Mahoney and by Thomas have shown that chief executives can have a marked effect a on firm's performance [58, 52]. But there is an important caveat, according to Pfeffer and Davis-Blake [45]. They showed that simply replacing a poor manager with another is not the answer. A competent replacement is required. They studied the effects of coach replacements on team performance in the National Basketball Association. Replacing a coach, alone, had little direct effect on team success. They did find, not surprisingly, that the competence of the new coach, as measured by experience in the NBA and success in turning around other teams, was related to the success of the team. Thus, those who select managers and coaches are faced with the problem of predicting success, a problem so difficult that millions of dollars and much time has been spent thinking, talking, and writing about it. This theorizing, speculation, and research about leadership has persisted for a long time, always with the same objective: to understand leadership in ways that make it possible to select persons who are likely to be effective leaders and to better train and develop leadership skills.

In this chapter, we focus on this problem of understanding what makes a leader effective. **Leadership**, as we define it here, is a "form of organizationally based problem solving, implemented in a social context, where an attempt is made to bring about goal attainment by influencing the action of other [organization] subsystems" [22]. This definition places leadership in the broad domain of influence, power, authority, and politics (discussed in the previous chapter), but in this chapter the focus is on leadership theory which, almost without exception, *focuses on individuals in organizational positions with legitimate authority to make decisions about others.*

In early research, leadership was studied as a collection of personal traits or characteristics of those identified as leaders. Later research emphasized leadership as a series of acts, or a behavioral repertoire, designed to help a group achieve its objectives. Since the mid-1960s, attention has been directed toward developing "contingency" theories of leadership; that is, theories that state effective leadership is a function of the situation in which leader and followers interact. These themes are the main thrusts of leadership theory and research discussed in this chapter. Specifically, we will discuss trait approaches, behavioral approaches, process approaches, and contingency approaches to leadership.

TRAIT APPROACHES

We often hear that leaders are forceful, tend to be very outgoing, and are persuasive. These common sense observations form the basis of the belief that personalities of effective leaders are different from non-leaders. **Trait theories** of leadership are based on this idea.

Studies have examined leadership factors such as age, height, intelligence, academic achievement, judgmental ability, and insight, all of which were thought to predict successful leadership. These studies were done in a wide variety of settings such as military units, business firms, student organizations, elementary schools, and universities. They led to a rather disappointing conclusion. No specific traits seem to be correlated with leadership in all situations. There are several explanations for such a result. First, just because a person has a particular trait is not a sufficient condition to be in a leadership position or a management job and be successful at it. The person must want the job *and* must want to be effective. Also, traits do not operate alone but in a constellation of other factors. Those who have such a constellation have an advantage over those who do not, and over those who have the similar constellation but do not want to be in a leadership or management position [4].

The second reason these research studies produce very divergent results is that the studies have been done in too many different situations. Traits may be related to effectiveness in certain situations but not in others.

Third, there is also the possibility that the trait research tended to focus on *specific* traits instead of more *general* factors. After a careful review of several hundred trait studies, Bass concluded that if specific traits were grouped into general classes of factors, there were differences between effective and ineffective leaders [4]. The general attributes that differentiated leaders from non-leaders follow:

1. *Capacity* refers to an individual's ability to solve problems, make judgments, and generally work harder. Specific traits are intelligence, alertness, verbal facility, originality, and judgment.

2. *Achievement* is the second general leadership characteristic. Effective leaders tend to do better in academic work, have more knowledge, and accomplish more in athletics than ineffective leaders.

3. *Responsibility* is another general characteristic possessed by effective leaders. The specific traits that fall into this category are dependability, initiative, persistence, aggressiveness, self-confidence, and a desire to excel.

4. *Participation* and involvement are higher for effective leaders than for ineffective ones. Effective leaders tend to be more active and more sociable, have greater capacity to adapt to different situations, and show higher levels of cooperation than less effective leaders.

5. *Status* is also an attribute of leaders. It shouldn't be surprising that effective leaders have higher socioeconomic status and are more popular than less effective ones.

6. *Situational factors* such as the goals to be achieved and the intelligence, skills, needs and status of the followers are related to which different attributes affect leader effectiveness.

LEADER MOTIVE PATTERN

An important approach is McClelland's **leader motive pattern** [40]. This is a configuration of personality dimensions that have been found to be related to managerial effectiveness. The personality configuration is (1) power needs that are higher than affiliation needs and (2) high power inhibition [38, 39] (see Chapter 7). Low affiliation needs suggest that the person does not require interaction with, or positive acceptance by, others. Power inhibition means that the person has discipline and self-control in the use of power.

McClelland and Boyatzis found in AT&T that "senior managers in jobs that do not focus on engineering aspects of the business who (1) are concerned about influencing others, (2) are less concerned about being liked, and (3) have a moderate degree of self-control are more likely to succeed" than senior managers without this pattern [40]. These results are impressive because the personality evaluation of the managers in the study was done eight and sixteen years before the measure of success was assessed. In a study of a service firm, the leader motive pattern of branch managers was also found to be related to the importance and status of branch offices [10].

BEHAVIORAL APPROACHES

Behavioral approaches to leadership attempt to relate what a leader *does* to leader effectiveness, whereas the trait approach focuses on what a leader *is*. How many times did he or she discipline an employee? How often did the leader communicate with employees? There are two classes of behavior that have received much attention in the leadership literature: (1) decision influence behaviors and (2) task and social behaviors.

DISTRIBUTION OF DECISION INFLUENCE

Many studies have been conducted on how the distribution of decision-making influence between superiors and subordinates is related to the performance and satisfaction of individuals and work groups. Some of the important work in this area was done over 50 years ago by Lewin, Lippitt, and White [34]. They developed a classification of leader behavior that was based on the sharing of decision making between a leader and a follower. Leader behavior was described in the following terms:

Autocratic Leadership. In **autocratic leadership**, the leader makes all decisions and allows the subordinates no influence in the decision-making process. These supervisors are often indifferent to the personal needs of subordinates. For example, when setting goals an autocratic manager would assign a worker a task or a goal without any discussion with the worker. The manager simply meets with subordinates and gives them a set of goals that the superior prepared [8].

Participative Leadership. Participative supervisors consult with their subordinates on appropriate matters and allow them some influence in the decision-making process. Participative leadership is not punitive and treats subordinates with dignity. The participative leader might set goals with subordinates after talking with them to determine preferences. For instance, a manager might communicate departmental goals to subordinates in a meeting. Using this information, subordinates would then develop their goals, or the superior might develop goals for the subordinate and later meet to arrive at some mutual agreement about the subordinate's goals.

Laissez-Faire Leadership. In **laissez-faire leadership** supervisors allow their group to have complete autonomy. They rarely supervise directly, so that group members make many on-the-job decisions themselves, such as what jobs they want to do. With such an approach, subordinates set their own goals with no managerial inputs and work toward them with no direction.

Effective groups have had autocratic leaders and participative leaders [4]. Participative leadership is associated with higher levels of subordinate satisfaction. Those who work for participative leaders are less resistant to change and show more organization identification than those who work for autocratic leaders. The laissez-faire style has not been studied as much as the autocratic and participative styles, but the results are consistent, showing that subordinate satisfaction and performance under laissez-faire are lower than under the participative approach but higher than under the autocratic approach [4].

Type of Situation. One of the weaknesses with this research is that situational differences were not studied. In some situations, unilateral decisions might be more effective than a participative decision process. If so, how can you know what approach is most likely to get good results? According to Maier, the right amount of subordinate influence depends on two factors that constitute an effective decision: *quality* required in a decision and its *acceptability* by subordinates [37].

Quality of a decision is the degree to which technical and rational factors are critical to a good decision. It is usually an objective characteristic that can be measured against some technical standard, such as cost or feasibility. When decision quality is the most important dimension of a problem, a directive approach works.

Acceptability of a decision is the extent to which those who must ultimately carry it out like the decision and are willing to implement it. The acceptability dimension of decisions is usually subjective, not objective. It is emotional and attitudinal. When acceptability is a crucial factor, participative decision making is more effective.

By combining the quality and acceptability dimensions, Maier was able to show how influence could be shared by leaders and followers to make better decisions. In addition, the Vroom-Yetton model (see also Chapter 13) provides another way to determine subordinate involvement in decision making [57]. These approaches to decision making are important because, first, they clarify the role of subordinate influence in decision making. Second, they provide the conceptual groundwork for contingency theories of leadership, which we discuss later in this chapter.

TASK AND SOCIAL BEHAVIORS OF LEADERS

Two very important programs of research on leader behavior were conducted at Ohio State University and the University of Michigan. The work centered on whether effective leaders emphasize task activities and assignments *or* tend to concentrate on trying to keep good relationships and cohesion among group members, or do *both* of these things. You will recall that in groups, task functions and socioemotional functions are the two key sets of activities.

The Ohio State Studies. From the late 1940s through the 1950s, a group of researchers at Ohio State conducted extensive studies of leadership and effectiveness in industrial, military, and educational institutions. They developed instruments to measure leadership and evaluated factors that might determine group effectiveness. Two leadership behavior dimensions consistently emerged from these studies:

1. **Consideration** is the extent to which the leader is likely to have job relationships characterized by mutual trust, respect for subordinates' ideas, and consideration of their feelings. Considerate leaders tend to have good rapport and two-way communication with subordinates.

2. **Initiating structure** is the extent to which the leader is likely to define and structure his or her role and those of subordinates toward goal achievement. High initiating structure leaders play an active role in directing group activities, communicating task information, scheduling, and trying out new ideas.

Most studies show that consideration is generally related to high employee satisfaction; it is related much less often to high performance, although it is occasionally. In some studies, initiating structure has been found to be related to job satisfaction but less often to high productivity, low absenteeism, and low turnover [4].

The Ohio State studies had a profound impact on leadership thinking and research. Wide use has been made of the scale, called the Leader Behavior Description Questionnaire (LBDQ), for measuring consideration and initiating structure. Concepts from these studies have become part of the conventional wisdom about leadership and are the basis of many programs to train leaders [6, 25].

The Michigan Studies. At the Institute of Social Research at the University of Michigan, researchers conducted a number of studies in offices, railroad settings, and service industries. From early studies, they concluded that leadership behavior could be described in terms of two styles: a supervisor may be production centered or employee centered. In **production-centered leadership**, the supervisor was primarily concerned with achieving high levels of production and generally used high pressure to get it. He or she viewed subordinates merely as instruments for achieving the desired level of production. In **employee-centered leadership**, the supervisor was concerned about subordinates' feelings and attempted to create an atmosphere of mutual trust and respect.

Early interpretations of the Michigan research concluded that the most effective leadership style is employee centered—that employee-centered supervisors are more likely to have highly productive work groups than production centered supervisors. This is an important difference between the Ohio State and Michigan studies. In the early stages of the Michigan studies, leaders were described as engaging in behavior that was *either* production centered or employee centered while the Ohio State studies attempted to characterize an individual on *both* dimensions [50]. The Ohio State and Michigan researchers used somewhat different measures, however, which makes their studies less directly comparable.

A later study at Michigan by Bowers and Seashore refined the concept of leader behavior [7]. They found four supervisory behaviors, reflecting task and social dimensions, associated with satisfaction and performance in a study of 40 agencies of an insurance company. These four basic supervisory behavior dimensions are:

1. *Support*. Behavior that enhances someone else's feelings of personal worth and importance.

2. *Interaction facilitation*. Behavior that encourages members of the group to develop close, mutually satisfying relationships.

3. *Goal emphasis*. Behavior that stimulates an enthusiasm for meeting the group's goals or achieving excellent performance.

4. *Work facilitation*. Activities that help achieve goal attainment by doing things such as scheduling, coordinating, planning, and providing resources such as tools, materials, and technical knowledge.

Inconsistencies and Issues. One strong conclusion can be drawn from these studies. Making a distinction between task-oriented leader behavior and person-oriented behavior of leaders seems to be a useful way to describe the ways leaders act. This distinction shows up in many different studies and suggests that the concepts may be a valid way to describe leader behavior.

But there are some unresolved issues with this approach, as you can figure out from the previous discussion. Although the results were a little more consistent than with trait research, they still varied. This stimulated efforts to reformulate leadership theory to account for situational factors, as is done in contingency theories.

Another important question is the direction of causality. That is, is it the behavior of the leader which causes higher performance, or is it possible that follower performance causes the leader to act in certain ways? Much of the leader behavior research consists of field studies that use correlational methodology, which does not prove causality.

Some research supports the idea that leader behavior may be a result of the group's performance as well as affecting it. One very convincing study was done by Lowin and Craig [36]. They designed an experiment in which they hired managers for part-time student work groups. Prior to employment, the applicants were introduced to one of the workers and asked to supervise him for a period of time. In some cases, the worker was said to be "very competent," but in other instances, the applicants were told that the worker was less competent. Those who managed the "competent" worker did not supervise him closely and engaged in more "consideration" and less "initiating structure" behaviors. Those who managed the less competent worker were more directive. After reviewing studies of this type, Bass concluded that leader "consideration both increases the satisfaction of subordinates and is increased by it [4]. The initiation of structure by the leader (if structure is low) improves the subordinates' performance, which, in turn, increases the leader's subsequent consideration and reduces the leader's initiation of structure" [4].

PROCESS APPROACHES

Trait approaches and behavioral approaches focus mainly on the leader, what the leader is or what the leader does. Some recent theories try to explain the "processes" by which a relationship develops between leaders and subordinates. One such theory is called Transformational Leadership Theory. Another is called Vertical Dyad Linkage Theory.

TRANSFORMATIONAL LEADERSHIP THEORY

Transformational leadership theory is an attempt to explain how leaders develop and enhance the commitment of followers. In this approach, transformational leaders are contrasted with transactional leaders. In **transactional leadership**, the leader and subordinate are viewed as bargaining agents, negotiating to maximize their own position [14]. The subordinate's motivation to comply with the leader is self-interest, because the leader can provide payoffs, perhaps both economic and psychological, that are valued by the follower. There are several important assumptions underlying the transactional view of leadership [14].

1. Human behavior is goal directed and individuals will act rationally to achieve those goals.

2. Behaviors that pay off will persist over time, while those that do not pay off will not persist.

3. Norms of reciprocity govern the exchange relationship.

The style of the transactional leader is to [4]:

1. *Use contingent rewards.* Rewards are associated with good performance and accomplishment.

2. *Manage by exception.* The leader acts when he or she (1) anticipates that performance is likely to deviate from standards or (2) takes action when standards are not met.

3. *Take a hands-off approach.* The leader acts in a laissez-faire manner, abdicating and avoiding responsibility.

Transformational leadership deals with the leader's effects on the followers' values, self-esteem, trust, and their confidence in the leader and motivation to perform "above and beyond the call of duty" [29]. The transactional leader's influence is derived from the exchange process, but it is different in an important way from transformational leadership. Transactional leadership works *within* the context of the followers' self-interests while transformational leadership seeks to *change* that context [4].

The transformational leader's influence is based on the leader's ability to inspire and raise the consciousness of the followers by appealing to their higher ideals and values. This occurs because the transformational leader has charisma, and engages in particular behaviors as well. Specifically, Bass suggests that a transformational leader [4]:

1. *Is charismatic.* The charismatic leader creates a special bond with the followers. The leader is able to articulate a vision with which the followers identify and for which they are willing to work (see Chapter 15).

2. *Is inspirational.* The leader creates high expectations and effectively communicates crucial ideas with symbols and simple language.

3. *Practices individual consideration.* The leader coaches, advises, and delegates to the followers, treating them individually.

4. *Intellectually stimulates followers.* The leader arouses them to develop new ways to think about problems.

Figure 16.1 illustrates some task behaviors, social behaviors, influence techniques of transformational leaders, and corresponding subordinate behaviors and feelings. The *task behaviors* of the leader are the heightening of task goals, articulating paths to achievement, and proposing innovative strategies. Subordinates become aware of new possibilities, have increased feelings of self efficacy, are willing to work longer and harder, have higher task identification and stronger achievement motives, and more emotional involvement with the work. The *socio-emotional behaviors* of the leader involve showing enthusiasm and trustworthiness, acting in ways to increase group cohesiveness and being approachable and available. The subordinate response is to identify with the leader and the mission, to try to emulate the leader, to feel increased desire to stay in the group, and to admire and trust the leader. The leader's *power* tends toward the charismatic type (see previous chapter), socialized power, unconventional behaviors, and different emotional appeals to subordinates. The subordinates tend to respond with more involvement, trust, compliance, and commitment.

☐ **FIGURE 16.1**   *Transformational Leader and Subordinate Behavior and Attitudes*

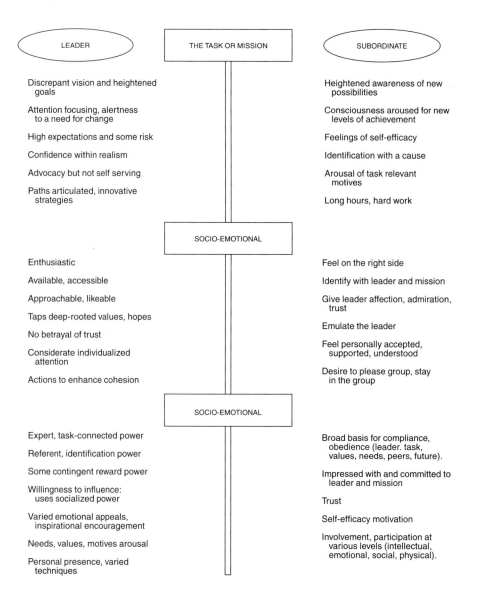

In work organizations, transformational leaders may have strong effects. We have already mentioned several important executives (Chapter 15) who fit the description of the transformational leader (for example, Iaccoca of Chrysler, Perot of EDS, and Mary Kay of Mary Kay Cosmetics). All of them were able to build or change organizations in dramatic ways and, at the same time, obtain very high levels of commitment from others in the firm.

Transformational leadership effects have also been demonstrated in several studies [1, 3, 5, 12, 24, 48]. Seltzer and Bass interviewed subordinates about the leadership of their superiors and found that transformational patterns were very strongly related to desirable organizational outcomes [48]. Similar results were found in a study of naval officers [59]. Howell and Higgins studied champions, or advocates, of new technologies [31]. Those who were perceived as technological champions tended to exhibit transformational leader behavior patterns.

The concept of transformational leadership raises some interesting questions. First, because of the focus on follower commitment to the leader rather than organization performance, what happens if there is a divergence of interests between the transformational leader and other important stakeholders, such as stockholders? Some evidence shows that in the absence of stockholder influence, executives manage the firm in their interest, not the owners'. Rather than maximizing owner return, they may increase the size of the firm in ways that increase the owners' risk [55]. Thus, a transformational leader may manage a firm ineffectively from the stockholders' perspective.

Another question is whether it is possible to develop a transformational style. There is some research, though it is currently rather limited, which suggests that it is possible to develop a charismatic style through training. In a laboratory study, Howell and Frost gave actresses scripts that portrayed charismatic leaders, structuring leaders, and considerate leaders [30]. The emotional state, body language, facial expressions, and other symbolic cues were described and learned for the charismatic role. The charismatic leader was able to get high productivity from the experimental group. Subjects generated more alternatives and were more satisfied with both the task and the leader.

VERTICAL DYAD LINKAGE (VDL) THEORY

The **vertical dyad linkage theory**, focuses on the relationship between the leader and the subordinate in a different way from other models [11]. In some approaches, the leader is measured by his or her responses to some form of psychological measurement instrument. For example, achievement motivation and power motivation are assessed by the responses to the Thematic Apperception Test [38]. In other approaches, leader style is measured by descriptions of the leader by subordinates. For example, initiation of "initiating structure" and "consideration" behaviors are measured in this manner. In VDL theory, responses from *both* the leader and the subordinate about their relationship are considered.

The VDL approach is based on the assumption that leadership can be understood in terms of role relationships between managers and subordinates, members of a vertical dyadic relationship, in an organization. It is in the interest of managers to ensure that the role relationships are well defined since managerial success depends on subordinate performance. Therefore, managers and subordinates "negotiate" these role relationships through a variety of formal and informal processes that occur primarily in the early period of role development [13].

Through this role negotiation process, the leader develops different relationships with different subordinates. In VDL theory, the agreement between leaders and subordinates about the degree of trust in the relationship, subordinate competence, loyalty, and similar factors is measured. Leader-member relationships are classified into "in-group" and "out-group" categories depending on the level of agreement in the dyad. In-group relationships between leaders and subordinates are close, the leader spends more time and energy in them, role participants have more positive attitudes toward the job, and there are fewer problems than in out-group relationships [13].

The research shows that the quality of the linkage affects some subordinate behaviors and perceptions. Liden and Graen found out-group subordinates spent less time on decision making, did not volunteer for extra assignments, and were rated lower by subordinates [35].

Kozlowski and Doherty studied how the quality of supervisor/subordinate relations affected perception of the organizations climate [33]. They found that subordinates who had high quality relationships with supervisors had more positive perception about the climate. Also, their climate perceptions were similar to the supervisors, and there was greater consensus about the climate than was the case for subordinates who had low quality relationships with supervisors. There is little evidence, however, that the nature of the supervisor/subordinate relationship is related to subordinate performance [13].

VDL theory may be a very useful way to study the relational aspect of leadership. While in-group or out-group status may not be related to the subordinates' performance, it seems to be related to several other important aspects of life in organizations. It could be, for example, that the nature of the relationship is an important predictor of subordinate advancement. Further, it may help define more specifically the critical dimensions of the leader-subordinate relationship. It also emphasizes the evolution of that relationship, which has received little attention in the other leadership literature.

CONTINGENCY THEORIES OF LEADERSHIP

Contingency theories of leadership attempt to account systematically for situational factors and leadership effectiveness. The three most prominent contingency theories are Fiedler's contingency theory of leadership, the path-goal theory, and the Vroom-Yetton model discussed in Chapter 13 [16, 15, 27, 57]. These theories attempt to specify how a leader's or manager's behavior is related to effectiveness in different circumstances. This kind of work on leadership provides us with more specific prescriptions about how a manager should function in different types of situations.

☐ CULTURE AS A LEADERSHIP CONTINGENCY

A good illustration of the role of culture on subordinate characteristics and expectations as they are related to the effectiveness of management behavior is provided by Hofstede (1980). He discusses how managers from different countries react to management by objectives, depending on cultural backgrounds. MBO, popularized in the United States, stress mutual goal setting between a superior and a subordinate. In Germany, the emphasis that has developed in MBO is on team objectives and mutual goal setting. This is because the German culture, according to Hofstede, is characterized by tendencies to avoid uncertainty and risk (which can be done by clear goals) and by preferences for small power differences between superiors and subordinates (which come from mutual goal settings).

In France, when MBO was first introduced in the late 1960s, it met with wide acceptance. This is because, at the time, there were powerful, but very brief, pressures to democratize organizations that were very autocratic. Eventually, however, MBO lost its popularity. The reason, according to Hofstede, is that a fundamental value of the French, which pervades their culture, causes them to accept great differences in power between superior and subordinates. MBO would reduce power distance, and it would also depersonalize authority because managers would have internal personal goals, not externally set goals. As a result of the clash between the suggested practice of MBO and the cultural values of the French, managers were unable to effectively use MBO to provide direction to lower-level staff in organizations.

FIEDLER'S CONTINGENCY MODEL OF LEADERSHIP

In 1967, Fiedler proposed a theoretical explanation, called **Fiedler's contingency model**, of how *leadership orientation*, the *group setting*, and *task characteristics* interact to affect group performance. There are three important things about this theory. First, it was the first theory to systematically account for situational factors. Fiedler integrated situational factors such as relationships between the leader and the group, task structure, and leader power into a theory of leadership.

Second, Fielder's concept of leadership considers the "leader's orientation," *not* leader behavior. This orientation is a function of leader needs and personality. Although this may affect a leader's behavior, it is the leader's orientation toward those with whom he or she works that determines how effective the group is. Therefore, consistent with personality theory and trait theories of leadership, Fielder believes that leadership orientation is somewhat stable and not easily changed.

Third, because leadership orientation is relatively stable, it is not likely that a leader will change orientations when confronted with different situations.

These are different from the implications of other models which suggest that a leader must change the way he or she manages, depending upon the situation. Fiedler does take the position that leader orientation, like personality, is stable and not easily changed. This does not mean that a leader cannot behave in different ways, only that either directive or supportive behaviors are more preferable to him or her.

There is some very nice evidence that a person can change behavior in different situations. For example, when a critical, stressful situation exists at work, the supervisor is likely to act in a directive way with subordinates. In a low-stress situation, the same supervisor may be much more "considerate." This was demonstrated in a study of supervisors' behavior under both stressful and nonstressful conditions [23]. When stress was low, the supervisors were less directive and tended to reward subordinates more. When situations became threatening, the supervisors became more directive and were less likely to reward subordinates. Fiedler and Chemers also showed that leaders can sometimes change their behavior from directive to supportive and vice versa [19].

Situational Variables. There are three situational factors in this theory: (1) *leader-member relations*, (2) *task structure*, and (3) *position power*. These determine the amount of situational control that a leader has [17]. The more that these factors are present, the more control the leader has over the situation. The level of situational control determines whether or not a particular leader orientation will be effective.

1. *Leader-Member Relations.* **Leader-member relations** refer to the amount of trust a group has in the leader and how well the leader is liked. When leader-member relations are good, there is usually high satisfaction with work, individual values are not in conflict with organizational values, and there is a good deal of mutual trust between the leader and the group. When relations are bad, mutual trust is lacking. Group cohesiveness may be low, making it difficult to get members to work together. If group cohesiveness is high but leader relations are bad, the group works together to sabotage the organization and the leader.

2. *Task Structure.* **Task structure** is the extent to which jobs (tasks) are specified. A job with high task structure is spelled out in detail—the worker knows what the goals are and how to achieve them. A worker has little leeway in doing the job and must "follow the instructions." For example, the telephone salesperson who works at a computer terminal has very high task structure. For the whole workday, the person sits at a terminal, answers the phone, enters the order, enters the customer's name and other relevant information, then completes the sale.

   Low task structure is present when the objectives of the task or the way it is to be done is somewhat ambiguous. With low task structure, the person must decide how to perform a task each time it is to be done. For example, a machinist may work in the tool room of a factory and be responsible for making a wide range of different parts needed to keep equipment operating. It is also generally thought that the work of managers and many professionals is unstructured.

3. *Position Power*. The amount of position power is a critical factor in this theory. High **position power** exists when a manager has much legitimate authority, which means that he or she can make important decisions without having them cleared by someone at higher organization levels. Low position power means that the manager has only limited authority.

Leader Orientation—The LPC Scale.   Fiedler's leadership concept is a very specific kind of orientation toward others with whom the leader has worked. The leader's orientation is determined by whether or not *the person the leader least likes to work with* is viewed in a positive or a negative way. This orientation toward others is one aspect of the person's motivational hierarchy. It is not a leader behavior, but does reflect a behavioral preference [19]. Those who have positive views of least preferred co-workers are more likely to be disposed to act in more considerate ways. Those with negative views are more likely to focus on tasks, not people.

The leader's orientation is measured by the **Least Preferred Co-worker (LPC) Scale**. A person is asked to think about someone that he or she worked *least* well with, then indicate whether he or she has positive or negative feelings about the least preferred co-worker. "They may produce a very negative description . . . or a relatively more positive description of the least preferred co-worker" [19].

High LPC leaders tend to have favorable views of their least preferred co-workers. They are people-centered and more positively oriented toward the feelings and the relationships of people in the work group. These leaders are able to see some positive things in the people they least like to work with. This type of leader wants to be accepted by others, has strong emotional ties to people in the workplace, and has higher status and self-esteem and is more likely to act in a considerate way [19]. **Low LPC leaders** have more negative views of least preferred co-worker. They are more oriented toward the task, and personal relationships tend to have secondary importance for them. These leaders have tendencies to be directive and controlling and to make subjective, rather than reasoned, judgments about those who work with them.

Leader Effectiveness.   Either Hi LPC or Lo LPC leadership orientations can be effective, depending on the situational control that the leader has [17]. A leader has high **situational control** when (1) leader-member relations are good, (2) there is high task structure, and (3) the leader has high position power. Low situational control occurs when there are (1) poor leader-member relations, (2) low task structure, and (3) the leader has little position power—in this case, obviously, the situation is not a favorable one for the leader. Moderate situation control means the situational characteristics are mixed. Some work to the advantage of the leader (for instance, high position power) whereas others do not (poor leader-member relations).

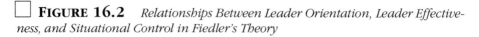

☐ **FIGURE 16.2** *Relationships Between Leader Orientation, Leader Effectiveness, and Situational Control in Fiedler's Theory*

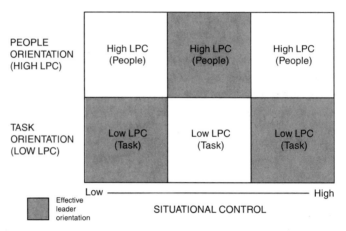

These levels of situational control require leaders with different LPC orientations, as shown in Figure 16.2. The low LPC leader, with a strong task orientation, is most effective when situational control is either very low or very high. Weak situational control is good for the low LPC leader. The group may fall apart or it may not attend to the task requirements unless the leader exerts a good deal of direction. When situational control is strong and the conditions are favorable, the low LPC leader is *also* more effective. The group may be willing to accept the task-oriented leader since success is assured because of their own performance and the vigilance of the leader.

The high LPC leader is most effective when there is moderate situational control. In these cases, the high LPC may be more effective in motivating group members to perform better and to be cooperative toward goal achievement. The lower LPC leader does not have tendencies to do those sorts of things. The low LPC would probably exert pressures to work harder to produce more, which may counteract good performance.

Much research has been done on this approach since the theory was introduced. Meta-analysis of these studies show fairly strong support for it [43, 51].

Implications for Organization Effectiveness. Fiedler's Contingency Theory of leadership carries a simple message about improving organization effectiveness: if the organization is not achieving good results, then replace the leader or change the situation. For example, task structure can be increased or decreased. Jobs can be made more routine and simple or be enlarged and the task structure reduced. The position power of a manager can be increased by delegating more authority and responsibility, or it can be reduced by taking them away. Leader-member relationships may be improved through any number of different training and group development methods.

Cognitive Resource Theory. A serious weakness of leadership theory, in general, is that leader ability is not considered in the various models. With the exception of intelligence, a proxy for problem solving ability, leadership theory has focused on traits, behaviors, and situational properties. Fiedler and Garcia have addressed this matter with **cognitive resource theory** [20]. This theory, a modification of Fiedler's Contingency Theory, integrates a set of trait-like dimensions, called cognitive resources, into his model. Cognitive resources are the person's intelligence, job competence, and technical knowledge and skill that can be used in the task of managing.

Cognitive resource theory is based on the assumptions that (1) managers communicate their plans and strategies to subordinates through directive behavior and (2) that smarter and more experienced leaders can make better decisions than those less intelligent and less experienced. However, intelligent and experienced leaders will not be effective across all situations. For example, "leader experience contributes to performance only in stressful conditions, while leader intelligence contributes only under stress-free conditions" [18]. The reason for this is that under stress the experienced leader can fall back on "a large repertoire of previously learned automatic behaviors and . . . will perform better than a less experienced leader who lacks a large repertoire" [18]. In the stress-free condition, the leader can resort to normal problem solving behavior, based on intelligence. However, as Fiedler notes, "When someone starts shooting at you, it is safer to obey the primitive impulse to run rather than to stop and consider alternative options" [18].

The more complete set of relationships between leader cognitive resources and group performance is outlined by Fiedler and Garcia in the following propositions [20]:

1. Leaders under stress will divert their intellectual abilities from the task to focus on other problems not related to the task. Therefore, under stress, the intelligence of leaders will not correlate with group performance.

2. The intellectual resources of directive leaders are more highly correlated with group success than the intellectual resources of non-directive leaders.

3. Since leader directions will not be implemented unless the group complies, the relationship between leader intelligence and performance is higher when the group is committed to and supports the leader than when it does not.

4. If the leader is non-directive and the group supports and is committed to the leader, the intellectual abilities of the group are related to group performance.

5. The intellectual abilities of the leader contributes to group performance to the extent that the group's task requires those abilities.

6. Under conditions of high stress, especially interpersonal stress, the leader's job relevant *experience*, rather than intellectual abilities, will be related to group performance.

The research support for cognitive resource theory is, in the main, reported in Fiedler and Garcia and the theory has not been extensively tested by others [20]. However, Vecchio found support for the hypothesis that leader intelligence was more strongly related to group performance for directive leaders than for non-directive leaders [56]. Murphy, Blyth, and Fiedler showed that group performance was higher when leaders who had technical training were more directive, but that technically trained groups performed better when the leaders were non-directive [42].

PATH-GOAL THEORY

Path-goal theory has a unique aspect that differentiates it from other leadership theory. It links leader behavior to performance using the expectancy theory of motivation [27, 28].

The basic idea of path-goal theory is shown in Figure 16.3. In order to get desired organizational results, certain tasks must be performed. The results are the goal; the tasks are the path. When appropriate tasks are performed, the goals are achieved. When the goals are achieved, rewards for the individual should follow. The role of the leader is to ensure that the path to the goal is clearly understood by the subordinate and that there are no barriers to the achievement of the goals. There are two key propositions in path-goal theory [21].

1. Subordinates will view a leader's behavior as acceptable and satisfying if it is either an immediate source of satisfaction or will lead to future satisfaction.

2. Leader behaviors will be effective if (a) they make satisfaction or subordinate needs contingent on good performance and (b) they provide guidance, support, and rewards that are not present in the work situation.

☐ **FIGURE 16.3** *Basic Premise of Path-Goal Theory*

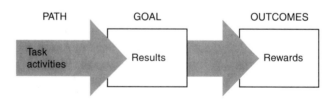

Leader Behaviors. In path-goal theory, there are four different types of leader behavior which affect outcomes and reward [28].

1. **Directive leadership** is the style in which the leader gives guidance and direction to subordinates about job requirements. The leader defines the work roles of group members, determines and communicates performance standards to them, and manages using specific policies, procedures, and rules. Directive leadership is similar to the Ohio State concept of initiating structure.

2. **Supportive leadership** is a style in which the leader is concerned with the needs of those who report to him or her. The supportive leader is friendly and approachable. Members are treated as equals. This set of behaviors is similar to the style called consideration.

3. **Participative leaders** act in a consultative style. They seek advice from subordinates about problems and consider these recommendations seriously before decisions are made.

4. In **achievement-oriented leadership**, leaders set challenging goals for their work groups. These leaders expect their groups to perform well and communicate this to subordinates.

Contingency Factors. Leader behavior interacts with two contingency factors to affect subordinate performance and satisfaction. The contingency factors, shown interacting with leader behavior in Figure 16.4 are (1) subordinate characteristics and (2) environmental factors.

☐ **FIGURE 16.4** *Basic Factors in Path-Goal Theory*

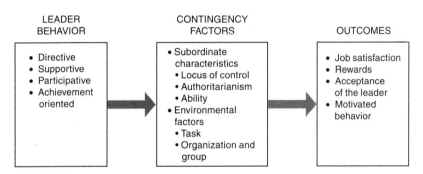

Three *subordinate characteristics* affect how subordinates perceive the leader's behaviors. These are (1) locus of control, (2) authoritarianism, and (3) ability. Those subordinates with an internal locus of control tend to react more favorably toward participative leadership. Directive leadership is more satisfying to subordinates with an external locus of control. Participative leadership styles are more acceptable to subordinates who are low in authoritarianism, whereas those high in authoritarianism react more positively to directive leadership. Those subordinates with high ability will see directive leadership as unnecessary and undesirable, and will react unfavorably to it.

The *environmental factors* are (1) the task and (2) the organization and group. These may affect performance and satisfaction in several ways. First, the level of task certainly (or task structure) determines the clarity of the path to the goal. When tasks are uncertain, a more directive style of leadership may be more effective. Second, extrinsic rewards are located in the organization and the task environment. Third, significant environmental barriers to performance may exist. Figure 16.5 shows how these environmental factors are related to the task (for example, the path and the goal). It also shows that the role of leader in path-goal theory is to increase task valences and reward valences, remove barriers, and ensure that the right level of task certainty exists.

☐ **FIGURE 16.5**   *Leader Role in Path-Goal Theory*

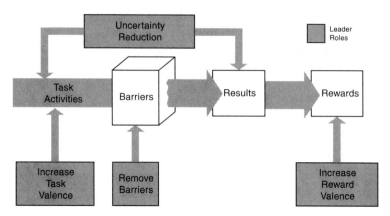

What Leadership Style?   The leader's role in path-goal theory varies, depending on the situation. First, the leader must reduce uncertainty by clarifying expectations about the desired results or the way to get them (task uncertainty). Second, the leader should remove barriers to performance. If something gets in the way, the leader must try to eliminate it. Lastly, the leader must attempt to increase the subordinates valence for the task itself, the achievement of the goal or both.

From Figure 16.5, you can make the following predictions about what leadership styles would be most effective. If there is a high level of task certainty because the subordinate knows how to do the job or because the task is very routine, then the path to the goal is clear. The best leadership style here is supportive, not directive. Directive leadership may increase performance because there is added pressure to produce, but it may lead to decreased job satisfaction because of close supervision.

When there is high uncertainty about the task or the goal to be achieved, the leader must clarify them. When the subordinate is uncertain about the best way to do a job, the manager should give instructions. If the goals are not clear to the subordinate, then they should be spelled out. When there is high task uncertainty, the most effective leadership style is to be directive.

Research on Path-Goal Theory.   Path-goal theory is a complex view of leadership. With four different types of leader behavior, three subordinate characteristics, and two environmental factors, it is very difficult to evaluate the whole theory. Most research tests some specific proposition from path-goal theory, and the results are mixed, partly because of the difficulty in testing the theory. However, when path-goal hypotheses are tested in carefully designed studies that reflect the conditions outlined in the theory, the results are more encouraging. Schreisheim and DeNisi tested some facets of the theory in a bank and in a manufacturing company [47]. They found that directive leader behavior was related to subordinate satisfaction with supervision exactly as predicted by the theory. Subordinates who worked in relatively routine jobs were dissatisfied with more directive leadership while those who worked on less structured jobs liked it more.

☐ **PATH-GOAL
THEORY IN PRACTICE** _____

Two years ago, Joe Bond was hired as a production superintendent in the new Nelson Appliance manufacturing plant. This plant was designed with the most advanced equipment available and according to some of the ideas of participative management and self-directed work teams. The combination of new technology and more human-resource-oriented management would, the management of Nelson believed, make the plant efficient and highly competitive.

Joe was hired because he had the reputation of being the best start-up supervisor in the industry. He had been through five other starts, and in each case his groups always seemed to develop fastest, and they achieved production quotas, both in quality and quantity, more quickly than other groups.

Joe is a trained machinist. He developed some basic skills in electronics by attending evening courses at a community college and self-study. He has no formal engineering training, but with his experience and knowledge, he has excellent production instincts.

There was never any doubt about Joe's technical competence, but there were some reservations in the mind of Paul Gerrity, the plant manager, about whether or not Joe could work with the high-involvement management style that Nelson Manufacturing intended for the plant. Gerrity had a long talk with Joe to discuss these concerns and to impress on him that the plant was not going to be one of the "iron-fisted" plants that were common in the industry. Joe told Gerrity, "I'll manage this team the right way. Don't worry." But still Gerrity wasn't sure.

Gerrity watched Joe as the new plant started. Joe worked very differently from the other production supervisors. He systematically rotated all the new employees around to all the jobs in his unit. Each one had to get the feel of every job. The other supervisors allowed much less rotation.

Another thing that Joe did was to attend all training sessions on the equipment with his team. These training sessions were usually taught by the machine manufacturers, and they were very important in getting the workers' skill levels raised. After each training session, Joe would meet with the team to discuss problems that had not been thoroughly solved.

Joe's team also spent the most time of any on maintenance. When there was a breakdown, Joe would shut down the machine and fix it right. Many of the other supervisors wouldn't do that. They would figure out some way to keep the machine running during their shift and let the next shift worry about fixing it. As a matter of fact, Terry Golden, who was the

☐ PATH-GOAL THEORY . . .

supervisor of the work team that was on the floor before Joe's team, told the personnel manager it was great to have Joe's team follow his. "That way," Terry said, "I can get the production, and I know that the equipment will be in good shape when we get there the next day."

This went on for six months, and during that time Paul Gerrity was surprised to see that Joe's production was the lowest of the teams, and it was also hard for Gerrity to understand why Joe's team didn't complain about him. After all, Joe was reputed to be a "tough supervisor." The team's quality was always high because Joe never allowed the equipment to run "out of spec" like the other supervisors. He would fix it, so he had few quality problems. Still, his group had the poorest production record. One time when Gerrity complained to Joe about production, Joe said, "We don't run as much as everyone else because we keep fixing their mistakes." Gerrity became angry and pushed Joe a little hard. Joe told him, "I'll manage my group my way. If it's not what you want, I can leave."

About eight months after the plant opened, the productivity of Joe's group began to increase. The team maintained its quality level, but output went up six months in a row. Within 15 months from the plant opening, Joe's team was usually number one, and never below number two, in production and quality.

Joe Bond's approach to managing can be understood in terms of path-goal theory. His training and coaching clarified how the work was to be done properly, and his firm stand on quality left no uncertainty about what results were expected.

SUBSTITUTES FOR LEADERSHIP

The image of the leader in leadership theory is of a person who is able to influence others to act toward organization objectives. This image is reinforced by the popular press, television, and films" [41]. However, we know that other factors such as ability, intrinsic motivation, the nature of technology, and the structure of the organization can affect performance and satisfaction of members. In fact, in some instances, these factors may be even more crucial than leadership [32, 53]. They can serve **substitutes for leadership** because they, not the action of the leader, contribute to success or failure [32]. Suppose that effectiveness of a group depends on (1) performing the task and (2) good working relationships among members. From a leadership behavior perspective, "initiating structure" could provide the members with knowledge about how to perform the task. Good working relationships can also develop because the leader exhibits a "considerate" style of behavior.

But there are other ways that task knowledge and good relations can be present, and they are substitutes for the behavior of the leader. Task knowledge may be present because the group members know how to do the job or because there are specific procedures that are well known by the members. These work in place of "initiating structure." There may be good working relationships because of work group norms, because all the workers are friends, or for many other reasons. These are substitutes for "consideration."

There are three sources of leadership substitutes: the subordinate, the task, and the organization. Specific substitutes are shown in Table 16.1. This table shows that if a person gets feedback because the task itself allows him or her to make a judgment about how well things are going, there is no need to have a manager give feedback.

☐ **TABLE 16.1**   Some Substitutes for Leadership

Subordinate Characteristics	Task Factors	Organization Dimensions
Ability	Repetitiveness	Formalization
Experience	Clarity	Availability of special staff
Background and training	Task-provided feedback	Work group cohesiveness
Professional orientation		Spatial distance between the leader and the group
Indifference toward organization rewards		

Source: S. Kerr, and S. Jermier, "Substitute for Leadership" *Organizational Behavior and Human Performance*, 1978, 22, 375-403 [32].

The concept of substitutes for leadership is important for two reasons. First, it suggests that contextual control (discussed in the previous chapter) is an alternative to *active* leadership to get obtain good results. For example, selecting competent and motivated people is one way, and job enrichment is another. In fact, the High Involvement Organization (see Chapter 8) is meant to be a substitute for leadership, trying to improve performance with intrinsically motivating work, supportive working conditions, and a pay structure which provides incentives to learn new skills. However, it takes leadership and the use of power to create leadership substitutes and the conditions for them to operate effectively in organizations. The development of HIOs, as one particular example, call for extraordinary leadership in all phases of formulation and implementation.

Second, there are implications about the interaction of leadership, leadership substitutes, and the nature of the organization. The various factors that act as substitutes will not have similar effects in all organizations [54]. For example, in mechanistic organizations, the task itself will provide clarity, formalization will provide direction, and lower-level workers will be indifferent toward organization rewards. In organic organizations, however, task competence, high intrinsic task motivation, and cohesive work groups will be more powerful substitutes.

It is also likely that the effects of leadership substitutes vary by organization level [54]. At higher levels in mechanistic organizations, socialization and experience are likely to be more powerful factors that affect performance than at lower levels. At lower levels, formalization and technology may be stronger substitutes.

SUMMARY

Organizations are concerned with leadership because of the need to select and promote individuals into management positions. The manager's role is to get the work of the organization done through the effective use of physical and human resources. Therefore, we believe that an effective manager should be a good leader.

Although there is no doubt about the close relationship between leadership and management, there is more to it than simply understanding the role of the leader/manager. In previous chapters, we have shown that there are many reasons why people are willing to cooperate to achieve organization goals. Many of the reasons are only incidentally related to the superior-subordinate relationship. For instance, the broad shape of the psychological contract is probably constructed in early socialization, before one joins an organization.

However, it is important to know how situational factors, the work setting, and the characteristics of the subordinate interact with the personality and the behavior of a manager/leader to affect the level of individual and organization performance. In this chapter, we have discussed several theories of leadership that illustrate this. Path-goal theory and Fiedler's work explain leadership phenomena with a greater number of situational factors than had been used in earlier approaches. VDL theory contributes to understanding leadership because of its focus on the relationship between the leader and the subordinate. At the end of the chapter, however, we show how contextual control of members can operate through substitutes for leadership, relating leadership back to the subject of power, discussed in the previous chapter.

☐ KEY CONCEPTS

Achievement-oriented leadership	High LPC leaders	Path-goal theory
Autocratic leadership	Initiating structure	Position power
Behavioral approaches to leadership	Laissez-faire leadership	Production-centered leadership
Cognitive resource theory	Leader-member relations	Situational control
Consideration	Leader motive pattern	Substitutes for leadership
Contingency theories	Leadership	Supportive leadership
Directive leadership	Low LPC leaders	Task structure
Employee-centered leadership	LPC scale	Trait theories
Fiedler's contingency model	Participative leadership	Transactional leadership
		Transformational leadership theory
		Vertical Dyad Linkage theory

☐ STUDY QUESTIONS

1. Define leadership. How is it different from the concept of political activity discussed in Chapter 15?
2. What are trait theories of leadership? Why are they deficient as explanations of leadership?
3. How do behavioral approaches differ from trait theories of leadership?
4. How do contingency theories of leadership differ from trait theories and behavioral theories?
5. What are the contingency factors in the path-goal theory? In Fiedler's theory of leadership? Compare and contrast Fiedler's theory with path-goal theory.
6. Can you apply the concepts from the substitutes for leadership to a situation in which you have had to work?
7. Analyze the leadership style of the President of the United States using at least two different theories of leadership.
8. How can you integrate some idea about charismatic power (Chapter 15) with the concepts of leadership?
9. How would the substitutes for leadership vary by type of organization (see Chapter 2)? By level of organization? For professionals compared to indifferents compared to organization-oriented personality types (see Chapter 4)?
10. What is the important difference between VDL theory and other approaches? Relate this approach to topics considered elsewhere in the text, for example, the Good Enough Theory of Promotion or attribution theory.

CASE

☐ THE DENTAL MANAGEMENT ROUNDTABLE

Dr. Kim Smithson, the head of the state committee on dental practice improvement, was the moderator of a panel on the leadership and supervision at the annual state convention of the American Dental Association. He invited two old friends, Dr. Tom Sims and Dr. Douglas Harris, to participate because both are outstanding dentists and have very successful practices. Kim believed they could provide some important insights to the other dentists attending the convention. After an introduction by the Program Chairperson, Kim announced the format for the panel discussion. "Drs. Sims, Harris, and I have decided that the best way to proceed is that I will interview each of them. After a series of questions that I will pose to each of them, we will be open to questions from the audience. Dr. Sims will be first, then Dr. Harris."

Smithson:	When I visited your office, I noticed you have two other dentists working with you. Are you partners?
Sims:	No, they are employees. They get a certain percentage of my net collections. With this compensation system, they get more than the average dentist in private practice.
Jackson:	This payment procedure helps to motivate them?
Sims:	Yes, it does. That is one reason for it.
Smithson:	You also have your own laboratory technician who makes, dentures, bridges and inlays.
Sims:	That's because, in addition to general dentistry, I specialize in trauma work, and we need a full-time person.
Smithson:	Trauma work?
Sims:	Yes, many of my patients need mouth reconstruction because of automobile accidents. These patients are referred to me by other dentists. This work is quite challenging. It's a help to have the technician in the office all the time because we bring him in when a patient is being examined. He can get a good look at the patient's whole mouth, general appearance, the color of the teeth, and so on. This is a big advantage for technician in doing the dental work.
Smithson:	How many dental assistants do you have?
Sims:	I have eleven. They are not all working at the same time, however.
Smithson:	Do they work 40 hours a week?

☐ THE DENTAL MANAGEMENT . . .

Sims:	No, they work a 4 day week, which is less than assistants at a lot of other places. This is one reason why they stay with me for so long. I haven't had an assistant leave me for over two years.
Smithson:	Do the assistants rotate among the different dentists?
Sims:	No. Each dentist has his own assistant. However, whenever one is not busy, he or she is supposed to help out somewhere else.
Smithson:	Do you have much trouble among your staff? Fighting, arguments, etc?
Sims:	Yes, some. You know how people are.
Smithson:	What do you do? Do you step in?
Sims:	No, I tell then to work things out for themselves. I never get involved because if I do, the staff might begin to think I am playing favorites and get angry.
Smithson:	Do you usually do that? Let them work things out for themselves?
Sims:	Yes, for nearly everything. They work out their own schedule, their own vacation periods, and so on. They always come up with a plan that is satisfactory with them. I think it's best if they do these things themselves. They know what they want.
Smithson:	Do they ever have any trouble reaching a decision?
Sims:	Yes, but they always do.
Smithson:	How about selection and training? How do you do that?
Sims:	For me, selection is not a big problem. Most of my staff have been with me for a long time, and they seem to be very happy with me. If I needed somebody in the past, my present assistants can usually find someone for me.

As for training, I believe in cross training. All my staff have worked as a receptionist, clerk, assistant, and so on. This gives us flexibility, and they understand each other's problems better. |
Smithson:	How about pay?
Sims:	Their pay is at the going rate for the region. Sometimes they might get a little more for a shorter work week, which is flexible for them.
Smithson:	Have you ever fired anybody?
Sims:	Yes, once I had an assistant who just could not get along with the others.

531

☐ THE DENTAL MANAGEMENT . . .

Smithson: Your practice is quite large. How long has it been this size?

Sims: I have built it slowly to this point. Now we are crowded for space. I moved into my present suite, which actually is very large, several years ago, thinking that I would need the space because I had a practice about this size in mind.

Smithson: Your patients must be satisfied.

Sims: Yes, they are. They get a lot of personal attention in my office. I'm a strong believer in that. I make sure I talk to every patient I can, at least for a few minutes, whenever I can. I also make sure every patient gets some treatment, now matter how small, on every visit, even for the first one. At the first visit, I scale their teeth, which helps me to learn more about them and their problems.

              I try to impress on my staff that patients want somebody to be interested in them and their welfare. This works. I have patients who come from out of state to me.

Smithson: Do you feel that it is important to give your assistants attention, too?

Sims: Absolutely. My assistants want me to take an interest in them and their problems. They want to be accepted. To feel part of something.

Smithson: How have your patients responded to several dentists? Do you trade off patients?

Sims: Yes, we do. If somebody is busy, another dentist fills in.

Smithson: From the way your office seemed to operate when I visited you, I would say you had a very efficient operation. Is that right?

Sims: Yes I do. I'm quite happy with it. But, I have good people. The most important thing to remember in running a successful operation is to have good people. You get good people by providing good salaries and by training and motivating them.

Smithson: Why are they motivated to do good work?

Sims: Because the work is interesting and because here we all have an interest in each other's work. We review each other's work all of the time. Knowing that somebody else is going to look at your work motivates you to do your best.

Smithson: What if somebody thinks that something with a patient should be done differently. Do you discuss this in private?

☐ THE DENTAL MANAGEMENT . . .

Sims:	No, I believe in open disagreement, even in front of the patient. We don't fight about it. We discuss it. Of course, I am the boss ultimately.
Smithson:	Do you mean to tell me that the dentists and the assistants all have an open discussion about what to do about a particular problem a patient has right in front of them?
Sims:	Yes, that's right. That's what we do. And the group discussing a patient's particular problem may include some of the other dentists as well as the assistants and lab technician.

Dr. Smithson thanked Dr. Sims, then turned to Dr. Harris.

Smithson:	You also have quite a large staff.
Harris:	Yes, I do. I didn't always have as many as I do right now. With my system now, however, I need them all. After a patient sees the receptionist, he or she is routed around the office to various work stations to provided necessary personal information and get information about the procedures that will be done. Then the patient pays. A tag is attached to the patient so that the staff knows exactly what is to be done. Then the patient is routed to the various work stations where we work on them.
Smithson:	How do you select your staff?
Harris:	I've never had any trouble finding good people. That's because I pay them at least 20 percent more than they earn anywhere else.
Smithson:	Why do you do that?
Harris:	Because I want the best staff possible. I run a tight operation here. I demand a lot from a person as compared to what he or she might have been used to in the past. The staff must keep very busy every minute of the day, so I figure I've got to pay them more to get the ones I want. I want individuals who are ambitious, who are willing to work extra hard for more money, who are trainable, and who will do what they are told. In addition, my staff must do things here they don't do in other places. I also want them to have operating room experience, if possible.
Smithson:	Why?
Harris:	Because of the work I do in my practice. An assistant or an auxiliary here must not become upset at a lot of blood. Things happen, we have emergencies, it gets messy, sometimes patients might vomit and so on.

☐ THE DENTAL MANAGEMENT

Smithson:	Does all your staff have operating room experience?
Harris:	Not all, but most of them do. I have two former nurses. The others have worked for oral surgeons.
Smithson:	How do you recruit them?
Harris:	Usually with ads in the newspaper, but I have hired some whom my present auxiliaries have known.
Smithson:	Do you have a probationary period?
Harris:	Absolutely. If they are not satisfactory at the end of three months, I get rid of them. Actually, if they are really bad before the end of the probationary periods, I tell them that they are not working out and let them go immediately. If I decide to keep them after three months I give them a substantial bonus at that time.
Smithson:	Do they have permanent jobs then?
Harris:	Not necessarily. I fired two auxiliaries who had been with me over a year.
Smithson:	Why?
Harris:	One started fighting with some of the other auxiliaries. In the other case, the auxiliary started slacking off. With my practice, I can't tolerate those sorts of things. You've seen how we operate. We are on the go all of the time; so we can't put up with less than full attention to the job.
Smithson:	How do you keep your staff motivated?
Harris:	This isn't a problem. After all, they are getting paid more in my office, and they want to keep their job. They know I'll let them go if they don't keep up. Also, it's not like they are working in an office where there is just filling of teeth. We do serious work which involves a great deal of responsibility for the well being of the patient.
Smithson:	Do you think you attract an unusual type of employee here?
Harris:	I know I do. They are more motivated and trustworthy than the typical dental assistant.
Smithson:	Do you supervise them directly? Give them orders, that sort of thing?
Harris:	Just during operations. I have a lead auxiliary who handles all the details of who is to do what, what their schedules are and so on.
Smithson:	Would you say that the status position of the employees to each other is highly related to their salary?

☐ THE DENTAL MANAGEMENT

Harris: Yes, because that in turn is related to the complexity of their duties and to their experience. The auxiliaries working with the dentists directly earn the highest salaries.

Smithson: Do you intervene in any disputes among the staff?

Harris: No. I tell them I won't tolerate any bickering and trouble.

Smithson: Do you talk to the auxiliaries about their personal problems and their ambitions or things like that?

Harris: Not very much. You saw how busy I was when you visited my offices. Sometimes a staff member will come to me and ask if she can upgrade herself, and I give them a chance to do so whenever possible. Actually, I like my employees to have the ability to do many of the jobs we have to do around here so that they can fill in for each other when necessary.

QUESTIONS

1. What are the main differences in the leadership styles of Drs. Sims and Dr. Harris?
2. Which do you think is the most effective manager, based on the theories discussed in the chapter?
3. Are the "substitutes" for leadership different in the two practices? What are they? How are they different?

REFERENCES

1. Avolio, B.J., Waldman, D.A., and Einstein, W.O. Transformational leadership in a management game simulation. *Group and Organization Studies,* 1988, 13(1), 59-80.
2. Barsoux, J.L. and Lawrence, P. The making of a French manager. *Harvard Business Review,* 1991, 69, 58-67.
3. Bass, B.M. *Leadership beyond expectations.* New York: Free Press, 1985.
4. Bass, B. M. *Bass and Stogdill's handbook of leadership: Theory, research, and managerial applications.* New York: The Free Press, 1990.
5. Bass, B.M., Avolio, B.J., and Goodheim, L. Biography and assessment of transformational leadership at the world class level. *Journal of Management,* 1987, 13(1), 7-19.
6. Blake, R.R., and Mouton, J.S. *Building a dynamic corporation through grid organization development.* Reading, MA: Addison-Wesley, 1969.
7. Bowers, D.G., and Seashore, S.E. Predicting organizational effectiveness with a four-factor theory of leadership. *Administrative Science Quarterly,* April 1966, 11, 238-63.

8. Carroll, S.J., and Tosi H.L. *Management by Objectives: Applications and research*. New York: Macmillan, 1973.

9. Chen, C.C., and Meindl, J. R. The construction of leadership images in the popular press: The case of Donald Burr and People Express. *Administrative Science Quarterly*, 1991, 36, 521-551.

10. Cornelius, E.T., and Lane, F.B. The power motive and managerial success in a professionally oriented service industry organization. *Journal of Applied Psychology*, 1984, 69(1), 32-9.

11. Dansereau, F., Graen, G., and Haga, W.J. A vertical dyad linkage approach to leadership within formal organizations—A longitudinal investigation of the role making process. *Organizational Behavior and Human Performance*, 1975, 13, 46-78.

12. Deluga, R.J. Relationship of transformational and transactional leadership with employee influencing strategies. *Group and Organization Studies*, 1988, 13, 456-467.

13. Dienesch, R.M., and Liden, R.C. Leader-member exchange model of leadership: A critique and further development. *Academy of Management Review*, 1986, 11(3), 618-34.

14. Downton, J.V. *Rebel leadership: Commitment and charisma in the revolutionary process*. New York: Free Press, 1973.

15. Evans, M.G. *The effects of supervisory behavior on worker perceptions of their path-goal relationships*. Ph.D. dissertation. New Haven: Yale University, 1968.

16. Fiedler, F.E. *A theory of leadership effectiveness*. New York: McGraw-Hill, 1967.

17. Fiedler, F.E. The contingency model and the dynamics of the leadership process. In L. Berkowitz, ed. *Advances in experimental social psychology*, 2nd ed. New York: Academic Press, 1978, 59-111.

18. Fiedler, F.E. Time based measures of leadership experience and organizational performance: A review of research and a preliminary model. *The Leadership Quarterly*, 1992, 3, 5-21.

19. Fiedler, F.E., and Chemers, M. *Leadership and effective management*. Glenview, IL: Scott, Foresman, 1974.

20. Fiedler, F.E., and Garcia, J.E. *New approaches to effective leadership: Cognitive resources and organization performance*. New York: John Wiley, 1987.

21. Filley, A.C., House, R.J., and Kerr, S. *Managerial process and organizational behavior*. Glenview, IL: Scott, Foresman, 1976.

22. Fleishman, E.A., Mumford, M. D., Zaccaro, S. J., Levin, D. Y., Krothin, A. L., and Hein, M.B. Taxonomic efforts in the description of leadership behavior: A synthesis and functional interpretation. *The Leadership Quarterly*, 1991, 2, 245-280.

23. Fodor, E.M. Group stress, authoritarian style of control, and the use of power. *Journal of Applied Psychology*, 1976, 61, 313-18.

24. Hater, J.J., and Bass, B. M. Superiors' evaluations and subordinates' perceptions of transformational and transactional leadership. *Journal of Applied Psychology*, 1988, 73, 695-702.

25. Hersey, P., and Blanchard, K. *Management of organizational behavior*. New York: Prentice-Hall, 1988.

26. Hofstede, G. *Culture's consequences: International differences in work-related values*. Beverly Hills, CA: Sage Publications, 1980a.

27. House, R.J. A path-goal theory of leader effectiveness. *Administrative Science Quarterly*, 1971, 16, 334-38.

28. House, R.J., and Mitchell, T.R. Path-goal theory of leadership. *Journal of Contemporary Business*, 1974, 4, 81-97.

29. House, R.J. and Singh, J.V. Organization behavior: Some new directions for I/O psychology. *Annual Review of Psychology*, 1987, 38, 669-718.

30. Howell, J.M., and Frost, P.J.A laboratory study of charismatic leadership. *Organizational Behavior and Human Decision Processes*, 1989, 43, 243-269.

31. Howell, J.M., and Higgins, C.A. Champions of technological innovation. *Administrative Science Quarterly*, 1990, 35, 317-341.

32. Kerr, S., and Jermier, J. Substitutes for leadership: Their meaning and measurement. *Organizational Behavior and Human Performance*, 1978, 22, 375-403.

33. Kozlowski, S.W.J., and Doherty, M.L. Integration of climate and leadership: Examination of a neglected issue. *Journal of Applied Psychology*, 1989, 74, 546-554.

34. Lewin, K., Lippitt, R., and White, R.K. Pattens of aggressive behavior in experimentally created social climates. *Journal of Social Psychology*, 1939, 10, 271-99.

35. Liden, R., and Graen, G. Generalizability of the vertical dyad linkage model. *Academy of Management Journal*. 1980, 23, 451-65.

36. Lowin, A., and Craig, J. The influence of level of performance on managerial style: An experimental object lesson on the ambiguity of correlational data. *Organizational Behavior and Human Performance*, 1968, 3, 440-58.

37. Maier, N.R.F., Hoffman, L., and Read, W.H. Superior-subordinate communication: The relative effectiveness of managers who held their subordinates' positions. *Personnel Psychology*, 1963, 16, 1-12.

38. McClelland, D.A. *Power: The inner experience.* New York: Irvington, 1975.

39. McClelland, D.A. *Human motivation.* Glenview, IL: Scott, Foresman, 1985.

40. McClelland, D.A., and Boyatzis, R.E. Leadership motive pattern and long-term success in management. *Journal of Applied Psychology*, 1982, 67, 737-43.

41. Meindl, J.R., Ehrlich, S.B., and Dukerich, J.M. The romance of leadership. *Administrative Science Quarterly*, 1985, 30, 78-102.

42. Murphy, S.E., Blyth, D., and Fiedler, F. E. Cognitive resources theory and the utilization of the leader's and group member's technical competence. *The Leadership Quarterly*, 1992, 3, 237-254.

43. Peters, L.H., Harke, D.D., and Pohlman, J.T. Fiedler's contingency theory of leadership: An application of the meta-analysis procedures of Schmidt and Hunter. *Psychological Bulletin*, 1985, 97(2), 274-85.

44. Pfeffer, J. The ambiguity of leadership. *Academy of Management Review*, 1977, 2, 104-12.

45. Pfeffer, J., and Davis-Blake, A. Administrative succession and organizational performance: How administrator experience mediates the succession effect. *Academy of Management Journal*, 1987, 29, 72-83.

46. Reinganum, M.R. The effect of executive succession on stockholder wealth. *Administrative Science Quarterly*, 1985, 30, 46-60.

47. Schreisheim, C., and DeNisi, A.S. Task dimensions as moderators of the effects of instrumental leadership: A two-sample replicated test of path-goal leadership theory. *Journal of Applied Psychology*, 1981, 66, 589-97.

48. Seltzer, J., and Bass, B. M. Transformational leadership: Beyond initiation and consideration. *Journal of Management*, 1990, 16, 693-703.

49. Smith, M., and White, M. C. Strategy, CEO specialization, and succession. *Administrative Science Quarterly*, 1987, 32, 263-280.

50. Stogdill, R.M. *Handbook of leadership: A survey of theory and research*. New York: Free Press, 1974.

51. Strube, M.J., and Garcia, J.E. A meta-analytic investigation of Fiedler's contingency model of leadership effectiveness. *Psychological Bulletin*, 1981, 90, 307-21.

52. Thomas, A.B. Does leadership make a difference to organizational performance? *Administrative Science Quarterly*, 1988, 33, 388-400.

53. Tosi, H.L. When leadership isn't enough. In H.L. Tosi and W.C. Hamner, eds. *Organizational behavior and management: A contingency approach*. New York: John Wiley, 1982, 403-11.

54. Tosi, H.L. *The environment/organization/person contingency model: A meso approach to the study of organizations*. Greenwich, CT: JAI Press, Inc., 1992.

55. Tosi, H.L. & Gomez-Mejia, L. The decoupling of CEO pay and performance: an agency theory perspective. *Administrative Science Quarterly*, 1989, 34, 169-189.

56. Vecchio, R.P. Theoretical and empirical examination of cognitive resource theory. *Journal of Applied Psychology*, 1990, 75, 141-147.

57. Vroom, V.H., and Yetton, P.W. *Leadership and decision making*. Pittsburgh: University of Pittsburgh Press, 1973.

58. Weiner, N. and Mahoney, T. A. A model of corporate performance as a function of environmental, organizational, and leadership influences. *Academy of Management Journal*, 1981, 24, 453-470.

59. Yammarino, F.J., and Bass, B. M. Transformation leadership and multiple levels of analysis. *Human Relations*, 1990, 43, 975-995.

Chapter 17
*Organization
Change and Development*

Ames National Bank is one of the largest in the southwestern United States. Like most large banks, it was quite highly centralized with a strong emphasis on formal lines of communication through a rather rigid hierarchy. While the managerial and professional ranks have an interest in lifelong careers in the bank, most lower-level employees plan to work for a short term. Like most banks in recent years, competitiveness with other financial institutions had greatly increased.

Recently, Beth Williams, a vice president, had some problems requiring immediate attention. The first problem was with a subordinate manager, Bill Cantril. Two of his subordinates had quit the bank recently. This was quite a loss because the bank had spent considerable time and money training them. They had complained about Bill's management style. He had been abrupt with them and frequently criticized them, sometimes in front of others. He rarely praised them for a job well done. When Beth raised these cases with Bill, he said that if the bank gave him decent subordinates, he wouldn't have to chew them out. He refused to admit there was any trouble with his style of management. Beth knew better because Bill had always had a reputation of being a difficult boss, but she knew he had great technical competence which the bank needed.

Beth's other problem was with an employee suggestion system that had been installed as a demonstration project in her unit about eight months previously. The idea for the suggestion system came from a senior bank official who had recently visited other banks that had such systems in place. He thought it would work quite well for generating ideas from employees for improving efficiency and productivity. Improvements were needed. Labor costs were high for a bank, clerical and reporting errors were increasing, and cooperation had broken down between several departments. An external consultant had recommended that the new suggestion system be installed in one unit to see how it worked, and Beth had volunteered. She worked hard with the Human Resource Department and the consultant to set up the program. Some eight months later, however, very few worthwhile suggestions had been received. Most focused entirely on improving working conditions for the employees—flexible hours, decor, custodial services, and so forth. Beth was afraid that the senior manager who had started this system would blame her for its failure. She wondered if the bank should start over with a new design.

Beth's problems are typical of managers who are pressured to change something. But sometimes the results are disappointing, as in Beth's case. Sometimes the objectives are achieved, but perhaps not fully. To have successful change, it is necessary to know why they are necessary and what factors facilitate or inhibit change attempts. In the case of Ames National Bank, it would be useful for Beth to know how the personality of individuals, their degree of organization commitment, and the organizational structure and culture could affect the success of her change efforts. In this chapter, we explore why a change effort might succeed or fail. We will also discuss some approaches which are effective in achieving individual, group, or organization-wide change.

SUCCESSFUL CHANGE AND ORGANIZATIONAL EFFECTIVENESS

Successful change today is associated with greater organizational effectiveness. This is partly because the movement toward globalization of business worldwide has greatly increased competitiveness. Firms everywhere now face far more global competition than formerly. Competitors are often very efficient, putting pressure on others to improve their own productivity. In addition, the rate of technological change is now very high. This fosters new products and the processes for making them. There have also been significant changes in the political-legal environments of firms, and in the social environment from which the firms import its human resources.

Trends in technology development and manufacturing systems are now causing managers to restructure organizations and become more flexible [12, 35]. The conclusion is inescapable: organizations must be masters of change. McGill, Slocum, and Lei have identified a number of U.S. firms that seem to have mastered managing the change process and, as a result, have performed very well in recent years [28]. These firms include British Petroleum, Whirlpool, Eastman Kodak, Arthur Anderson, and Taco Bell. These companies have a style of management called "generative learning" which allows them to quickly respond to a wide variety of environmental changes. These organizations encourage initiative, experiment, exhibit openness, and take risks with new ways of conducting business.

A CHANGE MODEL

An approach to the change process is shown in Figure 17.1. Pressures for change may be directed at an individual, a group, or an organization. The change can be planned and systematic or more informal and reactive. Systematic change efforts are often designed and implemented by consultants, whereas informal and reactive change efforts occur on an everyday basis as managers carry out their job responsibilities. Figure 17.1 also shows that some change methods are more appropriate for individuals, others for groups, and yet others for an entire organization. We will discuss these methods in this chapter, describing how they can be used and how effective they might be.

FIGURE 17.1   *A Basic Change Model*

KEY STAGES IN CHANGE PROCESS / PRESSURES TO CHANGE	Individual	Group	Organization
Create motivation to change	• Training need analysis • Performance feedback	• Modeling • Survey research	• Action research • Pilot study analysis
Use appropriate change method	• Training of individuals • Individual counseling	• Group training • Team building	• Change task forces • System audits
Reinforcement of change	• Positive reactions • Supervisory praise • Performance success	• Group praise • Improved functioning • Performance success	• Improved functioning • Praise by other organizations • Performance success

TARGETS OF CHANGE

THE FOCUS OF CHANGE PROGRAMS ARE OFTEN A MOVING TARGET

A discouraging feature of change programs that involve an attempt to catch up with competitors in the marketplace lies in the fact that such competitors are often moving ahead on a variety of fronts. If companies catch up with such competitors in some respects, there is the problem of the target moving ahead in other areas requiring a constant and never ending change process.

A good example in the attempts of U.S. manufacturers to catch up to Japanese competitors. Such U.S. manufacturers have now improved so much in recent years that the Japanese no longer have a clear lead in many areas and even may have fallen behind in some such as reliable delivery. This was revealed in a survey by Deloitte & Touche consultants of 900 U.S. and Japanese companies with respect to their key manufacturing strategies. While the gap between U.S. and Japanese firms has closed significantly in such areas as strong supplier relationships, durable products, rapid delivery, and having broad distribution channels, the Japanese, already having a high degree of expertise in these areas, have moved on to other competitive advantages.

☐ THE FOCUS OF CHANGE . . .

The survey indicated that the Japanese now have been focusing more recently on such competitive factors as more and better product features, flexible factories, expanded customer service, and rapid outpourings of new products. Here the gap between the U.S. and the Japanese firms tends to be fairly substantial reflecting the fact that Japan has pushed for changes in these areas over the past ten year period. The use of sophisticated computer technologies has helped the Japanese manufacturers to make important positive changes in these areas.

From Stewart, T.A. (1992) "Brace for Japan's Hot New Strategy." *Fortune*, 126(6), 63-74 [43].

RESISTANCE TO CHANGE

Resistance to change may be traced to individual, group, or organizational characteristics. To take a specific example: a consultant had revised an organization's performance appraisal system several times. There was deep resistance to changing the existing system in spite of the fact that it was well known that it was not working well. A general fear of the unknown and a preference for the known appeared to be operating. Supervisors may have felt that a new system would prove even more difficult to use than the present one. They may have thought that their subordinates' performances will look worse under a new system, which might reflect back on them. They may also have feared that they would have to face new problems and decisions for which they lacked experience. Finally, changing may simply not be worth the trouble—the gain is not worth the pain.

Organization Culture and Power as Barriers to Change. The organization culture and power structure help to maintain stable behavior patterns in organizations (see Chapters 3 and 15). They are self-reinforcing and potentially significant barriers to change. After all, the very nature of change may put them in jeopardy. It is therefore likely that the change efforts will not work unless they are compatible with the organization culture and the power structure. This is a very well-documented reason why many change efforts fail. Quite often, for example, a top management group decides to decentralize decision making, giving more responsibility to lower-level managers. This requires a climate of trust and willingness to delegate. In an organization that has a political organizational culture, a lack of trust, and strong centralized decision making, decentralizing will be very difficult.

The effects of the organizational power structure on change are described by Rosabeth Moss Kanter in her book, *The Change Masters* [23]. She describes a, company she calls Chipco, a high-technology computer company. In Chipco, the human resources manager decided to ask the company to establish task forces made up of managers from different specialties within the plant. These task forces would tackle various plant-wide problems. The manager's superior provided an initial grant to get the project going. She was able to sell her plan to many managers. She obtained support from some outside consultants. She soon found, however, that some important managers in the plant, including the plant manager, were opposed to the project. They had serious reservations about how well the project would work and its impact on other aspects of the company, such as the existing structure, the compensation system, and so on. Eventually, the project was successfully implemented, but it took a great deal of persuasion and endorsement by strong political forces. It became very broadly accepted and institutionalized after it produced innovative solutions to some of the company's most serious problems.

Change Interdependencies.   Change programs often focus on changes in tasks, people, technology, or structure. In task changes, the duties assigned to individuals are changed. In people changes, an attempt is made to alter individual knowledge, attitudes, or skills. Technological change focuses on the machinery, procedures, work flows, or materials. Structural rearrangements focus on changing how members are grouped together or on the systems and procedures that the organization employs to guide and direct interactions. However, to change any one of these means that the others are very often affected as well. These **change interdependencies** may cause an effort to eventually fail, even though a desired change in one of the factors had initially taken place.

The McKinsey 7-S model shows that key interdependencies exist among seven factors that are major determinants of organizational success (see Figure 17.2) [32, 33]. The structure of an organization, whether it is organic or mechanistic, must fit the style of management (directive versus democratic), the shared values of organization members (toward collaboration and innovation), and the staff (abilities of people). The strategy of the organization (market focus) must be congruent with the organization's skills (unique organizational abilities) if the organization is to be successful. The systems employed by the organization (reward, control) must be congruent with the type of people employed and their characteristics as well as being compatible with the way people are grouped together by the organization's structure. When one of these elements is changed, others will be affected.

☐ **FIGURE 17.2**   *The McKinsey 7-S Framework*

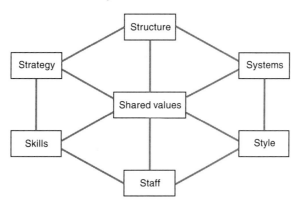

PRESSURES FOR CHANGE IN ORGANIZATIONS

Pressures for change may be internal or external to the organization (see Figure 17.3). When organization performance is unsatisfactory, for example, pressures may come from many stakeholders. These pressures are often conflicting. Stockholders may demand improved earnings and dividends at the same time that environmental protection groups want the firm to spend dollars on costly antipollution activities. Pressures to change come from the various environments of the organization, more so in recent years since many changes have occurred in the economic, technological, political, and social environments of organizations.

☐ **FIGURE 17.3** *Pressures for Change*

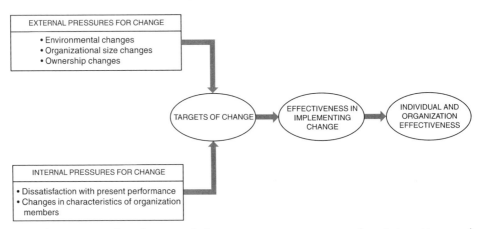

These internal and external change pressures are complex, interactive, and dynamic. Changes in one environment can produce changes in several other environments and to internal organizational operations. For example, a major change for U.S. automobile companies was the rise in gasoline prices after the Middle East oil embargo of 1973. As the price of gasoline skyrocketed and shortages occurred, the consuming public began to demand smaller, more fuel-efficient automobiles. This opened up opportunities for foreign automobile manufacturers which already had experience making them. As foreign automobiles entered the market, U.S. firms were motivated to change their existing product lines to form joint ventures with foreign manufacturers and to sell foreign made automobiles under their own names. This required enormous modifications in company operations. Entire plants, including personnel, technical processes, and administrative procedures, had to change in order to compete more successfully against global competitors. Another result was significant reductions in the U.S. workforce and political pressures to impose quotas against foreign automobile companies. This in turn encouraged foreign manufacturers to locate in the United States to avoid the quotas. New problems arose in managing plants in a new culture. The imbalance of trade in automobiles between the United States and Japan worsened the trade deficit with Japan, causing political frictions. This may have helped to open some trade opportunities in Japan for other U.S. manufacturers such as aircraft producers.

Another illustration of how external pressures interact with internal changes is the case of a U.S. manufacturer of power tools. It was necessary to make significant modifications in some of its production facilities because of inroads into its markets by a foreign competitor. The U.S. firm adopted new cost-reducing machine technologies that were more easily adaptable to shifts in customer demands. Other internal changes were also required when sales of the firm's power saws declined because high interest rates had caused a decline in new home sales. At about the same time, the company was fighting an antitrust suit by the U.S. government over an acquisition. Problems in its international plants arose when the value of the dollar declined relative to foreign currencies. This affected the value of inventories and the prices of components. While all of this was going on, it had to deal with social problems resulting from changes in the composition of its work force in its domestic plants. For example, like other firms, the increased work force participation of mothers has created pressures to modernize benefits. An increase in the number of foreign-born non-English speaking workers in some of the plants created pressure to make a number of adjustments. Attempts by the company to deal with all of these issues led to a change in management. A top management team was brought in from another industry which then set about revamping managerial practices and policies in many areas.

Organization growth also leads to change. Managerial styles, organization structures and systems, and the procedures that were appropriate for a small organization may be quite inappropriate for a larger one [15, 45]. Small, centralized firms may be decentralized; then as they grow, they become more centralized. If they become very large, they may have to decentralize again, but in a different way. Over time, managers of the large organization have to change their focus from entrepreneurship and innovativeness to efficiency and cost control, and to achieving harmony along the many diverse interest groups in the organization [40]. Managers are needed with a perspective that fits the company's stage of growth.

Change in ownership also induces organization change. Thousands of mergers and acquisitions have taken place in U.S. industry in recent years. Typically in such takeovers the acquired organization must adopt the management styles, philosophies, and systems of the acquiring organization, often in a very short period of time (see Chapter 3). Changes in ownership where the new owner is a foreign company create special adjustment problems for organizations since here there is often a culture clash. The compromises and adjustments that have to be made are often especially severe [9, 19, 25].

Perhaps the most common internal change pressure is dissatisfaction with performance. Undesirable levels of outcomes such as quantity, sales, cost of operations, or quality can all trigger pressure to change. Dissatisfaction with employee turnover or performance failures may also instigate change efforts.

TARGETS OF CHANGE

Sometimes pressures to change may focus on a single individual (see Figure 17.1). When the individual is the target, the goal is usually to improve performance or to change attitudes.

The focus of attention may also be the group or the unit. In order to obtain better performance from a unit, it may be necessary to have the unit function differently. Suppose a research and development unit has a disappointing record of new product ideas. Perhaps the members aren't cooperating enough. This can seriously hinder the effectiveness if interdependent tasks are required to solve challenging problems. Sometimes the problems of change are the relationship between two or more units, as when a marketing department is not working effectively with a personnel unit.

Finally, the target may be an organization-wide change, such as a change of the budget system, organizational goals and strategies, or the organizational culture. This is often accomplished by change efforts that might begin with individual, move to the group level, and then on to organizational level changes.

KEY STAGES OF SUCCESSFUL CHANGE

Successful change depends on getting through the key **stages of the change process** in a systematic manner. The first stage is the development of motivation to change among those who are initiating it and those who are implementing it (see Figure 17.4). Motivation to change depends on two basic questions: (1) Is it worthwhile to change? and (2) Can the change be successfully carried out? In determining whether it is worthwhile to change, a calculation, at least in a rough sort of way, must be made of the positive and negative outcomes associated with not changing relative to the outcomes associated with changing.

 **FIGURE 17.4** *Determinants of Motivation to Change*

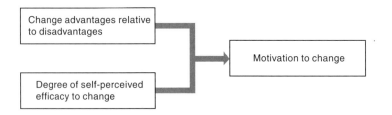

Motivation to change also requires that those involved believe that it is possible to change and that a change effort will be followed by success. Increasing the motivation to change involves building **self-efficacy**, the degree to which an individual believes it is possible to achieve a particular performance level or behavioral standard [2]. Self-efficacy can stem from a variety of personal experiences. One source is someone's actual achievements. When a task is performed successfully, the person gains a sense of enactive mastery and will feel capable of performing that way again.

One way to facilitate self-efficacy is to structure the work setting to ensure that the individual has an opportunity to gain **enactive mastery** by performing successfully. Self-efficacy can also develop from vicarious learning, or modeling (see Chapter 4). In organizational change programs, appropriate models should demonstrate the desired behaviors to the targets of change. Verbal persuasion and other types of social influence may contribute to a heightened sense of self-efficacy for change by convincing the change targets that they are capable of engaging in desired behaviors.

The second key stage (see Figure 17.5) when sufficient motivation to change exists is use of an appropriate change method. Not all change methods are equally effective. Techniques for knowledge change are different from those for changing skill. Methods for changing individual behavior may be completely ineffective for achieving change at the group level.

The third key stage in successful change is **reinforcement of change**. New behaviors, working relationships, procedures, and so forth must result in rewarding positive, not negative, outcomes. Otherwise, the individuals, groups, or organizations will revert to previous conditions or look for new ones.

☐ **FIGURE 17.5** *Key Stages in Effective Change*

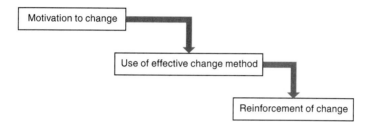

THE NEED FOR IDENTIFYING CAUSES OF BEHAVIOR

As indicated earlier many attempts at change are created by a perception that something is not satisfactory. In such change attempts, it is very important to correctly identify the real causes of the problem. For example, some companies may attempt to reduce absenteeism or turnover by changing organizational conditions in such a way that job satisfaction is improved. This assumes that the causal relationships between organization conditions, job satisfaction, and absenteeism/turnover are as shown in Figure 17.6. There is some research evidence that job satisfaction is correlated with absenteeism and that changing organizational conditions can result in changes in job satisfaction. However, without knowing exactly which conditions in the specific organization are affecting job satisfaction, it is risky to start any change effort. For instance, some research shows that job satisfaction is related to both the individual's life satisfaction and state of mental health [41]. Job satisfaction of individuals tends to remain the same even when such individuals change jobs several times and move from one organization to another in spite of the fact that the organization situations encountered are different. The same is true of performance. Performance differences may be affected more strongly by individual differences in ability and energy level. In such cases, organizational changes may do nothing to improve performance unless they involve hiring persons with more skill [41].

☐ **FIGURE 17.6** *An Assumed Causal Sequence Between Organization Conditions, Job Satisfaction and Performance.*

INDIVIDUAL CHANGE

Many change methods are directed at individuals. Of course, if enough individuals change, a unit and the organization itself would be changed. If the individuals targeted for change are important in the organization, then only a few may need to be changed to improve an entire unit or organization [1].

CREATING MOTIVATION TO CHANGE IN INDIVIDUALS

Often individuals are self-motivated to change. They may receive negative evaluations from others or suffer failure. They recognize that present performance is unsatisfactory and should be changed to avoid adverse consequences.

Both formal and informal performance feedback provide individuals or groups with information about how their performance compares with some previously developed standard. First, feedback facilitates good performance by reminding the individual or group of the performance standard: poor performance may result because organization members simply do not know what is expected of them. Second, feedback has reinforcing effects. This was the case in the positive reinforcement program at Emery Air Freight [14]. Supervisors were given instruction workbooks that described various types of rewards ranging from a smile to very detailed praise.

Reinforcement can also be self-administered when employees see that they are making progress toward a goal. Feedback systems can be designed to allow for self-monitoring. At Emery Air Freight, most workers were given checklists to record their performances throughout the day.

METHODS OF INDIVIDUAL CHANGE

Many different approaches for individual change have been developed over the years. Indeed, programs for changing a person's health (mental and physical), habits (eating, alcohol consumption, and so on), and competencies for careers are a major industry in the United States. In organizations, common individual change programs include coaching and mentoring, individual counseling, and training. Training is also used as method for group change and, for that reason, will be discussed in more detail later in this chapter.

Coaching and Mentoring.   One informal type of training is **coaching**: a superior provides advice and guidance to subordinates. Another is **mentoring**: a mentor is an older and more experienced organization member who helps a younger, less experienced person in the organization learn to navigate in the world of work [26]. This older person does not have to be the direct supervisor of the younger person. Some organizations have a more formal mentoring program in which mentors are assigned to proteges, but most mentoring arrangements are informal and carried out so as to meet the needs of the two parties [10]. Mentoring can be of special value to those who are often excluded from organizational networks, such as women and minorities. Through mentoring, they can obtain valuable information that they would not normally receive in addition to having a champion who can make their talents visible to upper ranks in the organizational hierarchy [31].

Counseling. Counseling is the core of employee assistance programs [16, 20, 38]. These programs help employees cope with many different types of problems including employee stress [37]. Counseling is a problem-focused interaction process with the object of stimulating learning, growth, and changed behavior [21]. Outside the work setting counseling is typically utilized for helping individuals cope with emotional problems. In the work setting, it is usually directed at helping employees cope with work-related issues, such as relationships with superiors, salary issues, and absenteeism. It has become more important recently in preparing people for career transitions such as retirement, in managing staff cutbacks in organization restructuring, and in helping individuals get more realistic perceptions of their job opportunities with a view to improving their satisfaction [44, 45].

Counseling may lead to different outcomes for the person. Davis lists several of these that can help achieve change [13].

1. *Advice.* The counseling interaction can result in a course of action that may help an employee deal with his or her problems. Acceptance of the advice is obviously the critical difficulty.

2. *Reassurance.* The counseling interaction can build the employee's self-confidence or sense of efficacy for coping with difficulties.

3. *Communication.* Counseling can uncover causes of employee problems that have not been noticed by the managers. In this sense, counseling is a form of upward communication that may result in change.

4. *Release of emotional tension.* Emotional release from the tensions and frustrations can result from counseling. This may be an important first step in personal problem solving.

5. *Clarified thinking.* The problem may be the result of an individual's emotions not being congruent with the facts of the situation. The counselor may be able to help the employee realize that minor incidents are being unrealistically magnified and that the employee's perceptions or conclusions in the problem situation are not warranted by the facts.

6. *Reorientation.* The counselor can help an employee change basic goals and perceptions, perhaps by recognizing personal limitations.

The employee can adopt a more realistic assessment of his or her personal reality.

Counseling can have a shallow or a deep focus. That is, it can aim at obtaining some reasonably simple behavior changes, or it can be an approach to produce fundamental changes in the personality or to alleviate significant emotional difficulties. In this latter case, counseling is better called psychotherapy. Most organizational counseling programs are of the shallow type; though some firms have professionals available when necessary [45]. When a firm does wish to use managers as counselors, they should be restricted to dealing with work problems and trained so that they understand the counseling role, the scope of the problems they can handle, and their limitations in dealing with more serious mental health matters.

Counseling will work when it results in the individual wanting to change, if it builds the individual's confidence in his or her ability to change, when the counseling method is appropriate for the type of problem, and if the counselor provides reinforcement in the desired directions of change.

There are three different styles of counseling. In **directive counseling**, the counselor listens to an employee, decides what should be done, and then actively directs the employee to do it. Although it can produce useful results, directive counseling can lead to dependency. The subordinate's feeling of self-confidence in solving his or her own problems in the future is not enhanced. In **nondirective counseling**, the counselor listens to an employee's problems. The counselor acts as a reflector of the employee's problems. By expressing them, the employee eventually begins to understand them. The non-directive counselor's role is to motivate the employee to solve his or her own problems. This approach may take much time and require counseling skills that the average supervisor does not have [13]. **Cooperative counseling** involves mutual and cooperative exchange of ideas between a supervisor and a subordinate to solve problems.

Counseling need not necessarily take place in a formal, planned manner. It can be done during any interaction between supervisors and subordinates. Thus, it may occur during a meeting for a performance appraisal interview, or it could occur informally, as in the cafeteria at lunch.

The research on the effectiveness of employee counseling shows that it can lead to changes and improvements [8]. In one study, 80 percent of the employees who had undergone counseling reported that their situation had improved and 74 percent were content with the treatment received [48]. In another, a group of frequently absent employees reduced its level of absenteeism after counseling [39].

GROUP CHANGE

Sometimes the focus is on changing groups. These groups may be intact organization units such as departments and project teams, or organizational level groups, such as first-line supervisors.

MOTIVATION FOR GROUP CHANGE

Often when groups are the target of change, methods are used in which group pressure or group acceptance play an important role. A person may change not only because he or she wants to change, but also because it is perceived that group members want him or her to change. Reinforcement for the change is also likely to come from other group members. Motivation for group change may also occur when group members are failing to complete tasks, are engaged in conflict, or have other interpersonal tensions. It may also be that the group needs new skills, for example, in effective teamwork.

APPROACHES TO GROUP CHANGE

Many of the specific approaches to developing groups and improving their performance have been discussed in Chapter 8, such as managerial motivation strategies. Without exception for groups, the change methods rely on the influence effects from groups on individuals which were discussed in Chapters 10 and 11. Identification with others, cohesion, pressures toward conformity, social facilitation, and the strength of group norms combine with the subject matter of the training to produce change. Here we discuss the more generic types of group change processes.

Training. There are a number of different training methods which may be used individually or in combination to change knowledge, attitudes, or skills. The *lecture method* involves one-way communication. The *case study* approach uses complex situations, usually written in the form of the cases at the end of each chapter in this book, which the students must analyze. The *discussion method*, in which everyone participates in the training effort, is widely used. *Business games* and *simulations*, which attempt to create actual business situations in which the participants make decisions and can see the effects of these decisions, are often used as well. In *programmed instruction*, trainees teach themselves at their own pace by following a prescribed sequence of exposure to concepts and information. *Role playing*, in which the participants act out an interpersonal simulation, is often used for skill development and attitude change.

There are a number of principles for conducting training [49]. The first is ensuring trainability. Individuals must have sufficient ability and motivation. Second, an optimum training environment is important. Participants must be able to practice the new behaviors and skills. The material must be learned well enough in training so that it can be transferred, even under adverse conditions, to the work setting. It is very important to maximize the similarity between the work setting and the training setting to ensure the transfer of training. Third, participants should be given knowledge of the results of training. This makes the material meaningful, allows trainees to proceed at their own pace and takes individual differences into consideration.

SOCIAL LEARNING APPROACHES

Social learning theory has been applied very effectively in changing the behavior of groups (see Chapter 4). Latham and Saari studied supervisors (see Figure 17.7) who were trained to relate more effectively to subordinates [27]. **Vicarious learning** and **behavioral modeling** were an important aspect of this program. The supervisors were first divided into a trained group and an untrained group. The trained group went through eight training modules. Each module focused on a different aspect of supervisory behavior: (1) orienting a new employee to the job, (2) providing recognition to deserving employees, (3) motivating poor performers, (4) discussing poor work habits with subordinates, (5) discussing potential disciplinary actions with subordinates, (6) reducing employee turnover, (7) handling the complaints of employees, and (8) overcoming resistance to change.

☐ **FIGURE 17.7**   *Group Social Learning: The Latham and Saari Program*

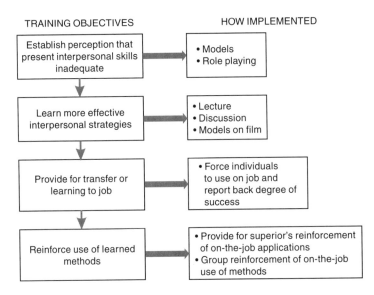

Each module was conducted in a two-part segment once a week. Each training module followed the same format. The first step was to have the trainers explain the topic and show its significance. In the second step, the targeted group was given three to six principles for handling the interpersonal problems considered in the program. These principles were first shown in a film then demonstrated by a supervisor model in a realistic factory setting. The third step was to have the training group discuss the competence of the supervisor in the film in handling the situation. In the fourth step, the trainees practiced the principles by role playing. Fifth, the trainees received feedback about their role playing performance from the other trainees. Sixth, each trainee was required to try out the newly learned behaviors on the job the next week and report back to the group how well the technique worked. The seventh step involved the trainee's boss reinforcing the use of the new behaviors in the job setting.

When this training was completed, the performance of the trained supervisors was compared with the performance of the untrained group. The performance of the supervisors participating in the program was significantly better than that of those who had not been trained. The next year the untrained group was trained, and the differences between the two groups vanished.

TEAM-BUILDING APPROACHES

Team building focuses on any defined work group. Teams may be family groups consisting of a boss and subordinates, a colleague group such as the regional sales managers of a company, or a project team with members from different specialized departments [3]. Team building is a difficult and time-consuming process. Its effects may also take a long time to be obvious.

Team-building efforts are often begun with a self examination. A consultant asks each group member, "What can be done to increase the effectiveness of the operations of this team? What are the obstacles to achieving this?" Answers are analyzed and then fed back to the team members. The feedback helps to motivate the group to change since problems that hinder group effectiveness are identified. These problems then can be converted into solutions by the group. Then the group sets goals to carry out these solutions. In the goal-setting approach to team building, participation in the group's decisions enhances commitment to problem solutions [5].

☐ ACTION LEARNING

Managers often have trouble learning in a typical management development program because of the way the material is taught to them. Action learning may have much higher acceptance among managers because it involves learning by doing and because it focuses on solving real organizational problems. It does not involve a passive approach to training which managers do not like. A typical action-learning group consists of six to ten managers who work on assigned projects provided by clients who have a genuine interest in the outcome of the group and need an outcome within a particular period of time.

While in the action-learning groups, managers also spend time on the underlying group processes involved in their deliberations. They question the assumptions they are making and also focus on issues of implementation and weaknesses. Some follow-up surveys of managers who have experienced this training format indicates that this approach can result in increased openness to behavior of others and the values of the organization.

However, this approach to training is not easy to use. It requires the full backing of the top level of management in the organization. It also

☐ **ACTION . . .**

requires a willingness of units to provide the groups with real significant projects to accomplish. In addition, any solutions to the problems discussed to the group must receive full consideration from the clients who provided them.

From Raelin, J.A. & LeBien, M. (1993). "Learning by Doing," *HR Magazine*, 38(2), 61-70 [36].

A particular type of team building, called sensitivity training or T-Groups, emphasizes improving the interpersonal competence of group members [5]. Members are taught to share their feelings with one another, to communicate with others in a non-evaluative way, and to provide social support. This type of training is especially useful for organization family groups such as a project team or a department. The family group is more difficult to work with than, say, a group of strangers, because there is a greater threat to cooperation if the family group members have difficulties in training that might damage their personal relationships.

ORGANIZATION CHANGE

Change efforts that focus on the whole organization fall into the broad category of **Organizational Development (OD)**. They usually involve an attempt to change through an organization-wide program in which most workers, managers, and professionals participate [18, 22, 29]. Organizational development is concerned with planned change. In other words, change is to be anticipated, planned, and consciously designed rather than approached in a crisis mode when a problem occurs. Often an attempt is made to produce different organization structures and cultures to support any new systems or approaches introduced. This is because in organization development, it is assumed that all organization functioning involves a number of organization components working together. To change any part of the system requires sensitivity to adjustments across the entire system as in the McKinsey 7-S model.

The change program is usually executed by organization members who collaborate with change agents. **Change agents** seek to enhance the capacity and motivation of those in the organization to learn, improve, and change through their own efforts in the future. They emphasize development through human growth and improvement. OD practitioners often have training in the behavioral sciences [47]. Because of their background, they emphasize diagnosis and the use of specific behavioral technologies in helping individuals, groups, or organizations to reach a more successful mode of functioning [34].

ORGANIZATIONAL ANALYSIS

Organization-wide change programs are often begun with some type of action research showing where and why a particular system is not working as well. **Survey feedback** is an action research method fairly widely used in organization development. The survey feedback approach begins when an organization recognizes that it has problems. This provides the initial motivation to change, but organization members still must have confidence that improvements can be realized from the program. A pilot program can provide such assurance by demonstrating in one part of the organization that a system change can be successfully implemented and can produce improvements.

☐ CHANGE AT AT&T

Some AT&T managers feel that the U.S. government did the company a favor when, one decade ago, it forced the company to create seven new independent regional operating companies and allowed the company to keep only its long distance business and Western Electric, its equipment manufacturer. This traumatic event forced the company to change in countless ways which have made it far more flexible and responsive to the new environmental realities and perhaps a far more effective company in general. Since the breakup in 1984, its stock has quadrupled in value, it has maintained its sales revenue, and its profits are moving upward. AT&T has been broken down into a number of businesses that must grow and be profitable. They have invested in a number of other high technology companies such as NCR and McCaw Cellular Communications with products related to their business, moved to internationalize their business, and made drastic changes in their competitive strategies, organizational structures, and management processes. With respect to changes in management approaches, they have created structures that encourage cooperation among separate businesses such as cross unit teams, created a corporate statement of company values, created more harmonious ties with its unions, changed its management styles and many of its human resource management practices. With respect to such human resource management practices, there is now recruitment from outside as well as inside, and no longer can employees be guaranteed a lifetime job. No longer the bureaucratic monster with considerable inertia, the company now is highly flexible and able to move quite rapidly to take advantage of opportunities, technological or market, which present themselves. Part of the reason for this new speed and flexibility comes from the independence granted to its various new business units. Of course, all of these changes have meant a dramatic change in the types of behaviors required of its employees given the very different organizational culture created by the new AT&T.

From: Kirkpatrick, D. (1993) "Could AT&T Rule the World?" *Fortune*, 127(10), 54-46 [24].

A **organizational needs analysis** is usually done with a survey, using interviews or structured questionnaires, to identify what should be changed. The survey may reveal problems with performance, employee morale and absenteeism, or failure to achieve unit or organizational goals. The problems identified may also be perceptual or emotional. Once specific problems are identified, different remedies may be initiated to change behaviors, perceptions, attitudes, or other unsatisfactory conditions.

ORGANIZATIONAL CHANGE METHODS

Organizational development efforts may be designed and implemented using any of the change methods discussed in this chapter or in Chapter 8. For example, team building, positive reinforcement programs, Management by Objectives, and High-Involvement Organization Strategies have been implemented and been found to be effective in both public and private organizations. The important aspect of any of these approaches is that they systematically involve organization members throughout the whole change process and that they are based on **action research**. For example, Figure 17.8 shows the steps in an action research change program carried out in a firm by external consultants. The external consultants formed a group made up of managers from the company's executive committee to work with them. This helped to ensure the credibility of the change efforts and the solutions that were developed. Two members of this group were designated as internal advisers to assist the consultants in designing approaches to study the problem and to help implement the solution. Internal advisers are useful for their knowledge of the organization and its history. They can help ensure that changes are compatible with the organization's culture, history, personnel, and existing practices. The external consultants then gathered data by interviews and structured questionnaires. These data were evaluated, summarized, and presented to the top management project group. But while the data were being collected, this group was trained with respect to various issues involved in the change. They were shown what existing research, theory, and practice suggested about the forces influencing the change effort. When they received the summarized survey feedback data about current problems, they then began developing solutions with the aid of the consultants.

REINFORCEMENT OF ORGANIZATIONAL CHANGES

The final step in planned change is to follow up to ensure that the change has been effective. This follow up could take several years and many modifications may be made before a desirable level of effectiveness is achieved. In the survey research program described in Figure 17.8, there were four separate assessments over a six-year period and, each time, modifications in the system were made as a result.

☐ **FIGURE 17.8**   *An Approach to Organizational Change*

A. The organization or unit perceives it has problems with an existing system and calls in an external consultant.

B. Consultant forms a top management system task force (those with influence and motivation).

C. A group of internal advisers is formed (those with prestige and competence).

D. An organizational audit is conducted to determine current problems with the management system (e.g., communication, performance levels, motivation, intergroup relations, leadership).

E. Top management group and internal advisers are trained.
   1. Training for top management group focuses on broader aspects of program (e.g., long-range planning, policy implications, need for top management support).
   2. Training for internal advisers focuses on implementation issues (e.g., training, answering questions users pose, superior-subordinate goal setting).

F. Results of audit in D above are provided to both top management group and internal adviser group.

G. Group of internal advisers is aided in developing a program tailored to organizational needs.

H. Internal advisers develop the program and communicate to top management group.

I. Top management task force forwards suggestions for change to internal adviser group.

J. Internal adviser group finalizes program with aid of external consultant and obtains approval of top management group.

K. Pilot testing, revision, orientation, and training program are conducted.

L. Program is put into effect. External consultant monitors top management program sessions and activities. Interal advisers monitor middle- and lower-management program sessions and activities.

M. External consultant conducts organizational audit no longer than one year later and feeds results back to top management group and internal advisers.

N. Modifications in program are made by internal advisers and approved by top management.

O. Above steps are repeated at a later time.

Improved organizational results can also be reinforced through feedback showing that revenues, costs, quality, and quantities are better than before. Feedback from other organizations may also be helpful. In several cases in which the results of an OD project results were written up and widely disseminated [11, 46], the firms were frequently visited by teams from other organizations wishing to improve their own systems with a similar solution [11, 46]. The recognition from these other organizations increased acceptance in the organization where the change was originally implemented.

EVALUATION OF ORGANIZATION CHANGE PROGRAMS

To change individuals, groups, or organizations takes time and money. There are also hidden costs, such as political issues that make change and improvement difficult when they are not resolved. For these reasons, it makes sense to try to determine whether or not the change program was effective.

Change programs can be evaluated in very sophisticated ways. These evaluations involve very complicated measurement techniques, statistics, and research designs. The manager can get help from professionals when it is needed but can look at other factors as well. Beer has described a number of factors to be considered by a manager in judging the effectiveness of a change program and whether it was worthwhile [6]. What is most critical and most important will depend on the organization's situation at the time. Those threatened with bankruptcy do not have the luxury of evaluating the effectiveness of a change by waiting to look at long-term performance improvements.

There are a number of difficult problems in evaluating change. First, it is difficult to isolate the effects of the change. Suppose, for example, that team building is used to improve relationships between the research group and the manufacturing units and, while the training is being conducted, a new manager is assigned to the research group. It may be difficult to separate the effects of the new manager from the effects of the training. Second, there is often a time lag between development and evaluation. Both external and internal forces could effect the measured results which would increase the problem of separating the training effects from the other forces. Timing also complicates other issues. For example, some positive changes may not occur quickly, but take more time. If the assessment is made before the effects take, an incorrect inference of no impact will be made. Third, it is often difficult to specify what to measure. For instance, while the ultimate goal of much training is improved economic performance, the training itself may focus on attitudes and group relationships with the assumption that improvements in them will increase profitability. In this case, assessing changes in profitability may be the wrong measure since it is not likely to be easy to tease out the effects of the training. Fourth, in complex OD programs, it is possible that several changes are introduced with several different methods. In this case, it is almost impossible to know which method, or combination of methods, produced effects when they occur.

However, there have been many studies on the effectiveness of change and development methods, and the results of this research has been evaluated with meta-analytic techniques. For example, training programs and goal setting programs have stronger effects on productivity than most approaches [17]. Large scale OD interventions which involved redesigning work and implementing autonomous work groups were next most powerful [17]. Another analysis showed that the use of self-directed work groups resulted in 38 percent more productivity than when they were not used [4]. The effects were also very durable. They persisted over several years, though they were much greater in the first 2 years following the intervention. These large scale OD interventions were also much more effective in changing satisfaction and attitudes [17]. The effects were also greater outside the United States. Beekun estimated that non-U.S. countries were over a 100 percent more productive than U.S. firms after an intervention [4].

Neuman, Edwards, and Raju [30] are not so positive, however. While they do find some effects, they caution that they may be situationally specific. This could mean that the results are likely to be affected by the particular configuration of factors which make up the intervention. This is certainly consistent with the analysis of the effects of gainsharing plans on organizational performance by Bullock and Tubbs [7]. These OD interventions were more effective when employees were involved in the design of the plan, there were employee involvement practices, and a participative management philosophy in the organization.

SUMMARY

Organizations are subject to pressures from the outside environment and from inside the organization itself. From the external environment there are pressures to change because of new regulations, new competition, ownership changes, and simply from organizational growth itself—systems and personnel that were appropriate at one time are no longer appropriate. A major pressure for change also comes from dissatisfaction with present performance. Other change pressures stem from changes in the characteristics of people, changes in technologies or internal systems employed, or the personal objectives of powerful managers.

Organizational success is affected by an organization's ability to change when this is required. Successful change requires having the necessary motivation to change, using an effective change method, and reinforcing the change after it occurs so that it stabilizes and endures.

There are many individual change methods. Counseling and mentoring are two important approaches. Training is used for both individual and group change. Over the years, a great deal of knowledge has been obtained on how to train effectively. Counseling programs can result in a number of positive outcomes, depending on individual needs in the particular situation.

Group change focuses on entire groups or organization units. In group training, the interdependencies among individuals in a group and the importance of any new behavior being reinforced and supported by other group members are recognized. Thus, the whole group is trained together so that the members can support one another in their efforts to change.

Many organization-wide change approaches focus on changing a particular system used throughout the entire organization, such as a performance appraisal system or an inventory system. One widely used approach is survey research, in which organization members collaborate with outside experts in devising a new program to solve organization problems.

Change is easier if the organization has a climate or culture that is generally supportive of change. Successful changes require effective communication in which concerns and expectations flow easily up and down the organization. There should be a climate of trust in the organization, especially between workers and management, that will help them cope with the risk, uncertainty, and fear that often accompanies organizational change.

☐ KEY CONCEPTS

Action research	Enactive mastery	Reinforcement
Behavioral modeling	Mentoring	of change
Change agents	Nondirective	Self-efficacy
Change	counseling	Social learning theory
interdependencies	Organizational	Stages of the change
Coaching	development	process
Cooperative	Organizational	Survey feedback
counseling	needs analysis	Team building
Directive counseling		Vicarious learning

☐ STUDY QUESTIONS

1. What recent changes in the environment of the university have affected its operations? What responses are required from the modern university to react to these changes? Are all universities the same in terms of having to respond to such change pressures? What types of universities would be different?

2. We have indicated that an organization must change in response to its members just as members must change to adapt to the organization. What does this mean? Give some examples of how organizations must adapt to their members.

3. Everyone has been subject to training, both informal and formal, throughout life. List the types of training you have been subject to. Then indicate which of these types of training have been most effective in changing you. Why have these types of training been most effective?

4. Think of a time in the past when your efficacy for performing a particular task or activity was quite low as you perceived it at the time. Did this self-perceived efficacy change? In what direction? What happened to make it change?

5. For training to be effective, it should be reinforced. How is the training received in many college courses reinforced? What could colleges and universities do to reinforce more effectively any training they might carry out?

6. Social learning theory emphasizes learning through the observation of others. List the models that have been an important factor in things you have learned in the past. Which of these models has been most significant to you in learning something?

STUDY...

7. Change efforts directed at individuals, groups, or organizations may be effective in the short run but may not be in the long run. List some examples of change programs at the level of the individual, group, or organization that might be effective in the short run but not in the long run. List some examples of change programs that could be effective in the long run but not in the short run.

8. List two pieces of legislation passed by the U.S. Congress that involved attempts to make changes in the functioning of our society. Indicate if you think these were fairly successful or fairly unsuccessful. What were some of the factors that had an impact on the success of these programs?

9. What societal problems that presently exist should be the subject of a change program? What type of program might work to correct this problem, given what we know about successful change?

CASE

HAMMOND ENGINE COMPANY: PART I

Bob Shack and Steve Williams, both consultants with McAndrews and Company, had just finished teaching an all-day management development session for the Research and Development Division of the Hammond Engine Company, one of the nation's largest manufacturers of diesel engines. Participating in this particular day's program were upper- and middle-level managers from the division, as well as Hal Connors, the division head, and Ed Pinter, the personnel manager.

In the morning, Bob Shack and Steve Williams had conducted some formal training. In the afternoon, the upper- and middle-managers were separated into two groups to discuss the implications for practicing what they had learned that day and how their relationship with the other group of managers could be improved. At the end of the afternoon, the two groups of managers, together, decided on policy and procedure changes for the division.

The whole change effort was planned by Bob Shack, who worked with other consultants on the project. It was designed to respond to a survey of all managers and professionals that Shack had done months earlier. The survey had identified a number of problems in this division. There was high stress among the managers and professionals due in part to the considerable ambiguity about each individual's major responsibilities and because of a lack of sufficient structure in the organization. The training program design involved the development of materials that focused on the causes of the organization's problems as revealed by the survey. This material was first used in working with the top management group. These

☐ HAMMOND ENGINE COMPANY . . .

managers were asked to determine how they could change the practices and how they could change their own behavior to solve these problems. A good deal of time was spent on developing the acceptance and commitment to these changes by the top group. Then they worked on developing a new set of relationships with lower-levels of management. A similar process would occur for each lower management level, until all organizational levels were trained and had worked out its relationship with the next lower level.

QUESTIONS

1. Evaluate the effectiveness of the change program according to the chapter discussion.
2. Can the training program be designed to reduce stress and ambiguity identified in the survey?

HAMMOND ENGINE COMPANY: PART II

At the end of the day, after one of the training sessions, Bob and Steve were preparing to leave for the airport to head back to Chicago. They were approached by Hal Connors, the division head.

Hal:	How do you think it went today?
Bob:	Just great!! Why, you people made about five policy changes alone in the afternoon.
Hal:	I'm uneasy. I just don't know. Those policy change decisions could have been made at a much lower cost in executive time. Maybe there were some side benefits.
Bob:	I think so. Now your middle managers know more about how you look at things, and you certainly got a lot of feedback from them on some of the things they think are wrong with this organization.
Hal:	By the way, I was looking at a report from our marketing research department. I have a feeling things might get pretty bad here after the first of the year. Acme has decided to make their own diesel engines for their trucks. The sales to Acme are a big share of our business.
Bob:	Oh!! (Apprehensively).
Hal:	I was thinking that I may have to cut back personnel in the division. How could I go about this?
Bob:	Well, naturally you will have to use some ratings. It all boils down to judgment.

HAMMOND ENGINE COMPANY . . .

Steve:	If you are going to use judgment, I suggest it be collective judgment. Something like this has to be done just right, with no favoritism or bias. I would suggest three to five raters, in order to maintain accuracy and fairness. The staff should be rated on the skills and knowledge needed the most now, and in the future.
Bob:	And perhaps you had better exempt all those with over 15 years of service.
Hal:	Why?
Bob:	Because it's just not right to let them go after they have been here that long a time.
Hal:	Hell, I didn't hire them! Why should I have to bear the cost of my predecessor's mistakes?
Bob:	It just isn't right to change the rules now if they were told they were okay before.
Steve:	How about the morale effects? I guess it all depends on how bad they are. You should use some sort of weighting system in your evaluations: so much for potential, so much for seniority, and so on.
Hal:	It might be good for performance to let a few older ones go. Okay, let's say it's mostly the young men who will go. Should they be selected from all those hired recently, or should we do it department by department? If we rate all the young people together, we will wipe out engineering and not touch research.
Bob:	Do you put your best people in research initially?
Hal:	Yes. This is one big problem. You boys have a plane to catch. You better leave or you will miss it. We'll work up something on this and let you see it when you return.

QUESTION

1. What should the criteria be for layoffs if such are necessary? Explain.
2. What are the possible connections between layoffs and training and development efforts of the division. Can the two be compatible?

HAMMOND ENGINE COMPANY: PART III

Some two years later, Steve Williams happened to run into a manager from Hammond Engine Company. After discussing the general state of affairs at Hammond, Steve asked the manager about Acme's decision to make their own diesel engines and, as a result, forcing Hammond to lay-off some personnel. The manager said that Acme eventually gave up on the idea of making their own diesel engines because they could not obtain the technical knowledge to do it. They simply could not find enough diesel engineering experts to make this project work and therefore no layoffs were needed. On the other hand, back at Hammond, word leaked out that there were committees making up lists of those who were to be laid off, and that frightened many employees. Not only was there some fear of receiving a layoff notice but also fear that the company's future might not be as bright as once was anticipated. This perception, in turn, caused a number of the best employees to quit in order to avoid the actual layoffs. The company, therefore, lost many employees that it did not want to lose.

QUESTIONS

1. What are the implications when organizations go through this kind of change?
2. What can Hammond do to manage this type of situation in an effective way?

REFERENCES

1. Argyris, C. *Six presidents: Increasing leadership effectiveness*. New York: John Wiley, 1976.
2. Bandura, A. Self-efficacy mechanism in human agency. *American Psychologist*, 1982, 37, 122-47.
3. Beckhard, R.B. *Organizational development: Strategies and models*. Reading, MA: Addison-Wesley, 1969.
4. Beekun, R.I. Assessing the effectiveness of sociotechnical interventions: Antidote or fad? *Human Relations*, 1989, 42(10), 877-897.
5. Beer, M. *Organization change and development: A systems view*. Santa Monica, CA: Goodyear Publishing, 1980.
6. Beer, M. The technology of organization development. In M.D. Dunnette, ed. *Handbook of industrial and organizational psychology*. Chicago: Rand McNally, 1976, 937-93.
7. Bullock, R.J., and Tubbs, M.E. A case meta-analysis of gainsharing plans as organization development interventions. *Journal of Applied Behavioral Science*, 1990, 26(3), 383-404.
8. Cairo, P.C. Counseling in industry: A selected review of the literature. *Personnel Psychology*, 1983, 36, 1-19.

9. Carroll, S.J. The changing nature of human resource management systems in the U.S. and their implications for U.S. based Japanese companies. In K. Takeuchi, ed. *Proceedings of Conference on International Management Practices*, Tokyo Keizai University, 1992, 352-363.

10. Carroll, S.J., Olian, J.D., and Giannantonio, C. Mentor reactions to proteges: An experiment with managers. *Best Papers Proceedings of the Academy of Management*, annual meetings, Anaheim, CA, 1988, 273-76.

11. Carroll, S.J., and Tosi H.L. *Management by Objectives: Applications and research*. New York: Macmillan, 1973.

12. Davidow, W.H. & Malone, M.S. *The virtual corporation*. New York: Harper/Collins, 1992.

13. Davis, K. *Human behavior at work: Organizational behavior*. New York: McGraw-Hill, 1981.

14. Fairbank, J.A., and Prue, D.M. Developing performance feedback systems. In J. A. Frederiksen, ed. *Handbook of organizational behavior management*. New York: John Wiley, 1975, 281-99.

15. Filley, A.C. A theory of small business and divisional growth. Ph.D. dissertation, Ohio State University, 1962.

16. Gerstein, L.H. & Bayer, G.A. Counseling psychology and employee assistance programs. Previous obstacles and potential contributors. *Journal of Business and Psychology*, 1990, 5(1), 101.

17. Guzzo, R.A., Jenne, R.D & Katzell, R.A. The effects of psychologically based intervention programs on worker productivity: A meta-analysis. *Personnel Psychology*, 1985, 38, 275-291.

18. Hawley, J.A. Transforming organizations through vertical linking. *Organization Dynamics*, 1984, 9, 68-76.

19. Hofstede, G. *Culture's consequences: International differences in work-related values*. Beverly Hills, CA: Sage Publications, 1980a.

20. Hosie, T.W., West, J.D., and Mackey, J.A. Employment and roles in employee assistance programs. *Journal of Counseling and Development*, 1993, 71(3), 355.

21. Hunt, R.G. *Interpersonal strategies for system management: Applications of counseling and participative principles*. Monterey, CA: Brooks.Cole, 1974.

22. Jick, T.D. *Managing change: Cases and concepts*. Homewood, IL: Irwin, 1993.

23. Kanter, R.M. *The change masters*. New York: Simon & Schuster, 1983.

24. Kirkpatrick, D. Could AT&T rule the world? *Fortune*, 1993, 127(10), 54-56.

25. Kluckholn, F.R. The study of culture. In D. Lerner and H.D. Laswell, eds. *The policy sciences*. Stanford, CA: Stanford University Press, 1951.

26. Kram, K.E. *Mentoring at work: Developmental relationships in organizational life*. Glenview, IL: Scott, Foresman, 1985.

27. Latham, G., and Saari, L.M. Application of social-learning theory to training supervisors through behavioral modeling. *Journal of Applied Psychology*. 1979, 64, 239-46.

28. McGill, M.E., Slocum, J.W. Jr., and Lee, D. Management practices in learning organizations. *Organizational Dynamics*, 1992, 20, 5-16.

29. Murphy, S.E., Blyth, D., and Fiedler, F.E. Cognitive resources theory and the utilization of the leader's and group member's technical competence. *The Leadership Quarterly*, Fall 1992, 3, 237-254.

30. Neuman, G.A., Edwards, J.E., & Raju, N.S. Organizational development interventions: A meta-analysis of their effects on satisfaction and other attitudes. *Personnel Psychology*, 1989, 43(3), 461-476.

31. Olian, J.D., Carroll, S.J., & Giannantonio, C.M. Mentor reactions to proteges: An experiment with managers. *Journal of Vocational Behavior*. In press, 1993.

32. Pascale, R.T., and Athos, G. *The art of Japanese management*. Boston: Little, Brown, 1981.

33. Peters, T.J., and Waterman, R.H. *In search of excellence*. New York: Harper & Row, 1982.

34. Porras, J.I. & Robertson, P.J. *Organizational development: Theory, practice, and research*. In M.D. Dunnette, & L.M. Hough, eds. *Handbook of industrial and organizational psychology*. Consulting Psychologists Press Inc., 1992, 823-895.

35. Port, O. & Smith, G. Quality, small and mid-size companies seize the challenge—not a moment to soon. *Business Week*, November 30, 1992.

36. Raelin, J.A., and LeBien, M. Learn by doing. *HR Magazine*, 1993, 38(2),61-70.

37. Sadu, G., Cooper, C., and Allison, T. A post office initiative to stamp out stress. *Personnel Management*, 1989, 21(8), 40.

38. Schneider, R.J. & Colan, N.B. The effectiveness of employee assistance program supervisor training: An experimental study. *Human Resource Development Quarterly*, 1992, 3(4), 345.

39. Skidmore, R.A., Balsam, D., and Jones, O.F. Social work practices in industry. *Social Work*, 1974, 3, 280-86.

40. Smith, K.G., Mitchell, T.R., and Summer, C.E. Top-level management priorities in different stages of the organization's life cycle. *Academy of Management Review*, 1985, 10, 799-820.

41. Staw, B.M. Organizational psychology and the pursuit of the happy/productive worker. *California Management Review*, 1986, 27(4), 40-53.

42. Staw, B.M., and Ross, J. Expo 86: An escalation prototype. *Administrative Science Quarterly*, 1986, 31, 274-97.

43. Stewart, T.A. Brace for Japan's hot new strategy. *Fortune*, 1992, 126(6), 63-74.

44. Van Fleet, D.D., Griffin, R.W., and Moorehead, G. *Behavior in organizations*. Boston: Houghton Mifflin, 1991.

45. Wagner, J.A. III, and Hollenbeck, J.R. *Management of organizational behavior*. Englewood Cliffs, N.J.: Prentice Hall, 1992.

46. Walton, R.E. How to counter alienation in the plant. *Harvard Business Review*, 1972, 50, 70-91.

47. Warrick, D.D. *Managing organization change and development*. Chicago: Science Research Associates, Inc., 1984.

48. Weissman, A. A social service strategy in industry. *Social Work*, 1975, 5, 401-403

49. Wexley, K.N., and Yukl, G.A. *Organizational behavior and personnel psychology*. Homewood, IL: Richard D. Irwin, 1984.

Chapter 18
Organizational Behavior in the Global Context

Gary Katzenstein, just receiving his MBA and M.S. in Computer Science from U.C.L.A. but with only limited Japanese language skills, took an assignment at Sony in Japan [32]. He encountered so many adjustment problems that he felt he had to resign long before even a year was up. The adjustment problems came about because he could not accept what Sony required of him. Despite his advanced degrees, he was treated like a new college graduate trainee with a general undergraduate degree. He was even forced to attend computer programming classes on methods which he already knew because of his advanced work in computer science. When he tried to talk to individuals outside his immediate group, he was rebuffed. Similar difficulties arose when he attempted to lunch with women within his work department. He also resented the rules in the company dormitory where he was forced to live. The gate to the dormitory was closed at ten each night. To stay out overnight, he had to sign out indicating where he was going and leave a telephone number where he could be reached. When he took a four day vacation he believed he was entitled to, his supervisor became very angry and forbade his work colleagues to have anything to do with him. He was ostracized until he apologized to the human resource department. The informal requirements to work on weekends, the boring and very routine work he was assigned, and the long compulsory meetings all served to make this work opportunity a very unpleasant experience. Ultimately, he was forced to leave the company.

Situations like this are easily explained. Gary Katzenstein could not adjust to the Japanese culture, a problem that is faced by more and more employees as foreign assignments or jobs in foreign companies in their home country become more common. American manufacturing companies, banks, insurance companies, consulting firms, service companies, and universities now have facilities and employees in various overseas locations. Many of these companies (for example, Black and Decker, IBM, and Xerox) sell more products outside than inside their U.S. market. Similarly, a large number of foreign firms have established major operations within the United States, the best known of which are Nissan, Mazda, Toyota, Honda, and BMW in the automobile industry. There are now about 3,000 Japanese firms (about 600 factories) located in the U.S. and a recent survey reported that 30 percent of the major Japanese firms intend to establish operations in the U.S. by the end of the 1990s [30].

But internationalization is more than just the establishment of offices and plants in foreign countries. Investors from all over the world have also acquired substantial holdings in U.S. firms. The British are examples. British Airways has a major equity position in USAir, and Grand Metropolitan PLC has a large interest in Pillsbury. Table 18.1 lists the acquisitions of 225 U.S. firms by foreign investors for which the purchase price exceeded ten million dollars [16]. Of course, U.S. firms are similarly involved in other countries and, in fact, have far more operations in other countries than foreign firms have in the United States.

TABLE 18.1   Acquisition of U.S. Firms by Foreign Firms (1979-1989).

Country of Acquirer	Total Sample*
Australia	9
Canada	31
U.K.	80
France	15
Hong Kong	5
Japan	18
Netherlands	11
New Zealand	3
Sweden	5
Switzerland	16
Germany	13
Other	19
Total	225

*In each of the 225 sample acquisitions, the foreign acquirer paid more than $10 million to acquire a majority stake in a publicly held U.S. firm.

GLOBALIZATION

With all of this international activity, it should not be surprising that more than two-thirds of the heads of major companies in the world believe that their future economic success depends upon how effective they are in meeting foreign competition and that their revenues will be increasingly affected by the results of their foreign operations [43].

☐ MOBILIZING FOR GLOBAL EFFECTIVENESS: THE CASE OF FIAT

Fiat, the giant Italian automaker, largely operates in the very protected Italian market. It has recently started an internationalization program. As Giovanni Angelli, chairman of the company said, "Globalization of competition compels us to developing our internationalization." The Fiat group is the largest in Italy and one of the largest in the world. In 1989, it employed almost 300,000 people and had locations in 56 countries. It had been in business for 90 years producing not only automobiles but also marine engines, airplanes, tractors, and railcars.

Fiat's internationalization program gradually evolved into a number of action steps. First, to become a true international company, the organization decided that it had to study itself to identify its strengths and weaknesses as they could affect globalization. It also had to develop a strong internal culture for the company, something that might help to hold its many diverse managers together. The company also had to foster the openness necessary to accept other cultures and approaches. It had to acquire foreign firms in some cases and participate in joint ventures with foreign firms to move into certain businesses in particular countries. More specifically the company decided to recruit graduates in engineering and economics who desired careers in international business. These individuals would be assigned two year tours of duty in other countries. Existing company management development programs had to be devised to incorporate material on internationalization and foreign language training. An English language course for recent graduates was developed consisting of 100 hours, instruction given over a five month period. The company is attempting to achieve more consistency in its international operations by developing an integrated program for selection, training, job evaluation, and performance appraisal.

From "Managing Internationalization at Corporate Level: The Case Study of Fiat" by Giuseppe Audia, SDA Bocconi, Milan Italy 1991 [5].

The **globalization** of business has enormous implications for managing the human assets of a firm. Companies must be concerned with the attitudes, values, expectations, motivations, and typical behaviors of employees from other cultures. Globalization means that different cultures confront, and must adapt to each other. There are other serious legal and cultural constraints which must be recognized. Consider just the differences in laws that govern human resource management practices in the countries described below:

Holland. Like most western nations, Holland has many laws regulating the employment relationship. In Holland, the laws are strict and cover quite a number of areas. Firms in Holland must not discriminate and, in fact, must

569

employ disadvantaged workers at a proportion of the workforce between 3 and 10 percent. It is very difficult to fire an employee once they pass the probationary period, working on Saturday and Sunday is prohibited for most industries, and employees generally receive five weeks of vacation a year. Management is required to consult with employee elected work councils on any major decision affecting the workforce. Paid maternity leave is required. Currently Dutch companies are attempting to shift responsibility for human resource management from the staff departments to line managers [28].

Italy. In Italy, the government is heavily involved in the economy. Three large state holding companies own large segments of industry in sectors such as food processing, banking, and airline travel. The labor relations system is highly regulated. There is a high degree of unionization and trade union confederations negotiate with employer associations with respect to pay levels, holidays, hours, and working conditions. In Italy, a high proportion of managers, including some senior managers, belong to unions. Workers have job protection rights and termination indemnities.

Outside of the state owned companies and the large private firms, there is a large sector of small and medium-sized family owned companies. Many of these are affiliated with cooperatives, especially in the area around Bologna. Many Italian companies, which focused on protected internal markets in the past, are beginning to pay more attention to globalization strategies.

Germany. In Germany, employers must gain the consent of elected worker work councils before they can appoint or dismiss employees, set working hours, require overtime, or even change the prices of lunches in the company cafeteria. Germany has perhaps the most highly regulated system of labor relations in the world. This has forced German managers to use management styles that are very informal, collegial, and participatory in spite of stereotypes to the contrary. Most German workers are affiliated with industry wide trade unions. It is very difficult to terminate employees. Most promotions are filled from within the firm. German companies are known for their enormous investments in training. The length of the work week has recently been reduced by collective bargaining agreements in most firms, and this has caused firms to use part-time workers, flexible working hours, and overtime to more fully use the expensive new technologies employed by many German firms in recent years [3].

Denmark. In Denmark, workers have more benefits than in virtually all other European nations. The Danes are among the most highly paid in Europe, work a maximum of 37 hours a week and have such benefits as paid parental leave. Working conditions and pay are negotiated by a national employers' association and the trade union confederation. Most human resource practices in Denmark are administered by line managers rather than specialized staff departments. Training and development is very extensive in Danish companies [4].

France. Like other European countries, France has a large body of laws and regulations regarding employment. Employees cannot work for more than 39 hours without overtime, receive 30 days of vacation a year, have mandatory maternity leave, a minimum wage, and compulsory profit sharing for firms.

Trade unions and work councils are the rule in French plants. As in other European countries, French HRM managers have been shifting some HRM responsibilities to line managers while adopting an adviser role to these line managers [7].

China. In a communist country such as China, HRM practices are tightly controlled by the central government. Workers in China have traditionally been assigned to companies by the government without regard for the company's needs. This results in overstaffing, which is very expensive because the companies must provide extensive training, housing for the workforce, and health and medical care benefits as well. The central government decides on the rate of pay by comparing descriptions of jobs to national standards. Chinese managers must negotiate all decisions with trade union representatives and the Office of Internal Security, which represents the ruling communist party in the company. Typically, managers must periodically sit with subordinates and discuss their performance weaknesses. At the present time, experiments with profit based company bonus systems are being carried out. Recently, in special zones of China, the firms have been allowed great flexibility in managing their workforce. At this writing, given the rapid changes in the Chinese economy, it is impossible to predict the structure of HRM practices in the future [34].

Japan. Human resource management practices in large Japanese companies are very different from those in small- and middle-sized companies. In the larger companies, employees receive much higher pay, benefits, and job security. Laws governing HRM in Japan are very similar to those in the United States since they were originally established by U.S. occupational forces after World War II [23]. These laws are widely ignored and not strongly enforced, especially those dealing with limitations on hours and bans on employment discrimination of women and the disabled.

Japanese companies have traditionally used extensive training, early retirement (age 55 to 60), and have generally made pay increases and promotions on the basis of seniority. Japanese HRM departments tend to have a great deal of power.

The larger Japanese companies generally hire new employees only from among recent middle school, high school, and college graduates. They do not, generally, hire more experienced employees unless they have needs for certain specialists.

Employees are hired either for permanent jobs or for temporary jobs. In recent years, there has been a significant increase in the use of temporary workers to increase flexibility. Women were, in the past, generally hired as temporary employees, but recent government pressure has led to an increase in the number of permanent female workers [46].

ORGANIZATIONS IN CULTURES

Culture, in the broad sense, refers to the social context within which humans live. We would expect culture to have an effect on the very nature of organizations in which people work, and it affects the ways in which individuals perceive and respond to the world. **Culture** is:

patterned ways of thinking, feeling, and reacting, acquired and transmitted mainly by symbols, constituting the distinctive achievements of human groups including their embodiments in artifacts. The essential core of culture consists of traditional, . . . ideas, and especially their attached values [33].

Culture is a kind of collective software or "programming of the mind that distinguishes the members of one human group from another. . . . It is to human collectivity what personality is to an individual." [24]

Differences in national culture emerge from a constellation of forces within a nation to which a particular people must adjust. These forces are a product of a nation's history, geography, resources, climate, and other factors. [24] For example, when the United States was settled by Europeans in the 17th and 18th centuries, they found almost unlimited resources and land. They could spread out, be individualistic, and develop practices which wasted resources. On the other hand the Japanese, with little arable land and with few natural resources, had to band together in more structured communities. They had to be more frugal in their use of resources for building homes and for obtaining food. Cooperation was especially necessary with the wet agricultural methods for growing rice which required collective effort in building irrigation systems. Farming practices in the U.S. could be quite different. Although some cooperation was needed, much of the work could be done by a family itself [24].

Other factors can be important in shaping a culture. For example, a people subject to instant execution for minor offenses by members of a warrior class such as in Japan (as well as in several other countries) may develop an unusually high deference to authority.

What emerges from these forces is a set of dominant values and beliefs that govern human behavior and facilitate human relationships. These are so fundamental that their presence and effects make them invisible to its members. It is this invisibility that makes culture so powerful—it drives behavior, perception, and judgment often without the person's awareness. It is the most subtle type of control.

For a country, its dominant values can be called the national character, or the **modal personality** [24]. The modal personality refers to the degree of homogeneity and strength of the dominant personality orientations in the society. The modal personality is a result of socialization, the process through which a society instills its members with basic values and beliefs. These form the bases for accommodation in the society. Their acquisition begins early in life. They are the bases for individual control because an overwhelming number of the society's members accept them. Of the many different values acquired through socialization, some of the more important are those related to work, ways of responding to authority, and power orientations.

It is within the context of the national culture that the organizational culture develops. As we have already noted in Chapter 3, the company's history, beliefs of its founders, the values of the dominant coalition, the technologies, the strategies, and other factors are important. Thus, while two similar firms in a country would be subject to the same national cultural influences, their separate experiences will lead to differentiated organizational cultures. For example, the Sony corporation has a different organizational culture than the older and more established Mitsui, the oldest Japanese large trading company. This is due, in part, to the fact that Sony was established about three hundred years later than Mitsui when economic and cultural conditions were quite different. Sony could not rely upon employees hired directly from schools and universities for its talent as other companies did because it needed experienced managers and professionals immediately. Therefore, it developed the practice of hiring some employees from other Japanese companies, a rare practice among large Japanese companies.

DIFFERENCES IN NATIONAL CULTURES

There are different ways to characterize national cultures. One interesting approach is the use of **cultural metaphors** [17]. These metaphors are situations, events, or circumstances that occur in a culture and that capture and clarify its essential elements. For example, the symphony orchestra is the metaphor for Germany. Not only is Germany a musical nation with many orchestras, but the country operates like one. In a symphony orchestra, conformity is valued, rules are established, and each person is expected to work for the good of the whole. In business, as the orchestra, strong leadership is preferred, but it should be exercised in such a way that there is considerable delegation of power and decision making to subordinates. The opera is the metaphor for Italy, a country in which drama and emotions are so often intensely felt that they cannot be easily contained within the individual. Among other metaphors for culture are the Japanese Garden, the Turkish coffee house and the Israeli Kibbutz.

The "density" of the social context is another way to view culture [21, 22]. There can be high context and low context cultures. In a **low context culture**, typified by individualized and somewhat fragmented cultures such as Switzerland, Germany, and the United States, people tend to use mechanical extensions of themselves (for example, computers, telephones, and radios) to acquire information and relate to one another. In a **high context culture**, people have a high emotional involvement with each other and information flows more indirectly from person to person or from the social system to the person (China and Japan are examples). In a high context society, individuals can communicate a great deal of information with few words because individuals know what is expected. The socialization processes in high context cultures tend to be more intensive and extensive since there is much to learn about appropriate interactive behaviors.

The Hofstede Model. Geert Hofstede has conducted the most extensive research on cultural differences [24, 25, 26]. In his first important study, he surveyed several thousand managers from more than 40 countries who worked in a large U.S. firm [24]. That the managers worked for one firm is particularly important since it means that the results he obtained are less likely to be due to differences in organization cultures. In a second study, a sample of students from 23 countries were the subjects [27]. These studies resulted in five dimensions which can be used to characterize the modal personality of a national culture. These dimensions differentiated one culture from another and are the basis of attitudes and behaviors, organization practices, and social practices such as marriages, funerals, and religious ceremonies. These five dimensions are:

1. Uncertainty avoidance
2. Power distance
3. Individualism-collectivism
4. Masculinity-femininity
5. Long vs. short term patterns of thought

Uncertainty Avoidance.   High risk and ambiguity make some people uncomfortable. Societies high in uncertainty avoidance tend to prefer rules and to operate in predictable situations as opposed to situations where the appropriate behaviors are not specified in advance. Those with high **uncertainty avoidance** prefer stable jobs, a secure life, avoidance of conflict, and have lower tolerance for deviant persons and ideas. Japan scores higher than the United States on uncertainty avoidance while both score higher than Sweden. Thus, in Japan there appears to be far less tolerance for deviations from accepted behavioral practices than in the United States while Sweden is generally considered to be a very tolerant society. These differences are reflected in many educational and training programs in Japan devoted to learning the customary behaviors for all types of social situations including how to bow, how to eat certain types of foods, how to behave at a funeral, and so on. Some Japanese managers have been known to hire private detective agencies to find out what others in the company think about them, apparently to reduce the uncertainty of not knowing exactly how they stand.

In nations low in uncertainty avoidance such as the U.S., there is less acceptance of rules and less conformity to the wishes of authority figures than in high uncertainty avoidance nations such as Germany and Japan [9]. For example, lateness and absenteeism are more serious issues in Japan than in other countries such as Sweden where uncertainty is more acceptable.

Power Distance.   Power is the ability of one person to affect or control another. **Power distance** is the degree to which differences in power and status are accepted in a culture. Some nations accept high differences in power and authority between members of different social classes or occupational levels while other nations do not. For example, the French are relatively high in power distance while Israel and Sweden score very low. In Israel and Sweden, worker groups demand and have a great deal of power over work assignments and conditions of work [2, 14]. French managers tend not to interact socially with subordinates and do not expect to negotiate work assignments with them. The French sense of power distance is exemplified by the experience of a French MBA student in a U.S. firm. She was surprised to find on the first day of her internship in an American company that some workers called the manager by his first name and talked with him about their weekend activities. She felt that this would rarely happen in a French factory.

There are some other consequences of power distance differences. For example, in low power distance countries such as the United States, powerful individuals can be forced out of their position or can be successfully challenged by less powerful individuals or groups [9]. This is not likely to happen in a high power distance country. Also, there is generally less acceptance of status differences in low power distance nations. In the low power distance country, individuals feel less discomfort and stress when disagreeing with one's boss. One study showed that in a high power distance culture, Hong Kong, individuals were less upset when they were insulted by high status individuals than in a low power distance culture, such as the United States. Finally, in high power distance societies, managers feel that they must have specific answers to questions raised by subordinates about work. Laurent, in a cross-national study, found that only 10 percent of the Swedish managers thought it important to have precise answers to subordinate questions, but 65 percent of the Italian managers, 45 percent of the German managers, and 30 percent of the English managers thought so [35].

Individualism-Collectivism. **Individualism-Collectivism** refers to whether individual or collective action is the preferred approach to deal with issues. In cultures oriented toward individualism (such as the United States, the United Kingdom, and Canada), people tend to emphasize their individual needs and concerns and interests over those of their group or organization, while the opposite is true in countries which score high on collectivism (e.g., Asian countries such as Japan and Taiwan). Often firms in collectivist societies will make decisions without regard for the personal needs of those affected if it is thought that the decision is good for the organization. For instance, employees may be arbitrarily transferred to other locations with little concern for how such a transfer will affect the person or the family. This happened to a Taiwanese manager who was directed to enter an MBA program in the United States. He went against his wishes because his wife was about to have a child. When the child died in birth, he was not allowed to return to Taiwan. He was told that it was not in the company's interest to allow him to do so and that he should just learn to bear with the situation.

In a collectivist society, one is supposed to interact with members of his or her group. It is almost impossible to perceive a person as an individual rather than one whose identity comes from groups that individual is associated with [9]. For that reason, before visiting a collectivist society, it is useful to carry business cards which clearly identify one's organization and status within that organization.

Certain work behaviors may also be affected. For example, in an individualistic society such as the U.S., there is a tendency for persons to shirk when tasks are assigned to a group as opposed to when tasks are assigned to individuals. This tendency toward social loafing was not present in the collectivist country of Taiwan [19].

Masculinity-Femininity. The **masculinity-femininity** dimension is defined in terms of values associates with stereotypes of masculinity (such as aggressiveness and dominance) and femininity (such as compassion, empathy, and emo-

☐ COLLECTIVISM AT JAPAN INK AND CHEMICALS CO: THE ORIENTATION PROGRAM

Japan Ink and Chemicals was founded in 1908 as a producer of printing inks but later diversified into a variety of chemical products after World War II. It has sales offices around the globe and joint ventures to improve its distribution capabilities. The company has facilities in Indonesia, Korea, Hong Kong, Kenya, Mexico, China, Taiwan, the United States, Malaysia, and other countries. One of the problems in managing such a worldwide operation is in attempting to achieve some sense of overall company unity. The company's orientation for new employees is one means to achieve this. New employee orientation programs in Japanese companies are very important. They often involve learning the company anthem, inspirational talks by the chairman of the company, and the recital of a pledge to make the orientees into official employees with all the rights and obligations that creates.

The Japan Ink orientation program started off on a freshman day that occurs when the colleges admit freshmen for their first semester's work. This date is said to reflect a historical situation in which military recruits started their military careers and other societal institutions had to adjust to that. Thus, all Japanese companies start their orientation programs at the same time. These different groups of employees sat in assigned seats and were grouped by educational level. The dress of the various groups was quite different. The recent college graduates all had on very nice suits which looked brand new and expensive. The high school graduates who were to be factory workers were often in jeans. The young women who were to be office workers dressed in a variety of outfits from informal to more professional looking outfits. Each group tended to keep to themselves and only communicate within their own group.

All of the groups received the same general overall training during the first week of the orientation program. The entry level professional and managerial level employees were then given special orientation programs for another month that related more specifically to their future careers. The first week of training consisted of lectures on various topics: the history of the company, the company's many products, the rights of employees, and the benefits the company provided. Etiquette was also given a great deal of attention including how to speak to others correctly (the Japanese language has many levels of politeness which must be mastered), how to bow appropriately, and how to speak to customers. A whole day was spent on the company's TQM (Total Quality Management) program. A great deal of stress was placed on keeping internal company "customers" satisfied. The employees were told about the 500 quality circles in the company, how these groups operated, and what the expected behaviors for QC members were.

☐ COLLECTIVISM AT JAPAN INK AND CHEMICALS CO: . . .

A lot of attention was paid to such things as the importance of eating a good breakfast, the value of exercise and other activities to maintain health, and the importance of going to bed early. They were urged to carefully plan the best route to work to get to work on time. Some of those in attendance thought that this part of the program was somewhat demeaning or insulting. Employees also showed varying levels of attention. The young women seemed to be the most bored and spent considerable time fixing their hair, adjusting their makeup, and similar activities. Attempts were constantly made to excite the orientees. Each day they had to give a collective hello to start the day and were constantly asked to be more enthusiastic. By the end of the week, they gave the morning greeting in a much more enthusiastic manner than when they started on the first day.

tional openness). While there is some disagreement over the exact meaning of this dimension [2], it does appear that there is a higher degree of assertiveness and less concern for individual needs and feelings in more "masculine" nations. There also seems to be a higher concern for job performance and a lower concern for the quality of the working environment in more "masculine" nations. According to Hofstede, countries that score high on the masculinity dimensions such as Japan, Germany, and the U.S. tend to emphasize achievement, growth, and challenge in jobs [24]. In the more feminine scoring Scandinavian countries such as Sweden and Norway working conditions, job satisfaction, and employee participation are emphasized. Countries scoring high on masculinity also tend to have more sex differentiated occupational structures with certain jobs almost entirely assigned to women and others to men.

Long vs. Short Term Patterns of Thought. In his original study of managers, Hofstede found only the four dimensions above [24]. This fifth, **Long vs. Short Term thought patterns**, that he found from a student sample is one which he believes is a fundamental cultural difference between western and Asian nations [26]. The long term orientation, characteristic of Asian countries, reflects an orientation toward the future, belief in thrift and savings, and persistence. The short term orientation, a western cultural characteristic, reflects values toward the present, perhaps even the past, and a concern for fulfilling social obligations.

In countries with a long term orientation, planning can be expected to have a longer time horizon. Firms are willing to make substantial investments in employee training and development, there will be longer term job security and promotions will come slowly [29, 39]. Firms will also seek to develop long term relationships with suppliers and customers [2].

Other research on cultural differences has revealed somewhat similar factors as those uncovered by Hofstede [24, 26]. Several of these studies, along with Hofstede's, have been carefully reviewed and integrated into a classification of culturally similar country clusters [40]. These country clusters, or cultural groups, share somewhat similar modal personalities, language, geography, and religion. The similar country clusters are shown in Table 18.2. The Anglo cluster values low to medium power distances, low to medium uncertainty avoidance, and high masculinity and individualism. Both Latin clusters showed high power distance preferences, high uncertainty avoidance, and had high masculinity scores, but on individualism, the Latin Americans scored lower than the Latin/Europeans.

☐ **TABLE 18.2** Clusters of Nations Grouped by Culture [40]

ANGLO GROUP
United States, Australia, Canada, New Zealand, United Kingdom, Ireland, South Africa

LATIN AMERICAN GROUP
Argentina, Venezuela, Chile, Mexico, Peru, Columbia

GERMANIC GROUP
Austria, Germany, Switzerland

LATIN EUROPEAN GROUP
France, Italy, Spain, Belgium, Portugal

NORDIC GROUP
Finland, Norway, Sweden, Denmark

NEAR EASTERN GROUP
Turkey, Iran, Greece

FAR EASTERN GROUP
Malaysia, Singapore, Hong Kong, Philippines, South Vietnam, Indonesia, Taiwan, Thailand

ARAB GROUP
Baharain, Abu-Dhabi, United Arab Emiirates, Oman

UNIQUE CULTURES
Brazil, India, Japan, Israel

There are important differences within each cluster, though. For example, Hall says that the English and Americans are two great "peoples separated by the same language" [20]. One difference is in how they use space. In the United States, the location of one's home and office is an important cue to status, whereas in Britain social class is the crucial factor. Another difference is the way privacy is sought. An American who wants to be alone will go into another room and separate from others using a door. The English mostly become quiet, even in the presence of others.

ORGANIZATIONAL CONSEQUENCES OF CULTURAL DIFFERENCES

There are important ways in which cultural differences may be observed in organizations. For example, since people in Anglo cultures prefer less power distances than those from Latin countries, this will alter the manner in which subordinates interact with higher level managers. In cultures that are high in uncertainty avoidance and low in power distance, as in Israel and Austria, organizations run effectively by clearly defining roles and procedures rather than by actively using the hierarchy [2]. In several countries, high uncertainty avoidance is combined with high power distance. Such is the case in Singapore and Mexico where organizations are modeled after the traditional family and the head of the family has very high power. Loyalty is expected in return for protection. Organizations are viewed as pyramids where the lines of communication are very vertical, not horizontal, and the hierarchy is more actively used [2].

MANAGERIAL PHILOSOPHY

Cultural differences will be reflected in **managerial philosophies**. For example, an analysis of the managers from different countries who work for a large multinational U.S. corporation showed that

> German managers, more than others, believed that creativity is essential for career success. In their mind, the successful manager is the one who has the right individual characteristics. Their outlook is rational: they view the organization as a coordinated network of individuals who make appropriate decisions based on their professional competence and knowledge.

> British managers hold a more interpersonal and subjective view of the organizational world. According to them, the ability to create the right image and to get noticed for what they do is essential for career success. They view the organization primarily as a network of relationships between individuals who get things done through influencing each other through communicating and negotiating.

> French managers look at the organization as an authority network where the power to organize and control the actors stems from their positioning in the hierarchy. They focus on the organization as a pyramid of differentiated levels of power to be acquired or dealt with. French managers perceive the ability to manage power relationships effectively and to "work the system" as particularly critical to their success [35].

Ouchi, in **Theory Z**, shows how cultural differences and managerial styles translate into organization practices in Japanese and U.S. firms [39]. In Japanese firms, promotions come slower and only after careful evaluation. For example, in the largest Japanese firms the average Japanese CEO is 64 years old and joined his company in 1945 while in the largest U.S. firms, the average CEO was 57 years old and joined his firm in 1955 [31].

579

Japanese managers expect more cooperation and harmony from workers than American managers [6]. Workers are not managed through strong managerial controls but through implicit, subtle social controls based in a culture where the work organization is a fundamental part of their life. Japanese managers are far more likely to consider enthusiasm rather than ability in making work assignments to subordinates while the U.S. managers were far more likely to stress ability over enthusiasm [6].

Transplanting a managerial philosophy from one culture to another can create complications. The Japanese philosophy and style of management has become a model which others have tried to emulate. Firms all over the world have sought to increase worker involvement, implement quality circles, and reduce the number of organizational levels. Managers in other countries have met with different degrees of success, partly because the Japanese style of management is often inconsistent with their culture's dominant values. For example, Hayao Nakamura was appointed in 1993 to be the managing director of Ilva, the state owned steel group in Italy which was having profitability and production problems. Nakamura is a Japanese citizen who worked for Nippon Steel in Italy for many years. His appointment drew unusual attention because he was the first foreigner named to such a senior post in Italy's very large state operated economic sector. After three months, unsatisfied with the rate of improvement, Nakamura made a strong appeal to the workforce telling them that "L'azienda e' casa tua," "The company is your home,"—a very Japanese, but not a very Italian approach. It remains to be seen what the effects of his appeal will be.

The experience of firms in the United States that sought to adopt the Japanese approach led to a realization that it must be modified to fit the dominant cultural values of the work force. This is nicely illustrated in a study of Japanese-owned firms in the United States. Workers of Japanese origin, whose early socialization resulted in exposure to Japanese values, were more favorably inclined to the paternalistic practices common in Japan than were the U.S. workers, who had different socialization experiences [36].

Organization design. Because the process of organization design involves human choice, cultural values will shape the decisions that produce organization structures. Table 18.3 shows how the cultural dimensions might affect the organization structure. For example, high power distance means greater acceptance of strong authority systems, high status differentials, and willingness to accept orders from superiors so in countries such as Mexico, Venezuela, and Brazil organizations will have more centralized authority, more organization levels, more supervisors, and a wage structure in which white-collar and professional work is disproportionately more highly valued. A study that compared the organization properties of 55 American and 51 Japanese manufacturing plants in the same manufacturing industries show how cultural dimension affect organizational structure [36]. The Japanese plants had more specialization of labor, taller hierarchical structures, and more formal centralization of authority. However, there was also real decentralization of decision making: workers had many opportunities to make important contributions to

☐ **TABLE 18.3**   Organizational Characteristics and Cultural Values in
Various Countries

Low Power Distance Dimension High	
(Austria, Israel, Denmark, Sweden, Norway)	(Philippines, Mexico, Venezuela, India, Brazil)
Less centralization	Greater centralization
Flatter organization pyramids	Tall organization pyramids
Fewer supervisory personnel	More supervisory personnel
Smaller wage differentials	Large wage differentials
Structure in which manual and clerical work are equally valued	Structure in which white-collar jobs are valued more than blue-collar jobs.

Low Uncertainty Avoidance Dimension High	
(Denmark, Sweden, Britain, United States, India)	(Greece, Portugal, Japan, Peru, France)
Less structuring of activities	More structuring of activities
Fewer written rules	More written rules
More generalists	More specialists
Variability	Standardization
Greater willingness to take risks	Less willingness to take risks
Less ritualistic behavior	More ritualistic behavior

Low Individualism-Collectivism Dimension High	
(Venezuela, Columbia, Taiwan, Mexico, Greece)	(United States, Australia, Britain Canada, the Netherlands)
Organization as "family"	Organization is more impersonal
Organization defends employee interests	Employees defend their own self-interests
Practices are based on loyalty, sense of duty, and group participation	Practices encourage individual initiative

Low Masculinity-Femininity Dimension High	
(Sweden, Denmark, Thailand, Finland, Yugoslavia)	(Japan, Austria, Venezuela, Italy, Mexico)
Sex roles are minimized	Sex roles are clearly differentiated
Organizations do not interfere with people's private lives	Organizations may interfere to protect their interests
More women in more qualified jobs	Fewer women are in qualified jobs
Soft, yielding, intuitive skills are rewarded	Aggression, competition, and justice are rewarded
Social rewards are valued	Work is valued as a central life interest

☐ **TABLE 18.3**   Organizational Characteristics . . .

Short   Long Term—Short Term Patterns of Thought   Long

Short Term Patterns of Thought (United States, France, Russia)	Long Term Patterns of Thought (Japan, Hong Kong)
Shorter term focus	Strategic long term emphasis
Organizational socialization left to society	Formal organizational schemes for thorough organizational socialization
Focus on results in negotiation	Focus on the process in negotiation

Source: From E.F. Jackofsky, J.W. Slocum, Jr., and S.J. McQuaid, "Cultural Values and the CEO: Alluring Comparisons," *The Academy of Management Executives*, 1988, vol. 2, no 1, pp, 39–49 and J.C. Child, "Culture Contingency and Capitalism in the Cross-National Study of Organizations," in L.L. Cummings and B.M. Staw, eds., *Research in Organizational Behavior*, vol. 3 (Greenwich, Conn.: JAI Press, 1981), 303-56 [12, 29].

solving problems they faced in their daily tasks. The structure of the manufacturing plants in Japan also appeared to be less rigidly tied to operations technology than in the United States. The organization of the production subsystems, probably with very similar technologies, is different, reflecting cultural differences between the two countries.

THE MEANING AND PERCEPTION OF ORGANIZATIONS

Different organization structures may have different effects and implicit meanings because the elements of structure (authority relationships, job definitions, and so forth) are interpreted against different values. Trompnaars and Inzerilli examined these interpretations in studies of the way managers from nine countries perceived the organization in which they worked [45]. The study assessed whether the managers saw the organizations as *social models* or *rational models*. In the rational model view, organizations are seen as logical and impersonal with authority structures based on rational criteria and seeking specific technoeconomic goals. The social view defines organizations in terms of personal relationships and authority structures based on status with diffuse goals. Managers from the United States described organizations in rational terms. At the other extreme, a group of Venezuelan managers described organizations from the social point of view. Managers from the Netherlands, Sweden, Austria, and Greece had perceptions closer to those of the U.S. managers. Managers from Italy, Spain, and Singapore had perceptions similar to those of the Venezuelans.

RELATIONSHIPS AMONG ORGANIZATIONS

Culture affects the way organizations relate to each other. The most obvious example is how dominant economic values, such as those derived from capitalistic versus socialistic philosophies, drive competitive or cooperative behavior of firms. Another example is the way organizations that are dependent on each other manage their relationships. For instance, in the United States when one firm is a long-term supplier for another, there is usually a contractual relationship between them. This is consistent with both legal requirements and the cultural values in the United States. A different kind of relationship among organizations is found in the Prato region around Florence, the center of Italian textile production. The organization of this textile industry is unique because there are no large, vertically integrated plants that perform the production function from beginning to end. Instead nearly 20,000 firms, most of them very small, perform very specific, specialized functions. Some process new wool, others reclaim old wool. Some spin, others dye; some clean and others cut. All in all, the industry is highly fragmented, but these firms have developed close working relationships. This results in such effective coordination that the wool production process is quite efficient. In large part, this effective coordination stems from basic cultural values. It is based as much on social linkages as on the conventional types of interorganizational linkages common in the United States. Many of the small firms in the Prato region are owned and managed by relatives from an extended family. Italians have a deep sense of family and strong loyalties to the region of the country in which they live.

SUPERVISION AND LEADERSHIP

There has been much research on differences in leadership and supervisory styles. For example, Child reports on differences in leadership styles in the United Kingdom, Germany, and France [12]. In Germany and France, leadership and control tends to be more centralized. German managers want to be informed about everything that is going on, and they show less interest in their subordinates. In the United Kingdom, managers delegate and decentralize more, they have a greater interest in their subordinates and, unlike the Germans, they want to be informed only about exceptional events.

These results are relatively consistent with the power distance values in these countries, a cultural dimension which Hofstede believes has important implications for leadership and supervision [24]. Power distance differences would predict, for example, that supervisors in countries such as India and Mexico (high power distance) will act autocratically and paternalistically. Subordinates will accept status differentials between themselves and their supervisors and will not object to differences in privileges and benefits. In low power distance companies (for example, U.S., Israel, Sweden and Denmark), there is more participation in the workplace. Subordinates are likely to want to be consulted on important issues, prefer a democratic mode of supervision, and are likely to resent high status differentials and "unfair" privileges for those who manage them.

GROUP BEHAVIOR

The individualism-collectivism dimension may be the most useful one to understand cultural differences in group behavior [44]. Nations high on collectivism will emphasize group factors more so than countries high on individualism. Cole has shown that formal assignments to work in groups are used most frequently in Japanese firms, next most frequently in Swedish firms, and less in U.S. firms [14]. This perfectly fits the sequence of collectivism scores for these three countries [24]. As an example, Japanese companies use quality circles much more than U.S. firms. In 1987, there were at least 250,000 official quality circles, Japan involving more than 2 million members. The number of unregistered quality circles has been estimated to be five times that number. Furthermore, the groups are much more effective than similar U.S. groups [14].

Culture also affects the willingness to participate in formal groups. In the United States, about 15 percent of employees appear to be willing to participate in quality circle programs while in Japan the figures are often more than six times this figure [14].

The individual-collectivist dimension also appears to affect the level of performance in groups. Early found that those from a culture with high individualism had lower performance when they were working in groups than when working alone [15]. Those from a collectivist culture performed better when they were working in a group which was relatively cohesive and with which they identified. They did not perform as well working alone or when in a group with which their identification was low.

The reasons for using and empowering groups differs in these nations, again conforming to basic cultural values. For example, the U.S. and Sweden are more egalitarian than Japan. In these two countries, the purpose of group work assignments for ordinary workers are (1) democratization and (2) humanization. In Japan, work groups are more tightly controlled by management and are created simply for improving efficiency [14].

MOTIVATION

Some have argued that motivational theories developed in the United States are not applicable in other cultures [2, 25]. Properly considered, we believe that these theories can be very useful. Without exception, all process theories of motivation apply, with the same limitations as in the U.S. For example, a behavior which is positively reinforced in Cairo, Egypt will be repeated just as a positively reinforced behavior in Cairo, Illinois would be. What will differ is the specific nature of the reinforcer. Thus, supervisory recognition may be a very strong positive reinforcer in the United States, but have less reinforcing effect in another country. The content theories of motivation have more problems when applied cross-culturally. For example, Job Design Theory (see Chapter 8) which focuses on the desirability of enriching individual jobs does not work as well in more collectivist countries where the focus is on group task assignments [2]. In cultures that are high on collectivism, the achievement motive may not be such a dominant cultural value as it is in highly individualistic societies [37]. In fact, in some languages, such as Italian, there is no direct translation for the word achievement.

This means that effective motivational techniques are culture-specific. For example, in Asian countries (high on collectivism) there is a heavy reliance on group meetings as a device for inspiring employees to commit themselves to company goals and plans. A study of almost twenty thousand workers in a large U.S. company operating in 46 different countries found major differences in worker preferences [41]. In English speaking countries, individual achievement was more strongly emphasized than security. French speaking countries tended to place greater importance on security and less to challenging work than the English speaking countries. In northern European countries, leisure time was more important, there was higher concern for the needs of employees and less for the needs of the organization. Latin countries, Germany, and southern European countries put more emphasis on job security and fringe benefits. Japanese employees put a stronger emphasis on good working conditions and a friendly work environment.

Compensation practices also vary by country, driven by cultural values and local laws, most importantly the marginal tax rates [1]. CEOs in the United States are the highest paid in the world, though American managers and workers at lower organizational levels do not receive such wage premiums relative to their European counterparts [1]. The pay of Japanese CEOs is more closely tied to stock returns and earnings while for U.S. CEOs pay is more closely linked to sales growth [31]. Managerial pay seems to be becoming a bit more homogeneous across different cultures, changing in response to the increased influence of multinational firms. For example, Japan, France, and Germany have high uncertainty avoidance scores, which suggests that compensation systems would avoid performance incentives which would increase pay risk and uncertainty. However, German companies are beginning to implement more performance-based incentives for managers and workers, French firms are designing compensation systems which include long term incentives and performance-based bonuses, and Japanese firms have begun to use performance bonuses [10].

CROSS-CULTURAL COMMUNICATION

Of all the areas of organizational behavior, communication is among the most troublesome. Effective communications are universally difficult because people have different values and, therefore, different perceptions. As a consequence, they do not always agree on the meaning of words and could easily have dissimilar styles of expressing themselves. In a cross-cultural situation in particular, it is easy to see how difficult and complex communications might become.

☐ PROFESSIONAL EMPLOYMENT: INTERNATIONAL BARRIERS

The globalization of companies continues to have an impact on the employment of all kinds of workers around the world. According to the Wall Street Journal, professional employees in America are beginning to suffer job erosion of the kind that lower-level workers have faced for years. A former Lockheed electrical engineer, for example, was unable to compete for a job at Intel near his home in California because Intel was only hiring Irish engineers, at significantly lower wages, in its new plant in Ireland. Jobs that were once open to Americans are sometimes now given

☐ **PROFESSIONAL EMPLOYMENT . . .**

to highly skilled nationals in Asia, the former Soviet bloc, and Europe. In some cases, foreign nationals are being temporarily assigned to projects in the United States, also to keep costs down. Overseas, money is not always the issue; hiring locals in their own country takes advantage of their knowledge of laws, markets, and other relevant business conditions. The number of applications to bring foreign professionals into the U.S. is also increasing. This puts further stress on the employment opportunities and pay levels of Americans seeking work. Professional status offers no protection against foreign competition, even though foreign companies often prefer to hire American professionals for work in the United States and overseas.

Many professional areas are not effected by these conditions, and professionals are still a privileged group. Threats to their jobs in no way compare to those experienced at blue collar levels. Nevertheless, the appetite for using foreign professionals may increase. AT&T, Boeing, and Minnesota Mining and Manufacturing have stepped up efforts in this way in areas such as product development, customer support, design and engineering, manufacturing, and sales. Lower costs and local national knowledge and experience continue to provide incentives to these companies. Foreign professionals are often well prepared to assume demanding jobs in the experience of some companies like Komag, Inc., who opened a new operation in Malaysia.

Zachary, G.P. "White Collar Blues." *Wall Street Journal*, March 17, 1993, p. 1 [47].

One would expect communications within a single culture to be less burdened with problems, but it is deceiving to think that using one language would solve **cross-cultural communication** problems. For example, English is widely spoken around the world. This makes many Americans feel that they can get along quite well in other countries so long as they deal with individuals who can speak English. This is a mistake for reasons beyond differences in values, perceptions, word meanings, and styles of communicating. Wide misunderstandings can easily arise between individuals from nations that have English as the primary language [18]. Of course, misunderstandings are far more likely when English is not the primary language of the parties involved.

Communication differences across cultures may vary because of the openness or willingness to provide necessary information, speed of communication, and how information is evaluated. These communication process choices differ even among people from cultures that are not too dissimilar. In a study of communication patterns among German, French, and American managers, Americans were seen as the most ethnocentric in their attitudes [22]. They discounted what those from other countries said more so than vice versa. Also, the German mode of communication is slow and ponderous compared to the

French resulting in slower decisions. In a study of France, Japan, and the United States, it was found that the Japanese subjects were least willing to make personal disclosures to others while the French had the greatest willingness to express conflict [42].

The context of communication also makes a difference [38]. In Japan, one must interpret communications not only in what the message itself says but in such things as the physical environment in which the communication takes place, or the rank of the person doing the communication. It is necessary to attend to any behavior beyond the message itself, such as body posture. When the Japanese are negotiating, they seek to understand the other party before they are willing to arrive at a contract or agreement, while Americans are more interested in completing the task [13]. These different orientations make for a very difficult negotiation.

Some ways to improve cross-cultural communication include showing respect verbally and non-verbally, being nonjudgmental, avoiding ethnocentric conclusions, showing empathy, and striving for accuracy [2]. Communications are better when the parties know and are concerned about the effects that culture can have on their interaction. Some research shows that Americans have less cultural sensitivity than individuals in other countries especially European nations [22]. Part of this may be caused by the fact that most Americans speak only English and do not have much experience living in other cultures. Most educated Europeans and Asians speak English, and perhaps other languages, in addition to their own. The Europeans are also more likely to travel and experience other cultures than Americans.

SUMMARY

The problems of globalization involve much more than strategic decisions to expand operations in overseas locations or to participate in joint ventures with foreign firms. Organizations must learn to manage the multicultural diversity that goes along with operating internationally. Organizations must have personnel who can function effectively in different cultures and with the ability to manage individuals from different cultures in various locations in the world. This means that it is necessary to understand how cultures operate to affect behavior and performance.

In this chapter, we have identified differences in cultural dimensions which seem to have important implications for what happens inside multicultural organizations. These dimensions, which have been found to be useful ways to differentiate culture are the degree (1) to which a nation emphasizes an individual or a group orientation, (2) that there is appropriate power distance among individuals, (3) to which masculine versus feminine ideals are valued, (4) of the desire to avoid uncertainty, and (5) of the society's basic orientation toward the short versus the long run. These factors affect the dominant managerial philosophy, approaches to the design of organization structures, the way organizations are perceived, communication patterns, motivation, and leadership styles.

☐ KEY CONCEPTS

Cross cultural
  communication
Culture
Cultural metaphors
Globalization
High context cultures
Individualism-
  collectivism

Long vs short term
  thought patterns
Power distance
Low context
  cultures
Managerial
  philosophies

Masculinity-
  femininity
Modal personality
Theory Z
Uncertainty
  avoidance

☐ STUDY QUESTIONS

1. How has globalization impacted the educational experiences you have had recently? What changes do you see occurring in the curriculum, student body, and other factors related to the educational process?

2. How do you think the new globalization of business will impact on your career? Given this, what implications are there for you with respect to managing a successful career?

3. Think about some foreign students you have met or observed recently. What differences in their behaviors or thought patterns did you notice that vary from most individuals in your own nationality group? What underlying cultural differences may be reflected in these behaviors or thought patterns?

4. Some say that one's own culture is invisible to those who are in it. Do you believe that statement is true? Take a position on this issue and provide arguments for it.

5. Which three aspects of your own group's culture do you believe will facilitate doing business in the next three decades?

6. Which three aspects of your own group's culture will be most detrimental to doing business in the next three decades in your opinion?

7. Consider the possibility of being sent to an overseas post for three years. What types and amount of training would you like to receive before moving overseas?

8. Of the several countries mentioned in this chapter along with some of their characteristics, which sounds like it would be the easiest for you to live in while conducting business for an American company? Give reasons for your choice.

9. What do you think is going to happen to the human resource management practices used in different countries to manage their workforces? Are they going to start becoming more similar, stay the same, or become more different? Give reasons for your answers.

10. What are the origins of human resource management practices in various countries other than culture? Which of these is most important? Give reasons for your answer.

CASE

☐ SWEDISH MATCH—
CONSUMER PRODUCTS GROUP

Mr. Gunnar Christiani could not help but smile as he read the April 1, 1987 announcement that laid on his desk. Swedish Match had just concluded negotiations to acquire Wilkinson Sword. Wilkinson Sword, a British based corporation, specialized in the production and marketing of shaving products and garden tools. Strategically, Swedish Match's acquisitions of Wilkinson Sword made good sense. Wilkinson not only added to Swedish Match's dominance of the world wide matches market but also provided Swedish Match an opportunity to expand into new businesses outside Sweden.

Of one thing Mr. Christiani was certain, the acquisition of Wilkinson Sword would have a major impact upon his goal to implement a human resource planning system within the Consumer Products Group. Mr. Christiani became Vice President of Human Resources of Swedish Match's Consumer Products Group on August 1, 1986. Prior to joining Swedish Match, he held various personnel positions with Volvo and for eight years held a staff position with the Swedish Graduate Engineer's Union. The primary reason he had left Volvo, world renowned for its management practices, was to seek a new professional challenge. It was becoming increasingly apparent that this objective was being more than met.

Since assuming his responsibilities as Vice President of Human Resources, Mr. Christiani had spent considerable time traveling in Europe, Southeast Asia/Pacific, and South America to meet with local managers and discuss their international operations. In addition, he sought their views on the group's human resource management function and how the function might assist them. The Consumer Products Group employed *approximately 65 expatriate managers*. Approximately 20 of these managers were located at group headquarters in Nyon. The remaining were scattered throughout the world at various Swedish Match Consumer Products Group locations. While a majority of Swedish Match's expatriate managers were Swedish, other nationalities were also represented.

While being recruited by Swedish Match, Mr. Christiani was told that the human resource function within the Consumer Products Group was undeveloped and had been neglected for a number of years. Mr. Massimo Rossi, President of the Consumer Products Group had, however, assured Mr. Christiani that a dramatic change in the role of human resources within the Group was necessary. Mr. Rossi stated further that only with the establishment of sophisticated human resource policies and programs could the Consumer Products Group hope to reach its newly established strategic goals.

Foremost among existing human resource needs was the development of a human resource planning system. With companies directed by expatriate general managers scattered around the world, it was essential that the

☐ SWEDISH MATCH . . .

Group monitor the flow of its managerial resources. As previous experience had amply shown, failure to do so resulted in reduced operating efficiencies and managerial turnover. This problem was acutely visible in the Lighter Division. During the preceding ten years, the Lighter Division had been headed by ten different general managers.

Swedish Match and the Consumer Products Group.   Founded in 1917, Swedish Match was an international industrial corporation with business activities concentrated on home improvement, consumer products, packaging, and chemicals. The acquisition of Wilkinson Sword brought Swedish Match's worldwide employment to 35,000. Personnel were located at approximately 100 worldwide corporate affiliates. Corporate sales in 1986 were approximately 10.9 billion Swedish krona. Percentage sales by region were: Sweden, 26%; Nordic countries excluding Sweden, 19%; Europe excluding Nordic countries, 26%; United States, 15%; and other regions, 14%. Income after taxes in 1986 was 351 million Swedish krona and return on equity was 15.0%.

Swedish Match was organized into six Groups: Tarkett (flooring), Doors, Kitchens, Consumer Product, Akerlund and Rauding (packaging), Alby Chemical, and other activities. Each group operated with considerable independance. The Consumer Products Group was formed on January 1, 1986, through the merger of the former Match Group and Akerlund and Rausing's Consumer Division. The Consumer Products Group had operating companies in 35 countries and 18,000 employees. Group sales in 1986 were approximately 3.3 billion Swedish krona, approximately 30 percent of corporate sales.

The Consumer Products Group was comprised of three divisions: the Match Division, the leading match manufacturer in the world; the Lighter Division that was the producer of Cricket, Poppel, and Fuedor disposable lighters, ranked among the three largest disposable lighter manufacturers in the world; and the Paper Products Division that produced disposable table products, gift wrapping paper, greeting cards, and carrying bags. Through internal growth and acquisition, the Paper Products Division had experienced the most rapid expansion within Swedish Match during recent years. Exhibit 1 presents an organization chart for the Consumer Products Group.

The Consumer Products Group was formed to consolidate all fast moving consumer products that were marketed together under one umbrella. In industrialized countries, Akerlund and Rausing's Consumer and Match Group products were often sold through the food trade. This fact was expected to lead to considerable integration advantages in sales and distribution. Specifically, potential synergies exist in common warehousing and deliveries, common management and administration, and a common sales force in the marketing companies.

☐ SWEDISH MATCH . . .

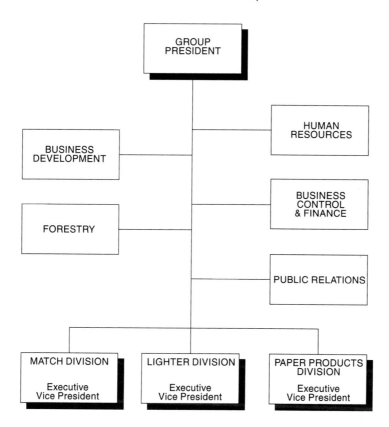

SWEDISH MATCH
Consumer Product Group

Human Resource Planning. Mr. Christiani was far from having developed a comprehensive human resource planning system to meet the needs of the Consumer Products Group. He had, however, identified a number of human resource planning issues that he believed warranted attention. One issue that concerned him was the movement of expatriate managers within the Group's subsidiaries.

General managers of Swedish Match's foreign operation were, in most cases, outside Europe expatriates. The Consumer Products Group included approximately 60 foreign subsidiaries. Expatriate assignments were normally for a two to three year period. These assignments could, however, be extended. Given the number of foreign subsidiaries within the group, and the length of expatriates' assignments, there was a constant worldwide movement of group managers. Like many other multinational corporations, Swedish Match had learned, often the hard way, that the successful placement of expatriates within foreign subsidiaries was

591

☐ Swedish Match . . .

a difficult task. In some cases, managers were unable to adapt to the foreign culture. In other cases, managers culturally adapted, yet were managerial ineffective. Normally, an expatriate was accompanied by his/her family, therefore, increasing the number of persons required to make a successful cultural adjustment.

The effective management of expatriates' careers by Swedish Match was even more difficult than it was for some multinational corporations. Because the Swedish Match Consumer Products Group did not possess a large domestic market and because it maintained a relatively small corporate staff in Stockholm, it was not possible for expatriate managers to have periodic home assignments. Furthermore, the movement of managers across groups within Swedish Match was very limited.

The management of expatriates' careers was further complicated by the interdependency of foreign assignments. At times, job assignments of three or four managers hinged upon whether a single manager accepted a new assignment. As might be expected, some subsidiary assignments were viewed as more attractive than others. For example, while few managers objected to assignments within Western Europe or the United States, positions in some Asian and African based subsidiaries were often difficult to staff. A related question concerning the placement of expatriate managers concerned the time spent in developing countries versus developed countries. Extended assignments in developing countries, at times, resulted in managers losing touch with new developments in their fields.

Mr. Christiani concluded that the Group was not managing the flow and placement of its expatriate managers with the attention this process deserved. On two occasions since joining the Consumer Products Group, Mr. Christiani had received phone calls from subsidiary managers requesting to know their next assignment. In both cases, he was unable to answer their request. One manager responded that if he did not receive an answer soon he would consider leaving the corporation.

Two additional issues pertaining to the placement of expatriates were the danger of managers "going native" and the difficulties of placing non Swedish expatriate managers at corporate headquarters in Stockholm or within Swedish affiliates. Because Swedish is seldom spoken outside Sweden, managers from other countries found such assignments almost impossible.

Swedish managers, on the other hand, frequently resisted reassignment to Sweden for other reasons. Certain managers simply enjoyed the excitement associated with foreign assignments, while other managers became strongly attached to certain countries and life styles they found there. Given Sweden's high tax rates, most managers found it financially attractive to remain abroad. To date, neither Sweden Match nor the Consumer Products Group had developed a policy to deal with this issue.

☐ SWEDISH MATCH . . .

A challenge even greater than managing the career paths of expatriates within the three Divisions of the Consumer Products Group involved the movement of managers across Divisions. The Consumer Products Group was formed to capitalize on the synergies which existed between the three Divisions. Achieving these synergy objectives required not only market integration, but also the integration of managerial resources. Historically, however, the movement of managers across division boundaries was very infrequent. An explanation commonly given to explain this lack of management mobility across divisions was that each division has a unique culture. Thus, it was argued that managers accustomed to one division's culture had difficulty adapting to another division's culture.

The Match Division, for example, was perceived to be Swedish in culture with a strong manufacturing orientation. It was also viewed as having a flat organizational structure, which resulted in decentralized decision making. On the other hand, the Lighter Division was regarded as having a French culture and viewed as having a more centralized structure leading to a top down style of management. Finally, the Paper Products Division had a very entrepreneurial culture. Representative of the lack of cross division movement of managers was the fact that during a recent period of rationalization, excess managers in the Match Division were not offered positions in the other divisions, even when vacancies existed.

Beyond the issue of effectively managing the movement of managers within the group were questions concerning the recruitment of future managers. A fundamental question was what type of individuals the group should recruit. Historically, the Consumer Products Group was dominated by the Match Division. In fact, many people felt that the Match Division was the Consumer Products Group. Over time, the dominance of the Match Division declined. In the 1950's, the Match Division accounted for approximately 90 percent of Sweden Match's revenues. By the mid-1980s the Match Division accounted for approximately ten percent of corporate revenues. During the era of the Match Division's dominance, engineering and manufacturing skills were viewed as the prerequisites for a successful managerial career. Given the Group's changing portfolio of products, a number of people argued that marketing skills were increasingly critical to individual and organizational success.

Equally important to selecting potential managers with the appropriate skills, was the necessity of developing and retaining potential subsidiary managers. In this area, the *Consumer Products Group had not been particularly successful.* Between 1982 and 1985, the Match Division hired eight new employees in managerial career track positions. Six of these individuals left the organization. It was estimated that this turnover cost the group approximately five million Sweden krona. Explanations of why these individuals left the corporation, to some degree, varied from case to case.

☐ SWEDISH MATCH . . .

A theme voiced by several individuals who left pertained to career uncertainly. Several young, potential managers stated that they were uncertain what career track lay ahead of them and what options existed. Mat Lindroth, a financial analyst within group headquarters, voiced the perception of a number young employees. He stated that the group was viewed as fluid and flexible in its operation. As a result, the Consumer Products Group presented good career opportunities for people who were self-starters and who were also comfortable managing their own careers. However, he noted that not all people met these criteria. Several of his friends that he mentioned had left the group because they felt a lack of career structure and guidance.

Prior to the acquistion of Wilkinson Sword, Mr. Christiani had developed several tentative proposals to improve human resource planning within the Consumer Products Group. The acquisition of Wilkinson Sword, however, fundamentally expanded and complicated the scope of the human resource planning challenge.

Wilkinson Sword, previously a wholly owned subsidiary of Alleganhey International, with total employment of 8,500 had operations in approximately 20 countries. With this acquistion and many new managers, the need for human resource planning drastically increased. Along with the increased numbers, Wilkinson Sword and Swedish Match possessed very different organization cultures. While Swedish Match's culture was heavily Swedish, Wilkinson Sword's culture was heavily Anglo Saxon/English. In addition, there were other important differences between the two companies. Unlike Swedish Match, Wilkinson did not encourage their managers to gain international experience. Rather, they relied on local managers to manage their operations. These local managers seldom were asked to accept international assignments. A final important difference between the two companies was their organizational structure. Swedish Match was organized largely around products. On the other hand, Wilkinson Sword relied largely upon a geographical organization structure.

A final issue that Mr. Christiani had to consider was the low morale that existed at Wilkinson Sword. During the period that it was owned by Alleganhey International, Wilkinson Sword felt it had been poorly treated both with respect to corporate attention and resources. As a result, turnover was high and morale low. On the other hand, most Wilkinson Sword employees were pleased with Swedish Match as the buyer. For many years there had been good relations between Swedish Match's Match Group managers and managers in the Match Operations of Wilkinson Sword.

Despite these obstacles, Mr. Christiani realized that strategically the acquisition of Wilkinson Sword was in the best long term interest of Swedish Match. The acquistion of Wilkinson Sword enabled Swedish Match to

☐ SWEDISH MATCH . . .

enter new product markets. This diversification was particularly important in light of a five to ten percent annual decline in the volume of matches sold in developed countries. Furthermore, the acquistion of Wilkinson Sword enabled Swedish Match to achieve additional economies of scale. Finally, certain potential synergies existed between Swedish Match and Wilkinson Sword products. For example, many individuals hoped that Wilkinson's shaving products and Swedish Match's lighters could utilize similar distribution channels and production technology.

Mr. Christiani fully realized that many of the anticipated benefits of the current acquisition could only be achieved by the development and implementation of an effective human resource planning system. As the date of his first anniversary with the Consumer Products Group approached, he was certain that Mr. Rossi and the presidents of the various divisions of the Consumer Products Group would be expecting to learn his thoughts pertaining to the introduction of a comprehensive human resource planning system, particularly given the recent Wilkinson Sword acquistion.

QUESTIONS

1. How important is the transfer of managers in Swedish Match?
2. What are the main differences in country cultures that Swedish Match must recognize as it considers the international movement of its managers?
3. Why do the managers have a sense of inequity when they have a foreign assignment coming up?
4. What can Swedish Match do to increase the movement of its managers across the various divisions of the Consumer Products Group?

REFERENCES

1. Abowd, J.M. and Bognanno, M. International differences in executive and managerial compensation. Unpublished paper, Center for Advanced Human Resource Studies at Cornell University, Ithaca, New York, 1993.
2. Adler, N.J. *International dimensions of organizational behavior.* Boston: PWS-KENT Publishing Company, 1991.
3. Arkin, A. At work in the powerhouse of Europe. *Personnel Management,* 1992, February, 32-35.

4. Arkin, A. The land of social welfare. *Personnel Management*, 1992b, March, 33-35.
5. Audia, G. Managing internationalization at the corporate level: The case study of Fiat. Unpublished Paper, Milan, Italy, SDA Bocconi, 1991.
6. Baba, M., Hanoka, M. Hara, H., and Baba, K. *Managerial behavior in Japan and the USA: A cross cultural survey*, Japan Productivity Center, 1984.
7. Besse, D. Finding a new raison d'etre. *Personnel Management*, 1992, August, 40-43.
8. Bond, M., Wan, K., Leung, K., and Giacalone., R. How are responses to verbal insults related to cultural collectivism and power distance. *Journal of Cross Cultural Psychology*, 1985, 16, 11-127.
9. Brislin, R. *Understanding culture's influence on behavior.* Fort Worth: Harcourt Brace Jovanovich, 1993.
10. Brooks, B.J. Trends in international executive compensation. *Personnel*, 1987, 64(5), 67-70.
11. Caplan, J. It's the climate that counts. *Personnel Management*, 1992, April, 32-35.
12. Child, J.C. Culture contingency and capitalism in the cross-national study of organizations, in L.L. Cummings and B.M.Staw, eds. *Research in Organizational Behavior*, vol. 3 Greenwich, Conn.: JAI Press, 1981, 303-356.
13. Cohen, R. *Negotiating across cultures.* Washington, D.C.: U.S. Peace Institute, 1991.
14. Cole, R.E. *Strategies for learning: Small group activities in American, Japanese, and Swedish industry*, Berkeley: University of California Press, 1989.
15. Early, P.C. East meets west meets mideast: Further explorations of collectivistic and individualistic work groups. *The Academy of Management Journal*, 1993, 36(2), 319-348.
16. Eun, C.S., Kolodny, R. & Scheraga, C. *Cross-border acquisitions and shareholder wealth: Evidence from U.S. and foreign stock markets.* Working paper, University of Maryland at College Park, College of Business and Management, 1992.
17. Gannon, M.J. *Cultural metaphors: Capturing essential characteristics of 17 diverse societies.* 1993, Chicago: Sage Publishing.
18. Garcia, O. and Otheguy, R. *English across cultures, cultures across English.* New York: Mouton de Gruyter, 1989.
19. Grabrenya, W., Wang, Y.J., and Latane, B. Social loafing in an optimizing task: Cross cultural differences among Chinese and Americans. *Journal of Cross Cultural Psychology*, 1985, 16, 223-242.
20. Hall, E.T. *The hidden dimension.* New York: Doubleday, 1969.
21. Hall, E.T. *Beyond culture.* Garden City, N.Y.: Doubleday, 1989.
22. Hall, E.T. and Hall, M.R. *Understanding cultural differences: Germans, French, and Americans.* Yarmouth Maine: Intercultural Press, 1990.
23. Hanami, T. *Managing Japanese workers.* Tokyo: Japan Institute of Labour, 1991.
24. Hofstede, G. *Culture's consequences: International differences in work-related values.* Beverly Hills, CA: Sage Publications, 1980.
25. Hofstede, G. Motivation, leadership and organization: Do American theories apply abroad. *Organizational Dynamics* Summer , 1980, 2, 42-63.

26. Hofstede, G. Cultural constraints in management theories. *Academy of Management Executive*, 1992, 7(1), 81-94.

27. Hofstede, G. and Bond, M.H. The Confuscius connection; From cultural roots to economic growth. *Organizational Dynamics*, 1988, 16, 5-21.

28. Hoogendoorn, J. New priorities for Dutch HRM. *Personnel Management*, 1992, December, 42-48.

29. Jackofsky, E.F., Slocum, J.W., and McQuaid, S.J. Cultural values and the CEO: Alluring companions. *Academy of Management Executive*, 1988, 2:1, 39-49.

30. JOEA *A survey report on international staffs.* Japan Overseas Enterprises Association, 1989, May.

31. Kaplan, S.N. Internal corporate governance in Japan and the U.S.: Differences in activity and horizons. Unpublished paper, University of Chicago, 1992.

32. Katzenstein, G. *Funny business: An outsider's year in Japan.* New York: Prentice Hall Press, 1989.

33. Kluckholn, F. and Strodtbeck, F. *Variations in value orientations.* Evanston, Ill.: Row, Peterson 1961.

34. Laaksonen, O. *Management in China during and after Mao in enterprises, government, and party.* New York: Walter de Gruyter, 1988.

35. Laurent, A. The cross-cultural puzzle of international human resource management. *Human Resource Management*, 1986, 25:1, 91-102.

36. Lincoln, J.R., Hanada, M., and McBride, K. Organizational structures in Japanese and U.S. manufacturing. *Administrative Science Quarterly*, 1986, 31, 338-64.

37. McClelland, D.A. Toward a theory of motive acquisition. *American Psychologist*, 1965, 20, 321-23.

38. Mead, R. *Cross cultural management communication.* Chichester: John Wiley & Sons, 1990.

39. Ouchi, W. *Theory Z: How American business can meet the Japanese challenge.* Reading, MA: Addison-Wesley, 1981.

40. Ronen, S. and Shenkar, O. Clustering countries on attitudinal dimensions: A review and sythesis. *Academy of Management Review*, 1985, 10(3), 435-454.

41. Sirota, D. and Greenwood, M.J. Understanding your overseas workforce, *Harvard Business Review*, 1971, (Jan.-Feb.), 53-60.

42. Ting-Toomey, S. Intimacy expressions in three cultures: France, Japan, and the United States. *International Journal of Intercultural Relations*, 1991, 15, 29-46.

43. Towers Perrin Co., *Priorities for competitive advantage.* New York: Towers Perrin, 1992.

44. Triandis, H., Brislin, R., and Hui, C. Cross-cultural training across the individualism-collectivism divide. *International Journal of Intercultural Relations*, 1988, 12, 269-289.

45. Trompenaars, F., and Inzerilli, G. Perceptual models of organization structure in different cultures. Unpublished paper. Lausanne, Switzerland: IMEDE, 1985.

46. Whitehill, A.M. *Japanese management: Tradition and transition.* London: Routledge, 1991.

47. Zachary, G.P. White collar blues. *Wall Street Journal*, March 17, 1993.

Index

617